BA in Leader
and Management

BA in Leadership and Management

Skills for the Workplace
Student Yearbook, 1st Year

Andrew Maund

Los Angeles | London | New Delhi
Singapore | Washington DC | Melbourne

Los Angeles | London | New Delhi
Singapore | Washington DC

SAGE Publications Ltd
1 Oliver's Yard
55 City Road
London EC1Y 1SP

SAGE Publications Inc.
2455 Teller Road
Thousand Oaks, California 91320

SAGE Publications India Pvt Ltd
B 1/I 1 Mohan Cooperative Industrial Area
Mathura Road
New Delhi 110 044

SAGE Publications Asia-Pacific Pte Ltd
3 Church Street
#10–04 Samsung Hub
Singapore 049483

Editorial arrangement © Andrew Maund, 2018

Chapter 1 © Mike Metcalfe 2006
Chapter 2 © Suzette Dyer, Maria Humphries, Dale Fitzgibbons and
    Fiona Hurd, 2014
Chapter 3 © SAGE Publications Inc. 2016
Chapter 4 © SAGE Publications Inc. 2017
Chapter 5 © T. V. Rao 2016
Chapters 6, 7, 8 and 9 © Gopal K. Kanji and Mike Asher 1996
Chapters 10 and 11 © V. Kumar 2013
Chapters 12 and 13 © Gautam Mahajan 2016
Chapter 14 and 15 © SAGE Publications Inc. 2012
Chapter 16 © Mohamed Branine 2011
Chapter 17 © Mats Alvesson 2013
Chapter 18 © David Coghlan 2016
Chapter 19 © Stewart R. Clegg, Martin Kornberger and Tyrone Pitsis 2015
Chapter 20 © Joanne Roberts 2015
Chapter 21 © The Music Educators' Journal 2014
Chapter 22 © Jennifer Mencl and Scott W. Lester 2014
Chapter 23 © The Association for Business Communication 2006
Chapter 24 © Psychological Reports 2011
Chapter 25 © Meera Alagaraja and Rod Patrick Githens
Chapter 26 © Australian Council for Educational Research 2017
Chapter 27 © SAGE Publications 2017
Chapter 28 © SAGE Publications 2017
Chapter 29 © John A. Miller 2017
Chapter 30 © American Association for Adult and
    Continuing Education 2013
Chapter 31 © Pedro F. Bendassolli 2016
Chapter 32 © SAGE Publications 2014
Chapter 33 © IMI SAGE Publications 2014
Chapter 34 © SAGE Publications 2009
Chapter 35 © IMI SAGE Publications 2014
Chapter 36 © IMI SAGE Publications 2016

First published 2018

Typeset by: C&M Digitals (P) Ltd, Chennai, India
Printed in the UK
Printed on paper from sustainable resources

British Library Cataloguing in Publication data

A catalogue record for this book is available from
the British Library

ISBN 978-1-5264-6279-4 (pbk)

MIX
Paper from
responsible sources
FSC
www.fsc.org   FSC® C011748

Contents

PART 1

DEVELOPING WORKPLACE
CRITICAL THINKING

Using System Thinking to Critique

Metcalfe, M.

I can think of the phenomenon of a chicken, as a chicken or as a system. As a chicken it is like a picture, an object, a large bird, feathers, two legs and a face. As a system it is a process, things go into it and come out of it, food, water and DNA are transformed into a scratching machine, eggs, feathers, a sandwich and a parent. (See Figure 2.1, source unknown).

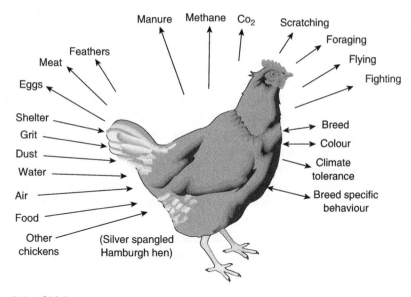

Figure 2.1   Chicken as a system

Transforming

At its simplest level system thinking involves thinking about something as part of a system that has inputs and outputs, which transforms things from one form to another (food to eggs), using various components (stomach, uterus, skin, etc.) which interact with each other to assist the transformation. The workings of the human body could replace the hen as an example of a thing being thought of in systems terms; the respiratory sub-system works with the dietary systems, the nervous sub-system and the blood circulatory sub-systems to assist the whole system, a critiquer, to transform a written passage into an insightful critique.

Critique the following passage by identifying the system depicted in the passage:

- **Identify the object under consideration as a system (a process).**

- **What are the inputs, the outputs, the components?**

- **What is transformed from what to what?**

In our global mechanised world it is almost impossible to appreciate the human lives that go into everyday things. Imagine the thousands of people's working lives that have gone into getting a tin of baked beans onto the supermarket shelf. I've been a bean counter (accountant) in a bean factory. It was huge, old, cruddy, and located in the miserable urban decay of the back streets of London, surrounded by disused canals and railways. Twice around its perimeter was literally a marathon. When the raw beans came into the factory they had to be sorted into big ones, little ones, and black ones and white ones. Have you ever noticed that the beans in your tin are identical in size? They do not grow them like that. The bean trucks arrive with beans from all over the world – Canada, India, South America – arriving at street level to unload onto conveyor belts which move the tons and tons of raw beans indoors to rows of automated sorting machines. Under these sorters are chutes for the rejected beans which drop down into the basement where some lonely old man passes his day slowly attaching and removing large sacks to and from the ends of these chutes. When the sacks were full he would load them onto trailers ready to be sent to the piggeries. You can imagine the life of this lonely little bloke who worked in that miserable basement room, no windows, cigarette hanging out of his mouth, withered, bent over, newspaper open at the sporting page, cheap radio in the background, thirty-five years' service, punctual in taking his tea breaks, so typical of the slave classes grateful to secure a regular job in the globalised economy. He was most likely comfortable enough with the job, the boss rarely visited and he was not out in the winter weather. So long as the job got done no one would ever notice he existed. One day someone was walking past the entrance to this part of the basement and noticed piles of beans bulging up the stairwell. This looked unfamiliar so an investigation was started. It took some time and considerable bean shifting to establish what had happened. The poor man had died. The beans had kept coming, filling the room, burying him and eventually overflowing up the stairwell.

One system that I identify is that of the bean factory, in particular the bean sorting part of the factory. The inputs were raw beans, labour and capital equipment in the form of trucks, conveyor belts, sorting machines and chutes. The outputs of the bean sorting system are acceptable beans, and, down the chute, rejected beans en route to the piggery. The old man was a component in this system, one that moved the reject beans from the chute to the piggery trailers; he is the only human component identified. Mixed raw beans are transformed by the machinery and the person into sorted beans.

Thinking of the passage in system terms has introduced a new image that can be used in a critique of the passage. In a system view, the man is a component, not a feeling human being to be protected from social forces greater than himself. He is dehumanised, compassion is excluded through association. A system view has the man as a victim oppressed by mass consumerism and the machinery of large-scale manufacturing. The man is presented as a product of his environment. In the criminal law courts we do not do that. We prosecute individuals as individuals, not as components in a social system. While your childhood, your social environment and your role in a criminal syndicate may be mitigating circumstances, you as an individual are considered responsible for your actions. This would be a non-system view.

The main advantage of system thinking is to shift thinking from the object to an interrelationship of components; from the old man to the manufacturing system he is merely one part of. That insight, that he can be seen as a standalone individual or as a component in a system, provides the first level of critique using system thinking. This is a similar switch from cognitive psychology to social psychology. From the early 1960s to the mid 1990s psychology placed emphasis on the individual, on the importance of an individual's personality, cognitive styles and intelligence to deal with situations. Researchers like Milgram (1992) and those interested in small-group performance started to show that human behaviour is very situational. Much of what we do is because of the situation we are in and who we are with. For example, attitudes to risk are very different when at home compared with when attending a race meeting. Seeing someone as part of a system goes a long way to seeing them differently.

A further example of view shifting by using system thinking comes from problem solving. If a group of people are blaming each other for some problem, then it is sometimes possible to see things differently if someone suggests the problem is not any one person's fault but rather a fault of the system. Plagiarism has been debated in this way. Is it the individual 'loser's' fault or rather an obvious outcome of an education system that has made class sizes too large, required students to compete for very high scores, made lecturers too busy to set more novel and non-repetitive assignments in the context of rapid text communication through email, the Internet and word processors. My point is not that either view of plagiarism is right but that by switching from an individual view to a system one a more insightful critique is possible. The baked beans man might have been seen as getting all he deserved for not eating better, getting more exercise, making more effort to improve his education and for not making an effort to develop relationships at work or home.

The dimension of transforming can also be used to consider the passage as a whole. How does the passage transform the readers? Perhaps they have a better idea of the effort in human lives that goes into their everyday foods. What are the inputs and outputs of the passage; are these validated? The inputs include the author's experiences and care for the lives of workers; are these inputs reliable? The story may be told for humour, not for compassion. The outputs include the conclusion to the passage. What is it? Perhaps, that most people live very ordinary lives.

Connections

System thinking has a few different dimensions which are related in the sense they aim to change the way you think about things. A new viewpoint provides a new way of critiquing. The next dimension outlined here is centred on the idea of 'connections'. The components in a system are connected. The bean sort is connected to the chutes, my heart is connected to my liver, the accounts department of a university system is connected to the teaching schools, and the tax collection department in the Westminster system of government is connected to Parliament. Ackoff (2000), a long-standing writer on the use of system thinking to come up with innovative solutions to problems, emphasises the importance of using 'connectivity' to shift people's appreciation of a situation. He often draws on the example of car parts. If you own a Toyota Corolla and need a new carburettor then you would not buy a Rolls-Royce carburettor as a replacement. It would be inappropriate given the other components in your Corolla as a system. A component needs to be thought of in terms of how it connects with other components. For people a little less mechanical, these connections are called social networks. Rather than seeing a person as an entity it is possible to focus on their social network. Who do they know, how often do they see them and what do they talk about? At work, or socially, they may be the focal point of a tightly connected group of twelve people, or rather they may be loosely connected to two rather distinct social groups so occasionally act as a 'liaison person' between these groups.

This focus on connections can be used to see a passage differently, to critique it. Critique the two passages below in terms of connections:

There is a story told around the British Rolls-Royce engineering works that Boeing, the American aircraft company, once very carefully sent Rolls-Royce what you and I would describe as an aluminium drinking straw. It was about a foot (30 cm) long, with a hole down the middle about 2 millimetres in diameter, like a drinking straw.

(Continued)

(Continued)

Boeing had machined this thin rod out of a block of aluminium and then drilled it down the centre. Boeing sent it to Rolls-Royce as proof of its precision engineering skill. I gather aluminium is not an easy metal to use for this sort of high-precision machining and drilling work, partly because it is hard to get a very pure sample. Drilling out the 'straw' required some very specialised vacuum chamber lathe equipment.

Rolls-Royce's version of this story was that after examining this work and admiring it, the engineers re-drilled it down the centre so as to enlarge the centre-hole diameter. They then made and slotted a smaller brass 'straw' as a lining inside the aluminium one, such that the original internal diameter of the aluminium straw was not changed. It looked like a silver straw lined with a brass straw. Then they sent it back.

A few years back, men wearing earrings upset an inordinate number of people. An institutionalisation of this concern included the procedure for a blood bank collection agency. In the days before quick, cheap blood testing for HIV (AIDS) the agency responsible for screening blood donations was concerned with how to minimise the risk of collecting infected blood. The agency issued instructions to the nurses doing the screening to discreetly vet the male donors for any physical indication of homosexuality. One suggestion was that they should check to see if they were wearing an earring in their left ear. This was to be discreetly noted on their record card so their blood donation could be quickly disposed of when they left the clinic. The marked card then became a permanent record of someone being a possible homosexual at a time when there was considerable social and legal discrimination against homosexuals.

Apparently, the practice of working men wearing earrings is quite old. It has been suggested that sailors either started or popularised the practice. The understanding was that if a sailor was washed overboard and drowned, whoever found the body was rewarded for giving the body a decent burial with the gold in the earring.

Critiquing these passages using the 'connections' stance could stimulate numerous different critiques. The one that comes to my mind is that they present two worlds linked by a common object. In the first passage the two worlds are the British Rolls-Royce engineering company and the American Boeing engineering works, two worlds linked with a common respect for precision engineering, symbolised ironically by a metallic drinking straw. It does not matter how true it is; the message is one of respect for the pursuit of engineering expertise. In the second passage the male earring provides the link from a sad present involved in avoiding death from AIDS to a sad past where sailors sought a respectful burial. Using this connections stance on the baked beans story may suggest a man isolated from fellow humans by a mechanised manufacturing system, his only connections being with machines that are indifferent to his personal needs.

This system dimension of connections can again be used to think about the article as a whole. What is the article connected or not connected to? Perhaps you think both articles are men's histories, not connected to women. Perhaps, for the more quality minded, they make you think about quality, of engineering skills and of transfusion blood. Do they remind you of something else you have read or seen?

Purposeful activity – intentional minds

Critique the following passage, in terms of participants' purposeful activity.

At the end of the Second World War there was the massive problem of moving the British economy from a war footing to a peacetime one. Numerous manufacturing plants had been changed from making domestic products to instruments of war. Planes, tanks and gun manufacturing were employing millions of people. In order to assist with the changeover, temporarily, manufacturers were instructed to keep making their war output until a smooth transition could be thought through. A period measured in months was imagined. Adding to the complication were two wartime requirements for armament manufacture. The first was a decentralised manufacturing process to avoid risk of an entire production process being ruined by one bombing raid. The parts for the guns, tanks, etc., were made in small plants all over the country. Second was the need for secrecy, which meant that no one plant had an overall appreciation of the supply chain of these weapons. Orders came from coded 'customers' and deliveries were made to small warehouses from where they were picked up when the supplier was not present. So, it is easy to see how the oversight was made. During the transition period those responsible for the collection of the battle-ready product were instructed rather than to dispatch them to a military unit, to deliver them back to the iron smelting foundry which was at the beginning of the supply chain. This caused little concern to the iron smelting foundry. It had always included 'rejected' weapons and melted them in with raw iron ore. It made rods and bars to supply to the sub-assembly manufacturers. So, as a temporary measure, the supply chain was a closed loop. Manufactured goods were delivered to customers who were paid to deliver them to the iron foundry.

The Second World War ended in 1945. In 1984 it was discovered that one of these closed loop supply chains was still operating. Somehow in the millions of arrangements for closing down the loops, and given the secrecy of the supply chain, this one was missed. For nearly twenty years the government had been paying for a particular type of field gun to be made, stored for a while and then melted down to be made into another gun, and so on.

What made this passage a little 'humorous'? Given the suggestion to look out for purposeful activity perhaps you identified that the temporary manufacturing system had lost its *purpose*, or rather that the *intent* of the post-war administrator had gone astray. The original intent, the driving force, behind the administrators setting up the closed loop supply chain was to keep people in employment for a few months while the peacetime economy was established. Consideration of 'purpose' is another dimension of system thinking. Separately, evolutionary philosopher Daniel Dennett has written about *The Intentional Stance* (1989), pointing out that this is perhaps a unique characteristic of the large human brain. The concepts of purpose and of intention are similar. They have to do with having an appreciation of why, the explanation, the reasoning, the driving forces, for wanting to do something. They differ from goals, targets, objectives, visions and missions which are perhaps more about 'what' rather than 'why'.

A passage can be critiqued in terms of its purpose (or the author's intentions). What were the 'driving forces' behind writing the supply chain passage? The great thing about this simple question is that a moment's thought makes you reply, 'it depends'. In the context of this chapter it is to provide an example from which 'purpose' can be discussed. If told in a pub, then the purpose would have been to amuse. If told as part of a government policy meeting its purpose might be to argue for more decentralised policy oversight. Moreover, within the passage, the issue of 'purpose' changes. The purpose, driving force, of the closed loop supply chain was to smooth the transition to a peacetime economy. This sounds like good policy. However, over time this purpose diminished in its reasonableness. Therefore, critiquing a passage using the 'purpose' stance encourages thinking about 'driving forces' but also about the numerous different points of view involved.

Appreciating purpose or intent is an emergent property of intelligence; it is part of being self-conscious. Boulding (1956), one of the seminal qualitative economists, argued that simple systems cannot be said to be engaged in purposeful activity. Does an alarm clock have any 'driving forces'? He suggests not. A human can give the clock's designer a purpose, to make a device to wake people up on time, and perhaps the owner's purpose is not to be late for work. In the weakest form a radar-guided missile system may be said, by some, to have 'driving forces' in terms of its electronic feedback circuits re-targeting the missile as the target tries to evade it. Moving up the scale of complexity, does a jelly fish or a dog have driving forces? It would seem to be easy to say they have genetic ones to eat, reproduce, and so on. Given our language skills, other 'higher order' driving forces may have emerged from the large human brain, such as the ability to predict the purpose or driving forces of others. It allows us to predict which way a hunted animal might go by our appreciating its driving forces; the animal must be feeling hot, hungry, thirsty, want to protect its young, may be trying to mislead us. This can become, 'If I do this then they will do that.' So, perhaps, critiquing by thinking about the driving forces of others is a unique human act.

Use the 'purpose' stance to critique the following passage, focusing on the purposes of the participants in the story rather than the author.

My high school was a naval training school in North Wales. Above the entrance of the school was a quote from its most famous ex-pupil and poet, John Mansfield. It was, 'We went down to the sea in ships, the lonely sea and the sky.' He knew what he was talking about. One of the interesting things about this old-fashioned British private school was the mental state of the officer–teachers. Many of them were ex-merchant-navy seamen. I was at the school in the early 1960s so many of these officers had spent the Second World War in the convoy system going back and forth across the freezing U-boat-infested North Atlantic. Apart from some of the images recounted in books and films like *The Cruel Sea*, most people have little appreciation of how dreadful the war in the Atlantic was for these seamen. It was boring, stormy, cold, dangerous – just plain miserable. Many merchant seamen spent the war ploughing back and forth from Europe to North America carrying war materials. One of our officers was teaching us about lifeboats, their design specifications, the regulations on provisions, and so on. There was a bit of a rumour among the cadets that this particular officer had nearly perished in a lifeboat full of nurses which was lost in the North Atlantic after their ship had been torpedoed. Now to 14-year-old cadets this sounded like utopia; in those days nurses meant young women. But once when we managed to get the officer to talk about the experience it soon became clear from his white face, and slight shake, that it was a dreadful and harrowing experience. He had to deal with the cold, the thirst, the hunger, the fear, in an overloaded, unstable, waterlogged boat, responsible for issuing rations and deciding who he would allow into the boat and who not from those hanging on the sides. Rescue could not be assumed, and many of the nurses had been badly burnt or choked by the fuel oil that spread on the sea surface after a ship was torpedoed. He could have only been in his twenties at the time. When he was eventually rescued everyone just laughed at his good fortune of being lost at sea with a boatful of young women.

The participants in this passage who would be self-conscious enough to be considered as purposeful and as being able to appreciate the purpose, drivers or intent of others I identify as: the cadet, the officer–teacher and the nurses. While there are numerous purposeful actions going on, including survival, one that I feel may provide a novel critique of this passage is that of *learning*. This may be used to critique the passage by identifying conflicts in the intent to learn or by identifying a common purposeful activity. My critique of this passage is, therefore, that all the participants can be seen to have a common desire, that of wanting to learn. The cadet's purposeful action for talking to the officer–teacher can be interpreted as wanting to learn about the risks of a future life at sea. The officer's driving force can be seen as *learning* how to live with the experience he had in the lifeboat: teaching the next generation of sea-goers not to romanticise the experience of a sinking ship. The driving force for the nurses in the lifeboat can be seen as *learning* the rules of survival from the young officer in charge of the lifeboat; how are they to deal with the others in the lifeboat, the life and death decisions, the hunger, the cold and the feeling of helplessness? The passage can be seen as a learning story.

Analyse and synthesise

Another dimension of system thinking which again involves shifting your point of view involves zooming in (analysis) and zooming out (synthesis) of the situation depicted in a passage. In the lifeboat passage, *analysis* of the situation would involve thinking about the details in the situation, such as weather conditions for the lifeboat, the rations, the numbers of people and their injuries. *Synthesising* the situation involves zooming out of the scene to get a new, wider view. This may result in your thinking about the overall strategy of the war in the Atlantic, perhaps its effectiveness, looking for statistics on how many ships were sunk over what dates. What were the survival rates of crews of torpedoed ships? This information could be a comparison with casualties and conditions for soldiers fighting on land at that time. The critique would reflect on the passage from this wider view.

Critique the following passage using the stance of first analysing the situation, then synthesising it.

> Crossing the Pacific in an old merchant ship used to include film-shows on deck, at night, to take advantage of the tropical sea breezes. Not a mosquito in sight, but the problem with the tropics is that you get a lot of rain showers. From the bridge of a ship these appear as columns of water falling from individual small dense clouds. When a film was being shown it was the duty of the person on the bridge to steer the ship so as to avoid these showers, and so avoid the crew getting soaked. The ship moved at about 17 knots, and the shower clouds often moved at much the same speed, criss-crossing the course of the ship. It required a good sense of timing to adjust the ship's course by a few degrees in anticipation of the path of a shower cloud to neatly weave around all the columns of water. On a warm tropical night, with one of those huge full moons, all alone in the middle of the Pacific, it was a slow-motion ballet, an excellent memory.

The analysis may include commenting on the physical possibility of a 17 knot ship out-running a shower squall. Alternatively it might ask about the safety to other shipping or the damage being done to dead-reckoning navigational calculations given the repeated change of course. An overhead awning may have been more sensible. A synthesis might have drawn analogies with airliners changing their altitude to avoid turbulence when passengers are being served a meal. It may be the same as people in a car choosing a longer but scenic route over a boring but quicker highway.

Again this dimension of system thinking can be used to compare the entire passage with something else you have read or seen. Perhaps some phrase in the passage reminds you of something (analyse), or you see the passage as the same as a group of other passages (synthesise).

Boundary

Critique the following passage by noting what is included and what is excluded. What is the boundary?

> We rented a farmhouse from a wonderful man, Ron, who farmed sheep in New Zealand. When my young daughters saw newborn lambs wandering about his farm bleating for their mothers they asked him if they could feed them, make them pets. Quite rightly he pointed out that if they did that when the lamb and mother were in a good relationship they could be responsible for the mother rejecting her own lamb. However, there was often a lamb or two whose mother died and he would find one for them to care for. Many of these orphan lambs died despite all good intentions, either because they also turned out to be very weak after the birth or because they had failed to get that crucial first feed from their mother. I gather this sets up the stomach of the lamb. However, a little later in life these pet lambs face yet another risk because a few months of being hand-fed by humans scrambles their survival instincts. Untamed sheep know to run away from people. Pet lambs know the opposite. They run towards people who call out to them, thinking there is a free feed about. So, some less-than-desirable people know that if they are driving past a mob of sheep and fancy a feed it was well worth just standing at the edge of a paddock and calling out. The non-pet lambs run away but the pet lambs run towards whoever is shouting. When close enough they got banged on the head and quickly thrown into the car boot.

One of the other dimensions of system thinking, and perhaps what really separates it from the assumptions of the physical sciences, is 'boundary'. A system is bounded; it includes some things and excludes others. The education system includes schools, universities and lecturers but excludes emergency services. Anything known about a system only applies to that system. The education system may be having a funding crisis while the emergency services systems could be over-funded. What is known is not universal; rather it is bounded by the definition of the system under consideration.

The boundary is chosen by the person thinking about a system. When thinking about an organisation as a system the most common way of bounding it is by legal employment and ownership relationships. These are recorded in its financial records. However, when thinking about product supply chains, a different boundary may be used. Sales staff's relationships with suppliers, and the buyer's relationship with suppliers, may be included and administrative staff excluded. By shifting the boundary a new view of the system comes to mind. Another example would be first thinking about your family as a system with parents, children and relatives as the components. Then change the boundary and think just about children as a system in their own right. The components may now include school, television and friends. This process of changing how you view a system is similar to the idea of zooming in and zooming out (analysis and synthesis) discussed above. However, it encourages more options in terms of views by redefining systems in terms of focusing on the components of one system, making these into a new system view. In the family system, children are at first only one component of the system. Then the boundary is changed and children are then thought of as an entire system in their own right.

Returning to the pet lamb passage, the life of pet lambs in this part of New Zealand might be chosen as the system boundary. In this view the lambs are seen as central, vulnerable and under attack from inadequate mothering and hungry passers-by. By imagining new systems from these components other systems emerge, e.g. the 'other' lambs, farmers and the passers-by as systems. From each of these systems as a viewpoint a different critique of the passage is possible. For the farmers the pet lambs are not financially viable owing to the cost of the hand feeding and the risk of theft. From the view of the other lambs, the pet lambs are 'spoilt', unable to sustain themselves in the world. From the view of the passers-by, they could argue they are only weeding out of the gene pool those with mothering problems, as nature was trying to do in the first place. They are discouraging the farmer from being tempted to breed from the lambs when older.

The boundary dimension of system thinking may also be used to critique the entire passage as a story. What can be bounded in with the passage? What group of stories does it remind you of? What stories are totally different?

Critique questions

The above discussion might be summarised into a series of questions you might ask yourself about a passage.

Transforming (inputs and outputs)

- What are the inputs and outputs of the passage?

- What processes are involved in the passage?

- What gets transformed from what to what in the passage?

- Why is it transformed?

- How is the reader transformed?

- Are the outputs of the passage, the conclusion and recommendations fully justified?

Connectivity

- What is linked to what in the passage?

- Is there an identifiable social network in the passage?

- What is the passage connected to?

- What is its place in the literature, discipline or topic?

- What else has the author done?

- What does the passage remind you of, how does it sit with what else you know?

- What other evidence is available?

- What ripple effects will it have on wider systems?

- What do you see as the wider system on which it will have the largest impact?

- What genre, enquiry tradition and school of thought is it from?

Purpose

- What are the driving forces behind the actions of those in the passage?

- What is the driving force of the author?

- How else might the author's purpose (intention) have been achieved?

Analyse and synthesise

- **Do the details (facts) in the passage seem plausible?**

- **What details are missing or too inexact to be meaningful?**

- **What is similar to the passage?**

- **What does the passage remind you of?**

Boundary

- **Is the passage complete, does it present a self-contained story?**

- **How can the passage's contents be seen differently by rebounding the story around components of the passage?**

- **Are all the issues and concepts raised well defined and scoped?**

Summary

This chapter has suggested that a passage, written or spoken, can be critiqued using the dimensions associated with system thinking. These were transformation, connections, purposeful action, analysis and synthesis, and boundary. There are other dimensions to system thinking so these are only indicative of how a problem-solving stance might be turned into a critique stance. Examples of how the dimensions discussed might be applied were provided, although, again, this can only be thought of as indicative. For more on system thinking see Midgley's four-part collection (2003).

Exercises

1 **Critique the passage below using system thinking dimensions.**

One night we heard a crash outside. We guessed yet another car had driven off the winding road that passed by our house. Normally they went over the small 6 foot (2 metre) precipice into the tide trying to avoid driving into the cliff face on the other side of the road. We rushed out to help and found a car sitting in a few feet of seawater with the driver calmly at the wheel staring forward.

continued

continued

The local farmer, the nicest man you could meet, came up and told us not to worry, he knew the man in the car. He was drunk. The farmer waded out and knocked on the window offering to help. The driver slowly looked around and then suddenly started to shout, 'I don't want any bloody help from you, I'd rather bloody drown.' The farmer then waded back and with a smile said that there had been a misunderstanding between the two of them some years before.

Apparently, the farmer had been out helping with the birthing of new lambs when an unknown Red Setter had come bounding up to him very excited by the new lambs. A dog's presence worried the ewes, which meant they might abandon their lambs. Things got worse when the dog picked up a lamb and ran off. A short while later the dog returned and took another lamb. Naturally, the farmer went off to the village pub to ask if anyone knew the dog. The local lads, mostly farmers themselves, were angered by the report of a rogue dog. There were strict laws about dogs not being allowed near sheep at lambing time. Although the farmer tried to settle them down they rushed out, got their guns and waited in the paddock until the dog reappeared. They duly shot it.

That night the farmer got a knock on his door and the distressed owner of the dog was standing there holding two healthy lambs he had found in his front garden. He knew nothing of the shooting so was concerned that his dog was not at home. Clearly the man was extremely fond of his dog, very anxious for any news. The farmer explained that the dog had been shot. The man went ballistic, calling the farmer all sorts of names. It was the dog owner who was in the car, sitting waist deep in the tide.

2   **Critique the passage below using system thinking dimensions.**

A Consultant's Report

This report has been prepared in response to the question: 'Why did the chicken cross the road?'

Deregulation of the chicken's side of the road was threatening its dominant market position. The chicken was faced with significant challenges to create and develop the competencies required for the newly competitive market. MBA Consulting, in a partnering relationship with the client, helped the chicken by rethinking its physical distribution strategy and implementation processes. Using the Poultry Integration Model (PIM), MBA Consulting helped the chicken use its skills, methodologies, knowledge, capital and experiences to align the chicken's people, processes and technology in support of its overall strategy within a Program Management framework. MBA Consulting convened a diverse cross-spectrum of road analysts and best chickens along with MBA consultants with deep skills in the transportation industry to engage in a two-day itinerary of meetings in order to leverage their personal knowledge capital, both tacit and explicit, and to enable them to synergise with each other in order to achieve the implicit goals of delivering and successfully architecturing and implementing an enterprise-wide value framework across the continuum of poultry cross-median processes. The meeting was held in a hotel by the sea setting, enabling and creating an impactful environment which was strategically based, industry focused, and built upon a consistent, clear and unified market message and aligned with the chicken's mission, vision and core values. This was conducive towards the creation of a total business integration solution. MBA Consulting helped the chicken focus its change in direction.

Source: unknown

3   **Critique the passage below using system thinking dimensions. Hopefully you will provide a different critique from when this passage was used in the argument chapter.**

Few people will know where Invercargill is, the New Zealand one that is. It is a little town on the very southern tip of the real 'God's Own Country'. It must be a contender for the town closest to the Antarctic. For people growing up there in the 1950s and 1960s it must have felt fairly isolated despite the lovely countryside.

This story involves a young lad, about 11 years old, trying to make a little pocket money from a paper-round. You need to imagine a paper-round in Invercargill in those days. It involved going from one fairly remote house to another, often before dawn in the cold and rain. He did this lonely chore on his heavy old bicycle. One morning the lad arrived at the newsagent to pick up his papers and there was this dog he had never seen before sitting outside the newsagency. He noticed how very friendly it was, so he gave it a few strokes. On the way out the dog was still there, still being friendly, so the boy encouraged it to go with him on his lonely round. The dog looked extremely pleased and full of life. When the boy threw the first newspaper onto the porch of a house, the dog ran and fetched it back. It turned out to be a very long morning.

2

Gender, Race and Class Diversities in the Workplace

Dyer, S., Humphriews, M., Fitzgibbons, D. and Hurd, F.

Learning Objectives

To gain a growing understanding of the attractiveness of diversity management (DM) and the degree of emancipation this can deliver in the context of a wider and deeply embedded, competitive, market-orientated institutional logics, in this chapter we will:

- compare and contrast notions of equality, equity and fairness;
- examine the doctrines of equal employment opportunities (EEO) and affirmative action (AA) and their limitations;
- examine the emancipatory claims of diversity management.

CRITICAL CONCEPTS

Programmes of *equal (employment) opportunities* (EEO) and *affirmative action* (AA) are hard-won institutional responses to evidence of prejudice, racism, sexism and other forms of institutional discrimination that belie the claim for universal participation and empowerment of both neo-liberal and democratically orientated societies. This response has been overshadowed by a discourse of *diversity management* (DM).

EQUALITY, EQUITY AND DIVERSITY MANAGEMENT

[C]omparative findings suggest that members of Western, educated, industrialized, rich, and democratic societies ... are among the least representative populations one could find for generalizing about humans ... Overall, these empirical patterns suggest that we need

to be less cavalier in addressing questions of human nature on the basis of data drawn
from this particularly thin, and rather unusual, slice of humanity. (Henrich et al., 2010)

Henrich and colleagues (2010) invite us to think about the populations that
have been researched, and the misleading generalisations that have been drawn
from such research and become embedded as knowledge or truth about some
aspect of our humanity. The sampling has been taken from a very thin slice of
humanity! The influence of this selection bias has gained some attention in
management literature and teaching. The discussion of human diversity has
found a place in most textbooks for students who aspire to manage other people. What remains problematic, however, is the still deeply embedded precon-
ceptions about 'normal people' from which many management theories have
taken their shape.

Much of the empirical work that underpins model-making for theories in
organisation behaviour or human resource management, for example, was conducted on populations of workers that were most readily accessible to the
researcher. Researchers themselves were most likely to be Western-trained academics, often white and male, rarely openly gay, and most likely to have been
trained in one of the positivist sciences. Workers or workforces were the objects
of their research. The personal particulars of the people they studied might or
might not have been deemed important to the researcher. In the case of the
famous Hawthorne studies, gender blindness might be an apt description of the
researchers' considerations (Bendl, 2008; Emandi, 2012). Needless to say, this
resulted in some significant biases in the generalisations of research findings
and their applications to the management of employment.

We concur with, but do not rehearse in this chapter, the claims that are now
well supported in the literature that race, sex, sexual orientation, age, religion,
levels of physical (dis)ability and even perceived physical attractiveness make a
difference in terms of how people are treated and what individuals may anticipate as possible or not (Byrne, 1971). Their (self)-perceived identity, too, will
have an impact on the opportunities and the hurdles they experience and the
power they (believe they) can muster to manifest their hopes, to meet their
responsibilities and to access and protect their human rights to the means with
which to generate a flourishing life.

The intentional distinction between the words 'work' and 'paid employment'
has been discussed in previous chapters. In this chapter, we explain our emphasis on this distinction more fully. We revisit the use of these words when we
reconsider the unpaid work that subsidises the economic measures we are
expected to see as the indicators of global well-being. The way this discussion
plays out in typified areas of unjust organisational discrimination is where we
now refine our focus. Who gets to be employed, how and under what conditions
are increasingly challenged when it seems that people categorised *in one way*
appear to have more or less access to the jobs of influence and high rewards or
when categorised *in another way* may find themselves relegated to insecure,
unsafe, low-paid and dirty work. We examine more closely the influences that

may foster or inhibit the equal opportunities that are assumed to be a necessary dynamic in neo-liberal markets and in the organisation of Western democratic nations more generally. We suggest that the equal employment opportunities (EEO) and affirmative action (AA) programmes have been overshadowed by a discourse focused on diversity management (DM), a discourse that is attractive because it appears to make good business sense. What if EEO and AA approaches to demonstrable inequality of outcomes result in some form of proportional representation of diverse people in all occupations and in all institutional positions of the system? Has justice been served?

WORK AS A UNIVERSAL HUMAN RIGHT AND DUTY

Access to employment is codified as a universal human right in the United Nations Universal Declaration of Human Rights, the International Labour Organization Convention on Equal Pay and Discrimination, and the United Nations Convention on the Elimination of All Forms of Discrimination against Women (CEDAW). The redefinition of work as a human right not only raises issues in employment contexts, but is now so closely associated with the form of development being imposed on people the world over that we have reason to reconsider these instruments of emancipation in a more critical light. A broad-brush picture drawn from global statistics would suggest that in the global economy white men hold a disproportionate number of the well-rewarded jobs. Women from non-white gene pools, if they reach the labour market at all, hold a disproportionate number of the insecure and low-paid jobs. The old, the frail, the diagnosed disabled and increasingly the young seem also to have difficulty attaining secure, safe and well-paid employment. A finer grained examination will show some variation in this pattern, but not sufficiently so to dismiss the depiction of this disparate access to employment as invalid. While in Chapters 4 and 5 we examined the diverse ways in which human populations experience employment, and perhaps become defined by (in)access to employment, in this chapter we look more closely at how the diversity of human beings is managed to systemic benefit.

Historically, characteristics of the scope and design of many jobs assumed the unencumbered, white, able-bodied, male employee as the standard against which all others might be assessed. This is changing. There are two significant lines of reasoning about this change that need closer attention: (i) there will not be enough white males to hold all the jobs that need doing; and (ii) work, now redefined as a universal human right, must not only *be* accessible to all human beings, but it is being made *the duty* of almost all people to secure such employment as the most legitimate way to achieve a livelihood. Efforts to manipulate the relationship of diverse people with the ever-changing needs of the global economy, as discussed in Chapters 3, 4 and 5, has generated some significant differences in outcomes in distinctly patterned ways. Where these patterns are suspected to be the result of discrimination, both neo-liberals and more radical theorists agree that action is needed. Not all agree on what those actions should be. EEO programmes have proliferated for several decades. Their necessary corollary, AA, is often demonised. The issues of unequal inclusion and exclusion, however, seem intractable. Explanations as to why these EEO and AA approaches have not achieved their projected employment outcomes have been framed by some as 'the wrong focus' and by others as 'historically incomplete'. We have argued elsewhere that these approaches to diversity management have been allowed to be marginally successful in order to dissipate dissent and to ensure hegemonic integrity (see, for example, Humphries and Grice, 1995; Gatenby and Humphries, 1999a, b, 2000; McNicholas and Humphries, 2005; Humphries and Verbos, 2012).

Questioning the efficacy of equal employment commitments is among the more difficult exercises for students of management. Such programmes seem so enlightened to their advocates and so necessary to their enactors. How can they be deemed so pernicious to their critics? The critique of EEO and AA programmes can be vociferous – but for many different reasons. In Chapters 3 and 4 we examined the systemic changes in the global political economy and the significant impact of these changes on the structure, location and conditions of paid employment. We argued in those chapters that the changes we have examined contribute to the disparate outcomes in terms of who gains access to paid work and the level of remuneration associated with such employment. That disparate employment outcomes are experienced by particularly vulnerable groups within the global economy; for example, women, minorities, migrant workers and indigenous people. We now examine the rhetoric of equality (of opportunity) as it is shaped, supposedly in the interests of such vulnerable people.

The measurement of livelihoods, primarily framed in income terms, demonstrates radical disparities among nations, among individuals within nations, and among employees within and across occupations. The generation of an outcry by some against such disparities makes good sense – in a way. One proffered solution embedded in the philosophical positioning of neo-liberalism, as well as in policy initiatives promoted by the World Bank, the International Monetary Fund, the International Labour Organization, the OECD, the United Nations and many governments throughout the world is that all people must become more actively engaged in paid employment. The view that access to paid employment is a means to achieve social justice and to relieve poverty, as well as being a fundamental human right, are embedded in a number of United Nations and International Labour Organization conventions generated from the United Nations Universal Declaration of Human Rights endorsed in 1948 (see www.universalrights.net/main/creation.htm). These values are made explicit or implied in the constitutions of various democratic jurisdictions and are increasingly espoused in many corporate mission statements, particularly, but not only, by those corporations explicitly committed to the United Nations Global Compact introduced in Chapter 1.

A call to focus on local or distant poverty and the attractiveness of market remedies to alleviate this poverty is a good place to start thinking about the connection made between the notions of emancipation and paid employment. It seems such a reasonable connection to people who have long assumed its validity. Demonstrating that some people are living on less than a dollar a day (or below a specific poverty line determined in a particular jurisdiction) invites justification for (further) economic development of a particular Western capitalist type and pressure for the poor or poorly paid to improve their circumstances through paid employment – no matter what non-monetary riches such development may undermine or what the cost of this 'work' on offer may be. Women and men, people from various ethnic affiliations, experience efforts for their development differently. In the global economy, it is white men who continue to hold a disproportionate number of the most lucrative and influential jobs. White women have made some inroads into such careers. In general, a patterned outcome holds firm.

People jostling for jobs in our own communities – economic refugees subletting mattresses in Russia's basements in a desperate attempt to send money home to their dependents in Central Asia; Greek farming families pressured off their small landholdings by the stroke of a policy pen to make room for the more 'efficient' agri-businesses; South Americans looking north for livelihoods; seasonal workers whose opportunities are framed by politically controlled economic aspirations; and rural peoples flushed into cities to provide the labour for the booming or struggling industries – are diverse in many ways, but they also have much in common. Within each context, gender, age, race and so on, will have a specific manifestation. The patterns of their struggles suggest to critical theorists that their situation is systemically generated and the shaping of their situation goes well beyond anything they can be held personally responsible for. The eradication of almost all other forms of achieving a livelihood and the vagaries of where employment is to be found constitute a systemic pressure to search for, accept and remain engaged in employment – no matter how grim the conditions of work.

Advice on how to do so is prolific in the literature. Dani Monroe (2013) is a recent example of an expert in explaining the relationship of diversity and organisational change to the bottom line, the value of the hidden talents of their workforce, and the importance of resourcefulness, resilience and resolve. According to the publisher's promotional material, through Monroe's book, managers will 'learn to recognise *and mine* some key, fundamental leadership traits that are essential for a competitive business' (emphasis added). The way such mining plays out has diverse consequences. This invites closer scrutiny by liberals and radicals alike. The rhetoric of equal rights to participation and inclusion – a conceptualisation of equality framed as 'equal (employment) opportunity' (EEO) – is purportedly the insurance that all will have the opportunity to compete and be rewarded based on merit, two of the implied values of capitalism we question in this book. The outcomes of employment are demonstrably unequal. That this inequality takes specific patterns wherever the capitalist mode of development is undertaken invites an examination of potential systemic discrimination and selective privilege, dynamics deemed unacceptable in a meritocracy.

THE CIRCLE OF PRIVILEGE AND RESPONSIBILITY

Professor Jones has enjoyed her time in Hong Kong. Initially, she was angry at her husband, Ted, for taking a posting so far from her family in Germany. Now she was glad she had conceded. Here in Hong Kong they were able to secure two good maids to look after their children, to ensure the house was spotless, food cooked, and the car was cleaned. With domestic responsibilities reduced to supervision, she had been able to complete her PhD and gain significant research experience at the local university. Now Ted had taken a job in China and she was pleased to have scored a position as professor, a position well above the rank she might have achieved in Germany. In China, they would need only one maid. Which one could she most easily take with them? Which one would be most easily discarded? Both, she thought, had been lucky to have had time in her household. Both had improved their English. Both had been able to keep in touch with their families because of the generous phone allocations she had provided for them. Perhaps she could let them decide. After all, both were now in a better position to improve their circumstances than they were before she hired them.

Despite a significant challenge to the integrity of this blunt categorisation, we are each defined as either male or female. Even though biological sex and social(ised) gender categories are of much greater diversity than this two-option category suggests, census and employment forms are examples of where we must all affiliate with one identifier or the other. This is a further example of the confessing of identity we introduced in Chapter 5. Space constraints mean that we cannot cover all forms of discrimination in employment in this chapter. Thus, seemingly biologically determined but socially defined gender differences are the main thread of diversity discussions in this chapter – with the added emphasis that women and men, of course, are not 'homogeneous categories'.

Race, class, religion, sexual preferences, age, physical strength, intellectual agility, geographical location, number of dependants and so many other aspects of their being affect a person's ability to engage in paid employment. The race of privileged women also needs scrutiny because those who have experienced racism have been writing about white privilege for decades. From their worldview, it is self-evident that white people have directly and indirectly benefited from historic and contemporary processes of colonisation and institutional racism. Came (2012) reviews the emerging field of whiteness studies that seeks to make whiteness visible. She calls on a landmark essay on the subject by McIntosh (1988) who describes white privilege as a collection of unearned assets, an invisible weightless knapsack of white privilege that has special provisions such as: 'maps, passports, codebooks, visas, clothes, tools and blank checks' that can be cashed in at any time. McIntosh (1988: 1) explains 'whites are taught to think of their lives as morally neutral, normative, and average, and also ideal, so that when we work to benefit others, this is seen as work which will allow "them" to be more like "us".' In examining privilege, McIntosh and Came both maintain that it is necessary to confront the myth of meritocracy, the realisation that certain doors are opened and closed for people through no virtue of their own (Came, 2012: 88).

CREATING FAIR EMPLOYMENT

Paid Employment as a Fundamental Human Right

Access to decent paid employment is deemed a fundamental human right within the United Nations Universal Declaration of Human Rights (1948), by the International Labour Organization and in the United Nations Convention on the Elimination of All Forms of Discrimination against Women (1979, CEDAW). For example, Article 23 of the Universal Declaration of Human Rights states that everyone has the right to work of their own choosing, protection from unemployment, to fair and safe working conditions, equal pay for equal work, and pay levels that ensure 'for himself [sic] and his family an existence worthy of human dignity' which is to be supplemented by social protection if necessary. Moreover, Article 24 stipulates that 'Everyone has the right to rest and leisure, including reasonable limitation of working hours and periodic holidays with pay' (www.un.org/en/documents/udhr/).

The right to equal remuneration for equal work of equal value between men and women is further codified and more clearly defined in Article 1 of the International Labour Organization's Equal Remuneration Convention 100 (1951) where equal pay is to be based on rates 'of remuneration established without discrimination based on sex' (ILO, 1951). The International Labour Organization's Discrimination (Employment and Occupation) Convention 111 (1958), Article 1, defines discrimination in employment as: 'any distinction, exclusion or preference made on the basis of race, colour, sex, religion, political opinion, national extraction or social origin, which has the effect of nullifying or impairing equality of opportunity or treatment in employment or occupation' (ILO, 1958). Of the 183 ILO member nations, Conventions 100 and 111 have been ratified by 168 and 169 members respectively (ILO, 2011). More recently, a number of ILO conventions have been signed that seek to address discrimination in employment in a number of areas; for example, on the basis of sexual orientation, age, ethnicity, disability, indigenous status, parental status, including pregnancy, and marital status (ILO, 2007).

The United Nations CEDAW specifically addresses the persistent discrimination experienced by women in the political, social and economic realms. The focus of the CEDAW is to extend fundamental human rights that have been codified in various United Nations' documents and conventions to women by promoting equality of treatment between men and women in all areas of life. Embedded in the CEDAW is the recognition that discriminatory practices against women are perpetuated through legal, cultural and religious practices. The CEDAW also recognises that women's reproductive role has an impact on their access to employment. Article 11 of the CEDAW specifically focuses on eliminating gender discrimination in paid employment and incorporates many features embedded in the Declaration of Human Rights and in a number of ILO conventions. In Article 11, work is deemed to be 'an inalienable right of all human beings' (United Nations CEDAW, 1979).

As of October 2011, there were 187 parties to the CEDAW. To secure this right, Article 11 promotes equality of opportunity and treatment between men and women in all areas of the employment process. This begins with enabling women to freely choose work which is meaningful to them, through to apply-ing the same criteria in the selection, training, job evaluation and promotion processes, and ensuring equal pay for work of equal value, job security, paid sick leave and access to safe work environments, and social security in times of sickness, unemployment and retirement. How most people do not experience such freedom is discussed in Chapters 4 and 5. We assume that this must then be an aspirational position. Much energy, however, is going into achieving equal representation of women and men at all levels in all occupations. Such activity *is*, by definition, affirmative action. Opinions vary about what shape such action might be allowed to take. Perhaps most controversial and perhaps most effective are the instigation of mandatory quotas.

Anti-discrimination and Quota Legislation

To engage with any equalising activities is to engage with *affirmative action*. For many neo-liberal idealists, this is to corrupt the free workings of 'the market'.

DISCIPLINING THE QUOTA QUEEN

Lani Guinier served as Professor (and Chair) of the Afro-American Studies Department at Harvard University. In April 1993, President Bill Clinton nominated Lani for the position of Assistant Attorney General for Civil Rights. In the process of selection, President Clinton was informed that her interviews with senators were not going well and he was urged to withdraw the nomination (Geoff, 2012). Lani was branded a 'Quota Queen' – the kiss of death for any political career. By affiliation, she would become a career impediment for Clinton and his supporters. President Clinton took the advice of his elected officials and withdrew her nomination.

Despite the influential ideological preference for non-intervention in the free market as the arbiter of merit and outcomes, many nations have implemented minimum anti-discrimination and various forms of equal pay legislation as a means to redress the differentiated outcomes experienced by certain groups in society (Bell, 2007; ILO, 2011; Shore et al., 2011). Examples include the United Kingdom (Wells, 2003), the United States (Kohl et al., 2005), New Zealand (Harcourt et al., 2005) and European Union member nations (Lawson and Gooding, 2005).While such legislation differs around the world, it typically reflects the demographic features identified above. That is, the target groups or aspects identified in anti-discriminatory legislation have come to include women, people with disabilities, religious affiliation, sexual orientation, age, political affiliation, HIV/AIDS status, ethnicity, nationality and race (ILO, 2011).

Some countries – for example, Spain (ITUC, 2009) and Norway (Casey et al., 2011) – have extended anti-discrimination legislation to include quotas for women board membership. Hole (2010) reports that the implementation of a quota system in Norway has improved women's participation on boards from 7 per cent in 2003 to 38 per cent by 2008. Other nations – for example, New Zealand (Casey et al., 2011), Australia and Germany (ILO, 2011) – have minimal anti-discrimination legislation that underpins exhortations to voluntary development of internal policies to redress disparate employment outcomes between women and men. Increasingly visible is the rising concern about high and growing levels of youth unemployment and its gendered expression. Some analysts suggest that the class divide that has been the concern of Marxists and the gender divide that preoccupies feminists should be broadened to examine the intergenerational struggle for the means of life. The law as it stands everywhere and the policy responses that are emerging seem not to be stemming the rise in youth disaffiliation in Europe – with its attendant risks to social stability. While some organisations have implemented particular processes to achieve compliance with anti-discrimination legislation more recently, there is a different type of willingness to develop diversity strategies because employment of 'the best person for the job' regardless of their biological characteristics is deemed to make good business sense, an issue we now turn to.

MORPHING EEO AND AA INTO 'DIVERSITY MANAGEMENT'

Embedded in the business case for greater achievement of workplace diversity is a recognition that significant changes in the demographic composition of the workforce and customer base have occurred in recent decades. One source of this change is through global outsourcing of business activities in terms of the location of goods and services provision and the development of global markets as discussed in Chapters 3 and 4. In turn, this globalising process has significantly changed the ethnic, religious, language and nationality features of workforces and customer bases (Watson et al., 2009). Increased migration patterns have had similar effects on the demographic features of more localised communities, workforces and customer bases (ILO, 2010). In addition, many localised labour forces have been affected by an exponential growth in the number of women in the labour market (Lee et al., 2007) and, in many countries, by ageing workforces (ILO, 2011). Youth unemployment has reached a level so high in various places that calls for urgent interventions are amplifying, particularly in Europe where such calls are motivated at least to some extent by fears that youth, left in such dire circumstances, may be increasingly attracted to neo-Nazi-style, right-wing groups.

These changes in the demographic make-up of communities, labour forces and customer bases have some commentators arguing that diversity management takes on new meanings involving cross-border interactions between managers and workers with different backgrounds, cultures and languages (McVittie et al., 2008; Watson et al., 2009). In this environment, Ashkanasy and colleagues (2002) conclude that emotional intelligence and diversity management skills are required to be efficient, to retain customers and remain competitive. These types of discussions, now well embedded in some areas of management education and practice, might cover such concerns as, for example, the appropriateness of employing men in early childhood education or as assistants in women's underclothing retail. Equally controversial is the idea that bringing more women to the tables of power would enhance the likelihood of more peaceful and just negotiations (Myers, 2013). These kinds of examples rely on complex and inappropriate stereotyping.

At the organisational level, diversity management is offered as a solution to improve organisational performance and productivity in light of the demographic changes (Richard, 2000). In support of this view, a number of reports show that companies with women board members achieve profits that are higher than industry averages (*Catalyst*, 2004; Rosener, 2009). Applied to the national level, Goldman Sachs chief economist Tim Toohey reported that closing the gap between male and female workforce participation rates in Australia, and increasing women's participation rate in non-traditional, male-dominated and growth industries, would boost the economy by $180 billion (Ferguson, 2011). Applied to other nations, Toohey estimated that such an increase in women's participation rate would lead to GDP rises of 10 per cent in the United States, 20 per cent in Italy, 12 per cent in Germany, 11 per cent in Britain and 8 per cent in Sweden.

A number of explanations are offered as to why workforce diversity leads to improved productivity and profits. One argument embedded in human capital theory is that effective diversity management widens the potential pool of candidates, leading to hiring more skilled and qualified individuals (Meier et al., 1999; McVittie et al., 2008). A flow-on effect is the creation of diverse workgroups, who, it is argued, can draw upon their individually unique talents, skills and abilities reflective of their backgrounds. In doing so, such groups are believed to make better and more innovative decisions because they are less susceptible to 'group think' (McVittie et al., 2008).

A more recent analysis of why workforce diversity improves organisational performance and profits is tightly linked to the increased ethnic diversity within communities and customer bases resulting from globalisation and migration. The ILO (2011) estimates that workforces are made up of as much as 8–20 per cent of ethnically diverse workers. We note but will pass over the observation that all women have ethnicity and that this statistic vindicates the claim of white blindness we have made earlier. From this pragmatic perspective on ethnic diversity, it is argued that customer attraction, service and retention are enhanced by ensuring a match between the demographic composition of the workforce and that of the surrounding community (Andrews et al., 2005). Jackson and colleagues (2003) argue that there is a significant body of similarity-attraction literature that confirms people prefer to engage with those similar to themselves. Put another way, people have an aversion towards engaging with others who are perceived as dissimilar to themselves. Paradoxically perhaps, a heterogeneously diverse workforce enables the maintenance of homogeneous relationships between demographically similar employees and customers. It is this homogeneity in the relationship that is believed to enhance customer attraction, retention and service because of the comfort experienced by dealing with someone who shares a similar background, language or culture. Indeed, Andrews et al. (2005) conclude that a mismatch between workforce ethnic diversity and the demographic composition of the community had a negative association with organisational performance. Ashkanasy et al. (2002) suggest that matching workers and customers is particularly important in service organisations, as shared understandings enable service workers to understand and respond to customers. In turn, performance is said to improve because of increased customer loyalty and retention, and customer attraction through word-of-mouth advertising (Anderson et al., 1994; Wangenheim and Bayón, 2007).

BANKING ON GOOD DIVERSITY MANAGEMENT

Sheeba and her friend Marcus have worked at the same bank for some years. Their path up the professional ladder has been pretty similar. Now, however, a very senior job has become available in marketing. Sheeba and Marcus both want the job very much. The manager, Su, who is to make the decision, is facing a quandary. On the one hand, Sheeba has shown a great sensitivity to the cultural diversity of the community this bank serves. Marcus, however, is a man. Many of the bigger clients the bank wants to attract show a significant preference for dealing only with men. No one has spelled this out to Su. He just knows this in his gut, a gut feeling no doubt well informed by the subtle and not so subtle jokes that are exchanged at the swanky professional club he drinks at. On balance, it may be best to go with Marcus. Sheeba's personal capacities to challenge his decision are probably not as solid as those of Marcus. That in itself is worth a consideration. Sheeba, after all, has been comparing notes with Marcus in the tearoom about the plans each has to start a family – and that too is worth a thought.

While a number of scholars assert links between workforce diversity and increased productivity and profits, as discussed above, evidence of such a relationship in empirical research is a mixed bag (McPherson, 2008). For example, in their meta-analysis of 63 studies, Jackson et al. (2003) found limited and inconclusive evidence to support the claim that ethnic workforce diversity increases organisational performance. This conclusion was supported by Jehn and Bezrukova (2004). Others highlight that there may be a negative relationship between organisational performance and workforce diversity. Williams and O'Reilly (1998) show that ethnically diverse workgroups can experience miscommunication, conflict and poor cohesion, leading to lower group and, therefore, organisational performance. Richard (2000) points out that this might be so because effective diversity management requires supportive organisational structures and strategies. Shore et al. (2011) also suggest that such negative results might be partially explained by the initial emphasis of diversity strategies which focused on increasing the proportions of target groups within organisations, with little emphasis placed on integrating and including them within the organisation. They propose that it is timely for diversity management strategies to move beyond a preoccupation with numbers and move towards developing inclusive strategies that enable the valuing of diverse input.

EEO, AA AND MANAGING DIVERSITY

Combined, equal employment opportunity (EEO), affirmative action (AA) and the more recent diversity management (DM) provide the legal, philosophical and practical frameworks aimed at achieving a diverse workforce and avoiding costly challenges to discriminatory practices. Moreover, the philosophical and practical methods associated with these three approaches are advocated as mechanisms to help comply with anti-discrimination legislation, by some groups seeking to achieve human rights and fairness through access to paid employment (e.g., ILO, 2011), as well as by those who view diversity management as a means to enhance business performance.

AA has often related specifically to legislated quota systems and, as an approach, has its roots in the United States, though, as noted above, it has been adopted more recently in a number of jurisdictions as a means to enhance the entry of women into senior leadership positions (Burgess et al., 2009; ILO, 2011). While variations can be found, definitions of EEO typically embed many of the human rights issues apparent in the Declaration of Human Rights, the CEDAW and the ILO conventions discussed above. For example, such definitions include notions of eliminating explicit or implicit barriers throughout all aspects of employment, including recruitment, selection, training, pay and rewards, career development and promotion to ensure that decisions throughout the process are based on individual merit and fairness. By doing so, EEO, then, is deemed a means to enhance an individual's ability freely to choose work that is of interest to them. Similarly, many definitions make explicit links between EEO and the business case presented above, by promoting the proposition that an individual's ability to choose work of interest that reflects their skills to personal productivity will enhance motivation, loyalty, commitment and organisational performance.

A number of nations combine a legislative approach with a voluntarist approach to achieving workforce diversity. For example, some countries specify a limited range of target groups, or apply anti-discrimination legislation to specific sectors or to specific organisations based on, for example, size (Burgess et al., 2009; Dyer and Hurd, 2011). Organisations or sectors that are not specifically covered by EEO or AA legislation may be encouraged to adopt practices that enhance worker diversity. This approach is most closely aligned with the notion of managing diversity (Burgess et al., 2009). Thomas (2001) suggests that while anti-discrimination legislative approaches provide the entry of target groups into the workforce, managing diversity practices provide the means within which to enhance the productivity and development of the newly created diverse workforce. In many ways, this reflects the view of Burgess and colleagues (2009) that the management of diversity is more closely aligned with the business case, and Shore and co-workers (2011) who argue that, while the initial focus of diversity was to increase target group numbers in non-traditional fields of employment, the task now is to include and value diversity within the organisation.

Regardless of whether codified in law or taken up as a voluntary initiative by organisational leaders, there are a number of practices that have been recognised and promoted as facilitating the achievement of equal employment outcomes and effective diversity management. Topical among these are the development of work–life balance initiatives, many of which focus on various forms of flexibility around start and finish times of work and the location of jobs. More longstanding initiatives include sexual harassment and bullying policies, and the development of informal and formal mentoring and networking relationships (Tremall and Nierenberg, 2006). However, despite the significant and sustained interest in enhancing EEO at the level of the United Nations and at national and organisational levels, disparate employment outcomes continue based on gender, ethnicity, race, religion, sexuality and so on (ILO, 2011).

EXPLAINING DISPARATE EMPLOYMENT OUTCOMES

Research continues to show that a number of organisational practices continue to affect the allocation and rewards associated with work, and how workers are treated within the organisational context. For example, women and minorities are still more likely to be hired into positions that are not linked to formal (and informal) career paths. Women continue to experience discrimination surrounding maternity and are more likely to experience sexual harassment in the workplace (ILO, 2011).

Structural explanations look beyond organisational practices to consider why disparate outcomes continue. For example, women still perform the majority of the unpaid work in the home which directly affects their ability to participate in paid employment on an 'equal footing' to men. The structural explanation also highlights the connection between globalisation, changes in economic and political policies and the low wages attributed to the jobs held primarily by women. In the global economy, women feature as the low-wage workers in manufacturing and services, and even where women compete directly in the same domain as men, their wages are often much lower than their male counterparts (see, for example, recent publications by the OECD, the United Nations, the ILO, or your own nation's income statistics). The current structure of employment divides workers globally through outsourcing specifically to less-expensive but appropriately skilled labour. Women have been particularly vulnerable in this process, as employment has shifted globally to where the cheaper, often female labour force can be sourced.

Combined, these structural considerations provide evidence to support the argument that patriarchal values are embedded in, produced and reproduced within the global economy. Moreover, the way that paid and unpaid work is structured, organised, allocated and rewarded acts to produce and reproduce traditional male-breadwinner/female-caregiver roles within the home, regardless of how couples might prefer to organise themselves and their families. Because men are more likely to be paid more, couples may by necessity divide their work load to maximise the income to the family, and by doing so reproduce the structural constraints that affect women's ability to engage in paid employment. Thus, notions of freedom of choice to make individual decisions with regard to employment, and to be rewarded according to merit achieved on an apparent level playing field, become more myth than reality, but a myth supported by what might appear at face value to be rational choices made by well-informed individuals and by organisational work–life balance initiatives aimed at enhancing women and men's working lives.

MEET THE TEACHER

Jesse is a teacher. This week it is 'meet-the-teacher' week at her school. On these days, Jesse will be at school from 8 a.m. to 8 p.m. Her own little daughters, Ella (8) and Rebecca (5), will be free from their class from 1 p.m. for two afternoons that week. The day before the first 'meet-the-teacher' day, Jesse's friend found her in her classroom looking anxious and upset. An administrator had just delivered a set of documents that required her to provide new measurements of children's achievements to complete quality assurance documentation urgently required by the Principal for a funding application. The documents appear to have little to do

(Continued)

(Continued)

with the good teaching of children. The school, however, could certainly do with the extra funding the Principal is seeking. In the interests of the children, Jesse believes that she had better complete the forms. She realises that this week she would be at school for an additional two evenings and also parts of the weekend to cope with the backlog of work. Jesse misses her children and her children miss her. At home, the laundry is building up. Housework has been put aside for precious time with Ella and Rebecca. It all seems so huge! Jesse cannot afford to work part-time. Her Mum would love to help her, but she has her own job issues to contend with, including an intercity commute to manage her job and other family commitments, commitments that include some care for her own increasingly frail mother. Jesse wishes she, Ella and Rebecca could visit their grandmother more often. There just is not the time to do so. Is *this* what the liberal feminists Jesse had admired in college had intended to achieve?

Underpinning the discussion of employment are particular definitions and (de)valuations of paid and unpaid work. Work is recognised in the United Nations Universal Declaration of Human Rights and the CEDAW as an inalienable human right. A definition and valuing of paid and unpaid work can be found in the United Nations National Accounting System. Paid work is valued according to the dollar amount this work contributes to national economic and financial wealth, and is recorded in gross domestic product figures. In contrast, unpaid work – for example, that which is done in the home, including raising and nurturing children – is defined as not contributing to the financial wealth of a nation, and hence is deemed of little or no value (Waring, 1999). These definitions and values of paid and unpaid work are embedded in the WTO, the IMF and the World Bank, as well as OECD policy initiatives, and can be discerned in many national-level legislative frameworks, as well as being manifest in social and economic policies. Importantly, GDP figures help determine budget allocations; moreover, by these definitions, the majority of women's work the world over is not accounted in GDP figures, and hence much of women's contribution to society is ignored by their governments, and, as a result, by proxy, men's contribution is deemed more valuable to society.

From a critical perspective, an analysis of the assumptions embedded in the way work is defined, structured, allocated and rewarded not only helps to highlight which particular set of meanings and practices have become taken for granted and common sense, but, importantly, how those meanings shape, produce and reproduce power relations within society. Developing this line of reasoning, we argue that the philosophical underpinnings of EEO and AA provide a liberal solution to a fundamentally neo-liberal problem. That is, at the philosophical level, EEO and AA advocates focus on the individual and the removal of all artificial barriers preventing such individuals, regardless of race, gender, ethnicity, parental status and so on, accessing the employment of their choice and that which they are capable of performing. This focus on individuals and paid employment is in harmony with the neo-liberal philosophical position that individuals ought to be responsible for looking after the self through paid employment, and, again, regardless of race, gender, ethnicity, parental status and so on. However, as part of a greater commitment or subjugation to neo-liberalist ideals, many nations have withdrawn their legislative as well as philosophical support for full employment policies achieved by legislation or policy pressures. Market-orientated rules governing employment relationships, including enabling offshoring, as discussed in Chapters 3 and 4, prevail. As a set of initiatives, EEO or AA policies and practices cannot create employment, but having such policies and practices in place gives the appearance that disparate employment outcomes can be attributed to individual success and failure in the market. Such an approach ignores the systemic practice of vulnerable groups drawn in and pushed out of employment along with boom–bust cycles (Burgess et al., 2009) and the growing power of business to determine the conditions, location and reward associated with work within the global economy.

CONCLUSION

The sense of duty to find and maintain employment for one's personal survival and the care of one's dependants is a fabricated necessity that is easily manipulated by the powerful to serve their interests. The vast array of values and beliefs, of personal and group identities, of desirable skills and attitudes, of geographical locations, and of access to power are just some of the diversity considerations to be managed. Despite claims to valuing diversity, through the imposition of a kind of mono-cultural, instrumental and functional notion of humanity, workers are generally treated as atomised labour widgets in patterns of employment devised to provide flexibility for the system's changing needs. Many are held entranced by a delusional metaphor of the self-actualising man (and some kind of enabling woman who probably also needs a job). Even very self-aware and self-directed people can be challenged, re-configured and re-harnessed to the interests of 'globalisation'.

EEO and managing diversity have been depicted in this chapter as a neo-liberal solution to a neo-liberal problem, that of shifting the emphasis from employment as a fundamental and inalienable human right to that of an individual responsibility. In the context of a global economy, based on patriarchal and neo-colonialist values and underpinned by structural unemployment, EEO and managing diversity, embedded with merit principles, shift the responsibility of obtaining employment and the blame of not obtaining employment onto individuals and therefore abdicate responsibility from governments to address structural and social inequalities to the individual.

TALK BOX   STEPPING IN 'GOOD OLE BOY POOH'

From an email conversation in 2012 between two professional women, each in an institution with explicit EEO and anti-discrimination policies:

'I stuck my foot in some "good ole boy pooh" this week! I went to the worst presentation I have ever seen given by a candidate for a job in our department. In the supposedly confidential feedback process we were required to contribute to, I said as much. I was told by the colleague whose office is next to mine that my opinion was totally inappropriate. My comments were obviously forwarded to him, and probably to the job candidate too. It turns out that they are friends! I might as well paint a target on my back. It will be open season on me if he gets the job – or maybe even more so if he does not! It is so ugly. And here I am fretting over it and emailing you about what a mess I have made when I should be getting my next project out. So this is how unqualified males get hired over more qualified minorities or women!'

- Does the 'danger' in the story hinge on the gender of the three main characters?
- Are you aware of similar incidences where an under-qualified 'in-group' member achieved employment?
- What are the implications from (i) a human rights perspective; (ii) an EEO perspective; (iii) an AA perspective; and (iv) a business case perspective?
- How much energy, distraction and demotivation are generated by various forms of discrimination at work, in education and elsewhere?

Tricky Questions

- Organisational behaviour texts tell us that, in selection interviews, decisions are often made in the very first few minutes of an interview. What dynamics may be at play in those early minutes?
- Researchers in management education have found that the same piece of written work assumed to be written by a male attracts higher scores than if the work has been attributed to a female. What does this indicate for all aspects of careers in management, politics and media, in particular, but in other careers as well?
- 'Passing for' and 'coming out' are two terms used by people who, through certain biological features, can 'pass for' members of the dominant group. 'Coming out' (or being 'out-ed') has significant career implications. Can you find examples of courageous people who 'came out' to 'call out' those who are part of a repressive regime of discrimination, subtle or covert? What were the consequences of their actions? Examples may include the US military 'Do not ask' policies.
- In a system that is competitive, does not have room for all, but is the only or main means to a livelihood, what does/should happen to those for whom there is no room?

ment flexibility. If 'equality' or even 'proportional representation' is
deemed to have been achieved within the current structural environment (e.g.,
those in paid employment reflect personal identity characteristics in proportion
to their presence in the composition of the community) what would we have
achieved? How do 'ousted' groups/individuals take care of their survival needs?
- What would have to occur to achieve the human rights and social justice principles inherent in the ILO position on access to paid employment? What concerns does this position not adequately address?

ADDITIONAL RESOURCES

Berg, N. and Lien, D. (2002) Measuring the effect of sexual orientation on income:
evidence of discrimination. *Contemporary Economic Policy*, 29: 394–415.
Humphries, M.T. (2011) The bully in the workplace. In J. Marques, S. Dhiman and
J. Biberman (eds), *Stories to Tell your OB Students*. New York: Palgrave-
Macmillan. pp. 60–2.
Jackson, S., Brett, J., Sessa, V., Cooper, D., Julin, J. and Peyronnin, K. (1991) Some
differences make a difference: individual dissimilarity and group heterogeneity as
correlates of recruitment, promotions, and turnover. *Journal of Applied
Psychology*, 76: 675–89.
Keough, L.J. (2006) Globalizing 'postsocialism': mobile mothers and neoliberalism
on the margins of Europe. *Anthropological Quarterly*, 79 (3): 431–62.
Komisar, L. (2013) At the end, Betty Friedan broadened her vision (www.
thekomisarscoop.com/2013/03/at-the-end-betty-friedan-broadened-vision/;
retrieved 10 September 2013).
Pines, A.M., Lerner, M. and Schwartz, D. (2010) Gender differences in entrepre-
neurship: equality, diversity and inclusion in times of global crisis. *Equality,
Diversity and Inclusion: An International Journal*, 29 (2): 186–98.
Sacks, J. (2002) *The Dignity of Difference: How to Avoid the Clash of Civilisations*.
London: Continuum.
Thomas, A. and Humphries, M.T. (2011) Alternative futures filling the empty signi-
fier with the rhetoric of emancipation: drawing women into the market – a case
in point. Paper presented at the 7th International Critical Management Studies
Conference, Naples, 11–13 July.
Waring, M. (1995) Who's counting? Marilyn Waring on sex, lies and global econom-
ics, dir. T. Nash (www.nfb.ca/film/whos_counting; retrieved 14 September 2013).

REFERENCES

Anderson, E., Fornell, C. and Lehmann, D. (1994) Customer satisfaction, market
share, and profitability: findings from Sweden. *Journal of Marketing*, 58 (3): 53–66.
Andrews, R., Boyne, G., Meier, K., O'Toole, Jr, L. and Walker, R. (2005) Representative
bureaucracy, organisational strategy, and public service performance: an empirical

analysis of English local government. *Journal of Public Administration Research and Theory*, 15: 489–504.

Ashkanasy, N., Hartel, C. and Daus, C. (2002) Diversity and emotion: the new frontiers in organisational behavior research. *Journal of Management*, 28 (3): 307–38.

Bell, M.P. (2007) *Diversity in Organizations*. Mason, OH: South-Western.

Bendl, R. (2008) Gender subtexts: reproduction of exclusion in organizational discourse. *British Journal of Management*, 19 (1): 50–64.

Burgess, J., French, E. and Strachan, G. (2009) The diversity management approach to equal employment opportunity in Australian organisations. *Economic and Labour Relations Review*, 20 (1): 77–93.

Byrne, D. (1971) *The Attraction Paradigm*. New York: Academic Press.

Came, H. (2012) Institutional racism and the dynamics of privileges in public health. PhD thesis, University of Waikato, Hamilton, New Zealand.

Casey, C., Skibnes, R. and Pringle, J.K. (2011) Gender equality and corporate governance: policy strategies in Norway and New Zealand. *Gender, Work and Organization*, 18 (6): 613–30.

Catalyst (2004) The bottom line: connecting corporate performance and gender diversity. *Catalyst* (www.catalyst.org/knowledge/bottom-line-connecting-corporate-performance-and-gender-diversity; retrieved 10 September 2013).

Dyer, S. and Hurd, F. (2011) Gendered perceptions of corporate restructuring and community change in a single industry town. *NZ Sociology*, 26 (1): 68–88.

Emandi, E.M. (2012) Conflicting views of women in Hawthorne. *Gender Studies*, 12 (2): 147–56.

Ferguson, A. (2011) A call to get more women working. *The Age* (www.theage.com.au/national/a-call-to-get-more-women-working-20110826-1jem1.html; retrieved 10 September 2013).

Gatenby, B. and Humphries, M.T. (1999a) Defining careers. *International Career Journal*, 2 (3/4).

Gatenby, B. and Humphries, M.T. (1999b) Exploring gender, management education and careers: speaking in the silences. *Gender and Education*, 11 (3): 281–94.

Gatenby, B. and Humphries, M.T. (2000) The more things change, the more they stay the same: reconstructing gender through women's careers. *Australian Journal of Career Development*, 9 (1): 45–53.

Geoff, K. (2012) Susan Rice: This Decade's Lani Guinier. The Root (www.theroot.com/blogs/blogging-beltway/susan-rice-lani-guinier-sisters-witch-hunt; retrieved 28 September 2013).

Harcourt, M., Lam, H. and Harcourt, S. (2005) Unions and discriminatory hiring: evidence from New Zealand. *Industrial Relations*, 44 (2): 364–73.

Henrich, J., Heine, S.J. and Norenzayen, A. (2010) The weirdest people in the world? *Behavioral and Brain Sciences*, 33 (2–3): 61–135.

Hole, A. (2010) Government action to bring about gender balance (www.20-first.com/406-0-a-personal-account-of-the-quota-legislation-in-norway.html; retrieved 10 September 2013).

Humphries, M.T. and Grice, S. (1995) Equal employment opportunity and the management of diversity: a global discourse of assimilation? *Journal of Organizational Change Management*, 8 (5): 17–33.

Humphries, M.T. and Verbos, A. (2012) Decoupling equality, diversity, and inclusion from liberal projects. *Equality, Diversity and Inclusion: An International Journal*, 31 (5/6): 506–25.

ILO (International Labour Organization) (1951) *Equal Remuneration Convention No. 100.* Geneva: ILO.

ILO (International Labour Organization) (1958) *C111: Discrimination (Employment and Occupation) Convention, 1958 (No. 111)* (www.ilo.org/ilolex/cgi-lex/convde.pl?C111; retrieved 28 September 2013).

ILO (International Labour Organization) (2007) *Equality at Work: Tackling the Challenges.* Geneva: ILO.

ILO (International Labour Organization) (2010) *Global Wage Report 2010/11: Wage Policies in Times of Crisis* (www.ilo.org/wcmsp5/groups/public/---dgreports/---dcomm/---publ/documents/publication/wcms_145265.pdf; retrieved 10 September 2013).

ILO (International Labour Organization) (2011) Equality at work: the continuing challenge. Global report under the follow-up to the ILO Declaration on Fundamental Principles and Rights at Work. International Labour Conference 100th Session. Geneva: ILO.

ITUC (International Trade Union Confederation) (2009) *Gender In(equality) in the Labour Market: An Overview of Global Trends and Developments.* Brussels: ITUC.

Jackson, S., Joshi, A. and Erhardt, N. (2003) Recent research on team and organisational diversity: SWOT analysis and implications. *Journal of Management,* 29 (6): 801–30.

Jehn, K. and Bezrukova, K. (2004) A field study of group diversity, group context, and performance. *Journal of Organizational Behavior,* 25 (6): 703–29.

Kohl, J.M., Mayfield, M. and Mayfield, J. (2005) Recent trends in pregnancy discrimination law. *Business Horizons,* 48 (5): 421–9.

Lawson, A. and Gooding, C. (eds) (2005) *Disability Rights in Europe: From Theory to Practice.* Oxford: Hart.

Lee, S-H., McCann, D., Messenger, J.C and International Labour Organization (2007) *Working Time around the World: Trends in Working Hours, Laws and Policies in a Global Comparative Perspective.* London: Routledge/Geneva: ILO.

McIntosh, P. (1988) White privilege: unpacking the invisible knapsack. Working paper 189. *Peace and Freedom,* 10 (2): 1–2 (www.areteadventures.com/articles/white_privilege_unpacking_the_invisible_napsack.pdf; retrieved 10 September 2013).

McNicholas, P. and Humphries, M.T. (2005) Decolonisation through critical career research: Maori women and accounting. *Australian Career Development Journal,* 14 (1): 30–9.

McPherson, M. (2008) *Diversity and Equality: Evidence of Positive Business Outcomes and How to Achieve Them. A Review of the Literature.* Auckland, NZ: Equal Employment Opportunities Trust.

McVittie, C., McKinlay, A. and Widdicombe, S. (2008) Organizational knowledge and discourse of diversity in employment. *Journal of Organizational Change Management,* 21 (3): 348–66.

Meier, K., Wrinkle, R. and Polinard, J. (1999) Representative bureaucracy and distributional equity: addressing the hard question. *Journal of Politics,* 61 (4): 1025–39.

Monroe, D. (2013) *Untapped Talent: Unleashing the Power of the Hidden Workforce.* Basingstoke: Palgrave Macmillan.

Myers, D.D. (2013) Viewpoint: what if women ruled the world? *BBC News Magazine,* 8 March (www.bbc.co.uk/news/world-21661744; retrieved 10 September 2013).

Richard, O. (2000) Racial diversity, business strategy, and firm performance: a resource-based view. *Academy of Management Journal*, 43 (2): 164–77.

Rosener, J. (2009) Women on corporate boards makes good business sense (www. womensmedia.com/lead/87-women-on-corporate-boards-makes-good-business-sense.html; retrieved 10 September 2013).

Shore, L.M., Randel, A.E., Chung, B.G., Dean, M.A., Ehrhart, K.H. and Singh, G. (2011) Inclusion and diversity in work groups: a review and model for future research. *Journal of Management*, 37 (4): 1262–89.

Thomas, R. (2001) From affirmative action to affirming diversity. In *Harvard Business Review on Managing Diversity*, pp. 1–32. Boston, MA: Harvard Business School.

Tremall, S. and Nierenberg, S. (2006) 'Blending in' vs. 'sticking together': women of color use differing strategies for informal networking, catalyst study finds (http://catalyst.org/media/blending-vs-sticking-together-women-color-use-differing-strategies-informal-networking; retrieved 10 September 2013).

United Nations CEDAW (1979) United Nations Convention on the Elimination of All Forms of Discrimination against Women (www.un.org/womenwatch/daw/cedaw/text/econvention.htm#article11; retrieved 10 September 2013).

Wangenheim, F. and Bayón, T. (2007) The chain from customer satisfaction via word-of-mouth referrals to new customer acquisition. *Journal of the Academic of Marketing Science*, 35 (2): 233–49.

Waring, M. (1999) *Counting for Nothing: What Men Value and What Women are Worth*. Toronto: University of Toronto Press.

Watson, B., Spoonley, P. and Fitzgerald, E. (2009) Managing diversity: a twenty-first century agenda. *New Zealand Journal of Employment Relations*, 34 (2): 61–76.

Wells, K. (2003) The impact of the Framework Employment Directive on UK disability discrimination law. *Industrial Law Review*, 32 (4): 253–73.

Williams, K. and O'Reilly, C. (1998) Demography and diversity in organisations: a review of 40 years of research. In B.M. Staw and L.L. Cummings (eds), *Research in Organisational Behavior*, 20: 77–140. Greenwich, CT: JAI Press.

3

What is Organizational Behavior?

Scandura, T.

A CRISIS OF LEADERSHIP?

Recent polls conducted by the Gallup organization show that about 70% of people who hold full-time jobs in the United States either hate their jobs or have "mentally checked out."[1] This is a large impact considering that an estimated 100 million people work full-time in the United States. Workers who hate their jobs cost their organizations millions of dollars in low productivity. Even worse, many of the Gallup survey respondents reported actively engaging in destructive behavior by spreading their dissatisfaction throughout their organizations. One of the most important things the Gallup study found is that the source of dissatisfaction is not pay or the number of hours worked, however.

Most employees in Gallup's study reported that the reason for their disengagement from work was their boss. And this is not new. This study was a follow-up of an earlier study conducted from 2008 to 2010, which showed similar discontent with work and leaders. Why? Isn't there something that can be done to improve the well-being, motivation, and productivity of people at work? Is anyone working on addressing the concerns of the workforce? The answer is yes. There is a field of study called organizational behavior (or sometimes called OB for short) that studies the challenges leaders face in the workforce. Unfortunately, much of the knowledge that could help leaders improve the experience of work is tucked away in scientific journals that few managers have the time to read.

The goal of this book is to help you become an effective leader—not the kind of leader described in the Gallup poll that produces discontented workers. You can choose to be a leader who understands the fundamentals of OB—how to motivate followers, resolve conflicts, lead teams, and even help them manage stress during change. For example, effective communication is essential for leadership, and this is covered in Chapter 11. After reading this textbook, your approach to leading others will be grounded in the most important and current research conducted on organizations.

Learning Objectives

After studying this chapter, you should be able to do the following:

1.1. Define the concept of organizational behavior (OB).

1.2. List and give examples of the four sources of information used in evidence-based management (EBM).

1.3. Define critical thinking, and explain the critical thinking skills leaders need.

1.4. Describe the scientific method used in OB research.

1.5. Discuss four types of outcome variables studied in OB.

1.6. Compare the levels of analysis in OB research.

1.7. Develop plans for using OB research to improve employee job performance.

Get the edge on your studies at
edge.sagepub.com/scandura
* Take the chapter quiz
* Review key terms with eFlashcards
* Explore multimedia resources, SAGE readings, and more!

$SAGE edge™

WHAT IS ORGANIZATIONAL BEHAVIOR?

Learning Objective 1.1: Define the concept of organizational behavior (OB).

OB is defined as the study of individuals and their behaviors at work. It is an interdisciplinary and multilevel research area that draws from applied psychology, cultural anthropology, communication, and sociology. This textbook draws upon all of these areas with a focus on applied social psychology. Social psychologists study the behavior of individuals in groups, so it makes sense that the study of how leaders influence people and their OB is grounded in this field of psychology.

OB is a relatively young field in comparison to areas in the field of medicine—and even psychology from which it draws. There were management practices in place since the early 1900s with Frederick Taylor's approach to "scientific management," which was the study of how work could be designed to make production work (particularly assembly lines) more efficient.[2] Most scholars agree, however, that OB (in contrast to management) started with the Hawthorne studies (conducted between 1927 and 1932), which led to a focus on the role of human behavior in organizations. The Hawthorne studies were two studies conducted by Australian-born psychologist Elton Mayo at the Western Electric Company near Chicago.[3]

Mayo spent most of his career at Harvard University and was interested in how to increase productivity in assembly lines. The first study was designed to examine the effects of lighting in the plants on worker productivity. However, the research team had a surprise. Productivity *increased* rather than decreased even though the lights were being dimmed. Perplexed by this finding, the research team interviewed the workers and learned that the workers appreciated the attention of the research team and felt that they were receiving special treatment. And then productivity *declined* after the researchers left the plant. This has been called the Hawthorne effect and refers to positive responses in attitudes and performance when researchers pay attention to a particular group of workers.

The second Hawthorne study was designed to investigate a new incentive system. However, instead of the incentive system increasing workers' production, the social pressure from peers took over and had more impact on worker productivity. Workers formed into small groups and set informal standards for production, requiring coworkers to reduce their production so pay was more equal among the group members.

The Hawthorne researchers concluded that the human element in organizations was more important than previously thought, and they learned that workers want attention. This is still relevant today. For example, recent work demonstrates that when employers provide gifts to employees (termed *empathy wages*), it elicits feelings of gratitude from them.[4] The "human relations" movement followed the Hawthorne studies, and OB emerged as a distinct field of study in the 1950s. Today, OB researchers have PhDs from psychology departments (in the area of industrial and organizational psychology) and business schools. They teach from the research base on OB and conduct research that addresses important challenges facing organizational leaders today.

Applied Social Psychology

Applied social psychology is the study of how people interact in groups and addresses significant challenges facing leaders today. Trends such as the need to compete in a global marketplace, organizational restructuring, and rapid changes in technology have resulted in the need to lead through change. OB is an applied field of study aimed at problem solving for organizational leaders. For example, OB researchers study how stress affects employee well-being. Another example is how a leader's vision affects follower motivation and performance toward goals. A third example is how frustrations with one's boss might lead to an employee quitting the organization (this is called turnover). Low productivity and turnover cost organizations millions of dollars. Beyond the impact on costs, employee well-being is a major concern for forward-thinking organizations today. OB researchers develop guidelines that directly address such challenges. Based on research, leaders can make better decisions to make their organization more effective and better places to work. In sum, the goal of OB as a field is to improve the functioning of the organization and how employees experience their work.

From Theory to Practice

OB is an applied science, so first it is necessary to briefly review what science is all about. The goals of science—any science—are as follows:

1. Description: What does the process look like?
2. Prediction: Will the process occur again? And when?
3. Explanation: Why is this happening?
4. Control: Can we change whether or not this happens?

For example, the forecasting of toy sales during the holiday season is an important process for the planning of manufacturing runs. Marketers have an understanding of why children want a particular toy (in other words, a theory) and can describe the colors and features of the toy. This theory is also fairly high on explanation since scientists have some understanding of why children want a particular toy. Prediction is important since marketers need to project with some accuracy what the demand will be for their products. However, sales forecasts are not always accurate, resulting in stock shortages (remember Tickle Me Elmo?) or the production of too many toys that must be sold at discounts. In this example, the science is moderate for prediction. For control, one could say that the science is low because there are many reasons why a toy may not sell that are outside of the organization's control (e.g., a better product from a competitor suddenly appearing on the market). This example illustrates why theories are so important to science. The better the initial understanding of why children want a toy, the better the marketing research department should be able to predict the demand for it. Theories are also important to OB as a science since theory is translated into leadership practice and this will be discussed next.

The phrase "there is nothing as practical as a good theory" has been attributed to social psychologist Kurt Lewin. Theories build upon prior research and extend into new areas of importance to leaders. A researcher generates hypotheses about human behavior in organizations and then gathers data to test it. Research eliminates the guesswork about what will work (or not work), and this helps leaders solve the problems they face every day. The ability to translate research to practice has been termed evidence-based management (EBM).

EVIDENCE-BASED MANAGEMENT

Learning Objective 1.2: List and give examples of the four sources of information used in evidence-based management (EBM).

Proving
Management
Matters

The term *evidence-based* was originally employed in the field of medicine to guide how doctors make decisions regarding patient care. EBM improves a leader's decisions by disciplined application of the most relevant and current scientific evidence. Although many definitions of EBM are available, this is the most frequently quoted and widely used:[5] EBM means making decisions about the management of employees, teams, or organizations through the conscientious, explicit, and judicious use of four sources of information:

1. The best available scientific evidence—for example, research published on OB
2. The best available organizational evidence—for example, interviews or surveys completed by people in an organization
3. The best available experiential evidence—for example, the intuition of the leader and his or her expert opinions
4. Organizational values and stakeholders' concerns—for example, stock price or groups that focus on whether the organization employs environmentally friendly practices

How can a leader use these sources of evidence to make better decisions? The following standards may be applied by leaders using EBM to ask questions and challenge their thinking about their organizations:[6]

1. Stop treating old ideas as if they were brand new. This has resulted in a cynical workforce that may view innovations from leaders as short-term fads (e.g., positive changes such as total quality management, teams, and engagement). Progress cannot be made by treating old ideas as new ones; cynicism could be reduced by presenting ideas that have been able to "stand the test of time" as best practices rather than new ideas.
2. Be suspicious of "breakthrough" studies and ideas. Question whether some new ideas in management are really breakthroughs, and be wary of claims about new management principles that may be either overstated or understated.[7]
3. Develop and celebrate collective brilliance.[8] In theory, a diverse collection of independent decision makers (although not expert) makes better predictions on the average compared to an expert decision maker. In a sense, this is how a Google search operates. Each click on a link serves as a "vote" for the agreement of the search term with the link. While Google guards its algorithm for how they do this specifically, the number of click-throughs determines the order in which you see a website in your search results. Google is thus gathering the collective brilliance of Internet users. See the following box for another method that may be used to develop collective brilliance: the Delphi decision-making method.

Using the Delphi Method to Harness Collective Brilliance

The Delphi method is a systematic decision-making technique that employs a panel of independent experts. It was developed by the RAND Corporation in the 1950s for the U.S. Department of Defense as a decision-making tool. Here's how it works. Experts are given a proposal and complete an assessment of it over several rounds. These experts can be co-located, or they can be dispersed geographically and submit their ideas from anywhere in the world electronically. After each round, a facilitator provides an anonymous summary of the experts' predictions or problem solutions from the previous round as well as the rationale each expert provided. Participants are encouraged to revise their earlier solutions in light of the replies of other members of the group. Over time, the expert panel converges on the best solution or prediction. This technique allows a leader to gather information from a wide range of expert sources to make better decisions, thereby utilizing the wisdom of many (or collective brilliance).

Discussion Questions:

1. How should experts used in a Delphi decision-making process be selected? Would paying experts influence their participation in the process and/or the outcome?
2. To harness collective brilliance using Delphi, how many decision makers do you think should be invited to participate? In other words, is there a minimum number to gain a broad enough perspective? How many is too many?
3. Do you feel that this process is worth the time and effort to improve a decision? Why or why not?

Sources: Dalkey, N., & Helmer, O. (1963). An experimental application of the Delphi method to the use of experts. *Management Science, 9*(3), 458–467; Delbecq, A. L., Van de Ven, A. H., & Gustafson, D. H. (1975). *Group techniques for program planning: A guide to nominal group and Delphi processes.* Glenview, IL: Scott, Foresman; Hsu, C. C., & Sandford, B. A. (2007). The Delphi technique: Making sense of consensus. *Practical Assessment, Research & Evaluation, 12*(10), 1–8.

4. Emphasize drawbacks as well as virtues. An interesting example of this is the marketing of an energy drink called Cocaine. Cocaine contains three and a half times the amount of caffeine as Red Bull. It was pulled from U.S. shelves in 2007, after the FDA declared that its producers, Redux Beverages, were marketing their drink as an alternative to street drugs, and this was determined to be illegal. The FDA pointed to the drink's labeling and advertising, which included the statements "Speed in a Can" and "Cocaine—Instant Rush." Despite the controversy, Redux Beverages continued to produce and market the beverage in limited markets and online.[9]
5. Use success (and failure) stories to illustrate sound practices but not in place of a valid research method. For example, Circuit City went bankrupt in 2009 but was a "great company" in the now-classic book *Good to Great*. What happened to Circuit City? Alan Wurtzel, the former CEO and the son of the founder, saw the threats coming from Best Buy and Amazon in the early 2000s, and he knew the company was headed for decline. "After I left, my successors became very focused

Data and
Critical
Thinking

on the bottom line—the profit margin," Wurtzel told a group at the University of Richmond. "They were too focused on Wall Street. That was the beginning of the end," said the former CEO as he recalled the rise and fall of the great company.[10] The lesson here is that no matter how great a company is, care must be taken not to simply copy what they do in today's changing business environment. There is no substitute for a careful analysis and diagnosis before embarking on a search for solutions.

6. Adopt a neutral stance toward ideologies and theories. An example of this is that most management "gurus" are from North America (e.g., Peter Drucker, Tom Peters, Ken Blanchard). This is not to say that their ideology isn't useful. However, in a global world, EBM demands that we question whether ideology developed in North America applies abroad. EBM would also suggest that we search for theories developed overseas to locate experts from other countries with important ideas.

In making important organizational decisions, the leader may include information gathered from one or all the four sources described previously in the definition of EBM. This can result in a lot of information. So how can a leader sort through it all and determine what is most relevant to the problem at hand? The answer lies in critical thinking, a process that has been developed for over 2,500 years, beginning with the ancient Greeks and the Socratic Method, which is the process of learning by questioning everything. Critical thinking skills are applied to sort through all of the information gathered and then prioritize it (and even discard evidence that appears to be invalid or irrelevant to the problem).

WHAT IS CRITICAL THINKING?

Learning Objective 1.3: Define critical thinking, and explain the critical thinking skills leaders need.

Critical thinking can be defined as follows: "Critical thinking calls for persistent effort to examine any belief or supposed form of knowledge in the light of evidence that supports it and the further conclusions to which it tends."[11] Critical thinking involves using justification; recognizing relationships; evaluating the credibility of sources; looking at reasons or evidence; drawing inferences; identifying alternatives, logical deductions, sequences, and order; and defending an idea. Critical thinking requires the decision maker in an organization to apply a complex skill set to solve the problem at hand. A set of guidelines for critical thinking is shown in Table 1.1.[12] Critical thinking is, in short, self-directed, self-disciplined, self-monitored, and self-corrective thinking. It requires rigorous standards of problem solving and a commitment to overcome the inclination to think that we have all of the answers.[13]

When it comes to asking questions, some of the best ideas come from a book by Ian Mitroff called *Smart Thinking for Crazy Times: The Art of Solving the Right Problems.*[14] Mitroff warns us about solving the wrong problems even though leaders solve them with great precision in organizations because they don't ask the right questions. He provides the following list of the basic questions facing all organizations (and ones we should be asking frequently if we expect to gain buy-in from employees for the implementation of their solutions):

- What businesses are we in?
- What businesses should we be in?
- What is our mission?
- What should our mission be?
- Who are our prime customers?
- Who should our customers be?
- How should we react to a major crisis, especially if we are, or are perceived to be, at fault?
- How will the outside world perceive our actions?
- Will others perceive the situation as we do?
- Are our products and services ethical?

Critical Thinking Questions: Why does asking these questions improve employee buy-in for the implementation of plans? Are there other questions you feel are important to ask?

In OB, there is a systematic method to answer questions. As the field was developing, scholars adopted much of their methodological approach from the physical sciences to address problems and opportunities faced by organizational leaders.

THE SCIENTIFIC METHOD

Learning Objective 1.4: Describe the scientific method used in OB research.

How do OB researchers know what they know? As discussed earlier, it begins with a problem to solve. For example, a problem might be a leader's concern that only about 50% of their employees are satisfied with their work. First, the leader reviews the available knowledge on job satisfaction (i.e., the scientific evidence from EBM) and learns that the way that supervisors treat followers may improve job satisfaction.

Based on theory, the leader forms hypotheses, or predictions, regarding what might improve job satisfaction. An example of a hypothesis is "A leader's appreciation of workers' efforts will lead to increased job satisfaction." The next step is to collect observations from the organization. This might be, for example, through interviews with employees or surveys completed by employees. Once data are collected, the hypothesis is tested with statistical techniques.

The basic research process described previously is depicted in Figure 1.1. As noted in the introduction to this chapter, OB is an applied field, and this is underscored by the typical outcome variables that are studied. Researchers focus on outcomes that are of interest to leaders in organizations such as employee job satisfaction and productivity. Next, the types of outcomes typically studied in OB research will be reviewed.

Increasing
Productivity

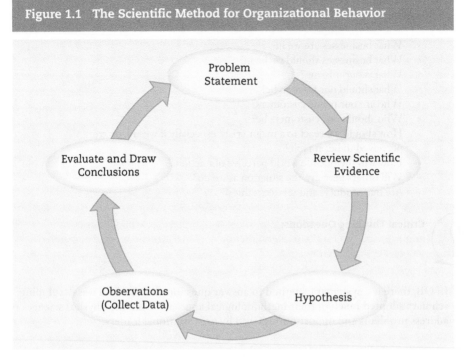

Figure 1.1   The Scientific Method for Organizational Behavior

Problem
Statement

Review Scientific
Evidence

Hypothesis

Observations
(Collect Data)

Evaluate and Draw
Conclusions

Source: Ashford, S. J., Blatt, R., & Vandewalle, D. (2003). Reflections on the looking glass: A review of research on feedback-seeking behavior in organizations. *Journal of Management, 29*(6), 773–779. p. 775.

OUTCOME VARIABLES IN ORGANIZATIONAL BEHAVIOR

Learning Objective 1.5: Discuss four types of outcome variables studied in OB.

In the preceding example, leader appreciation of workers is the independent variable. Worker engagement is the dependent variable (i.e., it *depends* on the independent variable: leader appreciation). Since OB is an applied science, the outcome variables studied are typically variables that leaders are interested in improving. There are four broad groups of outcome variables studied: performance, work-related attitudes, motivation, and employee withdrawal.

Performance

Productivity (or job performance) is one of the most important outcomes in OB. Performance can be actual performance as collected in organizational records (e.g., the number of forms correctly processed in an insurance company) or it may be rated

Hawthorne
Studies on
Employee
Performance

by supervisors and/or peers (e.g., the supervisor rates the follower's work quality on a scale of 1 to 7, with 1 being poor and 7 being outstanding). Organizational citizenship behavior (OCB) is the worker's willingness to go above and beyond what is required in their job descriptions to help others at work.[15,16] While OCB is an important outcome variable, it has also been shown that OCB predicts individual and organizational outcomes as well.[17]

Work-Related Attitudes

The measurement of work-related attitudes is an important aspect of OB research and job satisfaction has long been studied as an outcome variable. For example, there is a measure of job satisfaction dating back to 1935 that is still employed in organizational studies today: the Hoppock Job Satisfaction Blank shown in Table 1.2.[18] Another contemporary outcome variable that is gaining research attention is employee engagement.[19] Employee engagement can be defined "as a relatively enduring state of mind referring to the simultaneous investment of personal energies in the experience or performance of work".[20] In Chapter 4 of this book, you will learn more about these and other work attitudes and how they are studied in OB research.

Motivation

Classic views on motivation describe both extrinsic and intrinsic motivation as being equally important. Extrinsic motivation is based on the rewards from the organization's compensation system such as pay and bonuses. Intrinsic motivation, on the other hand, is related to the value of the work itself.[21] As with attitudes, motivation has been studied as an outcome variable but also as an independent variable that predicts productivity. Prosocial motivation is a new concept of motivation[22] that assesses the degree to which employees behave in a way that benefits society as a whole. You will learn more about motivation and rewards in Chapters 7 and 8 of this book.

Employee Withdrawal

As noted earlier, an employee quitting the organization is costly in terms of the money and time spent to recruit, hire, and train replacements. There is much research in OB on the reasons why employees think about quitting (turnover intentions) and actual turnover.[23] The availability of outside employment opportunities is a factor, but thoughts of quitting may be related to other outcomes such as lower job satisfaction and engagement. And if the economy improves and the job market improves with it, workers may eventually leave for other opportunities. Another costly form of employee withdrawal is absenteeism, since workers may not come to work when they are dissatisfied and there are few alternative jobs available.

Critical Thinking Questions: Is employee productivity the most important outcome variable? If not, what outcome(s) do you think is/are more important?

Job Crafting

LEVELS OF ANALYSIS IN ORGANIZATIONAL BEHAVIOR

Learning Objective 1.6: Compare the levels of analysis in OB research.

Individual behavior in an organization may be influenced by processes at different levels in the organization.[24] The most basic level is the individual level. For example, an individual's personality and experiences would explain much of their behavior, and differences in these variables among people would help explain why people behave differently. Other differences between people's behavior occur at the dyad (or two-party) level. An example would be a mentor and a protégé. Still, other sources include group and team level influences on individual behavior. An example would be a team that has high-performance norms that encourage a team member to perform at their best. Additional influences on individual behavior may come from the organizational level. For example, in organizations with strong cultures, the cultural characteristics can have a profound influence on an individual member's behavior. To illustrate this, one needs to look no further than the U.S. Marine Corps. The Marine Corps has a strong culture that includes pride and this inspires Marines to excel (this is evident in their recruiting ads: "The few, the proud, the Marines") (you will learn more about organizational culture in Chapter 14 of this book). There is also the industry level of analysis where comparisons are made across different industries (this is more typical for research in strategic management than OB). However, this level is included here to provide a complete listing of levels of analysis in organizational research. All levels may influence employee performance in organizations and this is discussed in the next section.

HOW ORGANIZATIONAL BEHAVIOR CAN INCREASE EMPLOYEE PERFORMANCE

Learning Objective 1.7: Develop plans for using OB research to improve employee job performance.

The chapters in this book will address all of the levels that may influence individual behavior and show how processes at one level may affect processes at another level. For example, a positive organizational culture may increase the commitment of individuals to their work and, in turn, their performance. Table 1.3 provides examples of hypotheses at the different levels of analysis discussed previously. This table illustrates how OB research at all levels may help leaders improve employee performance.

Critical Thinking Question: Which level(s) do you think have the most influence on individual behavior in organizations and why?

Table 1.3	Examples of Levels of Analysis in Organizational Behavior Research
Level	Example Organizational Behavior Hypothesis
Individual	The personality characteristic of conscientiousness is positively related to employee performance.
Dyad	High-quality relationships with bosses lead to higher employee performance.
Group and team	Team conflict is negatively related to employee performance.
Organizational	A strong, positive organizational culture is positively related to employee performance.
Industry	Employee performance is higher in the financial services industry compared with government organizations.

TOWARD MORE EFFECTIVE ORGANIZATIONAL LEADERS: PLAN FOR THIS TEXTBOOK

There are numerous challenges facing leaders of organizations today. Most organizations are experiencing rates of change unlike anything we have seen in the past. External pressures have been created from mergers, downsizing, restructuring, and layoffs as organizations strive to remain competitive or even survive. Other external forces are global competition, product obsolescence, new technology, government mandates, and demographic changes in the workforce itself. Internally, leaders must effectively communicate to followers, peers, and bosses. Managing poor performance is one of the most challenging tasks a manager must do. As noted at the beginning of this chapter, addressing the pervasive problem of worker disengagement will be a challenge for leaders in the years ahead. The changes organizations have undergone have resulted in followers who are filled with cynicism and doubt about their leaders. And the ethics scandals in business have fueled the perception that leaders have lost the credibility to lead their organizations in a principled way.

By now, you have realized that OB is a problem-focused discipline aimed at making organizations more effective. Your ability as a leader will be enhanced through knowledge of the theory and applications from OB research. Each chapter will review the essential and most current theory and research and relate it to how you can develop your leadership skills. At the end of each chapter, there are tools for your "toolkit," where you will directly apply the theories through cases, self-assessments, and exercises. At the end of this chapter, the Toolkit Activity is a personal leadership development plan, where you can apply the concepts and research covered in the textbook to your own development as a leader by setting goals and specific behavior strategies to meet them. For example, a student who set a specific goal to improve their coaching of other students that they tutor in accounting would formulate specific coaching behaviors and commit to engaging in them once per week. To gain feedback, the student would have the tutored students rate their coaching behavior by providing a yes or no answer to the following statement after each tutoring session: My tutor provides specific knowledge that has improved my accounting performance. Since leaders are expected to be coaches, this process should help the student improve their coaching skills for the future.

Figure 1.2 shows an overview of the entire book and how the material is tied to the themes of leadership development. This chapter has provided an overview of EBM and critical thinking that should be applied to all of the following chapters. The next

Figure 1.2 Framework for This Textbook

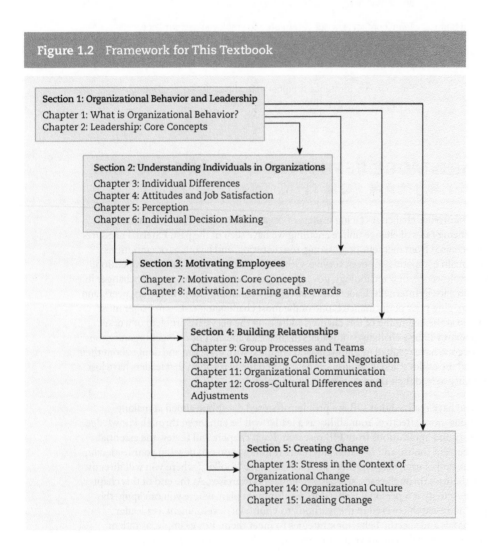

chapter (Chapter 2) will discuss the fundamental leadership theories that will guide you for the remainder of the book. Next, the importance of understanding individuals in organizations is covered in Chapters 3 through 6 including individual differences, job attitudes, perception, and decision making. The role of leaders as motivators is covered next in Chapters 7 and 8, motivating and rewarding followers. Following this, the role of leaders as relationship builders is covered in Chapters 9 through 12, covering the topics of teams, conflict, organizational communication, and leading across cultures. Finally, the role of leaders as change agents is discussed in Chapters 13, 14, and 15, which cover managing stress during change, organizational culture, and leading change. As you read this book, refer back to this figure as a map of how to organize the vast amount of theory and research on OB that has been generated for decades. It won't seem so overwhelming if you can place the material in the five broad groupings as shown in the figure. This first chapter and the next one will comprise Section I, which is an overview of OB and core concepts in leadership.

LEADERSHIP IMPLICATIONS: THINKING CRITICALLY

The goal of this book and your OB course is for you to become a more effective leader in organizations. Critical thinking has already been applied to the OB literature since this book includes the most relevant and evidence-based theory and research. You are encouraged to apply your own critical thinking based upon your own experiences with behavior in organizations and your study of this book. To aid in this process, you will find Critical Thinking Questions to challenge you to think critically about the material throughout the book. You may choose to read further from the Suggestions for Further Reading or conduct your own research on topics you find particularly interesting. Complete the assessments and exercises in the Toolkit Activity sections to apply the material to your own leadership development. The Case Study encourages you to apply organizational science to a real-world problem. The Self-Assessment will allow you to test your experiential evidence—what you already know about OB. By studying the chapters and completing the activities, this book should serve as a point of departure for your growth as you become an effective organizational leader with a broad understanding of behavior in organizations.

$SAGE edge™

edge.sagepub.com/scandura

Want a better grade? Go to edge.sagepub.com/scandura for the tools you need to sharpen your study skills.

KEY TERMS

absenteeism, 12
applied social psychology, 4
critical thinking, 8
employee engagement, 12
evidence-based management
  (EBM), 4

extrinsic motivation, 12
Hawthorne effect, 3
industry level, 14
intrinsic motivation, 12
job performance, 11
job satisfaction, 12

organizational behavior (OB), 2
organizational level, 14
prosocial motivation, 12
turnover intentions, 12
turnover, 12

SUGGESTIONS FOR FURTHER READING

Gill, J., & Johnson, P. (2010). *Research methods for managers* (4th ed.). Thousand Oaks, CA: Sage.

Mitroff, I. (1998). *Smart thinking for crazy times: The art of solving the right problems.* San Francisco, CA: Berrett-Koehler.

Surowiecki, J. (2004). *The wisdom of crowds.* New Yor NY: Random House.

TOOLKIT ACTIVITY 1.1

Personal Leadership Development Plan

As you study the evidence-based research in this textbook, use the following development plan to tie the concep to specific action plans and measurable outcomes for each chapter.

Name: _____

Date: _____

Leadership Development Plan

Goal	Connection to Course	Behavior Strategies and Frequency (fill in below)	Measurable Outcome
1	1A	1B	✓ 1C.1
		2B	✓ 1C.2
2	2A	2B	✓ 2C.1
		2B	✓ 2C.2

Goal	Connection to Course	Behavior Strategies and Frequency (fill in below)	Measurable Outcome
3	3A	3B	✓ 3C.1
			✓ 3C.2
		3B	

PLAN DETAIL

Complete the following for each of the goals listed previously.

1. **Goals**—This section is where you enter your development objectives. These objectives should be written so they read as goals you desire to achieve—for example, "I want to improve my team communication skills."

   A. **Connection to course material**—This section is where you tie each of your development objectives into the material you learned in this course. This will reinforce course material and help translate it into practice. For example, you would write a few paragraphs relating the exercises or material on communication to why you find your listening skills to need development. Be specific (e.g., cite exercises, articles, material from text or lecture). Fill out this chart: 1A to 3A.

   B. **Behavior strategies and frequency**—This section is the "how" portion. How will you achieve your goals? How often will you perform these tasks? This is the heart of your development plan. You should create specific strategies that will push you toward the completion of your goals—for example, "Practice active listening once a day." Fill out this chart for each goal: 1B to 3B.

GOAL: 1B

Timeframe	Behavior Strategy to Practice	Time Required
All the time	❑	
Weekly	❑	
Biweekly	❑	
Monthly	❑	

GOAL: 2B

Timeframe	Behavior Strategy to Practice	Time Required
All the time	❑	
Weekly	❑	
Biweekly	❑	
Monthly	❑	

GOAL: 3B

Timeframe	Behavior Strategy to Practice	Time Required
All the time	❑	
Weekly	❑	
Biweekly	❑	
Monthly	❑	

C. **Measurable outcome**—This section helps you measure your success toward each goal. If you are achieving your goal, how would you notice the change in your leadership? Specifically what will improve? How will you measure it? Develop or find a metric—for example, "I will have the person who I listen to fill out an evaluation of my listening skills, rating them on a 1 (poor) to 5 (excellent) scale" (1C to 3C).

Note: You can have more than three goals in your plan. Just be sure to complete all sections.

CASE STUDY 1.1

Organizational Science in the Real World

The skills and techniques of research are valuable to an organization's leaders. The following case study illustrates how research can be used to solve a challenge facing a government organization.

In 2012, the state of Florida implemented the federal government's decree that individuals applying for or renewing their driver's license must provide a number of documents to verify their identity. Resulting from the REAL ID Act of 2005, these measures were set forth by the federal government to help develop a national identity database through the Department of Motor Vehicles (DMV; or Bureau of Motor Vehicles [BMV] depending on the state) to not only prevent identity theft but also prevent terrorists and illegal immigrants from accessing identities. Phase 1 of the act had to be completed by 2014, with the target completion of all the phases by 2017.

But that was not the only change Florida was making to its driver license processes. The state of Florida merged the state's DMV with each county's tax collector in 2011. County tax collectors are often small organizations with 100 employees or fewer working at a handful of offices in each county to serve its patrons. Previously, tax collectors' offices handled vehicle registration, license plates, property taxes, and hunting and fishing licenses. The DMV handled only driver's licenses and identification cards. The purposes of this merger were to save money for the state, save time for citizens, and make the entire process easier. Thus, most DMV employees were not retained when the organizations were merged. Therefore, tax collector employees had to be trained on a host of new processes and procedures within a short period of time.

After these initiatives were rolled out statewide, the general manager of one county's tax collector offices noticed a number of changes. Turnover skyrocketed. Large numbers of employees began to exit where previously they worked for the organization until they retired. Similarly, only 1 of 6 new hires was retained for greater than 6 months prior to the changes.

Customer service declined. Before the merger, customers typically handled their transactions within half an hour or less. However, driver's licenses take significantly longer. Because the REAL ID Act requires documentation to be scanned into state and nationwide databases, it takes about an hour to apply for or renew licenses if there are no problems or delays. This has resulted in excessive wait times for customers. The tax collector tried to address this issue with requiring appointments for those seeking driver's licenses. However, not all patrons made appointments; instead, they continued to just show up, creating delays for those with appointments. While these patrons were denied and offered to schedule an appointment, they often became belligerent and sometimes verbally abusive to the staff.

Customers were often upset and irritated not only by the excessive wait time but also by the amount of documentation they had to produce. They were also upset by having to renew driver's licenses in person whereas previously they could renew by mail or the Internet. Tax collector employees were still friendly and polite with customers, but there was definitely some underlying tension and more complicated transactions. The camaraderie and morale among employees deteriorated.

Now it is your turn. Imagine that you are the office manager and are trying to solve the organization's problems. You simply can't revert the business back the way it was before the state's mandated changes, and you're not sure what needs to be fixed and where to go in the future.

Discussion Questions

1. How could research help this small organization? What would you hope to gain as the manager?
2. What dependent variables should you, as the manager, consider researching? Why?
3. Think about the research designs discussed in the Appendix on Research Designs used in OB at the end of the book. Which one(s) do you think would be appropriate for the manager to use? Would there be any benefit to using multiple methods, and if so, in what order would you conduct the research studies?

SELF-ASSESSMENT 1.1

Assessing Your Experiential Evidence

Some students think organizational behavior (OB) is common sense. Are the following statements true or false? The answers follow.

	True	False
1. A happy worker is a productive worker.	___	___
2. Larger teams perform better because there are more people to do the work.	___	___
3. Performance appraisals have high accuracy.	___	___
4. People perform better when asked to do their best.	___	___
5. When trust is broken with your leader, it is best to take the blame and apologize.	___	___
6. Money is the best motivator.	___	___
7. Leaders should treat everyone the same in their work group.	___	___
8. A work group can be "moody."	___	___
9. Group spirit improves team decisions.	___	___
10. Conflict in organizations should be minimized.	___	___
11. Models developed in the United States will work anywhere.	___	___
12. It's best to commit to a course of action and follow through no matter what.	___	___

Answers

	True	False
1. A happy worker is a productive worker.	_X_	___

What is important is what the worker is happy about. But generally, happier people are more productive. You'll learn why in Chapter 4.

	True	False

2. Larger teams perform better because there are more people to do the work. _X_

No. In fact, larger teams underperform due to increased conflict, free-riding, and other group dysfunctions. Research shows that there is an optimal group size for high performance, and you will learn what it is in Chapter 9.

3. Performance appraisals have high accuracy. _X_

No. There are a number of perceptual biases that can affect how a leader evaluates followers. You need to be aware of them so you can guard against these errors, and you will know about them after reading Chapter 5.

4. People perform better when asked to do their best. _X_

While this seems intuitive, people actually achieve higher performance when the leader gives them a specific goal rather than a "do your best goal." You will read more on the motivating properties of goals in Chapter 7.

5. When trust is broken with your leader, it is best to take the blame and apologize. _X_

No. Research on trust repair shows that admitting guilt may not be the best strategy. You will learn what the research shows you should do in Chapter 2.

6. Money is the best motivator. _X_

While this may surprise you, pay may actually decrease intrinsic motivation. You will learn about how to best reward employees in Chapter 8.

7. Leaders should treat everyone the same in their work group. _X_

Research on the leader–member exchange (LMX) model of leadership shows that effective leaders treat each follower differently based upon their skills, motivation, and need for development on the job. You will read more about this in Chapter 2.

8. A work group can be "moody." _X_

What? Yes, it can. Multilevel research has shown that negative affect (a "blue" mood) can be aggregated to the group level—and it affects group functioning. You will learn more about this in Chapter 3.

9. Group spirit improves team decisions. _X_

While cohesion can be a positive force in teams, it does not always result in the best decisions. Too much group spirit can result in groupthink and impair a group's decision making. You will read about this and other group dysfunctions in Chapter 9.

10. Conflict in organizations should be minimized. _X_

Actually, research shows that some conflict can be healthy since it can generate interest and challenge for followers. In Chapter 10, you will learn more about how to harness conflict and channel it toward increased motivation.

11. Models developed in the United States will work anywhere. _X_

Research on cultural differences indicates that we need to consider cultural values before we generalize research findings from one country to another. You will learn about cross-cultural differences in Chapter 12.

12. It's best to commit to a course of action and follow through no matter what. _X_

While it is important to commit to goals, research shows that escalation of commitment to a failing course of action is a decision trap. Learn how to avoid this and other traps in Chapter 6.

How did you do? Did you feel that you had to guess at some of these? OB research takes the guesswork out of being an effective leader! So keep reading!

HAVE LEADERS LOST THEIR FOLLOWERS' TRUST?

Each year, Richard Edelman conducts a global survey on which people and institutions we trust and how much we trust them.[1] Edelman is the president and CEO of the world's largest public relations company. In 2014, they surveyed over 33,000 respondents in 27 markets around the world and measured their trust in institutions, industries, and leaders. This year, only 50% of survey respondents reported that they trust business. While half of the respondents generally trust "business," they don't trust "business in general." The loss of trust in organizational leaders appears to be a global concern. For example, South Koreans are the least likely to say that they generally trust business leaders (only 36% reported having trust in business). However, the results indicate that respondents from the United Arab Emirates (UAE) were the most likely to trust business (85%). In the United States, 60% of respondents reported trusting business, a slight increase from last year's trust barometer (58%). Given these findings, it is no surprise that trust has emerged as a major concern globally and for research in organizational behavior (OB). The role of trust and how to repair it when it is broken will be covered later in this chapter.

As mentioned in Chapter 1, the objective of this textbook is to develop leadership skills. In this chapter, we will review the essential theories of leadership—both classic and contemporary—that you will use to guide your thinking about OB. It is important that you grasp these core leadership concepts because the textbook refers back to them in future chapters. This chapter will not cover all theories of leadership, but it focuses on the ones that have the strongest research base and/or best applicability to OB today. For a more comprehensive treatment of leadership theories, you can read a textbook by Northouse.[2]

Learning Objectives

2.1: Define *leadership*, and explain the difference between being a manager and being a leader.

2.2: Compare the elements of transactional and transformational leadership.

2.3: Illustrate the leader–member exchange (LMX) model with an example.

2.4: Explain why trust is important and how to repair it.

2.5: Compare and contrast power and influence, and provide an example of each.

2.6: Explain why political skill is important for a leader to be effective.

2.7: Describe ethical leadership, and explain its importance.

2.8: Compare and contrast authentic and servant leadership.

Get the edge on your studies at
edge.sagepub.com/scandura
• Take the chapter quiz
• Review key terms with eFlashcards
• Explore multimedia resources, SAGE readings, and more!

$SAGE edge™

PART
2

KNOWLEDGE AND INFORMATION MANAGEMENT FOR THE WORKPLACE

Knowledge Acquisition, Retention and Transfer

Roberts, J.

If you have knowledge, let others light their candles at it.

Margaret Fuller

It is clear from the previous chapters that knowledge is complex and its management is no easy task. However, before knowledge can be managed, it must be acquired. Once it has been acquired, its management necessitates methods to retain it within the organization as well as mechanisms for its transfer between internal members and relevant external parties – such as customers and suppliers. For knowledge to be a source of competitiveness for an organization, it must be applied. Hence knowledge must be transferred to and absorbed by relevant individuals and groups, so that they may apply it purposefully to sustain and improve the competitive performance of the organization. Knowledge, in and of itself, will not provide a competitive advantage; it is only when it is applied that this potential is released. The main purpose of this chapter is to explore the acquisition, retention, and transfer of knowledge from the perspective of managing knowledge for competitiveness. Negative consequences that could result, both for individuals and for society, from the drive for competitiveness through knowledge management practices will also be highlighted.

The ability of an organization and its members to acquire, retain, and transfer knowledge is influenced by the nature of the knowledge involved, as well as by the capacities of the organization's workforce and infrastructure, including its technological resources. The processes of knowledge acquisition, retention, and transfer will be examined from the standpoint of both explicit and tacit knowledge. A key point that we need to recognize is that these types of knowledge are interdependent; hence examining the transfer of explicit or tacit knowledge independently will not suffice. It is necessary to expose the symbiotic nature of these forms of knowledge. Moreover, an exploration of the transfer of knowledge requires a recognition that this process occurs at various levels; within an organization, this implies that it occurs between individuals, groups, and departments. Knowledge transfer within the organization is labelled 'intra-organizational knowledge transfer'. Furthermore, organizations engage with clients and suppliers as well as with competitors, sector-specific organizations and business, and regulatory institutions. In so doing, they transfer knowledge to external parties. This kind of knowledge transfer is labelled 'inter-organizational knowledge transfer'.

The chapter considers knowledge acquisition, retention, and transfer one by one. Clearly these are often interlinked, and these connections are highlighted here. In relation to the retention of knowledge, the chapter reviews issues concerning its protection – specifically, intellectual property rights (IPRs). The importance of trust and information and communications technologies (ICTs) as facilitators of knowledge transfer is also examined.

Knowledge acquisition

A key element related to the acquisition of knowledge is creativity and innovation (taken together as one), in the sense that knowledge is acquired through the development of new knowledge in the organization. This type of knowledge acquisition forms an important aspect of knowledge management, so much so that it will receive detailed consideration in Chapter 5. For the purposes of this chapter, the kind of knowledge acquisition to be explored is acquisition from the external environment. Organizations acquire knowledge through the employment of new workers who bring knowledge with them or through existing workers who absorb knowledge from the external environment. Organizations may also acquire knowledge through mergers and acquisitions, or else through the purchase of knowledge-intensive services like consultancy, research and development (R&D) outsourcing, and externally provided training programmes. In addition, knowledge may be acquired through the purchase of access to databases or machinery and equipment in which knowledge is embedded.

The various different channels through which an organization obtains knowledge can favour particular types of knowledge. For instance, the organization may purchase a database of information concerning potential clients, from which its members can extract information and combine it with their existing knowledge to produce new knowledge that supports the organization's competitiveness. This example illustrates the acquisition of explicit knowledge in a codified form, through a commercial exchange. Similarly, a consultancy company may provide a report on a particular aspect of the organization's market or management structures. Here again, knowledge is embedded in a codified form. Furthermore, its acquisition can be of benefit to the organization only if that knowledge is applied.

An example that illustrates these types of knowledge acquisition is the purchase of services from the customer science company Dunnhumby Ltd, employed by Tesco in the mid-1990s to build its databank of customer information through the Tesco Clubcard. To obtain a Clubcard, a customer must provide items of personal information such as address, telephone numbers, age, gender, size of household, household members' ages, and household dietary requirements. When the customer presents the Clubcard at the checkout, the information on the items purchased is collected along with the date, time, and location of the transaction. In return for engaging in the data collection process, customers are given rewards, for instance discounts off specific goods and vouchers that can be used on all purchases. Through the Clubcard initiative, Tesco has accumulated a vast set of information on customers and their purchasing habits that can be mined to develop knowledge from which it is possible to build better customer experiences and to foster loyalty. It is estimated that Dunnhumby Ltd has helped to save Tesco some £350 million a year (Brown, 2010). Indeed, such is the importance of Dunnhumby to Tesco's success that it is now wholly owned by the global supermarket giant.

According to its website, Dunnhumby analyses data from over 660 million customers worldwide, to gain valuable insights about their desires, locations, and price preferences.[1] In this way Dunnhumby is able to assist client companies in meeting the needs of their customers. Information is extracted from the data collected through mechanisms such as the Tesco Clubcard. It then becomes knowledge when it is considered in the context of existing knowledge about customers. Through the employment of companies like Dunnhumby Ltd, organizations acquire explicit knowledge through commercial exchange. Such exchanges involve the movement of knowledge in codified forms like reports, which may be accompanied by the movement of people – for example, to deliver the findings of a report or to consult with the client company.

When compared to the acquisition of explicit knowledge, the acquisition of tacit knowledge usually involves greater emphasis on the movement of people and their interaction within and outside of the organization. For instance, the employment of new staff may bring novel know-how to the organization; or existing workers may develop their own tacit knowledge through engagement in external personal and professional communities, and then they would use it in their employment. Accountants and marketers, for example, engage in the networks that exist around their professional associations, like the Chartered Institute of Management Accountants or the Chartered Institute of Marketing. By attending conferences, seminars, and workshops hosted by these professional associations, they acquire new knowledge, which can be brought to bear on the work that they perform in the organization.

Mergers and acquisitions can also be an important mechanism for gaining access to tacit bodies of knowledge, because they usually involve the acquisition of individual workers and groups. Of course, explicit knowledge is also acquired in this way; for example, the knowledge embodied in patents, databases, and machinery may be among the assets acquired. Nevertheless, tacit knowledge can be more difficult for an organization to acquire and transfer through its members. This is because tacit knowledge resides within individuals or groups and its acquisition, retention, and transfer are dependent on the social interaction between individuals, which is mediated by sociocultural norms and practices that are beyond the organization's direct control.

Acquiring knowledge is one thing; to benefit from its acquisition, an organization must possess the capacity to absorb and apply this new knowledge. Cohen and Levinthal refer to this feature as 'absorptive capacity', which they define as an ability 'to recognize the value of new external information, assimilate it, and apply it to commercial ends' (1990: 128). Building on this conceptualization and on earlier ones, Zahra and George go further, arguing that absorptive capacity is 'a set of organizational routines and processes by which firms acquire, assimilate, transform, and exploit knowledge to produce a dynamic organizational capability' (2002: 186). From their perspective, the ability to absorb knowledge can be divided into a *potential* absorptive capacity – the ability to acquire and assimilate knowledge – and a *realized* absorptive capacity – the ability to make use of the knowledge that has been absorbed. There is, then, an important distinction between acquiring and applying knowledge.

The motivation to absorb new knowledge is driven by the benefits that its application can provide. While an organization's absorptive capacity is based on prior related knowledge, ultimately it depends on its employees' absorptive capacity (Cohen and Levinthal, 1990). Individuals within organizations can thus have important roles in facilitating the realization of the benefits from the acquisition, assimilation, transformation, and exploitation of external knowledge. This is especially the case for individuals with roles that have gate-keeping or boundary-spanning functions. Hence, such individuals are in positions of power with regard to influencing what knowledge is acquired by the organization and what knowledge is neglected or ignored.

Alongside the individual's role in developing a firm's ability to acquire and absorb knowledge, it is also necessary to consider the organization's internal processes and its relationships with external parties. For instance, Lane and Lubatkin (1998) found that the ability to absorb knowledge between organizations depends on the similarity of knowledge bases, high informalities, centralization of research activities, similar compensation practices, and joint research communities. Moreover, they argue that the organization's ability to learn can be more significant than R&D investment in terms of the organization's competitiveness.

Many of the challenges evident in the acquisition of knowledge are also present for recipients in the knowledge transfer process. For this reason further consideration will be given later in this chapter to the acquisition of knowledge in the context of knowledge transfer. However, in the next section we turn to the challenges of retaining knowledge once it has been acquired.

Knowledge retention

According to the knowledge-based view of the firm (Grant, 1996), knowledge is the most important source of competitive advantage because it is both difficult to imitate and socially complex. Yet the knowledge capabilities of an organization only provide an important source of sustained competitiveness if access to them is restricted. If a particular knowledge base is widely available, there is no distinctive advantage to be gained through its acquisition. Therefore, to fully exploit the benefits of newly acquired knowledge that holds the potential to offer competitive advantage, an organization must restrict its use, thereby preventing its widespread dissemination. Alternatively, the organization could gain a proprietary right over the use of the knowledge in order to control its diffusion beyond the organization's boundaries. When referring to knowledge retention, then, it is important to consider how one stores and protects knowledge so as to prevent or control its widespread dissemination. Consequently this section considers the mechanisms employed to store and protect knowledge and how these mechanisms vary according to the explicit or tacit nature of knowledge.

Before going on, however, it is important to note that knowledge that is valuable today may hold little value tomorrow. Knowledge can quickly become outdated. For example, the introduction of new products such as the iPod in the recorded music sector, or of new business models like Amazon's online retailing platform, has significantly changed the dynamics of competition in the respective markets. As a result, the knowledge advantages held by competitors have been rapidly eroded. Consequently, while organizations can develop systems to retain and protect knowledge, radical innovations in the external environment can undermine their efforts. It is for this reason that organizations must, alongside these efforts to retain and protect knowledge, invest in the acquisition of new knowledge through creativity and innovation.

The idea of storing knowledge suggests that it can be accumulated for current and future use. Through codification, knowledge can be stored and therefore disseminated across time and space. The codification of knowledge is not just of significance to businesses but to society as a whole. Knowledge is stored and transferred from one generation to another through training and sophisticated systems of education as well as through the libraries, actual and virtual, upon which these systems depend. Knowledge is also stored and transferred through language and cultural norms and practices and routines. To be able to access the knowledge available in a library, it is necessary not only to understand the idea of a library and the books that it may hold, but also to be able to read in the language in which knowledge is codified in the pages of the books or on the visual displays. Without knowledge of the code – that is, the language – and without the ability to read the written language, codified knowledge is inaccessible. For instance, the capacity to access knowledge embedded in ancient Egyptian hieroglyphs was lost until the discovery of the Rosetta Stone in 1799, which contains the same inscription in both ancient Greek (a known language) and ancient Egyptian hieroglyphs. Through a process of translation and decoding that took scholars over 20 years, ancient Egyptian hieroglyphs became known once again, thus enabling access to the traces of knowledge left by this ancient civilization.

Libraries are systems of managing knowledge through the collection and storage of codified knowledge and data. In this capacity, libraries are information management systems. Until the widespread diffusion of the computer, information management was very much concerned with the collection of material, namely paper-based documents, files, and records. In fact information management systems range from the address book, which collects the names and contact details of loved ones, friends, work colleagues, and business associates, to the British Library, which holds copies of every book published in the United Kingdom and Ireland – and much more. The widespread distribution of computers in the 1980s gave rise to sophisticated information systems comprised of networks of information technology (IT) hardware and software, which are used to collect, filter, process, and distribute data. As computing power has increased exponentially, so too has the capacity of information systems. In today's world of multimedia-enabled smart mobile telephones, the Internet, cloud computing, and social media, information management systems have reached into every aspect of business and social life.

Access to knowledge on the scale now possible is of huge benefit, because such access has the potential to contribute to increased productivity and creativity in the workforce. Those seeking to solve problems are now able to draw on an enormous body of information and ideas. The combination of codification and computing power assists in the creation of new knowledge, making possible the analysis of data in ways that were previously unthinkable. For instance, the application of computing power to assist in the decoding of the DNA in the human genome project has given rise to a rapidly developing body of knowledge concerning genetics and to the introduction of gene therapies for an increasing number of medical conditions. The scope offered by the computer for the analysis of information and data is enormous and seemingly endless. Consequently, computer-based methods of collecting, collating, analysing, storing, and transmitting information are being applied to an increasing number of areas of economic and social activity.

Yet the codification of articulable knowledge ultimately depends upon the economic incentives to undertake the process of codification. Where knowledge is changing rapidly, leading to speedy redundancy, the benefits of codification may not be sufficient to cover the costs involved. Moreover, if codified knowledge can be easily replicated and applied in competing organizations, resistance to codification may be employed as a means to protect knowledge. In addition, as Cowan and Foray (1997) note, technological change can affect the economics of codification. For instance, the development of new languages may allow the codification of knowledge previously thought inherently tacit; or our ability to create models of phenomena and activities may be extended, perhaps with the assistance of ever-growing computing power. Furthermore, changes in the technologies of coding and decoding may improve, as may the technologies of storage, recording, and diffusion of messages. By reducing the cost and expanding the scope of codification, technological developments promote the codification of knowledge.

In the early development of knowledge management practices, the codification of knowledge was viewed as an important mechanism to spread knowledge of best practice throughout the organization, and in this way to retain knowledge when individuals left the organization. An organization cannot own its workforce, yet individuals or groups hold much organizational knowledge that is important. How can an organization secure such knowledge? It must do so either by earning the loyalty of its members or by extracting the knowledge from members and embedding it in machinery, databases, and routines. The strategy of deskilling workers can be traced back to the time and motion studies of Frederick Winslow Taylor (1911) in the late nineteenth and early twentieth centuries. By observing and analysing the flow of work, Taylor sought to identify and codify the best way to achieve a particular task and thereby improve labour productivity. In the process of applying such scientific management methods, knowledge is extracted from workers and this ensures that the best working methods are available across the whole organization. However, the bargaining position of the workforce is reduced, because the organization's managers are able to retain and deploy knowledge previously in the sole possession of its workers.

However, the codification of work processes does not always capture all the knowledge required to complete a job successfully. Julian Orr's (1996) study of photocopier repair technicians at Xerox PARC, *Talking about Machines: An Ethnography of a Modern Job*, serves to highlight the deficiencies of knowledge management strategies focused solely on codified knowledge. The Xerox technicians studied were supposed to be able to find in the company's repair manuals all the knowledge required to repair a copier machine. In the process of repairing Xerox machines, which are complex pieces of equipment that are affected by their particular environment and by the way they are used, technicians encountered problems that were not fully accounted for in the manuals. Nevertheless, they learned to overcome these problems through learning by doing and through engaging in the community of Xerox technicians during their regular breakfasts and lunches together, where they exchanged knowledge by recounting 'war stories' from the field. In this way the technicians developed knowledge in a social context, as they shared their experiences with, and learned from the experience of, other community members.

Hence it is not always possible to extract all relevant knowledge from the workforce through codification. Indeed the knowledge of some highly skilled sections of the workforce is difficult to articulate and not easily codified. Besides, if such workers are to be productive, they must have a high level of autonomy, because they handle highly idiosyncratic knowledge, which is difficult or costly to codify. The knowledge possessed by such employees can only be secured within the organization by safeguarding their loyalty. Organizations must therefore provide favourable working conditions and remuneration packages for highly skilled workers; they must also develop communities around key workers with a view to embedding their knowledge within the organization.

Knowledge management strategies focused purely on building up codified knowledge resources neglect knowledge applied in practice. That is, knowledge as an object is prioritized over knowing in practice. Nevertheless, as Orr's study of Xerox technicians demonstrates, the relationship between knowledge and knowing in practice is an important one. Certain skills cannot be gained solely from a database or manual. As the educational reformer John Dewey (1938) argued, learning occurs through practical experience and social interaction. Emphasis on one to the detriment of the other can diminish the success of efforts to manage knowledge.

Davenport, De Long, and Beers (1998) identified four objectives that generally characterize knowledge management projects: to create knowledge repositories; to improve knowledge access; to enhance the knowledge environment; and to manage knowledge as an asset. The application of technology can help in the achievement of these objectives when it is combined with the necessary human elements. Although data can be captured, processed, and disseminated through technological means, knowledge requires people to create, reveal, share, and use it. Because of this human component, a flexible, evolving structure, accompanied by an organizational climate that motivates knowledge creation, sharing, and application, is essential to any knowledge management strategy.

Despite recognition of the importance of the human dimension in knowledge management, there is a widespread drive towards codifying knowledge across the economic and social spheres of society (Roberts, 2001). Economic and technological forces are promoting this trend; and they are accompanied by political and social influences. In part, the drive towards codifying is symptomatic of the increased emphasis on accountability and on the measurement of performance in all sections of the private and public sector, which has accompanied the rise of neoliberal market economies. In a book in this series, Chris Grey (2013) explores the impact of this trend on management. Performance is very difficult to measure and assess in the predominantly service-based economy that characterizes industrialized countries. Moreover, the setting of performance targets may be quite subjective. The achievement of targets requires knowledge of performance that can be captured and codified in order to demonstrate that targets have been reached. Targets therefore become skewed towards activities where performance can be easily measured, with the consequence that areas where performance knowledge is not conducive to capture and codification are neglected. The imposition of performance targets can thus undermine performance in its wider sense. In sectors like healthcare, what counts as performance can lead to results that are incompatible with the idea of compassionate care. The case of the Mid Staffordshire hospital scandal in the United Kingdom provides an example: at a time when poor care was found to lead to the deaths of 300 patients a year, the head of the country's National Health Service, Sir David Nicholson (who subsequently resigned), is reported to have praised this hospital trust for making progress towards its targets (*The Telegraph*, 2013). Strategies that attempt to assess performance must recognize the importance of tacit knowledge and of knowing in practice and must acknowledge the inherent difficulties of measuring performance through systems that rely solely on the codification of knowledge.

Recognizing the importance of both explicit and tacit knowledge is crucial for an organization that seeks to manage and retain its knowledge advantages. A further challenge is how to prevent knowledge from leaking out (Liebeskind, 1997). Clearly, different forms of knowledge have different levels of mobility, and therefore varied potentials to permeate through the boundaries of the organization. Explicit knowledge, for example, can be disseminated beyond the boundaries of the organization in the codified form of instruction manuals, directories, blueprints, software, and so on. Tacit knowledge can move across an organization's boundaries, being embodied in individuals or groups. Codified knowledge is generally more easily replicated than tacit knowledge. For instance, a manual can be photocopied or downloaded from a company intranet at little cost. Given the ease of replication, such knowledge can be readily and widely distributed. In contrast, acquiring tacit knowledge may involve recruiting new staff or supporting existing staff to engage in periods of practice-based learning. The leakage of knowledge from the organization through the loss of staff can, to some extent, be addressed through the use of legally binding confidentiality agreements (also known as non-disclosure agreements), which restrict an employee's use and dissemination of company-owned 'confidential information'. Nevertheless, retaining knowledge can be a major challenge for organizations.

One method of protecting the company's knowledge is to stake a proprietary claim to that knowledge by securing IPRs over a specific area of knowledge (see Box 4.1 for a definition of intellectual property). The current IPR system was originally developed during the Industrial Revolution, when it was intended to reflect knowledge embedded in tangible innovations like the steam engine on the spinning jenny. The purpose of an IPR regime is to ensure that those who invest time, effort, and resources in the development of a new product or service are able to recoup their investment and enjoy a return on their effort. Importantly, an appropriate IPR system provides incentives for the development of new knowledge. However, the current system is poorly equipped to protect knowledge embedded in intangible assets or in the workforce.

Box 4.1   What is intellectual property?

The World Intellectual Property Organization defines intellectual property (IP) as:

Creations of the mind: inventions, literary and artistic works, and symbols, names, images, and designs used in commerce.

IP can be divided into two forms:

1. Industrial property, including inventions (patents), trademarks, industrial designs, and geographic indications of source; and
2. Copyright, which includes literary and artistic works such as novels, poems and plays, films, musical works, artistic works such as drawings, paintings, photographs and sculptures, and architectural designs. Rights related to copyright include those of performing artists in their performances, producers of phonograms in their recordings, and those of broadcasters in their radio and television programmes.

Source: Adapted from World Intellectual Property Organization (2013), 'What is Intellectual Property?', http://www.wipo.int/about-ip/en/index.html, accessed 13 May 2013.

Nevertheless, as the importance of knowledge to the competitiveness of firms grows, so too does the incentive to protect commercially valuable knowledge. Ownership of knowledge may be secured in a number of ways, from secrecy to copyrights, trademarks, and patents. The drive towards securing and defending IPRs in the form of patents is nowhere more evident than in the high-tech sector, where there is, for instance, an ongoing battle between Apple Inc. and Samsung Electronics over patent infringements related to their touch-screen mobile devices (Bradshaw and Mundy, 2012). Indeed Apple Inc. is not only diligent in the enforcement of its patents but also renowned for the level of secrecy it maintains over the development of new products: its employees work under tight security, which is meant to prevent the diffusion of information within the organization and beyond (Stone and Vance, 2009).

Although knowledge embodied in industrial processes and products or creative expressions can be protected by the patent system or by copyrights, for some types of knowledge assets the best form of protection is secrecy in the form of trade secrets. One of the best known trade secrets is the recipe for the soft drink Coca-Cola, which is held in a purpose-built vault in a permanent exhibit at the World of Coca-Cola in Atlanta (Stafford, 2011).

The effectiveness of the IPR system is being challenged by the increasing significance of innovations embodied in intangible assets. A growing number of services and products either require a digital component like software or are themselves entirely digital (recorded music and films fall in this category). These digital products can be easily replicated and disseminated through the Internet, enabling a new model of distribution. However, digital products and services can easily be copied and distributed illegally. There is, for example, a large number of illegal peer-to-peer file-sharing services like The Pirate Bay, founded in Sweden in 2003, through which members share copies of digital products, from films and music to books and video games. Successful efforts to prosecute in the courts those who establish such communities have led Internet service providers (ISPs) to block access to their websites and services – but with little long-term impact. For instance, even though the founders of The Pirate Bay were found guilty of facilitating the illegal downloading of copyrighted material and sentenced by the Swedish court to a year in prison and a fine of £2.8 million in 2009 (Farivar, 2012), such is the tenacity of those involved in this peer-to-peer community that new routes, or proxies, to connect to the service were rapidly developed to overcome the blocking activities of ISPs. Hence copyright infringement is difficult to police in sectors where outputs are digital.

Furthermore, the increased speed of new-knowledge creation in sectors characterized by short product cycles makes the IPR systems redundant in these areas. Competitiveness is achieved by engaging in continuous new-knowledge production rather than by protecting an existing body of knowledge. The software sector provides a good example. In order to speed up the production of new software, companies are increasingly turning to open innovation, a process whereby they work with competitors, the Open Source Software (OSS) community and user groups to develop new software products. For instance, IBM uses the OSS software Linux and has donated more than 500 software patents to the Open Software Foundation while funding Linux's development to the tune of $100 million annually (Leadbeater, 2008: 97).

Nevertheless, the IPR regime remains vital in many other sectors, including biotechnology and pharmaceuticals, where large investments are required to develop new products. In such sectors, recouping product development investments through a period of monopoly profits remains important for long-term sustainability. Therefore, despite the IPR regime's weaknesses but in line with the growing significance of knowledge as a source of competitiveness, there has been an upward trend in the scale of worldwide patenting activity. The number of patent applications grew from just over 1.05 million per annum in 1995 to more than 2.35 million in 2012; over the same period the number of patents granted increased from just over 400,000 to over 1 million (World Intellectual Property Organization, 2013: 45 and 48).

The monopoly rights awarded by the IPR system over a certain body of knowledge may prevent or postpone further creativity and innovation in the area concerned. IPRs serve to privatize and monopolize knowledge, so that its benefits are restricted to those who can afford to participate in knowledge markets. Moreover, the use of IPRs to appropriate knowledge previously available freely is a global phenomenon with major negative socioeconomic consequences. Well-known examples are the patenting of the components of traditional medicines from industrializing countries by the large pharmaceutical companies and the promotion of patented seed varieties by agri-business (Alonso, 2007; Shiva, 2007). Due to such developments, traditional medicines and seed varieties that were once available at low cost have now acquired prices that make them out of reach for the communities that originally produced them.

Moreover, the high cost of securing and protecting IPRs under the current regulatory system gives large multinational corporations (MNCs) an advantage over smaller firms in the race for knowledge commodification. As Lessig (2004) demonstrates in relation to the passage of the Sonny Bono Copyright Term Extension Act in the USA, the lobbying activities of large MNCs like the Disney Corporation have been influential in the development of IPR law. Not surprisingly, then, there is also much debate about the validity, nature, and scope of IPRs (see, for instance, Boldrin and Levine, 2008). Once knowledge is privatized through the IPR system, its use becomes restricted to those who can pay for the right to use it. As we will see in Chapter 5, the commodification of knowledge has consequences for creativity and innovation.

Methods of knowledge retention depend on the nature of the knowledge to be retained. While individuals and groups within the organization hold tacit knowledge, explicit knowledge may be held in the codified form of manuals and patents. Different types of knowledge require different forms of knowledge retention and different protection strategies. Retaining tacit knowledge requires embedding knowledge within communities and ensuring that remuneration and work conditions are conducive to the retention of key experts and of the communities within which they work. In contrast, the retention of codified knowledge may necessitate the use of legally enforceable IPRs like patents or copyrights, or the use of secrecy. The purpose of efforts to retain knowledge within the boundaries of the organization is to secure competitive advantage. However, securing competitiveness may also require the ability to transfer knowledge both within an organization and across several organizations.

Knowledge transfer

The challenges of knowledge transfer

Within the literature on knowledge management various terms are used to refer to the diffusion of knowledge from one party to another. The terms 'exchange', 'transfer', and 'sharing' knowledge are sometimes used interchangeably. In addition, scholars writing from different perspectives tend to prefer some terms over others. For instance, scholars in the field of economics may speak about knowledge exchange or transfer where scholars in organization studies are more likely to speak of knowledge sharing. 'Knowledge sharing' suggests a mutual exchange of knowledge; but at any single point in time the shared knowledge may be travelling in only one direction, while over any period of time a bidirectional flow of knowledge may occur. 'Exchange of knowledge' suggests a more formal movement of knowledge in exchange for something – perhaps other knowledge or other assets. Moreover, the term 'exchange' suggests a market transaction. 'Knowledge transfer' derives from the idea of technology transfer and may also involve a formal exchange of resources. Knowledge, like technology, may be transferred under licence for a one-off fee, for ongoing royalty payments, or in a combination of both. Hence the notion of knowledge transfer incorporates the idea of knowledge exchanged in return for some other asset (or for other knowledge). We can also talk of knowledge transfer when the process does not stimulate a return flow of resources. For this reason I adopt here the concept of 'knowledge transfer', using it to refer to all the forms that the movement of knowledge between parties can take and recognizing that knowledge transfer can occur through formal market exchanges or through informal sharing practices.

Knowledge transfer occurs when knowledge is diffused from one individual or group of individuals to others. Knowledge can be transferred through processes of socialization, education, and learning. It may be purposefully transferred, or it may occur as an outcome of other activity. Organizations and institutions have a central role in facilitating knowledge transfer. For the transfer of knowledge for commercial purposes, the relevant organizations and institutions are firms and markets, together with the legal and commercial institutional arrangements within which they operate. While firms can be viewed as repositories of knowledge, they are also active in promoting the transfer of knowledge through the activities of management and (more generally) personnel, as well as through the establishment of routines.

Knowledge may be transferred both between departments and groups *within* organizations and *beyond* the boundaries of organizations – either deliberately or surreptitiously. Some knowledge may be sticky and may flow less easily within and beyond the organization. Discussions of 'sticky knowledge' focus mainly on the challenge of moving knowledge between individuals and groups *inside* organizations. For instance, Eric von Hippel (1994) outlines the difficulty of transferring knowledge between research labs and engineering departments, while Gabriel Szulanski (1996) identifies the 'stickiness' of knowledge in efforts to circulate 'best practice' from one part of an organization to another. Additionally, where knowledge is a source of power for individuals or groups, its transfer may be impeded by the incentive to hoard it (Liebowitz, 2008).

When knowledge transfer takes place, one party acquires knowledge; therefore the entire problematic that knowledge acquisition generates is also relevant to knowledge transfer. For instance, the successful transfer of knowledge requires that the recipients have sufficient absorptive capacity. The form of the transfer will depend on the nature of the knowledge involved – that is, on whether it is tacit or explicit. The transfer of knowledge, like its acquisition, will involve learning. Tacit knowledge whose learning is time-consuming will be harder to transfer than explicit knowledge with a widely accessible code.

The transfer of knowledge through market exchange presents a number of difficulties. Chapter 1 discussed the public-good nature of much knowledge, particularly its non-rivalrous and non-excludable character. These properties influence the way in which knowledge is transferred. On the one hand, the non-rivalrous character of knowledge encourages its widespread distribution, since knowledge is a kind of resource that does not diminish in quantity when it is diffused. This idea is captured in the quotation that opens this chapter. Knowledge is like a candle in that sharing the flame to light someone else's candle does not diminish your own flame; moreover, codified knowledge is easily and rapidly replicated and spread. On the other hand, because knowledge is non-excludable, the fear of losing the advantage that new knowledge gives may discourage organizations from exposing it to others. Although the quantity of knowledge does not diminish through diffusion, if the value of knowledge lies in the organization's exclusive access to it, this value will rapidly fall as the knowledge in question is diffused beyond the boundaries of the organization.

The measurement of the transfer or 'flow' of knowledge is a difficult task. Two proxy indicators of embodied diffusion and disembodied diffusion are often used. The first involves the introduction into the production process of machinery, equipment, and components that incorporate new technology and knowledge. The second involves the transmission of knowledge, technical expertise, or technology in the form of patents, licences, or know-how. In both cases, the value of the transfer can be measured in terms of the costs involved. However, knowledge transfers also occur through the movement of personnel, the purchase of consulting services, foreign direct investment, intra-firm transfers, joint ventures, mergers, acquisitions, and cooperative research agreements. The knowledge transfer component of such activities is not always clearly distinguishable. Arguably the most important dimension of knowledge transfer is the role of people in initiating and facilitating such processes within and between organizations, through person-to-person communication. Consequently, everything that encourages or inhibits interpersonal communications affects knowledge transfer.

Trust and knowledge transfer

Knowledge transfer through market transactions presents difficulties that arise from the asymmetric distribution of the information concerning the transaction between buyer and seller. The Nobel prize-winning economist George A. Akerlof considered the problems of asymmetric information in the used-car market in his seminal paper 'The market for "lemons": quality uncertainty and the market mechanism' (Akerlof, 1970). The asymmetrical distribution of information can be exploited in markets where it is difficult for buyers to judge quality prior to purchase. An unscrupulous car salesperson may emphasize the positive aspects of a used car while neglecting to convey its weaknesses. Once the buyer has purchased the car, the weaknesses will become apparent through use and the buyer may find that they have bought a 'lemon'. Problems of asymmetric information also arise in markets for knowledge, because assessing its value requires access to it, which can only be achieved once the knowledge has been purchased and absorbed. Hence, trust in the knowledge provider is required. Trust may be gained through repeated transactions – in other words it is built gradually, on the basis of experience, or it is supported through formal institutional structures. So, for instance, students taking a programme in knowledge management do not know its value until they have completed it. They may feel that the programme is of little value while they take it; and sometimes they do not see any benefits until much later, when they come to use the knowledge gained in that programme. Students put their trust in the reputation of the professors who teach them – whose knowledge is based on formal qualifications and research expertise – and in the standing of the department and institution in which they study.

National and global university league tables like the *Times Higher Education* World University Rankings, international accreditation systems like the European Quality Improvement System (EQUIS) for business schools, and reports from national bodies like the United Kingdom's Quality Assurance Agency for Higher Education help students to determine the reputation of universities and of their various departments.

While indicators of the quality of knowledge exist in sectors such as education and medicine, this is not the case in all fields. In some areas the difficulty in appreciating the value of knowledge hinders the latter's efficient allocation through the market. Market failures in the transaction of knowledge provide a rationale for vertical integration. Yet knowledge is often developed interactively and transferred through networks within and beyond the boundaries of the organization. Networks offer an important means through which knowledge may be transferred and produced; and this represents an alternative to the traditional markets–hierarchy dichotomy. Networks are increasingly recognized as important entities for the development and circulation of knowledge. Where networks exist outside the organization, they depend on self-regulation through social capital, which includes trust and reputation.

Through codification and the appropriate contractual arrangements, explicit knowledge may be transferred in a tangible embodiment such as blueprints or patents, in machinery, as part of licensing or franchise agreements, or in trade between agents. But tacit knowledge often requires considerable time to be acquired through learning by doing. As noted in Chapter 3, because knowledge is often made up of both tacit and codified elements, codified knowledge alone may fail to facilitate the successful transfer of knowledge. Hence there are elements of knowledge that can only be transferred successfully through a process of demonstration, which is facilitated by face-to-face contact between the transmitter and receiver. Harry Collins' (2001) research on the measurement of the quality factor in sapphire confirmed not only the importance of demonstration in the process of knowledge transfer, but also the significance of trust – which is evident in the personal relationships between the scientists studied.

As Francis Fukuyama (1995) has argued, the level of trust between individuals, among organizations, and within society as a whole influences the nature of economic activity in terms of the character of organizational structures and the degree of economic prosperity. Trust influences the level of risk and uncertainty arising from the transaction of commodities within organizations and in the market. Although trust is a valuable commodity, it cannot be acquired in the market because, as Arrow notes, 'if you have to buy it, you already have some doubts about what you've bought' (1974: 23). Although a rather elusive concept, trust is highly important for the efficient operation of a knowledge-based economy, since the market exchange of knowledge gives rise to a high level of risk and uncertainty. These risks and uncertainties are reduced by the presence of a high level of trust.

Taking a strictly rational approach, Casson defines trust as 'a warranted belief that someone else will honour their obligations, not merely because of material incentives, but out of moral commitment too. It is assumed that such moral commitment is rational because it generates emotional rewards' (1997: 118). More broadly, Lazaric and Lorenz (1998: 3) argue that three conditions are common in definitions of trust and, together, provide a basis for a general definition. First, trust is to be identified with an agent's belief rather than with their behaviour or action. Second, trust is to do with beliefs about the likely behaviour of another (or others) who matter for the decision-making process of the person who holds those beliefs. Finally, trust pertains to situations where the complexity of the relationship, or the fact that it is marked by unanticipated contingencies, precludes having recourse to complete contracts with third-party enforcement. Clearly the market exchange of knowledge – particularly tacit knowledge – is not always amenable to enforcement by contract; hence the importance of trust in the transfer of knowledge.

Importantly, trust is influenced by the social context; and the levels of trust present in the economic environment vary between cultures and nations. This is of particular importance to cross-border knowledge transfer, whether in the market or within the boundaries of the firm. If shared expectations are to be built, the development of trust between agents from different cultural or national backgrounds will necessitate a higher investment than the development of trust between agents who share a common background. High levels of face-to-face contact and a process of socialization are usually required to establish and reinforce a relationship of trust and confidence between agents. Furthermore, the richness of face-to-face contact can help counterbalance the communication difficulties that may arise from differences in culture and language.

Over time, an agent engaged in the market transfer of knowledge will develop an appreciation of their trading partner's social context. Together, the two will establish their own social norms and mutual expectations, thereby enabling the development of trust and, with it, successful knowledge transfer. The presence of a relationship of trust between individuals indicates the capacity for a high degree of mutual understanding, built upon a common appreciation of the social and cultural context. Both trust and mutual understanding, developed in their social and cultural contexts, are prerequisites for the successful transfer of tacit knowledge. The use of technologically mediated communication and knowledge transfer will be more successful between agents who share social, cultural, and linguistic characteristics (Roberts, 2000). It will be less effective when agents are from diverse backgrounds, particularly in the early stages of interaction, before mutually determined norms and practices have been established.

Technology and knowledge transfer

ICTs facilitate knowledge transfer through the exchange of data. Where knowledge can be codified, it can, with the use of ICTs, be distributed worldwide at the touch of a button, with little cost. But the transfer of tacit knowledge cannot be executed in such a simple fashion, since the transformation of knowledge into information and then into data will be incomplete. As a result, the transfer of tacit knowledge often requires proximity between the transmitter and receiver. The growing set of technologies of communication detailed in Table 4.1, which include videoconferencing and virtual project rooms, may aid the transfer of tacit knowledge. Nevertheless, technologically facilitated communication cannot yet replace direct face-to-face contact, which is often a prerequisite for the successful transfer of tacit knowledge. Moreover, given the importance of tacit knowledge as a factor that enables the assimilation of codified knowledge, face-to-face contact may well be a prerequisite for the transfer of much codified knowledge too. Finally, the need to establish a level of trust that can facilitate the transfer of knowledge also favours co-presence and co-location (Roberts, 2003).

Studies of the use of ICTs in the work of dispersed R&D teams, in which the transfer of knowledge and shared learning is vital, attest to the importance of face-to-face interaction. As Boutellier et al. (1998) note, sensory information, feelings, intuition, non-verbal communication, and context are largely neglected in communication facilitated through ICTs; this is due to a lack of person-to-person contact. Nevertheless, relational proximity, achieved through face-to-face interaction, can also be realized through a combination of technology-mediated communication and mobility of individuals (Coe and Bunnell, 2003). In some cases, a combination of occasional face-to-face encounters and technology-mediated communication may facilitate the development of a more trusting relationship with someone located on the other side of the world than with someone in the office next door.

Table 4.1 Examples of ICT services enabling information and knowledge transfer

ICT services	Comments
Electronic mail (e-mail)	For day-to-day project communication and the transfer of documents (including minutes and agendas of meetings, project reports, schedules, images, etc.).
SMS	A text messaging service component of phone, web, or mobile communication systems, which allows the exchange of short text messages between devices.
Instant messaging services	Microsoft's MSN Messenger.
Voice mail	Asynchronous audio communication.
Teleconferencing	Telephone discussions between more than two people.
Videoconferencing	Group meeting among geographically dispersed individuals (often formal). Videoconference rooms may be dedicated to particular projects, allowing for frequent use. Includes the use of the freely available Skype service as well as commercially provided systems.
Desktop videoconferencing	One-to-one meeting, or in small groups (often informal). May include shared computer displays and virtual project rooms.
CAD and CAM	For the transmission of specifications from design to manufacturing.
Discussion lists	Information can be shared and stored through questions and answers, knowledge that would otherwise remain solely with individual members of the organization.
Blogs	Single-authored or multi-authored informational sites published on the World Wide Web and consisting of discrete entries or 'posts', normally displayed in reverse chronological order. Many blogs use the open-source blogging platform WordPress.
Information databases	For common access to project data.

(Continued)

Table 4.1   (Continued)

ICT services	Comments
Shared drives on corporate networks and commercial file-hosting services	All manner of digital content can be shared through joint access to computer drives and folders within organizational specific Intranets, as well as through externally provided file-sharing services such as Dropbox.
Social media	Interactions among people in which they create, share, and exchange information, ideas, and multimedia content in virtual communities and networks (e.g. Facebook, Twitter, Instagram, Tumblr and Flickr). Allow quick communication between group members.
Websites hosting FAQ pages	Frequently asked questions and answers are captured and made widely accessible.
Wikis	A website that allows people to add, modify, or delete content via a web browser. Wikis use specialized wiki software and are usually created collaboratively (e.g. Wikipedia).
Virtual worlds	Computer-based simulated environment contexts in which interlocutors can engage in rich multidimensional communication (e.g. Second Life).
Groupware	Includes a range of the facilities listed above. Examples include IBM Notes and Domino (formerly Lotus Notes) and Microsoft Exchange and Novell GroupWise.

ICTs are becoming increasingly sophisticated and, in certain circumstances where the individuals involved in the transaction are highly attuned to their use, they may facilitate or support the transfer of tacit knowledge. For instance, members of the OSS community are engaged in developing and transferring knowledge as part of their activity. They are especially familiar with the use of ICTs and they work on codes that exist in abstract form. They engage in knowing in practice as they compose and revise code online. Hence they have a specialized knowledge of knowing code in practice, even though their work is always mediated through ICTs. Software programmers develop a shared aesthetic appreciation of the code they work with; for example, they commonly refer to code as elegant or beautiful (Oram and Wilson, 2007).

Programmers working together at a distance can share knowledge through an understanding of the elegance or beauty of the code in the same way in which the flute-makers studied by Cook and Yanow (1993) shared knowledge through the feel of the tangible instruments they co-produced.

This suggests that tacit knowledge can be transformed into information, which, when converted into data, may be transferred across distance electronically. However, this tacit-to-tacit knowledge transfer arises from the transfer of codified knowledge, which, when combined with the tacit knowledge of the receiver, gives rise to *new* tacit knowledge (Roberts, 2000). Tacit knowledge can then emerge from the assimilation and absorption of codified knowledge. In this way ICTs can enhance the transfer of knowledge by supporting the creation of tacit knowledge. ICTs increase the sharing of information and of information about sources of knowledge, as well as the sharing of knowledge about sources of information. However, in most cases ICTs alone fail to capture fully the conditions required for the successful transfer of tacit knowledge. Two individuals on different sides of the world can read the same codified knowledge embedded in a document delivered to them simultaneously through e-mail. However, these individuals cannot share tacit knowledge effectively, not even with the help of desktop videoconferencing, unless they are in a common social and cultural context. If this condition is fulfilled, they may *share* tacit knowledge by assimilating codified knowledge and thereby creating new tacit knowledge that will be largely – though not completely – the same. Indeed, if Michael Polanyi's (1958) view of knowledge as fundamentally centred on the individual is accepted, it is questionable whether individuals can share their tacit knowledge base in its entirety. The most that can be achieved is a high degree of overlap between the tacit knowledge held by persons who work together in a group.

Shared cultural expectations and beliefs about the behaviour and actions of others provide the basis on which to build a relationship of trust and mutual understanding. For ICTs to assist knowledge transfer across distance, the individuals involved must succeed in creating a virtual location in which they share a social and cultural–institutional framework. In a sense, co-presence is facilitated through a combination of ICTs and shared social and cultural understanding. Only then can technologically assisted methods of communication be used to optimum effect. The need to fulfil this prerequisite restricts the scope of technologically assisted communication as a replacement for face-to-face contact. Such communication may be a useful complementary device designed to reinforce communications achieved through face-to-face contact. However, face-to-face contact remains a vital element in the establishment of a relationship of trust, which is an important condition for the efficient transfer of knowledge – both in the market and within organizations.

Conclusion

This chapter has highlighted the human element needed in the acquisition, retention, and transfer of knowledge. Although explicit knowledge can be transferred in a codified form independently of humans, if organizations are to absorb and apply such knowledge, people must interpret it. Moreover, explicit and tacit knowledge are interdependent in the sense that codified knowledge must be interpreted with the help of tacit knowledge, and in the process of interpreting codified knowledge new tacit knowledge is created. The acquisition, retention, and transfer of knowledge involve creative processes, which will be examined in the next chapter.

An important lesson to take from this chapter is that the management of knowledge requires paying attention to both its explicit and its tacit dimensions. One without the other will lead to the inefficient and ineffective management of one of the most valuable resources that organizations hold. Managers must balance the desire to capture and codify knowledge against the need to recognize and retain tacit knowledge within the organization. Given the tacit forms of knowledge and knowing in practice, the challenge of managing knowledge becomes one of managing the workforce in an appropriate fashion. Moreover, the acquisition and transfer of knowledge depend upon interaction between people. Communication is much more than codified signals: it is complex and subtle. It is not possible to take people and their need for trust and mutual understanding out of the knowledge management equation. This is because knowledge is acquired, retained, transferred, and applied in a social context.

Note

1. Visit the site at www.dunnhumby.com/uk/what-we-do (accessed 13 July 2014).

PART 3

DEVELOPING RELATIONSHIPS AND WORKPLACE ACHIEVEMENT

Learning and Development

Lussier, R. N. and Hendon, J. R.

● ● ● LEARNING OBJECTIVES

After studying this chapter, you should be able to do the following:

7-1 Discuss the major difference between training and development and identify the common situations where training may be needed. PAGE 226

7-2 Briefly discuss the steps in the training and development process and the common challenges to the process. PAGE 229

7-3 Identify the three common learning theories and how they are used to create the four methods for shaping behavior. PAGE 233

7-4 Discuss each of the major training delivery types. PAGE 239

7-5 Briefly discuss the Four-Level Evaluation Method for assessing training programs and the three common ways we measure training success. PAGE 243

7-6 Discuss the term *career* and the three common methods of employee development. PAGE 247

7-7 Describe the concepts of gamification, digital learning, and micro-learning, and the reasons that they have become more critical in today's organizations. PAGE 254

Practitioner's Perspective

Cindy told the story of Jennifer, who had worked in the same position for 10 years. Jennifer had always been a valuable employee, but lately, her productivity and performance had started to decline. Her supervisor, Mandy, finally called her in to find out what was wrong.

After some hesitation, Jennifer said, "To tell the truth, I feel like I am in a rut. I just don't get the same satisfaction from doing my job that I used to get."

"I wish we'd had this talk sooner," Mandy replied, "but now that I know how you feel, there is something we can do. Let's take a look at some of the training opportunities coming up this quarter. Tell me what training classes you might be interested in taking."

What if Jennifer and Mandy never had that talk? Do you think Jennifer would have remained at her job? Chapter 7 looks at the ins and outs of managing and retaining talent through training and development.

SHRM HR CONTENT

See Appendix: *SHRM 2016 Curriculum Guidebook* for the complete list

E. Job Analysis/Job Design (required)

5. Training and development

Vocational and career counseling

Needs assessment

Career pathing

L. Training and Development (required)

1. Needs assessment

2. Competency models

3. Learning theories: Behaviorism, constructivism, cognitive models, adult learning, knowledge management

4. Training evaluation: Kirkpatrick's model

5. E-learning and use of technology in training

6. On-the-job training (OJT)

7. Outsourcing (secondary)

8. Transfer of training: Design issues, facilitating transfer

9. Employee development: Formal education, experience, assessment

10. Determining return on investment (ROI)

11. The role of training in succession planning

12. Human/intellectual capital

Q. Organizational Development (required–graduate students only)

2. Developing human resources

3. Emotional intelligence

4. Equipping the organization for present and future talent needs

8. Measurement systems

11. Organizational learning

13. Outsourcing employee development

16. Training employees to meet current and future job demands

T. HR Career Planning (secondary)

1. Definition of a career

2. Balancing work and life

7. Plateauing

9. Career development

Get the edge on your studies.
edge.sagepub.com/lussierhrm3e

- Take a quiz to find out what you've learned.
- Review key terms with eFlashcards.
- Watch videos that enhance chapter content.

LO 7-1

Discuss the major difference between training and development and identify the common situations where training may be needed.

THE NEED FOR TRAINING AND DEVELOPMENT

Now that we've made it through the process of selecting individuals into the organization, the next thing we need to do is train them to successfully work within the new environment and to do their new jobs. In all cases, new employees should get at least basic training about the organization and its routine processes as well as the training for the job they are going to be filling. We can't reasonably expect them to do a job successfully unless they're trained in how to do it; and there is a relationship between training and job satisfaction,[1] so we need to insure that the required onboarding training is completed. Offering training and development also generally decreases expensive turnover[2] and makes it less likely that employees will engage in neglectful behavior.[3] Training is costly though, so it must be done correctly to get sufficient benefits to outweigh the cost.[4]

Effective training and development are investments, not expenses, as they pay for themselves through competitive advantage and increased performance.[5] This is why companies worldwide are investing heavily in training and long-term employee development.[6] **Hudson Trail Outfitters** even rewards employees for completing training programs.[7] As managers' skills should also be developed,[8] leadership programs and courses are currently popular.[9] This is why best-practice companies (e.g., **GE, IBM**, and **Johnson & Johnson**) provide leadership programs.[10]

Training and Development

Before we get into the details of training and development, we need to understand competency models because training is based on the competencies we want employees to have. Competency models *identify the knowledge, skills, and abilities (known in HR as KSAs) needed to perform a particular job in the organization.* We can utilize competency models to identify what types of training a new employee or an employee changing jobs will need. We go through a process of identifying and providing the training, evaluating how well the employee has learned, and then assessing the training process itself using one of several options. We will discuss this in more detail in a little while, but for now, just remember that training is a critical piece in the education of each employee in the organization.

In this chapter, we will discuss both organizational training and employee development. The two are related but separate pieces of the organization's processes involving the management of its employees.

SHRM

L:2
Competency Models

Competency model Model identifying the knowledge, skills, and abilities (known in HR as KSAs) needed to perform a particular job in the organization

---

••• CHAPTER OUTLINE

Training *is the process of teaching employees the skills necessary to perform a job.* We train employees to provide them with the KSAs that they will need to succeed in their work for the organization. Training is primarily intended to be put to immediate use by the individual being trained. As an example, **Amazon** focuses on customer service, so it trains its employees by drilling them in what steps to follow when they get everyday questions and when fielding more unusual requests. To make sure everyone at Amazon understands how customer service works, each employee, including the CEO, spends 2 days on the service desk every 2 years.[11]

Somewhat in contrast to the training we do so that employees can do a new job or do an existing job better is the process of employee development. Both colleges and corporations have been criticized for not doing a good job of developing business leaders.[12] This is one of the reasons why this book focuses on developing HR *skills*, not just knowledge. Employee development *is ongoing education to improve knowledge and skills for present and future jobs.* So, employee development is designed to teach our workers how to move up in the organization in the future by becoming skilled at those tasks that they will need to know to move into higher-level jobs. Development tends to be less technical, and it is aimed at improving human, communication, conceptual, and decision-making skills in employees. To remain competitive in today's dynamic environment, organizations must have employees who maintain up-to-date knowledge and skills; and development plays an important role in this effort.[13]

When Is Training Needed?

To successfully determine what kinds of training need to be carried out within the organization, HR managers should begin by completing a *needs assessment*. We will discuss needs assessments in the next section. For now, let's review some common points at which we should probably complete a needs assessment and at least consider providing training to our people.

*NEW EMPLOYEE ONBOARDING.*Orientation, known better now by the term onboarding, *is the process of introducing new employees to the organization and their jobs.* New employees are often called *newcomers* in organizational entry;[14] and newcomer socialization done effectively during the onboarding process increases new employee job satisfaction and performance and reduces turnover rates.[15,16] Onboarding frequently emphasizes corporate values, culture, and strengths.[17] Organizations that have developed innovative onboarding programs include **Rover.com, Wipro, Rackspace, Bazaarvoice,** and **Google.**[18] This socialization process is important to both newcomers and organizations, as newcomers learn the ropes and understand what is expected from them in their work as they assimilate into the organization and attempt to become productive members.[19] Thus, job and career orientation have long-lasting effects on new employee job attitudes and satisfaction, behavior, work mastery, and performance.[20]

Onboarding is an introduction of the person to the company. What do we need to think about when we introduce somebody to the company? We need to think about introducing the new employee to all of the things that exist within the organizational society that they are entering. The process is very similar to someone moving to a different country and having to assimilate into a new culture. What do people need to know in order to be able to go about their daily lives, do the routine things that they need to do, and provide

Marriott is one of many companies that offer a variety of training programs to its employees. Training topics include leadership, management, and work-life balance.

SHRM
E:5
Training and Development

SHRM
Q:16
Training Employees to Meet Current and Future Job Demands

SHRM
Q:2
Developing Human Resources

Training The process of teaching employees the skills necessary to perform a job

Employee development Ongoing education to improve knowledge and skills for present and future jobs

Onboarding The process of introducing new employees to the organization and their jobs

for their own personal needs? Orientation should be designed to answer all of the questions necessary to allow new employees to integrate into the "society" that they are entering.

One of the first things an individual would need to know is what the laws, rules, and regulations are in the new society; so we need to introduce the new employee to the organization's policies and procedures, rules, and regulations. The second thing that people would probably want to know is how to act and interact with others in the new society. So in addition to introducing the employee to the job and how to perform it within the organization, we would want to talk to the individual about the underlying organizational structure, plus where to go and whom to talk to in order to get certain things done. Who should they talk to in their department if they have questions about their job or about how things are done within the department? Who should they speak with in other departments if they have questions that can't be answered within their primary workgroup, and when is it acceptable to go to individuals in other departments?

Next, they might want to know how they get the money that they need in order to survive in society. So we need to tell them about their pay and benefits, including whom to contact with questions. People entering this new society would also probably want to know how to stay safe as they go about their business, so we need to talk to them about safety in the organization. They would also likely need to fill out paperwork—to get a driver's license, to open a bank account, to identify who they are, and so forth. Similarly, certain paperwork is necessary for the organization to function successfully, so during onboarding we ask the new employee to fill out this paperwork.

As you can see, there are many different things that we need to teach someone entering our new society, so we can't legitimately perform the entire onboarding process in one day or a couple of hours. Effective onboarding of employees also results in lower turnover rates,[21] so orientation to the firm and the new employee's job should "last at least one year to ensure high retention say staffing and HR experts."[22] Here are a few examples of world-class companies with long onboarding programs: **Toyota** has a 5-week orientation, **Honda** has a 6-week orientation, and **Southwest Airlines** has a 90-day orientation.

However, in most organizations, the onboarding process is significantly shorter than this, and this is one reason that our organizations suffer significant early turnover of new hires. If our new employee is frustrated due to not knowing how to do the job, where to locate tools, whom to go to with a problem, or how to fix an issue with pay, the likelihood of that person leaving the organization goes up drastically. Many organizations could significantly reduce new-hire turnover by modestly increasing the onboarding and socialization period for new hires.

NEW JOB REQUIREMENTS OR PROCESSES. The second common point where training may be necessary occurs when jobs change in some form. Whether our employee is in the same job or is changing jobs and needs to learn new processes, if there is a significant change in any work requirements, we need to train the employee. The change may be based on discovery of new techniques or technologies to perform particular work to make the work more efficient. The organization may have changed its strategic direction; and as a result, some or all of the jobs within the organization may require new processes or procedures. In any of these cases or any similar situation where the change has significance for that job, we should go through the process of performing a training needs assessment. If the result of the needs assessment shows that training is necessary, then an appropriate training program can be designed and implemented.

REMEDIATION. The third common point at which managers need to investigate the requirement for additional training occurs when there has been some failure of an employee or some employees to perform successfully and meet organizational standards. Remediation *is the correction of a deficiency or failure in a process or procedure.* In remediation, we work to correct the actions of the individual or individuals responsible for the process or procedure so that they can successfully carry out the action in the future.

**WORK
APPLICATION 7-1**

Select a job you hold in the present or held in the past. Did you receive both training and development or just training? Explain in some detail why it was one or both.

**WORK
APPLICATION 7-2**

Briefly describe the orientation you received for a job. How could it be improved?

Remediation The correction of a deficiency or failure in a process or procedure

We don't want to make a common mistake, though. Remediation is not about assigning blame for a failure. The emphasis in this case should always be on correcting the actions of the employee to better serve both the employee's and the organization's interests. Organizational managers act just as a good physician or mechanic would act—by diagnosing the situation first and *then* taking appropriate corrective action to solve the problem.

EMPLOYEE DEVELOPMENT FOR ADVANCEMENT. The next point at which to evaluate the need for training is in situations where we are working to develop current employee skills and abilities so that employees can move into higher level jobs within the organization. Offering development opportunities generally decreases turnover.[23] As noted in Chapter 4, all organizations have a responsibility to plan for the succession of individuals in management and executive positions; and this planning is usually a function assigned to the HR department. Providing development opportunities and succession planning is the only way the organization can be sustainable over long periods of time. To successfully carry out a succession process, people at lower levels in the organization must be trained in the knowledge and skills necessary to be able to take on higher-level duties. One area getting particular attention today is training and development in ethics and social responsibility, in part because of the litany of ethical failures in scores of companies over the past couple of decades. While very few organizations will attempt to develop all of the employees within the firm, most organizations go through an informal or formal process of identifying high-potential individuals for development and, ultimately, advancement into managerial and executive slots.

Many 21st century organizations have rigorous development programs that include job rotation to various departments within the organization, classroom and on-the-job training, assigned mentors, and many other programs–all of which are designed to train employees and develop their capabilities for future use within the firm. Organizations that neglect succession processes and employee development can find themselves at a competitive disadvantage when senior personnel leave the firm through either retirement or resignation. It is critical that HR lead the process of planning for succession and employee development. Although in this chapter we will focus more on training than development (there are five major sections explaining training, followed by one section on employee development), both are important to the organization over the long term.

HRM in Action

Training

SHRM

L:11
The Role of Training in Succession
Planning

THE TRAINING PROCESS AND NEEDS ASSESSMENT

LO 7-2

Briefly discuss the steps in the training and development process and the common challenges to the process.

How are we going to go about training our employees? How do we know who needs what training, in what forms, and at what point? How do we determine whether or not the employee is ready and willing to participate in the training? Finally, how do we know that the training was effective? In order to answer these questions, we have to plan our training processes very carefully. We need to look at what's currently going on in the organization and how that differs from what needs to happen in the future to accomplish our strategic business goals. So training and development are another set of strategic HRM tasks. Once we do this, we can analyze the types of training that will be necessary to build new knowledge, skills, and abilities for our workforce.

Steps in the Training Process

This chapter is primarily organized to follow the steps in the training process. Let's take a look at how we go through the training process in Exhibit 7-1. We'll follow that up with a brief discussion of the steps and then provide more detail throughout the chapter.

Step 1: Assessing needs. We conduct a needs assessment to determine what training is necessary to improve performance. We will discuss this step in this section.

EXHIBIT 7-1   THE TRAINING PROCESS

Step 2: Selecting how to shape behavior. We select a method of shaping employee behavior based on learning theories so that we can change employee behavior to improve performance. We will discuss this step in this chapter's section "Learning and Shaping Behavior."

Step 3: Designing training. We design the training and development based on the needs assessment. We must determine which training methods we will use to shape employee behavior. We discuss this step in this chapter's section "Design and Delivery of Training."

Step 4: Delivering training. Before we actually conduct the training and development, we must select the delivery method. We also discuss the delivery options in the section "Design and Delivery of Training."

Step 5: Assessing training. After we complete the training, our last step is to assess how effective the training was at developing the needed skills. We do this by determining our success at shaping behavior. We discuss this step in this chapter's section "Assessing Training."

Interrelationship of the Training Process Steps. Note in Exhibit 7-1 that each of steps 2, 3, 4, and 5 has a double-headed arrow; this is because all the steps are so closely related and based on each other that they are commonly planned together before actually delivering the training. In other words, you are constantly thinking ahead and behind your current step in the training process. If the assessment of the training reveals that the behavior has not been shaped (changed) as needed, we may have to go back to step 1 and start the training process again.

Needs Assessment

The first major step in the training process, and probably one of the most important, is the needs assessment. A needs assessment *is the process of analyzing the difference between what is currently occurring within a job or jobs and what is required—either now or in the future—based on the organization's operations and strategic goals.* If a needs assessment is not done correctly, a training course may be poorly designed, or it may cover the wrong information. The wrong employees may be asked to participate in the training, or they may not yet be capable of absorbing the information in the training because of a lack of a knowledge base or skill set. We may end up creating a training program that's unnecessary, or we may fail to determine that an issue is based on poor performance rather than

Needs assessment
The process of analyzing the difference between what is currently occurring within a job or jobs and what is required—either now or in the future—based on the organization's operations and strategic goals

lack of knowledge. These are significant issues that we can avoid if we correctly go through the process of a needs assessment.

Similar to those good physicians and automobile mechanics that we just mentioned, organizational managers have to diagnose what may currently be wrong with a process so that they can successfully repair and/or tune the process up. If they don't do the diagnosis correctly, managers may create training solutions that don't solve the existing problem. So the manager has to go through a process of identifying where in a current sequence of events things are not working the way they should, or how they can be done more efficiently. Only by diligently going through the process of looking at that chain of events in the status quo can a manager identify where the process can be changed to improve organizational productivity and reach the organization's goals.

Challenges to the Training Process

As part of the needs assessment and in order to design training appropriately, we need to identify and discuss some common challenges to the training process. These include minimally prepared or unprepared workers, difficulty in identifying the return on investment provided from training, employee resistance to change and feelings of insecurity, matching the training to the strategic goals of the organization, and logistics issues—including scheduling and making locations available for training courses. Managers have to work through each of these challenges in order for training programs to be successful.

Unprepared Workforce. One of the most significant challenges to work process training is the fact that so many of the individuals being hired into the workforce are ill prepared in the educational basics, including reading and math skills. As we noted in Chapter 6, employers continue to hire substantial numbers of new entrants who have significant education but poor work skills, requiring additional company investment to improve workforce readiness.[24] In cases where the employees don't have the basic skills necessary to succeed, the organization must train them in those basic skill sets before they can be taught the advanced skills necessary to improve organizational processes.

Return on Investment/Cost Justification. Businesses today are naturally concerned with the return that they get from any corporate investment. Training is time-consuming and expensive,[25] and it is no different from any other investment. Executives expect and, in fact, require that training provide a positive return on investment (ROI). HR managers have become more familiar with the ROI calculation discussed in Chapter 2, and they use it to provide justification for the financial cost of training programs.

Resistance to Change and Employee Insecurity. Since this is not a change management text, suffice it to say that virtually all individuals resist changes to their routine. They resist for a variety of reasons—including insecurity, based on their concern that they may not be able to successfully adapt to the change in some way. This insecurity leads to resistance to change, and it can cause significant difficulty in the training process. Management must overcome resistance to change exhibited by the workers so that training can be successful.

Strategic Congruence. Strategic congruence is another challenge to the training process. One of the most critical requirements in corporate training programs is the need to ensure that the training furthers the strategic goals of the organization. Any training program that does not aim squarely at the strategic goals of the organization is difficult to justify in a corporate environment. As HR managers, we have to ensure that our training and development programs help to carry out the organization's strategy over the long term.

Scheduling. The last of our common challenges, scheduling, involves both the timing and the location of the training. As with most things, there's never an ideal time to schedule a training course, especially if it runs for several days or even weeks. The trainees have to leave their regular jobs undone for the period of the training, and the organization has to be able to operate without those trainees performing their normal tasks. In addition, the

WORK
APPLICATION 7-3

Do a simple needs assessment for a job you have or had. Be sure to state the competency model (knowledge, skills, and abilities) it takes to do the job.

WORK
APPLICATION 7-4

Think about the people you have worked with. What is your perception of the preparation they have had for the workforce?

WORK
APPLICATION 7-5

Think about the people you have worked with. What is your perception of their resistance to changes in their work routine?

training may require the use of physical locations that have special equipment or tools and that are available only for limited time periods during the year. These logistics issues may seem minimal, but they frequently create significant problems for the HR department in scheduling training courses.

Employee Readiness

As part of our needs assessment, the manager needs to evaluate the employees who would be taking part in the training. Employees may feel insecure about their ability to learn, and they may therefore be unwilling to participate in training for new processes. We must also evaluate whether the employees are physically and mentally ready to go through the training process successfully. In other words, are they *able and willing* to learn?[26] Do they have the skills and competencies necessary to succeed in this training process?

HR managers select employees who have the ability and willingness to be trained to succeed on the job.

ABILITY. We have to determine whether or not our employees feel that they are *able* to participate in the training process. They might feel that they don't have the background training necessary to succeed in training for a more complex process, meaning they may feel that their core set of skills needs to be improved before they can be successful in more intricate training. Self-efficacy *is whether or not a person believes that they have the capability to do something or attain a particular goal.* If the employee's self-efficacy is low, they may not believe that they have the ability to succeed in the training process. Regardless of whether or not it is true, if the employee *believes* they are unable to learn, then it is highly unlikely that they will be successful in any training process because they are unlikely to try.

If employees feel that they are unable to learn, then the job of the manager becomes one of upgrading the employees' abilities if necessary and then convincing them of their capabilities. In addition, the manager has to analyze the true abilities and limitations of each of the employees who may participate in the training process. Remember that each of us has physical abilities and intellectual abilities, but we don't all have the *same* physical and intellectual abilities. Again, it is management's job to diagnose and determine whether or not an individual has the abilities necessary to succeed in a training process, and not to put people into situations where their lack of specific abilities condemns them to failure.

What happens when people are put into situations where they are almost certain to fail? What happens to their motivation, morale, and job satisfaction? What most likely will happen to their productivity? If managers put people into this type of situation, we are almost assured of lowering their performance level rather than raising it. This is certainly not the way to get maximum productivity out of our workforce, so we want to avoid putting people in training situations where they are almost certainly going to fail.

WORK
APPLICATION 7-6

Describe your self-efficacy for a job you have or have had. How does or did your self-efficacy affect your job performance?

WILLINGNESS. The second major piece in the employee readiness equation is whether or not employees are *willing* to learn what's being taught in a training program. In other words, we have to determine their motivation to learn. Why would our workers not be motivated to learn? There are several potential reasons.

First, the individual may not feel that they need to learn a new process. If they feel that the current process is sufficient and that the new process won't improve their work environment, they may be unwilling to learn. If they feel that the training process is being done solely for political reasons (e.g., many workers harbor a false belief that programs such as diversity training and sexual harassment prevention training are motivated by the perceived need of the organization to be politically correct, even though this is not true), then

Self-efficacy Whether or not a person believes that they have the capability to do something or attain a particular goal

they may not be interested in the training. If the individual doesn't feel that the training is related to their job, they may not be motivated to learn. If the employee is concerned that their work will pile up while they're gone, they may not be motivated to train. If their coworkers or supervisors don't support the fact that the individual will have to be away from the job in order to go through a training course, and as a result put pressure on the individual, that person may not be motivated to go through the training.

A significant part of willingness to learn is based on the support the individual gets from the people around them, including coworkers, supervisors, and even family members. If one of your employees is going to be away from home for a period of several weeks and the employee's family members are opposed to this extended period of separation, it's extremely unlikely the employee is going to be willing to participate in the training. So the manager needs to make sure that the employee is willing to go through the training process.

LEARNING AND SHAPING BEHAVIOR

Step 2 of the training process consists of selecting how to shape or change employee behavior. To do this, trainers have to understand how people learn. So in this section, we begin by explaining learning. Then we discuss three basic learning theories used to shape employee behavior. Next, we put the theories together in Exhibit 7-2 and discuss how to shape or change employee behavior. Then we end with learning styles.

Learning

What is learning? Learning can be many different things; but in a business, we usually need to *know* that our employees have learned something that we are trying to train them to do. How do we know that they have learned a particular thing, then? We know because of changes in their behavior at work. So in our case, learning *is any relatively permanent change in behavior that occurs as a result of experience or practice.*[27] This is a good definition to use in the organizational learning process, due to the fact that it provides us with the visible evidence that individuals have learned something because they *change the way they act.*

People learn in multiple ways. We learn through trial and error, from the consequences that occur as a result of something we've done, and from the consequences of other people's actions. And what makes this process even more complex is the fact that different people prefer to learn differently. We all have preferred learning styles, and we like having the option to pick one style over another.

Learning Theories

Let's take a look now at three common learning theories: classical conditioning, operant conditioning, and social learning. Each of the three is useful for certain types of training.

CLASSICAL CONDITIONING. Classical conditioning was made famous by a physiologist named Ivan Pavlov. Pavlov became famous by causing dogs to salivate even when not in the presence of food. Pavlov proved that when dogs were conditioned to associate the ringing of a bell with being fed, they "learned" to salivate when the bell was rung. What does the fact that a dog would salivate on command have to do with human learning? At first glance, it looks a little silly. However, what Pavlov proved was that animals will react *involuntarily* to a stimulus in their environment if they associate that stimulus with something else. OK, but humans are not dogs, so do humans react involuntarily to a stimulus in the environment? Of course they do. Human beings react involuntarily to stimuli the same way all other animals do.

Have you ever walked down a row of restaurants in your hometown and smelled the aroma of fresh food being prepared, and that reminded you of a relative's home when they were cooking your favorite dinner? This pleasant memory may change your mood, and in

WORK APPLICATION 7-7

Do you like to learn new things? Describe your willingness to learn in college and to train on the job. Will you voluntarily sign up for company training and development programs that are not required for your job?

Learning Any relatively permanent change in behavior that occurs as a result of experience or practice

fact, it may change your behavior because of the feeling of well-being that it creates. Alternately, have you ever heard a sound that caused you to be afraid or to want to run away from it? Why does such a sound cause you to be afraid? If you think for a few seconds, you will probably realize that the sound indicates danger to you, whether you consciously realize it or not. You've been involuntarily conditioned to the feeling of danger associated with the sound. So, Pavlov's classical conditioning results in "direct, involuntary, learned behaviors." The behaviors are *learned* because you have changed the way you act due to some prior experience, and they are *involuntary* because you didn't intentionally learn to act in a particular way in response to the stimulus. Finally, the behaviors are *direct* because the learning occurs as a result of something happening directly to you.

OPERANT CONDITIONING. The second common learning theory is called *operant conditioning,* which is based on reinforcement. Again, most of us have heard of the individual who made this learning theory famous—B. F. Skinner. Skinner's theory of operant conditioning says that behavior is based on the consequences received from behaving in a similar way at an earlier point in time. In other words, if we acted in a certain way previously and received a reward, we will likely repeat that behavior. If, however, we acted in a particular way and received a negative consequence (punishment), then we will probably not repeat the behavior. Skinner tested his theory using his "Skinner box." He would put animals such as a pigeon or a rat in a box and provide a stimulus such as a light above a lever. If the animal chose the right lever, they were rewarded with food. If the animal chose the incorrect lever they would receive punishment such as a mild electrical shock.

Skinner showed that very quickly, the animals would figure out which lever to press in order to receive the reward. So, operant conditioning results in "direct, voluntary, learned behaviors." The subjects in Skinner's experiments *voluntarily* selected the lever that provided the reward, so they learned to behave in a particular way based on the *direct* consequences of their actions. So Skinner proved that animals will voluntary act in order to receive a reward and avoid acting in order to avoid receiving punishment.

WORK
APPLICATION 7-8

Give examples of what you learned in an organization through classical conditioning, operant conditioning, and social learning.

SOCIAL LEARNING. Our third type of learning, social learning, is similar in form to operant conditioning. The difference here is that we are not learning from the consequences of our own actions but from the consequences of the actions of another person. Social learning is also called vicarious learning. The word *vicarious* means "experienced or realized through imaginative or sympathetic participation in the experience of another."[28] So social or

---

7-1 APPLYING THE CONCEPT

Learning Theories

Review the three learning theories below and write the letter corresponding to each theory before the statement(s) illustrating it:

a. classical conditioning
b. operant conditioning
c. social learning

_____ 1. My parents continuously told me how to behave properly as I was growing up. Could that be why customers comment on my good manners and social skills?

_____ 2. I got caught smoking in a no-smoking area and was given a verbal warning. I'm not doing it again because I don't want to get into more trouble and possibly end up losing my job.

_____ 3. Shelly is a very hard worker, but I've never even seen her get as much as a thank-you for her performance. So why should I work?

_____ 4. After seeing what happened to Sean, you better believe that I'm keeping my goggles on when I'm on the job.

_____ 5. I completed the project ahead of schedule and did an excellent job. As a result, my boss gave me a sincere thanks and a $100 gift certificate to Amazon.com. I learned that it is worth putting in extra effort for the boss.

vicarious learning is experienced through watching the actions of another person and witnessing the consequences of those actions. In other words, if a young boy watches his sister receive a cookie as a reward for cleaning her room and he wants a cookie too, he may determine that the best way to get a cookie is to go clean his own room. This would be an example of social learning. Again, social learning is based on *voluntary, learned* actions on the part of the individual, but it is based on *indirect* consequences of the actions of another person.

SOCIAL MEDIA FOR SOCIAL LEARNING. Recent innovation in using social media has provided a new tool for applying social learning. We know that people learn from each other as much as or more than they do from formal training. This is one reason why OJT is used so much. Because this type of learning works so well, and because more than *3 billion* people worldwide are members of at least one social media site, we can utilize social media as a learning tool.

Social media is all around us today. It is also easy to adapt as a platform for organizational learning, especially a fairly new form called micro-learning that we will discuss in more detail in the Trends and Issues section of this chapter. We can discuss problems, provide video and/or audio step-by-step instructions, utilize team-based brainstorming sessions and problem analysis, and discuss complex questions with large groups of combined customers, employees, and managers. You will need to understand the applications of social media in a training and learning environment to successfully manage learning in today's organizations.

Shaping Behavior

We can use the three types of learning that we have just reviewed, especially Skinner's concept of operant conditioning, to shape the behaviors of the employees in the organization. In order to shape the behavior of our employees, we can provide reinforcement (rewards) or punishment or, as a third alternative, provide neither. Take a look at Exhibit 7-2. It shows four methods of shaping behavior. We can break these methods down into a process of applying a reward, removing a reward, applying punishment, removing punishment, or providing no response to the actions of the individual.

So, what's the value of understanding Exhibit 7-2 and the four methods of shaping behavior? If we understand each of the four methods, we can use them to cause workers to act in ways that are conducive to the improvement and ultimate success of the organization. Let's discuss each part of the exhibit.

EXHIBIT 7-2   SHAPING BEHAVIOR

(A) **Positive Reinforcement** Apply a reward	(B) **Punishment** Apply a noxious stimulus— Give bad consequence
(C) **Punishment** Remove a reward	(D) **Negative Reinforcement** Avoid or remove a noxious stimulus

Extinction (E) = The absence of a response,
designed to avoid reinforcing negative behaviors

Shaping (changing) behavior:
A, D = Increasing target behaviors
B, C, E = Decreasing target behaviors

Positive reinforcement. If we *apply* a *reward* (the upper left quadrant A in the exhibit), we're using the concept of positive reinforcement. Positive reinforcement *is providing a reward in return for a constructive action on the part of the subject.* For example, if our employees do something that improves the safety of workers in the organization, we may give them a bonus as a reward. This would be positive reinforcement. Applying a reward to a particular behavior is likely to cause the individual to perform that behavior, or similar behaviors, again. So our employees would be likely to provide other suggestions to improve our business operations because of the past reward. We should realize that positive reinforcement is the most commonly used method of shaping employee behavior when we train new employees to do their jobs and when existing employees need to learn new job requirements and processes.

Negative reinforcement. Our second option would be to *avoid or remove* a *noxious stimulus* (the lower right quadrant D in the exhibit), a process called negative reinforcement. Negative reinforcement *is the withdrawal of a harmful thing from the environment in response to a positive action on the part of the subject.* Negative reinforcement is commonly based on rules, with punishment being given for breaking the rules. A rule itself is not a punishment; it is a means of getting people to do or avoid a specific behavior, such as coming to work on time. But if the rule is broken, punishment is usually the consequence. An example of negative reinforcement working as intended would be you coming to work on time not because you want to be on time but because you want to avoid a punishment for being late. It can also be removing an employee from disciplinary probation for tardiness in response to their positive action of showing up for work on time for a period of time after being disciplined. Avoiding or taking away a negative consequence in response to a positive behavior is likely to cause the individual to perform the desired behavior again. We should realize that negative reinforcement is commonly used during the new employee orientation to make sure employees know the expected behaviors and the consequences for breaking rules. We certainly don't want to punish employees for breaking a rule that they don't know exists.

Punishment. In contrast to reinforcement, we may punish bad behaviors. Punishment is *the application of an adverse consequence, or the removal of a reward, in order to decrease an unwanted behavior.* One method of punishment would be to remove a reward (the lower left quadrant C in the exhibit) as a result of people doing something that they shouldn't have done. Think of taking away the car keys for a school-age driver who does something wrong. Or let's say that our organization has a policy of providing free parking for our workers in a crowded downtown area. We might take away the parking privileges of an individual who continually harasses other workers in the parking lot.

Alternatively, we can *apply a noxious stimulus* (the upper right quadrant B in the exhibit), which is also considered to be punishment. An example here would be suspending a worker without pay because of excessive absenteeism. By suspending the worker, we're applying a negative response. The negative response received by the worker is designed to cause a decline in the behavior that created such a response. So in other words, punishment can be the application of something bad (a noxious stimulus) or the removal of something good (a reward).

We should realize that punishment is not commonly used during training of employees; rather, it is commonly used when employees know how to do the job but just will not meet the job standards, or when employees break a rule and get disciplined for doing so. We will learn more about when and how to discipline employees in Chapter 9.

Extinction. We noted earlier in this section that there are four options for shaping behavior. What is the other option? The last option doesn't fit in the diagram itself, because it's the absence of reinforcement or punishment of any kind. Extinction *is the lack of response, either positive or negative, in order to avoid reinforcing an undesirable behavior.* You may have heard the phrase "Ignore it and it will go away." How does a lack of response cause behavior to be shaped in a way that we desire?

WORK
APPLICATION 7-9

Give examples of how an organization uses positive reinforcement, punishment, negative reinforcement, and extinction to shape employee behavior.

Positive reinforcement Providing a reward in return for a constructive action on the part of the subject

Negative reinforcement Withdrawal of a harmful thing from the environment in response to a positive action on the part of the subject

Punishment The application of an adverse consequence, or the removal of a reward, in order to decrease an unwanted behavior

Extinction The lack of response, either positive or negative, in order to avoid reinforcing an undesirable behavior

Employees will sometimes exhibit problem behavior to cause a reaction from the manager or fellow employees. The employee who exhibits the behavior may delight in causing others concern or consternation. For example, the male employee who continually asks his female manager about organizational sexual harassment policies in front of other workers to cause her discomfort as she explains the policy is most likely *intentionally* acting to cause her embarrassment. In such a case, the female manager may be able to ignore the stimulus behavior and provide no reinforcement. If the manager does so for a long enough time, the employee's behavior will most likely decline or go away completely, because it is not having the desired negative effect on the manager. We should realize that extinction is also not very commonly used because when we train employees, we don't usually ignore behavior in the hope that it will not be repeated—we correct it.

Shaping (changing) behavior. If you understand these methods of shaping behavior, they become powerful tools in your managerial toolbox for changing behavior to increase performance. These tools allow you to *cause* your employees to act in ways you want them to and avoid acting in ways that are detrimental to themselves, their division or department, or the organization as a whole. Now let's discuss how to increase and decrease behaviors to increase performance.

Increasing targeted behavior. If we want to cause the behavior to increase, then we want to use positive or negative reinforcement (quadrant A or D in Exhibit 7-2). Reinforcement, whether positive or negative, is designed to cause an increase in the targeted behavior.

Decreasing targeted behavior. If, on the other hand, we want to cause a particular behavior to decrease, we would use punishment (in either of its forms) or extinction (quadrant B, C, or E in Exhibit 7-2). Punishment and extinction are designed to cause a targeted behavior to decrease over time.

Learning Styles

As a last point in our review of the learning process, we need to briefly discuss various learning styles that people prefer to use. There are more than 70 learning style inventories available in the psychology literature and even some questionnaires that track learning style on the Internet.[29] There is, however, disagreement concerning whether or not we should use preferred learning styles in designing training, including work-related training.

7-2   APPLYING THE CONCEPT

Shaping Behavior

Review the following methods of shaping employee behavior and write the letter corresponding to each before the situation(s) illustrating it.

 a. positive reinforcement

 b. punishment—give bad consequence

 c. punishment—remove reward

 d. negative reinforcement

 e. extinction

____ 6. Betty used to give me that intimidating look when I assigned her a task she didn't want to do, and that behavior made me uncomfortable. So I just ignored it and didn't let her make me feel uncomfortable, and she stopped giving me the look.

____ 7. You know the rules. That behavior is going to cost you $25.

____ 8. You got that angry lady to calm down and leave the store as a happy customer. This behavior leads to keeping our customers. Thanks, keep up the good work.

____ 9. If you don't stop breaking the pricing gun, you will have to buy a new one.

____10. I know you like to get out of work for a while and get our lunches, but because you mixed up the order today, Santana will go tomorrow.

7-1   SELF-ASSESSMENT

Your Learning Style

Below are 10 statements. For each statement, distribute 5 points between the A and B alternatives. If the A statement is very characteristic of you and the B statement is not, place a 5 on the A line and a 0 on the B line. If the A statement is characteristic of you and the B statement is occasionally or somewhat characteristic of you, place a 4 on the A line and a 1 on the B line. If both statements are characteristic of you, place a 3 on the line that is more characteristic of you and a 2 on the line that is less characteristic of you. Be sure to distribute 5 points between each A and B alternative for each of the 10 statements. When distributing the 5 points, try to recall recent situations on the job or in school.

1. When learning:
   _____ A. I watch and listen.
   _____ B. I get involved and participate.
2. When learning:
   _____ A. I rely on my hunches and feelings.
   _____ B. I rely on logical and rational thinking.
3. When making decisions:
   _____ A. I take my time.
   _____ B. I make them quickly.
4. When making decisions:
   _____ A. I rely on my gut feelings about the best alternative course of action.
   _____ B. I rely on a logical analysis of the situation.
5. When doing things:
   _____ A. I am careful.
   _____ B. I am practical.

6. When doing things:
   _____ A. I have strong feelings and reactions.
   _____ B. I reason things out.
7. I would describe myself in the following way:
   _____ A. I am a reflective person.
   _____ B. I am an active person.
8. I would describe myself in the following way:
   _____ A. I am influenced by my emotions.
   _____ B. I am influenced by my thoughts.
9. When interacting in small groups:
   _____ A. I listen, watch, and get involved slowly.
   _____ B. I am quick to get involved.
10. When interacting in small groups:
   _____ A. I express what I am feeling.
   _____ B. I say what I am thinking.

Scoring: Place your answer numbers (0–5) on the lines below. Then add the numbers in each column vertically. Each of the four columns should have a total number between 0 and 25. The total of the two A and B columns should equal 25.

1. _____ A. _____ B. (5)	2. _____ A. _____ B. (5)	
3. _____ A. _____ B. (5)	4. _____ A. _____ B. (5)	
5. _____ A. _____ B. (5)	6. _____ A. _____ B. (5)	
7. _____ A. _____ B. (5)	8. _____ A. _____ B. (5)	
9. _____ A. _____ B. (5)	10. _____ A. _____ B. (5)	
Totals: _____ A. _____ B. (25)	_____ A. _____ B. (25)	
Style: Observing Doing	Feeling Thinking	

There is no best or right learning style; each of the four learning styles has its pros and cons. The more evenly distributed your scores are between the A's and B's, the more flexible you are at changing styles. Understanding your preferred learning style can help you get the most from your learning experiences.

Determining Your Preferred Learning Style

The five odd-numbered A statements refer to your self-description as being "observing," and the five odd-numbered B statements refer to your self-description as "doing." The column with the highest number is your preferred style of learning. Write that style here:

_____

The five even-numbered A statements refer to your self-description as being a "feeling" person, and the five even-numbered B statements refer to your self-description as being a "thinking" person. The column with the highest number is your preferred style. Write that style here:

_____

Putting the two preferences together gives you your preferred learning style. Check it off below:

_____ Accommodator (combines doing and feeling)
_____ Diverger (combines observing and feeling)
_____ Converger (combines doing and thinking)
_____ Assimilator (combines observing and thinking)

Some of the recent research, including a study done by Dr. Beth Rogowsky and her colleagues, says that although we do have preferred learning styles, there is no evidence that receiving instruction in that preferred style allows us to learn any better than receiving instruction in another style.[30] Others argue, though, that there is evidence that we learn better using individual preferred learning styles, if for no other reason than we are more comfortable with our preferred style.[31,32] Despite the disagreement, it pays us to at least understand the issue of individual learning styles because there is no evidence that training using preferred learning styles harm the learning environment, and using individual preferred learning style may even help the trainee learn better. HRM training and development experts might want to continue to review this research over the next several years to see how it ultimately affects student learning though.

Fleming learning styles. One of the common learning style inventories, by Neil Fleming, provides three primary learner options. These three options are *visual, auditory, and tactile learning.*[33] As you would think, visual learners prefer to have material provided in a visual format such as graphs and charts. Auditory learners, on the other hand, generally prefer to learn information based on hearing that information. Auditory learners tend to perform best in a historical classroom setting where the teacher stands in front of the class and teaches while the students passively listen. Finally, tactile learners prefer to learn by doing. Tactile learners want to physically perform a task in order to learn. Most of us use a mix of all three of the major learning styles. Therefore, a trainer should take each of the styles into account when creating a training program.

You should realize that we provide multiple tactile-learning application and skill-building opportunities in this book. Which of the three options do you prefer when learning something?

Kolb learning styles. A more complex learning style inventory was developed by David Kolb.[34] Kolb's model is probably the most accepted of the learning style models in use today.[35] To determine your preferred learning style, complete Self-Assessment 7-1.

DESIGN AND DELIVERY OF TRAINING

Recall that back in Chapter 1, we identified four important HRM skills: technical, human relations, conceptual and design (decision making), and business skills. Essentially, all of the training methods are used to develop specific skills that can be classified into one of these four skills categories. Once we have completed our needs assessment and selected how we plan to shape behavior, we are ready to complete step 3 of the training process: designing the training by selecting training methods and then delivering the training. So in this section, we will present which training methods to use based on which types of skills we are developing. Exhibit 7-3 presents the type of skills, the training methods appropriate for developing each skill, and descriptions of the training methods.

Before we actually conduct the training, in step 4, the HR department or other trainers also have to select the types of training delivery. The choice will depend to some extent on what information is being transferred, as well as on the options that are available to the particular organization. We also need to look at the best type of training to use in order to maximize transfer of knowledge while minimizing the cost of the training process. Each of the four training types has advantages and disadvantages that have to be understood to assign the correct option to a specific type of training program. In the next sections, we discuss our four options: on-the-job, classroom, distance, and simulation training.

On-the-Job Training (OJT)

On-the-job training (OJT) is done at the work site with the resources the employee uses to perform the job. The manager, or an employee selected by the manager, usually conducts the training one-on-one with the trainee. Because of its proven record of success, job instructional training (JIT)—a specific type of on-the-job training—is a popular training type used worldwide.

LO 7-4

Discuss each of the major training delivery types.

WORK
APPLICATION 7-10

Identify and describe the training method(s) used to train and develop you for a job you have or have had.

EXHIBIT 7-3   SKILLS AND TRAINING METHODS

Skills Developed	Methods	Description
• Technical Skills	a. Written Material, Lectures, Videotapes, Question-and-Answer Sessions, Discussions, Demonstrations b. Programmed Learning	• Questions or problems related to previously presented material are presented to the trainee in a booklet or on a computer screen. The trainee is asked to select a response to each question or problem and is given feedback on the response. • Depending on the material presented, programmed learning may also develop interpersonal and communication skills.
	c. Job Rotation	• Employees are trained to perform different jobs. Job rotation also develops trainees' conceptual skills.
	d. Projects	• Trainees are given special assignments, such as developing a new product or preparing a report. Certain projects may also develop trainees' interpersonal skills and conceptual skills.
• Human Relations Skills	e. Role-Playing	• Trainees act out situations that might occur on the job, such as handling a customer complaint, to develop skill at handling such situations on the job.
	f. Behavior Modeling	• Trainees observe how to perform a task correctly, by watching either a live demonstration or a videotape. Trainees role-play the observed skills and receive feedback on their performance. Trainees develop plans for using the observed skills on the job.
• Conceptual and Design/Business Skills	g. Cases	• The trainee is presented with a simulated situation and asked to diagnose and solve the problems involved. Trainees usually must also answer questions about their diagnosis and solution.
	h. In-Basket Exercises	• The trainee is given actual or simulated letters, memos, reports, and so forth that would typically come to the person holding the job. The trainee must determine what action each item would require and must assign priorities to the actions.
	i. Management Games	• Trainees work as part of a team to "manage" a simulated company over a period of several game "quarters" or "years."
	j. Interactive Videos	• Trainees can view videotapes that present situations requiring conceptual skills or decision making.

7-3   APPLYING THE CONCEPT

Training Methods

For each of the training situations below, identify the most appropriate training method. Use the letters a through j from Exhibit 7-3 as your answers.

____ 11. You want your customer service staff to do a better job of handling customer complaints.

____ 12. Your large department has a high turnover rate, and new employees need to learn several rules and regulations to perform their jobs.

____ 13. You need your new employees to learn how to handle the typical daily problems they will face on the job.

____ 14. You need an employee to conduct an Internet search to find out more about a new product you want to buy for the department; you want a special report.

____ 15. You want employees to be able to do each other's job when they take vacations.

____ 16. You want to improve your employees' ability to sell products to customers in the store so that customers don't end up leaving and buying the products online.

____ 17. You need to prepare middle managers to advance to upper-level managers. You are considering having them run a simulated company getting quarterly results.

MODEL 7-1   JOB INSTRUCTIONAL TRAINING STEPS

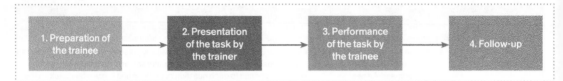

JOB INSTRUCTIONAL TRAINING (JIT). JIT has four steps, presented in Model 7-1 and described here.

SHRM

L:6
On-the-Job Training (OJT)

Step 1: Preparation of the trainee. Put the trainee at ease as you create interest in the job and encourage questions. Explain the task objectives and quantity and quality requirements, and discuss their importance.

Step 2: Presentation of the task by the trainer. Perform the task yourself slowly, explaining each step several times. Once the trainee seems to have the steps memorized, have the trainee explain each step as you perform the task. Prepare a written list of the steps in complex tasks and give a copy to the trainee.

Step 3: Performance of the task by the trainee. Have the trainee perform the task slowly while explaining each step. Correct any errors and be willing to help the trainee perform any difficult steps. Continue until the employee can perform the task proficiently.

Step 4: Follow-up. Tell the trainee who is available to provide help with any questions or problems. Gradually give the trainee more autonomy. Begin by checking quality and quantity frequently; then decrease the amount of checking based on the trainee's skill level. Watch the trainee perform the task and be sure to correct any errors or faulty work procedures before they become habits. Be patient and encouraging.

Even though OJT is fairly expensive on a per-person basis, many organizations still use it heavily because of the fact that it works very well. See Exhibit 7-4 for the advantages and disadvantages of OJT.

Classroom Training

Our second training option is classroom training. Classroom training is also a common form of training in organizations. To accomplish classroom training, the organization will create a training course—including content, instruction methods, lesson plans, and instructor materials—and provide all these materials to a qualified instructor who will teach the class.

Classroom training is generally very good for consistently transferring general knowledge or theories about a topic to a large number of people. It is generally not very good for teaching specific hands-on skills because of the passive nature of learning in a classroom. However, it is effective when using the same equipment that is used on the job. For example, many large banks have to train lots of tellers, and they conduct teller training in a classroom setting at headquarters, using an expert trainer so that the employees can go to the bank and actually begin work without any further training at the branch.

Employees are often given on-the-job training, especially in small businesses.

Let's do a quick review of some of the advantages and disadvantages of classroom training in Exhibit 7-5.

EXHIBIT 7-4 ON-THE-JOB TRAINING'S ADVANTAGES AND DISADVANTAGES

Advantages	Disadvantages
• Most people learn best by actually doing a job, in conjunction with how-to explanations.	• The one-to-one aspect of the training means that it is relatively high in cost on a per-person basis.
• The training can be immediately transferred to the job.	• Trainers may not know how to teach, may be unmotivated or unable to transfer their knowledge successfully, or may transfer their own bad habits to the trainee.
• Training occurs person to person on the actual job site and includes all of the incidental factors associated with the job.	• The training may be inconsistent unless trainers follow a standardized training plan.
• Training is done in an interactive environment, with feedback from the trainer.	• If the equipment being used is expensive, it may be dangerous to have trainees operating and potentially harming it because they are not yet skilled operators.
• The trainer is typically highly competent in doing the job.	• Training often disrupts the work environment.
• The instructor can customize the training to the trainee's needs.	

EXHIBIT 7-5 CLASSROOM TRAINING'S ADVANTAGES AND DISADVANTAGES

Advantages	Disadvantages
• Classroom training is a good method of providing consistent knowledge or information about a general topic to a fairly large number of people.	• Classroom training is often a passive environment, where the learner just absorbs the information provided.
• A significant number of students can be trained at the same time.	• The pace of the training may be too fast for some students and too slow for others, causing anxiety or boredom.
• Information provided to the trainees is typically more consistent than with OJT.	• It is more difficult to cater to different learning styles in a classroom setting than in OJT.
• Instructors are usually professional trainers.	
• Classroom training is less expensive than OJT, due to the fact that it's one-to-many training.	
• It provides a somewhat interactive environment, based on question-and-answer sessions.	
• It does not disrupt the actual work environment.	

Distance or E-Learning

Our third option is some form of distance learning—also called e-learning—in either a synchronous or an asynchronous format. *Synchronous distance learning* occurs when all of the trainees sign in to a particular Learning Management System (LMS) such as **Blackboard** or **Moodle,** or a corporate LMS, where their instructor then interacts with them and teaches the topics for the day. In contrast, *asynchronous distance learning* is a process in which the student can sign in to the training site at any point in time, and materials are available for their studies. The instructor may or may not be online at the same time as the student, but there's no dedicated connection between the two for the purpose of teaching the information. In many cases today, the student does not have to work through an LMS. They can learn using any number of free or low-cost apps for training in just about any field.

Distance learning, similar to classroom training, is valuable for teaching basic concepts and providing general information on the topic. There's typically even less interaction

EXHIBIT 7-6 DISTANCE TRAINING'S ADVANTAGES AND DISADVANTAGES

Advantages	Disadvantages
• Training may be available 24/7/365.	• There is a requirement for self-discipline on the part of the trainee. The responsibility for "getting" the information shifts from the instructor to the trainee.
• Students can learn at their own pace.	• A teacher in a standardized distance learning course often lacks the ability to respond directly to student needs and questions.
• There's no requirement for a physical classroom space, or necessarily for an instructor to be available at a particular point in time. No time is lost to commuting.	• In its basic form, distance learning often lacks the functionality to provide immediate feedback to students on their success or failure.
• The option is available to provide multiple media that can enhance the learning process by matching up with different learning styles.	• Distance learning programs tend to have high initial start-up costs due to the need to create voluminous online materials.
• Distance learning is a reasonably low-cost method of training, over time. Once the course is set up, costs to train additional students are fairly minimal.	• Student dishonesty is more difficult to identify, and testing usually has to be in open-book form.
• The training does not disrupt the actual work environment.	• There is a lack of social interaction, which can inhibit learning in certain fields.

between an instructor and trainees in this form than in classroom training. Let's analyze some of the advantages and disadvantages of distance learning in Exhibit 7-6.

Self-directed learning is a specific kind of distance learning. In self-directed learning, individuals go completely at their own pace, and they are able to study whatever aspects of the topic they think they need to study to be successful while leaving other parts of the training uncompleted. Massively Open Online Courses, or MOOCs, are primarily self-directed learning. Self-directed training tends to have all of the potential advantages and disadvantages of other forms of distance learning. The most significant issue in self-directed learning tends to be the fact that if individuals are not motivated to learn on their own, they will be unsuccessful because nobody else is going to follow their progress and push them to complete the training.

Simulations

The trend today is toward having more active involvement of participants and offering online simulation training and development.[36] A simulation is a training method whereby we may simulate a real-life situation to teach students what actions to take in the event that they encounter the same or a similar situation on the job. Some common examples of simulations are flight simulators, driving simulators, and firefighting simulations. Simulations would typically be used in situations where actually performing an action or set of actions could lead to significant financial cost (because of lost equipment) or could put the trainee in significant danger of injury or death.

In these types of cases, providing simulations makes much more sense than actually performing a particular task. Asking students to perform in a simulation will also generally cause them to go through the same set of emotions that they would go through in the real-life situation being simulated. Training through the use of a simulation allows the student to experience these emotions and learn to control them in order to resolve a complex and dangerous situation. Let's review the advantages and disadvantages of simulations in Exhibit 7-7.

ASSESSING TRAINING

The fifth and last step of our training process (Exhibit 7-1) is assessment. No matter what the training covers, we always want to evaluate whether or not it achieved the

SHRM

L:5
E-Learning and Use of Technology in Training

WORK
APPLICATION 7-11

Identify and describe the type(s) of training you received for a job you have or had.

SHRM

Q:8
Measurement Systems

LO 7-5

Briefly discuss the Four-Level Evaluation Method for assessing training programs and the three common ways we measure training success.

EXHIBIT 7-7 SIMULATION TRAINING'S ADVANTAGES AND DISADVANTAGES

Advantages	Disadvantages
• Simulation is a low-risk method of training individuals on how to react to a complex situation.	• Simulations can become "video games" to the student; and as a result, they may not be taken seriously.
• Generally, simulation is a very realistic form of training. Simulations can convincingly emulate actual physical situations.	• Simulation systems may be very expensive to create and/or maintain.
• Simulations allow the student to try out experimental solutions to a problem. If the solution fails, the simulation can just be reset.	• Complex computer-based simulations may require a very powerful and expensive processor in order to run.
• Results of the students' actions can be analyzed post hoc to determine whether or not different actions might have been more successful.	• Some processes cannot be simulated successfully due to a lack of knowledge of the details of the process.
• Simulation does not disrupt the actual work environment.	

shaped behavior identified through our needs assessment. Training can be designed to cause changes in a variety of employee attitudes and behaviors; and as a result, it can be assessed in a number of different ways, depending on what we were trying to accomplish. In this section, we present four assessment methods and how to choose an assessment method.

SHRM

L:4
Training Evaluation:
Kirkpatrick's Model

Assessment Methods

One of the most common assessment options, first identified by Donald Kirkpatrick, is called the Four-Level Evaluation Method.[37] It measures *reaction, learning, behaviors,* and *results.*

Reaction evaluations measure how the individual responds to the actual training process. Self-reporting measures are quick and common measures of training.[38] In reaction evaluations, the organization asks the participants how they feel about the training process, including the content provided, the instructors, and the knowledge that they gained by going through the process. They may also be asked about what new skills they have learned during the training process. This is the lowest level of training evaluation, and it is frequently discounted due to its subjectivity and because some people overestimate their capabilities.[39] After all, is the trainee the best person to evaluate the knowledge they've gained if that knowledge is brand new to them? Certainly, reaction evaluations are less rigorous than some other forms of evaluation, but they still provide the organization with valuable feedback concerning the learners' state of mind at the end of the training process as well as their attitude toward the process at its conclusion. Student course assessments are an example of reaction evaluations.

Learning evaluations are level-two measures designed to determine what knowledge the individual gained, whether they learned any new skills because of the training, and whether the person's attitudes toward their knowledge or skill set has changed as a result of the training. Learning evaluations are easily done using quizzes, tests, and even topic-based discussions. Learning evaluations help the organization evaluate the skill of the instructor as well as the change in the knowledge set of the trainee. If the instructor is inadequate as a teacher, it should show up in a learning evaluation measurement. We should also be able to see whether or not the individual gained knowledge of the subject because of the training process.

Behavior evaluations are the third level of evaluating training processes. Behavior evaluations are designed to determine whether or not the trainee's on-the-job behaviors changed as a result of the training. Behavior evaluations usually take the form of observation of the individual on the job, after completion of the training process. Did the process of going through the training have a direct effect on the individual's post-training job

The Four-Level Evaluation Method helps managers measure the effectiveness of employee training.

performance? The behavior evaluation is specifically designed to identify whether or not the individual is able to transfer the knowledge gained into new skills that they then use in their work.

Results evaluation is the fourth and final level of training evaluation. In a results evaluation, we try to determine whether or not individual behavioral changes have improved organizational results. In other words, we look at the organization's bottom line to determine whether or not productivity has increased. This is the level at which ROI is measured and evaluated to see whether or not the training has paid off for the company. However, ROI is not the only thing that we measure at this level. Other results that we may measure include increased quality of work, lower absenteeism and turnover, reductions in rework and scrap, lower on-the-job accident rates, and many others. What we're looking for in a results evaluation is concrete evidence that the training resulted in organizational changes that were valuable in some form.

Choosing Assessment Methods

Why not just evaluate all of our training programs at each of the four levels? The primary reason is that it costs the organization money to go through the evaluation process. So we don't want to evaluate something unless we need to. In fact, as we go from levels 1 through 4, the cost of evaluating the training process increases with each level. Let's identify when we might use each of the four evaluation levels.

Reaction evaluations (level 1) help us identify employee attitudes toward the training process. If, in fact, the training process has been designed to change employee *attitudes* such as motivation toward their work or satisfaction with their job, level 1 evaluation may be critical. The perception of the trainee in this case may be more important in changing their level of motivation and job satisfaction than any new skills that they actually learned.

Learning evaluations (level 2) are used if there's a need to evaluate more than employee attitude. We may wish to be certain that the trainee has gained a depth of knowledge of a particular issue to ensure that they are capable of putting their knowledge to use. For instance, to comply with federal harassment statutes, all US businesses need to ensure that their employees are trained on the concept of sexual harassment and how to avoid it. If we

WORK
APPLICATION 7-12

Which training assessment methods are used where you work or have worked? Give examples of the training and its assessment method.

SHRM

L:8
Transfer of Training: Design Issues, Facilitating Transfer

want to be certain that our employees know what sexual harassment is, we may choose to do a learning evaluation of that particular training session through giving a test.

Behavior evaluation (level 3) is needed not only to ensure that new knowledge has been gained but also to ensure that the individual knows how to apply that knowledge by acting in a certain way. Performing a behavior evaluation is the only way that we can truly measure whether or not the individual has transferred the knowledge gained into actions that will improve their performance. An example here would be training operators for a nuclear power plant. Determining their attitude toward their work and whether or not they have the innate knowledge necessary to perform the work is insufficient in this case. It would be critical to determine whether or not they could act correctly to maintain and operate the nuclear reactor, so we would observe their actual performance on the job. You can quickly see here that we need to be absolutely certain that they'll take correct action—in other words, that they will behave in the manner necessary to correct the failure.

Results evaluation (level 4) is the fourth and final level. In a results evaluation, we're trying to determine whether individual behavioral changes have improved organizational results. In other words, we're looking at the bottom line for the organization to determine if productivity increased. This is the level at which ROI will be measured and evaluated in order to see it the training has paid off for the company. However, ROI is not the only thing that we will measure at this level. Other results that may be measured include increased quality of work, lower absenteeism and turnover, reductions in rework and scrap, lower on-the-job accident rates, and many others. What we're looking for in a results evaluation is concrete evidence that the training resulted in organizational changes that were valuable in some form.

Measuring Training Success

One challenge in assessment is developing metrics to assess training.[40] Measurements of training have become significantly more important in the past few years. We now have the capacity to analyze large sets of data to find out how successful a particular approach is in creating a more skilled workforce. We also want to make sure we don't spend money without getting results. There are dozens of metrics for measuring training effectiveness, but let's take a look at a few of the most common measures here.

7-4 APPLYING THE CONCEPT

Training Assessment Methods

Review the following assessment methods and write the letter corresponding to each one before the situation(s) where it is most appropriate.

a. reaction evaluation
b. learning evaluation
c. behavior evaluation
d. results evaluation

____18. You are a software sales manager and you want your new sales reps to be able to demonstrate the various features of your software.

____19. You are a restaurant owner who installed a new food-ordering computer system with the objective of speeding up the time it takes to serve meals, so you need to train employees on how to use the new system.

____20. You are the HR manager and want to make sure that your staff understands what questions they can and can't legally ask during the selection process.

____21. You are the service desk manager at a retail store and need to train employees on how to effectively deal with angry customers when they return merchandise. You want the employees to remain calm and satisfy the customer.

____22. You are the HR manager responsible for diversity, and you develop a training program to help employees better understand each other and not use stereotypes so that they can work well together.

ROI (a results metric) is probably still the measure with the most meaning to those outside the HR department. Although it is sometimes hard to identify how to calculate ROI in a training situation (because of the difficulty of identifying the specific value of the gain), in at least some cases, it can be done quickly and easily. For instance, if a particular training program is designed to reduce *annual voluntary turnover rates* and it does so, the ROI measure would be as follows:

L:10
Determining Return on
Investment (ROI)

Average cost of turnover of one employee = $7,500

Annual voluntary turnover reduction after training = 8 employees

Total cost of training (course development, materials, instructor, etc.) = $25,000

$$\text{ROI} = \frac{\text{Gain form investment} - \text{Cost of investment}}{\text{Cost of investment}} = \frac{(\$7,500 \times 8) - \$25,000}{\$25,000}$$

$$\frac{\$35,000}{\$25,000} = 140\% \text{ ROI}$$

Customer satisfaction (another result) is another area where we may want to measure training results. If we perform customer service training and have baseline surveys on historical levels of customer satisfaction, we can compare those levels prior to and after the training to see whether customer satisfaction rates went up. This will not provide a direct dollar value for the training, but if the sales or marketing managers have data on "value per customer" provided to the organization and rates at which dissatisfied customers leave, and if these rates show lower *customer attrition*—then this can give us the means to do an indirect ROI calculation.

We may also want to evaluate *employee satisfaction* (reaction) levels after particular types of training—especially developmental training, which usually doesn't give us an immediate return on our investment. We will talk in detail about employee job satisfaction, and why and how we measure it, in Chapter 10. But for now, just remember that it is a predictor of absenteeism and turnover, which both cost companies lots of money. There are also strong correlations between job satisfaction and customer satisfaction as well as other positive organizational outcomes like *sales performance/revenue generation* (result), *individual productivity* (behavior), *accuracy/quality* (learning/behavior) of work, and others.

TALENT MANAGEMENT AND DEVELOPMENT

L0 7-6

Now that you have learned about the five steps of the training process, let's discuss developing employees. We should realize, however, that development programs also follow the same five steps of the training process, as the steps listed in Exhibit 7-1 state both training and development. Remember from the beginning of the chapter that employee development deals primarily with training workers for *future* jobs, not their current position. In this section, we discuss careers, common methods of employee development, and a model of career development consequences.

Discuss the term *career* and
the three common methods
of employee development.

Careers

What is a career? Is a career in the 21st century the same as a career in the 1960s or 1970s? Do individuals today go through just one or many careers throughout their work life? Half a century ago, a large percentage of people would spend their entire work life with one company. This obviously does not happen very often in modern organizations. In fact, there's much evidence that says that you will likely have several changes in career throughout your work life.

A Bureau of Labor Statistics survey that followed individuals born between 1957 and 1964 cited an average of 11 *jobs* per person in this group. The report defined a job as an uninterrupted period of work with a particular employer.[41] So, if we defined a career as we did in the 1960s and said that to have a successful career, you had to go to work after graduating from college, stay with that employer for 40 years while moving upward through a progression of jobs from lower levels to higher levels, and then retire with a pension, very few of us today would have a "successful" career. Obviously, then, the concept of career has changed.

So how do we define a career in the 21st century workforce? Douglas Hall defined career as a process where the person, not the organization, is the manager of the process. His definition states: "A career *is the individually perceived sequence of attitudes and behaviors associated with work-related experiences and activities over the span of the person's life.*"[42] Whew! Let's break this definition down into its subcomponents.

"Individually perceived." This definition of the term *career* relies heavily on the perception of the individual who is making the judgment concerning success or failure of the career. So, whether or not a career is defined as successful or a failure is determined within the individual's own mind. If you go through 4, or 5, or 10 different jobs in your lifetime, and if you perceive that as being successful, then you are a success. If you perceive it as a failure, then you have failed.

"Sequence of attitudes and behaviors." A career consists of both attitudes and behaviors, so it is not only *what* you do; it's also the way you *feel* about what you do and how well you think you've done over time. What is an attitude? Attitude is simply a positive or negative individual judgment about a particular situation. So your career involves not only the things that you do but also the way you think and how you feel about your progression of jobs over time.

"Associated with work-related experiences and activities over the span of the person's life." The definition of career involves not only the direct work that is done but also all work-related experiences and activities. So, even nonwork activities that are work related, such as training off-site, would be included in our definition of career. We can even extend this to the way your family and friends interact with you and your job, and we can say that any interaction of family, friends, and work could help define your career. This is one place where attitudes come into play. Your friends and family know how you feel about your job and how it allows you to interact with others or prevents you from interacting with others in different circumstances. Using this definition of career avoids the problem of having to confront the fact that by the 1960s definition, most of us would fail to have a *successful* career; and it also allows us to take into account the significant factors of perception and attitude.

Why Career Development?

Twenty-first century organizations need to provide our employees with reasonable career paths and career counseling so that they can achieve their personal goals over the course of their career. These services can create significant motivation in our workforce that, as we noted earlier, can lead to a major improvement in productivity and job satisfaction as well as lower absenteeism and turnover.[43]

The first factor that has caused companies to become more concerned with career development is the nature of jobs in a modern organization. Recall from Chapter 2 that many of our jobs are knowledge management jobs and that the individuals who fill these jobs have special skills. Because people with these special skills (human intellectual capital) are in short supply, the organization cannot afford to lose individuals with such abilities. So we spend significant amounts of time and money on developing them, which can help the organization reduce turnover of highly skilled employees.

Another issue is that the national culture of the United States has changed in the past 30 to 40 years, and the millennial generation of workers (many of you) have significantly different expectations of what they are going to be able to do in their careers than did their parents. millennial workers expect to have significant freedom at work to do what they think they need to do and make the money that they expect to make. Such high expectations create difficulty for organizations. We have to create policies and procedures that will not harm these individuals' initiative to work but that will also cause them to recognize the realities of the workplace. Through the process of career development, we can

T:1
SHRM
Definition of a Career

T:2
SHRM
Balancing Work and Life

E:5
SHRM
Training and Development:
Vocational and Career Counseling/
Career Pathing

T:9
SHRM
Career Development

L:12
SHRM
Human/Intellectual Capital

Career the individually perceived sequence of attitudes and behaviors associated with work-related experiences and activities over the span of the person's life show these younger workers how they can progress in their careers, be entrepreneurial, and reach their personal career goals.

The next major reason for career development is the significant continuing pressure that organizations are getting from governments to provide career paths for individuals who have historically been disadvantaged. Even though there are many different EEO laws on the books and we have had such laws for over 50 years, there's still a significant disparity between the number of Caucasian male managers and managers from all other groups.[44] Career development programs can create career paths for individuals who are members of these disadvantaged groups and who are qualified to go into management or other professional programs. This not only helps the individual employee; it also assists the organization in its diversity efforts.

Finally, good employee development and career planning programs can help the organization avoid productivity and disciplinary problems associated with employees who are stagnating in a particular job. This may be due to career plateauing. A career plateau *occurs when an individual feels unchallenged in their current job and has little or no chance of advancement*. If our employees feel as if their career has stagnated, they are more likely to become disciplinary problems. We may be able to avoid such problems by providing the opportunity for individuals to progress in their career over time.

There are many other reasons for career development, but these are some of the most common issues. So as you can see, there are a number of reasons why career planning has become a major issue to 21st century organizations.

──────── SHRM
T:7
Plateauing

Common Methods of Employee Development

So we need to develop our employees. How do we go about doing that? Can we outsource the development function to organizations with specific expertise in that field, or should we perform this function in-house? There are a series of common methods that organizations use, including the outsourcing option, or internal development through formal education, experience, and assessments. Let's go through a brief description of each of these options for development.

OUTSOURCING EMPLOYEE DEVELOPMENT. Based on a recent survey by **ADP**, "91 percent of large companies and 80 percent of midsized companies" say that outsourcing one or more HR functions provides "real value."[45] Outsourcing of the training and development function significantly lags other functions in the HR department, though.[46] Even so, modern organizations must evaluate whether or not outsourcing of the training and development functions makes sense. If the company can reduce costs for training and development as well as improve the quality of the development function, it may make sense for the organization to consider outsourcing of these functions.

Probably the most significant *strategic* issue in any outsourcing debate is whether or not the organization might lose control of key processes or functions that have historically been performed within the company. If training and development are critical functions within the organization that help us maintain or advance our competitive advantage over rivals, we can ill afford to outsource those functions.

──────── SHRM
L:7; Q:13
Outsourcing Employee
Development

FORMAL EDUCATION. Our first internal method of employee development, *formal education,* provides employees the opportunity to participate in programs that will improve their general knowledge in areas such as finance, project management, or logistics. These formal education opportunities include such things as degree programs at colleges and universities, short courses of study that are available from many different sources (including private training firms and public agencies), and courses in community colleges. Such formal education courses may be held with any of the training and delivery methods discussed earlier.

The intent of formal education programs is to provide the student with a specific set of information about a particular topic. Through formal education, we can provide

──────── SHRM
L:9
Employee Development: Formal
Education, Experience, Assessment

Career plateau When an
individual feels unchallenged in
their current job and has little or
no chance of advancement

programs for every individual within the organization, from the executives down to the first-line supervisors. At the executive level, we might send a strong midlevel manager from the company to a university executive MBA program. In contrast, at the supervisor level, the organization would probably want new first-line supervisors to go through courses that teach supervisory skills, leadership, coaching, and basic financial analysis. Many organizations pay part or all of the cost of formal education for their employees.

EXPERIENCE. Employee development programs that use experience as a method for developing the individual would seek to put the person through a number of different types of job-related experiences over time. Such an experience-based program might include job rotation to provide them with a wide range of experiences within the company. This allows the person to see more of what goes on within the organization and how each job ties to others.

Experience-based employee development might also include the use of coaches or mentors for the individual. The coach or mentor will work with the person to identify how these different job experiences help the individual to learn and grow within the organization.[47] Development using job experience can successfully be used from the executive level all the way down to the level of work teams within the organization. In fact, there's significant evidence that career experience, team experience, and job-related skills are all related to higher levels of team performance.[48]

In today's flatter organizations, it has become more difficult to climb the old corporate ladder. Plus, younger workers become bored doing the same job. Therefore, giving employees a variety of experience through lateral jobs that provide new challenges and experience, with pay raises, may help to keep employees satisfied and with the organization.

**WORK
APPLICATION 7-13**

State some of your career goals and the methods you will use to develop yourself to meet these goals.

EMPLOYEE ASSESSMENT. There are a number of different assessment tools that provide individuals with information about how they think, how they interact with others, and how they manage their own actions and emotions. These assessments provide individuals with information that allows them to understand better how they can manage others within the organization. Some of the more common measures include psychological assessments, emotional intelligence tests, and performance appraisals. Each of these assessments, if properly used, provides individuals with information that can be used to modify the way that they interact with others within the organization. We will review performance appraisals in the next chapter. However, let's take a look at the other two options now.

Psychological Assessments. These have gained significant acceptance within the workplace, and they include tests such as the Myers-Briggs Type Indicator (MBTI), the Birkman Method, and the Benchmarks Assessment tool. Each of the psychological assessment tools provides information about the person's style of thinking, interacting with others, management, and leadership.

SHRM

Q:3
Emotional Intelligence

The MBTI is probably the most common personality-type assessment used for employee development, but each of the tests has advantages and disadvantages compared to the other options. However, the validity and reliability of any of the common forms of psychological assessment have been questioned by various researchers.[49] Even with the weaknesses in validity and reliability, several of the personality assessment tools have been in use for many years and have shown legitimate real-world value in assessing the basic type of personality exhibited by individual employees within the organization.

Emotional Intelligence. Emotional intelligence is *the way that we identify, understand, and use our own emotions as well as the emotions of others to promote our working relationships.* It is an important part of human relations skills. Emotional intelligence is also referred to as an emotional quotient (EQ), making it similar to intelligence quotient (IQ). It is said that to be highly successful, a person needs a high IQ, a high EQ, and training on what to do to succeed.

Emotional intelligence The way that we identify, understand, and use our own emotions as well as the emotions of others to promote our working relationships

Emotional intelligence has also been described as "Our Most Versatile Tool for Success."[50] Author James Runde says, "What I found was that EQ was the secret sauce to career success."[51] We also now know that "regulating negative emotions is critical to peak performance"[52] in any work we perform, so how do we analyze EQ? The Mayer-Salovey-Caruso Emotional Intelligence Test (MSCEIT) is one of the more common tools used to measure emotional intelligence. The MSCEIT consists of four pieces: perceiving emotion (the ability to identify your own and others' emotions), the use of emotion to facilitate thought (the ability to use emotions to focus attention and to think more rationally, logically, and creatively), understanding emotion (the ability to analyze and evaluate your own and others' emotions), and managing emotion (the ability to adjust emotions of yourself and others).[53]

Here again, the validity and reliability of the tests are still in some question. However, as with personality assessments, there's at least some evidence in the business arena that higher levels of emotional intelligence provide employees with a greater chance of success as they move up in the organization.[54]

A Model of Career Development Consequences

Because the organization and the individual have joint responsibility for career planning and development, both will suffer significant consequences if the planning isn't done successfully. Individual employees go through a series of career stages as they progress through their work life. Within each of these stages, the employee has different needs that the organization must meet so the relationship between the two can remain stable and the worker will continue to be motivated to produce for the organization. Organizations must respond successfully to the individual employee based on the employee's current career stage.

Let's discuss the commonly identified stages of career development first identified by Donald Super and Douglas Hall.[55] You can see them summarized in the first section of Exhibit 7-8.

Exploration. The first career development stage, called the *exploration* stage, is the period of time during which the individual is identifying the personal needs that will be satisfied by a particular type of work, the types of jobs that interest them, and the skill sets necessary to be able to accomplish those types of jobs. This stage is usually identified as being between the ages of 15 and 24.

EXHIBIT 7-8   CAREER STAGES AND THE HIERARCHY OF NEEDS

Exploration	Establishment	Maintenance	Disengagement
• Meet personal needs • Identify interests • Evaluate skills • Tentative work choice	• Career entry • Building skills • Security/stabilization • Work relationships • Work contributions • Advancement	• Personal satisfaction • Continue advancement • Coach/mentor • Improve policies and procedures	• Lower output • Coach/mentor as desired • Balance between work and nonwork

MASLOW'S HIERARCHY OF NEEDS

Physiological	Safety/Security	Social	Esteem	Self-Actualization
• Air, food, water, sleep, etc.	• Physical shelter, physical security, financial security, stability, etc.	• Friendship, love, relationships, family, belonging to social groups, etc.	• Social status, recognition, self-respect, reputation, achievement, etc.	• Wisdom and justice—pass knowledge to others because *you* think it is valuable.

Establishment. The second stage, called *establishment,* is the period when the individual has entered into a career and becomes concerned with building a skill set, developing work relationships, and advancing and stabilizing their career. In the establishment phase, we see the individual begin to make significant personal contributions to their career in the organization and begin to create relationships or alliances with coworkers that allow them to become more secure within the organization. This stage is usually identified as covering approximately age 25 through the mid-40s.

Maintenance. This is the third stage of career development. The maintenance stage covers the period from the mid-40s to age 60 years old or older. In the maintenance stage, the individual typically continues to advance but begins to seek personal satisfaction in the jobs that they perform for the organization. This is the phase where we see individual employees begin to act as mentors or trainers to their younger coworkers and to act to improve the organization and its processes and policies because they see a need to do so.

Disengagement. Finally, the fourth stage is identified as the *disengagement* stage. This stage typically shows lower levels of output and productivity as the individual prepares for life after work. During this stage, because of the desire to balance nonwork with work activities, the individual may begin to choose to work only on efforts they feel are necessary or worthy of their attention. They may continue to mentor or sponsor other individuals in the organization as those others progress through their own careers. Obviously, this stage goes from the early 60s to whatever point at which the individual finally completely disengages from the organization through retirement.

You may be wondering why these career stages matter. Let's take a look now at the second part of Exhibit 7-8. We have added Abraham Maslow's Hierarchy of Needs below each of the career stages. It's rather surprising how closely Maslow's needs hierarchy matches up with our career stages. We could accomplish a similar matching process with many other motivation theories, but this one serves to illustrate why career stages matter so much to managers in the organization, and especially to HR management.

WORK
APPLICATION 7-14

Identify the level of career development you are on. Using Exhibit 7-8, but in your own words, describe your career stage and the Maslow motivational issues you are dealing with now.

What are people most concerned with at the earliest career stage or when they have to fall back to a lower level of work? They are typically most concerned with physical and safety/security issues, right? Are they physically able to get the *basic things* that they need in order to live and work—like money for shelter, food to eat, fuel for their car? Are they getting paid enough to *survive and be safe?* Then, as they get into the establishment and maintenance stages, they become more concerned with *social interactions* and then gaining *status and recognition* as organizational leaders. Finally, as they move to the disengagement stage, they are more concerned with higher-level esteem needs such as *self-respect, achievement* of personal goals, and being able to do the *things that they think are important.* So, we see people go through these different motivational points in their life as they go through their career. It's very interesting that the career stages follow almost exactly with what the motivation theories show us.

Now that we understand a little bit about the career stages that individuals go through during their work life and how those stages identify what might motivate workers in a particular stage, let's match those up with organizational HR strategies that are available to reinforce employee behavior. This will give us a general working model of how organizational HR strategies can create either positive or negative consequences for both the individual and the organization, depending on how the HR strategies are applied in a particular situation. Take a look at Exhibit 7-9. We have individual career stages identified on the left side of the diagram. On the right side are some of the major organizational HR strategies that are available. Depending on how the HR strategies are applied, and based on the individual's career stage and motivating factors, we end up with either positive or negative consequences to both the individual and the organization.

If we apply the correct HR strategy or strategies to an individual employee based on the factors that motivate the employee, we can improve each of the major organizational dependent variables that we identified in Chapter 1—job satisfaction, productivity, absenteeism, and turnover. In addition, there are several other organizational factors that can

EXHIBIT 7-9 CONSEQUENCES OF CAREER PLANNING

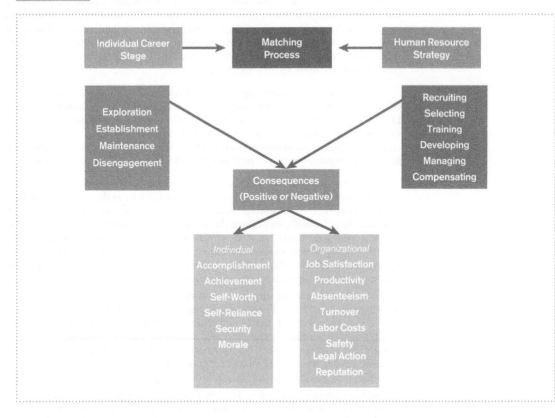

either improve or decline based on the application (or lack thereof) of the correct HR strategy. These factors include labor costs, organizational safety, employee lawsuits, and organizational reputation, among others. So as you can see, if the organization fails to apply the correct strategy to motivate the employee (based on the employee's current career stage), the consequences can be severe.

On the other side of the diagram, the consequences to the employee are equally significant. If the organization applies the correct types of HR strategies to develop the employee successfully over time, individual feelings of accomplishment and achievement increase, self-worth and self-reliance increase, the employee's sense of security increases, and their morale is likely to increase due to higher individual satisfaction levels. Again, if the strategies applied are unsuccessful, each of these individual consequences can become negative. After looking at the model, it should become obvious that successfully applying HR strategies to individual employees based on their personal motivating factors and career stage is critical to overall organizational success over time.

So now you know why it's so important to create career paths for our employees within the organization and provide employee development opportunities. If we do these things successfully, we end up with a series of positive consequences for both the organization and the individuals involved. We have better productivity, better job satisfaction and employee engagement, and lower absenteeism and turnover. However, if we fail to do these things successfully, a series of negative consequences can occur that ultimately cost both the organization and the individual time and money. Employee development is a critical piece in the organizational puzzle in order to provide long-term success.

LO 7-7

Describe the concepts of gamification, digital learning, and micro-learning, and the reasons that they have become more critical in today's organizations.

TRENDS AND ISSUES IN HRM

Let's take a look now at a couple of current trends and issues in training and development. The first trend involves the "gamification" of training and development and where it has been over the past several years, and the second looks at the issues of digital and micro-learning and their necessity in today's workforce.

Gamification—A Phoenix Rising?

A 2017 article by author Simon Parkin asks, "Was Gamification a Terrible Lie?"[56] Gamification continues to be a major trend in organizational training, but it has had its ups and downs in the past few years. Gamification is the process of designing and utilizing video, social media, and other game technologies to teach the player a business concept. It gained popularity a few years ago, but some early attempts did not provide the learning outcomes that were expected because of poor training design so it fell out of favor with some companies. Technology providers that jumped into gamification programs and apps, although they were not well versed in training and learning, have now washed out of the market though; and gamification is making a comeback in some circles. In many cases gamification is simply a new form of simulation training. It is being used for training in areas such as corporate values training, leadership development, customer service training, technical training, and more. It is also being used by a diverse group of organizations including **Unilever**, the **Department of Defense, Weight Watchers**, and **Nike**, so you can see that it isn't just useful in technology companies.[57]

Gamification is not a panacea for what is ailing a corporate learning and development program. There is at least some evidence that it does not improve long-term retention of concepts learned in training environments in all training situations. In fact, in some cases, traditional classroom learning has been shown to outperform various types of gamification or social learning.[58] What problems do we continue to see in learning using gamification? One issue has been the fact that gamification has been overhyped as a cure-all for training problems. Another common problem is that the player may become wrapped up in playing the game, and not understand *why* a result occurs, and will therefore miss the lesson to be learned. A third issue is poor game design—about 80% of them still fail to meet business objectives because the provider does not understand basic learning theories. However, one of the key challenges with training has always been to get people engaged in the process, and the evidence is mounting that gamification can help with engagement and ultimately get people to learn and retain key information for work.

The Corporate Learning Imperative

Employers today are concerned that their workers don't have the skills necessary to compete in modern organizations. In a recent Gallup poll, almost 90 percent of business leaders said that college graduates did not have the necessary skill sets for the workplace.[59] Other studies note that existing employee skill sets go stale at an alarming rate as well. Partially as a result of this lack of confidence in employee skills, US and European companies continue to increase their spending on internal talent development. Each year from 2010 through 2015 companies increased their spending on employee training, and that trend appears to be continuing.[60,61]

There is a problem with corporate learning environments though—no large blocks of time to learn. The average employee has about 25 minutes a week to "slow down and learn."[62] One manager noted, "Even TED Talks are now too long" in many cases![63] As a result of this problem, companies are exploring various forms of digital learning that can provide just-in-time content that is compact and valuable. *Digital learning,* according to Josh Bersin of **Bersin by Deloitte**, is "employee-directed, intelligent-machine driven, and brings "learning to where employees are."[64]

One solution to the problem of lack of time for training is micro-learning. Micro-learning is a learning form that uses "small, specific bursts" or chunks to learn a single piece of content that the user needs to know to solve a problem *right now.*[65]

Micro-learning as a form of digital learning allows around the clock access in many cases—whenever, wherever, however the employee wants to access it. Most micro-learning takes less than 5 minutes and includes a quiz.[66] Micro-learning "is effective, but limited," according to Stanford neuroscientist Priya Rajasethupathy[67]—it is designed to answer *specific questions, quickly,* during the course of doing the work—but it is one tool available for learning on the fly. However, other continued learning will be necessary for workers in modern organizations.

Life-long learning will continue to become more necessary.[68] Many times a professor will hear "I'll be glad when I graduate. I'll never have to go to class again" from one of their students and will chuckle. The professor knows that their student will be "going to class" constantly for the rest of their work life. Executives note that the average "shelf life" of skills associated with a college degree is 5 years.[69] HR managers will need to understand the new technologies available and the new ways that their employees learn, and will have to adapt to each challenge to enable the self-directed training that will become a more important part of the workplace.

Want a better grade?

Get the tools you need to sharpen your study skills. Access practice quizzes, eFlashcards, video and multimedia, and more at **edge.sagepub.com/lussierhrm3e.**

• • • DIGITAL RESOURCES

Training*

Training and Development

Experiential Learning as Management Development

Onboarding*

Bloom's Taxonomy

Effects of Training in Universal Design for Learning on Lesson Plan Development

Evaluating Training Programs*

Classical Conditioning

* premium video only available in the interactive eBook

••• CHAPTER SUMMARY

7-1 Discuss the major difference between training and development and identify the common situations where training may be needed.

Training is designed to provide employees with the knowledge, skills, and abilities (KSAs) that they need to succeed in their work for the organization. Training is primarily intended to be put to *immediate* use by the individual being trained. Employee development is designed to teach our workers how to move up in the organization in the *future* by becoming skilled at those tasks that they will need to know how to do to perform higher-level jobs.

The most common points at which managers should consider workforce training include new-employee *orientation*, which is used to acculturate new employees to the organization and its culture and to prepare them to do their own job within the organization; when *processes or procedures have changed;* whenever there has been some *failure to perform* successfully; or when *employee development* opportunities come up, allowing the company to develop current employees' skills and abilities so that they are able to move into higher-level jobs within the organization.

7-2 Briefly discuss the steps in the training and development process and the common challenges to the process.

The first step involves conducting a needs assessment to identify the type of training needed. The second step involves selecting how to shape employee behavior. The third step involves designing the training by selecting training methods. The fourth step involves selecting the delivery method and delivering the training. The last step involves assessing the training to determine if employee behavior has changed to improve performance—if not, return to step one. The steps are so closely related and based on each other that they are commonly planned together before actually delivering the training.

Common challenges to the training process include unprepared workers, difficulty in identifying the ROI provided from training, employee resistance to changes in processes and procedures, matching the training to the company's strategic goals, and logistics issues—including scheduling and locations available for training courses.

7-3 Identify the three common learning theories and how they are used to create the four methods for shaping behavior.

The three common learning theories are classical conditioning, operant conditioning, and social learning theory. Classical conditioning results in direct, involuntary, learned behaviors. Operant conditioning results in direct, voluntary, learned behaviors. Social learning is experienced through watching the actions of other people and witnessing the consequences of their actions, so it is voluntary and learned, but it is based on indirect consequences of the actions of others.

We can use the operant conditioning and social learning concepts of *reward and punishment* to create the four options for shaping behavior. These include positive reinforcement, negative reinforcement, punishment, and extinction. Positive reinforcement involves the application

of a reward in response to a person's behavior in order to increase the chances that that behavior will be repeated. Negative reinforcement involves the withdrawal of a noxious stimulus, or a negative thing, in response to a person's positive behavior to increase the chances that the behavior will be repeated. Punishment occurs either when a noxious stimulus is applied or when a reward is taken away in response to a negative behavior. Extinction provides no reinforcement, either positive or negative, to the actions of the subject.

7-4 Discuss each of the major training delivery types.

On-the-job training (OJT) is done at the work site with the resources the employee uses to perform the job, and it is conducted one-on-one with the trainee. In *classroom training,* the organization creates a training course and provides a qualified instructor to teach the class in a single location at a specific time. *Distance learning,* also called e-learning, allows the students to sign in to the training site and provides materials to them for their studies. There's typically less interaction between an instructor and trainee than in OJT or classroom training. *Simulations* mimic a real-life situation to teach students what actions to take in the event that they encounter the same or a similar situation in their job.

7-5 Briefly discuss the Four-Level Evaluation Method for assessing training programs and the three common ways we measure training success.

The four-level evaluation method measures *reaction, learning, behaviors,* and *results.* In *reaction evaluations,* we ask the participants how they feel about the training process, including the content provided, the instructor(s), and the knowledge that they gained. *Learning evaluations* are designed to determine what knowledge was gained by the individual, whether any new skills have been learned, and whether attitudes have changed as a result of the training. *Behavior evaluations* are designed to determine whether or not the trainee's on-the-job behaviors changed as a result of the training. In a *results evaluation,* we try to determine whether or not individual behavioral changes have improved organizational results. This is the level at which ROI will be measured and evaluated.

ROI, customer satisfaction and employee satisfaction were discussed as ways to measure training success. ROI and customer service are results metrics, while employee satisfaction is a reaction metric. There are strong correlations between employee satisfaction and customer satisfaction, and indirect relationships with ROI through individual productivity and accuracy/quality of work.

7-6 Discuss the term *career* and the three common methods of employee development.

Our definition of a career is "the individually perceived sequence of attitudes and behaviors associated with work-related experiences and activities over the span of the person's life."

Individually perceived means that if you perceive your career as being successful, then you are a success. If you perceive it as a failure, then you have failed. *Sequence of attitudes and behaviors* means that your career involves not only the things that you do, but also the way you think and how you feel about your progression of jobs over time. *Associated with work-related experiences and activities over time* means that even nonwork activities that are work related would be included in our definition of career. Using this definition of career avoids the problem of having to confront the fact that by the 1960s definition, most of us would fail to have a *successful* career.

The three methods of employee development are formal education, experience, and assessment. *Formal education* provides the opportunity to participate in programs that will improve general knowledge in areas such as finance, project management, or logistics. *Experience* as a method for developing the individual seeks to put the person through different types of job-related experiences over time. *Assessment* tools provide employees with information about how they think, how they interact with others, and how they manage their own actions and emotions.

7-7 **Describe the concepts of gamification, digital learning, and micro-learning, and the reasons**

that they have become more critical in today's organizations.

Gamification is the process of designing and utilizing video, social media, and other game technologies to teach the player a business concept. There is some evidence that gamification can engage the learners better than traditional learning in some cases and ultimately get people to learn and retain key information for work. Digital learning is "employee-directed, intelligent-machine driven, and brings "learning to where employees are." Again, engagement may increase if the company can provide the necessary training whenever and wherever the employee needs it. Micro-learning is one form of digital learning. It uses small, specific bursts to learn a single piece of content that the user needs right now, and again meets the learner when and where he or she needs the information. Each process gives information to solve problems that engages the employee better than some traditional forms of learning, in at least some cases.

••• KEY TERMS

career 248
career plateau 249
competency model 226
emotional intelligence 250
employee development 227

extinction 236
learning 233
needs assessment 230
negative reinforcement 236
onboarding 227

positive reinforcement 236
punishment 236
remediation 228
self-efficacy 232
training 227

••• KEY TERMS REVIEW

Complete each of the following statements using one of this chapter's key terms.

1. _____ identifies the knowledge, skills, and abilities (KSAs) needed to perform a particular job in the organization.

2. _____ is the process of teaching employees the skills necessary to perform a job.

3. _____ is ongoing education to improve knowledge and skills for present and future jobs.

4. _____ is the process of introducing new employees to the organization and their jobs.

5. _____ is the correction of a deficiency or failure in a process or procedure.

6. _____ is the process of analyzing the difference between what is currently occurring within a job or jobs in comparison with what is required—either now or in the future—based on the organization's operations and strategic goals.

7. _____ is whether people believe that they have the capability to do something or attain a particular goal.

8. _____ is any relatively permanent change in behavior that occurs as a result of experience or practice.

9. _____ is providing a reward in return for a constructive action on the part of the subject.

10. _____ is the withdrawal of a harmful thing from the environment in response to a positive action on the part of the subject.

11. _____ is the application of an adverse consequence, or the removal of a reward, in order to decrease an unwanted behavior.

12. _____ is the total lack of response, either positive or negative, to avoid reinforcing an undesirable behavior.

13. _____ is the individually perceived sequence of attitudes and behaviors associated with work-related experiences and activities over the span of a person's life.

14. _____ occurs when an individual feels unchallenged in their current job and has little or no chance of advancement.

15. _____ is the way that we identify, understand, and use our own emotions as well as the emotions of others to promote our working relationships.

••• COMMUNICATION SKILLS

The following critical-thinking questions can be used for class discussion and/or for written assignments to develop communication skills. Be sure to give complete explanations for all answers.

1. Is the currently available workforce really not sufficiently trained to participate in knowledge-intensive jobs? Why or why not?

2. Think of and then list all of the items that you think should be included in a new employee orientation. Briefly justify why each item should be included.

3. Briefly describe a job you have or had. (If you haven't had a job, think of someone you know well.) If you were to be

promoted, which training method(s) would you use to train the person to do your current job?

4. Which one of the primary delivery of training types would you use to teach basic accounting to a group of employees? Justify your answer.

5. Have you ever filled out an evaluation form for an employee training class? Which type of evaluation was it? What evidence led you to think it was this type?

6. Do you agree with the definition of a *career* presented in the text? Why or why not? How would you change it?

7. Which of the reasons for creating career development programs from the text do you feel are most valid, considering

the cost of career development programs? Justify your choice.

8. Which method of development, formal education, experience, or assessment do you think is most valuable? Justify your choice.

9. Identify and discuss two or three ways in which poor application of HR strategies (Exhibit 7-9) would create negative *employee* consequences.

10. If you were the lead trainer for your company, how would you go about trying to create an organization-wide commitment to sustainability? Why?

• • • CASE 7-1 DOING CRUNCHES AT NESTLÉ: CONTINUOUS IMPROVEMENT OF HUMAN ASSETS

With instant coffee, baby food, and bottled water in the mix, Nestlé crunches more than just chocolate. The world's #1 food and drinks company in terms of sales, Nestlé is also the world leader in coffee (Nescafé). It also makes coffee for the home-brewing system, Nespresso. Nestlé is one of the world's top bottled water makers (Nestlé Waters), one of the biggest frozen pizza makers (DiGiorno), and a big player in the pet food business (Friskies, Purina). Its most well-known global food brands include Buitoni, Dreyer's, Maggi, Milkmaid, Carnation, and Kit Kat. The company also owns Gerber Products. North America is Nestlé's most important market.(1)

Nestlé has over 2,000 brands, which are made in 418 factories located in 86 countries, and employees nearly 330,000 employees selling products in 191 countries.(2) How does one feed this growing concern? Mergers and acquisitions is one answer, yet that does not solve the skills-gap issue faced worldwide. The firm credits their success to their top-down/bottom-up approach to training.

Top-Down. Their Rive-Reine International Training Centre in Switzerland, since the late 1980s, has served as the focal point for mentoring and training from senior management. Trainee selection matches local domestic managers' candidate nominations, who hail from over 80 countries, with corporate-driven selection criteria usually resulting in a class of 15 to 20 nationalities from differing areas of expertise.

Who teaches these classes? "Course leaders" as they are called provide instruction to about 1,700 managers and are comprised predominately of highly experienced executives from numerous locations, with consultants teaching only 25% of the 70 courses offered per annum. The courses have two differing foci: internal operations and working with external stakeholders.

Executive Courses/Industry Analysis: This series of courses has been created to assist managers who attended management courses between five and ten years ago to develop the ability to identify and work with key external stakeholders (i.e., customers, competitors, suppliers). The focus is on industry analysis from the stakeholder's point of view and the actions they might take (i.e., What are our competitors' mostly likely actions and how do we counteract them?).

Management Courses/Operations and Business Value Chain: Two-thirds of the classes in this program are taken by managers who have been with the company 5 years or less. Here managers learn about the firm's business model (its internal operations) and the underlying values that drive that model.(3)

Bottom-up. An important factor in Nestlé's productivity is the skill set of entry-level workers. Employers invest in the skills of new entrants as an alternative to hiring more experienced people, partly

on grounds of cost but also for the opportunity to shape ways of working around specific technologies and processes and particular company values.(4)

For most employees at Nestlé to be successful, they must have a passion for learning, and their recruitment process emphasizes this. Once hired, employees' training is predominately "on-the-job" (OTJ), where an employee's supervisor serves as mentor, providing motivation and guidance to ensure employees' growth. Before training can begin, whether formally or informally, employees must possess the basic skill set necessary for continued learning (i.e., reading, writing, computer usage, oral communications, etc.); this is usually provided through an employee's schooling. In certain countries, their education may have been inadequate and the worker may decide to improve their skill set, especially in the area of communications. Special programs have been established to provide such training on a country-by-country basis. Once employees have acquired the basic skill set, individualized development formal training programs are created that increase workers' knowledge, skills, and abilities (KSAs). New employees with high school or university qualifications inevitably enter management-training programs in their local centers.

Local Training Centers. In addition to centralized training, residential training centers exist for many of their local operations—the net effect being that "people development" occurs predominately at local centers. This decentralized approach for employee training and development makes each manager accountable and directly involved in employee learning. Coaching and counseling skills are therefore emphasized where needed through a myriad of programs. Besides training current managers, local centers look to develop future managers by developing supervisory skills of ex-apprentices as well as technical personnel in the areas of IT management, maintenance and electrical engineering. Specialists are also "home-grown" through continuous training, given local market and employment conditions. Those seeking a purely administrative career path will find that OJT plays a critical role supported by in-house training. Even at the local level, outsourcing of training and education increases with an employee's rank and use of new technologies.

Production is one of the key success factors for Nestlé, and therefore employees (two-thirds of whom work in factories) need continuous OTJ on new factory technology and equipment; the faster the change, the greater the need for training. New technology also means learning how to work better and differently with others. Team and inter-team management training (including self-managed work teams) focusing on developing flex-manufacturing capabilities is needed in order to maximize equipment utilization.

Training methods are also changing with the times, especially related to the Internet. Distance learning, the use of information technology to deliver content, has led to the new methods of corporate instruction and special corporate training assistants and has allowed employees to obtain training and education that align with their life styles. For example, employees in Singapore are given the option to attend online, job-related night courses, which, if they lead to some formal qualification (i.e., certificate, diploma, degree), would qualify for cost reimbursement.(5)

The Singapore example indicates that although there is a commonality of training among local centers, training can be significantly different by location. New employees at Nestlé take management-training courses, but the approach of these courses varies widely by country. For example, in Japan the courses are short and usually last about 3 days each. In India, however, the programs run for 12 months. In West African countries, the management training programs run even longer, typically 18–24 months.(6)

Questions

1. For what purposes does Nestlé train and develop employees?
2. What challenges does Nestlé face in conducting their training programs?
3. Which skill sets does Nestlé focus on in their training programs?
4. What on-the-job training methods does Nestlé utilize in their training programs?
5. What forms of off-the-job training are available at Nestlé?

6. What are some of the ways that Nestlé's training programs address career development?
7. What trends in training and development is Nestlé utilizing, and what trends could they benefit from?

References

(1)   Oliver, L. (n.d.). Nestlé S.A. *Hoovers*. Retrieved April 26, 2017, from http://0-subscriber.hoovers.com.liucat.lib.liu.edu/H/company360/fulldescription.html?companyId=41815000000000

(2)   Nestlé: At a glance. (n.d.). Retrieved April 26, 2017, from http://www.nestle.com/aboutus/overview

(3)   Francis, A. (n.d.). Case study of Nestlé: Training and development. Retrieved April 26, 2017, from https://www.mbaknol.com/management-case-studies/case-study-of-nestle-training-and-development/

(4)   Nestlé: Business ownership of skills. (n.d.). Retrieved April 26, 2017, from http://www.nestle.co.uk/productivity/owning-the-skills-pipeline

(5)   Francis, A. (n.d.). Case study of Nestlé: Training and development. Retrieved April 26, 2017, from https://www.mbaknol.com/management-case-studies/case-study-of-nestle-training-and-development/

(6)   Ibid.

Case created by Herbert Sherman and Theodore Vallas, Department of Management Sciences, Long Island University School of Business, Brooklyn Campus

• • • CASE 7-2 GOOGLE SEARCH: BUILDING THE PROGRAM THAT WRITES THE CODE TO FIND FEMALE TALENT

Google Inc. took Web searching to a much more sophisticated level when it offered targeted search results from billions of Web pages, based on a proprietary algorithm that allowed for greater customization than did prior engines like Web Crawler and Dogpile. Employing more than 50,000 people, Google generates most of its revenue from advertising sales. In 2013, its net income was close to $13 billion, and the company showed 60% revenue growth between 2012 and 2014. Added to that, Google has been on the top of the *Fortune* "Best Places to Work" list since 2012.(1) Google is one of the best firms at making employees feel welcomed and supported; but being in the technology field, the company had become a "boys' club," with women constituting only 30% of its entire workforce.

Alongside Google, other Silicon Valley technology giants like Facebook, Yahoo, and LinkedIn recently disclosed their gender and racial diversity ratios in their workplaces. On average, Google's workforce consists of more than 65% males, 55% whites, and 35% Asians. The gaps between these numbers are even wider in technology-related positions. As shown in its May 2014 report, it employs only 2% blacks and 3% Hispanics. Google admitted that this problem required immediate action. Google's sharing of demographic information is a promising sign that it is willing to change, but action speaks louder than words.

Google took quick action and performed its own search. It found that women were losing interest in computer sciences as a career at an alarming rate. Only 14% of the computer science graduates were women in 2013, and surveys indicated that less than 1% of women expressed any interest in majoring in computer sciences

in college.(2) Google then recognized that it could not use traditional recruitment techniques to hire women since they were just not present in the labor pool.

Google also examined its own unique hiring processes and concluded that they were both difficult and tedious—women were not emerging through these processes, and Google could not just sit back and hope to gain new female employees from a labor pool that could not supply them.(3)

Google decided to be far more proactive in the area of women employee development and committed $50 million for both research and solution strategies. Its research indicated that if women were exposed to coding at an early age, they would more likely look favorably at a career path in computer science.(4) Google's research also noted that compared to the companies led by men, tech companies led by women achieved a 35% higher return on investment and 12% higher revenue.(5)

Google understood that its answer to this labor shortage, as well as to greater profitability, was to show young girls how interesting aspects of computer science could be, as well as how lucrative, and to inspire them to pursue a career in this field. Secondly, only 10% of the schools in the United States offered computer science courses, so access to this field was a major problem. To achieve its goal of more women in the workforce, Google initiated a project called "Made With Code" (MWC) that was designed to attract women to the sciences and, in the long run, diminish possible gender biases in its own organization, as well as in the field.(6)

MWC was launched as an event in New York City, with the participation of teenage girls from local public schools; famous female entrepreneurs; and many professional women who utilized coding in the film, music, and fashion industries. To increase exposure and inspiration, Google is working closely with producers and writers in the Science & Entertainment Exchange to have more female coders in movies and television series.(7)

With the MWC program targeting the people who normally did not have the access or the opportunity to pursue a career in computer science, Google provided accelerated tech-training programs to help them succeed in high-level tech jobs. Google did this by offering free coding classes online to pull extraordinary talent from the cities surrounding Silicon Valley.(8) It also provided workshops that fostered student collaboration on simple coding projects like 3-D printed bracelets. Research has noted that women thrive in team environments, and Google wanted them to understand that teamwork is the cornerstone of software development. To this end, Google gave an additional 3 months of free access to its Code School to women.(9) Google hopes that the outcome of its programs will increase younger girls' involvement in computer science and, in the long run, increase women's visibility in the profession and at Google.

Questions

1. What is a needs assessment, and how might Google use this tool to increase the presence of women in its workforce?

2. Some might argue that Google's "Made With Code" program has redefined the concept of employee development. Agree or disagree and provide an explanation supporting your position.

3. Explain how Google's particular situation demonstrates the relationship between employee recruitment and employee development, given the above discussion.

4. Explain how Google's "Made With Code" has become an integral part of its career planning.

5. How might the concepts of self-efficacy and reinforcement theory help us better understand schoolgirls' relative lack of interest in computer science?

6. Assume that Google is ultimately successful and receives more female applicants, whom it then hires. What suggestions do you have for managing this new talent pool?

References

(1) Hoover's Inc. (2014). Google Inc. *Hoover's Company Records: In-Depth Records.* Retrieved July 19, 2014, from Long Island University Academic Database.

(2) Lapowsky, I. (2014, July 1). Google and Square recruit girls early to tackle tech's gender problem. *Wired.com.* Retrieved from http://www.wired.com/2014/07/girls-coding/

(3) Warnes, S. (2014, July 1). 70% male, 50% white: Why Silicon Valley needs to diversify. *Mirror.* Retrieved from http://ampp3d.mirror.co.uk/2014/07/01/70-male-50-white-why-silicon-valley-needs-to-diversify/

(4) Mejia, P. (2014, July 11). Codes, not bros: Google pledges $50 million to ladies in tech. *Newsweek.* Retrieved from http://www.newsweek.com/codes-not-bros-google-pledges-50-million-ladies-tech-258298/

(5) Warnes, S. (2014, July 1). 70% male, 50% white: Why Silicon Valley needs to diversify. *Mirror.* Retrieved from http://ampp3d.mirror.co.uk/2014/07/01/70-male-50-white-why-silicon-valley-needs-to-diversify/

(6) Mejia, P. (2014, July 11). Codes, not bros: Google pledges $50 million to ladies in tech. *Newsweek.* Retrieved from http://www.newsweek.com/codes-not-bros-google-pledges-50-million-ladies-tech-258298/

(7) Ibid.

(8) Jones, V. (2014, July 8). How to hook up tech sector with talent. *CNN.* Retrieved from http://www.cnn.com/2014/07/08/opinion/jones-tech-minorities/

(9) Mejia, P. (2014, July 11). Codes, not bros: Google pledges $50 million to ladies in tech. *Newsweek.* Retrieved from http://www.newsweek.com/codes-not-bros-google-pledges-50-million-ladies-tech-258298/

Case created by Herbert Sherman and Theodore Vallas, Department of Management Sciences, Long Island University School of Business, Brooklyn Campus

• • • SKILL BUILDER 7-1 THE TRAINING PROCESS

Objectives

To develop your ability to conduct a needs assessment, to select how to shape employee behavior, to design a training program by selecting training methods, to select a method to deliver training, and to choose an assessment method

Skills

The primary skills developed through this exercise are as follows:

1. *HR management skill*–conceptual and design skills

2. SHRM 2016 Curriculum Guidebook–L: Training and Development

Assignment

As an individual or group, select a job and write out your answers. Follow the steps in the training process below to train a person to do the job.

Step 1: Needs assessment. Conduct a needs assessment for the job by developing a competency model identifying the knowledge, skills, and abilities needed to do the job successfully.

Step 2: Select how you will shape behavior. Be sure to specify if you will use positive reinforcement, punishment, negative reinforcement, or extinction. State the rewards and/or punishment.

Step 3: Design the training. Select and describe in detail the training method(s) you will use to shape the behavior.

Step 4: Deliver the training. Just select one of the four methods of delivery that you will use to conduct the actual training and describe how you will deliver the training.

Step 5: Assessment of training. Just select one of the four assessment methods and describe in detail how you will determine if the training did in fact shape the behavior.

Apply It

What did I learn from this experience? How will I use this knowledge in the future?

_____

_____

Your instructor may ask you to do this Skill Builder in class by breaking into groups of four to six and doing the preparation. If so, the instructor will provide you with any necessary information or additional instructions.

••• SKILL BUILDER 7-2 CAREER DEVELOPMENT

Objective

To begin to think about and develop your career plan

Skills

The primary skills developed through this exercise are as follows:

1. *HR management skill*–conceptual and design skills
2. SHRM 2016 Curriculum Guidebook–L: Training and Development

Assignment

Write out your answers to the following questions.

1. Do you now, or do you want to, work in HRM? Why? If not, what career do you want to pursue, and why?
2. If you want to work in HR, based on your self-assessment back in Chapter 1 or other knowledge, list your highest levels

of interest in HR disciplines. If not, what are your highest levels of interests, functions, or disciplines within your chosen career?

3. What methods of employee development (formal education, experience-internships and jobs, and assessment) are you using to prepare for your career?

Apply It

What did I learn from this exercise? How will I use this knowledge in the future?

_____

_____

Your instructor may ask you to do this Skill Builder in class by breaking into groups of two to three and discussing your career plans. If so, the instructor will provide you with any necessary information or additional instructions.

Defining and Building Competencies

Rao, T. V.

We have mentioned earlier in Chapters 1 and 2 that the performance of any given individual or performer depends on the individual's competence to efficiently execute the various tasks assigned to him/her. The person's commitment or motivation to do this is reflected in the effort he/she puts in and the organizational support available to help him/her successfully carry out various functions. The competencies required include knowledge, attitudes, skills, and so forth, which are needed for the person to effectively perform various tasks or activities, or KPAs and KRAs. Normally, technological competencies are ensured by corporations because they are aware of their employees' previous work experience, degrees, diplomas, and so forth. There are easy methods of ensuring technological competencies. For example, heart surgeries can only be performed by trained surgeons and software programs can only be written by trained software engineers. However, most jobs at the supervisory and managerial levels require different categories of competencies, including managerial (planning, organizing, mobilizing of resources, systems management, and so forth), behavioral (initiative, creativity, sociability, teamwork, self-control, and so forth), and conceptual (for example, the ability to forecast changes in the economy and their impact on a product a company is planning to make) skills. Competency requirements vary from job to job and from KPA to KPA, and in the same job from time to time. Therefore, to perform a given job well, an individual needs to first be aware of the required competencies and should possess them. Most performance management systems give weightage to such competencies in individual performers and assess the individuals annually. There are organizations that give a higher weightage to competencies and values than to accomplishment of results. It is very essential for every role-holder to be aware of the competencies required in an organization from the beginning of the year and to try to cultivate those that he/she may lack so that he/she emerges as a good performer. Identification and definition of competency is an equally important task like identification of KPA or KRA. Most organizations are impatient to let the employees identify competencies for each KPA or KRA and demonstrate those. They assume that once KRAs or KPAs are identified their job is done. However, several organizations take pains to identify and list the common and critical competencies that their employees need to have. The following are some competencies required by various organizations engaged in PM systems:

Core or Generic Competencies

1. Technical/functional competencies.
2. Commercial acumen.
3. Interpersonal skills and teamwork.
4. Proactive problem-solving and initiative.
5. Communication skills (listening, clarity of thought and expression, and written and verbal competency).
6. Positive attitude (viewing things positively, being optimistic, not being critical or cynical of everything, having the ability to look at the brighter side of change and various other decisions, policies, innovations, and so forth, and not being over-critical or critical all the time of people, events, and so forth).

Potential Factors or Competencies

The following are qualities that have become increasingly critical for higher level jobs and are meant to prepare executives to effectively fill such roles as they grow in an organization:

1. Ability to handle higher responsibilities including the following or more:
2. Vision and leadership.

3. Ability to assume responsibility and take decisions.
4. Execution.
5. Change management (openness to change, initiating and managing change).
6. Creativity.

Values

These include beliefs, behaviors, and actions that need to be exhibited by every employee:

1. Integrity and character, defined as coherence between thought, word, and deed.
2. Ability to speak fearlessly about what one feels (not having one thing in mind and speaking different things to please people or gain advantage of some kind or the other).
3. Ability to keep up promises or verbal commitments (doing what one says).
4. Customer focus.
5. Consistent quality.
6. Commitment to excellence.
7. Concern for people.

Some organizations change their requirements for executives from level to level. Others also change the weightages for KPAs and KRAs versus the competencies or attributes.

A good PMS helps individuals understand the competencies required for them to be successful performers from the beginning of the year and enables them to constantly review their performance, identify their competency gaps, and acquire the required competencies. Unless an employee has all the competencies needed to perform a given set of tasks he/she cannot be successful in accomplishing them, which frequently results in poor achievement of results. Therefore, continuous competency development is a critical requirement of the PM process. However, most employees do not realize this and sometimes unconsciously oppose their organizations' competency identification and development interventions. They seem to assume that competency-building is the exploitation of talent and challenge, sometimes by resisting the efforts of their seniors when they point out competency gaps and provide development opportunities to them. Competency development is a self-initiated effort and it is in the interest of every employee to develop themselves. In the following section, some inputs are provided for such self-management. I hope the reader will appreciate the scope of PMS for self-development and self-management through competency-building and future career growth.

The Effective Personality

An effective person is one who has a high degree of self-awareness. Such awareness is characterized by a good insight into one's strengths and weaknesses. In addition, effective individuals are constantly searching for opportunities to test themselves in new situations, gain more insights into their own personality, improve their strengths, and overcome their weaknesses.

One simple *model for self-awareness*, which is used widely, is the Johari Window (Luft and Ingham, 1973). Individuals' personalities and psychological worlds (attitudes, values, habits, knowledge, abilities, etc.) can be considered to comprise four parts in terms of their self-awareness and awareness of others. These include the following:

An *open* or *public self*, which consists of those aspects that are known to a person's self and also to others, for example, some of our strengths and peculiarities are known to us as well as to those around us (who keep observing and interacting with us). An individual may be an IT expert and everyone around him/her may know this. A good dancer knows his/her competencies as do those around him/her. A talkative person, an introvert, or a sociable person are all examples of how some of our qualities cannot be hidden and constitute our public self.

Only an individual is aware of his/her *closed* or a *private self* of which others are not aware. For example, one may have several strengths, weaknesses, and habits, which are not known to others because they may not like to talk about those. For instance, most people with rigid religious attitudes and prejudices are not likely to go around sharing their views. Interestingly, modesty also prevents people from sharing their strong points with others. As a result, talents exhibited in the early years go unnoticed in later ones, unless a situation is created where their existence is shared with others and opportunities are created to use them. An HRD manager in a company may have worked in an earlier company as a materials manager and may have done a great job in vendor development. However, since the person has been recruited to head HRD, he/she may never get an opportunity to apply his/her talent in the area of vendor development in the organization.

A *blind spot* refers to the part of individuals of which they are not aware, but of which others are. Some or much of what is perceived as our strengths and inadequacies may not be known to us. In relationship-valuing societies and cultures, such as in Asia, people normally tell you things that they know will please you and refrain from giving negative feedback. In such societies, people may have a sizeable chunk of blind spots. Individuals may take pride in considering themselves as flexible, whereas their behavior may be interpreted or experienced by their subordinates as inconsistent and unreliable (because of such people's constantly changing stands and views due to their creativity, which others may be adversely affected by and may perceive the changing ideas as their inconsistency).

People may have a *dark* or *hidden* part, which neither they nor others are aware of. This is because they have never gotten the opportunity to put themselves to the test and discover what they are capable of. During their entire lifetime, they may get the opportunity to discover only a small part of their potential.

1. Having a large area of blind spots impedes effectiveness.
2. Discovering more of the dark arena helps to bring out latent talent.

3. A high degree of awareness of one's strengths, weaknesses, and qualities helps in making conscious choices and enhances effectiveness.
4. Blind spots can be reduced by seeking feedback from others, accepting it, reflecting on it, and using it to improve oneself.
5. The talents of people who are in their private world to a large extent may not be available to others, since they may not be aware of the former's strengths. Such people may need to enhance their communication skills and let others know their competencies.
6. The dark arena can be reduced by people undertaking new tasks, activities, exploring new methods of working, experimenting, job rotation, and so forth. A high degree of action orientation and experimental and risk-taking attitudes need to be inculcated by such people. Pro-action and initiative are the most important prerequisites for this.
7. Leaders and effective managers and people constantly explore their dark arenas and attempt to reduce their blind spots.
8. 360-degree feedback is an effective tool for reducing blind spots, putting to use hidden talents and capabilities, and initiating actions to discover new areas or competencies.

OTHER DIMENSIONS OF PERSONAL EFFECTIVENESS

It matters very little whether you are an extrovert or an introvert, whether you are a reserved or socializing type, or whether you are a feeling or intuitive type of person. It is important to be aware of what your qualities are and how they affect you and contribute to the outcome of your actions. In other words, self-awareness is an important component of effectiveness. In addition to a high degree of self-awareness and continuous striving to enhance self-awareness, certain qualities contribute immensely to personal and managerial effectiveness. These include:

1. Action orientation—exploratory orientation.
2. Self-disclosure.

3. Receptivity to feedback.
4. Interpersonal sensitivity.
5. Self-confidence.
6. Internality and inner directedness.
7. Trustworthiness.
8. Inner core values such as honesty, sincerity, and truthfulness.
9. Goal orientation.
10. Drive and passion (for results, innovations, achievement, etc.).

Exploratory Orientation

People who take the initiative to keep experimenting with new situations are action-oriented and not afraid to make mistakes. They can take risks, are restless in their work, have high activity levels, like variety and change, and are likely to discover more and more of their potential. They keep applying themselves to many situations and actively make things happen. Such people can be called action-oriented explorers. Such explorers can discover more and more of their talents and benefit themselves and their organizations.

Self-disclosure

People who easily communicate with others about themselves; are frank and open; express their views, opinions, knowledge, and feelings freely, and share their knowledge and personal experiences with others (including subordinates, colleagues, and bosses) can be considered as the self-disclosing type. Such people constantly communicate with others and make an impact on them. This helps in generating data. Such individuals have more of an open and public self than a private one. Without an optimal amount of self-disclosure, we deny others the opportunity to know us and ourselves to get appropriate feedback. Low scorers are private individuals and may have difficulty in discovering themselves fully. At least it may be difficult for them to see themselves fully from the eyes of others. Such people make a limited impact on others.

Receptivity to Feedback

Those who seek feedback constantly or periodically, and try to find out about the impact they and their behavior has on others; those who take criticism sportingly, examine themselves and their behavior and try to learn from feedback, and those who value what others say about them, their actions, and behavior learn from feedback. They are likely to develop themselves and become more effective in the process. Those who are not willing to listen to the views, opinions and feedback from others and those who become defensive and are closed to feedback are likely to develop less. Receptivity to feedback is therefore an essential element of managerial effectiveness and growth.

Perceptiveness

Those who are sensitive to the cues and nonverbal communication of others, those who are perceptive of the impact of their behavior on others and are therefore sensitive about not saying and doing things that may not be appropriate, those who are sensitive to the needs and feelings of others, and those who make effort to understand other people or groups before saying anything are perceptive individuals. Such people are likely to utilize their time properly and make an impact on others. This makes them effective in most managerial settings.

Self-confidence

This refers to the self-concept or self-worth that individuals carry with themselves all the time. Confident people are able to accomplish many things. Self-confidence enables them to make use of their strengths, and to be open to feedback and experimentation. Self-confidence puts a glow on people's personalities and makes them attempt to do things and take risks. This is known as "approach orientation" by confident people and "avoidance orientation" by less confident ones.

Internality and Inner Directedness

This relates to people's tendency to do things on their own initiative and direction rather than merely doing them to comply with others' instructions or role expectations. Inner directed people are dictated by their inner selves and are likely to put more of their talents to use.

Trustworthiness

Trustworthiness or reliability and sincerity are hallmarks of effective people. They honor their promises and make statements they always mean and honor. Trustworthiness enhances the reliability of a person and creates a healthy society. It enhances confidence and both the inner and outer image of the individual.

Inner Core Values such as Honesty, Sincerity, and Truthfulness

These are values that give direction to life and also a sense of joy. They are essential for creating a healthy society, which is essential for healthy living.

Goal-orientation

Goal-oriented people are clear about what they want to do, where they want to put in their efforts, and consequently, reduce wastage of time. Goal-oriented individuals are likely to remain focused. If one knows what one wants to achieve, one has already come half way in achieving one's goal. Most people do not know what they want to achieve and, as a result, remain unfocused and waste a large part of their life.

Drive and Passion

These include a passion for results, innovation, achievement, and so forth. Goal-directedness gives direction and drive gives intensity. It reduces time and enhances the value of life. People with drive and passion can achieve the same things in less time than those with less of these attributes who have more time to do other things.

These are just a few qualities and attitudes that make an effective person. They are by no means exhaustive. There may be many more such as qualities including emotional intelligence and maturity, and psychosocial maturity which also contribute to effectiveness.

PMS: A Help for Management and Enhancement of Personal Effectiveness

Arising out of our educational system is the belief that personality development is a one-time effort; that it can be achieved through something like a crash course. However, there are no quick fixes in personal growth. The first step is to know oneself. The key is self-awareness—being alive to one's self, and to one's thoughts, behavior, and motivation through constant introspection, which is a lifelong commitment.

In Daniel Goleman's *Working with Emotional Intelligence*, emotional intelligence does not merely mean "being nice," but at times means bluntly confronting someone with the uncomfortable but consequential truth they have been avoiding. It means managing feelings so that they are expressed appropriately and effectively, and enabling people to work together smoothly toward their common goals.

The conditions for "personal effectiveness" in any given setting, therefore point toward an increasing need for the following:

1. *Self-awareness:* A basic emotional skills involves being able to recognize different feelings and giving a name to them. Equally important is to be aware of the relationship between thoughts, feelings and actions.
   Specifically, it relates to:

   - Emotional awareness: recognizing one's emotions and their effect.
   - Accurate self-assessment: knowing one's strengths and limits.
   - Self-confidence: a strong sense of one's self-worth and capabilities (Goleman, 1998).

2. *Empathy:* Getting the measure of a situation and being able to act appropriately requires an understanding of the feelings of others. Sensitivity/empathy helps us share each other's concerns and goals, and walk together toward a common goal of well-being instead of confronting and colliding all the time (Goleman, 1998).

3. *Ability to express emotions:* The ability to identify emotions in one's physical stages, feelings, and thought; the ability to identify emotions of others, in designs and works of art, etc. through language, sound, appearance, and behavior; the ability to express emotions and needs related to those feelings, the ability to discriminate between accurate and inaccurate or honest and dishonest expressions of feeling. (Singh, 2001)

4. *Ability to regulate emotions:* This refers to the ability to be open to feelings, both pleasant and unpleasant; to engage or detect from an emotion, depending upon its judged utility; to monitor emotions in relation to himself/herself and others, such as recognizing how clear, typical, influential, or reasonable they are; to manage his/her own emotions as well as those of others by moderating negative emotions and enhancing positive ones; to build rapport with various segments of society and create a network of people (Singh, 2001).

A precondition for personal effectiveness is increased self-awareness. But only understanding one's self does not make a person effective.

SELF-MANAGEMENT THROUGH PMS

In his article "Managing Self" (Harvard Business Review, 1999) Peter Drucker recommends that while building a life of excellence one should ask oneself the following questions:

1. What are my strengths? Know what you are good at. A person can only perform from strengths. One cannot build performance on weaknesses, let alone on something one cannot do at all. Analyzing feedback is the only way

in which you can identify your strengths. Write down the expected outcomes for your key decisions and actions and, 9 to 12 months later, compare them with the results. Place yourself where your strengths can produce results. Work to improve your strengths. Avoid intellectual arrogance— acquire skills as required. Remedy bad habits and be careful of your manners. Know what *not* to do—identify your areas of incompetence and avoid them.

2. How do I perform? As any personality trait, *how* a person performs is a given, just as *what* a person is good at or not good at. A reader prefers reading reports before meetings and discussions (for example, late US President Kennedy). A listener likes facing it and talking about the matter instead of reading and writing (for example, late US President Roosevelt). A reader cannot become fully a listener and vice versa.

3. How do I learn? A person may learn by reading, writing, doing, talking, listening to, or with a combination of these. One must always use methods that work. Do not try to change yourself too much. Instead, work harder to improve the way you perform.

4. What are my values? Ethics require that you ask yourself *what kind of person you want to see in the mirror in the morning.* Your personal value system should be compatible with that of the organization in which you work. Typical conflicts to avoid include an organization's commitment to new versus old employees, incremental improvements or risky "break- throughs," emphasis on short-term results versus long-term goals, quality versus quantity, and growth versus sustenance. In other words, *values* are, and should be, the *ultimate test* of your compatibility with an organization.

5. Where do I belong? Mathematicians, musicians, and cooks are usually mathematicians, musicians, and cooks by the time they are four or five years old. Highly gifted people must realize early where they belong, or rather, where they do *not* belong. Successful careers are *not* planned. They develop when people are prepared for opportunities because

they know their strengths, their method of work, and their values. Knowing where one belongs can transform an ordinary person—hardworking and competent but otherwise mediocre—into an outstanding performer.

6. What should I contribute? Given my strengths, methods, and values, what is a great contribution to what needs to be done? What results need to be achieved to make a difference? It is rarely possible to look too far ahead—*18 months* is ideal for achieving meaningful results and making a difference. Set stretched and difficult goals that are reachable. Gain visible and measurable outcomes. Define your course of action— what is to be done, where and how to start, and what are the goals, objectives and deadlines that need to be set

7. Responsibility of relationships: Bosses are neither the "title" on the Organization chart nor the "function." To adapt to what makes the boss more *effective* is the secret of "managing the boss." Working relationships are as much based on people as on work —co-workers are human and individuals like you. Taking the responsibility for communicating how you perform reduces personality conflicts. Organizations are built on trust between people who *understand* one another, which does not necessarily mean that they like each other.

Development requires acquisition of competencies. These competencies may be in terms of knowledge, attitudes, values, and skills. They may be in technical, management or human relation areas, or in conceptual and visionary thinking. As technologies, environments, and the profiles of organizations and people keep changing, enterprises are continuously faced with new challenges. Employees in supervisory and managerial positions need to face these challenges much more than those at lower levels. To face the challenge of the changing nature of jobs, to contribute one's best to an organization, and to pave the way for their career growth, supervisors and managers need to keep acquiring and sharpening their competencies. Therefore, continuous "competency development" is a "necessity." Most employees do not recognize this fact and take their development for granted. Every job provides learning opportunities for an interested individual. However, these opportunities may go unnoticed or unutilized if the individual does not learn. Organizations can be viewed as excellent learning communities for those interested in development.

CONDITIONS FOR DEVELOPMENT

For individuals to grow, the following conditions should be met or ensured:

1. They should be interested in developing themselves.
2. The organization should value employees' development and learning.
3. Employees should be clear about the direction in which they can develop.
4. They should make clear choices about the direction in which they would like to grow and develop.
5. They should make an attempt to become aware of the strengths and weaknesses that will help them move toward that direction.
6. Employees should be able to identify opportunities within and outside the organization for their development, including opportunities for overcoming their weaknesses and increasing their strengths.
7. They should identify mechanisms for using these opportunities and the support they need from their superiors and others for their development.
8. They should make focused efforts to develop.
9. They should review their progress periodically with the help of other people.
10. Reporting officers should enable an appropriate emotional and professional climate for the development of their juniors. While it is difficult to definitely identify conditions that will enable such a climate, openness, frankness and free exchange of opinions, mutuality, support and trust are likely to help.

Thus, promoting employee development is a function of employees and their reporting managers. Interpersonal feedback, communication, and periodic reviews are mechanisms that help employees to develop. However, these mechanisms may be dysfunctional if they are not used properly or if used in a ritualistic manner. A genuine concern for employees' development and a desire to help them are required. Reporting managers who believe that they are helping themselves by assisting their juniors to develop can facilitate development of a sense of independence and mutuality in their units.

Periodic reviews and counseling sessions are useful instruments for establishing mutuality—a condition essential for employees' development. Some of the skills required for development and counseling are outlined in the following section.

A high degree of initiative and activity makes people explorers. They apply themselves in new situations, do their work in different ways, experiment, take risks, and in the process *discover more and more of their own potential. Such individuals tend to reduce the* dark *of the* unknown *part of their personalities.*

A high degree of self-disclosure enables people to generate data about themselves for others to observe, recognize, react to, and evaluate and provide opportunities for themselves to make an impact on others. A managerial role requires individuals to make an impact on others, and without self-disclosure at an optimal level they may not be able to make this impact.

To assess the nature of the impact they have made and discover more of their strengths and weaknesses, individuals need to be receptive to feedback from others.

To be effective, they also need to have interpersonal sensitivity and tact and to understand the moods and feelings of others to increase the effectiveness of their own interpersonal and communication.

Proactively, self-disclosure, being receptive to feedback, and perceptiveness constitute the four important components of personal effectiveness. A high degree of personal effectiveness enhances managerial effectiveness.

PMS AND SELF-MANAGEMENT

When taken seriously, PMS can be an effective tool to enhance one's personal and managerial effectiveness. Organizations are platforms for people to apply, test, and develop their talent. KPAs and KRAs or any tasks or activities we perform require continuous application of our competencies. Organizations that give scope to employees to have some KPAs or KRAs on their own and the freedom to try out new methods are providing significant opportunities for their employees to apply and develop talent.

Performance planning is the time when managers or a performers can plan for self-discovery by taking initiatives and trying out tasks they have not performed so a far, or in using methods they have not used. Most organizations give scope to their employees to take risks within certain limits and discover themselves. Initiative and exploration are of use to organizations. In such circumstances, employees can discover a great deal about themselves.

Performance analysis, conducted periodically and discussed with seniors, colleagues, or juniors, provides people the opportunity to discover hitherto unnoticed strengths or areas of improvement.

Performance-related conversations and review discussions help in the receiving and giving of feedback and contribute to individuals' development.

Self-appraisal used in most PMS formats, if taken seriously, provides food for thought and helps to enhance self-discovery and self-awareness.

Discussions on competencies listed by organizations and performance-related conversations help to enhance employees' awareness and facilitate their plans to cultivate competencies.

SELF-APPRAISAL IN SELF-MANAGEMENT

Self-appraisal has an important role to play in employees' development. As we have seen in the previous chapters, development needs to be self-directed. Individuals are not likely to learn and develop themselves unless they make a conscious effort to identify possible directions of growth and continuously monitor this growth. For employees to develop their capabilities to perform particular functions associated with their roles, they must realize the importance of these functions in their roles as well as the links between learning to perform the functions and their future growth in (or outside) their organization. They must also know how they are performing these functions, their own capabilities and those they lack. They can discover this by performing these functions and receiving feedback from others about their performance levels and capability indicators. They can use this feedback and reflect on their experience to finally identify their capabilities and those they lack. They can then make plans to develop these capabilities with the assistance of their supervisors and others in the organization. Thus, individuals are always the focal point in determining their own development and improving their performance. Organizations provide a supporting environment and other facilities required for this development. It is in this context, that self-appraisal becomes an important step in the development and improvement of performance.

Self-appraisal should be a continuous process. More than their reporting officers, employees should take steps to continuously assess their performance, identify their strengths and weaknesses, keep a record of the efforts they make as well as their success and failure while performing different functions. They should also analyze the causes for their success and failures. While this process should go on continuously, individuals also should devote some time to reviewing their efforts, to assimilate and identify consistencies in their successes or failures, and prepare their development plans. The performance management period provides a formal opportunity for individuals to review their performance and growth over the entire year.

The following can be considered as the purpose for self-appraisal:

1. To provide an opportunity for employees to recapitulate:

   - The various activities they have undertaken in relation to different functions associated with their roles.

- Their achievements and failures with regard to these.
- The capabilities they demonstrated and those they felt they lacked in carrying out activities and the various managerial and behavioral dimensions they demonstrated over the year.

2. To identify their own development needs and plan their development in the organization by identifying the support they require from their reporting officers and others in the organization.
3. To communicate to their reporting officers their contribution, accomplishments, and reflections to enable them to view their appraisees' performance in the right perspective and assess it objectively. (This is a necessary preparation for performance review discussions and performance improvement plans.)
4. To initiate an organization-wide process of annual review and reflection to strengthen self-initiated development of managerial effectiveness.

Self-appraisal should start at the end of the performance period just before the performance review discussion takes place. It should start with the appraisees taking up their KPAs and objectives for the period and reflecting on their achievements and failures. They should have with them the notes they have maintained about events, critical incidents, and reflections during the period and use these to recapitulate their contributions as well as successes and failures. They can analyze their performance by using the guidelines suggested in the next chapter, "Performance Analysis." They can also assess themselves by using the organization's rating scales, if any. In addition, they should make brief notes of their reflections in their appraisal forms to communicate these to their appraisers.

The appraisees should also follow this process on behavioral and managerial dimensions. In addition, they should make suggestions about their identified developmental needs. The self-appraisal forms completed in this process should then be passed on to their reporting officers for their assessment and planning for performance review and counseling discussions. Appraisers should treat such self-appraisal reports received from their appraisees seriously. Appraisers normally do not get enough time to observe each of their subordinates closely. More often, they tend to form impressions about their subordinates on the basis of one or two of their striking failures. Sometimes, one or two successes may also leave a highly positive impression. It is necessary for appraisers to review every aspect of their appraisees' performance as well as behavioral and managerial qualities if they want to understand them and contribute to their development. The only way appraisers can get relevant information about their appraisees and their performance is by asking them about it. Data provided by appraisees through self-appraisal serves this purpose. Some appraisers are worried that their subordinates will only highlight their accomplishments and strengths, but not their failures and weaknesses. This perception is often wrong. However, even when it is true, appraisers do not need to worry because their appraisees have every right to highlight their accomplishments. Appraisers have the obligation to take cognizance of these in their appraisal. If there are failures and weaknesses the appraiser perceives, these can be pointed out during appraisal discussions. It should also be remembered that when appraisees only highlight their strengths and accomplishments, they are raising the expectations of their bosses of them for the subsequent period when more challenging goals can be set for them.

Therefore, self-appraisal can be a useful component of a development-oriented performance appraisal system if viewed seriously by appraisees and appraisers and used appropriately to generate a greater understanding of the former.

Self-Appraisal for Managerial Effectiveness

There are organizations where "self-appraisal" does not find place in the performance appraisal system. Often a small space is provided for the performer to write down his accomplishments or tasks assigned and results achieved. This cannot be called self-appraisal. In such cases executives often ask what should be done.

The author would like to assert that self-appraisal can be done independent of the performance management systems. Every manager should develop a discipline of reviewing his/her own performance as a manager at least once a year. Such reviews should be systematic and truthful. As no one else is involved in this process, the manager can say to himself/herself things that he/she may not like to share with others. Such a self-appraisal process may focus on the following questions:

1. What have I accomplished in the last one year?
2. How do I rate my accomplishments or contributions as against last year, and as against all that was possible this year?
3. What contributed to my performance? What factors helped me and what factors prevented me from doing better?
4. What are my own competencies and attitudes that helped me perform better and that prevented me from giving my best?
5. How are my attitudes affecting my growth and development as a competent manager?
6. What opportunities have I missed during the last year and how do I propose to use them this year if I face similar situations?
7. What support do I need from my seniors and from the organization to be able to make a better contribution?
8. What support do I need to develop my own potential and capabilities for the future?
9. What are my action plans for next year to become a more effective manager?
10. What do I want to communicate to my superiors to help them understand me better and also to help them to empower me for better performance?

Appendix

Self-Appraisal: A Format
Name:
Period: From   To

KPA for the period	Activities and targets	Accomplish-ments	Facilitating factors	Inhibiting factors	Action plans (Development actions, support requirements)

Customers' Contingency Table

Kanji, G. M. and Asher, M.

Method 9 Customers' contingency table

Purpose
To understand the needs of both internal and external customers for the fulfilment of customer satisfaction.

When to use
When a team is trying to learn the level of customer satisfaction of both internal and external customers. Failure to satisfy the customer may put the company out of business.

How to use
List both your internal and external customers and their needs, i.e. what they require; what they expect; and what would exceed their expectations. This can be generated with the help of brainstorming, mind mapping or a combination of both.

LEVEL OF CUSTOMERS' NEEDS

		Must	Expectation	Above expectation
	External	Receive product order	Easy to order Added value Helpful service	24-hour delivery Free shipping
CUSTOMERS	Internal	Receive correct information	Easy to deal with the process To be treated like a valuable customer	Full cooperation

Figure 1   *Customers' contingency table*

Benefits
It helps you to understand the association between your customers and their level of requirements.

Example
A customers' contingency table is shown in Figure 1. Here, *must* is the *minimum* customer requirement. Failling in this will cause dissatisfaction.

Relation Diagram

Kanji, G. M. and Asher, M.

Method 27 Relation diagram

Purpose
To illustrate the relationship between problems and ideas in complex situations. Also to identify meaningful categories from a mass of ideas when relationships are difficult to determine.

When to use
When a topic is so complicated that relations between different ideas cannot be established through conventional reasoning and the problem in question is exclusively a symptom of a more fundamental underlying problem.

How to use
The development of the relation diagram should be conducted in teams. The team writes each idea in a circle and clusters the circles in proximity to each other. It then identifies which idea strongly influences another and uses arrows to indicate the direction of influence. The results are evaluated by identifying ideas that have the most arrows entering or exiting.

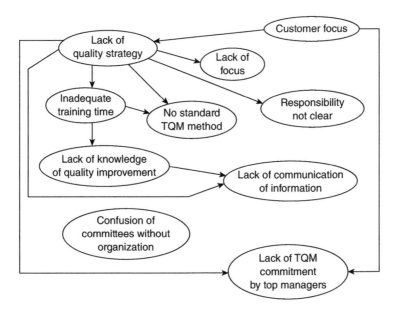

Figure 1   *Relation Diagram*

Benefits

It identifies relationship between problem and ideas in complex situations.

Example

Figure 1 presents the results of a team brainstorming session which identified ten major involved in developing an organization's quality plan.

Suggestion Schemes

Kanji, G. M. and Asher, M.

Method 67 Suggestion schemes

Purpose
To generate ideas for improvement.

When to use
At a later stage of a total quality process when there is a quality improvement plan in place and a mechanism for selecting ideas for action.

How to use
Suggestion schemes can seem deceptively simple and many fail because ideas are asked for without any mechanism being set up for decision-taking or communication of those decisions. The following are guidelines for running successful suggestion schemes:

1 Set up a steering group to oversee the process.
2 Delegate as far down as practical the decision on whether or not to implement the suggestion.
3 Give awards to supervisors and managers whose employees generate most ideas.
4 n the early stages go for quantity of ideas rather than quality.
5 To generate ideas in manageable numbers try to set themes for ideas and change the themes regularly.
6 Ensure that all ideas are acknowledged quickly and that the person generating the idea is told whether it is to be implemented and, if not, why not.
7 Look for reasons to say 'yes' rather than 'no'.
8 In the early stages be prepared for ideas to be about environmental aspects rather than operational ones.

Benefits
Suggestion schemes provide a way of moving to continuous improvement via small incremental changes.

Example
A head office function of a major service organization introduced a suggestion scheme as part of its total quality process. In the first year 18 suggestions per employee were generated and 90 per cent acted upon. The organization began a 'Suggestion of the month' and 'Suggestion of the year' award and the scheme flourished.

Hoshin Kanari

Kanji, G. M. and Asher, M.

Method 79 Hoshin kanri (quality policy deployment)

Purpose
To delight the customer through the manufacturing and servicing process by implementing the quality goals of the organization.

When to use
When objectives are identified at each level of an organization by top-down and bottom-up consultation and the overall goals of the organization have been set as specific targets.

How to use
1 Define short-term and long-term goals of the organization.
2 Identify the measurable goals.
3 Decide the critical processes involved in achieving these.
4 Ask the teams to agree on performance indicators at appropriate stages of the process.
5 Challenge every level of the process in order to force the organization to change the quality culture.
6 Organizational goals are to be used as measurable goals in order to make the employee understand the importance of the quality improvement process.

Benefits
It shows the employee what the overall goals of the organization are and where he or she fits in so that everybody pulls in the same direction towards clearly defined goals.

Example
Examples of goals set at different levels of an organization, making them evident in all organization processes, are as follows:

Level	Goal
Corporate	Delight the customer
Department	Reduce cost of poor quality
Maintenance	Reduce machine failure by 20 per cent
Manufacturing	Less than 3 per cent defect
Delivery	Less than 5 per cent late deliveries

Reference
Y. Akao (1991) *Hoshin Kanri: Policy Deployment for Successful TQM*, Cambridge, Massachusetts: Productivity Press.

PART 4

MANAGING PROJECTS IN THE ORGANISATION

Determining the Direction and Initial Specifications of a Project

Cobb, A. T.

INTRODUCTION

THE BALTIMORE PROJECT

John had no idea what was coming when he picked up his phone early one Monday morning at the corporate offices of Acme Auto Supply. Acme Auto is a midsized company that grossed more than $500 million in revenues last year and is gaining a reputation on Wall Street as an aggressive and growing company.

"Hey, John, you got a minute? I'd like to chat with you about a job I have in mind." It was Carol Byrnes, the director of John's division. Ten minutes later, John was getting comfortable in Carol's office and wondering what was on her mind. "You know, John, we are opening our new store in Baltimore come June 15th." "Yes, Ms. Byrnes, I've heard it's going to be some event!" "Well, that's right," Carol said. "That's why I called you. It's important that we open the store well because it is our first entry in this new market area.

In fact, we want this opening to exceed any of our others. The brass is looking to see how well the store starts out to determine the extent and pace of rolling out all our other planned stores in the Northeast corridor." "Guess that makes sense," John replied, trying to figure out why Carol was telling him all this.

"Well, John, I'd like you to take on the opening. I've talked to Ralph [John's boss] and a few other division folks, and we all are agreed you can handle this project. It means a lot to the organization and a lot to us in the division. If all goes well, it can mean a lot to you as well. Ralph can clear your plate of the Carlisle account, and we can give you Tom and, maybe, Alice to help. Can you run with this?"

What else could he say? "Sure, I'd love the opportunity." "Great!" Carol replied. "You'll need to draw up some plans for the 'Baltimore Project,' including a preliminary budget, and I'll want to review them, but let's have an initial talk tomorrow to see what you have come up with by then." Carol looked at her calendar. "Let's see, hmm, how about 3:00 tomorrow for an initial run through? I've got a half-hour slot open." "I'll see you at your office at 3:00, then," John replied, already beginning to get nervous about a high-visibility project dumped in his lap that he knew little to nothing about and that was only 6 weeks away from completion.

CHAPTER OVERVIEW

New projects can provoke more than a little anxiety even for those who deal with them often. This particular one is more than likely to do so. It is a high-visibility project; John has never opened a store before; and he has no idea how to get started. On top of it all, John wants to look good tomorrow for his meeting with Ms. Byrnes.

When any client brings a project to a project leader, the leader needs to develop an initial overview plan of the project: what the project is trying to achieve; who the important stakeholders are; and rough estimates of the work, cost, time, and other requirements of the project. Once done, the leader needs to review the project's initial plan with the key stakeholders involved and get their commitment to it. Preparing for this task is John's job for his next meeting with Carol. The steps John needs to take are the subject of this chapter.

We begin by examining the project's mission and some of the stakeholders who have an interest in it. We then focus attention on the project's more concrete objectives and its deliverables. Next, we address some of the other components of any project—its scope, resource, time, and cost estimates. These are brought together in the project's charter—the initial overview of a project's plan to be approved by the leader's superiors. We wrap things up by pointing out the other elements needed in a full project plan once the project charter is approved.

THE PROJECT'S MISSION STATEMENT

All projects have a mission. That mission is to help address some need, solve some problem, or seize some opportunity for a client. Constructing a formal mission statement helps leaders to understand and clarify the broader aims of a project, and mission statements themselves play a number of useful roles in it. Writing a mission statement is the first step project leaders need to take.

As a project leader begins to organize the project around its mission, it is important as well to identify the important stakeholders of the project. Who those stakeholders are, and what interests they have in the project, are important determinates of any project's success or failure.

WHAT IS A PROJECT MISSION STATEMENT AND WHAT ROLE DOES IT PLAY?

A mission statement states the purpose of a project—its general direction and aims. In a few sentences or paragraphs, it states what the project and its sponsoring clients are trying to achieve. Mission statements play a number of roles in a project, but two are very important. The first is that a mission statement helps establish and maintain the project's overall direction. The second is that it can help establish "common ground" among a project's stakeholders.

Provides Project Direction

Many people play different roles in a project and make a variety of contributions to it. All those roles and contributions are supposed to fit together in some way to produce what the project is expected to deliver. Mission statements help tie all these contributions together. In managerial terms, a mission statement helps provide unity of purpose and unity of effort in the project. It does so by clarifying the project's goals and requirements.

When a project team is first assembled, for example, the mission statement provides a common orientation to the project and its direction. As work is broken down and assigned, members can see how their efforts contribute to the project's mission as a whole. As a project moves forward, project members quite often work at different locations and narrow their project focus to their own particular jobs. The project's mission statement can help team members make sure their individual efforts will contribute to the team's goals for the entire project.

In a similar manner, those outside the project team can also assess their contributions in terms of the project's mission. Mission statements provide suppliers, consultants, regulators, and other external contributors with a common idea of the aims of a project and their role in it.

Establishes Common Ground

Mission statements that are designed with the principal stakeholders' advice and consent become a declaration of the stakeholders' common aim. As such, they provide common ground for those stakeholders' interests. That common ground can be used throughout the project to keep stakeholder ties strong, especially when unforeseen events arise and call for project changes. In these cases, the interests of different stakeholders may come into conflict, but mission statements help the principal stakeholders to keep their "eyes on the prize"—the project's ultimate purpose. During such times, the broader aims of a mission statement can provide a common "venue" where stakeholders can negotiate in good faith.

STAKEHOLDERS IN THE PROJECT'S MISSION

Any project will have a number of stakeholders—those who have an interest in the mission of a project or how it will be achieved and who can deeply affect it in some way. Success or failure of a project often turns on how well project leaders identify and work with these critical project stakeholders.

Important stakeholders in any project include the clients of the project and the host or performing organization in which the project is being done. The project team is an important stakeholder, as are the end users and various resource suppliers.

The Client

The project's client or customer[1] is the reason a project exists. It is the person or organization for whom the project is being conducted and who is paying for it. Every project is designed to address some need brought by a client, and the client is the ultimate source of funding and resources for the project. Clients' interests lie in having their needs met as much as possible, as quickly as possible, and, generally, for as low a price as possible.

The Host Organization

The performing or host organization[2] is the organization in which the project is conducted. The traditional model is that clients come to an organization to serve their needs. The organization, in turn, assembles project teams to do so. The interests of host organizations include making a profit from the endeavor and keeping the project and other parts of the organization running smoothly.

Organizations quite often undertake projects for their own purposes. Developing a new car model, for example, is a rather large project conducted periodically by automobile companies. Opening new markets (like John is helping to do), developing new products and services, conducting comprehensive studies of some aspect of an organization, and designing and leading organizational change are other common examples of projects conducted by organizations for their own benefit.[3] When organizations embark on such endeavors, project leaders are dealing with a stakeholder who is a client as well as the host organization and must address both sets of stakeholder needs at the same time.

The Project Team

The project team—the group of people who actually carry out project activities—is a critical stakeholder of any project, and the project leader will do well to look out for its interests even before it is assembled. Although project teams have many interests, an overriding one is simply to be able to do the project given the time and cost constraints and the products and services to be delivered. Other key interests are to have a smoothly running project with minimum disruption from changes and having the resources to do the job when they are needed.

End Users

End users are those ultimately intended to use or benefit from a project. Their interests focus on the utility of what is produced for them. The end users of the Baltimore Project, for example, are the intended customers of the Baltimore store. The gala opening will be successful only to the extent that potential customers are attracted to it. This, in turn, affects decisions about what kinds of advertising to use and the promotional incentives offered.

Suppliers

Projects often need suppliers to deliver the products and services that the team itself cannot supply. Many of these are provided by suppliers outside the host organization also called vendors, sellers, and subcontractors. The primary interest of outside suppliers is to increase their revenues by servicing the project. Often, their interests focus more on revenues than on other issues important to the project. Projects may also have internal suppliers within the host organization, however, who are called upon to help supply information, personnel, space, equipment, and the like. Quite often, the costs of these resources are not reimbursed. As one might imagine, this can set up a supplier-project relationship far different from one in which an outside supplier is paid for products and services. At the very least, project leaders need to be sensitive to the fact that supplies provided to the project often come at a cost to the internal supplier.

Dealing With Stakeholders

We have identified a number of stakeholder categories and will explore them and others much more in Chapter 7 as well as how best to work with them. For now, however, project leaders should remember that when they are dealing with stakeholders, they need to carefully consider their interests and concerns. In addition, leaders need to be aware of who are the key stakeholders for their projects. Key stakeholders are those who have the power and authority to make important decisions about the conduct and outcomes of the project. Although all stakeholders should command attention and respect, key stakeholders require extra time and attention.

As project leaders work through their mission statements and progress through the scoping of a project, they need to keep the principal stakeholders of the project in mind. These stakeholders often have conflicting interests that must be reconciled for the project to be a success. Although always a challenge, addressing those interests is far easier to do earlier in the project than later.

THE BALTIMORE PROJECT

It should not take John long to develop a workable mission statement for his project. A thoughtful review of those affected by the project will also point to its principal stakeholders. As a beginning, John's mission statement might state,

> The Baltimore opening is to be a gala event designed to attract Acme's principal customer base to view the products and services offered by the Baltimore store. The event will occur on or about June 15th.[4]

The stakeholders of this project include Ms. Byrnes and "the brass" in the host organization, who also play the role of clients of the project. Ralph,

John's immediate supervisor, is an important stakeholder as well. Other stake-holders include the manager of the Baltimore store and the end users the event is supposed to attract: the potential retail and business customers of the store. The project team includes John as project leader and both Tom and Alice as project members who were "volunteered" by Ms. Byrnes. Someone at the Baltimore store might also be recruited to play a role on the project team.

As the project moves forward, vendors will be added to the stakeholder list who will supply advertising for the opening (e.g., newspapers, radio) and supplies for the store itself as the site for the opening's events (e.g., caterers, performers, and store vendors who will demonstrate their prod-ucts to store customers).

John has laid out the general direction of the project and identified some of its key stakeholders. John needs to turn his attention now to the more specific objectives of the project and the specific products and services his project will provide to achieve those objectives—its deliverables.

THE PROJECT'S
OBJECTIVES AND DELIVERABLES

A few years ago, I was teaching a master's in business administration class about the basics of project management when an interesting event occurred. Project teams were presenting project proposals to other teams, who were acting in the role of clients. The project leader of one team finished presenting her team's proposal when one of the more experienced students began questioning her quite aggressively. "Would the project turn in a quality product, at cost, on schedule?" demanded the student/client. "Of course!" responded the project lead. "Will you guarantee satisfaction with the product?" After thinking for a moment, the project leader said, "Of course." At that point, the client turned to me and simply smiled—he had forced the project leader into an impossible posi-tion. No matter what was produced, it need not be "satisfactory" in the eyes of the client. The client could now make additional demands throughout the proj-ect on the grounds that it was not proceeding in a "satisfactory" manner.

At least two important lessons were learned that day. First, stakeholders have interests of their own that they pursue—sometimes very aggressively. Even if a stakeholder is not adversarial, honest disagreements can arise, and they usually come up "down the road" in projects, when things are tough to change. The second lesson was that although client satisfaction is always paramount, just what *will* satisfy a client should be hammered out *before* the project gets under way. "Of course," the project lead might have replied, "and we will work very closely with you in the planning process to specify what exactly will satisfy your needs before we begin the project."

Every project leader is faced with this same problem: What exactly can be done to satisfy the client—and can it be done on schedule and on budget? Once the general direction is given by the mission statement, the project's more specific objectives and deliverables need to be developed to help answer these questions.

WHAT ARE PROJECT OBJECTIVES AND DELIVERABLES?

Project objectives are those outcomes a project needs to achieve to fulfill its mission. John's project, for example, may well have a number of project objectives. One objective might focus on the effects of the event itself—what kinds of customers show up and how many. Another might focus on the advertising designed to get them to show up—who will it reach?

The project's deliverables are the specific products and services produced to achieve those objectives. Project deliverables include interim as well as final deliverables. Final deliverables include the products and services the project is to ultimately provide the client. Once these deliverables are provided, the project's mission is complete—the job is done. For example, John is likely to deliver some kind of advertising campaign for the project along with other final deliverables. Interim deliverables are products and services that support the development of final deliverables. For example, Ms. Byrnes might want John to produce reports on the effectiveness and costs of the various ways advertising can be done prior to her approval.[5]

ROLES PLAYED BY PROJECT'S OBJECTIVES AND DELIVERABLES

Project objectives and deliverables play a variety of roles in a project. One is that they help clients define their goals in concrete terms. Another is that they provide the project team with specific outcomes to achieve. Still a third role is that they force stakeholders to make hard choices and trade-offs as they pursue their interests.

Helping Clients Define Their Goals

When clients first present their projects—their needs, problems, goals, and ideas—they are often ambiguous at best. Developing a mission statement is an important first step in clarifying their aims. The process of developing project objectives and their deliverables moves the project forward another important step. It helps clients think through exactly what will address their needs given their resource and time constraints. Helping clients define their goals in concrete, "doable" terms is one of the most important services project leaders can provide.[6]

Providing Team Direction

Project objectives and deliverables also play an important role for the project team. Once specified, they can be translated into specific tasks needed to achieve them. Project teams can then use these tasks to direct individual and team efforts. Specificity is the key here, and the best objectives are SMART. They are Specific and Measurable. They are also Actionable—suggestive of the actions needed to achieve them—and Realistic—achievable even if challenging. Finally, they are Time-specific; they have a time frame within which they are to be achieved.[7]

Securing Stakeholder Agreement

Developing a project's objectives and deliverables also forces stakeholders to confront and work through their different interests. Projects often have a number of clients, for example, and each can have his or her own desires and interests. In John's project, Ms. Byrnes and the store manager are clients who are likely to have different desires and needs. In addition, clients will have different interests than host organizations, and project teams will have their own concerns as well. Developing a common set of project objectives and deliverables sets up a process by which different stakeholders must negotiate their interests to arrive at a specific set of concrete project outcomes. It also allows project teams and stakeholders to confront the hard choices earlier in the project rather than later, when adjustments are more difficult or impossible to make.[8]

THE BALTIMORE PROJECT

As stated earlier, John's project calls for at least two sets of project objectives. The first focuses on what the grand opening is trying to achieve—getting potential customers to show up for the opening. The second focuses on promotion—how to get them there. Acme Auto Supply primarily sells to two kinds of customers—to the retail "do-it-yourself" market and to professional auto mechanics. How many of each will actually show up during the grand opening would be a measure of the first project objective. The second project objective regarding promotion might set advertising targets to reach 80% of the general population within a 10-mile radius of the store and reach 99% of all auto repair shops within a 15-mile radius. The kinds of advertising and promotions used might differ, as well, between these two kinds of customers.

Given these objectives, project deliverables need to be developed to target those customers. Specific advertising and promotional incentives need to be designed, for example, that would interest them. Advertising by radio, local television, print media, and direct mailings are all possible deliverables that need to be considered for getting the message out.

Importantly, John will need to work closely with the store manager in this project. The store manager is a principal stakeholder with whom John will need to clarify promotional and other needs about the opening event itself (e.g., where it is to be held and whether refreshments and entertainment are to be provided). An example of John's project mission, some project objectives, and related, possible deliverables is given in Table 2.1.

Table 2.1 Illustration of John's Mission Statement, a Project Objective, and Its Deliverables

- Project mission: The mission of this project is to develop and stage the opening of the new Baltimore store. The opening is to be a gala event designed to attract Acme's principal customer base to view the products and services offered by the store. The event will occur on or about June 15th.
- Project objectives: [9]
- Promotion: The project's advertising will reach at least 80% of the general population within a 10-mile radius of the store, notifying them of the store's opening, the opening events, and any other promotional offerings. The project will also notify 99% of all auto repair shops within a 15-mile radius of the store about the store's opening, opening events of special interest to them, special services the store will offer to professional mechanics, and any special promotional offers targeting them.
- Customers attending: The opening events aim to attract at least 100 potential retail customers and representatives from at least 50% of auto repair shops within a 15-mile radius.
- Project deliverables: Advertising
- General population: Newspaper copy will advertise the opening of the store every day for a week prior to its opening. The copy will include a description of the event and coupons for promotional items (to be determined by store manager). Radio spots will be given about the store, its grand opening, and sale items (to be determined by store manager) on three of the area's most listened-to stations. These will include three spots per hour between 8 A.M. and 7 P.M. for 3 days prior to the grand opening.
- Business customers: Direct mailings to all auto repair shops within the specified radius of the store will be made 1 week before opening. In addition to information about the opening, several promotional items will be given to those who show up (to be determined by store manager). Personal visits by team members will be made to all auto repair shops with more than 10 mechanics within that radius. Phone invitations will be made to all auto repair shops with between four and nine mechanics. Additional promotional incentives will be given to mechanics and managers of the larger businesses (to be determined by store manager).

John will need to bring these ideas to his client and principal stakeholder, Carol Byrnes, and begin the process of specifying exactly what the project will produce for the company. Working with Ms. Byrnes to clarify what the project will deliver is his all-important first step. As said earlier, John will also need to work with other stakeholders, like the store manager and a wide range of outside suppliers (e.g., the print media, mass mailers, and caterers), about what is doable and the associated costs. Of course, John will need to keep in close communication with his direct supervisor, Ralph, about his need for time to work on the project and to keep Ralph generally informed about project progress. Finally, John would do well to identify and contact others who have opened stores in the past. Although this opening is to be unlike any other, consulting with them to explore action areas, deliverables, and what is achievable, and to get any "words of wisdom," will likely yield a great deal of useful information. These plans, too, he will share with Carol Byrnes in her role as a key player in the host organization. Finally, in the hours before his meeting with Ms. Byrnes, John might make a few phone calls to see if he can get some early figures and information to bring to his meeting. A listing of key talking points for that meeting is given in Figure 2.1. Some of those points also touch on needed project resources and costs and the project's timeline—the topics we consider next.

Figure 2.1 Talking Points for the Meeting With Ms. Byrnes

- Mission statement
  - Project objectives and deliverables (action areas)
    - Where held (venue)
      Held at the store. What would Ms. Byrnes like to see included in the opening?
    - Advertising
      Several outlets possible (direct mail, radio, TV, newspaper, etc.)
      Any preferences?
    - Other
      What kinds of attendance have been considered "successful" in past openings?
      Are there any other action areas/project objectives or deliverables that need attention?
- Stakeholders
    - Ralph (talk with prior to meeting to discuss any issues)
    - Ms. Byrnes as client and host sponsor
      Explore the components of a successful opening
      Any strategic and tactical advice on conducting the project?
      Any other managers I need to touch base with?

- Project team
  How much of Tom's and Alice's time can be devoted to the project?
  What are their backgrounds? When can they start?
  Whom do I need to work with to OK their work with me?
- Store manager
  Will need to work closely with him or her. Plan to contact soon.
  What is standard practice in these kinds of working relationships?
  Any advice?
- Others?
  Who else do I need to work with?

- Budget
  - Cost figures: Will develop based on similar openings. Does Ms. Byrnes have a figure in mind (keep options open)?
  - Other issues?

- Timeline
  - Possible effects on deliverables (e.g., venue and advertising)
  - Other issues?

- Other resource issues
  - Previous project leaders (whom can I contact?)
  - Authority/support (from Ms. Byrnes within organization)
    Who needs to be notified of the project and me as its leader?
    Can I come to Ms. Byrnes if I need someone to "run interference"?

PROJECT PARAMETERS: PROJECT SCOPE, COSTS, AND TIMELINE

The project's mission statement and objectives address what the project is trying to achieve. The deliverables address the products and services that will be produced to achieve them. Three other basic elements now require attention: the project's scope and the resources it will take to produce those deliverables, what they will cost, and how long it will take.

PROJECT SCOPE

The project scope includes all those tasks necessary to produce the deliverables required. A final project plan will detail those tasks in the form of a work breakdown structure (addressed in the next chapter). At this stage, however, some basic estimates can be made about the work that will be required and, importantly, the resources needed to support that work. Resources include all products and services that the project team will need in order to produce project deliverables. Resources related to promotional requirements and the opening itself, for example, will affect the costs of John's project. Estimates of these certainly need to be made. Three other kinds of resources also require attention, however, in ways that are often overlooked. These include human resources, information, and authority.

Human resources—the project team—are needed, of course, to work on the project's activities. Beyond personnel costs, however, project leaders need to consider the knowledge, skills, and abilities needed to perform work on the project and just who possesses them. Good human resources are notoriously in short supply, and the earlier project leaders can "lock them in," the better.

John's Baltimore project presents another, quite common issue with human resources. Members of his project team—Tom and Alice—were "volunteered" by Ms. Byrnes. When working with the store manager, John may find yet another person has been "volunteered" for his team. As early as possible, project leaders need to check out the knowledge, skills, and abilities of such resources as well as their true availability and commitment to project work. When personnel are drawn from other parts of an organization, their time is usually committed to other projects. Both they and their supervisors are rarely happy to give *their* time to *your* project.

Information is another often overlooked resource that needs to be acquired as soon as possible. Because projects are unique endeavors, information that can be helpful in planning and conducting them is invaluable. One excellent source of information is experience—one's own and that of others. Even before detailed planning begins, it serves leaders well to consider others who have experience in working on and leading projects similar to the one being considered. This would include potential team members, of course, but also others who might be able to shed some light on the project. Even a few "cold calls" can reap tremendous gains in information. Those who have labored in the "project trenches" are often quite willing and even eager to share a few stories. In John's case, reaching out to one or two others who have been project leaders for opening other stores would be well worth the time. Networking from those project leaders to others they might recommend may be helpful as well.

Another important resource for any project is the authority required to make the decisions needed in a project. Projects, for example, often need the help of others. The authority to acquire their help can work wonders when needed. Authority comes from those higher up in the host organization who will actively champion project work. Their support needs to be acquired early in the planning process and maintained throughout the life of the project.

Costs

Project costs are all the costs related to doing project work and acquiring its resource needs. For different reasons, project costs are always of concern to clients, the host organization, and project teams. Although ballpark figures tend to get discussed early on in projects, it is important to understand that early ballpark figures often determine stakeholders' expectations. Those expectations need to be handled carefully right from the beginning.[10]

Outside clients and even those in the host organization can underestimate true project costs. Outside clients, for example, tend to overlook a lot of project activities (e.g., the costs of simply administering a project) and underestimate the actual costs of project items (e.g., not considering Social Security, Medicare, and health benefits, among other personnel costs). Higher level managers in the host organization can also overlook cost items that are more apparent to project leaders working in the trenches (e.g., supplies, travel, overhead charges, equipment, and materials as well as administrative costs).

All this speaks to the fact that project leaders need to be very careful when dealing with project costs and the expectations of others. In John's case, he might get a reasonable ballpark figure by calling project leaders who have opened stores in the past, getting their final costs, and then adjusting for things like inflation and other items. This is called "top-down" or "analogous" budgeting, because it applies the costs of a similar project to the project at hand. The full costs, however, await "bottom-up" budgeting based on an accounting of all project tasks (these are addressed more fully in the next chapter).

Whether a project leader is asked to develop a project budget (as in John's case) or is given one by the performing organization, he or she needs to think through the implications in terms of deliverables and scheduled delivery very carefully and convey the implications to his or her manager and clients. This is a valuable service but one that often requires, at the same time, both tact and assertiveness.

Timeline

Like costs, the project timeline—the time allocated to get a project done—largely determines what *can* be done. Generally speaking, clients and host organizations want projects done as quickly as possible. Project teams, ever pressed for time, generally want more of it.

John's case is a typical one. Ms. Byrnes scheduled a hard completion date of June 15th without initial consultation with the project leader. That time horizon, however, might well affect some deliverables. A direct mail promotion, for example, might take more than 6 weeks to set up using standard operating procedures. Some equipment usually brought in for store openings may well be committed on that weekend by the vendors who supply it. Although more money can often speed things up or change the priorities of vendors, added costs, as we have seen, have issues of their own.

Project leaders need to make stakeholders aware of the implications of time demands just as they do for project costs. Like cost estimations, ballpark, top-down time horizons can be estimated from the times taken to complete similar projects. Nevertheless, each project is unique, and clients need to understand that time as well as costs will affect what deliverables are possible.

THE PROJECT CHARTER

Host organizations that routinely perform outside projects for their business often kick off a project with a project charter. A project charter is a thorough description of a project, and it formally authorizes the project to proceed. The idea of developing and using a project charter is a good one for all project leaders whether or not their organizations require one. A project charter can be as formal as those used in project organizations or as informal as a memo or e-mail that has been approved by the project sponsor—the manager with the authority to approve a project and commit organizational resources to it.

A project charter describes the project in enough detail that a sponsor can make an informed decision about whether it is worthwhile to commit resources to it. It describes the mission of a project and ties that mission to the broader organizational purpose(s) of the mission—why the project is worthwhile to the host organization. The project charter also lays out what will be needed for the project by first tying the project mission to the project's main objectives and deliverables. It then goes on to lay out expected timelines and enough cost information that all stakeholders can make an informed decision to move ahead. A project charter should also address what will be needed to make the project successful. Time and budget needs are based on time and cost estimates. Human and other resources needed are described. What levels of authority are needed to conduct project activities should be considered, as well as any other assumptions critical to project success (e.g., the availability of key personnel).

Just the production of such a charter will force the project leader to consider the important elements of the project at its initiation. The formal acceptance of the charter by key stakeholders, however, signals to the project leader that the project can, indeed, move ahead as planned. It signals, as well, that the project is a legitimate undertaking that has the full backing it needs to achieve its goals. Table 2.2 presents some key questions leaders can use as a check-off list when first developing a project. Although the questions are not exhaustive, they provide a jumping-off point for project leaders as they begin to put projects together for the first time.

Table 2.2   Initiation Check-Off List

There are many issues to consider when first planning a project. Listed here are a few of the more important questions leaders should ask themselves as they move through the project initiation process. The questions are meant to encourage project leaders to think through the issues involved and are meant to be used as a point of departure rather than as a comprehensive listing.

- What is the mission or purpose of the project?
- What are the key project objectives?
- What are the client's final and interim deliverables? Show extra care in the development of these; they are your "contracted" items. For example, are there any special quality requirements?
- What is the basic scope of project work that will need to be done? Consider work to produce the deliverables and any administrative requirements.
- What resources will be required? Consider human resources, material, equipment, facilities, and any other resource that may be needed. Include consideration of subcontracts for outsourcing. Consider any special arrangements that may be needed.
- What is the timeline for the project? Can the project be completed in that time?
- What is the budget for the project? Will it cover the costs required?
- What are the key areas of risk for the project in terms of deliverables, work requirements, costs, and time?
- Who are the key stakeholders of this project? What are their requirements? To what extent can they affect the project? Consider the client, higher management (including your direct supervisor), others on the project team, end users, external vendors, and internal suppliers of project resources. Make sure you have contacted all relevant stakeholders, whether or not they are key players. Make sure you have extended discussions with key players about their expectations.
- Whom can you quickly contact to get information about projects similar to this one? Ask about deliverables, project scope of work, timelines, budget, and special or unforeseen problems that arose that you should consider in your own risk assessments. Ask for referrals to others who have had similar projects whom you can contact.

(Continued)

- Have you developed a written charter of the project? Has it been approved by the key stakeholders of the project? Has it been formally accepted and approved by those in management who have the authority to approve the project and allocate funds and other organizational resources for its budget?

Once the charter is developed and accepted, it can be used as the basis for developing a full project plan. The project plan will nail down project specifics and guide the project through its life cycle. We will be attending to the other elements of the project plan in the following chapters, but it is appropriate now to specify just what goes into a project plan.

THE PROJECT PLAN

Before they begin actual construction, contractors need blueprints of the building they are to construct. So, too, do project leaders need their own blueprints of the project—the project plan. Project plans will vary in content, complexity, and detail depending on the projects they address. At the very least, however, a project plan should include a number of common elements.

- The project's mission statement: The mission statement lays out the general purpose of the project. The general purpose of the project needs to be tied to the broader objectives and mission of the host organization.

- The project's objectives: What the project is trying to achieve in specific terms. These are made relevant to the project's mission statement.

- All deliverables and quality criteria: Deliverables include both the final set of deliverables to be given to the client and all interim deliverables. If required, any quality criteria or other specifications for those deliverables should be included.

- A complete work breakdown structure: This is a complete specification of all project work that needs to be done—the project's scope. We cover this in Chapter 3.

- The project schedule: This is a schedule showing which tasks are to be done by what dates in the project. Typically, the schedule specifies the start and end or completion dates for all project tasks. We cover this in Chapter 4.

- All resources needed for the project: These include human resources, materials, equipment, facilities, and the like.[11]

- The project's budget: The budget should be laid out by project task so it can be used to control costs throughout the project as those tasks are performed.

- Risk assessments: Project risks include those that threaten the attainment of project objectives, push back project dates, increase project costs, or detrimentally affect project deliverables. These are addressed in a project risk plan, which we cover in Chapter 5.

The project plan, then, is really a series of project documents. Whether they are kept in three-ring binders or on a computer, project leaders will continuously refer to them as the project moves forward. They will also keep updating the plan as changes are required. They will add other documents to the plan as well—authorization for changes, sign-offs for work done, and the like. Keeping track of all these documents is an important administrative task for project leaders. They always seem to come in handy down the road and are often required by one or more key stakeholders.

As we finish this chapter, we see that our project charter has given us a good start at creating our project plan. Its purpose, after all, was to give stakeholders a ballpark idea of the project in enough detail to allow a decision to move forward and make a commitment to the project the leader had envisioned. We turn now to developing the work breakdown structure of the project plan and how it is used to make the more precise estimates leaders need of the resource, cost, and time demands of the project.

SUMMARY

All projects have a mission. That mission is to help address the problems and needs of the project's clients. Mission statements clarify the goals and aims of a project in those terms. As such, they help give general guidance to a project. They help to orient and direct project teams, for example, and anyone else who might work with or contribute to a project. When they are developed in concert with a project's principal stakeholders, mission statements provide a common understanding of the project that can help tie together the often diverse interests of stakeholders. This common ground can be used in bringing together stakeholders to negotiate matters of common concern as needed.

All projects also have a number of stakeholders who have a vested interest in the mission of a project. The client, of course, has a stake in the project solving his or her problem. The organization hosting the project has a stake in seeing the project run smoothly and, if appropriate, making a profit. The project team is a stakeholder, including the project leader. The team members want to see the project become a success, of course, but they would like not to be overstretched and overcommitted in doing so. End users are those who will ultimately use the output of the project. Suppliers are stakeholders, too. External suppliers make money from supplying a project. Internal suppliers, on the other hand, often have to supply resources to projects without compensation, putting a strain on the project-supplier relationship that needs attention. In all cases, stakeholders are people—people who can make decisions that can have an important effect on the project. Project leaders, then, need to be able to work with them successfully.

Once a project's mission has been clarified by its stakeholders, project objectives and deliverables need to be specified. Project objectives are specific goals that must be attained for the mission to be achieved. Deliverables are the products and services that will fulfill those specific goals. Project objectives and deliverables are better when they are SMART: specific, measurable, actionable, realistic, and time-specific.

Project objectives and deliverables help the client see the project in concrete terms, and they provide the project team with clear direction. They also help often diverse stakeholders negotiate concrete project outcomes that will satisfy their interests. Project leaders need to help their stakeholders come to agreement about what specific objectives and deliverables will satisfy them before moving ahead.

Once a project's mission, objectives, and deliverables have clarified its direction, project leaders need to make initial assessments of a project's work requirements or its project scope, its resource needs, its costs, and its timeline. All projects require resources to get them done, and an initial estimate needs to be made of them. Key among these are human resources—people with the knowledge, skills, and abilities to get the project done. In addition to all the other resources a project needs, two other, often overlooked, resources are information useful for the project and the authority to take the actions needed when conducting the project. A little time invested in attention to these resources can reap large benefits later.

All project stakeholders are interested in project costs—each for his or her own reasons and concerns. Initial ballpark estimates for projects will be needed, but care must be taken that the expectations of stakeholders are not inflated. Project leaders can often get an initial ballpark estimate by top-down or analogous estimating. To do so, a similar project is selected, its final costs are noted, and then they are modified to fit the specifics of the present project.

Stakeholders are also interested in the amount of time it will take to complete a project. As with cost estimates, a top-down time estimate can be developed from similar projects adjusted for present circumstances. Often both costs and a project's timeline are simply given to a project leader. In these cases, it is best for the leader to clarify the implications of such explicit and firm constraints on project deliverables.

Before a proposed project gets fully under way, the leader should develop a project charter. The project charter describes what the project is trying to achieve and how it intends to do so. It includes estimated costs and a project schedule or timeline as well as a description of needed resources. Once a sponsoring manager in the host organization or the leader's client formally sanctions the charter, the project has the agreement of key stakeholders to move forward the full planning and execution of the project.

The project charter is the first step in producing a project plan—the blueprint project leaders use to fully understand and run a project. At the very least, a project plan consists of a mission statement and the project's objectives. It should also contain a complete breakdown of all project work, along with a schedule of when specific tasks will be done. Resource needs require attention as well as a project budget. Finally, assessments need to be made regarding various risks to the project—threats to deliverables, costs, and time required for the project.

REVIEW QUESTIONS

1. Define and characterize mission statements. What roles do mission statements play for a project?

2. Describe how mission statements help to establish common ground.

3. What is a stakeholder in a project? Who are the stakeholders reviewed in this chapter, and what are their concerns or interests in a project?

4. What are the objectives and deliverables in a project? How do they differ from one another and from the mission statement? What roles do objectives and deliverables play for a project?

5. What are some of the key resources that need to be considered early in the development of a project?

6. How might ballpark estimates of project costs be developed early in the project? How should cost estimates be handled when working with the project's stakeholders?

7. What is a project charter? What forms can a project charter take? What are reasons that a project charter should be developed and used?

EXERCISE

1. Work individually or as a team to develop a project charter.

   a. Focus on a project that is relevant to you or your team.

   b. Focus on and define the basic problems the project will address.

   c. Identify the major stakeholders in the project and their interests.

   d. Develop a mission statement for the project and its major objectives. Develop one or more project deliverables for each project objective.

   e. Identify some of the key resources you will need for the project. Be as specific and concrete as possible given the needs of your project.

   f. Estimate the costs and time needed for the project. These estimates are for purposes of writing up the project charter only.

   g. Write up a one- to two-page charter for the project. Frame the charter as a proposal for approval by higher management in your host organization or by your client.

ENDNOTES

1. The Project Management Institute uses *customer* to indicate the client. Throughout this book, the term *client* is used.

2. The term *performing organization* is the one used by: Project Management Institute. (2008). *A guide to the project management body of knowledge* (4th ed.). Newtown Square, PA: Author. *Host organization* is the label preferred here, but *performing organization* is also used.

3. These kinds of projects, in fact, account for a great deal of the growth in the demand for project leaders.

4. A careful reader might note that the June 15th date set by Carol Byrnes has been changed to "on or about." Project leaders often take such constraints as "given" without question. Although Ms. Byrnes no doubt has this date in mind, further preliminary work may find it unacceptable. For example, some other event might be occurring on that date that would undermine the whole purpose of the opening (e.g., an automotive show attracting business users of the store or a NASCAR event attracting retail customers of the store).

5. In the development of a new product, for example, interim deliverables may include prototypes, testing, and marketing plans as well as the end product itself. Quite often, interim deliverables are required to decide whether to proceed with the project. We will see in the next chapter, as well, that the project can produce deliverables for itself in the form of planning and administrative products and services. Projects may also purchase some of their deliverables.

6. A common mistake, in fact, is for managers to simply dictate objectives to project leaders early on without carefully thinking them through. If so, project

leaders need to review the given objectives to see their full implications. These need to be brought to the attention of the manager privately and, hopefully, before the manager makes any public declarations of the project's objectives.

7. While the acronym "SMART" is a common one, the "A" has been used to refer to a number of goal criteria. *Achievable, accurate, agreed-upon,* and *action-oriented* are a few of them. I prefer *actionable* as it is least redundant and focuses attention on making things happen.

8. Using a "single text" procedure is one way of approaching this issue. The project leader lays out an initial listing of objectives and deliverables and lets the stakeholders discuss among themselves how to alter it. As they do so, the project leader facilitates negotiations with what can and cannot be done and addresses the interests of each stakeholder in terms of the project's mission. The stakeholders themselves, then, assume the responsibility for negotiating their own agreement.

9. These are two very different kinds of project objectives. The promotional objective is a performance objective—a measure of how well the advertising deliverable is to perform. The second objective—customers attending—is a measure of overall project success or the extent to which the deliverables produce what the client ultimately wants. Importantly, performance objectives of project deliverables are more under the control of a project than whether those deliverables will achieve other "downstream" aims. Any number of factors, completely out of control of the project team, can affect those kinds of objectives. For this reason, project leaders often try to limit project objectives to performance objectives or simply specifications of deliverables without regard to how well they are to perform. Clients, however, will judge a project in terms of how well deliverables meet their ultimate needs.

10. It should be mentioned that the costs of a project are very different from the price of a project. The costs of a project are borne by the host or performing organization. The price of a project is what the host organization charges the client and includes other associated overhead costs and profits to be made. Project leaders in host organizations rarely discuss costs with outside clients and are usually not involved in the pricing of a project at all.

11. Unique resources are particularly important to include. If you need a particular person to work on some task because of his or her singular expertise, that should be noted and arranged far in advance. The same goes for any special equipment, materials, and so forth.

KEY TERMS

Client: the customer—person or organization—for which the project is being conducted and the ultimate source of funds and resources for the project.

Deliverables: specific products and services produced to achieve project objectives.

End Users: the people who will ultimately use or benefit from a project.

Host Organization: the organization in which the project is conducted.

Key Stakeholders: stakeholders who have the power and authority to make important decisions about the conduct and outcomes of the project.

Mission Statement: a few sentences or paragraphs that state the general purpose and aims of a project—what it is trying to achieve.

Project Charter: a thorough description of a project used to formally authorize the project to proceed.

Project Costs: all the costs related to doing project work and acquiring its resource needs.

Project Objectives: specific goals or outcomes a project needs to achieve to fulfill its mission.

Project Plan: the "blueprint" that project leaders use to fully understand and run a project. It includes the project's mission, objectives, and deliverables. A work breakdown structure of work requirements is also included with the project schedule and budget to cover all project costs. All required resources are specified and assessments of foreseeable project risk provided.

Project Scope: all the tasks necessary to produce the deliverables required.

Project Sponsor: the manager within the host organization who has the authority to approve a project and commit organizational resources to it.

Project Team: the group of people who actually carry out project activities.

Project Timeline: the time required to complete a project.

Resources: products and services that the project team will need in order to produce project's deliverables.

SMART: project objectives and deliverables should be specific, measurable, actionable, realistic, time-specific.

Stakeholders: those people, organizational units, and institutions that have a vested interest in the project and can affect it in some way.

Suppliers: people who deliver the products and services that the team itself cannot supply.

Project Scheduling

Cobb, A. T.

INTRODUCTION

DR. HOWARD'S BIO-INFORMATICS PROJECT

"Be careful what you wish for." That saying kept running through Dr. Dan Howard's head as he looked at the project ahead of him. Dr. Howard, a professor at a large Eastern university, was awarded a $5 million, 5-year contract by the National Institutes of Health (NIH) to expand his award-winning work in bio-informatics. But it wasn't the bio-informatics research that bothered him now. It was the setup required before he could do the work! In his proposal to NIH, he allocated time and money to refurbish and convert a large facility at the university's research park into a fully functioning laboratory. Extensive modifications needed to be made on the structure itself, of course, but that was only the beginning. Equipment had to be purchased, delivered, set up, and tested. Supplies needed to be ordered and stored—some of them in special kinds of storage, and some with only a short shelf life. Special security had to be arranged as well—given the nature of his work—and the federal government would review security arrangements to make sure it was up to standard. He also had to hire and train a large contingent of administrative and laboratory staff to support the work of the lead scientists. And he had to do all this and more in just 4 months!

Chapter Overview

Although Dr. Howard's project might be in the category of "high science," the headache he faces here is common to many kinds of projects—how to arrange a lot of different jobs to come together smoothly through time. This chapter addresses that basic issue. Project work must be scheduled so that the different parts come together to produce whatever is needed at the right time. We begin our discussion of project scheduling by looking at different kinds of project schedules and the components that make them up. Next, we discuss how schedules are constructed, focusing on the construction of Gantt or bar charts. Finally, we explore some of the ways that project leaders use their schedules.

PROJECT SCHEDULES: TYPES AND COMPONENTS

The project schedule orders project tasks and events through time. It indicates when tasks should start and end and how long they should take, and it arranges them in a logical order. It is the principal tool project leaders use to keep track of a project: whether things are getting done on time, costs are being used according to budget, resources are being delivered as needed, and deliverables are being produced as promised. Schedules also help project leaders keep track of what tasks are coming up that may need attention and resources. At its heart, a project schedule is simply a list of when project tasks are to begin and end. Because some tasks must finish before other tasks can start, most project schedules tie these tasks together with dependencies—linkages that show how tasks are dependent on one another. As projects grow in complexity, their activities and dependencies grow into more and more detailed networks. As you can guess, all of this can get very complicated very quickly. As a result, a number of visual, mathematical, and computer tools have been developed that help project leaders organize and visualize the way project tasks must occur through time.

Types of Project Schedules

Three of the most common scheduling techniques are the Gantt or bar chart, the Critical Path Method, and the Program Evaluation and Review Technique.

The Gantt or Bar Chart

If you count nonprofessionals, Gantt or bar charts are likely the most commonly used scheduling tool because they are fairly easy to learn and can be used in even quite complex projects. Gantt charts illustrate project tasks as bars and place them across the days of a calendar. The length of the bar represents how long the task should take to get done. The beginning of the bar is placed on the calendar date where the task should begin, and the end of the bar shows when the task should end. If one task (e.g., staff training) depends on another task ending (e.g., staff hiring), the beginning of the dependent task's bar is placed at the end of the first task's bar because of that dependency. Sometimes, Gantt charts show arrows between these bars to illustrate their dependency.

Figure 4.1 presents a simple Gantt chart for ordering supplies in Dr. Howard's Bio-Informatics Project.[1] Figure 4.2 shows how Gantt charts can handle even more complex projects like the Bio-Informatics Project facing Dr. Howard. We will come back to this Gantt chart several more times to illustrate a number of points in this chapter.

Gantt charts are very good tools to use when trying to visualize a project's tasks through time and communicate that information to the project team and others. They are the most commonly used scheduling tool among nonprofessionals. They are fairly easy to learn and, with modern project management software, can be used to help plan and control quite complex projects.

Figure 4.1 A Simple Bar Chart—Ordering Supplies in Dr. Howard's Bio-Informatics Project

ID	Task Name	Week 1							Week 2							Week 3		
		S	M	T	W	T	F	S	S	M	T	W	T	F	S	S	M	T
1	Review Needs																	
2	Select Vendors																	
3	Order Non-perishables																	
4	Deliver																	
5	Store																	

NOTE: Figure 4.1 was generated using Microsoft Excel©.

The Critical Path Method (CPM)

A schedule of tasks can also be shown as a network of arrows and nodes. The arrows show task dependencies, and the nodes show where tasks intersect. Figure 4.3 shows a simple network diagram laying out a study Dr. Howard might conduct in his laboratory once it is set up. In this procedure, Dr. Howard has to spend some time setting up the study he will run. He then needs to do three experiments to compare with one another, each of which has two stages. Finally, he has to analyze the data he developed from them and write up the results in a project report. In the diagram shown in Figure 4.3, the study tasks are represented as nodes with information in them (i.e., the number of the task, the task name, and time needed to complete it). The arrows simply show the relationship between those tasks.[2]

The Critical Path Method (CPM) is a mathematical calculation that uses the time estimates for each task to develop the project's critical path, as shown by the double-line arrows in Figure 4.3. A project's critical path is that sequence of tasks that, together, will take longer than any other set of tasks to get the project done. Because the project cannot be done any earlier, the critical path determines the earliest end date for the project. Needless to say, this path will command a great deal of the project leader's attention, and we will return to it later. The CPM was created by the DuPont Corporation to aid in its chemical plant projects and has been shown to be very useful across a variety of complex projects. Appendix A discusses how a critical path is calculated using CPM.

The Program Evaluation and Review Technique (PERT)

The Program Evaluation and Review Technique (PERT) uses a network diagram similar to the CPM. It uses three different time estimates, however, for the completion of each task instead of just one: an optimistic time, a likely time, and a pessimistic time. Each task, then, has a probability distribution attached to its time estimate. Mathematical techniques like Monte Carlo simulations[3] can be used throughout the project to calculate the probabilities that the project as a whole—or subcomponents in it—will be completed as required. This technique was created for use in the development of the Polaris Missile Submarine. PERT is still used for very complex projects (e.g., those involving breakthrough technologies) in which time estimates are inherently more risky.

COMPONENTS OF PROJECT SCHEDULES

Project schedules have a number of components that make them up. Each component plays an important role in building an effective schedule.

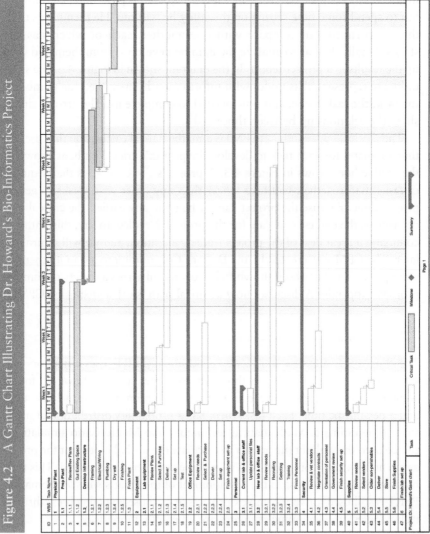

Figure 4.2   A Gantt Chart Illustrating Dr. Howard's Bio-Informatics Project

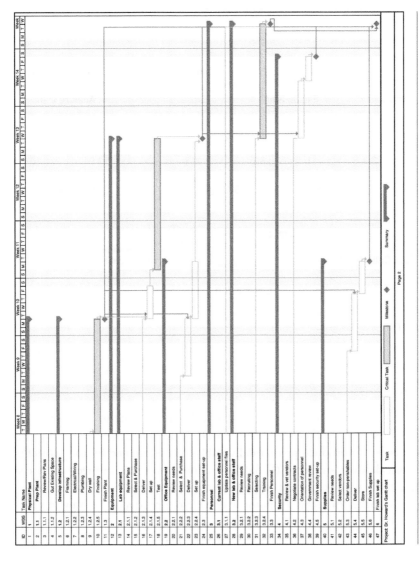

NOTE: Figure 4.2 was generated using Microsoft Project©. WBS = Work breakdown structure.

Figure 4.3   A Simple Project Network Diagram—Dr. Howard's Study

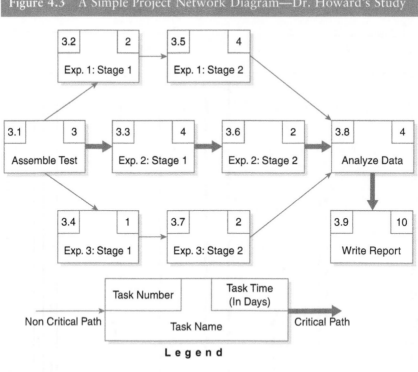

NOTE: Exp. = experiment.

Activities or Project Tasks

An activity is anything in a project that will require time to complete and usually money and other resources as well. Most often, activities are team tasks needed to produce project deliverables as determined by the project's work breakdown structure (WBS). Sometimes, however, project activities include tasks that lie outside what the project team is doing. For example, your boss, bank, or some regulator may have to approve something in your project before it can move forward. You want to make sure you include these kinds of external activities in your WBS and schedule as well.

Dependencies

Dependencies occur when one task is dependent on another task in some way. The most common form is the finish-to-start dependency, in which one or more tasks must finish before one or more tasks can begin. In Dr. Howard's project (Figure 4.2), for example, he must finish selecting new laboratory personnel (3.2.3) before their training (3.2.4) can start. Three other less common dependencies are "start-to-start," "finish-to-finish," and "start-to-finish" dependencies. In a start-to-start dependency, two or more tasks must start at the same time. When Dr. Howard is actually conducting experiments, for example, he may have to start two or more of them at the same time to get valid results. In a finish-to-finish dependency, two or more tasks must finish at the same time. Although the delivery of equipment might begin at any time for Dr. Howard's lab, for example, that activity must finish (i.e., be finally delivered to the lab) when the lab itself is finished so it can be moved in. Finally, a start-to-finish dependency signals that one or more tasks must start for one or more tasks to be finished.

Lag and Lead Times

Lag and lead times affect task dependencies in terms of the amount of time that must pass in one task before another task can be related to it. Lag time is the amount of time that must pass after work has been done on a task before work can start on a dependent, following, or succeeding task. Concrete must cure for a while, for example, before anything can be built on it. Dr. Howard's study in Figure 4.3 may show another example of lag time. Each of the three experiments may require growing bacteria in petri dishes. It may take only half a day to set up the growth, but the remaining time in Stage 1 for each experiment may be needed for the growth to reach maturity for that particular line of bacteria.

Lead time means something very specific in project schedules. It means that a following dependent task can begin before a beginning or preceding task has completely finished—it can "lead" the finish of the beginning task. In the construction of Dr. Howard's lab (Figure 4.2), for example, the wiring (1.2.2) and plumbing (1.2.3) can begin before all the walls are put up (Framing, 1.2.1). If the walls take 15 days to complete, the wiring and plumbing might begin when two thirds of the walls are completed, thereby leading the completion by 5 days.

Milestones

Milestones are important events in the life of a project but consume no time or resources. They are usually added to a project schedule to signal when some component of the project should have been completed. In Dr. Howard's project shown in Figure 4.2, for example, every major project component (e.g., [1] Physical Plant, [2] Equipment) has a "finish" scheduled as a milestone (e.g., 1.3, 2.3, 3.3). Often, milestones require some report or other deliverable to the client or to another stakeholder. If so, then it is important to remember that this kind of milestone must be preceded by activities that produce whatever is needed for the milestone and that they be included in the work breakdown structure, schedule, cost estimates, and the like.

The Project Network

Because a project ultimately depends on all project tasks being done at some point, all the project's activities and milestones will eventually be tied together in a complex arrangement of project tasks, known as the project network. Figure 4.3 of Dr. Howard's study shows a network as it is commonly conceived. All tasks are connected and eventually lead to the project's final goal. The Gantt chart in Figure 4.2 shows the bio-informatics project network, but rather than nodes and arrows, the Gantt chart uses bars and arrows to represent how the tasks connect to each other and eventually lead to the project's completion.

The Critical Path

Every project has a critical path—a sequence of tasks that will take longer to do than any other sequence of tasks. The project's critical path determines the earliest date the project can be completed. Because any change in the critical path affects the whole project, it commands a great deal of attention from project leaders. In planning, most risk assessments about the time it will take to do a task will be done along this path. If a leader wants to shorten the project completion date, he or she will work with the tasks scheduled along this path. While the project is being conducted, project leaders may take resources from an activity off the critical path and give them to an activity that is on the critical path to keep the project on schedule or to shorten the overall project—an activity known as "crashing."

The double-line arrows show the critical path in Dr. Howard's study in Figure 4.3. The critical path can also be shown in Gantt charts. In Figure 4.2, for example, the critical path is indicated by the solid gray bars in the diagram connected to each other with arrows—those are the tasks that make up the critical path. They must start and end as scheduled for the project to finish on time.

Slack or Float

Tasks that lie off the critical path have slack (also known as float). Those tasks can begin and finish later than scheduled without pushing back the completion time for the project as a whole. For example, take a look at the "Office Equipment" (2.2) task of selecting and purchasing of equipment (2.2.2) in the Gantt chart in Figure 4.2. It is scheduled to begin on the 2nd day of the project and will be finished in the following week. Delivery (2.2.3) of the equipment, however, cannot begin until near the completion date of laboratory construction some 8 weeks later. Selection and purchasing of office equipment, then, has a fair amount of slack. Dr. Howard may choose to put off that task until later and use its personnel for other, more pressing, project work.

HOW TO DEVELOP A PROJECT SCHEDULE: FOCUS—GANTT CHARTS

We will focus on developing Gantt charts because they tend to be the most useful for most projects. Before we begin, however, it would be a good idea to look at the Gantt chart of Dr. Howard's project in Figure 4.2. Although it might seem complicated at first, there are really just three basic parts to it. The first is the work breakdown structure in the left-hand column. This was produced using the approach to breaking down project work covered in Chapter 3. The work in Dr. Howard's project is clustered into five major components: (1) Physical Plant, (2) Equipment, (3) Personnel, and so on. Each of those project components contains all the project activities or tasks relevant to them. All these components and tasks are numbered in "outline form." The largest numbers are given to the largest project components (e.g., 1 Physical Plant). The smallest numbers within each component represent individual activities or tasks. Any numbers in between show how large project components are broken down into smaller project components (e.g., 1.1 Prep Plant and 1.2 Develop Infrastructure).

    The second major part of a Gantt chart is the project calendar. The days of the calendar are laid out across the top of the chart, and those days create columns down the rest of the chart. In Dr. Howard's Gantt chart, the days are clustered by week, and actual dates are often given for the project calendar. That calendar shows Saturdays and Sundays, as well as the days of the normal workweek. I like to include them to help visually keep track of the weeks in a project. Most often, however, they are not counted as project work time.

    The final part of the Gantt chart is the information that lies out across the project calendar. The most important information is given in the task bars that represent each project task. The length of each task bar is the time it should take to do the task. Where the bar is placed on the calendar indicates when the task should start and end. Those bars are also arranged in terms of their dependency on one another. If one task cannot begin until another task is done, its task bar is placed after that preceding task. That dependency is also shown in Dr. Howard's Gantt chart with arrows connecting the bars.

There are other, summary bars as well. They "summarize" how long related clusters of project tasks should take and when each task cluster should begin and end. Finally, you can see milestones on Dr. Howard's Gantt chart represented by diamonds. They indicate important dates in the project—usually when some larger component of project work should be done. Of course, many other kinds of information can be placed on the Gantt chart, but this is sufficient for most modest projects.

There are five basic steps to producing Gantt charts like Dr. Howard's. First, create a work breakdown structure in outline form. Second, review the times needed to complete each task. Third, determine the dependency between those tasks—what needs to be done first, second, third, and the like, so that other tasks can follow and build on the initial ones. Fourth, construct the project network of tasks across the project's calendar. Fifth, determine the project's critical path.

CREATE A WORK BREAKDOWN STRUCTURE IN OUTLINE FORM

As covered in Chapter 3, the WBS identifies the tasks that need to be done in a project. To create a Gantt chart, those tasks need to be arranged in outline form. The outline form is created to help keep similar, related tasks together. Dr. Howard's Gantt chart in Figure 4.2 provides a good example of a WBS in outline form in the chart's far left columns.

REVIEW TIME ESTIMATES

You may recall that when a WBS is developed, time estimates are made for how long the individual tasks will take to complete. Those estimates should be reviewed prior to the schedule's construction, and they should include such considerations as required lag time.[4] As was suggested in Chapter 3, it is a good idea to think about optimistic and pessimistic time estimates as well as your "best guess." The time risks of a project are a major threat to getting the project done on time and on budget and deserve extra attention.

DETERMINE TASK DEPENDENCIES

The next step to take is to determine how project tasks relate to one another—their dependencies. The most common dependency is the finish-to-start dependency—one task must finish before another can start.

It is helpful to start this task by looking within project job categories first. For example, in Dr. Howard's project in Figure 4.2, attention might be given to the Physical Plant first and to its related tasks. It is because these tasks *are* related that dependencies are likely to occur among them. In a similar manner, a first pass looking for dependencies would progress through all the other major project components.

Next, it is a good idea to step back a bit and consider how major project categories relate to one another. "Developing the Physical Plant" in the Dr. Howard's project, for example, is necessary before most other activities can be done within the finished laboratory. The last task of construction, then, needs to precede all those other dependent activities.

Construct the Network of Project Activities

The next step is to construct the schedule network itself. In Gantt charts, each task in the work breakdown outline is given its own row, and the tasks are clustered into project components of related activities. Recall that the columns to the right of the task listing represent time intervals in a project calendar—quite often, days of the week.

Initially, focus is given to individual project tasks. Task bars are drawn so that their length represents how long they will take to get done. Then they are placed on the calendar at the point of their earliest start date. As you place or draw the task bars across the project calendar, you need to keep in mind the dependencies between tasks—not starting a task, for example, before another, dependent task is finished.

When the bars for all project tasks have been placed on the calendar, higher order "summary bars" can be drawn to completely encompass the lower order tasks that make them up. These summary bars visually summarize and unite the project work beneath them into their higher order project components.

Once all the bars are placed on the project calendar, their dependencies can be shown by drawing arrows from the end of a preceding task to the beginning of a successor task that depends on it. In Gantt charts, the arrow goes straight across the row of the preceding task before it moves down to connect with its successor task. The length of the arrow indicates the preceding task's slack or float, as shown in Dr. Howard's project in Figure 4.2.[5]

Determine the Critical Path

Finding a project's critical path is rather straightforward, but the calculations involved can become quite challenging in complex projects. Project management software provides the best solution to this task. Nevertheless, project leaders should have a basic understanding of the process involved.

Recall that the critical path is the longest sequence of activities from the beginning of a project to its end. Because, eventually, all activities are connected to both the beginning and the end of the project, one path of project tasks will come up as the longest. The key to finding the critical path, then, is to trace the various paths of dependent activities in a project from its beginning to its end, always making sure to focus on the path that is taking the longest time to complete. To do so, keep adding the time it takes to do a task to the dependent task that comes next. Whenever two or more paths come together, choose the path with the longest time and begin tracing the next sequence of tasks from it. Eventually, this process ends with the last project task sequence. This process is known as a "forward pass" because you start at the beginning of the project, adding task times until you reach the end, and it results in two outcomes. The first is the amount of time it will take to finish the project—the sum of the longest sequence of task times. The second outcome is the identification of the longest sequence of tasks itself—the critical path. Any change in time for any of those tasks will affect the finish date of the project.

In critical path calculations, a "backward pass" is usually done as well. Beginning with the last task's finish date, subtract task times along task sequences. Doing so will indicate the amount of slack time between dependent tasks—none for those on the critical path and various amounts of slack for those tasks off the critical path. A more detailed description of the CPM is beyond the scope of this chapter, but Appendix A, "Calculating the Critical Path Using the Critical Path Method," demonstrates both the forward and backward pass and the calculations that result from them.

USING THE OUTPUT OF A PROJECT SCHEDULE

The project's work schedule plays a variety of roles for the project leader. These roles include helping visualize the project as a whole, revising the project's estimates, and making project adjustments. Finally, because the schedule arranges project tasks through time, it allows project leaders to command, control, and coordinate resource use and outcomes of the project.

VISUALIZING THE PROJECT AS A WHOLE

One of the most important benefits of the project schedule is that it provides a "whole picture" of the project. As we said in Chapter 3, the WBS provides a list of all the tasks, and if graphed appropriately, it can provide a picture of the project's structure as well (e.g., recall the Compliance Project graphed in Figure 3.1). The project schedule, however, is the only tool that arranges the project's tasks through time. At first glance, the Gantt chart of Dr. Howard's Bio-Informatics Project in Figure 4.2 might seem a bit confusing. Project leaders, staff, and others quickly learn to read such schedules, however, like orchestra leaders and musicians read music. In fact, project schedules are designed, in part, to help project stakeholders see the phases and dependencies within a project and to communicate with one another.

Project Phases

As one looks past the individual tasks to see the outlines of the project as a whole, the phases of the project begin to emerge. All projects are composed of tasks done through time, and clusters of them often have to be done before other clusters. These task clusters form the various phases and sub-components of a project. Different resources are likely to be needed in different phases, and each phase is likely to require different deliverables for the project as a whole. Who leads what activities may also change across project phases and project task clusters.

Project Dependencies

Another pattern that emerges from a project schedule is its network of task dependencies. These dependencies are shown as task "strings" through the project. The most commanding of these strings is the critical path—that sequence of tasks that determines the earliest completion date of the project. Possible project errors are riskier along this path because even a small problem here can affect the whole project. Tasks that lie off the critical path—although connected—are less critical to the timing of the project. Problems that occur with those tasks provide less risk to the project because their start and end dates are not as constrained—they have more slack. This slack in noncritical tasks, in turn, provides "wiggle room" for the project and its leader. Project schedules help make these task dependencies and risks very clear.

Communication to Stakeholders

Because the project schedule provides a graphical arrangement of all project tasks through time, it has the unique ability to provide both a broad understanding of the project as well as a more detailed calculation of the work required. As such, it makes for an excellent communication device for all stakeholders. The pace and timing of the project, for example, can be more easily communicated to clients. The most appropriate times for decision points, milestones, project reports, transfers of funds, and interim deliverables can be quickly and clearly communicated to clients with a project schedule. The project schedule is also useful in communicating with the host organization. When funds must flow to the project, when resources will be required, when updates make the most sense, and similar issues are all more clearly communicated with the help of project schedules. Those working on the project also use the schedule as a principal aid in communicating with each other. Different project team members can see very clearly when their work must begin and end. They can also have a clear picture of the project as a whole in addition to their part of it. This allows them to see where their work fits in with the work of others and how it will be used. Finally, internal and external suppliers can use the project schedule to see when their input is needed to make sure the right resources get to the right people at the right time.

Revision of Planning Assumptions and Estimates for the Project Plan

When a schedule is first produced, it aids in revising assumptions and estimates from the project's earlier planning stage. Those assumptions and estimates were made when the WBS was first developed—before consideration was given to how the tasks are connected to each other through time. When the schedule is developed and dependencies are determined, those estimates may need revision. Team members responsible for project components may notice tasks that need to be added or others that are not needed at all. Project staff may also be able to provide more input into resource needs, personnel, time estimates, and dependencies between tasks when studying the schedule.

Internal and external resource suppliers can use the schedule to confirm availability of resources or discuss adjustments that need to be made. Project leaders themselves may see things that they missed earlier in the planning phase. All changes, of course, have effects across the project. Because the schedule indicates what task sequences are most critical for getting the project done (e.g., those on the critical or near-critical paths[6]), particular attention can be given to the risk assessments of those tasks in particular.

Another assumption that needs to be checked is the level of resource use at any particular time in the project. When developing the initial WBS, resources are committed to tasks without regard to when they are to be used. When those tasks are scheduled at specific times, some resources may become overcommitted. Logistical problems may arise in the scheduling of equipment use and the flow of material. Personnel may also be overcommitted. For example, some team members may be scheduled to work more than 40 hours per week once tasks are arranged across time. Noncritical tasks with slack, then, can be moved forward or backward on the schedule to redistribute personnel and/or resources to help address this problem.

Project leaders typically spend a great deal of time revising and modifying the initial schedule to address issues and problems such as these. In truth, addressing all these matters can be quite frustrating. Project leaders need to keep in mind, however, that these issues are better confronted in the earlier planning stages rather than later on when they will cost more time and money and will provide even more frustration.

MAKING ADJUSTMENTS TO
THE PLAN THROUGHOUT THE PROJECT

Because projects are unique endeavors, leaders often find that adjustments need to be made while the project is under way to keep it on schedule and on budget. Project schedules allow project leaders to see the effects of any such adjustments they make. These effects can be seen even more clearly when using project management software. When resources are moved and times adjusted, the program can instantaneously update the resource use listings and the schedule, showing any changes in the critical path.

Project leaders quite often take resources from activities off the critical path and commit them to tasks on the critical path to help them reduce project risk, shorten project time, or keep the project on schedule if it is falling behind. If the project budget is in trouble, project leaders tend to look to tasks off the critical path for cutbacks. Although this is an acceptable approach to making needed adjustments, there are a number of problems that can emerge if the project leader is not careful.

First, resource shifts may lengthen other project tasks to the extent that a new critical path is developed. If a noncritical activity has only one day of slack, for example, shifting resources from it may lengthen its time horizon beyond that one day, making it critical (e.g., the plumbing task [1.2.3] in Figure 4.2 becomes critical with the addition of a single day and pushes the whole project back if it takes any longer). For these reasons, project leaders often conduct "sensitivity analyses" on their critical paths. One approach is to shorten time estimates of activities on the critical path to see if other task sequences become critical. Another approach is to lengthen estimates of tasks off the critical path to see if their task sequences then become critical. If the sensitivity analysis reveals any task sequences that have the potential of becoming critical, note should be made of them. Project leaders will need to pay as much attention to these near-critical tasks as they do to tasks along the critical path.

A second problem that can emerge when making adjustments in the middle of a project is an overuse of resources. It is not unusual, for example, that a member of the project team is working on several project tasks or both project and nonproject tasks at the same time. Looking at the work he or she is doing on only one project task can lead to the mistaken notion that the member can work elsewhere, resulting in overload. The same kind of overloading problem can arise with equipment and other resources. Careful tracking of scheduled resource use can help address this risk.[7]

A final problem emerges with what might be called "resource mathematics." Doubling the number of people working on a task, for example, rarely cuts task time in half. This is the case for at least two reasons. One is that increasing the number of personnel creates process loss. Problems with coordination, information sharing, "free riding," and the like tend to increase with more personnel. Another reason is that resources are often not smoothly interchangeable. It takes time to get up to speed, for example, when working on a new job. In addition, the knowledge, skills, and abilities of the new personnel may not fit as well to the new job's requirements.

COMMAND AND CONTROL

Still another key benefit of the project schedule is its use as a tool for project control. As a project network moves through time, a variety of project tasks must be done and resources used. Schedules help leaders manage those activities by clearly showing what tasks are currently in progress, who is working on them, and how close they should be to completion. Depending on the task's slack, project leaders know how much attention should be given to its on-time completion. As resources are used by the project, leaders can keep track and compare them to what was budgeted to keep control of project costs. (One tool used for cost control making use of the schedule is Earned Value Analysis and is discussed in Appendix B.)

Schedules also let project leaders look into the near- and farther term futures of their projects. Armed with the knowledge of what will be required, leaders can ensure resources are available; adjust schedules and tasks; and anticipate, analyze, and address potential problems. Table 4.1 presents a list of questions project leaders can ask themselves as they move through the process of creating a schedule. Although not exhaustive, it can provide a check-off list of some key things to consider.

Table 4.1   Schedule Check-Off List

Depending on its complexity, a schedule can be a fairly straightforward or difficult tool to construct. Without a schedule, though, leaders cannot manage their projects. Listed here are a few key questions leaders should ask themselves as they move through the process of constructing a schedule. The questions are meant to be used as a point of departure, to help encourage project leaders to think through the issues involved in creating a project schedule. Leaders should add other questions as they see fit. The assumption made here is that the schedule will be in the form of a Gantt chart and that a critical path will be developed.

- Have all the core and support activities been included in the schedule? Have they been grouped together along work process lines and arranged appropriately in an outline form?
- Have all other scheduled work tasks been included? Consider the initiation and delivery of outsourced work. Consider regulatory reviews if required.
- Have task time estimates been reviewed and confirmed? Have they been properly represented in the schedule?
- Have lag times been incorporated into those tasks that require them? Consider any task that needs time to rest or mature after active work has finished.
- Have all task dependencies been included and reviewed in the schedule?
- Can some dependent tasks incorporate lead time? Is it possible for a dependent task to begin before its preceding task is complete?
- Have project milestones been placed appropriately in the project schedule? Consider locating them at times of project component reviews and completions. Will milestones require reviews or reports? If so, schedule the required tasks and include them in the WBS, budget, and related planning documents.
- Has a critical path been determined? Have near-critical tasks been identified?
- Has task slack of noncritical project tasks been determined?
- Does the visual layout of the project schedule make sense? Does the schedule communicate to the leader and to others the overall flow of the project in ways that will make sense to them? Consider whether work processes are clustered together in ways that make sense to those who work in and interact within them. Consider whether project phases make sense. Consider project dependencies between large project components as well as specific work tasks.
- Have resource requirements been arranged according to their scheduled use? Is any resource overcommitted or undercommitted? Consider the workweeks and workloads of all project personnel. Consider the logistical requirements of all equipment and materials needed. Have arrangements been scheduled for their on-time delivery? Have any project task requirements of those arrangements been scheduled?
- Has the project budget been arranged in accordance with the project schedule of resource use and revenue requirements? How easy is it to determine whether the project is on budget at any particular time during the project?

SUMMARY

Project schedules are basic and invaluable tools for project planning and management. At its most basic, a project schedule is simply an arrangement of project tasks across time. Different kinds of schedules help project leaders build on this fundamental notion. Gantt or bar charts use bars to represent project activities, with the length of the bar representing the length of the activity. These bars are placed on a project calendar to show start and end times at certain dates. The Critical Path Method (CPM) is a tool that helps project leaders determine a project's critical path in a project's task network and the slack of those tasks that do not lie on that path. The Program Evaluation and Review Technique (PERT) accounts for time risks in projects by incorporating optimistic and pessimistic time estimates for tasks in addition to their likely completion times.

Project schedules have a number of components in common. All have project activities or tasks that are scheduled to begin and end at certain times. Most have milestones that represent important events in the life of a project. Whether shown on a schedule or not, project tasks are tied together by their dependencies—one must end, for example, before another can begin. Eventually, all project tasks are linked in some fashion, and those linkages can be represented in a project network of task dependencies shown by arrows connecting dependent tasks. One particular sequence of dependent tasks represents the critical path of a project—that sequence of tasks determines the earliest date the project can end. The dependent tasks on the critical path must begin and end no later than scheduled or the project gets pushed back. All other tasks have some degree of float or slack—their start and finish times can vary to some extent without the project completion date being affected.

Project schedules are constructed from the activities in the WBS, their time estimates, and their dependencies on one another. The first step in developing a Gantt chart is to break down the project's work and arrange it in outline form on a spreadsheet. The rows of the spreadsheet will be dedicated to the project's tasks and the columns to the project calendar—most often representing days. Second, estimations of the time to complete each task are made and reviewed. Third, dependencies between tasks are determined. Fourth, the Gantt chart is built by constructing and placing bars for each activity on the project calendar. The length of each bar is constructed to be as long as the time estimate of the task. It is placed where the task is to begin on the project calendar. Dependent tasks do not begin until their predecessor tasks are completed as required. Gantt charts often connect their bars with arrows showing task dependencies as well.

A project schedule serves a variety of purposes. One is that it helps the project leader to visualize the project as a whole with its various phases and dependencies. It also helps other stakeholders to visualize the project and serves as an excellent communication device to the project's clients, its host organization, and others. Another use of the project schedule is to help in the revision of project assumptions and estimates. Once it is seen as a whole, various stakeholders can review the tasks, assumptions, and estimates to assess any problems, additions, or opportunities for the project. The project schedule also is critical in project revisions and adjustments. From initial planning to the ending of a project, leaders are called on to make adjustments of one sort or another. The project schedule helps guide such adjustments by making clear how they affect other tasks, resources, and project time. Finally, project schedules play an important role in command and control of the project. They help project leaders focus their attention on critical tasks and resources as the project moves forward and allow them to keep track of how the project is progressing and using its available resources.

REVIEW QUESTIONS

1. What is a project schedule?
2. Describe the three kinds of scheduling techniques covered in this chapter.
3. What are the components of project schedules covered in this chapter?
4. Define and give examples of dependent tasks.
5. Define and give examples of tasks with lag and lead times.
6. Define and give examples of tasks that have float or slack in relation to other tasks.
7. What is a project's critical path? What role does the critical path play in project management?
8. Describe the process of developing a project schedule. Use either the Gantt chart or the CPM technique in your discussion.
9. What are the ways project schedules are used in projects?

EXERCISE

1. Work individually or as a team to develop a project schedule. In this exercise, you will build a Gantt chart.[8]
   a. Focus on a project that is relevant to you or your team.
   b. Develop a WBS for a significant portion of your project (if you developed a WBS for Chapter 3, you can use it for this exercise).

c. Display the WBS in outline form on sheets of graph paper (if you are using project management software, display the tasks in it). Leave a few rows above your WBS outline.

d. On a row above the beginning of the WBS, start numbering columns to the left of the WBS. These columns will represent the days of your project from Day 1 to the final day.

e. Estimate the time required to complete each task.

f. Determine any dependencies between tasks.

g. Draw a line to the left of each task representing the time it will take to accomplish. Begin with the first tasks that can be done. Start dependent tasks where required preceding tasks have ended.

h. Continue building your Gantt chart, keeping in mind dependencies and lag times.

i. When you are done, evaluate the project network you have created. Identify needs for required modification and opportunities to shorten the schedule.

ENDNOTES

1. This sequence of tasks is shown without regard to the other tasks in the larger project shown in Figure 4.2.

2. This is called an activity-on-node diagram because the activity or task is displayed in the nodes of the network. There are also activity-on-arrow diagrams, in which the task is labeled on the arrow instead of in the node. These are used far less frequently.

3. Monte Carlo simulation is named after Monte Carlo gambling wheels. Each "spin of the wheel" assumes a particular start and end date for project tasks. Computers can spin the wheel thousands of times very quickly and calculate the likely distribution of project times between the beginning and end of a project or any sequence of tasks within it. This is beyond the scope of this book, however.

4. I like to include lag time for such things as vendor delivery of purchases, inspectors showing up once notified, and the like.

5. When doing this by hand, arrows are usually optional. In more complex projects, they add valuable visual information and are easily constructed with project management software. In fact, modern project management software can make the process of developing project schedules a fairly easy one. Microsoft Project©, for example, facilitates constructing a work breakdown structure, estimating activity times, drawing bars, linking them with arrows, and placing them on a project calendar all at the same time when developing a Gantt chart. The Gantt chart of the Bio-Informatics Project in Figure 4.2, for example, is based on the output of Microsoft Project©.

6. A near-critical path is a sequence of tasks that are close to becoming critical. More attention is given to this issue shortly.

7. Project management software can help reduce this risk by keeping track of resource use at any point in time.

8. This exercise is designed to produce a Gantt chart. The exercise assumes that the reader is not using project management software. If the reader is using project software, disregard references to using graph paper and so forth. Instead of graph paper, spreadsheet programs can be used if project management software is unavailable.

KEY TERMS

Activity: anything in a project that will take time to complete and usually money and other resources as well. Most commonly activities are project team tasks, but outside activities or tasks are included as well.

Backward Pass: a process for calculating slack or float in a project based on calculations made on a forward pass through the project. See Appendix A for more detail.

Crashing: when project leaders take resources from an activity off the critical path and give them to an activity on the critical path to keep the project on schedule or to shorten the overall project.

Critical Path: that sequence of tasks that, together, will take longer than any other set of tasks to get the project done. The critical path determines how long a project will take.

Critical Path Method (CPM): a method for determining a project's critical path.

Dependencies: a task relationship that occurs when one task is dependent on another task in some way.

Finish-to-Finish Dependency: a task dependency in which two or more tasks must finish at the same time.

Finish-to-Start Dependency: a task dependency in which one or more tasks must finish before one or more tasks can begin.

Float: the amount of time that a noncritical task can wait to begin or finish without pushing back the completion time for the project as a whole. Also known as "slack."

Forward Pass: a process for determining a project's critical path. See Appendix A for more detail.

Gantt Charts: a type of project schedule that illustrates project tasks as bars and places them across the days of a calendar. The length of the bar indicates the time it should take for the task to be done.

Lag Time: the amount of time that must pass after work has been done on a task before work can start on a dependent, succeeding task.

Lead Time: the amount of time that a succeeding dependent task can begin before a preceding task has completely finished.

Milestones: important events in the life of a project that consume no time or resources. They often signal the completion of important project work.

Near-Critical Tasks: any task sequences that have the potential of becoming critical if small time adjustments are made to the tasks.

Program Evaluation and Review Technique (PERT): a network diagram that uses three different time estimates for each task or activity—an optimistic time, a likely time, and a pessimistic time for its completion.

Project Calendar: the calendar for starting and completing tasks in a project. In Gantt charts, the project calendar is represented by dates across the top of the chart, which are then used to divide the chart into columns. Task bars and other time-relevant information are then placed across those time columns.

Project Network: a complex arrangement of project tasks in which all tasks are connected by arrows and eventually lead to the project's final goal.

Project Schedule: orders project tasks and events through time. It indicates when tasks should start and end and how long they should take, and it arranges them in a logical order.

Sensitivity Analyses of the Critical Path: a method to determine if there are any near-critical paths in a project. Time is shortened on the critical path or lengthened on noncritical paths to see if other paths become critical.

Slack: the amount of time that a noncritical task can wait to begin or finish without pushing back the completion time for the project as a whole. Also known as "float."

Start-to-Finish Dependency: a task dependency in which one or more tasks must start for one or more tasks to be finished.

Start-to-Start Dependency: a task dependency in which two or more tasks must start at the same time.

Summary Bars: bars on a Gantt chart that summarize the length of time to complete a group of related tasks.

Task Bar: bar on a Gantt chart the length of which represents the time estimated to do the task.

PART 5

UNDERSTANDING AND ENGAGING THE CUSTOMER EXPERIENCE

13 Metrics for Engaging Customers

Kumar, V.

Find answers for...

- How do firms engage with their customers and derive value out of that engagement?
- What is customer engagement value (CEV)?
- What are the components of the CEV framework?
- How does the CEV framework help organizations?

A FIRM'S APPROACH TO CUSTOMER ENGAGEMENT

In the previous chapter, we discussed the need for firms to quantify the value derived from the customer engagement process. From a firm's standpoint, engaging with customers to derive tangible value out of the interaction is a tough task. However, many firms are successfully doing this today. How do firms actually engage their customers in today's competitive business world? The following paragraphs will discuss how firms engage with their customers through various examples from different firms.

Microsoft, in an independent study of nearly 1,000 Internet users, found that people prefer Bing's search results to Google's, two-to-one in blind comparison tests.[1] Capitalizing on this result, thereby spreading the news in the market, Microsoft launched the "Bing It On" challenge in October 2012. The "Bing It On" challenge was essentially an online and in-store promotion that involved customers comparing any five search results for Bing and Google side by side without knowing which is which, and picked the results that were the most relevant. Consumers who took the challenge in-store received a $25 gift voucher, which they could redeem for any product in the Microsoft store. As a follow-up to the promotion, Microsoft fielded a survey with approximately 4,700 consumers asking for their impressions of Bing before and after taking the challenge. The results showed that around 64 percent of people were surprised by the quality of Bing's Web search results. Over half of the people surveyed indicated that their impression of Bing improved after seeing Bing's Web search results next to Google's. Additionally, of people who identified Google as their primary search engine, 33 percent said they would use Bing more often after taking the Challenge.[2] Google undoubtedly still dominates the search engine market; however, with the "Bing It On" challenge, Microsoft is trying to engage customers and derive value out of this engagement.

Apple Inc. is engaging children through their education-related product offerings. The iPad's popularity among the younger age groups forced the acceptance of iPads as an effective learning tool for schools and colleges. As a step forward, Apple launched its interactive iBooks textbooks for iPad in January 2012.[3] With the world becoming increasingly digitized, children are the quickest to adapt to these technological changes. iBooks textbooks on the iPad offer an engaging solution for experiencing diagrams, photos, and videos for students. Students can dive into an image with interactive captions, rotate a 3D object, or have the answer spring to life in a chapter review. They can flip through a book by simply sliding a finger along the bottom of the screen; highlight text, take notes, search for content, and find definitions in the glossary. Also, carrying all their books on a single iPad is a convenient option for students. Phillip Schiller, senior vice president of worldwide marketing at Apple, said the iBooks provide a "more dynamic, engaging, and interactive" way for students to learn.[4] In addition to this, Apple's iBooks Author app enables anyone with a Mac to create and self-publish a range of books, including textbooks, cookbooks, history books, and picture books, and add engaging features to them. Apple engages their customers in a manner that creates a unique experience for its customers, which in return provides value to Apple with an increased appeal and user-base of the iPad and other Apple products.

While companies are increasingly participating in customer engagement activities to derive value for themselves, these activities provide a clear benefit to the customer as well. One of the leading consumer packaged goods (CPG) companies, Procter & Gamble (P&G) has been successfully running the "Have You Tried This Yet?" campaign for two years. This campaign is designed to highlight innovative products for self, family, and home.[5] In 2012, under the same campaign, P&G launched another leg—"The Great Try

Out," where 15 upcoming tastemakers in the categories of beauty, family, and home competed for a spot. They were called the "Trend Trio," earning the opportunity to be one of three program experts. This competition provided customers with a chance to be a part of selecting the Trend Trio. The Trend Trio acted like a brand ambassador for the various P&G brands, blogging and sharing tips to make customers' everyday life a little easier. The campaign enabled P&G to engage with its customers at a deeper level by providing the story behind their brand innovations. Customer interaction with the Trend Trio, selected by the popular votes of the customers themselves, built up trust and laid the foundation for a long-term engagement with the brand. P&G's attempt to bring their brands closer to their customers, through these third-party experts, is an excellent example of customer engagement with mutual benefits to the firm and the customer.

As seen in the above examples, firms spend a lot of time and resources in customer engagement activities, with an aim to convert a buyer's propensity to buy a product/service into an actual purchase. Customers' future purchases are dependent on their previous experience with the brand in question. As a result of a customer experience (good or bad), a customer is likely to form a perception about the brand (good or bad), talk about the brand to others (in positive or negative context), refer or not refer the brand to their close circle of people, and create a positive or negative influence on potential buyers to convert them into actual customers. All of these activities, in addition to the actual purchase, are of great importance to marketers. Hence, in addition to tracking purchase behavior of customers, marketers need to pay close attention to indirect forms of customer interactions like the ones mentioned above. Also, it is important for marketers to know that not all customers are equal. For instance, a customer may like a product and could make a purchase. However, does such a purchase obligate him/her to talk about the brand, in a sense, spread the word? Many customers may not engage in detailed conversations about the brands they buy or the services they use. So for a marketer, the real questions are (*a*) will customers refer the product to their close friends, (*b*) will they write about the product on their blog/social network, and (*c*) will they actively participate in product improvement initiatives offered by the firm? Even if the answer to all the above questions is yes, not all customers will end up contributing equally to the profits of the firm. Every customer is different and firms require a technique to identify and differentiate customers based on their differences. So, how does one maximize profits and identify this group of customers who not only directly contribute to the firm profits by their purchase but also make an indirect contribution to the firm profits by acting as brand ambassadors for the brand? Customer engagement principles have been studied for a long time but haven't been quantified yet and hence objective measurement and evaluation of customer engagement metrics is challenging. This chapter discusses a comprehensive, quantifiable, and forward-looking framework that will enable such measurement and evaluation of the value of a customer based on all aspects of customer behavior, i.e., purchase- and non-purchase–related contributions to the profit of the firm.

CONCEPTUALIZING CEV: AN INTEGRATED FRAMEWORK

Customer contribution to firm profitability occurs in two ways: (*a*) directly— through their purchases, and (*b*) indirectly—through their non-purchase reactions, i.e., by making referrals to potential customers, by influencing current and potential customers in their network, or by using their own experiences to provide review/feedback for improvements. Identifying the right set of customers who create value for the firm can be useful in trying to maximize profits. The CEV framework can be used to identify and evaluate the right customer, who is successfully engaged with the firm, and who generates value and positively contributes to the profits of the firm.

As discussed in Chapter 1, CEV is managed as a set of four dollar metrics, i.e., CLV, CRV or BRV, CIV and CKV, and one attitudinal metric—CBV. The conceptual approach for measuring customer engagement is comprised of five core dimensions and is shown in Figure 2.1. The framework incorporates recent trends in social media and the influence it has on marketing strategies, thus providing an effective and comprehensive tool to understand the value of a customer and his or her impact on the firm's future profitability. As seen in Figure 2.2, each component in the CEV framework can be applied to business-to-consumer (B2C) as well as business-to-business (B2B) settings. The following paragraphs will explain the CEV framework. For ease in understanding, the framework is discussed from bottom up.

In the business world, customers and businesses are interdependent. Customer actions, in terms of behavior, attitude, and network metrics, have an

Figure 2.1 The CEV Framework

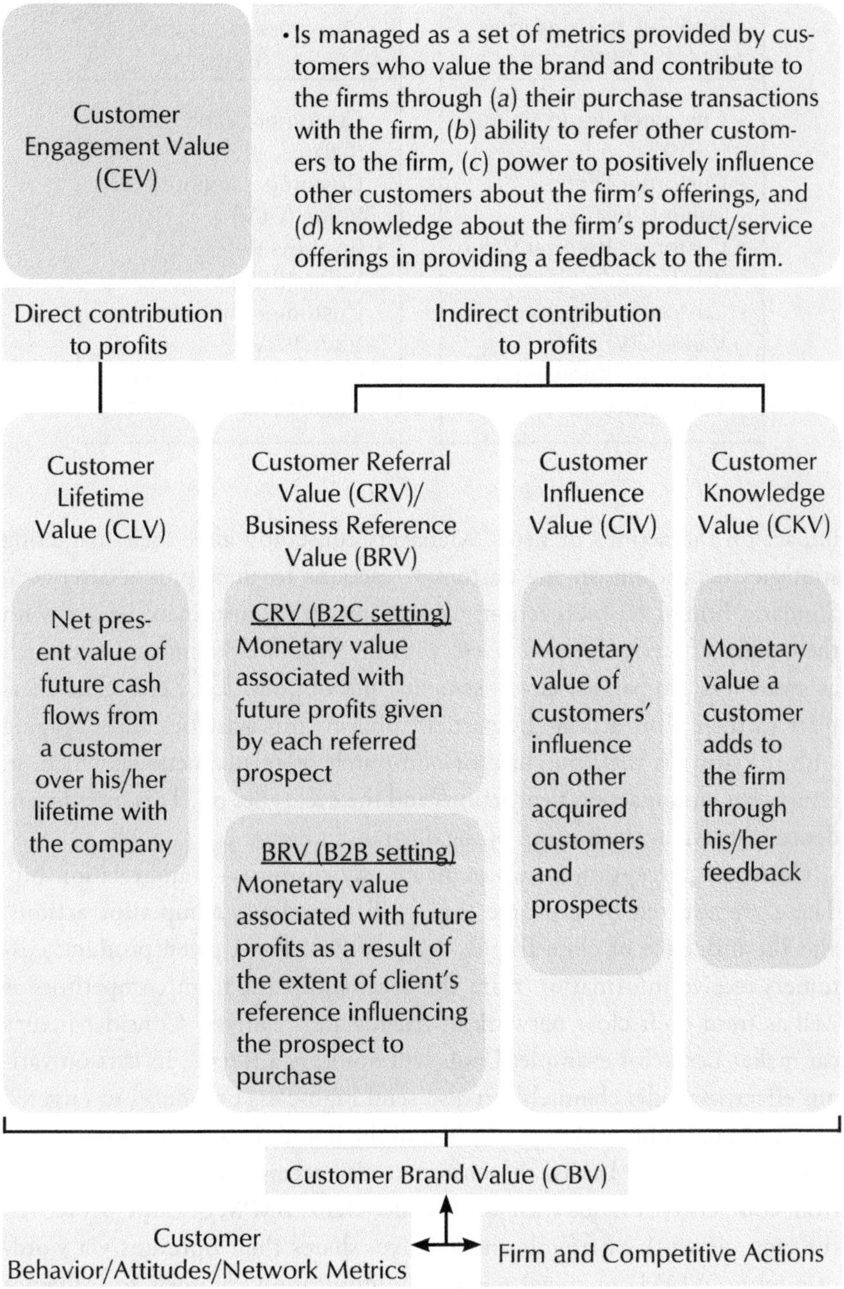

Customer Engagement Value (CEV)

- Is managed as a set of metrics provided by customers who value the brand and contribute to the firms through (a) their purchase transactions with the firm, (b) ability to refer other customers to the firm, (c) power to positively influence other customers about the firm's offerings, and (d) knowledge about the firm's product/service offerings in providing a feedback to the firm.

Direct contribution to profits

Indirect contribution to profits

Customer Lifetime Value (CLV)	Customer Referral Value (CRV)/ Business Reference Value (BRV)	Customer Influence Value (CIV)	Customer Knowledge Value (CKV)
Net present value of future cash flows from a customer over his/her lifetime with the company	CRV (B2C setting) Monetary value associated with future profits given by each referred prospect	Monetary value of customers' influence on other acquired customers and prospects	Monetary value a customer adds to the firm through his/her feedback
	BRV (B2B setting) Monetary value associated with future profits as a result of the extent of client's reference influencing the prospect to purchase		

Customer Brand Value (CBV)

Customer Behavior/Attitudes/Network Metrics ⟷ Firm and Competitive Actions

Figure 2.2   Five Core Dimensions of CEV Framework

Business to Consumer (B2C)	Business to Business (B2B)
• Customer Brand Value (CBV) • Customer Lifetime Value (CLV) • Customer Referral Value (CRV) • Customer Influence Vaue (CIV) • Customer Knowledge Value (CKV)	• Customer Brand Value (CBV) • Customer Lifetime Value (CLV) • Business Reference Value (BRV) • Customer Influence Vaue (CIV) • Customer Knowledge Value (CKV)

impact on the actions of firms. Managers constantly alter their marketing strategies depending on the customer reactions to their products/services. Similarly, firm or business actions have an impact on customers, i.e., (*a*) with the quality of products/services, (*b*) with the firm's marketing activities such as awareness campaigns, advertisements, promotions/deals, etc. Customers react to these firm actions by participating in firm activities and engaging with the firm via their purchase or non-purchase–related actions, which, in return, has an impact on firm actions and the cycle goes on. This interdependence is shown at the bottom of the diagram in Figure 2.1.

Customer perception is important for any customer–brand relationship. These are affected by multiple forces—firm actions, competitor actions, and the influence of close friends and relatives. For a given product, customers receive information from the focal company, from competitors as well as from their close network of friends and relatives. Consider luxury car maker Lexus for example; Lexus will not only advertise its cars on various effective media channels but also send high-class brochures to targeted customers to build on that perception of the brand. In addition to information received from Lexus, the customer also receives marketing messages from competitive brands such as Mercedes-Benz, BMW, or Audi. Moreover, the close network of friends and relatives shares their opinions via word-of-mouth (WOM) or social media communication channels to influence these customer perceptions. All these different forces act on the customer perception together. Customer brand value (CBV) captured under the CEV framework measures the value that the customer attaches to the brand as a result of all the marketing and communication messages delivered via different media. CBV is a multi-dimensional composite metric that measures the customer's brand knowledge, brand attitude, brand behavior intention, and brand behavior. It enables companies to devise appropriate strategies depending on where the problem exists—awareness, trust, or loyalty?

Based on the perceptions formed, a customer can engage with a firm in a myriad of ways. All these are captured under the CEV framework. The most important way a customer can engage with a firm is via his or her own purchase of a product/service. Customer engagement through their own transactions with the firm is captured under CLV. As seen in Figure 2.1, CLV is the metric that directly contributes to the profitability of the firm. The companies can use CLV to get the net present value of a customer based on his or her future transactions with the firm. The concept of CLV aids in understanding the quality of the length of stay of a customer with the firm during his or her lifetime.

A firm can encourage customers to buy more and more, which will increase the customer's CLV and thereby increase his or her contribution to profits. However, there are other levels of engagement that can indirectly contribute to the profits of a firm. The other three metrics—customer referral value (CRV) or business reference value (BRV), customer influence value (CIV), and customer knowledge value (CKV)—measure the indirect contribution of a customer to the firm profitability.

The customers can engage with a firm via firm-generated referrals programs. Referrals are a form of engaging customers with the firm in a B2C setup. Referral programs enable current customers to influence prospects via these firm-generated, incentivized referral programs. CRV within the CEV framework assists in quantitatively understanding the value generated through referrals and its impact on a firm's profitability. CRV measures the net present value a customer creates for a firm via his or her referrals, i.e., the value a customer generates by referring the firm's products to its potential customers. While referrals work in a B2C setting, B2B companies follow a different reference mechanism. In a B2B setting, client firms provide references to the seller firm, which influence the prospective client firms to purchase the product/service from the seller firm. BRV is the ability of the client firm to influence prospects to purchase. Since B2B reference functions differently from B2C referrals, the CEV framework captures them separately as BRV.

Are referrals the only way current customers can engage and influence potential customers? What about situations when there are no company-sponsored referral programs? Do customers stop talking about the brand within their close network of people? Obviously, customers talk about the good and the bad aspects of their experience with the brand, even if there are no incentivized referral programs. Today, customers influence each other via various social media platforms. A customer's interaction and influence on each other via social media channels such as Facebook, Twitter, MySpace, Foursquare, etc., have increased dramatically in recent years. The CEV framework captures this engagement—the influence of current customers on current customers as well as prospects via social media channels under CIV.

Another level of customer engagement is achieved when a current customer actively involves himself or herself in improving a company's product/service by providing feedback or suggestions. Customer review and feedback add great value to a firm. Moreover, from a firm's standpoint, knowledge and understanding of customer preferences is highly beneficial. It enables them to customize their product offering in line with the customer expectations. When a company implements the feedback or suggestion provided by a customer, that customer indirectly contributes to the profits of the firm as the improved product/service is expected to appeal to a lot more customers than before, thereby bringing more profits to the firm. The CEV framework captures this customer engagement under CKV. CKV is a metric that measures the value of this communication between customers and firms to improve their existing or potential products or services.

CBV is the attitudinal metric under the CEV framework that has an impact on the other four dollar metrics, i.e., CLV, CRV or BRV, CIV, and CKV, as illustrated in Figure 2.1. Customer perceptions of the brand (i.e., CBV) have an impact on the way customers purchase the product/service in the future, refer the brand to their close network of people, engage in social media channels to influence other customers, and get involved in providing feedback. These interactions between CBV and the other four metrics (CLV, CRV/BRV, CIV, and CKV) can be seen in Figure 2.1. These interrelationships will be explored in greater detail in subsequent chapters.

While there are methods and/or conceptual models for measuring the five metrics discussed in the previous paragraphs, an integrated approach to measure the CEV is still in its evolutionary stage. This is because CEV is not merely an aggregate of the four components (CLV, CRV, CIV, and CKV), but a metric that is correlated and constantly interacting within the four metrics. For instance, though CLV and CRV are separate metrics, they cannot be added up across all customers. An understanding of these five components of the framework and the interaction among these components will help senior level leaders in any business to understand and value customers for their contribution in the customer engagement process. The following sections of this chapter will explain the significance of each component of the CEV framework.

CUSTOMER BRAND VALUE (CBV)

In a firm, managers are often faced with a situation where they have to decide if they want to go down the path of selling their brand with the highest margin or treat customers as a valuable asset and focus on building and maintaining this asset. The actual question concerning managers is: which of these routes will result in maximum profitability for the firm? Building a strong brand would develop loyalty amongst customers, while a weak brand would drive customers to the competition.[6] Also, it may be difficult to evaluate the effect of brand building efforts on the customer base. In an ideal world, managers would work on brand building and customer building simultaneously. This balance can be made possible by establishing a link between brand and customer value. One way of looking at this would be "customer-based brand equity." Customer-based brand equity is defined as "the differential effect of brand knowledge on consumer response to the marketing of the brand."[7] In other words, customer-based brand equity is the summation of the customer's individual brand value (CBV). Conceptually, CBV refers to the total value a customer attaches to a brand through his or her experiences with the brand over time.[8]

Brand perceptions are built over a period of time, through various marketing activities that firms carry out to engage customers. From a company's standpoint, brand building activities are often used to increase brand presence in the minds of current and potential customers and thereby enter their consideration set for future purchases. CBV recognizes the attitudinal value of a customer based on his or her perception of the brand. It is a dynamic, multi-dimensional construct, which measures the contribution of each aspect of brand value, i.e., brand knowledge, brand attitude, brand behavior intention, and brand behavior to the lifetime value of that customer. According to this view, brand knowledge is not just the facts about the brand—it includes all the thoughts, feelings, perceptions, images, experiences, etc., that get linked to the brand in the minds of the customers (actual or potential, individuals or organizations).[9] CBV can thus be understood as a set of associations that customers make with the brand.

The starting point for any customer association with a brand can be attributed to brand awareness and brand image. These two metrics form the basic "Brand Knowledge" that creates a sense of trust and impacts the brand attitude of a customer. By influencing customer attitudes, firms can influence the brand behavior intentions and as a result, influence the brand behavior of that customer. A key aspect of brand behavior is "Brand Loyalty," which thereby impacts the brand advocacy and premium price behavior from a customer. In a day and age where customization is the buzzword around marketing of any kind of product, CBV provides managers with a tool to gain an in-depth understanding of the customer level metrics of brand awareness, brand image, brand trust, brand affect, purchase intention, and brand loyalty.

Sustained brand image and strong brand loyalty are key factors to the success of any brand in the long run. A brand like Harley Davidson is an excellent

Brand Perception

Source: Printed with permission from http://tomfishburne.com/ (retrieved on January 03, 2013).

example of the creation of a strong image. The brand enjoys a strong cult status in society. Its motto "Live to Ride, Ride to Live" echoes in the minds of its customers who are seeking to experience the adrenaline rush while riding their machines. Harley Davidson enjoys a strong image owing to the strong brand loyalty and brand advocacy by its loyal customers. With a clear vision to target the customer base seeking adventure and individuality, Harley Davidson does a good job of satisfying the needs of its customer base.

Companies like Samsung have walked the path of building brand value for their customers. Samsung's recent success in the United States has been a result of building brand awareness and positive brand image in the minds of current and potential customers. Having achieved initial success, Samsung's future profitability depends on (*a*) maintaining the current positive buzz around the brand, and (*b*) successfully influencing customers in the next two phases, i.e., brand attitude and brand behavior.

The concept of CBV can be applied to B2B and B2C companies. In B2C companies, the concept is more dynamic and companies are constantly tracking changes happening in the customer portfolio to effectively take appropriate measures. CBV, i.e., the customer's perceived value of the brand is what drives companies such as Apple, Google, Microsoft, and many others. The buzz around every new launch by Apple in recent times can be attributed to the high awareness and positive brand image of the brand. Thus, non-buyers of the brand also have a great amount of information about upcoming Apple products, which only amplifies the buzz around this brand. Oldsmobile, the General Motors (GM) brand, can shed some more light on this concept. Allen Adamson, a managing director at the corporate identity firm Landor Associates mentioned once that "what Oldsmobile ran into was an advertising problem. It failed to clearly define what is different about the brand." In the GM hierarchy of brands, Oldsmobile was supposed to be a sporty, upper-middle-priced division, a touch less expensive and less conservative than Buick and a bit pricier, more sophisticated than Pontiac brand. Such marketing gradations were more effective decades ago, when the US car market was less competitive. GM embarked on a campaign to shrink its cars to match what the company's leaders envisioned would be an era of $3-a-gallon gas and diminished expectations. The Oldsmobile division's reputation for innovative engineering took several hits ranging from quality problems with diesel engines to ineptly handled product decisions, such as putting Chevrolet engines in certain Oldsmobile models. It was a negative brand image that caused GM to park its Oldsmobile vehicle for good in 2000.[10] In spite of expenditures on promotions and advertising, a successful brand image could not be built, which forced GM to eventually stop production.

CBV in B2B companies will have to be looked at a little differently. In a B2B setting, brand value creates an image of the seller in the minds of the client. Hence, a lot of B2B companies use online websites as a tool to build an image which can aid in converting prospects into actual customers. Also, B2B companies have long-standing relationships with their customers and this relationship is built over time based on the perceived brand value. Many firms in a B2B setting say that they are not influenced by advertisements but data and client spending suggest otherwise. In the early to mid-1980s, IBM did not have a leading position in computer systems or pricing. In time, IBM built a strong brand image of quality, assurance, and sustainability. Once the image was formed, IBM could reap the benefits of this strong brand image in terms of stronger business in the future. "Big Blue" soon became the enterprise systems market leader because *you never got fired for buying IBM* (same with Cisco today).[11] IT Directors "bought" a relationship, company, reputation, service, people, and assurance. In other words, they bought the goodwill of the brand. The client firm most often weighs the benefits of doing business with the seller firm based on its reputation in the market, quality of its products and services, etc. This is the precise reason why big consulting firms have long-term client relationships, which last for over a decade. Once a brand value is established in the minds of the client firm, the relationship is expected to last longer when compared to a B2C firm.

Within the CEV framework, CBV offers a quantitative view of the customer perceptions of the brand. CBV interacts with the other components of the CEV framework to develop a good customer–firm relationship with high engagement value. This interaction effect of CBV with all the other four metrics is explored in the respective chapters of the book in greater detail.

CUSTOMER LIFETIME VALUE (CLV)

CLV is the fundamental metric under the CEV framework which directly contributes to firm profitability. CLV is a forward-looking metric that not only accounts for the contribution to profit, based on past purchase behavior of a customer, but also predicts the future value of the current customer as well as profits from prospective customers. In its simplest terms, CLV is a formula that helps marketing managers arrive at a dollar value associated with the long-term relationship with any given customer, revealing just how much a customer relationship is worth over a period of time. CLV helps marketers adopt the right marketing activities today to increase profitability tomorrow. It rewards not those who have been the best customers, but those who will be the best customers in the foreseeable future. Conceptually, CLV refers to the net present value of the monetary contribution of the profits associated with a customer's future purchases.[12]

Essentially, CLV enables a firm to treat individual customers differently and exclusively from each other, based on his or her contribution to the firm. By being able to quantify this value, firms are able to discern how much they can and should invest in a customer in order to achieve a positive return on investment (ROI) or maximized profitability. In addition to calculating CLV for a customer, firms can optimally allocate their resources to gain maximum returns using strategies that can help them maximize the CLV of a customer and ensure long-term profitable customer engagement. These strategies called "Wheel of Fortune" strategies will be discussed in greater detail in Chapter 4. CLV creates value not only for firms but also for customers. Customers get better products and services that are tailor-made to their needs as firms comprehend their needs better than ever before. In other words, customers have an incentive to remain loyal because their relationship with the firm is mutually beneficial.

The concept of CLV can be applied to both B2B and B2C companies. IBM, a leading multinational high-technology firm providing hardware, software, and services to B2B customers, implemented the CLV-based framework with an aim to maximize their profits. IBM used to measure customer profitability using a metric called Customer Spending Score (CSS), which was defined as the total revenue that can be expected from a customer in the next year.[13] Since CSS focused primarily on customer revenues and ignored the variable cost of servicing customers; in 2004, IBM felt the need to move to a better indicator for customer value measurement than CSS. IBM especially wanted to test the following belief, "when all the other drivers remain unchanged, can an increase in the level of contact with the right customers create higher value from the low-value customers?" A CLV-based framework allowed IBM to refine and improve their customer contact strategy. Using the CLV-based approach, IBM could (*a*) increase the return on their marketing investment by allocating resources toward customers who were most likely to provide value in the next year, (*b*) identify products to sell as bundles, and (*c*) reallocate the excess resources (after targeting the most likely customers who would buy in a given time period) to other prospects (acquiring new customers or reactivating dormant customers). Two major initiatives that were being considered based on the CLV management framework included (*a*) segmentation and profiling and (*b*) understanding customer migration.[14] They identified the right customers to target and optimally reallocated resources to profitable customers and saw a tenfold increase in their revenues in the following year.

Consider a B2C example of a fashion retailer wanting to maximize profitability not only at the store level but also at a customer level.[15] The retailer was seeking answers to the following questions: (*a*) What is the right metric to manage customer programs, for example customer loyalty programs? Can CLV outperform traditional metrics? (*b*) How can the CLV concept be applied to measure and manage customer value? (*c*) How can the CLV concept be applied to manage store performance? The CLV framework was implemented with an objective to maximize a customer's lifetime value, thus profits at the store level. After taking a step-by-step approach of the framework, it was observed that (*a*) at a customer level, the top 20 percent of their customers accounted for 95 percent of their profits. Careful analyses of results had indicated that the retailer was losing money with the bottom 30 percent of the customers. (*b*) At a store level, by implementing CLV-based strategies, this B2C firm realized a 42 percent increase in store revenue for the bottom 10 stores in one year and a 30 percent increase in the stock price or shareholder value compared to other B2C firms in this industry. This framework also recommended the firm to shift their management focus from managing customer relationship to managing customer value.

A firm can have customers with positive or negative CLV scores. After having realized their contribution to profit, firms might have the urge to fire customers with a negative CLV. Chapter 1 mentioned Sprint firing 1,000 customers from its pool of 53 million customers for calling the call center too often. AT&T also cancelled service to customers who made most of their calls while in roaming. Given the fact that the cost of acquiring a customer is significantly higher than retaining him or her; is firing a customer a good strategy for any firm aiming to maximize profits? Does one have the information regarding the future value of the present customer to effectively take such a decision? CLV allows firms to predict customer churn/attrition effectively by evaluating the two approaches, i.e., the "always a share" approach and the "lost for good" approach. Chapter 4 will discuss the CLV metric that can be used to optimally allocate resources, predict future purchases of customers, and reach the right customers with the right message through the most apt channels in detail.

CLV provides an excellent framework for managers who aim to maximize profits using a customer-centric approach to marketing. While CLV can measure direct and indirect components and can include all aspects of value creation by a customer; in practice and in academic literature, it is often identified only with the actual purchase behavior. A limitation of the CLV metric is that it fails to measure data on customer attitudes. The CEV framework provides a more robust understanding of customer value for firms to effectively manage customers, build loyalty among the core customer base and maximize profits for the firm. For a firm aiming to maximize profits, it is imperative to consider all levels of customer engagement. By calculating the CLV for all customers, firms can rank the customers on the basis of their contribution to the firm's profit.[16] This forms an important step under the CEV framework to evaluate the value of a customer and the direct contribution made by the customer to the firm profitability. By linking CLV to CBV, managers can (*a*) monitor the overall performance of the brand, (*b*) manage the brand at the segment level, and (*c*) manage the brand at the individual level.

CUSTOMER REFERRAL VALUE (CRV)

Do customers engage with the firm and impact profitability only with their own purchase? The answer is "no." As discussed in the earlier paragraphs, customers not only contribute directly through their purchase, but also contribute through indirect actions; one such action is referrals. The next step in the CEV framework is to look at a metric that deals with the indirect contributions made by a customer through their referrals. The concepts of WOM communication and customer referrals have been around for a while now. Researchers have conducted extensive studies to understand the implications of referrals on customer behavior. Depending on the level of engagement, customers are seen to be at different stages of contact with the firm. Companies spend a lot of resources in devising incentive-generated referral programs to increase penetration of their brand/product. Customer referral, especially WOM communication has been a widely accepted concept and is known to have an impact on the purchase of a product or service by potential customers. For a company spending a part of its marketing budget in referral programs, it is extremely important to know customers who have a high impact amongst prospects. Not all customers are willing to engage with a firm at a level where they not only contribute to profits of the firm by their purchase, but also communicate and refer potential customers to turn prospects into customers for the firm. An effective metric to measure this aspect of consumer behavior and its impact on profitability of the firm did not exist for practical use by companies. CRV was conceptualized with an aim to provide just that. CRV is the quantifiable measure of the type, quantity, and effectiveness of referrals or recommendations that an individual customer provides to others with regard to a particular product. Conceptually, CRV of a customer is the monetary value associated with the future profits given by each referred prospect, discounted to the present value.[17]

CRV enables managers to measure and manage each customer based on his ability to generate indirect profits to the firm.[18] CRV focuses on current customers turning potential customers in their social network into actual customers for the firm via firm-initiated incentivized referral programs. Customers are rewarded for the conversion of potential customers to actual customers as they indirectly contribute to the profit of the firm. The referrals are extrinsically motivated and hence customers can be looked at as nonemployee sales

The Power of "Word of Mouth"

Source: Printed with permission from http://tomfishburne.com/ (retrieved on January 03, 2013).

people who are compensated for contributing to the profit of the firm. CRV enables managers to value customers based on their indirect impact on the firm's profits from both the savings in acquisition costs and the growth of new customers who were referred to by a current customer.

Referrals can be successful or unsuccessful. Therefore, depending on the impact of referrals, CRV can be negative, positive, or zero, i.e., no impact on profits of the firm. A customer with a high CRV contributes to the profits in multiple ways (*a*) by his or her own transaction with the firm, (*b*) by converting prospects into actual customers and thereby the contribution to profit through that transaction, and (*c*) by savings in the customer acquisition cost of the prospect. Every action taken by the firm has an impact on the customer behavior toward the brand as well as the brand perception that the customers have. Negative actions by the firm promote bad referrals and can deter prospects from entering into any transaction with the firm in the future. It is important for firms to ensure that their brand equity is not diluted in the process of achieving maximized profits.

Over the years, many startups have been using referrals as their mode to create awareness and build the user base. Dropbox is one such startup that relied on referrals as their initial strategy. Drew Houston, cofounder and CEO of Dropbox, initiated a two-sided incentive program wherein the referrer and the referee both gain additional space in their account. Bank of America too had a similar referral program where they rewarded the referee and the referrer with $25.[19] Bank of America provided $25 for customer referral, $10 for a student referral and $50 for a business referral. After the referral program has been implemented, it is the key to identifying high impact customers who are influential or who have medium to high CRV, to be able to maximize their indirect contributions to the profits of the firm.

Customers who refer new customers to earn rewards on successful referrals are extrinsically motivated. That aids them to not only talk about their experience with the firm within their social network but also try and convert this WOM communication into an actual transaction. This generates value for the firms as well as customers. Hence, it is important to include the probability of conversion of prospects into actual customers and the cost savings due to each successful referral in the CRV framework. Also, it is important to factor in the possibility of the prospect having turned into an actual customer regardless of the referral and the partial impact of multiple referrals to the same potential customer.

In a B2C context, referrals are often a go-to strategy for marketing managers to increase the reach of their brand. Referrals are a great way to spread awareness for a brand in case of budget constraints in marketing and promotional activities. We see small brands using referrals increasingly to raise their user base and gain potential customers. For example, a small firm called Keku, headquartered in New York, provides cheap international calling services to its users. This company uses referrals to increase its user base. The referee and the referrer are awarded with additional talk time on their international calling plan as an incentive. Customers are happy to be rewarded and the company rejoices with every increase in penetration for the brand. Referrals are not only used by small companies but are successfully implemented by the big players in every industry depending on their marketing strategy.

CRV is definitely an important metric under consideration for any profit-maximizing firm. By linking CRV to CLV, companies can launch successful referral programs that also ensure customer profitability. It is critical for managers to understand the limitations of CRV to be able to effectively use the metric in their business. We will discuss a few important factors managers should keep in mind while incorporating CRV in the CEV framework[20]:

- Measuring CRV is only one method of finding out whether a customer can impact profitability by bringing in new customers to the firm and might not be applicable to all firms or industries.
- It is difficult for every business to have the ability to track referral behavior. If they do, managers should ensure that the systems in place have a reasonably long history of tracking customer referral behavior to estimate the customer value accurately.
- The method suggested under the CEV framework for measuring CRV only takes into account the extrinsic motivation of a customer to make referrals (i.e., through incentives) and does not try to determine which customers generate referrals through an intrinsic motivation.

Chapter 6 discusses the details of measurement, application and future of CRV in greater detail. For a company aiming to understand the value of a customer, measuring CRV and linking this to CLV of that customer is the next step. CRV captures the indirect aspect of the customer behavior through referrals under the CEV framework.

BUSINESS REFERENCE VALUE (BRV)

The purchase decision in a B2B setting is far more complex when compared to a B2C setting. Similarly, the reference in a B2B setting works differently from referrals in a B2C setting. For B2B businesses, in most cases, the use of client references is often the only tool seller firms have to build their business.[21] In a B2B client's words, "[the] list of references provided by the seller helps us to shortlist the seller firms. However, to decide on whom to buy from, we check at least a couple of references provided by the seller." Many companies have a database of customer reference cases on their website for potential customers. Some encourage customers to create "video success stories," which they use as references for potential customers. We often see most B2B companies incorporating testimonials on their website to provide confidence to potential customers. For instance, McKinsey mentions testimonials and video references on their website to encourage potential customers to use their consulting services. Although companies have adopted these measures for a long time now, they have not been able to measure the impact of such referrals to the profits of the firm. With this in mind, the concept of Brand Reference Value, i.e., BRV was conceptualized to be able to appropriately capture the value created by such references for the seller firm. Conceptually, BRV for a client is the monetary value associated with future profits as a result of the extent of a client's reference influencing the prospects to purchase, discounted to present value.[22]

BRV is guided by the following three components: (*a*) How much influence, in general, do references have on the prospect's adoption? (*b*) How much influence does a particular client firm's reference have on the prospect's adoption? (*c*) How profitable is the prospective client post adoption? BRV is an effective tool for managers to select the right references that can indirectly contribute to the profits of the firm. The drivers of BRV are discussed in greater detail in Chapter 6.

CUSTOMER INFLUENCE VALUE (CIV)

Referrals are not the only way current customers influence prospect behavior. By now we know that customers can have an impact on firm's revenue and profits based on what they feel and what they are prepared to communicate to others about the brand. This impact is, at times, more valuable for the company than just the purchase, as this influence brings in prospects for the firm. Researchers in the past have established the influence an individual can have on prospects and the significant role of WOM communication in a firm's marketing efforts.[23] However, firms do not have a metric to evaluate the impact of WOM in social media platforms pertaining to the return on marketing investments. Conceptually, CIV refers to the monetary value of the profits associated with the purchases generated by a customer's social media influence on other acquired customers and prospects, discounted to present value.[24]

The customer influences are usually intrinsically motivated by WOM activities that persuade and convert prospects to customers, minimize buyer remorse (to reduce defections), and encourage an increased share of wallet (SOW) of the existing customers. With an ever increasing social media network, customers are provided with a platform to openly communicate about customer experiences and thereby exchange views and reviews about a product or service. Companies need to value customers with high CIV who can bring in additional revenue to the firm by influencing current as well as potential customers. The CIV under the CEV framework provides a platform to measure this behavioral aspect of customer behavior.

The existing customer base is as important to a firm as acquiring new customers. Customer retention has been a key focus for many companies as the value created by existing customers over a period can have a huge impact on the profits of a firm. Rennlist, an international online community for Porsche, Audi, and BMW enthusiasts founded in 1998, is an example of customers engaging in an online world to share their views with other customers having similar interests.[25] Members of this group actively engage in discussions and share opinions on very specific aspects of the brand. These customers consider themselves a part of the company and evaluate the products offered by the company in great detail. There is an increase in the number of such forums in the online world today. Brand enthusiasts break the space barriers and openly discuss and influence other potential customers in an online community. Traditionally, customers consulted their close circle of family and friends for advice; today the social media and the Internet have drastically widened the consumer's network. Consumers are increasingly seeking reviews of products and services online before making that purchase decision. A firm needs to identify influential customers and evaluate the degree to which these customers are able to influence potential customers to enter into a transaction with the firm.

Social media marketing has taken center stage for most marketers today. With innumerable options and the abundance of information, it is tough for managers to optimally use social media marketing platforms to influence potential customers. CIV provides a straightforward step-by-step model to evaluate and measure the effectiveness of the influence a current customer has on customers in the social media setting. Chapter 7 discusses the quantifiable aspect of the CIV, its implications, and the linkage of CIV with other related metrics in greater detail.

Like CRV, CIV too involves WOM communication to influence prospects. Then, how different is CIV from CRV? The concepts of CRV and CIV are distinct. Hence, it is critical to understand the differences between them clearly, to be able to evaluate each metric individually.[26] These are illustrated in Table 2.1.

Table 2.1	Comparison between CRV and CKV

CRV	CIV
CRV measures the value a current customer brings to a firm by referring prospects and converting them into actual customers using traceable official communication channels like email or text message with individually identified codes.	CIV measures the value a current customer brings to a firm by influencing current and prospective customers in a social media setting.
Customers are extrinsically motivated through firm-generated incentive programs.	Customers are intrinsically motivated. Customers are engaged with a brand to the extent where they feel motivated enough to talk about the brand and thereby influence people in their social network who may or may not be current customers of the firm.
Customers are monetarily compensated. These are tangible compensations provided for the referrals.	Customers are not monetarily compensated but are given prizes (intangible or experiential).

(Table 2.1 Continued)

(Table 2.1 Continued)

CRV	CIV
The value can be positive, negative or zero. The marketing and servicing costs can be higher for the referred prospect than the revenue from the referred prospect, resulting in a negative CRV.	The value can be negative but these occurrences are less. CIV assumes negative values when a firm is dealing with deal-prone customers who buy only when offered a deal/promotion, which impacts firm profitability negatively.
A customer can be referred only once in his or her lifetime with the firm.	A customer can be influenced multiple times during his/her lifetime.
Generally, the total number of referrals made by a customer is fewer.	Total number of influences, on the other hand is much more.

Source: Printed with permission from V. Kumar, L. Aksoy, B. Donkers, R. Venkatesan, T. Wiesel, and S. Tillmanns, "Undervalued or Overvalued Customers: Capturing Total Customer Engagement Value," *Journal of Service Research, 13*(3), (2010): 297–310.

CUSTOMER KNOWLEDGE VALUE (CKV)

"Customization" is a key term in marketing today. Customers value a brand that can customize a product to their needs. Given that the failure rate of new products is between 40 percent and 75 percent,[27] firms should be particularly concerned about what their customers say they want and need. Highly engaged customers are more than willing to provide feedback to the firm for improvements or changes in their product offering. Similarly, from a company's standpoint, customer feedback provides great value to a company as firms gather knowledge about what their customers understand about their product and/or service offerings. This feedback can play a vital role in a company's new product development processes. If the companies listen to their customers, they can reduce the failure rate of products and also improve the service quality.[28] Delivering value to customers by understanding and incorporating their feedback gives companies an edge over their competitors.

Let us consider the example of Atlanta-based Delta Air Lines.[29] In 2011, they created an online forum called "Ideas in Flight" on a social media site (Facebook) to gain feedback from customers on how the airlines could improve the travel experience for its customers. According to the airlines, about one-fourth of the suggestions were small ideas that could be examined immediately, although the actual execution of the suggestions would still depend on many aspects. However, the fact that customers provided directions to the company for improvement increases the value of such customers for the firm. Several companies are now coming up with similar initiatives. However, companies are not able to assign a value for this feedback from customers and correlate it to the company's goal of profit maximization. CKV under the CEV framework provides a model to measure this customer knowledge and feedback and link it to the profits of a firm. Conceptually, CKV is the monetary value associated with the profits generated by a customer's feedback, suggestion or an idea to the firm over a period of time.[30]

In both physical and viral communities, customers leave traces of behavior and opinions (intentionally and unintentionally), which can be analyzed to improve a product and service as well as the various processes and methods that go into bringing it to the customer. Customers with a strong interest in the brand usually have extensive product knowledge and are actively engaging in discussions and forums to share their opinions.

An important component of obtaining customer feedback is to be able to utilize customer knowledge efficiently. In order to achieve this, firms need to establish a quick and easy medium of communication. Providing feedback should be natural, interactive, and effortless. For these reasons, social media is a particularly useful tool to maximize CKV.[31] We notice the increasing use of social media and such forums in business-to-customer companies involving customers in the new product development process across product categories; although, CKV extends its merit to not only new product development ideas but also to service creation and innovation. With customers spending 10 percent of their time online on social networking sites, engaging customers in a conversation through various platforms (such as the Facebook fan pages) is a great option for companies to explore.[32]

There are recent examples in companies who have failed to capitalize on the knowledge provided by customers. Two of the most innovative companies in the world today, Google and Apple, have failed in one of their attempts to be innovative and ignore the customer taste and preference and feedback. Let us explore Google first. "Google Buzz," a social network pitched against Facebook, focused on making the sharing experience very rich by integrating photos, videos, and links was launched in February 2010. It offered an easy solution to flip through photos and experience them the way they were meant to be seen: big and full resolution. And videos play online so you can watch them without opening a new window.[33] However, soon after its launch

Google buzz faced privacy nightmares.[34] Customers clearly did not want consolidation due to privacy concerns and hence this initiative did not take off as intended by its makers. As a result, Google decided to shut down Google Buzz.[35] Another technology giant, Apple, had a similar experience. Apple's "Mobile Me" service was intended to consolidate all mobile apps in one, but it did not get the reaction Apple desired from its loyal customer base.[36] In spite of having great visuals and usability features, the change was too drastic for customers to accept. However, there have been companies who have deployed marketing strategies based on customer feedback and achieved success in the market. Dominos was able to capitalize on the feedback provided to reinvent its brand after the drop in sales in 2009.[37] They took customer feedback and followed cues to drastically improve their product offering.

Customers with interest in the brand provide valuable feedback and suggestions from time to time. They are constantly communicating with the firm. It is the marketers who need to listen to the customer voice and thereby devise strategies to incorporate this feedback. Take an example of the Telecommunication industry, which is an extremely competitive industry for firms to operate in. AT&T faces stiff competition from other leading players like Verizon, Sprint, and T Mobile. Customers have often expressed their feedback in customer satisfaction surveys regarding AT&T's poor voice service and phone-based customer care. However, AT&T has failed to capitalize on this feedback attaining the last position in the satisfaction survey while its competitor Verizon attains the No. 1 ranking.[38] Companies have various ways of engaging customers to utilize customer knowledge of their product and service. Apple, for instance, has shared their software development kit to the common user to create his or her own application. With this, Apple stimulates cocreation amongst its customer base. Customers with appropriate knowledge are able to make useful applications, which create value for Apple as well as the entire customer base. The University of Texas, Austin recently launched a university wide program called "Ideas of Texas" to promote "creative problem solving" on the campus.[39] Members have been asked to "contribute ideas to enhance teaching, research, student life and the alumni experience, increase productivity, reduce costs and improve effectiveness. The members are also asked to review and vote on submitted suggestions so that at the end of the term, the administration can implement the winning and feasible ideas. The program received an overwhelming response with around 700 submissions, of which over 50 were implementable ideas.[40]

The top ideas are in the implementation phase. Once implemented, these are expected to enhance the overall experience and effectiveness, as per the program objective.

B2B companies have been a slow adopter of this feedback process from customers. However, the recent trend is encouraging. B2B companies are increasingly using social media to understand their core customer needs and are seeking feedback to improve their services. Some consulting companies, for example, have a feedback process built in at the end of the each project to gain insights to improve their service and better understand the gaps.

By consolidating all feedback data received from customers into a single centralized system and using that system across the organization, companies can gain valuable insights into what customers need, want and value most, as well as identify important trends and patterns in the data that contributes to the success of the business. As a result, the total value from a customer's engagement could evolve from the measurement of CLV, CBV, CRV or BRV, CIV, and CKV of that customer. This ensemble of metrics helps firms assess the degree (in value terms) to which a customer directly or indirectly impacts a firm or its product, with the goal of increasing the profitability of the firm.

By means of case studies and examples, Chapter 8 shall discuss the concept, measurement, and applications of CKV in greater detail.

Customer Feedback

Source: Printed with permission from http://tomfishburne.com/ (retrieved on January 03, 2013).

HOW DOES IT HELP ORGANIZATIONS?

Before we look at how the CEV framework assists organizations, it is important to understand the current economic environment and how it is impacting the consumer decision-making process. The economy today plays a crucial part in day-to-day decisions. With consumers being extremely cautious about their purchases, companies have an increasingly tough task to gain and retain customers, which affects their profit margins. With the added pressure of plunging sales, it is easier for companies to release coupons and distribute those using social media channels like Facebook, Twitter, Pinterest, etc. Companies fail to understand that although many customers may respond positively to such initiatives, the initiatives have a different impact on different customers. It is important to identify the right customer—existing or potential—who can add value to the firm by contributing to the profits over a period of time. Understanding and providing value to customers can help companies overcome the challenges posed by the economy by devising strategies that are targeted to the right customer who will not only add value by their purchase, but will also be a marketer for the brand and will spread a positive word about the brand to influence future prospects.

Companies now have a forward-looking approach, which enables them to understand the current value of a customer based on his or her current purchase behavior, the impact of this current behavior on future profitability for the firm, and the future contribution of prospective customers to the profit of the firm. Companies can continue to reward its loyal customers but now managers will have a better hold on which customer should be rewarded based on the customer value calculated using the proposed framework. This is an effective tool that can equip managers to be better informed about the customers they are dealing with and their contribution to the profit of the firm. The interconnected nature of these five key metrics make it that much more interesting for a manager to evaluate the value of a customer. Managers can use these concepts and frameworks to further their objectives for the brand, product, or service.

In addition to evaluating these metrics, companies can now maximize the profit for the firm and make customers market their product on the company's behalf in an efficient and cost effective manner. When companies understand the exact nature of each of these various elements, it is possible to develop and implement effective marketing strategies and ensure the efficient allocation of resources. Companies need to understand that customers are not only purchasing a product or service but are also increasingly partnering with the firm in creating a valuable brand for themselves.

CONCLUSION

The components that make up CEV can be determined by considering: (*a*) value of a customer's own transactions and corresponding CLV, (*b*) CRV generated by bringing in new customers via referrals thereby aiding in the acquisition process, (*c*) CIV generated by primarily influencing and encouraging existing customers to continue and/or expand usage post acquisition as well as encouraging prospects (individuals the firm is trying to acquire) to buy, (*d*) CKV created by providing knowledge and feedback to aid in the process of innovation, and (*e*) CBV created by the perception of the brand in minds of customers that helps in maximizing the CLV of the customer. The following chapters discusses each metric, details how they can be defined, and how they are different from one another so that managers can understand and apply the proposed concept in real-world situations to solve business problems faced by the brand/product or service.

NOTES AND REFERENCES

1. S. Fiegerman (2012), "Microsoft Asks Consumers to Compare Bing to Google Via a Pepsi Challenge," Message posted to http://mashable.com/2012/09/06/microsoft-bing-it-on-challenge/ (retrieved on January 03, 2013).
2. The Bing Team (2012), "Over 5 Million Have Visited the Bing It On challenge," Message posted to http://www.bing.com/community/site_blogs/b/search/archive/2012/10/02/over-5-million-have-visited-the-bing-it-on-challenge-35-of-google-primary-users-say-they-would-use-bing-more-after-taking-the-challenge.aspx (retrieved on January 03, 2013).
3. Apple, "iBooks Textbooks for iPad," http://www.apple.com/education/ibooks-textbooks/ (retrieved on January 03, 2013).
4. S. Shearman (2012), "Apple Launches Interactive Textbooks for iPad," Message posted to http://www.marketingmagazine.co.uk/news/1113101/Apple-launches-interactive-textbooks-iPad/ (retrieved on January 03, 2013).
5. Proctor & Gamble (2012), "Have You Tried This Yet? Returns to Showcase Innovative P&G Brands," http://news.pg.com/press-release/pg-corporate-announcements/have-you-tried-yet-returns-showcase-innovative-pg-brands (retrieved on January 03, 2013).

6. V. Kumar, A.M. Luo, and V.R. Rao, Connecting brands with customers: An integrated framework. Working Paper (as of 2013), Georgia State University.

7. K.L. Keller, "Conceptualizing, Measuring, and Managing Customer-Based Brand Equity," *Journal of Marketing*, 57(1), (1993): 1–22.

8. Kumar, Luo, and Rao, Connecting brands with customers: An integrated framework.

9. R.P. Leone, V.R. Rao, K.L. Keller, A.M. Luo, L. McAllister, and R. Srivastava, "Linking Brand Equity to Customer Equity," *Journal of Service Research*, 9(2), (2006): 125–138.

10. V. O'Connell and J. White, (December 13, 2000). "After decades of brand bodywork, GM parks Oldsmobile: for good," *The Wall Street Journal* http://online.wsj.com/article/SB97666277082301184.html (retrieved on January 03, 2013).

11. K. Randall, It's a fact: Strong brands drive B2B Markets. http://www.brandchannel.com/papers_review.asp?sp_id=1235 (retrieved on January 03, 2013).

12. V. Kumar, *Managing Customers for Profit: Strategies to Increase Profits and Build Loyalty* (Upper Saddle River, New Jersey: Pearson Education, 2008).

13. V. Kumar and J.A. Petersen, *Statistical Methods in Customer Relationship Management* (West Sussex, United Kingdom: John Wiley & Sons, 2012).

14. V. Kumar, R. Venkatesan, T. Bohling, and D. Beckmann, "The Power of CLV: Managing Customer Lifetime Value at IBM," *Marketing Science, 27*(4), (2008): 585–599.

15. Kumar and Petersen, *Statistical Methods in Customer Relationship Management* (2012).

16. V. Kumar, *Customer Lifetime Value: The Path to Profitability* (Hanover, MA: Now Publishers, 2008).

17. V. Kumar, J.A. Petersen, and R.P. Leone, "Driving Profitability by Encouraging Customer Referrals: Who, When, and How," *Journal of Marketing, 74*(5), (2010): 1–17.

18. V. Kumar, L. Aksoy, B. Donkers, R. Venkatesan, T. Wiesel, and S. Tillmanns, "Undervalued or Overvalued Customers: Capturing Total Customer Engagement Value," *Journal of Service Research*, 13(3), (2010): 297–310.

19. Bank of America Referral Program, http://www.maximizingmoney.com/banking-bonus-deals/bank-of-america-referral-program-25-personal-and-50-business-checking-bonuses/ (retrieved on January 03, 2013).

20. Kumar et al., "Undervalued or Overvalued Customers: Capturing Total Customer Engagement Value."

21. V. Kumar, J.A. Petersen, and R.P. Leone, "Defining, Measuring, and Managing Business Reference Value," *Journal of Marketing, 77*(1), (2013): 68–86.

22. Ibid.

23. Kumar et al., "Undervalued or Overvalued Customers."

24. V. Kumar, V. Bhaskaran, R. Mirchandani, and M. Shah, "Creating a Measurable Social Media Marketing Strategy for HokeyPokey: Increasing the Value and ROI of Intangibles & Tangibles," *Marketing Science* (Forthcoming).

25. Rennlist is a site for high-end sports car enthusiasts. http://www.rennlist.com (retrieved on January 03, 2013).

26. Kumar et al., "Undervalued or Overvalued Customers."

27. G.A. Stevens and J. Burley, "Piloting the Rocket of Radical Innovation," *Research-Technology Management*, 46(2), (2003): 16–25.

28. V. Kumar and Y. Bhagwat, "Listen to the Customer," *Marketing Research*, 22(2), (2010): 14–19.

29. Atlanta Journal Constitution. 25 December, 2011, *The Atlanta Journal Constitution*, Business section; December 8, 2011.

30. V. Kumar and Y. Bhagwat, "Listen to the Customer."

31. Ibid.
32. The Nielsen Company Global Faces and Networked Places: A Nielsen Report on Social Networking's New Global Footprint; March 2009.
33. E. Ho (2010), Google Buzz in Gmail. Message posted to http://gmailblog.blogspot.com/2010/02/google-buzz-in-gmail.html (retrieved on January 3, 2013).
34. M, Wood, (2010), "Google Buzz: Privacy Nightmare," Message posted to http://news.cnet.com/8301-31322_3-10451428-256.html (retrieved on January 03, 2013).
35. https://support.google.com/mail/bin/answer.py?hl=en&answer=1698228&ctx=mail (retrieved on January 23, 2013).
36. Apple's 'Mobile me', http://www.apple.com/support/mobileme/ (retrieved on January 28, 2013).
37. Domino's, (2009), "Domino's Pizza: Celebrating 50th Year Domino's Gives Itself a Makeover." http://phx.corporate-ir.net/phoenix.zhtml?c=135383&p=irol-newsArticle&ID=1366561&highlight= (retrieved on November 13, 2012).
38. Atlanta Journal Constitution. (December 8, 2011).
39. W. Powers, Jr. (2010). Letter to the University of Texas at Austin Community.
40. "Ideas of Texas," http://www.utexas.edu/president/ideas/ (retrieved on January 28, 2013).

Please Help Us Help You...

Kumar, V.

Find answers for...

- How can firms measure the value of the feedback provided by customers?
- How can firms encourage customers to provide a feedback?
- How can firms maximize the value derived from customer feedback?

INTRODUCTION: THE VALUE OF CUSTOMER KNOWLEDGE

While brands, logos, taglines, and jingles are common knowledge among customers about businesses, customers are known to possess a lot more knowledge about businesses than just these commonplace items. This suggests that businesses, in turn, have a lot to learn from their customers. Customers can prefer one business over another for certain products and services and it is important for businesses to know the customers' preferences, likes, and dislikes to help improve the business's offerings to attract and retain customers.

Understanding customer preferences is extremely valuable for any business and the knowledge thus gained by the business will serve as a vital ingredient for the success of its products and services. Customer feedback can be either business initiated or customer initiated. Businesses can initiate the customer feedback process through surveys. Typically, such surveys involve incentives for those customers who provide feedback. However, gaining a customer's knowledge about the business can be done in many ways but most notably through his or her involvement in the process. For example, Ben and Jerry's encourage customers to participate in the new product development process by sponsoring a contest where customers can suggest the "best new flavor." "Customer participation" can be defined as the extent to which the customer is involved in the manufacturer's new product development process.

With the ever-growing influence of the Internet, e-Commerce portals, and social networks, it is becoming easier for individuals to search for a certain product or service's merits, demerits, and popularity on the Internet before making the decision to buy the product or service. There is a long list of such helpful sites based on the industry, product, and service that customers can peruse to gain the information they seek. Some examples are google.com, amazon.com, yelp.com, epinions.com, CNET.com, and tripadvisor.com.

In the next sections, we will review three examples of how businesses manage their customers and how they use customers' feedback to improve their respective businesses. Domino's Pizza is the first example that highlights how it turned around its business from strong negative publicity by responding in an appropriate and timely fashion to what customers were saying about its business. The second example is about Zappos, an online shoe retailer, where the focus is entirely on customer satisfaction and how that strong culture within the business has helped it in its success. The third example will focus on Quirky.com, which is a website solely dedicated to collecting customer feedback on new product innovations.

"Show Us Your Pizza"—Domino's Pizza

Customer feedback is of great value to firms, as it allows them to learn what their customers think. This knowledge greatly aids the new product and service development process. When firms truly understand what their customers want and how to deliver their customers' expectations, they have an edge over their competition. Domino's Pizza had a very bad publicity when a couple of its employees posted a prank video on the Internet.[1]

After experiencing a year marked by stagnant sales, negative viral marketing, and customer dissatisfaction, Domino's Pizza embarked on a mission in 2009 to recreate its product, brand, and image based on customer feedback and demand.[2] In stripping the brand and product of all previous concepts, Domino's was highlighting "losing touch" with its customers as the primary reason for its recent struggles. The pizzas were no longer a reflection of customer requirements. In light of this, chief marketing officer Russell Weiner announced that they would be "creating a pizza to reflect what consumers are looking for."

In rebuilding its brand and product concepts, Domino's adopted a new company philosophy that was based on listening and responding to customer feedback. Even after remodeling their product concept and changing the recipe based on customer feedback, Domino's further showed their commitment to listening to customer feedback with the launch of www.showusyourpizza. com. This website allowed Domino's customers to upload pictures of their pizzas to the website (both good, and bad) that the company would then use to improve its products. While Domino's had to go through a bad phase and turn its business around by addressing the gap it had developed with its customers, the next story is about how a company has made "customer satisfaction" as the foremost goal and cornerstone of its business.

"My Expressions"—Tanishq

Tanishq, an Indian jewelry brand launched a promotion called "My Expressions" which acted as a platform for its customers to codesign a new jewelry line "Mia" for working women. The top 10 customer designs were considered for production and the customers were rewarded ₹100,000 each (around $2,200). Tanishq believed that through this promotion they would gain insights to customer's views about Tanishq's jewelry and at the same time find creative and smart designers who were ready to collaborate with Tanishq.[3]

"Culture is Everything"—Zappos

As Tony Hsieh, CEO of Zappos, is fond of putting it: "Culture is everything" and "if you get the culture right, most of the other stuff like great customer service, or building a great long-term brand, or passionate employees and customers will happen naturally on its own." What drives Zappos' culture is an obsession with superior customer service, and there is not a customer or employee that does not know it. Even in these hard economic times, Zappos is meeting internal revenue targets. This is a key challenge for the company in these difficult economic times without drastically reducing prices and diluting the brand for continued growth. Great customer service is what helped Zappos build a loyal customer base. Approximately 50 percent of Zappos. com orders are from existing customers, and an additional 20 percent are from new customers who were referred by existing customers.[4]

"Listening to Customers"—Shoppers Stop

Shoppers Stop, an Indian department chain store, firmly believes in listening to the customers. They believe that by listening to the customers, they will gain more insight into changing customer preferences and they will be in a better position to create products that would satisfy the customer needs. Also, by listening to customer feedback and by proactively addressing customer issues and queries, they feel they will be able build a strong base of loyal customers. The Shoppers Stop management strongly feels that two-way dialogues is the future of customer engagement and wants to capitalize on their customer feedback mechanisms.[5]

"Bringing Ideas to Life"—Quirky.com

One great example of seeking customer input for innovation and new product development is Quirky.com. Since its launch in 2009, Quirky is on a quest to rapidly change the way the world thinks about product development. Quirky engages participants to collaborate in every aspect of product creation—from ideation, design, naming, manufacturing, marketing, right on through to sales. Figure 8.1 outlines "The Quirky Process."

Quirky is a business that is initiated and driven by customer feedback through their Product Evaluation (BETA) program. Thousands of creative people around the world submit their ideas first to be evaluated by Quirky, and then website visitors vote for the ones with the most potential. They bring new consumer products to the market each week, by enabling a fluid conversation between a global community and Quirky's expert product design staff. The world influences the business in real-time, and then they share the revenue directly with the people who help Quirky make successful decisions.

All of the above examples from Domino's Pizza, Zappos, and Quirky emphasize the strong need for businesses to gather customer feedback and apply the knowledge gained for retaining and acquiring customers. Based on these examples, it is clear that there is a huge benefit for other businesses to embark on a journey to better understand their customers and how to value their customers' opinions and knowledge. For understanding the value that a customer brings in for a business in terms of the knowledge about the company's products and services, we need to have the same point of view of the company like the customer.

Figure 8.1 The Quirky Process

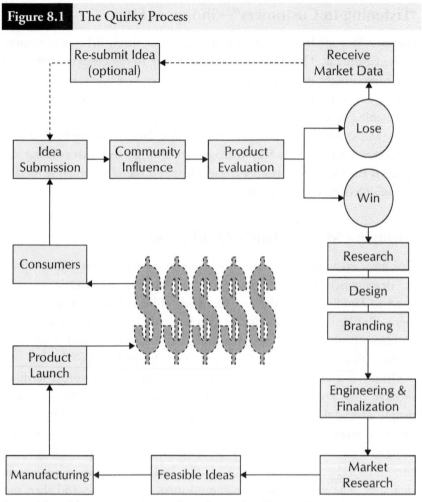

Source: Adapted from www.quirky.com/learn (retrieved on January 03, 2013).

This chapter introduces an approach to measure the value of customer knowledge and lists strategies that can be used to take advantage of the power of customer feedback/suggestion/idea known as customer knowledge value (CKV). As explained in Chapter 2, the monetary value a customer adds to the firm when the company implements a feedback, suggestion or an idea provided by that customer, measures the value of the knowledge gained from customers.[6] Using this knowledge, this chapter showcases how a customer feedback response strategy can be implemented to maximize and encourage CKV. The chapter will also present some examples of how CKV is used in businesses across various industries and then unravel the link between CKV and the other customer engagement metrics (CLV, CIV, and CRV).

DEFINING CUSTOMER KNOWLEDGE VALUE (CKV)

Customer knowledge value (CKV) can be defined as *the monetary value attributed to a customer by a firm due to the profit generated by implementing an idea/suggestion/feedback from that customer.* In some instances, customers can collaborate with the firm to produce new products and services. If more information of this engagement is known and made public, one can then create a separate metric called customer collaborator value (CCV). Here again, customer collaborator value (CCV) can be defined as *the monetary value attributed to a customer by a firm due to the profit generated by the new products/ services arising out of that customer's collaborative efforts with the firm.* In this book, we will focus on the CKV. Customers can add value to the company by helping understand customer preferences and participating in the knowledge development process. This knowledge can be used by the businesses to improve its offerings and innovate based on popular demands from the customers. Customer feedback/suggestions can serve as indicators to businesses about existing products and services and tell them if they are meeting customer expectations. Customer feedback not only identifies areas in need of improvement, but also helps provide suggestions and solutions for future upgrades and modifications. Additionally, such feedback mechanisms also offer new ideas for completely new products and services. This feedback has the potential to not only make the entire offering more attractive to existing and potential customers but also improve process efficiencies (e.g., reduced complaint management).

MEASURING CKV

The process of measuring CKV begins when the customer has ideas for developing a new product or refinements to the existing products. Customers may suggest ideas on their own accord or they could be business initiated. The entire process is summarized in Figure 8.2.

Figure 8.2   Conceptual Approach to Measure CKV

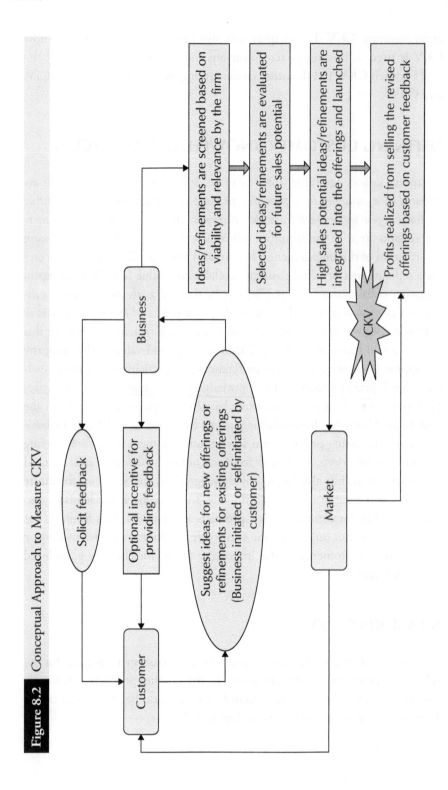

Customer initiated: In this world of social media, it is so easy for a customer to voice his review and feedback to a company about its product/service. It need not be prompted or paid. It could be just a simple "Tell us what you think" on the website that makes the customer share his experience about the product/service which is a rich insight and feedback. In some cases the idea can be from multiple sources (customers).

Business initiated: The business can initiate the idea generation in two ways. The first is to provide incentives upfront for customers to provide feedback. Businesses can reach out to their customers by simply soliciting via email, or by sending a survey or even by human interaction (in phone or in person). To make this process cyclical in nature, organizations typically provide some form of reward to encourage customers to continue to provide suggestions like these. The most common form of reward is monetary or op-portunities to win a monetary reward. For instance, Express, a clothing com-pany, launched a contest that entered a customer in a drawing for a $250 gift card for every clothing review he or she submitted.[7] For every picture a customer submitted wearing Express clothing, he or she would be entered five times in the drawing.

The second way of initiating idea generation from customers is a more involved form of reward. Here, the firms provide a share in profits from the sales of the new product. For instance, Brewtopia, a company that specializes in brewing customized beer for its customers, promised its initial members dividends based on how well the beer sold.[8] Perhaps the most involved re-ward mechanism is the one practiced by the software companies. For in-stance, Microsoft Corp. is planning to give developers who write software for Windows computers and devices a greater share of revenue sold through the company's upcoming Windows Store.[9] According to this new plan, as long as the software, or app, has made at least $25,000 in revenue, Microsoft plans to give developers an 80 percent cut. Additionally, if a Windows app has not reached the threshold yet, Microsoft will share 70 percent as well. Amongst its competitors, Apple now gives developers 70 percent of the revenue that apps bring in.[10]

To explain the CKV measuring strategy, let us expand on the Microsoft example. As the revenue is $25,000, and if the developers are going to get 80 percent out of it, it would be $20,000. One would think that the CKV is the remaining $5,000, but we have to factor in and deduct the marketing cost and other related expenses (say around $3,000). So, the

CKV attributed to the customer is the remaining $2,000. We have to be mindful that if the idea or development of the software was done by a group of four individuals (customers), the total CKV of $2,000 would be divided among the four customers and CKV of each customer would be $500.

In some instances, certain software companies have also let the customers/ users maintain ownership of the patent for the ideas suggested by them that eventually got integrated into the final product. In sum, regardless of the type of reward options, encouraging customers to provide feedback and suggestions for improvement does significantly contribute to the customer–firm engagement levels. The suggestions are then screened on the basis of practical applications and relevance to the company's product offerings. Suggestions that get past this stage are then evaluated for marketability. It is important to remember that *not all great ideas are market-friendly*. Therefore, the organization will evaluate the suggestions on the basis of generating future sales. The suggestions that show promise in generating sales will then be worked upon to be either integrated into the product development process (in the case of new ideas) or updated in the existing product offerings (in the case of product refinements). The profit that the organization realizes from the subsequent sales of these offerings is the knowledge value that can be attributed to the customer, or the CKV. If multiple customers had provided this suggestion, then, the value of the profit is divided among that number of customers and attributed to those individual customers as their CKV (as we explained in the Microsoft example).

Kissan, an Indian ketchup brand, started a new campaign "Welcome to Kissanpur—*where what you grow is what you eat.*" This campaign which was aimed at building brand, focused on customer engagement by getting customers to cocreate the product along with Kissan. The company first distributed tomato seeds glued on to newspapers along with an advertisement explaining the process of growing tomatoes. Customers were then encouraged to post the pictures of their tomato plants in the Kissanpur website and win a chance to get their names printed on the ketchup bottles. This is not exactly an example of cocreation but it certainly was an opportunity for Kissan to gain insights into the knowledge that its individual customers have about the brand (although it is not apparent if Kissan capitalized on this opportunity or not). The insight could help them measure each customer's brand knowledge value.

CKV MEASUREMENT STRATEGY

Since customer feedback gets initiated through multiple channels (to be discussed below) to generate good CKV measures for businesses, the following strategy is suggested as shown in Figure 8.3.

Customer Feedback Channel Identification

In this step, the business will have to analyze the various channels through which customers provide feedback and identify those channels that provide significant and quality feedback that the business can use. There are many ways that a business can keep an ongoing "listening ear" for customer feedback. Some very simple-to-use methods are:

- *On-site Surveys:* On-site surveys may be held by asking customers questions at the point of purchase. One way to do this is by using comments cards on display in stores (example: near checkout lanes or carts) or they can be inserted in the shopping bag along with the purchased goods. For example, "Shortly after Domino's Pizza founder Tom Monaghan opened his first outlet, he asked customers one question every night as they were waiting for orders. He wrote down the answers and learned that delivery was three times more important than issues such as price and service" (Small Business Tax Strategies 1). Although it can be time-consuming, this method does provide immediate feedback.
- *Online Surveys:* Another method of collecting customer feedback is through surveys. Mail surveys can be expensive and usually have a low response rate. This can be solved by providing a stamped survey postcard at the time of purchase saying something along the lines of "Thank

Figure 8.3   CKV Measurement Strategy

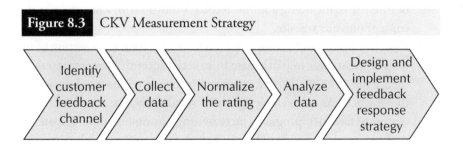

you for using (company name). To help us serve you better, please take a minute to answer the following questions" (Small Business Tax Strategies 1). More information can often be gathered through telephone surveys. Unfortunately, Caller ID has made telemarketing more difficult, so it may be a good idea to ask a customer if you may call them and what time would be most convenient. Online surveys seem to have a higher response rate than mail surveys and they are generally faster, inexpensive, and more convenient to customers. The only downside is that company surveys may get trapped in spam filters or considered illegal soliciting. Some sites such as opinionoutpost.com and surveysavvy.com not only give rewards for taking a survey but they also give rewards for referring new members for taking the survey.

- *Telephone:* The method best preferred by customers when an immediate response is expected (like a complaint or intricate matter). Assigning a toll-free (hotline) number is recommended and it is better to have a human touch to the customer service line rather than expecting the complaint to get resolved by automated machines.
- *Email/Fax:* Fax is now being sent as an email given the advantages of an email communication method. Email saves a lot of human interaction time and is also easier to deal with when sensitive issues are handled (especially when there is a dispute or negative experience). Businesses are using the latest Unique Code Embedded Technology to track email surveys. QuestionPro[11] is one such software in which business can track responses and send reminder emails, etc. The links in the email surveys allow real time responses. Survey respondents can even post their responses to social networks like Facebook, Twitter, or Google+. Once the responses are collected, analysis is done with many features such as real-time summary, trend analysis, etc.
- *Website Feedback Link:* The most important and popular since the boom of Internet is, including a simple feedback button with a box to write the content on your website.
- *Customer User Group:* Companies can invite a certain cross section of interested customers to participate in a special incentive program to share their experience or provide a general feedback of the product/service they launch. As an example, clothing retailer, Express, implemented a customer feedback program, incentivizing customers to participate actively in product design. They launched a contest in which customers

who submitted product reviews and pictures would be entered into a drawing that awarded a $250 gift card to the winner. The reviews and pictures allowed Express to see how customers were interacting with their products. Being able to identify trends in how people were combining different articles of clothing to form outfits could be cross-analyzed with demographics, seasons, and other customer characteristics. There are certain companies, such as the online T-shirt printing company Threadless Tees,[12] who take this idea a step further by encouraging fans to create their own clothing. Threadless Tees' model is entirely based on the concept of customer feedback as the customers are in total control of creating a product that is tailored to their individual demand.

- *Focus Groups:* Generally a group of 8–12 customers will meet to discuss a specific topic concerning the business. Focus groups can be difficult to run and may require a hired professional to lead and record the discussion.
- *Follow-Up:* Soon after the sale or service has occurred, calling customers (if the client base is relatively small) or emailing them with a satisfaction-questionnaire asking them to rate if the product/service expectation is met.

If you want to encourage feedback, try and offer customers a choice of feedback mechanisms to use. Also, make each method as easy as possible to use, for example, do not ask a long list of detailed questions and for telephone feedback, consider using a phone number. If the feedback is a specific complaint, do ask for precise contact details and make contact with the person as early as possible to address the problem. And be sure to review regularly, the pattern of comments and feedback you receive so that you can spot trends and identify aspects of your review where you may need to change or improve things.

Collecting customer feedback can help firms in (*a*) evaluating the performance of their existing products and services, (*b*) assessing how well they are able to meet customer expectations, (*c*) identifying areas of improvement in delivering products and services, (*d*) identifying suggestions and solutions for future product upgrades and modifications, (*e*) securing new ideas for new products and services, and (*f*) developing ways to reduce the failure rate of new and existing products. Firms can increase their profits when this valuable customer feedback is effectively implemented in product development and

CRM programs. Therefore, there is a financial value to be gained by utilizing customer insights and feedback. This strategic gain is termed as CKV and is attributed to the customer who provided the idea.

Data Collection

After identifying the channels, the business will have to come up with mechanisms of integrating the channels to collect feedback data. Customer feedback is a resource and it is wasted if not acted upon and used for improvement. By finding out and addressing customer concerns from the feedback, the companies gain a solid understanding of customer needs, wants, and issues. One thing to keep in mind is that various departments within an organization may be collecting customer data, but this data is often not unified. One department may have collected data for a specific purpose and not shared it with the other departments. This is another reason why it is important to set up and manage a customer feedback program. Streamlining and consolidating all feedback data can provide valuable insights into what customers need, want, and value most. For example, in order to understand and satisfy a customer's true needs and wants, LG Telecom in Korea created the voice of customer (VOC) organization. VOC incorporates both the positive and negative feedback by customers and knowledge to improve LG Telecom's service and product offerings.[13] If LG provides incentives for the feedback from its customers and formalizes the process of providing incentives, this would facilitate the tracking of the source of ideas to set the stage for computing CKV. Further, if LG can commercialize the ideas/suggestions/feedback that they get from the customers, then the roadmap for CKV can be implemented.

As a means to collect more data, companies can add a "feedback page" and link it to their company website, which describes the feedback process and the benefits of feedback that can encourage users to share their experience. This page could also have links connected to other popular review sites (like yelp.com) where customers can read about feedback of the specific product/service.

It is not uncommon for unsatisfied customers to go the extra mile to narrate their experience with a product while most satisfied customers do not even jot it down. It is all the more important to create a customer feedback process for happy customers as it can be difficult to manage negative feedback once they appear in the public. Receiving negative feedback is inevitable at some point; however, it is important to remember that consumers want to see feedback and not just positive reviews as it would look like as the company has edited/delete bad reviews. Consumers like to have information even if it is negative as it aids the buying decision. It is better to have a few standalone negative reviews (which have been solved and updated by the person who wrote the complaint) as consumers trust the legitimacy of the business and the feedback more when they see a mix of good and bad reviews.

Does negative feedback help? Let us take the example of the retail giant Wal-Mart and its attempt to handle negative feedback by censuring the negative comments. Needless to say it was just short of a disaster. Wal-Mart started a Fanpage/open forum on Facebook so that an open forum such as Facebook could revive their not so great public image. As expected, in a short time period they acquired a large number of fans for the page, but knowing the number of fans just did not yield any valuable and measurable data for Wal-Mart. As the fans base started growing, their engagement increased, and fearing the negative comments/feedback from the members, Wal-Mart restricted the "comments" option from their wall (page), which negatively impacted the image of the company. This essentially demeaned the whole point of creating a Facebook page. The fan page completely lacked interactivity and became just another place for Wal-Mart to advertise. So lack of planning and abandoning their brand image led the campaign to be unsuccessful.[14]

The key takeaway from this can be summarized as:

- Negative feedback gives a feeling of credibility to the existing positive reviews.
- Negative feedback can help potential customers move toward making a purchase decision as they feel they have zeroed down the product they want, knowing its pros and cons.
- Negative feedback gives businesses a chance to respond and show their superior customer service levels.

Instead of getting alarmed at negative feedback, we can use it to encourage customer engagement, which will become a vital part of marketing. Responding to negative feedback should be highly diplomatic and it is a good practice to have a plan to avoid future customers having to raise the "same issue" for which the negative feedback was given. The more feedback we get from the customers, the better we would be able to serve them to their satisfaction.

Online feedback: reach many, acquire more! When it comes to customers' opinions and the public sharing of those opinions with a huge online audience, there is little businesses can do—except ensure that their service is as good as it can be and to engage with their customers more than ever before. Even though local businesses don't have direct control over what their users write about them, they can influence the conversation and turn a potential threat into a great marketing asset.

Many local search engines, local directories, and local-social sites use customer feedback as a factor for how prominently they show a business in their results. Both the volume of feedback and the sentiment of the feedback received have an effect on how visible a business is and businesses that can successfully encourage their users to share positive reviews will benefit from reaching a wider audience.

Rating Normalization

Different channels may provide ratings from customers in different scales of measurement like "five-star rating scale," "10-point rating scale," "seven-point likert scale," etc. So businesses will have to adopt a standard way to normalize the data collected from the various channels to a "likert scale" of their choice that can be used for further analysis. Graphing the available data using advanced computer systems is another technique. It is easy to visualize a normal distribution, quadratic distribution, etc., by mathematical transformation and then use it to normalize your data.

Data Analysis: Feedback Response Strategy

Once data is accumulated in the repository, the business will need to analyze and classify the feedback data into useful information that can be used in generating CKV.

The feedback information retrieved by the company is business initiated or customer initiated and can further be classified in a classic 2×2 matrix. As shown in Figure 8.4, the type of feedback is represented on the x-axis (positive or negative) and the time to act on the y-axis (immediate or long term). A response for internal and external action is presented within the matrix. In order to analyze the genuineness of the feedback, the matrix can be completed with selected feedback received that is correlated with customer

Figure 8.4   Feedback Response Strategy

	Positive	Negative
For long-term action	• Internal Response: Send to R&D and Market Intelligence teams so that takeaway can be implemented in the upcoming product release(s). • External Response: Thank and reward (discount coupons) customers valuing their feedback. e.g.: Coke Freestyle Vending Machine	• Internal Response: Identify the root cause. Research should be done how to incorporate lesson learned from this negative review. • External Response: Provide alternate buying options from the product/service line and satisfy customer in future transactions. e.g.: Iphone 4 having signal problems and rectifying this same in future versions.
For immediate action	• Internal Response: Acknowledge the review and measures to meet and exceed expectation about the product/service. • External Response: Thank and reward (discount coupons) customers valuing their feedback. Encourage the customer knowledge value by increased interaction with these valuable influencers. e.g.: KLM Surprise	• Internal Response: Action should be taken at once to correct the issue and identify the root cause and eliminate reoccurrence of the same issue. • External Response: Damage control and measures to satisfy the affected customer assuring him for continuous support and service. Sending discount coupons and product replacements depending on the situation is recommended. e.g.: Netflix, Verizon

Type of feedback

interactions such as product returns and service calls with complaints during the same timeframe.

Feedback from popular sites (e.g., yelp, amazon, and mouthshut) can be collected and sorted out internally by a business. As we see, the review/feedback reaction can be positive and negative and the action that should be taken from the business side could be immediate or long term. Similarly, the action from the business side can be an internal, circular, or a decision and there will be an external response to the customer by means of a forum, email, or a social media website.

Feedback Response Strategy Design and Implementation

Now let us take some real-life examples of how certain companies have adapted this Feedback Response Strategy in their business and the implications to understand these strategies in detail.

Immediate Action (Positive Feedback): The Royal Dutch Airline, KLM, is going the extra mile with its social media efforts using creativity to create exciting, crowd-pleasing projects.[15] KLM has started an interesting campaign to connect with their customers called "KLM Surprise" at the Amsterdam Schiphol Airport. Designed to track "how happiness spreads," the campaign involves surprising travelers with unique gifts based on their social networking profiles. The way it works is when passengers check in at KLM's Foursquare,[16] a location-based social media site, the KLM Surprise team uses social networks such as LinkedIn, Twitter, and Facebook to find out information about the passenger. Most likely, anyone who uses Foursquare will have a presence on other social networks, providing the team with information about the person and his or her trip. The KLM Surprise team then uses this information to come up with a personalized gift to surprise the passenger. The team follows up by monitoring the conversation generating on social networks by that person and his or her friends. They also take photos of the people they have surprised and post them to the KLM Facebook page. The KLM team has surprised travelers with champagne, notebooks, a watch, and traditional Dutch foods. KLM is keeping tabs on the conversations generated through social media due to this campaign, and plans to evaluate its effectiveness afterwards, but has already said it may be used again in the future. The KLM Surprise campaign is definitely a unique way to get your customers talking positively about their brand, and a classic example of immediate positive action taken by a company using the customer knowledge they acquire.

Long-term Action (Positive Feedback): The idea behind Coca-Cola's freestyle "soft drink" dispensing machine is clearly CKV and is achieved in real time as the data is used for improvising the existing flavors and innovating new flavors.

Coca-Cola's new "Freestyle" Vending Machine[17] was introduced in 2009 as an experiment in Atlanta, Salt Lake City, and Southern California. It has become a revolutionary and interactive machine to customize drinks by mixing and matching different Coca-Cola brands and flavors. The new age touch screen soda fountain uses micro dosing technology that allows the right amount of flavoring for over 100 different drink combinations. Currently, there are over 600 locations around the country using Freestyle including fast-food restaurants, airports, movie theaters, college cafeterias, and theme parks. The machines are interactive and pleasing to the consumers, i.e., instead of levers for different sodas, they have a touchscreen, slick as an iPad, and the system provides daily detailed sales data back to Coke headquarters on flavor popularity, beverage consumption, peak times, popular locations and other data that Coke can use to access the machines to determine customer preferences and act on it.

Starbucks is another classic example of how social media and the Customer feedback mechanism are to be followed. Starbucks has a consumer portal where customers can share ideas or suggestions they have about how to improve the "Starbucks experience."[18] "My Starbucks Idea" takes the concept of crowd sourcing and opens it up to any customer willing to register. This also gives end users the ability to see what other people are suggesting, vote on ideas they agree with and even see the results. Starbucks' "Ideas in Action Blog" acts as a counterpart to the My Starbucks Idea website. This site is written by different Starbucks employees and talks about how they implemented, or are reacting to the suggestions and information from customers.

Immediate Action (Negative Feedback): Below, is a list of examples where the companies have acted upon the feedback given by customers.

Netflix's subscriber base had been on a reliably upward trajectory since it was founded more than a decade ago. The company—widely praised for making it easy to stream films and some TV shows via the Internet—was in the news for the wrong reason recently as the customers were unhappy about a pricing plan, which caused them to lose millions of customers. Finally, the business realized the value of customer feedback and revised the plan to what it was before.[19]

Similarly, Verizon Wireless canceled a planned $2 "convenience fee" for online and phone bill payments after a backlash from consumers.[20]

Long-term Action (Negative Feedback): In 2010, Apple's bestselling smart phone, IPhone Apple, received many complaints from its ever loyal customers about the call "droppings" and signal issues, and Apple released a free software update but it took several weeks to fix the glitch.[21]

IMPACT OF SOCIAL MEDIA IN CKV

All of these methods are an effective means of collecting data from existing customers. What about the noncustomers (i.e., potential customers)? By interviewing potential customers, we get to know about their mindset, why they want this product, and their expectations on the product/service like benefits, willingness to pay, etc. This will also give knowledge on their apprehensions in making the decision to buy a product. By offering trials of a product or service, potential customers may be picked up and useful information can be obtained through optional questioning before and after the trial. Offering an opt-in newsletter can also deliver more information to the customer and promote the future sale of the product being tested.

If a person uses the trial and does not proceed to purchase the product, offer freebies in exchange for a few minutes of his or her time, and talk to them about why he/she chose not to purchase. Continue offering these prizes until feedback starts becoming repetitive. If a product uninstaller is included, incorporate a question asking the reason for uninstallation. Other techniques include providing positive testimonials from existing customers to draw new customers and giving away free products in exchange for feedback.

Gathering data about why the business lost sales can help them create a product, which will be successful in market rather than something that can cause buyer remorse. With an increase in viral commerce and growing web-based communities, products and services are purchased, discussed, and spread at an accelerated rate. Through customers' viral participation with these products and services, companies can analyze and store all of the purchasing habits, comments, and feedback that are readily available. This information is important not only in terms of its cost-effectiveness and availability, but also in terms of the variety and the fairly indiscriminate method of diffusion that it provides. However, due to the volume of information and the vast digital space throughout which it is spread, any manual or case-by-case analysis of this customer feedback is impossible. It is therefore imperative that companies develop automated systems for extracting the knowledge from customer feedback. This process, known as "Opinion Mining" (OM), deals with gathering these customer feedbacks on products and presenting the findings in order to best accomplish certain objectives. Because of the varied findings (customer feedback), the methods and steps in OM keep changing with the objective.

An objective of getting the number of negative and positive reviews of a product, classifying those reviews as negative or positive would be the most crucial step. However, if the goal is to show customer feedback for each aspect of the product, it would be crucial to extract the feature aspects and analyze the overall sentiment for each feature. OM includes feature extraction, sentiment classification, and opinion summarization, with a particular emphasis on the sentiment that the customer is expressing, with various methods based on factors like linguistics and sentiment classification.

Social media has become an increasingly important (and free) method of collecting customer feedback. So many people use it religiously, and sites like Facebook and Twitter may be the most convenient way for them to voice a praise or complaint. Companies that neglect this are missing out on a huge opportunity to manage their customers and product. The companies that are still using call centers to address complaints are falling far behind. Not all customer care centers are open for 24 hours a day, whereas all social media networks are accessible 24 × 7. Customers don't care when your off hours are and they want to deliver their message at a time that is most convenient for them. As part of the exceeding customer service, customer queries and concerns should be responded to as quickly as possible including the feedback/comments which appear in social networking accounts.

ENCOURAGING AND MAXIMIZING CKV

Businesses can help boost the customers' knowledge about the products and services using their interaction toward the customers. Data derived from personal interaction unlike transactional data yields richer content and helps us know what customers do and why. It will also shed light on the reasons for certain decisions customers make. By encouraging customers to write a review or feedback, we get a clear idea of the source of problems they might have, preferences, and needs. Customer feedback provides the best channel to extract ideas for innovations and improvements the customers would like the business to adapt. Having a streamlined process and system to manage and encourage customer knowledge is crucial as this can help us design and launch new products in a timely manner and can aid businesses in keeping the customer loyalty and commitment intact. CKV focuses on capitalizing on information about customer needs to improve satisfaction and increase buying behavior. By encouraging CKV, we can steer the customer from taking the plunge of absorbing high costs and switching to competitors.

The Internet can also be an excellent means to maximize CKV. It aids in establishing contact with customers and it creates value by building a rapport with the customer base (both existing and prospective). We outline the distinct capabilities of the Internet as a platform for customer engagement, including interactivity, enhanced reach, persistence, speed, and flexibility, and suggest that firms can use these capabilities to engage customers in collaborative product innovation through a variety of Internet-based mechanisms. The customer needs to be given the opportunity to easily contact the firm to share his or her ideas or provide feedback. Firms must decide what level of involvement they would like from customers and use suitable social media channels to encourage such interaction with customers to promote this desired level of involvement. Without ease of communication, many valuable insights from the customer base will go untold. Firms should, therefore, take advantage of the Internet when creating initiatives to encourage customer feedback.

In addition to utilizing the Internet, firms should take into account the variety of motivations customers have for providing feedback. For example, some customers may inherently be reward seeking. They are extrinsically motivated and require some kind of compensation from the firm for their ideas and feedback. Firms can offer to buy ideas or can offer these customers a cut of the profits. Firms can also engage customers by sponsoring competitions. Some clothing stores allow aspiring fashion designers to submit their designs and then allow the public to vote on their favorite designs. The winner's design is subsequently manufactured and offered for sale (and the winner is provided monetary compensation). Other customers may be attention seeking and just want fame. Again, contests can provide an excellent means to retrieve their insights and provide them with public recognition. Some other ways to give recognition to the customer could be to name the new product after the customer or post pictures of the customer on the company website. Finally, some customers may only want to offer their direct input to the firm (product reviews) as information providers in contrast to aiding in the new product development process. It is likely that these customers are seeking monetary rewards instead of fame or recognition. As a result, CKV can be maximized when the firm makes communication with customers easy and accessible, provides some form of incentive (monetary or otherwise), and engages the customer in activities through which the customer can offer feedback and collaborate with the firm.

APPLYING CKV IN BUSINESS

An example of creating CKV through the new product ideas contributed by customers is Polyvore.com. This website lets users mix and match images from the web to create and share fashion outfits, interior designs, and other types of collages. The user-generated fashion creations in this website are created by a community of highly engaged stylists and trendsetters. Apart from providing a portal to display fashion creations, the website also lets other users rate the creations and provide comments. Additionally, for users interested in buying any creation listed on the website, the website directs them to other websites that carry the individual items displayed in the creations. All these features have not only enabled the online retailer to recognize and engage the fashion-savvy users, but also facilitated fashion houses and independent fashion designers to interact and gauge customer expectations and preferences. Luxury fashion brands and houses such as Bergdorf Goodman, Rebecca Minkoff, and Prabal Gurung have used Polyvore to engage with customers by offering special promotions including meet-and-greet and branded products. In fact, some of the creations suggested by users of the website have also been showcased in major fashion events across the country. The value accruing from all the customer-suggested creations is most likely realized by the fashion houses and designers by way of increased sales and profits. Additionally, for the website this has resulted in a strong growth in member base to around

6.5 million, who browse luxury products, seek fashion advice from fashion experts, and create collages showcasing their fashion inspiration.

In the airline industry, Delta Air Lines[22] actively seeks ideas from its customers regarding improvements to the airline's travel experience through its online forum called Ideas in Flight, located within their Facebook page. This initiative is part of a partnership between Delta and TED, the nonprofit organization devoted to "Ideas worth Sharing." Within the first few months in operation, this forum has received more than 1,000 ideas. Of the ideas collected so far, Delta has identified that nearly 70 percent of the ideas could become a part of the travel experience. Of that 70 percent, about a third can be tested immediately. The remainder would require much more time as they would be large projects. When Delta sees such ideas to fruition, the profits accruing from these ideas can be directly attributed to the respective customer(s) as their CKV.

Dell is another archetypal example of how CKV is being implemented. Dell IdeaStorm is a website launched by Dell on February 16, 2007 to allow Dell "to gauge which ideas are most important and most relevant to" the consumers. To participate, individuals must join the IdeaStorm community (at no cost) by selecting an anonymous username (you do not have to be a Dell customer to join). After registering, IdeaStorm members can propose ideas as well as comment and vote (promote and demote) on the ideas of others. When the articles are demoted, a "vote half-life" system is used to stop older ideas that are no longer receiving votes from appearing on the popular ideas page. Dell also modifies the half-life vote to prop up ideas that they feel need more exposure. As articles are promoted, their score is increased, allowing Dell to rank which suggestions and requests are considered most important by the website's users. Anyone submitting an idea agrees to give Dell a royalty-free license to use the idea with no restrictions. Dell's feedback response strategy is logged on a page and it demonstrates how they respond to each suggestion and that page is only changed when the status of an idea updates to "implemented" while the information on the ideas being worked on are kept under wraps. An empirical study of Dell's IdeaStorm community reveals that serial ideators (i.e., individuals submitting ideas on at least two separate occasions) are more likely than consumers with only one idea to generate an idea the organization finds valuable enough to implement, but are unlikely to repeat their early success once some of their ideas are implemented.[23]

Before we move on to find out how the components of CEV are inter-related, let us have a close look at the Customer Engagement Management by Hewlett Packard (HP),[24] an information technology leader, which was in the news recently for incorporating social media channels into existing contact center channels to provide organizations with a holistic view of their customers. According to HP, the new HP Social Enterprise Services help organizations quickly implement a social CRM program to improve communications and engagement with customers, while also helping them to better understand those customers. Organizations can rapidly deliver new products and services that are aligned with customer requirements by integrating social media strategy, process, information, analytics, and technology and high-performance contact center teams which establishes a solid competitive advantage. As part of the HP Customer Engagement Management, HP Social Enterprise Services provide two service models: HP Agent Services to engage with customers in social media channels and HP Social Media Analysis to mine the social web for information and insights on customers. Key features include: Listening Service—monitors a client brand or product in social media channels to identify new engagement opportunities); Analysis Service—leverages various analytics to gain insight into client, competitor and industry trends to refine the company's social media strategy; Routing Service—directs engagement opportunities to internal stakeholders, such as customer service, marketing, sales and product development for prompt action; Engagement Service—leverages insights derived from analytics to rapidly respond to customer inquiries and comments in social media channels; and Reporting Service—provides daily snapshots, weekly summaries and monthly reports of insights, analysis and opportunities to measure program success.

When bundled, HP Agent Services and HP Social Media Analysis allow clients to manage customer relationships more effectively by keeping pace with social media and analytical technologies.

INTERRELATIONSHIPS

Linking CKV and CLV

The examples of Polyvore.com, Delta, and many more such companies are classic indicators of firms shifting focus to actively seeking and working with the feedback provided by consumers. Companies are beginning to realize that customers not only provide value through their purchases, but also through their feedback about products/services. This section discusses the importance of realizing the value potential of customer feedback and illustrates the relationship between CLV and CKV.

Normally, customers with low CLVs have little experience with the product and/or they are likely to be unenthusiastic about the firm and, therefore, are likely to provide very little feedback to the firm. In other words, low CLV customers are likely to have a low CKV. Consequently, the higher a customer's CLV, the more are the opportunities for the company to receive input and, therefore, a higher CKV. However, at very high levels of CLV (an indication of a close fit between the company's products and a customer's needs), the customers are likely to be highly satisfied, and thereby have little incentive to communicate with the company. In other words, after a threshold point, high CLV customers are likely to have a low CKV.

While the above relationship between CLV and CKV is likely to be the dominant outcome in most situations, in a small number of cases, it is also possible that a customer with low CLV but one who is highly active through new product idea suggestions may be one of the firm's most valuable assets. This scenario would reflect that the company's offerings are not matched with the customer expectations and identify areas of development. This chapter highlights that the level of connectedness of customers to other prospects and customers can provide firms the capability to better assimilate information from their networks and hence the market when providing feedback, thereby increasing their knowledge value to the firm.

The relationship between CLV and CKV from what we infer is that customers with low CLVs have little experience with the product and/or they are not very enthusiastic about the firm. Hence, their involvement with the company or the product category is probably quite limited. These customers will be, therefore, neither able nor willing to provide new insights into the company on how to manage processes and how to improve its products. However, the higher a customer's CLV, the more positive that customer will perceive the company and its products, and the more are the opportunities for the company to receive input. Very high levels of CLV, however, are indicative of an almost perfect fit between the company's products and a customer's needs. Since these customers are highly satisfied, they would be expected to have little incentive to communicate with the company about how to further improve its products. These customers can, however, offer assistance to less experienced and knowledgeable customers if firms create a communication medium and motivate them to do so.

Linking CKV and CBV

We have seen how CKV is related to CLV. Chapter 4 has a detailed description of how CLV is related to other customer engagement metrics. Since what customers think of the brand and how they value the brand has a major role in making them provide a useful feedback about the product/service to the firm, we have developed a 2×2 matrix combining these two metrics (Figure 8.5). Marketers can implement this to maximize overall customer value and it can be used as a framework to strategically segment customers based on their individual CKV and CBV metrics.

A brief description of the recommended strategies for managing each of the four segments is described below.

Figure 8.5   The Relationship between CKV and CBV

	Honeymooners	*Partners*
High CBV	These customers value the brand highly but do not give valuable feedback to the firm about the product/service. *Strategy:* Encourage them to give feedback.	These customers value the brand highly and also help the company by giving feedback. *Strategy:* Nurture their relation as they give reference as well as think highly of the brand.
	Blankslates	*Consultants*
Low CBV	These customers do not value the brand, nor do they give feedback about the product or service. *Strategy:* Spend least unless they have high CLV.	These customers do not strongly value the brand but they do give feedback to the company on the product/service. *Strategy:* Promote the brand to these customers.
	Low CKV	High CKV

- *Honeymooners:* These clients have high CBV, which means they value the brand, but their low CKV indicates that they are not sharing their feedback with the firm. The recommended strategy would be to identify potential Partners and understand why they are not providing feedback. One reason could be that they have just started their relationship with the firm and do not have enough input to provide feedback. In this case provide necessary information to the firm and encourage them to give feedback. This could be achieved by sending emails to them with a feedback link, which will prompt them to get back to the business or one can ask them how they liked the product they purchased recently from the company.
- *Blankslates:* These clients have a low CBV and CKV. By this we mean that they neither provide feedback nor think highly of the brand. It is best to minimize marketing efforts on these clients except for the ones with high CLV, as the ones with low CLV, CKV, and CBV are not adding any value to the firm.
- *Consultants:* These clients have a high CKV and low CBV. This means that the client has a good understanding of the firm's products and services but does not think highly about the brand. For a mutually beneficial relationship, customers should value the Brand, know more about it and then share the feedback with the firm. The strategy to make these customers into "partners" is to promote the brand to them. Brand promotion can be done by sending promotional coupons and rewards for repeat buying.
- *Partners:* These customers have high CBV and CKV, which means they provide feedback to the firm and at the same time value the brand. These clients are valuable clients and it is recommended to nurture the relationship with them.

Linking CKV and CIV

It is observed that a customer's CIV will be strongly influenced by his or her online activities and social networking index like the reach of his or her blogging sites, number of active friends in Facebook, Twitter, etc., and also his or her interest in reviewing a product/service. All these activities are excellent channels through which feedback is gained which is translated to customer knowledge and can also act as a medium to influence peers. For example,

Netflix, an online DVD rental retailer, actively seeks feedback from its customers regarding their movie rental experience by observing what its customers are saying to each other. Customers are encouraged to review movies in their website to inform other customers. This information is then used by Netflix to refine the recommender systems that suggest movies to its customers. It is also not uncommon that customers react in extreme situations like when someone is very happy or upset about their purchase. When they are instantaneously happy it comes out as a positive comment or a feedback and if there is some kind of a disappointment either in a product or a service quality, it is expressed as a negative feedback. Although positive and negative evaluations generate valuable feedback for the firm and contribute to the generation of CKV, customers providing this feedback generally are at the extremes in terms of CIV. However, it will be interesting to study whether increased usage of social networking sites such as Facebook has decreased the polarizations of online evaluations. The ease of communication on such mediums may encourage more moderate evaluations.

Linking CKV and CRV

The relationship between customer referral value (CRV) and customer knowledge value (CKV) is very obvious as both depict the connectedness of the customer. The more connected a customer is, the more knowledgeable he or she will be about other customers' usage situations, problems, and solutions related to the firm's products. By soliciting feedback from a well-connected customer, a firm is able to tap into a much broader knowledge base as opposed to soliciting feedback from an unconnected customer.

The same connections to potential customers make it possible for a customer to effectively refer customers to the firm. Also, product experience, knowledge, and involvement enhance both the effectiveness of customer referral behavior and the value of any knowledge transfer between the firm and the customer. The relationship will be strengthened in cases where the firm acquires knowledge from customers through incentivized schemes; as such an action would trigger feedback from customers who are malleable to incentives. For example, Express, a clothing company, motivated customers to submit product reviews by entering them in a drawing for a gift card based on the number of reviews they submitted. It is likely that the company retrieved more knowledge from its customer base by motivating customers to submit reviews (provide knowledge) who normally would not have been inclined to do so.

Linking CKV and BRV

In real life, we see many firms providing references for the firms they do business with. They choose to do it via their website in various formats, audio/video testimonials, case studies, white papers, etc. The firms can also offer other businesses to call or contact them for references. All these add value to the selling firm as they increase the reputation of the firm's products and services and also proof of their consistent service. It also means that the firm that is providing the reference is very knowledgeable about the firm with which they are doing business. To understand this relationship better, we have developed a 2×2 matrix combining these two metrics (Figure 8.6).

A brief description of the recommended strategies for managing each of the four segments is described below.

Figure 8.6   The Relationship between CKV and BRV

	Low CKV	High CKV
High BRV	*Advertisers* These clients provide good references but do not give valuable feedback to the company about the product or service. *Strategy:* Find ways to encourage them to give feedback to the company.	*Collaborators* These clients give good reference and also help the company by giving feedback. *Strategy:* Nurture their relation as they give reference as well as feedback.
Low BRV	*Wallflowers* These are clients who neither refer nor give feedback to the business. *Strategy:* Minimize the marketing effort on these customers except for the ones with high CLV.	*Identifiers* These are clients who give extensive and valuable feedback about the products but do not add value by giving references to the business. *Strategy:* Find ways to make these customers give valuable references.

- *Advertisers:* These business clients have a high BRV, which means that they are referring the firm to other business but their low CKV indicates that they are not sharing their feedback with the firm. The recommended strategy would be to identify potential collaborators and identify why they are not providing feedback. One reason could be that they have just started their relationship with the firm and do not have enough input to provide feedback. In this case provide necessary information to the firm and encourage them to give feedback.
- *Wallflowers:* These business clients have low a BRV and CKV. By this we mean that they neither provide feedback nor provide referrals to the firm. It is best to minimize marketing efforts on these clients except for the ones with high CLV, as the ones with low CLV, CKV, and BRV are not at all valuing adding to the firm.
- *Identifiers:* These business clients have a high CKV and a low BRV. This means that the client has a good understanding of the firm's products and willingly shares feedback but their references are not adding value to the firm. For a mutually beneficial relationship, the firm should provide ideas/ avenues for the clients to give valuable references.
- *Collaborators:* These business clients have high a BRV and CKV, that is, they provide feedback to the firm at the same time refer the firm to other businesses as well. These clients are valuable clients and it is recommended to nurture the relationship with them.

CONCLUSION

As we have already described, customer knowledge value is the value that an individual customer can provide a firm through purchase behavior, opinion mining, and other feedback channels. In both the physical and viral communities, customers leave traces of behavior and opinions (intentionally or unintentionally), which can be analyzed to improve a product and service as well as the various processes and methods that go into bringing it to the customer. Being able to quantify CKV in a consistent fashion would allow companies to maximize the efficiency with which they deal with customer feedback, as well as how they implement it into changing their strategies and products. Being able to analyze, and then quantify the historical value of the feedback from each individual customer would allow companies to locate the customer feedback sources that are most likely to provide insightful feedback. This use could, and should, be broken down into individual product levels, with some customers having greater CKV regarding one product than another.

NOTES AND REFERENCES

1. Youtube (2009), "Domino's Pizza on Today Show," http://www.youtube.com/watch?v=xaNuE3DsJHM (retrieved on February 20, 2013).
2. V. Kumar and Y. Bhagwat, "Listen to the Customer," *Marketing Research—A Magazine of Management and Applications 22*(2), (2010): 14–19.
3. 5 Cocreation Examples, http://www.innovationmanagement.se/2012/02/24/five-co-creation-examples-e-on-coca-cola-mtv-tata-group-and-heineken/ (retrieved on April 4, 2013).
4. Gabbay, Nisan (2006, Sep 17), "Zappos.com Case Study: Why Shoes are Great for E-commerce … Yes, Really," http://langturn.com/translations/55?locale=pt (retrieved on September 9, 2013).
5. "How Shoppers Stop Is Wooing Customers the Social Way," http://marketingtransformation.informationweek.in/index.php/news/item/26-how-shoppers-stop-is-wooing-customers-the-social-way/26-how-shoppers-stop-is-wooing-customers-the-social-way?limitstart=0 (retrieved on April 1, 2013).
6. Kumar and Bhagwat, "Listen to the Customer."
7. Ibid.
8. Ibid.
9. CNS News, "Microsoft Pledges Windows Developers Generosity," http://cnsnews.com/news/article/microsoft-pledges-windows-developers-generosity-0 (retrieved on February 20, 2013).
10. Apple, https://developer.apple.com/support/ios/iad-network.html (retrieved on February 20, 2013).
11. QuestionPro, http://www.questionpro.com/collectyourdata/ (retrieved on February 20, 2013).
12. Threadless, http://www.threadless.com/ (retrieved on February 20, 2013).
13. Customer Insight Management 'LG' Craze," http://economy.hankooki.com/lpage/industry/200712/e2007122417275847580.htm. (The page is Korean but can be translated into English.) (retrieved on April 8, 2013).
14. Aline, Fatima (December 11, 2011). Let's Learn: Top 5 Social Media Campaigns That Failed Miserably. Message posted on http://blog.askoli.com/social-media-marketing/let%E2%80%99s-learn-top-5-social-media-campaigns-that-failed-miserably/ (retrieved on February 20, 2013).
15. Corina, Mackay (November 12, 2010) Royal Dutch Airline Gives Passengers a Surprise," Message posted on http://thenextweb.com/socialmedia/2010/11/12/royal-dutch-airline-gives-passengers-a-surprise/ (retrieved on February 20, 2013).
16. Foursqaure, https://foursquare.com/p/klm/3450621 (retrieved on February 20, 2013).
17. Cola-Cola, http://www.coca-colafreestyle.com/#!/100-brands/ (retrieved on February 20, 2013).

18. Starbucks, http://mystarbucksidea.force.com/ (retrieved on February 20, 2013).

19. Huffingtonpost (September 15, 2011). Netflix Price Increase Causes Bigger Subscriber Loss Than Expected. http://www.huffingtonpost.com/2011/09/15/netflix-price-increase-subscriber-loss_n_964026.html (retrieved on February 20, 2013).

20. Bloomberg (2011), "Posterior Marketing Response Parameters," http://www.bloomberg.com/news/2011-12-30/verizon-defends-2-convenience-fee-.html (retrieved on February 20, 2013).

21. IBN live (2010), "Apple Apologizes for iPhone 4 Signal Glitch," http://ibnlive.in.com/news/apple-apologises-for-iphone-4-signal-glitch/125891-11.html (retrieved on February 20, 2013).

22. Delta, https://ideasinflight.delta.com/IdeasInFlight/home.action (retrieved on September 9, 2013).

23. B.L. Bayus, "Crowdsourcing New Product Ideas Over Time: An Analysis of the Dell Ideastorm Community," *Management Science*, (2012). http://mansci.journal.informs.org/content/early/2012/11/02/mnsc.1120.1599.abstract (retrieved on February 20, 2013).

24. HP, http://www8.hp.com/us/en/business-services/it-services.html?compURI=1079486#.UQw6Px1fCxc (retrieved on February 20, 2013).

Why is Value Creation Important for CEOs?

15

Mahajan, G.

The various sections in this chapter are focused on why Value Creation is good for a CEO and his company, and why moving slowly away from the short term to the long term and focusing on the Customer and employees makes eminent sense. As CEO Polman of Unilever said, the focus on long term reduced share price volatility and increased it steadily for the long haul. The Customer Value Index will increase your Customer attractiveness (how attractive your company is to Customers) and will force you to be Customeric, because the Customer ratings could make or break your company.

CEOs must reinforce the principle that Value extraction can only happen if you Create Value.[1] So managers have to be taught to Create Value. The CEO has to create a Value Creating organization, for which an organogram has been shown later.

Experts then discuss why the CEO wants to be a winner and why he should Create Value. The CEO can use the Chief Customer Officer (CCO) as a Chief Value Creation Officer (CVCO).

Long-term Strategy Creates More Value than Short-term Focus

The CEO has to ask whether Value Creation is a flawed concept, particularly as it places the Customer and employees ahead of the shareholder. The Value Creation concept is not wrong when it suggests that doing good things for employees and Customers not

---

[1] Bharat Wakhlu, MD of Sikorsky India, said win-win means we share the same pie. In Value Creation, you grow the pie.

only makes excellent sense but also creates more long-term Value for the company and ensures its longevity.

Fortunately, many CEO leaders are supporting the Value Creation belief through thinking about conscious capitalism and delivering happiness.

Take Apple, for example. Steve Jobs used to say that Apple was in business primarily to make great products, not big profits. Ironically, that helped them make great profits. He told his biographer: "The products, not the profits, were the motivation," though he admitted that profits gave them the fuel for making great products. Naturally, if you create high Value, you get a higher price and higher profits. Which Apple is able to accomplish.

Amazon is another example. Jeff Bezos, its CEO, believed in long-term Customer focus, and these combined with internal drive became a Customer Value orientation. In his letter to shareholders, Bezos says that Customer focus brings in pro-activity and internal alignment for the Customer. Amazon's attempt is to impress Customers and not best competitors. Amazon's performance results really showed this to be true.

Recently, thought leaders were questioning the theory that had been drilled into CEOs' minds that Value Creation for shareholders is their goal. Not only that, but this goal has to be achieved in the short-term, and long-term thinking has to take the second place in the CEOs' rationale.

Many people have come out against this thinking. These include Lynn Stout, Professor of Corporate and Business Law at the Clarke Business Law Institute at Cornell Law School, John Mackey, once CEO of Whole Foods, and Paul Polman, the Chief Executive Officer of Unilever.

John Mackey coined the phrase "conscious capitalism". He states that while it is essential to make money, the company has a higher purpose, and this purpose goes beyond profit. The purpose could be Creating Value for society and the company's stakeholders: "They understand that their role is to serve the purpose of the organization, to support the people within the organization and to create Value for the all of the organization's stakeholders."

Paul Polman, talks about today's capitalism and how it has to be flawed, when it cannot be inclusive, when the poorest

3.5 billion people make less money than the richest 85 people, 1 billion people go hungry and we use 1.5 times the resources available in the world. He asks if we wonder about sustainability.

Lynn Stout worries about Value destruction for employees, taxpayers, and society, and for shareholders too, through a relentless focus on share price which can hurt not only the shareholder but also the enterprise. Instead of thinking that the purpose of a corporation is to create and delight Customers, it seems that CEOs think that the purpose of a Customer is to increase shareholder wealth. I believe those CEOs that do lose long-term success.

Lynn calls this "shareholder capitalism" which is robbery. She says companies have to think of enterprise prosperity versus profit of shareholders. Hence Customers have to be nurtured and must be at the center of the firm for the sake of the enterprise!

Conscious business is similar in thinking: Conscious businesses focus on their whole business ecosystem, creating and optimizing Value for all of their stakeholders, understanding that strong and engaged stakeholders lead to a healthy, sustainable, and resilient business.

They recognize that without employees, Customers, suppliers, funders, supportive communities, and a life-sustaining ecosystem, there is no business. Conscious business is a win-win proposition, which includes a healthy return to shareholders.

Lynn adds, during the last century as capitalism concepts grew, for the most part the professional manager viewed himself as a caretaker responsible for taking large public enterprises toward creating benefits for shareholders, employees, Customers, and society.

Unfortunately, linking managerial wealth to short-term profits has changed some of this thinking.

Lynn Stout talks of short-term gains that have harmed companies.[2] She cites that in the name of increasing shareholder Value, public companies have sold key assets (Kodak's patents), outsourced jobs (Apple), cut back on Customer service (Sears)

---

[2] Looking at the short term also means that the CEO may be looking at the issue from an incomplete context.

and research and development (Motorola), cut safety corners (BP), showered CEOs with stock options (Citibank), lobbied Congress for corporate tax loopholes (GE), and drained cash reserves to repurchase shares until companies teetered on the brink of insolvency (much of the financial industry). Some corporations even used accounting fraud to raise share price (Enron and WorldCom). Public companies employed these strategies even though many executives and directors felt uneasy about them, sensing that a single-minded pursuit of higher share prices did not serve the interests of society, the company, or shareholders themselves.

Thus, short termism harms shareholders and has to go!

In fact, corporations are legal entities, Lynn adds, with shareholders having a contract with the corporation as owning share of the stock. The corporation must fulfill its higher Value Creating purpose. And for this, they need a conscious culture that fosters love and care and builds trust between a company's team members and its other stakeholders. Conscious culture is an energizing and unifying force that truly brings a conscious business to life. Polman talks about the change in the shareholders psyche as Unilever moved toward long termism (shareholders approved). Stock price volatility reduced and long-term prices increased.

Lynn Stout states that it is time to recognize that the philosophy of "maximize shareholder Value" is just such a defunct economists idea.

Therefore, according to Polman, different leaders are required with the ability to focus on the long term, to be purpose-driven, to think systemically, and to work much more transparently and effectively in partnerships. He reiterates that long-term thinking gives increased profits, and it also means that you have to work with annual goals and meet them over the long term.

Sustainability, like not buying products from companies that rely on deforestation to produce edible oils, is a stand taken by many companies. This focus on sustainability is reaching a critical mass that will reduce deforestation and improve the ecosystem. This is an example of a higher purpose of an organization. Polman's focus on the environment and responsible business has made some shareholders wonder whether Polman worries more about the environment than about them.

Then you have Steve Denning, who presents yet another view about shareholder capitalism. Steve Denning wrote in Forbes a few years ago why the idea of maximizing shareholder Value, despite being pervasive in the business world and academia, is, as even Jack Welch admits, "the dumbest idea in the world." It has led to the very opposite of what was intended. It has systematically destroyed actual shareholder Value and morphed into something quite different: C-Suite capitalism, in which companies are being run principally for the benefit of the C-Suite, creating in the process a massive financial incentives bubble.

Lynn Stout in her book, *The Shareholder Value Myth: How Putting Shareholders First Harms Investors, Corporations, and the Public*, argues that shareholder Value is not only dumb and counterproductive, but it is legally unsound.[3]

Jesse Eisinger at ProPublica discusses what Lynn suggests:

> [W]hat the law actually says is that shareholders are more like contractors, similar to debt-holders, employees and suppliers. Directors are not obligated to give them any and all profits, but may allocate the money in the best way they see fit. They may want to pay employees more or invest in research. Courts allow boards of directors leeway to use their own judgments. The law gives shareholders special consideration only during takeovers and in bankruptcy. In bankruptcy, shareholders become the "residual claimants" who get what's left over.

Lynn calls for a return to "managerialism," where executives and boards of directors run companies without being preoccupied with shareholder Value. Companies would be freed up to think about their Customers, their employees and even start acting more socially responsible.

---

[3] http://dealbook.nytimes.com/2012/06/27/challenging-the-long-held-belief-in-shareholder-Value/?_r=0 (accessed February 15, 2016).

"Merely freeing the C-suite from any need to give special consideration to shareholders would be like throwing kerosene on a raging fire, argues Jesse. It would simply blow the financial incentives bubble even bigger, unless CEOs shun C-Suite capitalism.

"If anything, the voice of shareholders needs to be strengthened, not weakened."

"The era of managerial supremacy was not that successful then and would be more catastrophic now," says Nell Minow, a standard bearer of the corporate governance movement. "The idea of speaking of shareholders as owners is absolutely crucial."

She contends that the idea that shareholders wield too much power is laughable. Shareholders have increasingly been voting against directors only to see them reappointed. Recently, shareholders at a handful of companies have voted the majority of shares against the pay packages of chief executives—and have been ignored.[4]

Jesse continues, "Professor Stout's book is concerned about reining in excessive executive compensation but weakening shareholder influence is hardly the way to go about it."

Even today, most CEOs already say that "our Customers are number one," and "employees are our most important asset" and "we are committed to being good corporate citizens" and "our firm is committed to environmental sustainability." And yet everyone in those firms knows that when it comes to the crunch, what really matters in these firms are the short-term profits. Even though the management talks about multiple goals, it actually has a de facto single bottom line.

From Jesse's viewpoint, the fundamental point is that we have passed into an era of Customer Capitalism. Starting from Peter Drucker's 1973 insight that "the only valid purpose of a firm is to create a Customer," firms are now facing a marketplace of intense global competition where the Internet has shifted power has

---

[4] I think a shareholder agreement enforceable in commercial law should set the basis. Commercial law should place more emphasis on a transparent view of what that encompasses so that shareholders understand what they are buying into.

shifted from seller to buyer. The result is that the true bottom line of today's corporations is whether it is delighting its Customers by providing a continuous stream of additional Value and delivering it sooner.

This is a business argument, not just an appeal to philanthropy.

Jesse shows Figure 1.1 on how the financial-incentive bubble has caused damage to the economy.

Jesse concludes that the most powerful case for fundamental change from the doctrine of shareholder Value comes not from appeals to selflessness, which are unlikely to have much impact, but rather from the business case: the shift from shareholder capitalism to Customer capitalism makes a lot more money for the firm, the shareholders, the employees, and everyone else. Thus, Creating Value becomes important.

So the CEO has to decide whether his role is to make short-term profit to the detriment of everything else. He has to decide if his bonuses are more important than longevity. He has to decide whether he is good enough and smart enough to Create Value for all stakeholders while expounding a purpose for the corporation leading to long-term growth and wealth. Value Creation takes away this choice because it will impact both the short-term and the long-term results.

You have to create a company culture as Zappos did. Culture is about purpose: a commitment that the employee and Customers come first. It is about building a relationship with employees and a like–like experience for the Customer (all positive). Polman says that people are proud to work for companies with a purpose and the culture that employees, Customers, and sustainability come first, and they love a company that is prepared to make a difference and improve the quality of life.

If it works for Zappos (who, you know is famous for its Customer orientation) who grew exponentially with the employee/Customer culture, so can you.

Value Creation comes from a larger purpose than profits, and building a Customer culture and a company for the long term. And this will mean longevity for the CEO, too! Value Creation is a great mantra.

Figure 1.1: The Giant Financial-incentive Bubble

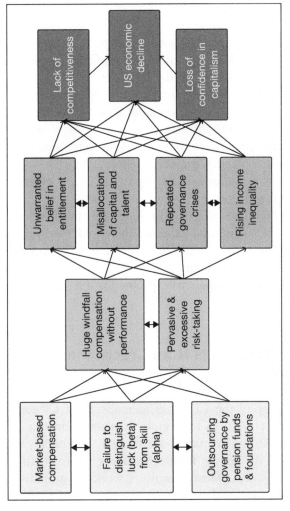

Source: Based on Desai, M. 2012, March. "The Incentive Bubble." *Harvard Business Review*. Available at: https://hbr.org/2012/03/the-incentive-bubble (accessed February 15, 2016).

Companies will become exposed to Customer-led ratings such as the Customer Value Index that Customer Value Foundation uses. Such ratings will rate companies for Customer attractiveness.

Value Creation Pointers

- Value Creation is for all stakeholders. The elements are: Customer, employee, partners, shareholder, and society; all considered, none neglected.
- Value Creation puts Customers and employees ahead of the shareholder (actually on a par with them). By doing so shareholder wealth increases.
- Short-term goals have to give way to long-term thinking. This leads to Value Creation
- Conscious capitalism puts the purpose of the organization beyond just profits.
- Paul Polman has shown that long-term thinking reduces share price swings and increases shareholder wealth.
- Short-termism is linked to managerial wealth, and this has led to Value destruction.
- Value Creation helps create profits for the short term and long term.

Why Value Creation Is More Crucial than Value Extraction?

Another philosophy the CEO has to embrace is: Create Value before you extract Value. Create more than you extract.

Today's MBAs and managers are trained to generally extract Value, extract the most from employees, from Customers, and from the system. Most executives work on administering, improving efficiency, making sure things are done effectively, and managing people to get the best out of them.

I learnt from a boss at Continental Can that extracting the most from and squeezing suppliers was harmful. He would ask how much difference it would make if the supplier got a little more. Analysis would show little difference. So we tended to be "fair." In return, the supplier rewarded us with loyalty and tended to bring improvements and ideas first to us. Our company would be the last to see a price increase.

How many MBAs are trained and attuned to create long-lasting Value?

How many are disposed to change the rules of the game? How many are willing to ask why are we doing these things or is there a better way?

You can extract Value to a limited extent. Unless you create more Value you cannot extract more Value. At some point there will be no more Value left to extract.

Here are some examples of Value Creation and Value extraction (read destruction) given by Tim O'Reilly of O'Reilly media:

> Consider this: when John von Neumann and his team at the Institute for Advanced Studies at Princeton developed the fundamental architectural approach of modern computing, they put their work into the public domain. When Paul Baran developed the fundamental concepts of packet networking that underlie the internet, he did the same thing. So too did Vint Cerf and Bob Kahn with the TCP/IP protocol, and Tim Berners-Lee with HTTP and HTML, the technologies that underlie the World Wide Web.
>
> These pioneers created enormous Value, yet they didn't capture very much of it for themselves. That was left for others who built on what they gave to the world for free.
>
> On the other side of the ledger, consider the Wall Street mavens who created new instruments to suck Value out of the financial system while damaging the economy as a whole, culminating in the 2008 financial crisis that the world is so painfully digging itself out of today.[5]

---

[5] The material is excerpted and referenced from the interview in ©2012 O'Reilly Media, Inc. and it is available at: http://www.forbes.com/sites/oreillymedia/2012/09/12/connected-company/ (accessed January 27, 2015). Dave Gray's book referenced in the interview. (Gray, D. 2014. *The Connected Company*. California: O'Reilly Publishing).

In fact these guys created more Value for themselves than for the people they supposedly helped. Greed and monetary power were major factors.

This is why MBA's should be taught to Create Value. In fact, Value Creation is one of the most important tasks of an executive, not just Value extraction (though they must do both). And Creating Value does not mean giving away things for free, but actually to get a Value for what you create, while also learning not to over-extract Value, or destroy Value.

So we need people who have degrees called Master's in Value Creation and Master's in Value Management and transform the company to Create Value for employees, Customers, partners, distribution channel, and thereby for the shareholder.

Later is the organization chart of the company of the future (Figure 1.2), taken from my book, *Total Customer Value Management: Transforming Business Thinking*. Everyone has a Value Creation role. This figure looks like an organogram you are used to, except that it assigns Value Creation roles to executives. This reminds them to also concentrate on Value Creation consciously and conscientiously.

Figure 1.2: Organization of the Future

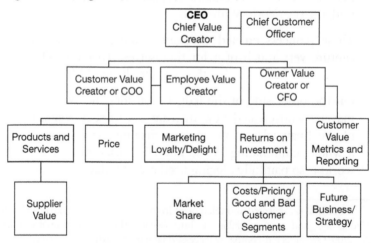

Source: First appeared in *Total Customer Value Management* by Gautam Mahajan, 2011. SAGE Publications, New Delhi.

Please note that the COO is the Chief Customer Value Creator and runs, in essence, a Customer department.

The MBA of the future will give general management courses on Value Creation, such as Value Creation for leaders, Value Creation and HRD, Value Creation and finance, Value Creation and IT. The MBA degree will be MVC or MVM (Master's of Value Creation or Master's of Value Management). The MBA courses could be merged with various disciplines like engineering and science so that students get an analytical and technical (or even humanities) background along with management.

Value Creation Pointers

- Create Value before you extract Value. Create more than you extract.
- Examples of Value Creation are the Internet as a free service.
- The company of the future has the CEO as the Chief Value Creator and the COO, renamed as Chief Customer Value Creator running a Customer department (what we used to call the operations department).
- Managerial greed leads to Value destruction (see 2008 financial crisis).
- Courses in Masters of Value Creation and Management are needed.
- Do not extract the most out of your system (includes Customers, employees, partners, and society). Create Value also for them.

Value Creation Is a Good Idea!

CEOs will find that few companies actively carry out and fewer colleges teach Value Creation. Practicing Value Creation will give the CEO a leg up over competition because they will be differentiating themselves, their companies, and their executives. Customers will perceive the change.

Why do colleges not teach Value Creation? The answer is that colleges themselves are in business and most businesses do not wish to upset the applecart. If it is not broke, don't fix it. This is so different from some of today's companies that must create innovation to survive and become Value Creators, like Apple, Whole Foods, Amazon, Ritz Carlton, and many smaller businesses Like Zane Cycles written up in the first issue (Vol. 1. No. 1) of the *Journal of Creating Value*.

Business progression is moving faster, and new ideas progress and die faster, unless companies are vigilant. (I said earlier that the average life of companies has fallen from 28 years to 12 years in the last 40 years.)

I had a great conversation with two leaders in the Customer Value field, Ray Kordupleski, the father of Customer Value Management and a professor at the University of Montana; and with Bob Thompson, President of CustomerThink.

Bob stated that many aspects of Value Creation are being taught in business schools. Topics like innovation and differentiation are examples. But no single B School teaches Value Creation as a discipline. Value Creation will bring together a whole new thinking and make MBAs upgrade themselves or graduate from being just good managers, good administrators, and efficiency experts. This is why companies land up with few Value Creators, and thus there is a need to change the education and B school paradigm and teaching Value Creation should be the prime role of a leader and general managers. Teachers should Create Value for the students while teaching and interacting with them. The B school program has to be modified to make Value Creation a general management elective. Current courses can be modified to show how to Create Value.

Ray told me that business leaders and CEOs want to win; they want to be the best (generally in creating shareholder wealth). To do this they have to attract and retain the best employees, Customers, partners, suppliers, and be the best with government and society. How do they do this? They have to Create Value across the organization and for the Customers and for society. They have to do this holistically and as a discipline. Then alone will they be the best in creating shareholder wealth. To be effective, business leaders must understand competition and the Value it creates, and be better than their rivals. Ray went on to say that business leaders must lose sleep over Customers as much as they do over profits. And if they do this, they will wake up to Creating Value as a mantra.

London Business School and the Wharton School are offering courses in Value Creation. Wharton also has two online courses in Customer Value. Stanford has a design for Customer Value and market success graduate certificate course, not a whole deal of courses at these top schools. B schools could help executives Create Value and in so doing Create Value for themselves.

Another example is the state of Colorado which has started to measure the Value they are creating for investors and what will create most Value for them (reported in the *Journal of Creating Value*, first issue [Vol. 1. No. 1]).

Moshe Davidow of Service2Profit and the Academic College of Tel Aviv Yaffo of Israel, and Colin Shaw of Beyond Philosophy felt we need Value Creation seminars and Value Creation courses for managers and faculty members taught by the world's best exponents in the field. What do you think?

I am in the process of designing a one year specialist program for Value Creation in MBA schools consisting of 18 courses, including practical intern courses. The courses cover many of the concepts discussed in this book in depth. Maybe this is a start for changes in MBA thinking. I have also given courses at IIT Delhi, Mandi and Gandhinagar and other places on Creating Value and setting up Value Creation Councils. Another initiative is the *Journal of Creating Value*. We have set up Value Creation Councils at some of India's biggest companies, consisting of the front end, Customer facing people, and staff people to support them.

Here are some proposed courses:

The Customer of the Future and the Company of the Future	Who is the Customer, how is he changing, what choices does he have, become Customer's trusted buying aide, fight concept of anonymous Customers
	How does the company become more adept, agile, and ambidextrous, employ social media scores and balance with brand scores, look at Customer Value Index, speed new products and increase gap over competition, physi-digi versus digi-physi, helping Customers buy versus sell, be available when and where needed

Value Creation Strategy: Use Customer and Stakeholder Strategy to Build Business Strategy	Build Customer strategy, who, where, when, and why. How to go after target, how to make him non-anonymous, strategies, products, and services to do so, differentiation by brand and social media scores, systemic changes to improve service
	Form teams and share Customers across company, and give Customer roles to everyone and put into key performance indicators (KPIs) and balanced score card. How to have a self-tuning strategy
	Use learning from stakeholder strategy especially owner and Customer strategy to build classical business strategy, incorporating Customer and market opportunities, willingness to change, best to next practices, self-tuning, adaptive, agile, and ambidextrous, rigid when needed, understanding Customer, market place and options and competitors. Differentiate in Customers eyes, marketing, and pricing to capture Value, training people to be Customeric. Practice Total Customer Value Management
Value Creation and Leaders	Understand and build purpose of company as distinct from profit. Agile, adept, ambidextrous, Customer-driven, the Chief Value Creator, important versus urgent work, priorities, flexibility, and managing of mind-sets, Value Creation, and dilemmas. Convert departments into Customer departments, measure Customer Value Index, and use for improvement and for reporting to board. Outsource routine work. Make operations department a Customer department, have Customer-related KPIs
	Balance shareholders needs and Customer's needs. Do not giveaway Value to Customer, ensure that you create optimum Value for all

(Continued)

(Continued)

Value Creation and HR	What is routine and essential work? Outsource routine work. Build concept of HR becoming a line department, strategic, and the Chief Employee Value Creator, and how to Create Value for the employee and the Customer role. Value Councils, Customer-centric circles, changing mind-sets. Changes of attitudes from receptionist to CEO (where do you see a great attitude when you enter a company?
Value Creation and Other Departments or Call this Value Creation and Operations	IT and Value Creation: make IT a line function. Finance and the Customer and Value Creation, manufacturing, marketing and selling, new products: how to ensure and measure Value addition and how to use Value to price
Zero Complaints	Source of complaints include poor information, poor service, unkept promises, no feedback, annoyance (the opposite of do not annoy), the importance of time, energy, psychic needs, image, etc.
	Getting an attitude and mind-set, Customer-centric circles, and ensuring systemic changes to ensure no more complaints. Ensure Bill of Rights being kept and the continuous Customer improvement programs.
	Importance of employees and partners to enhance Customer happiness, responsibility, and success, in short, creation of Value, and how to measure it. Improved Customer processes and systems, and agile updation.

Value Creation Pointers

- Many aspects of Value Creation are taught in business schools, such as innovation and differentiation.
- Value Creation should be taught as a discipline to graduate Value Creators.

- Today's MBA's are taught to be good administrators and efficiency experts. Value Creators go beyond this.
- Value Creation has to be done holistically and across the organization to attract the best talent, best Customers, and best investors.
- The best B schools are starting courses on certain aspects of Value Creation.
- Examples of possible courses are given.
- Set up Value Creation Councils in your organization to inculcate a Value Creation culture.

8 Signs Why Your Company Isn't Creating Value

Value Creation requires a distinctive and flexible mind-set. It is mentality driven by enhanced self-esteem, awareness, and proactiveness. It goes beyond just doing your job, it is doing something extra.

Value Creation is executing proactive, imaginative, or inspired actions that increase the net worth of products, services, or an entire business to create better gains or benefits for employees, Customers, partners, society, and shareholders. Value Creation stimulates executives and business leaders to generate improved Value for Customers, driving success for the organization and its stakeholders. The business of business is to Create Value for its ecosystem.

Value Creation creates Customer-conscious companies.

If Value Creation is so good and basic a management technique, why is it not being adopted in a universal fashion? Which of the following reasons is holding your company from using it? (If you are using Value Creation techniques, you would be aware of this! Are you?) You will find that smart people like you will be able to create more Value when you focus on doing so. There are several reasons:

1. You are captives to what you have been taught and what you have learnt.

You have been taught to be executives and hard driving at that to Create Value for the company.

Executives believe that Value Creation for the company means increased profits, typically by reducing costs, increasing efficiency, and trying to increase market share.

Executives are taught to forget that they are Customers too. You, therefore, find it difficult to think like an executive and a Customer at the same time. You do not have the flexibility to be both.

You have to take advantage of everything in your power to Create Value for the company. This could mean exploiting the employees, Customers, partners, society, and ethics, if you have to. This concept is undergoing a sea change, as executives now know the importance of employees, Customers, partners, society, and ethics (Values). But it has not gone far enough.

Too much stress is paid to systems and processes but not to mind-sets starting from the top to be Customeric.[6]

All these prevent us from adopting Value Creation in the proper manner.

2. In the last 20 years, CEO compensation has gone up much faster than profits, and is based on short-term profits. The lifespan of CEOs has gone down, making them look for quick wins.

More and more of the executive bonuses are now being based on short-term profits. Compensations through stocks and options have gone up sky high, which is huge motivation to make more money now. Why worry about the long run? The CEO may not last that long!

Figures 1.3 and 1.4 show that the lifespan of companies and executives is reducing and executive compensation is going up, especially through stocks and options.

The short-term thinking is against Customer Value Creation and Value Creation in general, except for Value Creation for the shareholder.

---

[6] Customeric is a word coined to show that a company has the Customer-in-center. The Customer is the center of its strategy, its focus. The company is Customer-centric, takes Customer responsibility, measures Customer data and lets Customer thought lead the business.

Figure 1.3: Median CEO Pay ($M, Constant 2011 $)

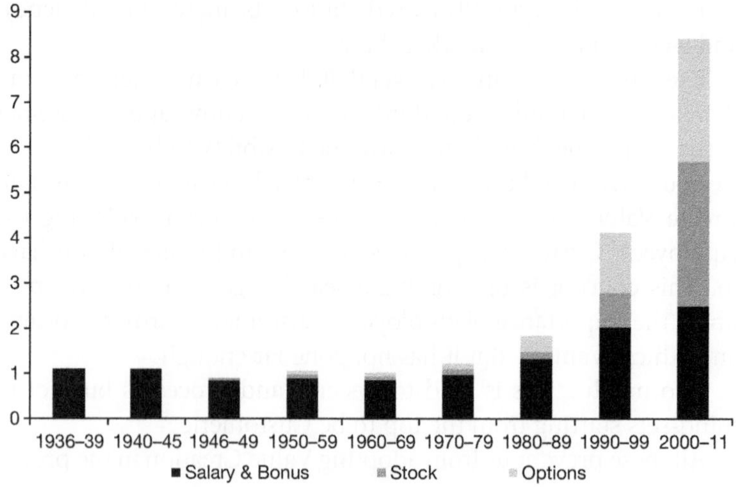

Source: Taken from James Montier "The World's Dumbest Idea".[7]

3. MBA and professional schools teach students to become executives, and teach them that shareholder wealth is the real purpose of the firm, then that is what they will practice. They do not understand that shareholder wealth is a result and not the purpose of the firm's existence. Inability to distinguish between urgent work and important work.

Shareholder Value is not necessarily shareholder wealth. Shareholder Value can mean much more than just profits. It could be a focus on employees and Customers or even societal Value. Shareholders are savvy people also.

Shareholder wealth (read profits) grows by increasing Customer Value Creation because it grows the loyalty and market share.

Profits are one measure of the success of one's investments, or a measure of the health of the investment. Generally, one invests for a purpose: to bring out a new technology, to be the best in the

---

[7] Available at: https://www.gmo.com/docs/default-source/research-and-commentary/strategies/asset-allocation/the-world's-dumbest-idea.pdf?sfvrsn=0 (accessed February 15, 2016).

Figure 1.4: Average Company Life and CEO Tenure

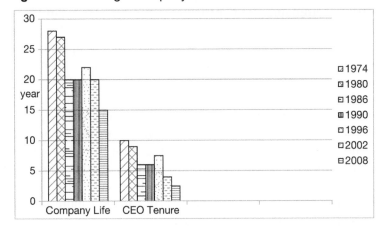

Source: Adapted by the author from James Montier.[8]

world, to be a leader in a segment, to be Customer admired, etc. Profits are a result of how you manage, how you take care of your environment consisting of employees, Customers, the partners, society, and the shareholders.

Too much time is spent on urgent work, with little attention to important work.

4. There is an overemphasis on efficiency, systems, and processes. Not enough thought is given to mind-set and attitudes, which are required to increase employee and Customer Value. These should be my priorities and the Customer priority is getting sufficient attention.

Mind-set comes from education and awareness, and wanting to Create Value rather than being forced to do so. Set up Customer-centric circles and Value Creation Councils. Even to be world class you must have the proper mind-set and flexibility.

The Customer priority is relegated to a more junior person.

---

[8] Available at: https://www.gmo.com/docs/default-source/research-and-commentary/strategies/asset-allocation/the-world's-dumbest-idea.pdf (accessed on March 7, 2016)

5. More time and emphasis is paid to correcting problems and settling complaints, rather than to get to zero complaints.

Every time there is a complaint, it takes away the Value you are providing. What are you doing to prevent complaints from happening? Why are you not finding systemic ways to prevent future complaints?

This requires a mind-set that works universally to avoid complaints, driving the business to a zero complaint state.

There is a feeling that complaints give you the opportunity to interact with a Customer. Surely, there are better ways to do so! Imagine, the waiter drops soup on you; a true cause for a complaint. Is this what you want as an interaction? No, it is an interaction you could do without. Better to find more positive ways of interacting with Customers.

6. Competition is doing the same thing, why change. Let's all make merry and get our bonuses.

Why do we need to be different? Because we will gain competitive advantage and be ahead of competition, rather than be followers.

7. Customer concepts apart from being executive-led are also embedded by consultants who in a race to get ahead come up with niche phrases like Customer Relationship Management (CRM), Customer Experience (CX), Customer Journey, Customer Effort, and so on, but mostly focus on processes.

There is confusion on basic definitions. So work is done in bits and pieces instead of a real sea-change as outlined in my book, *Total Customer Value Management: Transforming Business Thinking.*

You may not realize that a Customer journey requires an effort from the Customer and if the company is following the journey, there is an effort required from the company. You may not realize that the basic product and the service should provide the experience, and other experiences other than delightful ones are unnecessary. Thus, a good experience is when you are upgraded by an airline or being allowed to get free miles for lower points.

The reverse is having an experience such as cancelled flights. We do not want this experience. If it does happen, the Customer journey to get the problem solved should be minimal.

8. Employees and departments such as HR and IT are not taught to create true Value and remain staff functions.

Owners, managers, or employees must realize that companies place a Value on their functions and positions (what the company will get versus what it costs them to have the employee). Value is created when employees do something extra and go beyond what is expected of them. Employees add Value by doing things better than others. If actions are worse, employees destroy Value. Those that add Value get promoted and get better raises.

Employees destroy Value sometimes. Why would one wish to destroy Value? Unintentionally, unwittingly. Value gets destroyed, too, unconsciously.

Put your Customers at the center of your business decisions on making organizational changes.

Destruction of Value happens unconsciously just as creation of Value. If you created Value consciously and you understood this, you would work differently.

And companies, if they understood the true intent of shareholder Value and that there is a strong connection between Creating Value for employees and employees Creating Value for Customers to increase profits, they will embrace Value Creation as a mantra.

HR and IT have to change. HR has to look at Creating Value for employees and Customers. The policing tasks have to be outsourced to administrative departments. IT continues to be focused on doing tasks efficiently, and not leading the change to focus on Creating Value for Customers.

Value Creation Pointers

- Value Creation is a distinctive mind-set. It is mentality driven by enhanced self-esteem, awareness, and proactiveness. It goes beyond just doing your job; it is doing something extra.
- Value Creation creates Customer-conscious companies.

- Value Creation does not happen completely because you are captives to what you have been taught and what you have learnt.
- Employees are taught to forget that they are Customers and to become executives.
- Just focusing on Creating Value for the company reduces long-term wealth.
- Short-term and increased managerial bonuses in the last 30 years have reduced companies' life and CEOs' tenure.
- Set up Value Creation Councils and Customer-centric circles to change mind sets.
- Reduce focus on processes and systems and change company culture and mind-set.
- Departments such as IT and HR have to become line functions and add focus on Customers and employees. They should outsource routine work.
- If competition is doing the same thing, then it is an opportunity for you to go ahead of competition with next practices such as Value Creation.

From Value Grabbing to Value Creating: Lesson for Leaders

Delivering happiness, giftivism, and conscious capitalism all have common messages, one of which is "give forward."

That is, you Create Value for someone, often without thinking of a reward. When companies start to understand that they have a greater purpose than just to make profits, they move from being Value grabbers to becoming Value Creators. They realize that the company's purpose is to give to society and the world and, in the process, to employees, Customers, partners, and unions. In doing this, they are Creating Value for the stakeholders, and Customers in turn will help the company Create Value.

Imagine doing something out of the ordinary for the Customer, such as creating unexpected delight. The returns may not be immediate. In the long term the returns will become visible.

I remember when I came back to India after living in the US for around 20 years; I was deeply capitalistic. A good friend, an industrialist asked me for some ongoing help, and I suggested we first negotiate what I would get paid. Everything was measured in dollars and cents.

A few weeks later, I went to meet a famous lawyer about helping me with a case. He said he would. I asked him what his fees would be. He got angry. He said I know your family and your grandfather who had attended my wedding and I cannot take money from you.

I walked out quite dazed and chastened. I appreciated there was something called *lihaz* (respect and consideration for others, having a concern, and being considerate) in the Indian world.

The lawyer had given without any expectation from me. He got in me an admirer and a well-wisher in return.

And I learnt also to give forward, without expecting something in return. It is a satisfying experience.

This lesson is easier for individuals to accept. But when you make a corporate inanimate, it can only think in dollars and cents. Corporates are humans hiding behind the anonymity of the company, humans trying to be tough, and only concerned about profits. This is what happens when you convert from being just ordinary people to becoming company people.

Harvard Business School's Professor, Brian J. Hall, calls this paying forward. Pavi Mehta in *Giftivism* echoes the same and gives wonderful examples of giving without expecting returns or anything in return.[9] Brian Hall calls this Value Creating behavior and he goes on to say this is a requisite for successful leadership. Winning leaders have a Value Creation mind-set where they do good turns on behalf of the organization without expecting any returns.

Value Creation by definition increases Value and there is more to go around and share. The pie gets smaller or is shared by fewer when leaders are Value grabbers, who are trying to maintain their place in the organization by any means.

Value Creators also create happiness, and they share credit and profits. They tend to be team players and work for the team.

---

[9] https://www.youtube.com/watch?v=p_QLGvp_stI (accessed February 2, 2016).

Value grabbers tend to be Value destroyers in the long run. I remember when I worked with the University of Wisconsin to set up a campus in India, most Indian professors at Wisconsin were motivated by what they could get out of a campus in India, rather than the fact that an India campus would Create Value all around, for the State of Wisconsin, for the university and its stakeholders, and for India and Indian youth. By being Value seekers, they played a negative role.

Such people tend to be secretive, they get a sense of security by keeping their knowledge to themselves and not sharing it, because they fear they will lose out or others will become smarter than them. They destroy Value. And those who share knowledge encourage people to grow, and act as catalysts; those who teach people how to apply knowledge and Create Value are winners.

And this is true in negotiations. The "I must win at any cost" thinking, the thought of having it all and not leaving anything on the table are Value grabbing syndromes. Many purchasing people are either taught to win or their ego wants them to extract all they can from suppliers. When you ask them this is true, they will say, oh, no! We believe in a win-win with our suppliers. Carlos Cordon of IMD says this is often win-win for one side (the purchasing guy winning twice).

Purchasing people often do not try to create Value for their suppliers. The Value starved suppliers will seek to take revenge whenever they can. As an example, Nippon Steel starved Nissan during a steel shortage, causing huge losses.

I had a boss, who taught me the art of reverse negotiation. Negotiate hard but then give something away, that the supplier will remember.

I recall negotiating an annual plastic resin contract for 33.0 cents a pound when the going rate was 32.5 cents. My reasoning included that we needed the supplier's un-restrained support for new products, specification changes when required, and potential price increases. My purchasing director (who had negotiated the supplier down to 32.5 cents a pound) was aghast. But a few months later when the prices had gone up to 60 cents a pound, while our competition was forced to pay higher prices, we enjoyed lower prices for a period of time, a great competitive advantage.

Conscious capitalism suggests that companies should make the world a better place. Blatant denuding of the earth of its resources for short-term gain (like the illegal mining in the State of Haryana, in India; or the cheating in getting telecom licenses in India by Minister Raja and the companies he favored, or in getting illegal advantage in coal mining leases; or in the mortgage crisis in the US, born of greed) is Value and resource grabbing. Large-scale Value destruction occurs as a result. Conscious companies or conscious executives will not participate in Value grabbing.

Pavi Mehta tells of her family charitable Arvind Eye Foundation, and eye care hospitals, where every patient is treated equal. His or her ability to pay has no bearing on the treatment. Everyone pays what they want to (not what they can). And those that pay more than the treatment cost fund those who cannot pay. As an aside, Arvind's cost structure is very low, as the volumes are high, and the cost of consumables and equipment is low. An eye doctor conducts a cataract procedure every three minutes in an assembly line process.

Pavi talks about restaurants where this happens. Your meal is paid for and whatever you want to give for the meal is used to feed someone else. This is the paying forward concept.

Paul Polman of Unilever states that companies with a purpose beyond profits tend to create more shareholder wealth in the long run and have less fluctuation in share prices in the short run. Firms of endearment, a term coined by Raj Sisodia, David Wolfe, and Jagdish Sheth, that tend to have a purpose and practice conscious capitalism are shown to have 14 times greater returns than S&P companies, and 6.4 times the returns of good to great companies in 15 years.

McKinsey in "Redefining Capitalism" (written by Eric Beinhocker and Nick Hanauer) argues that capitalism has served the world well and has led to growth. However, CEOs and investors are at a crossroad today. Should the role of the business be to make money or advance the good for society? They conclude, "the essential role of capitalism is not allocation—it is Creation. Prosperity in a society is the accumulation of solutions to human problems." Ultimately, the measure of the wealth of a society is the range of human problems it has solved and how available it has made those solutions to its people.

Thus, argues, McKinsey, instead of celebrating wealth, we should celebrate innovative solutions to human problems. I would contend that if done well, creation of wealth is another result of doing the right things for society and other stakeholders.

Shareholder Value and profits are a result and a measure of how leaders work, not a goal. Such Value Creating leaders create happiness, not just profits, and are greatly successful.

Value Creation Pointers

- Value Creation by definition increases Value and there is more to go around and share.
- Delivering happiness, giftivism, and conscious capitalism all have common messages, one of which is "give forward" and, thus, Create Value.
- Giving forward and Value Creation is easier for individuals to accept. But corporates can also do this if they remember they are human and have employees who are humans.
- Winning leaders have a Value Creation mind-set.
- Value Creation by definition increases Value and there is more to go around and share.
- When leaders are Value grabbers, overall Value is decreased.
- Conscious capitalism and firms of endearment create higher shareholder returns.
- According to McKinsey, "the essential role of capitalism is not allocation—it is Creation. Prosperity in a society is the accumulation of solutions to human problems."

Leadership Training Not Effective: A Contrarian View

Recently, Pierre Gurdjian, Thomas Halbeisen, and Kevin Lane of Mckinsey in "Why Leadership-Development Programs Fail," outlined the reasons why leadership development programs fail. Some salient aspects they discussed are: $14 billion is spent in such programs. Sixty-seven percent of companies rank leadership development as the first three human capital priorities. Thirty percent of CEOs believe they lost international business opportunities because of poor leadership. Only 7% of the companies say their programs are effective.

Top business schools charge about $150,000 per person for such programs. Training of leaders is a big business and the trainers are often profit-led.

Wow, 93% of such leadership-development programs fail and yet companies still continue with such programs. With such appalling results, why do people try to look at seemingly obvious reasons for failure and are unable to reduce the failure rate?

If you couple this inexcusable training failure to the American Customer Satisfaction Index or ACSI score which has not improved in the last 20 years, since 1995 (score 74) to 2014 (score 76). What does it tell you? What does your leadership training do? It is failing in getting our leaders to be Customer-focused? The Customer is the real reason for a company being successful or not.

The companies' consultant advisors keep pushing them into new leadership-development programs, with new ideas like lets have programs that focus on companies needs and teach potential leaders how to manage two or three needs.

Other reasons for failure had to do with self-contemplation (or as Mckinsey puts it, reflection) versus hands-on training. The next was measuring the result of the programs and perhaps the most important was underestimating the mind-set.

Unfortunately, it is not the mind-set of the leader trainees but the trainers. (Ask yourself, if there is only 7% success, either selection of potential leaders is a problem or the trainer is a problem: he is teaching the wrong thing or the wrong way?)

As a contrarian, I am against training. I am for education and self-learning through reflection, catalyzed by the teacher, to help leaders understand how to Create Value, and for whom. Reflection, along with building self-esteem and confidence, and awareness are the first steps. Next is how to Create Value and for whom and how.

Obviously, Value is to be created for the employees (not mentioned in the paper other than to call leaders employees) and the Customer. The Customer is mentioned tangentially as "hunting for Customers" or for joint ventures in the essay.

The mind-set is most important, but again they are looking for a "leadership" mind-set not for a "Customer" mind-set. The current leadership-development mind-set is an inside point of view and not an external focus.

I think our current trainers have to unlearn, before they can teach new things. The leadership candidates have to unlearn all the gibberish on day-to-day stuff they have learnt, such as the leaders' role is to administer and to bring in efficiency and profits (these are the minimum the leader has to do, but he has to go beyond to Create Value). They have to forget what B schools taught them about crucial tasks and distinguish between urgent and important tasks and focus on the important ones.

They need to concentrate on becoming Customeric and creators of Value and not silent destroyers of Value.

Potential leaders have to develop a Customer mind-set. They have to understand that Customer scores and the Customer Value Index are edging out brand scores, when it comes to buying.

And as they reflect on this in their leadership self-development, they will soon come to a conclusion that they are in a people business, and they need to work with both internal people (partners and employees and unions) and external people (Customers whom they need to internalize).

Such business people understand changing social needs, the social media, and the changing world.

They understand the Value of creating employee Value. And they then develop or find specialists to aid them in tasks such as acquisitions of companies to improve the offerings to the Customer, such as developing or innovating new products that Customers can relate to, or services that wow Customers, and to find joint venture partners or new markets that are useful to Customers, and how to outsource routine work, and take critical management talent away from such work.

This then is the mind-set we want to inculcate. Forget whether we should make the leader aggressive (and if his mind-set is mild, to change that) or to make his mind-set innovative (even if he is a person that focuses on efficiency or stability) or to make him an internationalist.

Get the potential leaders to focus on people (most businesses should focus on people, employees, Customers, and partners), particularly Customers, and to find specialists who can help him with processes and systems, acquisitions, cost-cutting, increasing prices, entering more lucrative markets, finding talent, etc. Do not make him the one who does this but one who can lead and Create Value for the benefit of the Customer, the employee, and the company. This is true leadership creation.

Get the potential leader to focus on the Customer of the future and the company of the future. Teach him to be agile and adaptive to the changing world, and ambidextrous where he can offer both what the Customer wants and what the company has to offer. This will build the leaders of the future.

Value Creation Pointers

- Only 7% of leadership programs succeed: either selection of potential leaders is a problem or the trainer is a problem: he is teaching the wrong thing or the wrong way?
- Instead of training for a "leadership" mind-set, build a "Customer" mind-set.
- Leaders have to work with both internal people (partners, employees and unions) and external people (Customers whom they need to internalize). They are in the people business.
- Leaders must learn to Create Value.
- Leaders must be readied for the future, and become agile, adaptive, and ambidextrous.
- Leaders must outsource routine work, shy away from urgent work, and focus on important work.

Why Leaders Fail

In the last topic "Leadership Training not Effective: A Contrarian View," I quoted Mckinsey that $14 billion was spent on leadership development, and only 7% of such programs were effective. Mckinsey published a paper, "Decoding Leadership: What Really

Matters,"[10] on what makes good leaders. This was based on a survey of 81 large companies. They found that the top four traits of a leader were:

- Solving problems effectively
- Operating with a strong results orientation
- Seeking different perspectives
- Supporting others

Other traits in the answers included:

- Praising, champion-desired change, motivating, and bringing out the best in others.
- Making quality decisions, clarifying objectives, rewarding, and developing others.
- Communicating prolifically and enthusiastically, developing and sharing a collective mission.
- Facilitating group collaboration, keeping groups organized, fostering mutual respect, and on-task quality decisions.
- Staying composed and confident in uncertainty, recovering positively from failures, and differentiating among followers.
- Offering a critical perspective, having role model organizational Values.

Hardly exciting, a list that could have been made by MBAs, basically, employee- and team-related. Not one of these focuses on the Customer. Instead of focusing on the Customer, we have focus on making profits, organizational development, and problem solving. No wonder some leaders fail. They fail because these are not good enough in a highly competitive world.

And what about mind-set and thought processes? Not on the list!

---

[10] Feser, Claudio, Fernanda Mayol, and Ramesh Srinivasan. 2015, January. "Decoding Leadership: What Really Matters." *Mckinsey Quarterly.* Available at: http://www.mckinsey.com/insights/leading_in_the_21st_century/decoding_leadership_what_really_matters (accessed February 15, 2016).

No wonder, companies and CEOs are lasting for shorter times, and leaders are failing in this era of the Customer, fast product introduction, shorter product life cycles, social media, etc.

What would your top three or four traits be? Mine would be:

- A mind-set of Value Creation that goes beyond just looking at the obvious, such as processes, systems, and what we did in the past. Focus on important tasks.
- Focus on Customer and add Customer Value Creation. Look at the future with agility, adaptability, and ambidextrousness (being able to offer what the Customer needs along with what you have). Look at Customer scores such as Customer Value Index versus just the brand scores.
- Focus on employee and employee Value Creation.
- Have Values and be a Values role model (ethical, moral, fair). Have corporate consciousness (sustainability, ecology, societal).

All this will help you create shareholder Value.

Value Creation Pointers
Leadership traits: Leaders must

- Have a mind-set of Value Creation.
- Be Customer-focused and add Customer Value.
- Look at the Customer Value Index or Customer scores versus brand scores.
- Figure out important tasks and work on them, and do not get carried away by urgent (firefighting) tasks. Leave these to others.
- Be employee-focused and add employee Value.
- Have Values and be a Values role model (ethical, moral, fair). Have corporate consciousness (sustainability, ecology, societal).
- All this will help you create shareholder value.
- The 3As of agility, adaptiveness, and ambidextrousness will help you with the disruptive marketplace.

16

How CEOs Can Value Create for Customers

Mahajan, G.

If CEOs can create great Customer Value, they will build Customer Ambassadors and then follow and pamper them to get more business. We then talk about becoming part of a Customer's network. Value Creation and destruction for Customers is shown through examples. Lastly, the excuse given by managers that they have no time for Customers is debunked.

Customers As Ambassadors and Their Networks

People (and sometimes CEOs) mistake the term Customer advocate. A Customer advocate is one who works for your company but advocates and works to make the company Customer-centric and Customer-friendly.

Wiki says: Customer advocacy is a specialized form of Customer service in which companies focus on what is best for the Customer. It is a change in a company's culture that is supported by Customer-focused Customer service and marketing techniques.

If the Customer comes first (thanks to your Customer Advocates) and if you are truly Creating Value for the Customer, he will reward you with loyalty and referrals. Such Customer become your Customer ambassadors.

Examples of Customer Ambassadors are Mac, iPad, and iPhone users. They love these products and are ambassadors of Apple. They talk about the Apple products they own and make you want to own them.

In today's day and age of the social media, your interaction with Customers often become virtual ones! The social media becomes more important. How do you work with, follow, or use social Customer Ambassadors and network with them, and get them to refer other Customers to you?

Customers with "Social Value": Your Customer Ambassadors[1]

Most companies measure Customer's Lifetime Value. The equation includes the Customer's current buying, the expected rate of growth of his buying over the years, and the business obtained from the referrals he provides. Very often these referrals are more important than the Customer ambassador's own purchases. You need these Customers as your Customer ambassadors, and their Value as Customer Ambassadors can be immense.

How do Customers become your Customer Ambassadors? The necessary condition is that you create great Value for them over what your competition can. As an example, give them something to talk about, and go beyond the sale. Differentiate yourself. As Value increases (and Value is what it is worth to the Customer to do business with you and includes your products, the relationship, the image and brand, your people and service, and the price and non-price terms), they become more than just loyal, they become ambassadors. They want to promote your company and people and products.

A good Customer Ambassador recommends you to his network. A great Brand Ambassador also has a virtual social network where he can and does refer you.

This last kind of a Brand Ambassador has to be nurtured because his referral Value can be huge. As an example if he buys ₹100 a month, but refers 10 Customers who buy an average of ₹60 per month, he has referred ₹600 to you.

---

[1] Adapted from "Focus on Customers with 'Social Value'." Available at: http://www.forbes.com/sites/kellerfaygroup/2012/07/02/focus-on-Customers-with-social-Value/ (accessed February 3, 2016). Permission from Keller Fay Group.

Ask what made these people my Customer Ambassadors. How can I convert others to become Customer Ambassadors? There are many methods you might have used in the past such as asking for forwarding of marketing emails, rewards for referrals, or events where such Ambassadors can bring friends. Do something special for your Ambassadors.

Recognize that your best Customers are introducing you to their friends and making you part of their social circle. Give them your highest priority and rewards and treat them as special.

Creating Value from Your Customer's Network[2]

Today, the bulk of referrals are face-to-face, followed by telephones, and social media is a distinct third but growing. That is why you have to follow your Customer Ambassador there onto the net.

How do you Create Value from a Customers' network? We all know that if you have a great Customer network, it can lead to referral buying. How do you get to referral buying? A Customer network is your captive one which you normally manage through databases, CRM, and your website. The base database and network is your Customer network.

Your Customer's network is the network outside of your day-to-day control.

First, you can see the advantages of a Customer's network. If you use it intelligently, you can get the Customer to come to you directly, circumventing the normal means he would have used such as looking for the product on the net or going to a store to figure out whether s/he should buy from you or buy your products and services. Instead of this, they might use recommendations from friends, from social media like Facebook or Twitter. They look at what their influencers and friends have to say. They bypass some early buying steps. It is convenient for them and

---

[2] Partly adapted and with permission from Donal Daly, CEO at The TAS Group: "Creating Value for Your Customer's Network and Gaining from It." http://blog.the-tasgroup.com/donals-blog/Customer-network-Value (accessed February 16, 2016).

much easier for you to sell to them because they come with some positive pre-determined ideas. You should become a "friend."

How do you get to this point? First, you have to Create Value for your existing Customers. You have to create substantially more Value than your competition. Customers then reward you with loyalty and referrals. Creating Value means it is much more worth your Customers while to do business with you over competing offers. Your product, services, people, and marketing have to do better than competitions.

You also have to participate in the Customers' network. What is the social space that your Customers use? How do they surf the net looking for merchandize through their Customer network? How do you become a real (though background) part of this network? Can you become the Customer's aide in this interaction with his social space? How do you understand this interaction and how do you derive the data about this interaction or how do you monitor the Customer's network without invading his privacy? How can you influence him during this phase?

You need a data capture mechanism that captures referrals and Customers referring Customers. You can then start a special campaign for them. (You could also identify them from surveys as those who would definitely recommend, and by asking how many people have they recommended or can they suggest people we can contact. This can be added to your database.

Today, your first step is to be part of this social space, become one with them in this space, and become a trusted ally and part of the referral chain. Then price becomes less of an issue in the Value equation. You must start to understand what Value your Customers need in this space and for a Customer why he should (and make it easy for him) refer you. And how can you add Value (make it easier) for a Customer looking for a referral. What do you have to spend to eventually Create Value from your Customers' network?

But, the threshold is high—because in the end, for new Customers, you're going to ask them to do business with you. Being "like them" breaks down some barriers, but it is not enough. You must continually add more Value in the social universe than you expect to get in return. You are looking to recoup the return on the influence you have developed online later.

Value Creation Pointers

- You need good Customer advocates to Create Value for Customers and make your company attractive for your Customers to become your ambassadors.
- Customer ambassadors introduce you to new Customers and increase your business.
- Next get onto your Customers network. You need to add Value to the social universe.

No Time for Customers? Conduct a Task Audit

I discuss the importance of Customers, Customer Value, and Creating Value with CEOs and CXOs of companies of all sizes. We discuss how increasing Customer Value leads to increased profits. Many CXOs end the conversation saying, "What you are suggesting is important and certainly the Customer is crucial for us. However, we have too many other programs in place...." The Customer priority is generally low in these companies.

At first, I used to be mystified that the Customer was not that important to these companies and that they had no time for the Customer. So, I asked myself, what is more important? What tasks are they carrying out that are more significant? I then started to work with companies on a task audit (and these included India's largest companies). We looked at: (see Figure 3.1)

- Necessary and relevant work for the Customer.
- Necessary and irrelevant work for the Customer.
- Unnecessary and relevant work for the Customer.
- Unnecessary and irrelevant work: totally useless work.

As per definitions, *necessary work* is essential for, vital to, indispensable to, important to, crucial to, needed by, compulsory, required by, or requisite for the Customer (such as actual delivery of service). *Relevant work* is pertinent to, applicable or germane to, or appropriate to the Customer. This is work that can be eliminated without deterioration of present service or product (this could include improving products and services or cutting costs).

What work is the Customer willing to pay for? That would be termed as necessary and relevant.

The rest is all unnecessary or irrelevant. And unnecessary and irrelevant work is totally useless work (such as waiting for meetings to start).

Other work is business Value adding work.

We conducted research on tasks done by executives through questionnaires. Half of the executives answered the questions themselves and the other half with the researchers. Not surprising, the ones who answered the questions themselves found that 70% of their work was useful (either necessary or relevant to the Customer). The executives who filled the questions with the help of researchers found that only 50% of their work was useful. The rest of their time was on useless work (this makes sense, because people have difficulty in admitting that what they do is useless).

Examples of useless tasks are redoing reports, unnecessary meetings, waiting for meetings to start and, most important of

Figure 3.1: Mahajan Task Audit Quadrants

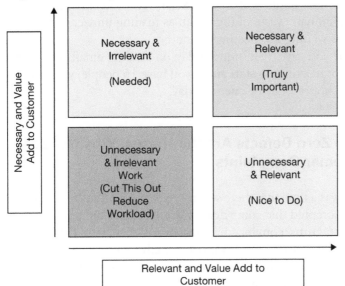

all, reading needless emails. If you spend 2 hours on emails, at least 30 minutes plus are useless. And if you are a department of 16 people, you are losing one man day on useless emails. Start thinking of this and eliminate useless work and start useful work for the Customer.

In *The Times of India*, March 8, 2013, they asked is "E-fatigue setting in? Firms may kill emails."

McKinsey is quoted as saying that employees spend 28% of their time reading, sorting, and sending emails every day.

CXOs, you have a choice of hiding behind the excuse of not having time, or doing something about it and in helping Customers get more Value. Act now!

Value Creation Pointers

- Many CXO's hide under the excuse of not having enough time for the Customer, or that they are doing so many things or they have other priorities.
- A task audit will reveal that 50–70% of the work is not necessary and relevant to the Customer.
- A task audit will make executives more productive and eliminate waste of time such as reading unnecessary emails or waiting for meetings to start.
- If you save 30 minutes a day on reading emails or waiting for meetings to start and if you have 16 people, you can save 8 hours a day or one man day.

When Zero Defects Are the Norms, Why Not Zero Customer Complaints

There was a time that there was no such phrase like "zero defects." It was accepted that some defects would always remain. But management gurus convinced management that zero defects were possible and also created competitive advantage.

Take safety. Hundred percent safety (or zero unsafety) is sought for. Why not zero complaints?

Today, it is accepted that Customer service is necessary, and good Customer service creates competitive advantage. Unfortunately, Customer service efficiency is measured by Customer satisfaction that measures transactions and not embedded feelings over a period of time as measured by Customer Value. Another measure is complaints per thousand interactions. Many companies are happy to have 10 or less complaints per thousand, or 1%. Some companies achieve 0.1% complaints. And they rest on their laurels.

Whenever a complaint gets escalated upwards to management, the general thought is to solve the complaint (and not always to the Customer's satisfaction). No one thinks about immediate systemic means to change processes and set procedures, so that these complaints do not occur in the future.

Much of this happens because the job of the managers is to solve the problem. They do not or are not asked to reach zero Customer complaints. If they were to look at the problem from this viewpoint, not only would the problem be solved, but also in future that complaint or Customer problem should not happen. Thus, ensure that information is easy to get and correct. Also, complaints are to be analyzed and root causes eliminated.

Let me give you an example from some of the most admired and large Indian companies.

I just bought overseas travel insurance on the net. Unfortunately, I had to extend the length of stay and consequently the number of days of insurance. The insurance was due to start a month from this time. I got on the phone and found that one number did not exist. The other one was difficult to get, and when I would get on and was made to answer many questions and listen to many unnecessary "ads," I would be put on hold for the next available agent. And then I would get disconnected. I had to go through a few iterations before I got to talk to an agent. No, the policy could not be extended (he did not know how). The best would be for me to cancel the policy and get a new one for a longer time period. So I requested cancellation. The agent could not tell me when I would get my refund. Almost 20 days later, I managed (through influence) to get the number of a senior executive. He was very apologetic. A few days later, I still did not have refund. So I sent an email again. This time an executive working for the company called me because his boss had asked him to help me get a refund. I had to fill a form for a refund. I told him I had not filled any form for getting the policy and why now, and why the call center had not told me about the form. To cut a long story short, he said he would arrange for a refund. The executives would never go back and get the problems corrected using software, processes, and procedures so that others would not have a problem, which would lead to zero Customer complaints.

Zero complaints are a worthwhile goal. Once you accept this, then you will start to work on it (conscientiously and consciously). This will reduce your complaints and costs, and increase profits.

A corollary of zero complaints is the reduction of unnecessary and irrelevant work. It will reduce unnecessary contact and effort with the Customer and make their journey shorter and more effective. Many of these problems happen because there is poor information; the Customer cannot understand a product or get adequate service, information on warranty, cannot find someone in the company, or has not got a reply. Or the Customer has a complaint and has problems with getting the complaint addressed. A start is to improve websites (many are inadequate and out of date) in order to reduce the Customer journey.

Another common reason for complaints is websites that have not been updated and have the wrong information, or the wrong information is given by the company people—certainly an area where there should be zero problems and zero complaints.

I urge companies to embrace the concept of zero Customer complaints and work on reducing problems for Customers. What a different Customer experience zero Customer complaints would bring! And it would improve your efficiency, reduce costs, and increase profits.

Value Creation Pointers

- Zero complaints are a worthwhile program to start.
- With changed mind-sets getting to zero complaints is possible.

- Many complaints are from error in information; ease of navigating websites and e-commerce, and systemic changes can eliminate these complaints.
- Some complaints are because of unnecessary Customer journeys.
- Zero complaints will also reduce unnecessary and irrelevant work.

5 Ideas for Creating Customer Value

When Don Hale of World of Customer Service asked me to suggest five tips on creating Customer Value, my first reaction was that everyone wants to focus on the things one should do. Working on Customer delight is easier than focusing on Customer disgust.

Much of the work that is done in Customer service is to give the Customer a good experience. Avoiding bad experiences are not given that much of a priority. There are processes and systems put into place to give a good experience and to make the Customers' journey more comfortable.

Despite this effort, all of us who are Customers (and that means every single one of us), still have persistent problems and heartaches in dealing with companies and service providers. Why is this?

Rather than answer the question, I suggest we look at typical problems and why they happen, and what might have prevented them from happening. We can then end this section with suggestions on the five tips.

Have you ever gone onto a website and found that you cannot get adequate or updated information? Take me as an example, I have often found that the addresses/phone numbers for offices are wrong and have landed up at a wrong office. Or there is no way to get updated information. Let's say, I deal with Joe Blow and I have his email, and Joe Blow leaves the company. I get an undelivered mail, and have no way of knowing who his replacement is. Try finding this information from the website (or at least to find the right person to get the information from). Often you are asked to fill in a form and submit it with your query but you get no response. Or you call the switch board (if any and provided you are not asked to punch an extension number or provided you don't have to wait an eternity), the person will ask who you are, why do you want to know, and so on. As if you are trying to steal the company's family jewels.

Or try using an Internet site for making a booking. Attempt making a hotel booking for two different types of rooms, an ordinary one and a deluxe one. You are not allowed to do so, and have to run the transaction twice. In India, the airlines offer you a minor discount (let's say ₹200 off on a ₹10,000 round-trip ticket) when you are booking online. Often the fine print does not show up. If it did show up and you could read it, you would find that if you had clicked this option you would lose cancellation rights. Or try filling out forms for overseas travel insurance where their form does not allow you to punch in your entire passport number (and the fine print there says wrong information will make the policy void).

I have told several senior executives of the insurance company about this and they all understand the problem but no one will react—"It ain't my job" syndrome at work. The problems related above have to do with lack of teamwork and poor communications. They also have to do with departmental silos.

The rules of the company look at the convenience of the company and not the convenience of the Customer.

Another example of the "not my job" syndrome, or the "I do not care" syndrome happened to me close to midnight at Marseilles airport. My flight was 3 hours late, and I went to pick up a Hertz car. Amex refused my payment. The Hertz lady was most helpful. She called Amex in Paris and asked for the card to be validated. The Paris lady could not, as this was a US card and could only be validated in the US. Could she connect me? No, she could not. Could she give me the US number? "Don't have it," she says. So I call Amex in India, get the US number and call the US and my card is validated.

Here is an example of an unnecessary Customer journey. Amex France could have seamlessly patched me to the US instead of extending my Customer journey unnecessarily. This is also an example of un-helpfulness, or of poor design of processes and systems.

I recently tried to book a hotel with a large group. They make you "chat" online with a rep. He then takes your information and sends it to sales, who come back to you at a snail's pace, causing you to become anxious, or wondering; Worse still, the payment I made through their gateway was for ₹20,999 but it showed on the Welcome Hotel site as ₹2,099,900! When I finally got through to them they said, "oh that is a decimal point error. Do not worry" (poor sap, me worrying about going broke, and it was only a decimal point error!) Who is going to ensure that the future Customers do not have this problem? Heaven knows!

Your payment transaction details response page:

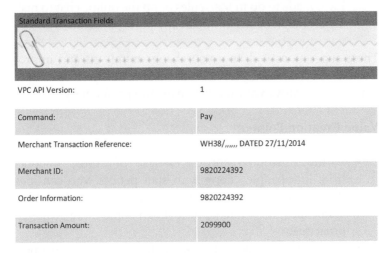

Standard Transaction Fields	
VPC API Version:	1
Command:	Pay
Merchant Transaction Reference:	WH38/,,,,, DATED 27/11/2014
Merchant ID:	9820224392
Order Information:	9820224392
Transaction Amount:	2099900

So what do we do? Here are my suggestions:

1. Form Customer-centric circles of cross-functional front-line people, along with staff people who can make things happen. These people will tell you about the problems that I have related above. This will also improve teamwork and help break silos. It will make front-line people more aware and proactive.
2. Have a communication system that allows you to update changes right away, and ensure the Customer has to make no unnecessary journey to get a new contact name or number or information.

3. Build in a Customers' Do Not Annoy (DNA) in the minds of your executives, not just the front-line people. Enable them (not empower them…empowerment without enabling information and tools is worthless) to put in processes and systems to prevent Customers from getting annoyed.
4. Give the convenience of the Customer the same, if not higher, priority than the convenience of the company, whether it is in refunds, cancellations, time, or energy. Reduce the Customer journey and avoid policies and actions (or inactions) that increase the Customer's journey.
5. Do not make the Customer anxious or keep him waiting, as I was made to do in Marseilles or on the online chat to make a reservation or when I made my hotel payment.

These suggestions will help you change mind-sets and improve Customer service and create more Value for your Customer, which will improve your market share and profitability.

Value Creation Pointers

- Form Customer-centric circles of cross-functional front-line people, along with staff people who can make things happen. This will also improve teamwork and help break silos. It will make front-line people more aware and proactive.
- Have a communication system that allows you to update and make systemic changes right away, and ensure that the Customer has to make no unnecessary journey to get a new contact name or number or information.
- Build in a Customers' DNA in the minds of your executives, not just the front-line people.
- Give the convenience of the Customer the same, if not higher, priority than the convenience of the company. Reduce the Customer journey and avoid policies and actions (or inactions) that increase the Customer's journey.
- Do not make the Customer anxious or keep him waiting.

PART 6

WORKPLACE CULTURE AND ORGANISATIONAL EFFICIENCY

PART   WORKPLACE CULTURE AND
6   ORGANISATIONAL EFFICIENCY

The Meaning and Importance of Managing Across Cultures

Branine, M.

━━━━━ LEARNING OUTCOMES ━━━━━

This chapter is designed to help the reader to:

1 Explain the triggers and drivers that have led to the emergence of managing across cultures;

2 Critically analyse interpretations of the concept of 'managing across cultures';

3 Outline the theoretical framework for the analysis of managing across cultures in diverse cultural settings.

Emergence of managing across cultures

Since the 1980s managing across cultures has emerged as a significant field of academic research and study. Its emergence is the result of a number of 'triggers' and 'drivers'. The triggers are those factors and events that raised the alarm about the importance of understanding cultural differences when operating in different countries; the drivers are those factors that resulted from, or contributed, to the triggers as shown in Table 2.1 below.

The triggers

First, we consider the triggers.

Table 2.1   The triggers and drivers of managing across cultures

Triggers	Drivers
Expatriates' failure to complete assignments abroad	Multinational companies
Recession in the 1980s	International competition
Economic development of Japan and South-east Asia	Regional economic integration
Economic development of China and India	Technical changes and flow of information
'Westernization' of Central and Eastern Europe	Trade and financial services
	Political and cultural influences
	Western management education and the use of English in business
	Reforms in developing countries

Expatriates' failure to complete assignments abroad

In international business, the first people to feel the crunch of working and living in different cultural settings are expatriates. Multinational companies (MNCs) depend on the knowledge and expertise of their expatriates to sustain the growth of their foreign investments (Bartlett and Ghoshal, 1989; Adler, 2002; Deresky, 2001). The role of an expatriate is to transfer the know-how, to control operations and to develop expertise in working in different countries. However, many expatriates have found it difficult to complete their assignments and this has created financial and operational problems for many MNCs. A number of studies reported that in the early 1980s as many as 70 per cent of US companies' expatriates did not complete their assignments abroad (Bartlett and Ghoshal, 1989; Evans et al., 1989; Adler, 2002; Deresky, 2001; Moran et al., 2007). Multinational companies started to feel the high cost failure of such. It became apparent that such failures originated in the expatriates' inability to understand the complexities of cultural differences and their consequent inability to successfully manage across cultures. Therefore many organizations have had to reconsider their recruitment, training and expatriation policies (Harris and Moran, 1991; Dowling, Welch and Schuler, 1999). Cultural awareness training has become a core subject in expatriates' pre-expatriation training.

Recession in the 1980s

The economic recession of the 1980s resulted in plant closures, mass redundancies and a sharp decline in international investments in the USA and Western Europe. Many US and European companies started to expand by shifting investments from home to a number of host countries, taking advantage of increased economies of scale and scope, and producing for different markets overseas in order to increase their profit margins. They benefited by shifting production from the west to the east and from the economically developed to the developing countries. They soon realized that they had to operate differently in the host countries. They had to introduce employment policies and practices that were more appropriate to the new socio-economic, political and cultural contexts. In order to gain competitive advantage, they have had to introduce international approaches to the employment, training, appraisal and reward of their increasingly culturally and nationally diverse workforce.

Economic development of Japan and South-east Asia

The emergence of Japan as a major industrialized nation in the 1970s, followed by South-east Asian countries, generated attempts to explain the causes of such success (Whitley, 1992; Chen, 2004; Tang and Ward, 2003). The success of Japanese companies was attributed to the management of their human resources and the implementation of manufacturing systems such as quality circles, just-in-time management and total quality management, as well as to the commitment and loyalty of their employees. Therefore, many large employers in the USA and Western Europe attempted to adopt Japanese production practices and employee relations policies with the aim of regaining competitive advantage they had lost in the world markets.

Moreover, the smaller economies – Hong Kong, South Korea, Taiwan, Singapore, Thailand and Malaysia – that followed in Japan's footsteps were known as 'tigers' because of their fast-growing and aggressive economic growth in the 1980s. While many Western countries experienced economic growth of less than 2 per cent, many South-east Asian countries grew at over 10 per cent. Therefore, many western companies became attracted to investing in South-east Asia. The move required not only the recruitment and development of employees who were inspired by and able to cope with the work ethics of Asian people but also an understanding of the socio-economic and political context in which people are employed.

Economic development of China and India

In late 1970s the government of the People's Republic of China (PRC) announced an open-door policy and began economic reforms aimed at moving the country from a centrally planned to a free market economy. Consequently the PRC became an increasingly important destination for foreign investment (Child, 1994; Nolan, 2001; Yan and Child, 2002). Companies investing in China have had to consider how to manage their resources in a country in transition between central planning and market economics. One of the major challenges for employers investing (most investments being joint ventures) in China is understanding Chinese culture and its impact on work and managerial behaviour (Tung, 1986, 2002; Easterby-Smith, Malina and Lu, 1995; Branine, 1997; Warner, 2003).

India has since the early 1990s embarked upon major economic reforms that have made it one of the largest stable and successful economies in the world. Foreign firms have been attracted by the formally educated and skilled workforce that is available throughout India. The recent move of some multinational companies' call centres from the US and Europe to India is an example of benefiting from an international labour market, though that has necessitated the introduction of cross-cultural training.

'Westernization' of Central and Eastern Europe

The end of the Cold War following the collapse of the communist bloc, the unification of Germany, and the dismantling of the Soviet Union has led to a gradual 'Westernization' of Eastern European countries. These developments have brought opportunities for multinational companies to expand their investments in central and Eastern Europe and in the former Soviet Union states. Many enterprises in the former communist countries have faced the need to implement economic reforms and to use Western ideas of free enterprise management. Polish, Hungarian and Czech companies, for example, no longer operate within the framework of national economic plans. The 'Westernization' process has required the transfer of market-related skills and management knowledge as well as investments from the US, Canada, Japan and Western European countries. However, for international investors to be successful in former communist countries they needed to understand local operations and to introduce locally responsive employment practices.

The drivers

Next, let us consider the drivers.

Multinational companies

Though multinational companies (MNCs) or transnational companies (TNCs) are not new, the rate by which they have developed since the 1970s has been extraordinary. Rapid increases in international activity have involved high levels of mergers and acquisitions, takeovers and joint ventures. While operating in different countries, MNCs have had to develop appropriate human resource strategies for attracting, recruiting and retaining local and international employees who are able to produce high-quality products and to provide high standards of services to meet the needs of customers in a competitive global market. There is no country in the world that has not been 'invaded' by multinational companies. Whether you are in the middle of the Sahara Desert or Siberia you can always find Coca Cola. As the number of MNCs increases the need for internationally minded managerial, professional and technical staff becomes greater and more attention has to be given to the way in which employees are employed, rewarded, trained and motivated to work effectively in different countries.

International competition

Many organizations have become similar in their distribution channels, technical standards and marketing approaches, products and production methods, giving customers similar choices worldwide. Increasingly, consumers from different countries are demanding products and services that are labelled world class. Customers are very much aware of the choices that are available to them at competitive prices. Therefore, local as well as international companies are being forced to compete on world-class standards to increase their chances of survival in uncertain business environments.

There is no one pattern of international competition because the forces that drive internationalization differ by industry, business, sector and location. However, the evidence from different international investors has shown that competitive successes or failures in the global market are strongly influenced by the quality of organizations' workforces (Peters and Waterman, 1982; Pfeffer, 1994; Ulrich and Black, 1999; Schuler, Jackson and Luo, 2004). Well-trained, skilled, and innovative employees can provide a competitive edge in markets where similar material and financial means of production are available. It is possible for almost any multinational company to acquire the necessary technology and capital, at a cost, but in many cases 'it is rather difficult to acquire a ready pool of highly qualified and highly motivated employees' (Sparrow, Schuler and Jackson, 1994: 269). The processes of obtaining and retaining the needed pool of skilled, motivated and highly qualified employees in different cultural settings require efficient management of resources across cultures.

Regional economic integration

The process of regional economic integration has driven the emergence and development of cross-cultural management. Trade relations between many countries have been improved by the establishment of bilateral and multilateral agreements, the creation of regional economic treaties such as the European Union (EU), the North American Free Trade Area (NAFTA) and the Association of South-east Asian Nations (ASEAN), and the involvement of international agencies such as the World Bank and the World Trade Organization (WTO). Economic integration and the commonality of regulations, as well as the equalization of taxes on a regional basis, have led to the development of common approaches to business and employment practices.

Technical changes and flow of information

Technical changes have led to the introduction of more productive and flexible working arrangements. The use of electronic control systems has made production and distribution processes more efficient, sophisticated and economic than before. For example, the advent of the internet has facilitated growth of international trade, international communications and easy access to information worldwide. Electronic mailing and information systems as well as the computerization of flight and shipping services are examples of current developments in information technologies. Customers can learn more about the goods they consume and many manufacturers are better informed about the needs of their customers. The international mobility of information has been enhanced by the integration of data processing and telecommunications networks on a global scale. Information can flow easily across borders, making geographical barriers less relevant and reducing the cost of travelling. Moreover, as information can be transferred quickly, rapid innovations can be effected in different countries, reducing lead times and product life cycles and increasing competition and cooperation between geographically dispersed organizations.

The speed and accuracy of information transmission are changing the nature of the international manager's job. Technology allows managers to access information and share it instantly. The internet is used increasingly by national and international companies for crucial HRM functions such as advertising job vacancies, contacting potential employees and online learning. The use of information technologies has led to an increasing demand for a workforce that is not just IT skilled but for also talented people with creative and innovative ideas as well as competency in languages.

Trade and financial services

Open trading between countries and instant availability of financial services has greatly facilitated global economic integration of capital markets. With the deregulation of financial services for international trade, it has become easier, faster and safer for companies to operate on the global scale. Many companies are no longer limited to capital sources within closed national boundaries. The global integration of national capital markets has led to freer flows of funds and easier investment between countries than at any time before.

As explained above, information technologies have facilitated international capital flows and provision of financial services to individual customers, suppliers and producers. Credit and debit card payments have led to virtual customers and virtual suppliers of worldwide products and services. The introduction of internet banking and the establishment of online businesses have opened up more opportunities for national and international, public and private companies to reach their customers, clients and employees in different locations.

Such developments have also created new challenges for MNCs as many small and medium size enterprises (SMEs) are trading internationally without requiring subsidiaries overseas. Consequently, managing diverse human resources across cultures has become important to all type and kind of organizations not just MNCs. There are examples of internationally successful companies that started with one person and his or her personal computer from the study in their own homes.

Political and cultural influences

Economic and political dependence of many developing countries on the west has led to the transfer of Anglo-Saxon and European education, political systems, technology, products, art works, and management theories to many countries of the world. Western cultural influences are evident globally and are embedded in people's daily encounters, from what we see and hear to what we consume in and outside our homes. People in developing countries have sometimes become more familiar with Western products, pop stars, film stars, football players, television presenters and politicians than with those in their own countries. Because of perceptions of Western progress, modernization, superiority and high standards, Western brands are sometimes preferred even when they are of poorer quality than those produced domestically. Here the role of the international media in advertising and promoting Western values is strong. This has strengthened a culture of capitalist consumerism and dependence on Western technology and investments.

Western culture is spreading around the world and penetrating people's lives everywhere. For example, in the Middle East the increasing presence of multinational companies is not only bringing requisite technology and management knowledge and skills from the west but also a culture of consumerism through their mass media advertising. Almost all major multinational companies of the world can now be found in the Middle East. Symbols of capitalism and Americanization such as McDonalds, Pizza Hut and KFC can be seen just metres away from the courtyard of the Holy Mosque in Mecca, Saudi Arabia. It is evident that the sustainability of increasing investments in different countries requires the employment and management of people with different cultural backgrounds and therefore the need to understand and implement cross-cultural management at both local and international levels.

Western management education and the use of English in business

Look at the composition of an MBA class in any American or British university and you get the picture of an ever-increasing internationalization of Western management education. More and more non-westerners are exposed to Western management education by attending courses at colleges and universities.

Moreover, the rapid dissemination of knowledge through international conferences, exchange programmes, publications, licensing, internet access and expatriation are narrowing the gap in the management 'know-how' between countries. Education has become one of the main drivers towards global integration as people are exposed to similar or the same knowledge and skills, and aspire to similar academic qualifications.

One way or another, management education is becoming universal. The management theories taught in MBA programmes, for example, in Chinese universities are likely to be the same as those that are being taught in MBA programmes in French, South African, Egyptian, Brazilian, Canadian or Indian universities. American and British management textbooks, which rarely make references to non-Western management experiences and practices, are adopted in universities, colleges and business schools throughout the world. What has made it even easier to disseminate such knowledge is the use of English as the international language of business. As more people are exposed to Western management knowledge and use English as their medium of instruction and as a means for business transactions, it becomes easier for companies to invest in different countries and therefore the drive to manage across cultures.

Reforms in developing countries

Many of the developing countries in Africa, South America and Asia have embarked on economic and political reforms that are aimed at liberalizing their economies and democratizing their political systems. Their socio-economic reforms have attracted increasing amounts of multinational investment. Economic reforms have led to large-scale privatizations of state-owned companies and to providing more opportunities for foreign direct investment. Many multinational companies have gained easy access to foreign assets and to overseas markets through direct ownership of foreign assets or forming joint ventures. The growth and expansion of international investments has driven the need for more knowledge and skills in managing across cultures.

ACTIVITY 1

What barriers or problems may be encountered by international managers seeking to manage across cultures?

The meaning of managing across cultures

So far we have seen the main reasons for studying the subject of managing across cultures and the major triggers and drivers for the emergence of the current widespread knowledge on cross-cultural management. We need now to consider of what 'managing across cultures' really consists. The subject is of course still evolving. Most of the available literature to date on managing across cultures or cross-cultural management (for example, Handy et al., 1988; Brewster and Tyson, 1991; Redding, 1994; Jackson, 1995; Hickson and Pugh, 1995; Gatley et al., 1996; Warner and Joynt, 2002; Budhwar and Sparrow, 2002a,b; Schneider and Barsoux, 2003; French, 2007; Browaeys and Price, 2008) has focused on the concept of culture and on the influence of cultural differences on doing business in different countries, rather than specifically on the process of *managing* across cultures. Though culture does indeed matter greatly in this context, the concept of culture is too complicated to be used in the kind of definition we require. The concept of culture and the different models of cultural differences will be discussed in the next chapter, where the context of managing across cultures is explained and critically analysed.

According to Adler (2002: 11), 'cross-cultural management explains the behaviour of people in organizations around the world and shows people how to work in organizations with employees and client populations from many different cultures'. Adler (2002: 11) adds that the aim of the study of cross-cultural management is to describe and compare organizational behaviour within countries and cultures, and to seek 'to understand and improve the interaction of co-workers, managers, executives, clients, suppliers, and alliance partners from countries and cultures around the world'. This description, however, concerns the study of cross-cultural management, rather than the process of managing across cultures.

Similarly, in the conventional literature on comparative management studies, the subject of managing across cultures has been assimilated to comparative management (see Negandhi, 1974; Ouchi, 1981), which in turn has been defined as a process of describing, analysing and discussing the policy and practice of management in two or more countries that makes it possible to see the main similarities and the main differences between them (Redding, 1994; Bamber and Lansbury, 2004).

It should be pointed out that the word 'across' in 'managing across cultures' implies, theoretically, having to go in between and within countries and cultures, and hence being able to observe, describe and analyse their similarities and differences. In practice, however, the process of managing across cultures is broader than comparative management because it implies (a) a broader understanding of the determining characteristics of national management systems and (b) the ability to distinguish between different systems and to learn from models of good (or bad) practice. This view of managing across cultures is supported by a number of recent studies. Some of these have focused on the ways in which national trends and characteristics, including socio-economic and political reforms, have influenced employment policies and practices in different countries (Brewster and Tyson, 1991; Budhwar and Debrah, 2001; Kamoche et al., 2004; Budhwar and Mellhi, 2006), while others have looked at aspects of management within and between countries by focusing on the impact of culture on business activities (Warner and Joynt, 2002; Schneider and Barsoux, 2003; Chen, 2004; French, 2007; Moran et al., 2007; Browaeys and Price, 2008). For instance, French (2007: 5) states that 'cross-cultural encounters might, for example, occur when companies decide to outsource work to new countries, or when organizations enter into new forms of networked relationships with overseas partners, or as a result of increased migration of labour'.

However, the study of managing across cultures should go beyond examination of the cultural encounters of multinational companies or of the similarities and differences between countries so as to determine the ways by which national differences have influenced employment policies and practices of different countries and the ways by which international companies have responded to them as shown in Figure 2.1 below. In this respect, Budhwar and Sparrow (2002b: 600) make the point that managers have become 'eager to know how human resources (HRs) are managed in different regions of the world' and added that 'in order to maximize cross-national management capabilities, we need to understand *how* people in different national settings respond to similar concepts within their particular functions' (p. 600).

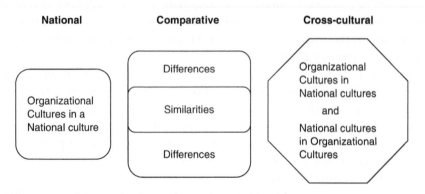

Figure 2.1   National, comparative and cross-cultural management

Managing across cultures is thus a two-way process that involves national and international employees and employers of different organizations in different countries and cultural settings. In this book, managing across cultures is defined simply as the process of *managing local employees globally and global employees locally*. This process involves a strategic approach whereby every employee is expected to act locally and think globally (see Figure 2.2 below). Understanding this process leads, not only to gaining knowledge of different national contexts and to comparing them, but also to international organizations learning the knowledge and skills of managing resources internationally in different national contexts.

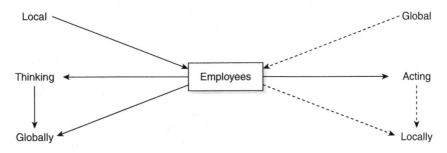

Figure 2.2 The process of managing across cultures

Managing local employees globally

It can be concluded from the drivers outlined above that the globalizing power of business has created common economic, technical and managerial imperatives, despite social, ideological and legal differences. Multinational companies have been the creators of cross-cultural management policy and practice, and have been the main drivers for international convergence rather than divergence. Multinational companies are the main contributors to the globalizing power of business as they have a significant presence in world business in terms of production, trade and employment.

However, one of the main challenges for international organizations in general and multinational companies in particular is to manage local employees globally, strategically and successfully in response to an ever increasing internationalization or globalization of business. The management of local employees globally requires, at least, the building of a global corporate culture that local employees can understand and identify with, and having a forward diffusion employment strategy.

Building a global corporate culture

Global corporate culture is the glue that can keep a global network of activities together (Rhinesmith, 1993). Corporate culture consists of shared visions, systems, mechanisms and processes. These four factors are created by the people on whom the organization depends, from the visions of the founding members or managing directors of the organization to the processes being carried out by employees at the shop-floor level. The building of a sustainable global corporate culture requires an international human resource development strategy that forms an integral part of corporate culture and that helps to create a global mindset in its key employees regardless of their place of work (Hendry, 1991; Srinivas, 1995). In other words, all employees become aware of the main features of that corporate culture and contribute effectively to the achievement of its objectives.

One of the main aspects of a globalising corporate culture is standardization of policies and practices throughout the organization (Bartlett and Ghoshal, 1998; Dickmann et al., 2009). Standardization throughout the organization enhances efficiency through the streamlining of production processes, employment policies, product development, and other activities. As more organizations engage actively in global operations, their activities are likely to lead to social as well as economic changes in societies around the world. For example, all employees working for McDonalds in London, Manhattan, Beijing or Moscow are expected to behave the same way and to serve the same products. The uniform, the grading stars, the service with a smile, the up-selling, the french fries, etc. are all standardized throughout the company in different parts of the world. However, standardization of operations, behaviours and products requires efficient training of local employees to carry out their tasks in the organization's way and the development of local and international managers to make sure that their organization operates in such a way. This process requires a forward diffusion of knowledge and skills and an HR strategy at the core of the organization's corporate strategy.

Forward diffusion of knowledge and skills

To ensure that local employees are successfully managed globally it is crucial to develop a global employment strategy that enables local employees to learn the knowledge and skills that make them globally employable. This process is very often referred to in the international management literature as 'forward diffusion' of knowledge and skills from the home to the host country (Edwards and Ferner, 2004; Edwards et al., 2005).

The forward diffusion of management theory and practice affects not only the local employees of a particular multinational organization but also employees of other indigenous and international organizations. For example, the Japanization of local industries through the increasing presence of Japanese MNCs has led to the adoption of employment policies and practices such as quality circles, total quality management, just-in-time management, pendulum arbitration, and single union representation by many non-Japanese companies in different countries.

=== **MINI CASE STUDY 1** ===

The Western Expatriate in West Africa

When asked about the working and living conditions of expatriates, Mrs Celia Ugboko, the managing director of a major petroleum company in West Africa, replied, 'Western expatriates are highly valued, highly paid, well respected and admired for their knowledge and expertise, commitment to their work, dedication, careful attention to detail, respect for time, and tolerance and sensitivity to other cultures. Our respectful treatment of foreigners has led to increasing numbers of Western and non-Western (third country) expatriates and has facilitated forward diffusion of Western management practices and policies to my country.'

Questions

1 Speculate on (a) the context in which the comment was made and (b) what might be the positive and the negative connotations of Mrs Ugboko's statement.
2 Judging from the manager's comment, what types of knowledge and skills do you think the local employees may learn from forward diffusion?

Managing global employees locally

Just as local employees have to be managed globally through the building of global corporate culture and the forward diffusion of knowledge and skills, global employees, mainly expatriates, have to be managed locally in order to achieve their assignment objectives successfully. Global employees, as home country expatriates or third country employees, have to understand the local working environment, the local employees, the local institutions and the local norms and values in order to work with or to manage the local workforces globally. In other words, global employees have to respond to the localizing power of culture and, very often, politics as well.

National differences in norms, values, traditions and beliefs, in levels of economic growth and development, and in institutional settings are the main sources for divergence in management policies and practices between societies. Though it is possible to assimilate organizational structures, to rationalize processes and to standardize products and services between countries, it is not, as Adler (2002) pointed out, easy to assimilate people's behaviour because of their culturally, economically and politically based differences. Therefore managing across cultures requires managers to be aware of the effects that these differences may have on their management policies and practices. They should be aware of the main national norms and values, of the national economic trends and organizational characteristics, and of the national institutions and the legal system.

National norms and values

National norms and values shape the ways in which organizations are designed and run in different countries because the degree to which people regard their work as a central life interest or as an onerous task is affected by their national values, norms and beliefs. The types of social relations and the power structure in family and society, the different norms and expectations related to leadership, social interaction and relationships, and perceptions of emotions differ significantly between countries (Hofstede, 1980a, 1991; Adler, 2002; Deal and Kennedy, 1982; Laurent, 1986; Whitley, 1992; Tayeb, 2003; 2005). As will be explained in more detail in Chapter 3, culture seriously matters in managing across cultures: cultural misunderstandings can easily cause business relationships to be broken, resources and time to be wasted, employees to be offended and international managers ashamed. Selmer (2001: 17) rightly states that 'not being able to interact with the host country nationals in daily life outside work makes expatriates ignorant about local thinking and mentality, which influences their ability to assess work situations and makes them develop erroneous assumptions about the people they are managing'. Therefore it is important for expatriates to interact frequently with the locals and to learn from the local values and norms. This process of national acculturation makes expatriates 'less surprised and frustrated by differences in non-work circumstances of the host country' (Selmer, 2001: 17).

When managing across cultures, international managers become more aware of social differences within individual countries and have to understand the impact of regional, tribal and other in-group and within-group alliances and differences in the way organizations are managed. Therefore, understanding the different norms, values and ways of life in the host country helps not only with the introduction of appropriate employment policies, but also the production of the right products and the provision of needed services. For example, Procter and Gamble faced problems of national preferences and differences when it developed the Visor washing power. It found that Germans generally preferred front-loading washing machines and they thought that the only way to clean white clothes was to use boiling hot water, while French consumers preferred the top-loading machines and did not think it was necessary to use boiling hot water to wash whites. However, the newly introduced Visor washing power was developed to clean whites best in cool water and in front-loading washers. It satisfied neither the Germans nor the French. According to Ulrich and Black (1999: 43), 'as the firm discovered, it is not easy to change people's deeply held beliefs on laundering their whites. Neither is it easy to get a nation to change from front-loading washing machines to top-loading ones'.

When managing across cultures it becomes apparent that what is moral or not, whether religious or just customary, is defined clearly in the relationships of people and is culturally specific. For example, respecting and protecting older people, hospitality, decency and pity, not wasting food and water, and even showing shyness and humility are common cultural values in many countries in the world, but some societies express them more openly than others. In Eastern cultures, it is very unlikely that a younger person would oppose the opinion of an older one. This does not mean, however, that talented and skilled young employees are denied respect and promotion. Therefore, international managers should be aware of such cultural values and take into account how their employees in a particular social context expect them to react and behave.

While emphasizing the importance of cultural awareness, we should also stress that international managers do not need to learn all the languages, convert to the religions of the host countries, or behave exactly like the local people (Torrington, 1994). This happens rarely. The process of managing global employees locally implies that international managers need a good understanding of the local norms, values, customs, history, geography and laws because these are among the main determinants of local identity and national pride. For example, until recently the expatriates who criticize or even refuse to attend a bull-fighting match in Spain may lose the support of local employees who see such a game as part of their national culture.

Host country values and practices have a significant influence on management practices and employment policies at all levels. Therefore, international managers will have to adapt to different working conditions and sometimes operate differently from the way they did in their home countries. For example, when working in African or Middle Eastern countries they may have to accept the hiring of friends and relatives, giving more consideration to trustworthiness and loyalty, and using red tape and cumbersome bureaucratic procedures, because such practices are customary in the host country and respected by the local managers and employees. Such differences should be seen as an opportunity to doing good business rather than a threat.

National economic trends and organizational characteristics

It has very often been argued that societies differ in their management systems according to their levels of economic growth and organizational characteristics (Lammers and Hickson, 1979; Hickson and McMillan, 1981; Ouchi, 1981; Hickson and Pugh, 2001). Countries with similar levels of economic growth and development may develop, and should at least be able to share, some managerial practices. A number of studies have concluded that the difficulties encountered by international managers in developing countries, when trying to implement Western management theories, occur mainly because such theories reflect the level of economic development of their inventors (Hofstede, 1980b, 1993; Srinivas, 1995). Hence, in managing across cultures, understanding the economic environment of the foreign operating country can help international managers to operate effectively when dealing with suppliers and customers, for example, and to predict trends and events that might affect their organizations' future performance.

Moreover, it is also important in managing across cultures to understand the main characteristics of organizations in the host country because the way organizations are managed differs from one society to another; depending on their structure, culture and process (Hickson et al., 1974; Ouchi, 1981; Hickson and McMillan, 1981). For example, in many African, Middle Eastern and South-east Asian countries, organizations are centralized and bureaucratic, and the delegation of authority is often made to relatives and trusted close friends. Misunderstanding of different organizational structures and management practices in the host countries can result in international managers making inappropriate business decisions, as seen from Mini Case Study 2 below.

National institutions and legal systems

A number of studies have found that patterns of national distinctiveness such as the country's history, its national and regional institutions, its political system and its legislative procedures have strong influence on management and employee relations (Whitley, 1992; Child, 1994; Chen, 2004). In managing across cultures, one of the most important institutions that international managers have to be aware of is the host country's education system. The types of education and training programmes delivered in a country are very likely to influence the structure and development of organizations, and to shape the nature and quality of its workforce. By understanding the education system and the types and levels of education in the host country it will be easier for international managers to decide how local employees could be trained and how easily technology can be transferred and implemented effectively. Also, it is important for international managers to understand how local employees learn in order to design appropriate training programmes for them.

The other important institutional factor in managing across cultures is the legal system of the host country. Being aware of international laws as well as host country legal systems and employment legislation is mandatory in cross-cultural management. Ball and McCulloch (1993: 370) argued that 'international business is affected by many thousands of laws and regulations on hundreds of subjects that have been issued by states, nations, and international organizations'. These laws can be divided into international and national laws, and they affect factors such as taxation, employment, trade relations, health and safety, imports and exports (including tariff controls), financial reporting, product liability, intellectual property, contracts, and currency control within and between countries.

Assessing and avoiding risks

The process of managing across cultures sits between the globalizing power of business and the localizing power of culture and politics. The problem in implementing such a process effectively lies in knowing the unknown. In this respect, it can be argued that the more is known by the international manager (expatriate) about the local working environment and the local employees, and the more the local employees know about the corporate culture and its operations, the greater and the better global integration and local responsiveness there will be and hence greater effectiveness in managing across cultures. The factors that facilitate the process of knowing the unknown are: the ability to assess and avoid risks by both local and international employees; and the encouragement of 'reverse diffusion' of management good practice from the host to the home country.

Although many countries have opened their doors to foreign investment, there are still problems of local acceptance that should not be underestimated in managing across cultures. When investing in a foreign country, MNCs should assess the risks involved in employing expatriates and local employees. It should be stressed that though the governments of many countries welcome foreign direct investment, they also have responsibility for protecting their own industries and citizens. Protectionism takes different forms, from trade barriers and quotas to employment restrictions, which MNCs have to be prepared for and deal with effectively. Moreover, the outcomes of inter-governmental conflicts, pacts and bilateral relations can have significant effects on managing across cultures.

Although many developing countries offer large market potential and exhibit strong economic growth, investing in them can be riskier than investing in industrialized countries. Most of the developing countries in Asia, Africa and South America have experienced complex and unstable political systems in their attempts to develop suitable frameworks and ideologies for their socio-economic development. There may also be financial and economic risks because of environmental (climate) changes, terrorism, international labour migration, fluctuations in demand for certain products, shortages in the supply of raw materials, international financial crisis, and so on, that international managers should be able to assess and avoid their impact whenever possible. Such risks have serious implication for the international operations of a firm and for the process of managing across cultures.

Local employees and governments should also be able to assess the risks of increasing presence of international corporate cultures and of forward diffusion of knowledge and skills from other countries. Local industries and business could be seriously affected by the direct international competition created by MNCs. The privatization of public utilities, mergers and takeovers could result in the restructuring of newly created companies and the downsizing of operations, resulting in mass redundancies in countries where unemployment, especially among the young people, is already very high. Another risk is the cultural influence of MNCs in countries that are already very receptive to Western capitalist norms and values. It will be seen from the relevant chapters of this book that the culture of consumerism, greed and competition is spreading throughout Eastern societies with increasing rapidity, partly, if not mainly, because of the spread of foreign investment in that part of the world.

MINI CASE STUDY 2

General Electric in Hungary

In the late 1980s the USA's General Electric Company (GE) moved into Hungary, which was then a communist state. It bought 51 per cent of the Tungsram Company, a producer of lighting products. It believed that it was making a good investment decision to take advantage of Hungary's move towards democracy and a free market economy.

What the company did not expect were the organizational problems that it encountered. Under years of communism there was a strong tradition of waste and inefficiency. There was no motive for individual employees to produce good-quality products. The concepts of customer care and customer satisfaction were alien to many Hungarian employees. The American managers thought that the Hungarian workers were too 'laid back' and the Hungarian employees thought that their American managers were 'too aggressive'.

It took eight years, $440 million and a 50 per cent cut in the workforce before the company began to make profits (Ulrich and Black, 1999).

Question

1 What are the main lessons for managing across cultures to be drawn from this case study?

Reverse diffusion of knowledge and skills

It is argued above that 'forward' diffusion is important for managing local employees globally and for global business integration. Equally, 'reverse' diffusion of management policies and practices from the host to the home country should be encouraged for managers to learn more about local management systems (Edwards, 1998; Edwards et al., 2005).

Reverse diffusion is part of the national identification process as international managers are informed of the national characteristics of organizations and managements in different countries. Ulrich and Black (1999) argued that one of the managerial competencies that may enable international companies to integrate and concentrate global activities while attempting to separate and adapt to local activities is to share learning and generate new knowledge from the local operations. Encouraging reverse diffusion of management theories and practices can lead to better understanding of the local working environment and to the development of appropriate approaches to managing across cultures.

Summary

1   The subject of managing across cultures has emerged in recent years as a significant field of academic research and study as a result of a number of triggers and drivers. Among the triggers are: the failure of expatriates to complete their assignments abroad; the economic recession of the 1980s; the rise and successes of South-east Asian countries; the openness of China and later India to the west; and the end of the Cold War and the 'Westernization' of Eastern Europe. The main drivers have been: the growth and spread of multinational companies; international competition; regional economic integration; technical changes and international mobility of information; open trading and availability of financial services; political and cultural influences; internationalization of Western management education with the use of English as the international language of business; and the liberalization and democratization of developing countries.

2   Most of the definitions of managing across cultures focus on the concept of culture and the effects of cultural differences on management in different countries. This book acknowledges the importance of culture and its effects on management and goes beyond the need to understand the similarities and differences between societies to see the process of managing across cultures as the management of local employees globally and global employees locally, including expatriates, host and third country employees, national and international employee regulations, and national and international employee and employer organizations.

3   The management of local employees globally requires, at least, the building of a global corporate culture that local employees can understand and identify with, and having a strategy of forward diffusion of knowledge and skills from the home to the host countries.

4   Just as local employees have to be managed globally, global employees, mainly expatriates, have to be managed locally in order to achieve their assignments successfully. Global employees have to understand the local working environment, employees, institutions, and norms and values in order to manage the local workforce globally.

5   The process of managing across cultures sits between the globalizing power of business and the localizing power of culture and politics. The problem in implementing such a process effectively lies in knowing the unknown. The more familiar the international manager (expatriate) is with the local working environment and local employees, and the more the local employees know about the corporate culture and its operations, the greater and better the global integration and local responsiveness. The factors that may facilitate the process of knowing the unknown are the ability to assess and avoid risks, and the encouragement of 'reverse diffusion' of management good practice from the host to the home country.

Revision questions

1 Discuss with the use of examples the main factors and events that have led to the emergence of cross-cultural management as a significant field of academic research and study.
2 What does 'managing across cultures' mean? Elaborate your answer by referring to at least two contrasting definitions.
3 What do you think are the main things that international organizations can do to be successful in (a) managing global employees locally and (b) managing their local employees globally?

References

Adler, N. (2002) *International Dimensions of Organizational Behaviour*, 4th edn, Cincinnati, OH: South-Western College Publishing/Thomson Learning.
Ball, D.A. and McCulloch, W.H. (1993) *International Business: Introduction and Essentials*, London: Irwin.
Bamber, G.J. and Lansbury, R.D. (eds) (2004) *International and Comparative Employment Relations*, 4th edn, London: Sage.
Bartlett, C.A. and Ghoshal, S. (1998) *Managing Across Borders: The Transnational Solution*, 2nd edn, London: Century Business.
Branine, M. (1997), 'Change and continuity in Chinese employment relationships', *New Zealand Journal of Industrial Relations*, 22(1): 77–94.
Brewster, C. and Harris, H. (1999), *International HRM: Contemporary Issues in Europe*, London: Routledge.
Brewster, C. and Tyson, S. (eds) (1991) *International Comparisons in Human Resource Management*, London: Pitman.
Briscoe, D.R. and Schuler, R.S. (2004), *International Human Resource Management*, 2nd edn, London: Routledge.
Browaeys, M.J. and Price, R. (2008) *Understanding Cross-cultural Management*, Harlow: Prentice-Hall/Financial Times.
Budhwar, P. and Debrah, Y.A. (eds) (2001) *Human Resource Management in Developing Countries*, London: Routledge.
Budhwar, P. and Mellahi, K. (eds) (2006) *Managing Human Resources in the Middle East*, London: Routledge.
Budhwar, P. and Sparrow, P. (2002a), 'An integrative framework for determining cross-national human resource management practices', *Human Resource Management Review*, 12(3): 377–403.
Budhwar, P. and Sparrow, P. (2002b) 'Strategic HRM through the cultural looking glass: mapping cognitions of British and Indian HRM managers', *Organization Studies*, 23(4): 599–638.
Chen, M. (2004) *Asian Management Systems*, 2nd edn, London: Thomson Learning.
Child, J. (1994) *Management in China in the Era of Reform*, Cambridge: Cambridge University Press.

Deal, T.E. and Kennedy, A.A. (1982) *Corporate Cultures: The Rites and Rituals of Corporate Life*, Reading, MA: Addison-Wesley.

Deresky, H. (2001) *International Management: Managing Across Borders and Cultures*, London: Prentice-Hall.

Dickmann, M., Müller-Camen, M. and Kelliher, C. (2009) 'Exploring standardisation and knowledge networking processes in transnational human resource management', *Personnel Review*, 38(1): 5–25.

Dowling, P.J., Festing, M. and Engle, A.D., Sr (2008) *International Human Resource Management*, 5th edn, London: Thomson Learning.

Dowling, P.J., Schuler, R.S. and Welch, D.E. (1994) *International Dimensions of Human Resource Management*, 2nd edn, Belmont, CA: Thomson International and Wadsworth.

Dowling, P.J., Welch, D.E. and Schuler, R.S. (1999) *International Human Resource Management: Managing People in a Multinational Context*, 3rd edn, Cincinnati, OH: South-Western College Publishing.

Easterby-Smith, M., Malina, D. and Lu, Y. (1995) 'How culture sensitive is HRM?: A comparative analysis of practice in Chinese and UK companies', *The International Journal of Human Resources Management*, 6(1): 31–59.

Edwards, T. (1998) 'Multinationals and the process of reserve diffusion', *International Journal of Human Resource Management*, 9(4): 696–709.

Edwards, T. and Ferner, A. (2004) 'Multinationals, national business systems and reverse diffusion', *Management International Review*, 24(1): 51–81.

Edwards, T., Almond, P., Clark, I., Colling, T. and Ferner, A. (2005) 'Reverse diffusion in US multinationals: barriers from the American business system', *Journal of Management Studies*, 42(6): 1261–86.

Evans, P., Doz, Y. and Laurent, A. (1989) *Human Resource Management in International Firms*, London: Macmillan.

French, R. (2007) *Cross-Cultural Management in Work Organisations*, London: CIPD.

Gatley, S., Lessem, R. and Altman, Y.(1996), *Comparative Management: A Transcultural Odyssey*, London: McGraw-Hill.

Handy, C., Gordon, C., Gow, I. and Randlesome, C. (1988) *Making Managers*, London: Pitman.

Harris, P.R. and Moran, R.T. (1991) *Managing Cultural Differences: High-performance Strategies for a New World of Business*, Texas: Gulf Publishing.

Harzing, A.W. and Ruysseveldt, J.V. (2004) (eds.), *International Human Resource Management: An Integrated Approach*, 2nd edn, London: Sage.

Hendry, C. (1991) 'International comparisons of human resource management: putting the firm in the frame', *The International Journal of Human Resource Management*, 2(3): 415–40.

Hickson, D.J., Hinings, C.R., McMillan, C.J. and Schwitter, J.P. (1974) 'The culture-free context of organization structure: a tri-national comparison', *Sociology*, 8: 59–80.

Hickson, D.J. and McMillan, C.J. (eds) (1981) *Organization and Nation: The Aston Programme IV*, Aldershot: Gower.

Hickson, D.J. and Pugh, D.S. (1995) *Management Worldwide: The Impact of Societal Culture on Organizations Around the Globe*, London: Penguin.

Hickson, D.J. and Pugh, D.S. (2001) *Management Worldwide*, 2nd edn, Harmondsworth: Penguin.

Hofstede, G. (1980a) *Culture's Consequences: International Differences in Work Related Values*, London: Sage.

Hofstede, G. (1980b) 'Motivation, leadership and organization: do American theories apply abroad?', *Organizational Dynamics*, Summer, 1980.

Hofstede, G. (1991) *Culture and Organizations: Software of the Mind*, London: McGraw-Hill.

Hofstede, G. (1993) 'Cultural constraints in management theories', *Academy of Management Executive*, 7(1): 81–94.

Jackson, K. and Tomioka, M. (2004) *The Changing Face of Japanese Management*, Routledge: London.

Jackson, T. (1995) *Cross-Cultural Management*, Oxford: Butterworth-Heinemann.

Kamoche, K.N., Debrah, Y., Horwitz, F. and Muuka, G.N. (eds) (2004) *Managing Human Resources in Africa*, London: Routledge.

Kanter, R.M. (1995) *World Class: Thriving Locally in the Global Economy*, New York: Simon & Schuler.

Lammers, C.J. and Hickson, D.J. (1979) *Organizations Alike and Unlike: International and Inter-institutional Studies in the Sociology of Organizations*, London: Routledge & Kegan Paul.

Laurent, A. (1986) 'The cross-cultural puzzle of international HRM', *Human Resource Management*, 25: 91–102.

Moran, R.T., Harris, P.R. and Moran, S.V. (2007) *Managing Cultural Differences: Global Leadership Strategies for the 21st Century*, 7th edn, Oxford: Butterworth-Heinemann.

Negandhi, A.R. (1974) 'Cross-cultural management studies: too many conclusions, not enough conceptualizations', *Management International Review*, 14: 59–72.

Nolan, P. (2001) *China and the Global Business Revolution*, London: Palgrave, New York: St.Martin's Press.

Ohmae, K. (1990) *The End of the Nation State*, New York: Free Press.

Ouchi, W.G. (1981) *Theory Z: How American Management Can Meet the Japanese Challenge*, Reading, MA: Addison-Wesley.

Peters, T. and Waterman, R. (1982) *In Search of Excellence*, New York: Harper & Row.

Pfeffer, J. (1994) *Competitive Advantage Through People: Unleashing the Power of the Workforce*, Boston: Harvard Business School Press.

Redding, G.S. (1994) 'Comparative management theory: jungle, zoo or fossil bed?', *Organisation Studies*, 15(3): 323–59.

Rhinesmith, S.H. (1993) *A Manager's Guide to Globalization: Six Keys to Success in a Changing World*, Chicago: Richard D. Irwin.

Rosenzweig, P. M., Nohria, N. (1994) 'Influences on human resource management practices in multinational corporations' *Journal of International Business Studies*, 25(2): 229–251.

Schneider, S.C. and Barsoux, J.L. (2003) *Managing Across Cultures*, 2nd edn, Harlow: Prentice-Hall/Financial Times.

Schuler, R.S., Dowling, P.J. and De Cieri, H. (1993) 'An integrative framework of strategic international human resource management', *International Journal of Human Resource Management*, 4(6): 717–64.

Schuler, R.S., Jackson, S.E. and Luo, Y. (2004) *Managing Human Resources in Cross-Border Alliances*, London, Routledge.

Selmer, J. (2001) 'Adjustment of Western European vs. North American expatriate managers in China', *Personnel Review*, 30(1): 6–21.

Sparrow, P., Schuler, R.S. and Jackson S.E. (1994) 'Convergence or divergence: human resource practices and policies for competitive advantage world-wide', *The International Journal of Human Resource Management*, 5(2): 267–99.

Srinivas, K.M. (1995) 'Globalization of business and the third world: challenges of expanding the mindsets', *Journal of Management Development*, 14(3): 26.

Tang, J. and Ward, A. (2003) *The Changing Face of Chinese Management*, Working in Asia Series, London: Routledge.

Tayeb, M.H. (2003) *International Management: A Cross-cultural Approach*, Harlow: Prentice-Hall/Financial Times.

Tayeb, M.H. (2005) *International Human Resource Management: A Multinational Company Perspective*, Oxford: Oxford University Press.

Torrington, D. (1994) *International Human Resource Management: Think Globally, Act Locally*, Hemel Hempstead: Prentice-Hall.

Tung, R.L., (1986) 'Corporate executives and their families in China: the need for cross-cultural understanding in business', *The Columbia Journal of World Business*, 21(1): 21–6.

Tung, R.L. (2002) 'Managing in Asia: cross-cultural dimensions', in Warner, M. and Joynt, P. (eds), *Managing Across Cultures: Issues and Perspectives*, 2nd edn, London: Thomson Learning, 137–42.

Ulrich, D. and Black, S. (1999) 'Worldly wise', *People Management*, 5(21): 42–6.

Warner, M. (1995) *The Management of Human Resources in Chinese Industry*, Basingstoke: Macmillan and New York: St. Martins Press.

Warner, M. (ed.) (2003) *Culture and Management in Asia*, London: Routledge Curzon.

Warner, M. and Joynt, P. (2002) *Managing Across Cultures: Issues and Perspectives*, 2nd edn, London: Thomson Learning.

White, M. and Trevor, M. (1983) *Under Japanese Management*, London; Heinmann.

Whitley, R.D. (1992) *Business Systems in East Asia: Firms, Markets and Societies*, London: Sage.

Yan, Y. and Child, J. (2002) 'An analysis of strategic determinants, learning and decision-making in Sino–British joint ventures', *British Journal of Management*, (13): 109–22.

Organizational Culture and Leadership

Alvesson, M.

Leadership often seems to be used as a rather straightforward and uncomplicated concept. But, like culture, it easily captures 'everything and nothing' and is often used in extremely vague and all-embracing ways. We need to think about more precise understandings of how the term 'leadership' should be used. In this chapter a cultural approach to leadership is developed. This includes the organizational cultural framing of leadership as well as how the action of 'leaders' influences the meanings, values, ideas and feelings of others.

What is Leadership?

There is a wide spectrum of definitions of leadership. Yukl (1989) says that 'the numerous definitions of leadership that have been proposed appear to have little else in common' than involving an influence process. This takes place within an asymmetrical relationship: the leader is exercising influence over the follower. Yukl himself defines leadership 'to include influencing task objectives and strategies, influencing commitment and compliance in task behavior to achieve these objectives, influencing group maintenance and identification, and influencing the culture of an organization' (p. 253). This definition is probably more thoughtful than many others in the literature. But one could very well substitute the word 'culture' for 'leadership' and have a definition of culture. Or swap leadership and strategy. One could also replace leadership with organizational structure, job design, social identity or something else. As mentioned in Chapter 5, Weick (1985) has used this trick to show how some definitions of strategy and culture are roughly the same. Despite the shortcomings of definitions and the similarities of what many popular terms refer to, in practice they trigger different meanings and lead to different lines of thinking, related to the context in which the terms are used.

'Leadership' is typically defined in general terms. The ambition is to say something of relevance across quite diverse settings, and frequently to discover the formula for effective leadership. The diversity of relations, situations and cultural contexts in which superior–subordinate interactions take place means that a coherent definition with universal aspirations may tell us relatively little in terms of the richness and complexity of the phenomena it supposedly refers to. It is then rather difficult to claim that 'leadership' as a general term and object of study stands in a clear relationship to a particular, distinct group of phenomena that can be conceptualized in a uniform manner. The efforts to capture variety through variables such as personnel orientation and initiating structure are not very helpful. There are two interrelated problems: the social worlds of interest to leadership researchers do not easily lend themselves to neat categorization and ordering, and language use has its limitations in relation to the goal of fixing meaning through definitions. In addition, leadership is very much a matter of how people involved view the subject matter.

Understanding leadership calls for careful consideration of the social context in which processes of leadership take place. Leadership is not just a leader acting and a group of followers responding in a mechanical way, but a complex social process in which the meanings and interpretations of what is said and done are crucial. Leadership, then, is closely related to culture – at the organizational and other levels. Understanding what a farm manager in Kenya, a female senior police officer in the USA and a Greenpeace spokesperson in Russia are trying to do in their relationships with people supposed to be following them, and even why Brutus betrayed Caesar, calls for a careful consideration of the specific cultural context of these relationships and interactions. This context includes the societal, occupational and organizational – which all frame specific leader–follower interactions.

What is defined as 'leadership' calls for not just a theoretical definition but also close consideration of what a particular group mean by leadership and how it relates to leaders and leadership. For different groups, leadership has different meanings and values. Generally, and at the risk of overgeneralizing, it is a common impression that while North Americans seem to rate leadership favourably, many Europeans have for some time been somewhat less enthusiastic, possibly as a result of their experiences of the 1930s and 1940s, when leaders such as Hitler, Mussolini and Stalin demonstrated how dangerous strong enthusiasm for the leader can be. Leadership may lead to followers being enchanted by the leader, ceasing to think autonomously and following routes leading to disaster. Some of the US enthusiasm for leadership has, however, been exported recently and leadership is today a hot topic more or less globally.

Although it may appear slightly stifling in countries with more egalitarian – and less hero-worshipping – traditions, many people in the USA seem to favour an ideology of celebrating strong, individualistic, masculine characters who can lead (Den Hartog and Dickson, 2004; Lipman-Blumen, 1992; Prasad, 1997). A typical view here is the leader as a commander – strong, in charge, superior, heroic, capable of bringing others up to standard (Spicer, 2011). Although recent developments may have included a de-masculinization of management as teams, networks and knowledge are seen as increasingly salient features of contemporary organizations (Fondas, 1997), still-popular approaches such as transformational leadership assume that the strong and powerful heroic leader exercises very significant influence on the followers clearly in need of the vision, the inspiration, the identification and the support provided by the great leader – see Hartnell and Walumbwa (2011) and Sashkin (2004) for illustrations of such a view, and Alvesson and Spicer (2011) and Bolden et al. (2011) for critiques.

US researchers strongly dominate leadership research, giving popular views an imperialistic overtone. Apart from avoiding the universalist aspiration coming from US dominance, there are other good reasons to clearly consider national variations. There are also significant variations between different sectors, organizations, workplaces and groups within societies regarding their attitude to leadership, including regional differences (Jones, 2005). From a cultural point of view it is vital to consider how leadership must be understood from the 'natives' point of view', given the meanings, values and expectations of the local, organizational setting in which people place themselves and/or are ascribed positions of leader and follower (or manager and subordinate) and then co-produce leadership (or something else).

Compared with people in business, researchers – at least outside the leadership field – tend to ascribe less significance to leadership in explaining performance and other outcomes in companies. Instead broader external forces and organizational conditions are viewed as much more central (Pfeffer, 1978). Within leadership studies, some researchers emphasize the attributions of causal powers to people in managerial positions assumed to be responsible for good or bad outcomes (Meindl, 1995). Most people, it is argued, are not willing to fully consider ambiguities or complex interactions as involved in the production of outcomes, but are eager to find a human being responsible, and this means a strong inclination to attribute significance to people believed to be in leadership positions. Expectations, reputation, impression management and pure projections matter. We in a sense invent leaders and leadership.

There is, however, a general trend to ascribe more and more significance to leadership as a way of solving organizational problems also in sectors that traditionally have downplayed the role of leadership, such as schools, churches, hospitals and universities. We live in an age celebrating leadership, and politicians, managers, other organizational practitioners and academics tend to drive or be driven by this broad trend. This is in a sense quite odd, as there is also the general understanding that people are well educated and individualistic and therefore would be able to manage without being that dependent on 'leaders' providing direction and support. One reason for this celebration of leadership is the general tendency to want to make what we do more impressive and nice-sounding in order to raise status and self-esteem. While management and managerial work may sound boring, leadership and leaders have a much more uplifting, grandiose flavour, easier to sell to people in organizations and to students for writers, consultants and educators wanting to market their books, courses and 'people improvement' activities, type 'leadership development programs' (Alvesson, 2013).

Of course, there is variation and debate also within academic camps about the meaning and relevance of leadership. One approach is to listen to various groups and organizations and find out when and why the 'natives' talk about leadership, what they mean by it, their beliefs, values and feelings around leadership and different versions and expressions of it (Fairhurst, 2009; Kelly, 2008). One can, for example, probably identify leadership-oriented organizational cultures where the interest in, space for and/or emergence of leaders , with a capital 'L', is less significant or even absent, for example as a consequence of a strong professional ideology or bureaucracy. The military and the university may exemplify this variation. Leadership may, by some groups, be seen as negative. An emphasis on leadership may, for example, be seen as related to authoritarianism, elitism and non-professionalism ('qualified people need no boss to tell them how to think and behave'). Or it can be viewed simply as interference: rather than getting on with the work in a way you see fit you are required to go to meetings, listen to the manager and be expected to follow his/her ideas and suggestions. A study of high-tech companies indicated a desire to be autonomous and minimize exposure to leadership. People were more inclined to turn to competent colleagues for advice and support than to managers who were often not specialists in at least some of the subject areas for which the people studied wanted support in the form of dialogue and guidance (Blom and Alvesson, 2012).

Leaders and leadership can then be seen as organizational symbols, with the orientations towards them not treated as 'facts' about leadership 'as such', but more as clues to understand organizational cultures. Does 'leadership' (or managerial work), in specific organizations, refer to the strong and decisive decision-maker, the superior technician or professional, the team-builder and coach, the educator and developer of people or the result-oriented number cruncher carefully monitoring and putting pressure on people to perform? How people talk and in other ways express sentiments about leaders and leadership (managers and managerial work) then indicates wider cultural patterns on human nature, social relations, hierarchies, power, etc. This approach would partly avoid the difficulties in defining leadership once and for all, valid over time and space.

Still, I refrain from restricting leadership studies to solely tracing the meanings and use of leadership vocabularies among people in organizations. Some theoretical ideas about what leadership as a theme may refer to are important to give some direction to one's understanding. Given the tendency of many people talking about leadership – including many academics – to include almost everything, there is a risk that a study of language use may lead to the result that leadership talk may move in all directions, which can make it difficult to say much more than that there is this variation. There is also a risk that many people uncritically share a tendency to overemphasize leadership – and neglect the significance of those supposed to be led, as well as the context. Generally, any good understanding needs to consider the leader (and also ask if this is a good way of capturing a person in a managerial job) and his or her possible impact on the (individual) follower and group, and vice versa, within a wider set of considerations, including followers (or co-workers disinclined to follow), relationships and cultural and social context. Leadership is very much a relationship and formed in interaction between various parties involved (Collinson, 2006; Ladkin, 2010). Consequently, moving an interest in leadership from a standardized conception of the subject matter – expressed, for example, in questionnaire studies measuring the leader (values, behaviour) – to a greater sensitivity to cultural contexts and the meanings of leadership interaction, while still having some idea of what leadership is broadly about, seems appropriate.

Bias towards abstract and thin studies of leadership

The leadership literature is enormous, but the academic work suffers from a heavily positivist bias and favours laboratory experiments or questionnaire studies that almost by definition neglect the organizational cultural context of leadership. It is revealing that in Yukl's (1989) and House and Aditay's (1997) extensive review articles on leadership research, the word 'culture' is mentioned in passing only a few times, and then as something that is changed as an outcome of 'transformational leadership' (Yukl) or as national cultures possibly influencing leadership (House and Aditay).

Most studies of leadership focus on how a person identified as a leader is (perceived as) behaving or interacting with a group of subordinates and/or broadly is 'managing' the organization. In most systematic academic studies, the leaders lead small groups of people. As organizational culture typically refers to a larger context than a small group it is not something that the typical small-group leader has a significant impact on. (One may talk about small-group culture, but this misses the point of the culture idea referring to wider and historically related meaning patterns.) Senior managers lead, however, entire or large parts of organizations and then the situation with regard to organizational culture becomes different. There is some interest in top leaders' influence on organizational culture in the literature. Frequently, the founder of the organization has been the target of attention (e.g. Pettigrew, 1979; Schein, 1985). A few studies have taken an interest in leadership in relationship to cultural change (Trice and Beyer, 1993). In these cases the leader is viewed as somebody who exercises a more or less far-reaching influence on culture. In the management literature, there are many statements such as 'organizational leaders instill their values, beliefs, and assumptions within an organization' (Hartnell and Wallumbwa, 2011: 232), with no (credible) empirical back-up, perhaps reflecting ideological conviction rather than careful investigations of organizational practices. Apart from the lack of realism in many cases, there is the problem that *if* this form of leadership were successful, it may lead to a vision and set of values that are 'installed' but do not really draw on an organization's existing set of orientations and sense of purpose, possibly leading to a vision that 'can become a tyranny, the dream of a dictator, imposing his or her will on the organization and its members' (Bolden et al., 2011: 86). People may comply with but not really share or be committed to the ideals and guidelines propagated by the top person.

There are not many good accounts of what leaders do and how followers/subordinates react to and act on the initiatives and efforts to exercise influence (Trice and Beyer, 1993). There are plenty of more popular writings on leadership, with a preference for hero portraits and anecdotes, which score higher on entertainment value than on intellectual depth and insights. Autobiographies of famous executives in business are generally far from trustworthy, as well shown by Hansen (1996). Also in the academic literature rather thin descriptions prevail. Trice and Beyer (1993) provide an account of Lee Iacocca, who started as president of Chrysler during the late 1970s when the company was in deep trouble. Iacocca is frequently described as 'a designated leader whose leadership drastically turned around an organization's culture' (p. 271). At the time, most people thought that Chrysler, with its huge debts and heavy losses, would not survive. But Iacocca generated 'a vision of a new Chrysler – one free of debt and actively competing in the national and international markets' (p. 271) – which mobilized managers and other employees in the company. He proposed and succeeded in getting the government to guarantee a very large bank loan, in return for agreeing to give the federal government a sizeable amount of control in monitoring the company. He also succeeded in getting the president of the US auto workers' union appointed to the company's board of directors. In addition he prepared and delivered television commercials that phrased his vision in simple, convincing language to both the public and Chrysler's personnel. This was at the time seen as radical, but the response was positive. At one time, he cut his salary from $360,000 to $1 per year. By 1983, 'he had dramatically eliminated debts, produced deep cutbacks, manufactured a profitable new car, and paid back the government-guaranteed loans a year early' (p. 272).

Trice and Beyer believe that Iacocca 'turned around' Chrysler's organizational culture, but their account does not say that much about how this was done. According to at least some of his subordinates, Iacocca had the ability to 'switch on, to light up' so they 'wanted to go back to the office and work some more, to put in another couple of hours' (Lacey, quoted in Trice and Beyer, 1993: 271). It is unclear to what extent this affected culture (patterns of meanings and ideas in the organization) – which is something other than people feeling (temporarily?) inspired to put in some extra work time. The 'vision' referred to above seems to be very general and lacks distinctiveness: being 'free of debt' and 'actively competing' are basic conditions in business. Getting loan guarantees from the government, appointing a union leader to the board and negotiating salary and benefit cuts with the union does not necessarily involve culture that much, although negotiating the meaning and appropriateness of these moves draws upon culture, and the outcomes can be seen as involving a symbolic dimension through which broader shared meanings may be changed. The union leader on the board may symbolize a more consensual orientation in management–worker relations, and unions taking a higher level of responsibility, although it is uncertain whether this was understood in this way and even more whether this led to significant cultural changes on a broader scale. Some of the other arrangements and outcomes (e.g. securing loans) can be seen as crisis management which do not necessarily imply cultural change at all.

Whether organizational culture did change or not is impossible to say based on the account, and Trice and Beyer's claim of the culture being 'turned around' seems to be speculative. Temporary reactions to threats of bankruptcy are not the same as cultural change. What is needed is a careful study of how organizational members broadly responded to the initiatives and arrangements of Iacocca and other senior managers. Also needed is research on any lasting consequences, for example in terms of new orientations to the company, to salaries, to union responsibility for the company, to competition, to how 'debt' is understood. In the absence of any good indications on this, we cannot really say anything about the possible effects of Iacocca's leadership on organizational culture. Getting people to temporarily adjust to difficult circumstances is not necessarily the same as cultural change. Most of his acts, such as negotiating loans and salaries, do not really concern leadership in any distinct sense, but refer to other aspects of management. While claiming to address leadership and organizational culture, in this case Trice and Beyer do not say that much about either.

Apart from the 'thinness' of most accounts of leadership in relationship to organizational culture, this example also illustrates a one-sidedness in the assumptions on how culture and leadership interact. In Trice and Beyer's narrative the 'leadership' is a product of Iacocca, his reading of the corporate situation and context and his charisma. Organizational culture, to the extent that these authors treat it, is portrayed just as an object which is reformed through acts of leadership. That organizational culture may frame leadership, and that any possible effect of leadership is a consequence of how people interpret and give meaning to various examples of leadership, are hardly addressed. Iacocca's salary cut to $1 is of interest not in itself, but in terms of how it is read by various groups in the company. If it is seen as a publicity stunt, a signal of temporary sacrifice under extraordinary but short-sighted conditions, or as a symbol of long-term corporate solidarity, the consequences are very different. It is here, on this interpretive level, that culture enters the picture, but this seems to be lost by Trice and Beyer – as well as by most other authors, not only pop-management writers but also academics.

As with other examples of critique delivered in this book, this is not intended to be an exercise in fault-finding. The full realization of a cultural framework calls for an understanding of what may go wrong in efforts to conduct cultural analysis. An awareness of how aspirations of illuminating organizational culture may drift into focusing on the level of behaviour – rather than the level of meaning – is important. Generally, it is tempting and easy to cut corners and see superficial material as indicators of organizational culture and cultural change. The lesson here is that leadership as well as organizational culture calls for precision and depth in order to be understood, and much richer accounts than those typically produced are needed.

Two examples of rich studies of leadership

I will briefly refer to two studies of leadership that take managers' intentions and acts (but also the subordinates' interpretations of these) seriously. One is a study by Smircich (1983c) in which the CEO of an insurance company based on the merger of two companies tried to strengthen cooperation within the new company. He devoted much time to team-building and encouraged the open sharing of viewpoints in the management group. He also launched the wheel as an organizational symbol, intended to make people move together in a synchronized way. But all this did not seem to affect the 'real' differences in orientations and commitments among people in the organization. Despite the encouragement, at least on the espoused level, to present 'genuine' opinions and feelings, the tricky issues were never seriously aired in meetings. The wheel metaphor did not work. It was reinterpreted in accordance with the understanding of the situation that people held, but was not aired in settings such as management team meetings. People said that the company was like a four-wheel van, but with all the wheels moving in different directions and at different speeds. The symbol then created an opposite effect from that intended: rather than making people adopt the idea of cooperation and support a shared orientation, it confirmed and reinforced their feelings of a diversity of orientations and objectives characterizing the different parts of the organization.

Another case is described by Hentze (1994). A young manager from a German corporate group was appointed as the production director of a French subsidiary in the printing industry. One intention was to strengthen the bonds between different parts of the group. The new director was well educated and had modern ideas about participative management. He succeeded a very experienced French manager who had worked his way up from the bottom and had superior knowledge about many aspects of the production technology of the company. The French predecessor had a direct, paternalistic style, dealt with his subordinates on an individual basis, had clear ideas about what should be accomplished and was fairly outspoken on what he perceived as positive and negative results. The new production director was several times told about the personality and style of his predecessor and he was well aware that he represented something very different. He believed in participative management and management by objectives, explained the principles to his subordinates and started to implement this type of management. After some time he was convinced that it was working – production results did not indicate otherwise, and a few managers left the company during his first months, but he carefully investigated their motives and concluded that they were not related to workplace issues.

But then the CEO of the company, the boss of the production director, received a letter from one of the production director's immediate subordinates, an experienced manager for whom the production director had much respect and with whom he thought he worked well. This manager, having been in the company for a very long time, expressed great concern about the state of affairs as well as the future of the production department. He emphasized the good intentions and qualifications of the new production director, but compared him unfavourably with the predecessor, whose direct, autocratic style and superior technical knowledge had been greatly respected. People felt much uncertainty about the purpose of all the management meetings that the new director had initiated. This led to endless discussions without conclusions and decisions: in one month about a quarter of the working time of the managers was spent in management team meetings. People lacked direction and felt that they were being asked to solve problems without much support or clarification as to what exactly they were supposed to do. Uncertainty led to anxiety – failure was at least under the previous director expected to lead to direct consequences such as people being informed about their bad performance in very clear terms.

The failure of the new production director can be ascribed to a lack of congruence between his management style and the expectations and assumptions of the people around him. They expected from a senior manager decisiveness, technical expertise and a strong mastery of the situation. They were also used to responding to relatively detailed instructions and to doing so on an individual basis. Even though people broadly understood the principles of the new management style, they did so only on a superficial level and did not value it. Meetings and discussions were seen as endless talk that seldom led anywhere, as taking time and energy from 'real work' and as a poor 'surrogate' for the director informing people what to do. Group discussions also worked against a deeply ingrained understanding of responsibility as an individual matter. As expressed in the letter to the CEO by the frustrated manager: 'at the end of the day we are only responsible for our own area of work'.

The deeper meanings of participative management and teamwork thus did seem to be lost in the managerial practices of this case: subordinates taking initiative and actively contributing with their expertise and ideas, people having some degree of shared responsibility – across levels, but also between people on the same level (management team) – and the group being an important unit in problem-solving and decision-making. To fully understand and work accordingly to these ideas calls for a deep understanding of them, also involving emotional adaptation.

Both cases illustrate that managers with good intentions and working according to what is today recognized to be good managerial practice may fail. The deep meanings associated with the cultural context they operated in were never touched upon in their acts of leadership – at least they did not connect positively to these meanings. Instead the cultural frameworks of the subordinates led to negative responses – the meanings intended by the managers and the meanings interpreted by their subordinates went in very different directions. The deep meanings leading to irony and distance in the first case, and worry, confusion and a feeling of waste of time and absence of direction in the second case, implied failures in leadership. Our own extensive in-depth research indicates that leadership efforts often do not lead to the intended consequences (e.g. Lundholm, 2011; Sveningsson and Larsson, 2006).

The selected cases powerfully illuminate that we need to take the meanings and interpretations of the subordinates seriously to understand leadership. Also the practical action of managers – at least when the 'voluntary' obedience of subordinates is called for (which is what leadership refers to) – calls for careful grounding in, and continuous interpretation of, what is on the minds of the subordinates and how they relate to the ideas and arrangements of the leader. The cases point to the need as well as difficulty to grasp 'in-depth meanings' and look at intentions, responses and social context.

Varieties of Leadership

Managers and leaders – instrumental and cultural?

Frequently, leadership is given a very broad meaning and includes almost everything that a manager or an informal leader does, as illustrated by Trice and Beyer's text scrutinized above. But managers clearly do much more than engage in leadership. As the great majority of managers are subordinated to more senior executives or are accountable to various constituencies there are clearly elements of a manager's work time that cannot meaningfully be defined in terms of leadership. Actually, with a precise and constrained view on leadership (see below) it may well be that leadership only happens occasionally.

A note on the relationship between managers and leaders (management and leadership) might at this point be called for. Of course, not all leaders are managers – they may be political leaders or informal leaders. A distinction can be made between designated leaders, with a formally based position, including rights and obligations, and emerging leaders, entirely based on support and legitimacy among the followers. In recent years many authors have proposed a distinction between managers, who rely on their formal position and work with bureaucratic processes such as planning, budgeting, organizing and controlling, and leaders, who rely on their personal abilities, work with visions, agendas and coalition building, and mainly through non-coercive means affect people's feelings and thinking (e.g. Kotter, 1985; Zaleznik, 1977). Managers then can be 'merely' managers or can also be leaders. Zaleznik (1977: 71) views the influence of leaders as 'altering moods, evoking images and expectations, and … establishing specific desires and objectives …. The net result of this influence is to change the way people think about what is desirable, possible and necessary.' Leaders are then heavily involved in what Pfeffer (1981a), reviewed in Chapter 4, refers to as symbolic management. In comparison, managers are much less omnipotent types.

According to Jackall (1988), arguing along similar lines to attribution theory, it is common for top managers to be described as 'leaders' by their subordinates and others, while managers at lower levels are seldom viewed as worthy of this label. This is not so much a matter of personal attributes as of social position. The formal social position makes people interpret and relate to the position-holder in a specific way. A story was widely told in IBM about how the founder Thomas Watson once, when accompanied with a group of executives, was stopped by a young female employee and asked to follow safety regulations, which he did, stopping his escort of managers from giving the young employee a reprimand for telling the top person what to do (Martin et al., 1983). The significance attached to Watson obeying safety rules like everybody else illustrates that the formal position adds considerable 'mystique' to the person, and makes his or her act appear in a radically different light from that of the common people (Mumby, 1988). How cultural values and expectations determine and constrain the chances of people emerging as 'leaders' is illustrated by the resistance of physicians in hospitals to administrators being relabelled as managers. For administrators to appear as – be labelled as or seen as – 'leaders' would be very difficult, given this culture, and of course the political interests it is fused with (Parker, 2000). Physicians, like many other professionals, are often not interested in reinforcing the status of a function and group of people that may reduce their autonomy.

I am not denying the possibility of leaders having the far-reaching influence proposed by advocates of the leader with a capital 'L' beyond the formal powers of the managerial position. It is, however, possible that most managers having a personal and non-coercive influence beyond pure 'management' are mixing elements of management and leadership and that the latter element is far from unconstrained by formal position and bureaucratic constraints, but typically intertwined with management. The following definition of the two concepts captures this:

> Management can get things done through others by the traditional activities of planning, organizing, monitoring and controlling – without worrying too much what goes on inside people's heads. Leadership, by contrast, is vitally concerned with what people are thinking and feeling and how they are to be linked to the environment, to the entity and to the job/task. (Nicholls, 1987: 21)

In practice, managers frequently to some extent rely on plans; they coordinate and control and use bureaucratic means. But they also try to create commitment or at least acceptance for plans, rules, goals and instructions. Making people understand the purpose of, and create meaning around, what should specifically be done may transgress any clear distinction between management and leadership. At the same time, with the exception of talks in which the manager-leader tries to energize the masses, it is rare with acts of leadership addressing thinking and feeling and making connections between tasks and broader contexts on a very general level, outside operations. As Grint (1997) has emphasized, leaders with no resources or activities other than pure persuasion (convincing talk) may be quite weak: 'naked, friendless, money-less, and technology-less leaders are unlikely to prove persuasive' (cited by Fairhurst, 2009: 1623). Managers affect thinking and feeling in connection to managing specific tasks and goals, thus making 'leadership' and 'management' difficult to differentiate in practice. This view allows a combination of the two elements which I believe we can find in the activities of most (contemporary) managers and organizations.

Nevertheless, leadership is not productively used if it is supposed to cover everything that managers do. Everything that does not involve interaction with or indirect communication to subordinates falls outside leadership even if the activities could be seen as salient in management. In the case of Iacocca discussed above, securing financial resources by obtaining a loan guarantee was a principal task for a president, but this did not mean it was an exercise of leadership, in any specific sense. And also in relationship to subordinates, parts of management have very little to do with leadership, for example when there is a strict behavioural and/or output measurement focus.[1] Leadership thus calls for a strong ingredient of management of meaning (Smircich and Morgan, 1982), in which the shaping of the ideas, values, perceptions and feelings of people is included. However, there is the risk that this is interpreted as 'a lofty and slightly nebulous' notion, quite divorced from mundane, immediate, instrumental and material concerns (Bryman, 2004: 754). As hardly any managers spend most of their time preaching visions and values, but are involved in the concerns Bryman refers to, it is important to relate management of meaning to these and see how the latter is played out in or possibly decoupled from specific mundane, instrumental acts. Arguably, a lot of leadership efforts are not consistent – with managers displaying diverse and incoherent agendas, priorities and activities, sometimes partly integrated or at least bridged over, sometimes creating ambiguities and undermining specific management of leadership projects aiming to manage meaning (Alvesson and Sveningsson, 2003).[2]

This meaning aspect points to the fact that leadership is by definition seen as 'cultural', that is, leadership must be understood as taking place in a cultural context and all leadership acts have their consequences through the (culturally guided) interpretation of those involved in the social processes in which leaders, followers and leadership acts are expressed. This, of course, does not imply that leadership means a significant impact on or capacity to shape and change culture at will. Leadership draws attention to the consequences within and through cultural meanings informing the thoughts, feelings and actions that leaders provoke. As stated, cultural impact may lead to fragmentation, confusion and ambiguity rather than the forming or strengthening of integrated and coherent shared sets of meaning. We will touch upon this below and return to it in Chapter 8, addressing culture, fragmentation and ambiguity.

Management – as different from leadership – is also cultural in the sense that interpretation and meaning are central here – as in all social life. But management typically addresses 'simple' and taken-for-granted meanings; the level of thinking and feeling should be 'passed quickly' in control efforts, leading to predictable responses at a behavioural level. Management then is not primarily targeted at a cultural level as an 'end' or as a significant site where a lot of things – thinking, sense-making – take place. Management as a mode of control is then thought to be able to bypass culture in its operations and minimize the involvement of values, unfocused thinking, and feeling. This is similar to Geertz's (1973) distinction between culture and social structure, where management would deal with the latter and leadership is targeting culture.

Returning to the case of Iacocca, most of the activities mentioned did not seem to refer to a genuine concern with people's thinking and feeling in the organization, but more with public relations work and instrumental issues. Getting people to accept cuts in salaries and benefits is mainly a managerial project, but it also includes an element of leadership. This is the case especially if the project does not stop with reducing costs and the workers grudgingly feel that they have no choice but to accept, but if the negotiations and communication around the issue lead to the workers developing an understanding and support for the outcome. It is interesting to try to grasp the creation and maintenance of a 'cost-conscious' culture and the development of a particular sentiment towards sacrifice and responsibility here. Understandings within various communities around issues like this illustrate the fine distinctions between finance and culture, between management and leadership.

The ambiguity of leadership – a case of leadership or anti-leadership?

Leadership has traditionally been described in terms of the traits of leaders or as a particular behavioural style. Occasionally, the need for a situation-dependent leadership style has been suggested. It is more fruitful to see leadership as an act or set of acts within a social process. This decoupling of leadership from a premature marriage with what a particular designated (or self-appointed) person does allows for a more open view. It also encourages one to pay attention to the meanings of all the people involved. It is then far from always clear if a particular act performed by a manager – or someone else – is productively described as leadership or not.

I will now present a glimpse of an event – a ritual – in a division of a Swedish industrial company (Alvesson and Björkman, 1992), with relevance for the interpretation of leadership. This organization is primarily populated by engineers or marketing people with an engineering background. Every third month there is an informational meeting for the 40 or so managers (here broadly defined, including marketing personnel and supervisors) in the division. When Gustaf, the head of division, started with these information meetings not all the 40 or so people invited appeared and those who came sat rather widely distributed in a meeting room capable of hosting a larger group. Gustaf then emphasized that the meeting was obligatory ('please inform me if you can't attend', he wrote in the calls for the meeting) and asked people to take the front rows, thus sitting close to each other.

At the time of our study no such encouragement is necessary. Most people attend and they take seats close to each other. Whether this reflects a new 'genuine' orientation or is a matter of behavioural compliance is difficult to say. All those present are men, with the exception of the female personnel manager and the secretary. Gustaf, the divisional manager, stands at the door and welcomes all the participants. During the introductory speech he gives a 'soft' impression, appears friendly and rather informal. The agenda is characterized by several speakers and Gustaf adopts a relatively low profile. He could have done some of the presentations himself, and on the original agenda his name appeared as speaker on some themes, but then he chose to let someone else take the centre stage. The atmosphere is informal and friendly. Sometimes Gustaf jokes with people and sometimes he is the object of their jokes. When the controller presents the results he uses Gustaf's picture aimed at showing changes in results on different markets in a pedagogical manner: 'Now we go over to Gustaf's own picture, the quantum physics diagram.' (Everybody laughs.)

After some comments, Gustaf asks the audience:

'Everybody laughs at me and this diagram. Do you find it unclear? I think it is rather revealing.' Some people reply:

'At first glance it looks quite difficult (laughter), but when you have looked at it some time .... It is easier for me as I am colour blind.' (More laughter.)

During the break, Gustaf serves coffee together with his secretary and the personnel manager. The overall impression from the meeting is one of community rather than formalism and hierarchy.

An interesting question is whether this is a case of leadership or not. It could be argued that this is the opposite of 'real leadership'. Gustaf is abdicating from a position as a leader, refraining from using the situation in order to exercise active influence on his subordinates. All the jokes about him and his diagram can be seen as undermining his authority and weakening the asymmetry which by definition characterizes the relationship between leader and subordinates. The situation is mainly characterized by various people providing information about results and different problems that the company is working with. It thus has the character of information giving, rather than an opportunity for the leader, through rhetorical skills and charismatic appearance, to frame the minds, values and feelings of followers. In this sense one could say that Gustaf expresses 'anti-leadership' more than what is conventionally, and perhaps stereotypically, seen as leadership with a capital 'L'.

But it is also possible to view the set-up and Gustaf's behaviour as fully in line with leadership as defined by Yukl at the beginning of this chapter. Gustaf is downplaying hierarchy, putting the emphasis on community, an open climate and the free flow of communication. He also encourages other people by asking them to be responsible for presentations, which can be seen as strengthening their status, work identities and motivation. By placing himself more as a host than an authority figure he sets the tone for others. Gustaf exercised cultural influence through delegation, emphasizing the value of everybody, underscoring social values, etc. The information meeting thus expresses Gustaf's agenda of building an integrated organization through cultural means in which the traditional scepticism and antagonism between different functions – in particular marketing and production – can be overcome and a shared divisional identity and organizational community be developed.

An understanding of leadership then calls for consideration of not only the behaviour involved – through just observing what takes place at face value it may well be seen as the absence of leadership – but also the ideas and intentions. Through grasping the logic of the manifested social processes, we may see this as a case of leadership. But we also need to consider the reactions of those that Gustaf tries to influence. Intentions and behaviour are neither sufficient nor even the most vital components – the interpretation of and meanings of subordinates are really what matters, as these are basic for the responses to and effects of leadership acts.

In the case of Gustaf actions like the information meeting appeared to be positively responded to by his subordinates. People praised his social attitude and interest in trying to create shared orientations among the entire division. But whether this had any deeper impact and led to significant effects on organizational performances is of course very difficult to tell.

This case illustrates the need to take not only the actions of the leader into account, but also the ideas and intentions behind them, and in particular the interpretations and reactions of subordinates. Understanding leadership calls for the consideration of social process and cultural context; that is, descriptions must be relatively rich or thick. The case also illustrates that what can be seen as leadership is an open issue. In informal, everyday settings it is even more uncertain what should productively be seen as leadership. In the case of Gustaf the manager-structured set-up and his senior position make the leadership label appear appropriate, but it is well worth considering whether the use of the 'absence' of high-profiled leadership simultaneously can be understood as anti-leadership or as a particular version of leadership. The trick of sensitively grasping what goes on may sometimes be best accomplished by transgressing established vocabularies or at least by showing the uncertainties and tensions involved.

Leadership in the context of organizational culture

The relationship between leadership and culture is complex. Given the view on leadership expressed above – in which leadership deals with meanings, thinking and feelings rather than having a narrow behavioural focus – leadership may even be defined as agents working through culture as the medium and target of action. Leadership is a culture-influencing activity, 'the management of meaning' as Smircich and Morgan (1982) expressed it. This does not necessarily mean that leadership creates or drastically changes culture, only that leadership is a cultural manifestation influencing other cultural manifestations, such as shared understandings of objectives, technologies and environment.

In the interplay between leadership and organizational culture, different kinds of relationships and emphases are possible. In 'pro-leadership' management circles – such as most consultants, practitioners and some popular academics – leadership is seen as having a far-reaching impact on the cultural values and orientations of organizational members. Many leadership writers emphasize the far-reaching capacity for CEOs, founders and other senior actors to produce, control and change culture. It is assumed they have the ability to 'define the parameters of the corporate culture' (Kets de Vries, 1994: 78) and that transformational leaders 'construct cultures that foster effective management of change. They do this by defining and inculcating in organization members the belief that they can affect, if not control, their environment, including government regulation, market competition, and technological change' (Sashkin, 2004: 194). We can then talk about assumptions about 'leader-driven organizational cultures', where a leader is influential in establishing or turning around certain core ideas, values and meanings.

The strongest case for leader-driven organizational creation or change is made by adherents of charismatic individuals in organizations, charisma being a key quality also for so-called transformational leadership, turning self-centred people into committed organizational members positively attached to the leader and working for the best of the organization (Burns, 1978; Diaz-Saenz, 2011). To qualify for the label 'charisma' a top position seems to be required, at least for those writing about it. Charismatic leadership emerges from the extraordinary influence exercised by a person, typically being able to get support for a radical vision, often in the light of a crisis, from a group of dedicated and more or less spellbound followers. They are willing to suspend critical thinking and disbelief and develop strong faith and emotional energy in the project of the charismatic leader. Charismatic leadership often involves the creation of something new. The best-known examples are from the political and religious spheres. Gandhi, Hitler and some leaders of religious sects are illustrative examples. In the corporate sphere, the space for charismatic persons is probably much more restricted, partly due to the sobering impact of market mechanisms and competition and the possibility for most people to switch jobs. Trice and Beyer (1993) do, however, refer to some examples of persons they think were or are 'genuine charismatics', including Iacocca and Steven Jobs, the founder of Apple. I will later in this chapter discuss a case of founders of a company who were attributed charismatic characteristics by their followers.

While many leadership enthusiasts of the 1990s were keen to emphasize the charismatic leader, the ideal leader of today is for many a different kind of hero; the soft-spoken, yet hard-working, tenacious and skilled leader who does not crave the spotlight so much, as he or she is eager to give space and recognition for the achievements of his or her colleagues (Collins, 2001). Charismatic leaders, it is now argued, rarely stimulate others to grow, but make the organization heavily dependent on themselves by fostering followership – instead we are told that leaders should strive to bring longer-term corporate aspirations to fruition, by creating sustainable organizations with first-class employees (e.g. Collins, 2001). (Many still emphasize the charismatic boss as an ideal, highlighting his or her positive impact on employee motivation.)

Founders of organizations – whether seen as charismatic or not – are frequently viewed as also founders of cultures or at least significant sources of a set of values which the organizational members adapt and reproduce (e.g. Schein, 1985). Founders of organizations in a sense start from scratch, having a significant influence on the particular combination of people employed, choosing the direction of the company and thus frequently being able to put an imprint on the shared ideas, beliefs and meanings that develop during the formative years of the company.

Although senior persons may be able to put a relatively strong imprint on an organization (or parts of it) under special circumstances – crises, changes in circumstances calling for basic reorientation, particularly favourable preconditions for strategic choice contingent upon market position and/or changes in the industry – it is debatable whether top executives normally can be seen as 'captains of culture'. Arguably, culture forms leadership rather than, or at least as much as, the other way around (Alvesson, 2011a). This is the case at least for the large majority of people designated as or emerging as leaders. As Biggart and Hamilton (1987: 435) put it: 'All actors, but perhaps leaders especially, must embody the norms of their positions and persuade others in ways consistent with their normative obligations.'

In a sense societal and business cultures set limits for the kind of managerial behaviour and arrangements that have a chance to be approved of. There are subgroups in society, such as religious sects, criminal groups and others, that deviate from broadly shared orientations and here there is space for leadership that would lead to sanctions in more 'open' contexts. Most organizations are, however, exposed to societal cultural values. This is accomplished through mass media attention, through the inflow of people carrying cultural orientations picked up in education and at other workplaces, and through organizational members being citizens affected by the ideas and values expressed in various extra-workplace situations. Cultures in organizations are also affected by the interaction with suppliers, customers, authorities and others. All this counteracts a strong workplace-level deviation from the shared cultural understandings within a society or an organizational field that makes cooperation possible. When Iacocca reduced his income to $1 per year for some time and appeared on television with messages about the company, this was innovative, but of course it appealed to broadly shared values rather than challenging or changing them. What a senior manager or other kind of leader does must in a fundamental sense be perceived as in line with some broadly shared values. As a lot of what executives do – in business life characterized by profit orientations, harsh competition and often greed (indicated by rapid increases in CEO salaries and benefits, leading to ever-widening gaps between their pay and that of their workers) – is at odds with some social values (including fairness, but also often honesty, coherence, rationality, democracy and ecology), they need to draw attention to what broadly is seen as good and natural and away from those values that one's actions are not in accord with.

Culture can be seen as a repertoire of positively and negatively loaded meanings. To be perceived as successful, leadership involves trying to attach positive meanings to one's intentions, acts, arrangements and outcomes and steer away from people – within and outside the organization – ascribing negative meanings and beliefs to what one is up to. In the case of Gustaf above, drawing upon and invoking values such as making people grow, participation and building organizational community and identity make his acts appear in a favourable light. On the other hand, if Gustaf were evaluated in terms of ideals such as establishing authority, being in control, giving direction, the leader as a great communicator, etc. the verdict would be less positive.

Culture does not only limit, frame and prescribe leadership on a general, societal level, but also *within* organizations. Any particular organization represents a mix of general societal and industrial expectations and ideas, and of local, more or less organization-specific ones. Organization-specific cultural ideas and meanings in various ways direct and constrain managerial behaviour and leadership. Senior managers pass on – or modify – organizational culture through being role models, using selective recruitment to managerial positions and through sanctioning or discouraging deviations. Also subordinates have a strong impact on how leadership is shaped. If we disregard the use of 'pure' power – breaking the will of people through the use of the whip (threats of being fired, etc.) – leadership means having some kind of appeal to people, to their hearts and minds. Visions, instructions, suggestions, goals and constructions of corporate reality must be perceived as legitimate and meaningful. The actions of the leader must then be fine-tuned to the frameworks and norms of those who are to be influenced. In this sense the subordinates as a collective – sharing certain cultural ideas – 'decide' what works in terms of leadership. This of course does not mean that the leader is totally subordinated to a given set of orientations or is forced to adapt to a specific style and just reproduce a given set of meanings and ideas. The leader can change these – though gradually – and in order to do so must proceed from an appreciation of people holding certain ideas, values and preferences. The leader is involved in the negotiation rather than the imposition of new or revised orientations on people. Cultural change then tends to be gradual, partial and an outcome of social processes in which a group of subordinates have as much if not more to say than the leader.

It is not uncommon for managers to be located in between values and norms held by senior managers and those promoted by their subordinates. 'Top management' culture – sometimes seen as corporate culture – and 'functional cultures' (associated with production, R&D, personnel or marketing) frequently differ and may conflict, and here leadership may partly be a matter of negotiation between different kinds of normative frameworks and views on corporate reality.

The need to deal with both overall organizational requirements and the orientations of the subordinates can be illustrated by the case of a US Coastguard officer who found his men – mainly college graduates whose expectations, interests and motives were at odds with the routines and lack of discretion of military life – bored and negative. Instead of trying to impose military discipline in a traditional way, he made a deal with his men about more discretion and certain liberties in exchange for more positive behaviour (Wilkins, referred to in Trice and Beyer, 1993). This case illustrates, among other things, how the values and orientations of a group of subordinates trigger a change in 'leadership' (if this is the right label in the case) so that it resonates better with their values and meanings.

I assume that most people expected to exercise leadership in their jobs are much more strongly influenced by organizational culture than they are involved in actively producing it. Apart from structural conditions (job task, resources, position, formal rights, etc.), which to some extent are cultural manifestations and have consequences through the cultural meaning attached to them, the cultural context guides the manager as to how leadership should be carried out. This is done, for example, through prescribing that 'leadership' goes beyond relying solely on formal authority, and involves influencing the ideas, values and orientations of subordinates on how they should interact with managers, say, in terms of the appropriate degree of subordination. This can range from marked to (almost) non-existent.

The 'culture-driven' nature of leadership is neglected in most of the literature and in talk by management gurus and practitioners. This is to some extent because the cultural dimension has traditionally been marginalized in leadership research. More significant, however, are the ideological overtones of a lot of talk on leadership. There is a broad tendency, in leadership research and among practitioners, to stress the manager (the 'leader') as a superior, unidirectionally interacting with subordinates, but neglect that almost all managers also are subordinates and thus have a hierarchy above themselves (Laurent, 1978). There is a desire among many people to ascribe strong impact to leaders, reflecting a need to see somebody as responsible for different outcomes, good or bad (Meindl, 1995; Pfeffer, 1978). This fits the self-image of many managers and reinforces their status and claims for high wages, prestige and authority in companies and society. Management writers, teachers and consultants would probably find their market smaller and less sympathetic if they argued for the significance of factors other than management and leaders, as well as the complexity and ambiguity of accounting for performance. Generally, the strong faith in leadership, the attribution of causal powers to it and the heroization of leaders may be seen as interesting cultural manifestations – reflecting socially invented 'truths' and being worthy of investigation.

Sometimes external dependencies and structural restrictions for leadership are noticed, but the phenomenon of 'cultural subordinacy' has not been treated seriously in leadership research. Leadership as the adaptation, mechanical reproduction, reinforcement, creative variation and/or rejuvenation of dominating cultural orientations in organizations is a potentially fruitful line of thinking.

To sum up, culture is often seen as affected by the leadership of the founders in particular, but also of senior managers to some extent and under certain conditions – at least if they are 'charismatic' persons. Leaders are said to work *on* culture rather than to work *within* culture. In the present book, leadership is understood rather as taking place within and as an outcome of the cultural context. Of course, under extraordinary circumstances leaders may transcend parts of existing cultural patterns or even contribute to the creation of culture. Also in such cases cultural context and cultural constraints must be considered. A precondition for changing culture is to connect to it. The next section will treat different kinds of leadership as creating – versus being created by – organizational culture.

A case of initiator-leadership and follower-leadership

I now return to the case of the computer consultancy company, CCC, that I addressed in previous chapters, and first treat leadership during the formative years of the company and then also address the notion of charisma. I will then provide an account of leadership in a post-formative phase. (For details of the study, see Alvesson, 1995.)

Leadership during the foundation and expansion of the company

The three founders of CCC headed it for the first 7–8 years of its (at the time of my study) 10-year history, and exercised a very strong influence on the ideas, beliefs and values that subsequently characterized the organization.

According to the subordinates the founders exhibited energy, enthusiasm, easy availability and an engaging and supporting attitude to the employees.

> One had a management that was very engaged. You had direct contact with the management. The management always was ready, always was available and always listened. You always got a motive.

The founders expressed a strong interest in the employees. Good performance was noted, acknowledged and communicated within the organization. Often a bottle of champagne was opened to celebrate the achievement.

The founders succeeded in tying together the everyday life of the personnel with the company's activities on a larger scale. The personnel felt that they were a part of the centre of the company, not only in different consultancy projects, but also in ideas and business developments, including contracts on new projects, joint ventures and acquisitions of companies.

> When we had morning meetings one of the owners was always there. We got a lot of inside information. On the present development, etc. We felt very much a part of what was happening.

The founders broadened the sphere for social influence that leadership in corporations is normally about. Through 'dramatization' of passing on information, employees felt close to the running of the company and a part of an inner, trusted circle. Through frequent participation in social activities, also outside normal working time, the leisure time became to some extent a part of corporate life, to the benefit of experiences of community and knowledge sharing.

As we will see below, the orientations that the founders powerfully promoted were shared broadly in the organization and also guided the work of subsequent managers. The founders may well be seen as initiators of an organizational culture. For their subordinates this was partly a consequence of the charismatic qualities of the founders. It may be tempting to emphasize the heroic qualities and the leader-driven nature of cultural patterns in the company, but, as stated, it is important to consider also the social and cultural context in order to avoid a one-sided understanding. The computer consultancy business was, at the time, young and expanding. Of course not all companies were successful, but the expansion possibilities facilitated the distribution of positive, interesting information and a dynamic atmosphere. In CCC, as in the rest of the industry, mainly relatively young and well-educated people were employed, providing a good ground for feelings of organization-wide community, an interest in social activities after work and so on. Swedish societal patterns are comparatively informal and non-hierarchical, providing a value-basis for interaction between hierarchical levels. CCC was not entirely unique in the cultural orientations that developed but showed some resemblance to other companies in the industry. The founders still were, compared to most other managements, highly influential in creating and shaping a particular version of organization culture, with significant impact on corporate development as well as on the work-life experiences of the personnel.

Charisma at CCC

Most of the literature and common talk on charisma in management contexts devolves on a limited number of public figures (Bryman, 1993; Trice and Beyer, 1993). Fame and mass media attention may contribute heavily to their aura and make their cases very special and perhaps of limited relevance for the understanding of less atypical managerial situations.

The founders of CCC were not media celebrities. Nevertheless, for the people in the company they scored highly in terms of charisma:

> They are looked upon as gods. They are never criticized. People look up to them.

> Christer [one of the founders] radiates enthusiasm. He can turn some damnable setback into something positive. He has exceptional charisma. Everyone wants to talk to him.

> The employees then developed strong faith and loyalty for the founders and would make efforts beyond what is common in working life.

> You could go through fire and water for the founders.

> You felt you were part of it. That making the extra effort was worth it.

CCC's founders meet at least two of the characteristics of being charismatic leaders: they were deemed to be exceptional by the followers and enjoyed great personal loyalty. A third characteristic, having a mission or vision, is somewhat more ambiguous in this case. For Weber, who developed the idea, 'the bearer of charisma enjoys loyalty and authority by virtue of a mission believed to be embodied in him' (quoted by Bryman, 1993: 292). This is a bit difficult in business life, as the 'mission' (ultimately to make profit) may be less capable of quickening the pulse for most persons in a commercial organization. Iacocca's 'vision', discussed above, was for example rather pale. Nevertheless, for some of the people at CCC, the business concept and the way the founders ran the company had considerable attractiveness (Chapter 5). A fourth criterion for charisma to appear, according to some authors (e.g. Trice and Beyer, 1993), is that the leader faces and solves a crisis of some kind. In a 'cool' situation, followers are less inclined to see the leader as so exceptional, to grant him or her so much authority and/or to be so devoted. In the case of CCC, there were of course occasionally significant problems, but no major crises for a long initial period. On the contrary, things went well: the company grew quickly and was successful in all respects during the time when the founders were so deeply admired.

Charisma is often understood as a personal trait, although certain circumstances may be called for in order to make the followers inclined to see the person as truly exceptional and be strongly devoted and loyal. Crises and anxiety help. When leaders in business must attend to a lot of administrative duties as part of normal management practice or when results are no longer good, the perception of the leader as charismatic may vanish. To understand charisma it is important to consider not only the leader's qualities and his or her behaviour but also the context and the characteristics of the followers. It is perhaps better to see charisma as a quality in the relationship between a person and a group following him or her or even as a perception or attribution of the group. A person seen as charismatic may well have certain qualities – self-confidence, rhetorical skills, knowledge, personal courage, an original idea – but this in itself does not lead to people responding with deep devotion. Whether a Ghandi, Martin Luther King, Iacocca, Jim Jones (leader of a religious sect that committed collective suicide) or Hitler are seen as charismatic or not is mainly a matter of social situation, cultural context and characteristics of the followers.

In the case of the founders of CCC one may, in addition to personal qualities and a thought-through and systematically applied leadership style with a strong appeal, also point to charisma-facilitating conditions. One can ask how they managed to be perceived as charismatic, which is by definition the same as being successful as leaders in the sense of having far-reaching influence and being able to get a high level of loyalty and work motivation.[3]

One important element here is to (choose to) be in a business in an expanding market. Being successful increases the chances of being perceived as charismatic. For a person wanting to be perceived as charismatic this is an alternative to following the more conventional path of facing and solving a difficult situation and thereby appearing as a saviour for a group ('the crisis route'). Another important aspect concerns recruitment. It is more difficult to appear as charismatic for a diverse audience, with different values and inclinations to interpret and react to talk and other forms of action. CCC's recruitment policy strongly facilitated a good spirit within the organization. Many of the employees were a part of the contact network of the three founders – who knew a lot of people – and were consequently personally known by the founders from earlier workplaces or in other ways. The average age of the personnel was low.

There is a general tendency for new organizations to start by recruiting a homogeneous group of people in order to lay a good foundation for confidence and mutual understanding (Kanter, 1977). In relation to leadership, a homogeneous group of followers makes it much easier to adapt a style and tailor a message that all respond to in a similar way.

The people recruited may have been inclined to respond to the ideas, practices and personal style of the founders in a highly positive way and perhaps be positively disposed to ascribe charisma-like qualities to the founders.

In order to understand charisma – the chief criterion being what subordinates see as exceptional qualities in leaders and a willingness to turn themselves into devoted followers – then several aspects need to be considered: not just the personal characteristics of the leaders and their leadership style, but also the socio-economic situation and the orientations of the followers. The relations being formed in the CCC case were not simply charismatic persons triggering certain reactions, but a more complex interplay between the characteristics of those involved (including young subordinates), favourable context (the rapid growth of the market) and processes involving an effective leadership style and intensive interaction (including attention, feedback and open praise of the personnel, frequent social events outside work, etc.).

Post-founder leadership

This history of leadership at CCC provides the background for the common features of the exercise of leadership within the company at the time of my study – 10 years after it was founded and 2–3 years after the founders had withdrawn from the operational management of the company. The patterns initiated by the founders continued to be distinct to the company. Group cohesion, friendship, 'have fun at the workplace', openness and generosity with information to the employees, etc. were important values.

From the view of CCC's management an important task was to create a totality, to get the parts of the company together. What may be referred to as social integrative leadership is a matter of inducing a common orientation and direction in the operative units (the subsidiaries, project groups and individual consultants), and to contribute to the identification with the company and a feeling of loyalty, and to achieve social cohesion both at the micro level, within work groups and subsidiaries, and at the overall level, within the company as an entity. Social integrative leadership does not primarily address technical and operative issues. It is a matter of transferring ideas, meanings and orientations that counteract the disintegrative tendencies inherent in consultancy work. It facilitates convergence in thinking, feeling and acting which increases the chances of people staying in the company, getting along and being able to cooperate efficiently within and between units.

Social integrative leadership is partly a matter of boundary keeping. The key group in CCC was the subsidiary managers – heading units of 30–50 people. (When a subsidiary grew and employed more than 50 persons, it was divided up into two units.) The company prided itself on its decentralization and very flat organization. In consultancy companies, as in some other service companies, the boundaries between company and customer were often unclear. The projects were carried out on behalf of the client, in cooperation with the client's personnel and often at the client's workplace. This could trigger loyalty conflicts, and identity problems might follow from this:

> You are out there with the customer and keep your face. But you easily get into problems with loyalty. And if you are to be on the right side of the border you have to go home occasionally and discuss the situation ...

For subsidiary managers it was then important to create and maintain strong social bonds between the company and the consultants:

> If you are working for a customer all on your own you have a tremendous need to have contact with your manager. To feel that you are not only earning money, but that you also are a person and important as such.

The subsidiary manager was important here as a representative of, and symbol for, the company as well as having a personal relation with the consultants. It was, CCC people thought, important that he or she was both respected and well liked. A related important aspect concerned the internal social cohesiveness and atmosphere within the company. The subsidiary managers should be socially active and express a positive and engaged spirit. The expectations in the company were high in this regard.

I will now give two brief illustrations to show how what may be viewed as leadership in CCC was exercised, in ways aiming to ensure that the right values and orientations were accomplished. Both illustrations are from the recruitment and selection process, which at CCC (but also more generally) reproduce and reinforce culture through selectivity in who is employed and also what the process signals to the newcomers. One example came from observations of a manager, responding to calls on a recruitment advertisement. Having described the company and the jobs and answered questions, he asked the persons calling – if they were interested in applying – to write to the company and say something about themselves and their qualifications, what they wanted and what they were like as persons. He asked them not to send academic grades, etc. He was not interested in formal documents. This signalled an informal approach, in which trust is indicated. It also communicated that it was personal characteristics and orientations, rather than technical skills or the job as best carried out in a depersonalized way, that were valued in this company.

In another example, also from the recruitment process, a manager asked personal questions like 'are you religious?', 'are you jealous?' and 'is it important for you to speak the truth?' He also talked with the potential employee's spouse about the job, what it might mean in terms of travelling, being away from home, etc. before an agreement to employ the interviewee was made.

In the second case there was also an emphasis on the informal as well as a broader view of the personnel in the workplace. The manager went far beyond what is traditionally conceived of as being part of the work role. This indicated that his and the company's interest in the personnel went much further than how to solve computer problems between 8 a.m. and 5 p.m. Openness and informality as well as the importance of the personal life and the link and overlap between work and home life were stressed. The new employee and his/her spouse were also expected to commit themselves to the demands of the company in terms of overtime, travelling, etc.

Dominant values in the company meant that there were certain local institutionalized expectations on managers. These were related to the style and values of the founders that had left a strong imprint on the organization as a whole:

> There is an opinion, a certain education that you get on how to be a manager in this company and that comes from the old leaders, the founders of the company. The leaders are seen as very important, to be a sort of cultural carrier and to be an ideal for the personnel. As a leader you must participate in all social arrangements. You should preferably be the funniest of all, you should be visible all the time and give a direction to the company and the personnel in the way you wish the company to function, offer nice parties and tell stories and things like that. (Subsidiary manager)

One manager expressed this as 'in CCC you only employ managers that can become buddies with their consultants' and 'the employees expect to have a beer with the CEO'. The personnel had more or less the right to veto candidates for subsidiary manager positions. One externally recruited manager failed to live up to expectations about providing information. He tried to put up a smokescreen around a bad financial result during his first year to keep it from the subordinates. They found out, and this contributed to their successfully demanding his removal from the company.

In this company there was a rather strong and explicit cultural framing of leadership at the organizational level. Top management, but perhaps even more so the personnel, had certain values and expectations on management and leadership to which the managers had to respond in order to be credible, legitimate and effective: to be active in social arrangements, to downplay status and prestige and emphasize close and informal social relationships, put personnel and team building into focus. As a manager you were part of and a key player in an organizational community. All this breaks with traditional hierarchies. For managers, this was a constraint but also a guiding framework in their leadership.

CCC was, of course, like all companies, unique in many ways. It was at the time of the study a young and, in terms of cultural orientations, very distinct and high-profiled organization. Many other companies incorporate perhaps less distinct, less espoused and more taken-for-granted ideas, beliefs and expectations. Still, there are institutionalized cultural orientations carried by superiors, colleagues and subordinates which means a selectivity in terms of who is recruited to and allowed to stay in managerial positions, and cultural rules for the kind of leadership that is seen as acceptable and that people respond positively to. The case of CCC illustrates how organizational culture shapes leadership, thus reversing the opposite logic characterizing the formative years of the firm, where founders had a strong impact on organizational culture.

Summary and Conclusions

In this chapter I have tried to make four interrelated points on leadership. A cultural understanding of leadership calls for an appreciation of local meaning. Leadership can be defined as about influencing the construction of reality – the ideas, beliefs and interpretations of what and how things can and should be done, in the light of what the world looks like. An understanding of leadership calls for the nuanced interpretation of the relation and context of interaction between superior and subordinate. But not all aspects of this interaction are best understood as leadership. Many researchers suggest a distinction between manager and leader. The leader then supposedly relies less on formal means and addresses 'substantial' concerns, but exercises an influence through the heads, hearts and values of people. However, managers always – in some way or another – 'manage' culture. Even strongly bureaucratic and number-crunching managers, not having management of meaning in mind, reinforce rule- and measurement-focused cultures and thus affect thinking, feeling and values. Also non-managerial organizational members contribute to cultural formation/reproduction, but typically from weaker positions.

A second point concerns the balance between academic *a priori* definitions of leadership and openness to the meanings of the people being studied. It is important to be somewhat careful in imposing a particular definition on leadership and instead be open to the meanings ascribed to 'leadership' by the natives. Interesting themes then become when, how and why do the people in an organization talk about leadership. What meanings – coherent, varying or contradictory – are expressed around leadership and what particular acts and arrangements are seen as leadership? What hopes, fears and expectations are there? How do people react to various styles and acts seen as expressing leadership? What is perceived as leadership?

Who is seen as a 'leader'? Which metaphors for leadership seem to inform understanding of this phenomenon – commander, coach, visionary? Interpreting the local meaning of leadership offers a route to an understanding of organizational culture. And vice versa.

If one wants to understand leadership it is a good idea to put less emphasis on the leader and what he or she does and more on how people relate and respond to managers' actions. The effect-triggering element in leadership is less what the leader does *per se* than how subordinates perceive, interpret and react to the leaders' actions. One and the same behaviour may, for example, be read as 'authoritative' and 'capable of making a decision' or 'authoritarian' and 'outdated', with very different implications for legitimacy, trust and motivation on the part of the subordinates. Here cultural meanings form a framework for the interpretation and assessment of managerial acts, and form the basis for how managers and subordinates negotiate shared meanings around the doings of leadership.

A third point concerns the influence of culture on leadership. As leadership is normally not carried out from a sociocultural point zero, but always takes place in a context of already developed meaning patterns – those of the leader and those of others – there is always a strong element of cultural determination of leadership. Promotion is often dependent on being adapted to dominant orientations of senior managers, which means that managers typically fit into corporate culture and tend to carry on rather than deviate from dominant patterns. Most leadership is culture-driven in the sense that shared beliefs and norms inform the manager how to act. Culture here may refer to the organizational level, but also societal, industrial and occupational cultures may be central. Leadership is then better seen as 'within' rather than 'outside' culture. Within culture-driven leadership the skilful manager may exercise considerable influence. Cultural constraints are seldom very strict, but may give rather broad parameters. Sometimes the acts of managers and informal leaders also more independently shape elements of culture. More significant examples of culture-shaping leadership (leadership-driven cultures) are rare, but in certain situations – particularly when organizations are founded, and during major crises, where a significant portion of key personnel are replaced – the situation is more open to the reframing of ideas, beliefs and meanings.

This brings us to charisma and a fourth point. In those examples where powerful leadership appears to have a strong impact on the radical transformation of culture, it is often viewed as charismatic leadership being in operation. When a person is ascribed charisma it means by definition a far-reaching preparedness to let oneself be influenced by a person. The question is under what circumstances followers can be moulded so strongly that they radically transform their frameworks and beliefs through the impact of a big leader. In business and public administration this is probably rare, and claims of the charismatic president turning round an organizational culture sometimes seem rather exaggerated – as I tried to demonstrate in the case of Iacocca. To understand charisma, as with other forms of leadership, not only the charismatic superhero, but also the context and the orientations of the subordinates need to be considered.

To sum up this chapter, I am arguing that the leadership of managers (and even more so of informal leaders) is typically strongly constrained by, and draws upon, the cultural and ideological context(s) of the organization. New ideas and initiatives are more likely to succeed if they are broadly in line with the dominant values and understandings. Recognizing that there are exceptions, leaders are normally better understood as 'transmitters' than as 'masters' of culture. Managers may more or less intentionally, more or less skilfully act as 'cultural engineers'. They are typically significantly more influential in the ongoing reproduction and revisions of cultural meanings than other organizational members.

Notes

1 Some authors do, however, include a broad spectrum of highly diverse orientations, tasks and behaviours in leadership (e.g. House and Aditay, 1997).
2 One wonders if managers and others supposed to do leadership receive that much help from, for example, popular leadership theories expressing an ideal, normative view of the subject matter, as they are out of touch with any realistic appreciation of organizational reality. This is sometimes messy, political and focused on the delivery of short-term results and adapting to the will of one's boss (Jackall, 1988; Watson, 1994), often involving subordinates not so inclined to accept the ideas and suggestions of their managers (Lundholm, 2011) and often characterized by pressing administrative and technical work allowing little space and time for leadership, apart from in event-driven, reactive forms (Alvesson and Sveningsson, 2003; Holmberg and Tyrstrup, 2010).
3 As Trice and Beyer (1993) point out, charisma also has some considerable drawbacks. The strong emotions and the bracketing of critical thinking in relationship to the leader may lead to irrationality. There is also a strong risk of disillusion when the high expectations on the leader are no longer met. Even though charisma means highly influential leadership, companies do not necessarily benefit from charismatic leaders.

19

Experiencing the Organizational Underworld

Coghlan, D.

Leslie reported that one day a member of staff whom the newly appointed assistant manager had only met joked with her about some grey hairs she had. She asked him to stop but he continued to the mirth of the listening staff and to her embarrassment. She was later overheard to say that he would regret what he had done when he read the next week's roster. When the roster was published several days later his working hours had been cut considerably.

The organizational underworld is the organization's dynamic life below the waterline in the lily pond image, the back region in Goffman's work or what is sometimes called 'the workplace within'. As presented earlier, the formal frontstage life is marked by rationality while the back region is marked by culture, meanings, attitudes, experiences, feelings, relationships, rumour/gossip, power, politics, etc. It is this covert life that makes organizations different from one another, and interesting and exciting to work in and to study. As organizations frame themselves in terms of mission, strategy and markets, they are also centres of a theory of action, hidden meanings, symbols, assumptions, feelings and covert behaviour. As an insider you have access to the back region and your insider inquiry opens up understanding of what might be going on. In this chapter you are invited to bring your experience to bear on seeking insight into the underworld of your organization. There are very many subjects that could be explored under the heading of the organizational underworld. Several are selected for attention here: the effect of its theory of action, how emotion is handled, the role rumour and gossip play, humour and joking, lying and, finally, demotivation and its outcomes in defensive behaviour. There may be other subjects that you choose to pursue yourself.

THEORY OF ACTION

In Chapter 1 the notion of a theory of action was introduced. What a theory of action emphasizes is how organizations have a *theory-in-use*; that is, the theory that is actually employed, usually tacitly, and is unrecognized by the people employing it. Argyris found that most organizational *theory-in-use* is grounded in an implicit disposition to controlling, winning and to avoiding embarrassment. The assumptions are: be in unilateral control, win and do not lose, suppress negative feelings and behave rationally. The action strategies that follow such assumptions are aimed to protect and defend the self against embarrassing situations by speaking in inferred and attributed categories thereby engaging in a defensive reasoning mindset to explain actions and to implement future actions. The consequences are routines that promote protectiveness, self-reinforcing behaviour, escalating error and ultimately increased defensiveness and decreased effectiveness. But because these routines are unquestioned the decreased effectiveness may not be noticed. Have you noticed situations backstage where your colleagues discuss a current problematic issue and make comments in the vein of 'of course the boss doesn't want to know'?

As Argyris explains defensive routines are thoughts and actions that are used to protect individuals, teams and organizations from dealing with reality. They are reinforced by organizational members who would prefer if these routines didn't exist but defend them as being necessary and part of being in the 'real world'. The routines are based on untested inferences that organizational members make. Organizational members reach conclusions that they believe they have tested carefully, but they haven't because they have been framed to make them untestable because they are privately held. In terms of what was discussed in Chapter 2 organizational members have climbed the Ladder of Inference. 'The boss doesn't want to know' is such a conclusion that is based on an inference. Accordingly, such routines are not discussable and that they are not discussable is itself not discussable. Organizational learning, which we will explore in Chapter 7, is inhibited because what cannot be discussed is kept hidden and is undiscussable.

In summary, an organizational theory of action produces consequences that people do not intend when they deal with difficult problems. It leads them to hold other people or the system responsible for errors rather than examine their own responsibility. They may exhibit collective *Child* self-protective responses to threats that are exhibited in organizational games. It enables errors to be repeated skilfully and organizational black holes in which information is driven underground are created.

Take a reflective pause and see if you can catch signs of defensive routines in your organization. This is not easy to do but is worth attempting so as to gain insight into the hidden world of your organization.

REFLECTIVE PAUSE

Reflecting on your organization:

- What is undiscussable in your organization?
- What makes it undiscussable?
- Can the fact that it is undiscussable be discussed?
- What is preventing what is undiscussable being discussed?

Standing back from any particular incident, what insights have you about your organization's action theory? Can you verify these insights?

EMOTION IN ORGANIZATIONS

As noted in Chapter 1, while the formal organization assumes that the only emotion that exists in the organization is goodwill based on satisfaction, motivation and energetic commitment towards the organization's goals, experience shows that organizations are arenas of feeling and emotion. This is not surprising. People are people and the affective side of their lives does not get put aside when they come to work. Similarly, relationships have rich affective dynamics and they also are part of work relationships. You like working with some people and not with others. You make friends at work. Some events at work may make you frustrated or angry; others have you enthusiastic. You have disagreements and conflicts which arouse strong emotion. In TA terms your *Parent* and *Child* are evoked and you may have to work hard to stay grounded in your *Adult* and judge when it is appropriate to be in a different ego state.

Organizations have an emotional life and this emotional life is intrinsic to their cultural wellbeing. Emotions can be a source of motivation and demotivation. For example a climate of organizational confidence or anxiety can aid or inhibit collaborative work and output. Emotions are often the first response to change. Reading emotions is a management capability. Mostly it involves being attuned to emotions that are being expressed (explicitly) or repressed and being empathic rather than rushing in to suppress or to rescue. It is easy to be emotional when the emotions are happy ones, such as celebrating a birthday, someone getting married or having a baby but it is much more difficult when we are confronted by the uncomfortable emotions of anger, alienation or grief.

For example, Bento explores how organizations have difficulty in coping with grief. She notes that organizations allow bereaved people a few days to deal with the death of loved ones, according to a sliding scale of love: so many days for a partner, for a child, a parent, a friend. Then after that period, with an awkward pat on the back, the bereaved worker is expected to 'get over it'. Any subsequent expression of grief is deemed inappropriate. Yet people cannot turn expressions of grief on and off. While you may be embarrassed to find a colleague in tears at his/her desk, it is harder when you see the person keeping an impassive demeanour and acting out grief indirectly through moodiness, making mistakes, being late and being unapproachable. A Transactional Analysis perspective could be that a collective *Child* is at work where unpleasant emotions are kept out so that there's a false happiness.

ENVY AND JEALOUSY

While the terms are sometimes used together, envy and jealousy are considered to be distinct emotions. Envy occurs when a person lacks another's perceived superior achievement or possessions and either desires it or wishes the other didn't have it. Jealousy occurs in the context of relationships, occurring when a person fears losing an important relationship to a rival. Envy and jealousy may be benign whereby you may desire the qualities of the other but don't wish that the other didn't have them or lose them. They may be malicious where there is a desire to put the other down. In TA terms envy and jealousy are *Child* responses.

EMOTIONAL LABOUR

Emotional labour is a feature of many contemporary organizations. By emotional labour is meant that the expression of feeling is imposed on particular role functions so as to portray a positive perception, irrespective of the particular feelings that an individual may have at the time. Indeed the expressed feelings may clash with inner feelings. There is a requirement that frontline employees of Disney, McDonald's and airlines portray a happy disposition and display a positive attitude constantly. Debt collectors may be under an obligation to portray a stern if not a nasty disposition. The popular notion of 'good cop, bad cop' is an artificial construction that forces both to play a role that may be other than how they may be actually feeling about the situation at hand.

The notion of emotional labour has particular relevance to front-line service staff who are at the organization–customer interface and who are representing the organization to the public. In Goffman's terms it is frontstage activity. Does it involve surface or deep acting on the part of the employee? Surface acting involves playing a part and simulating emotions that you don't actually feel, particularly by adopting the outer behaviour of facial cues and using specific gestures. Deep acting involves you trying to feel the emotion you think you have to feel (a *Parent* response) as you psych yourself into the role. The positive outcomes are selling more products, dealing with complaints more effectively and generally ensuring that customers return. The dysfunctions are that you may experience a dissonance and feel false and hypocritical in a way that may eventually lead to alienation, low self-esteem, depression and stress (a *Child* response).

Take a reflective pause to review your experience in your organization.

REFLECTIVE PAUSE

Reflecting on your organization:

- What pressure is there on your work colleagues (and yourself) to portray a happy and helpful disposition all the time?
- From your backstage experience do your work colleagues put it on as surface acting or do some try to internalize the emotions they are 'supposed' to portray? What outcomes do you observe for those individuals?
- Does having to play a role in emotional labour evoke your *Child* in you?
- What happens when an individual lets the mask drop and reacts to a customer in a manner that is undesired by the organization? How does management react? Are there consequences for that individual?

Standing back from any particular incident, what insights have you about your organization? Can you verify these insights?

RUMOUR AND GOSSIP

While organizations have formal communication channels, such as memos, briefings, bulletin boards, intranets, newsletters, social media and so on, there are also informal communication channels through which employees pass on information through networks of colleagues and friends. This is typically referred to as the grapevine that spreads information, which may be true or false, factual or speculative. In these instances we are referring to rumour and gossip.

Rumour and gossip are important vehicles for informal communication. What is interesting about rumour and gossip is that they are indirect communication, characterized by something like 'I can't remember who told me but have you heard?' The source of the information is not easily identifiable and you might wonder why this information is being spread around. The commonly accepted understanding of rumour is that it is talk that is unsubstantiated by authority or evidence as to its authenticity or truth. It is often regarded as synonymous with hearsay. Popularly regarded as idle talk or trivial chatter, gossip ordinarily carries with it the presumption of having some basis in fact.

Sometimes rumour is distinguished from gossip and other times they are indistinguishable. The basis of rumour is information that is unsubstantiated; it is more public and widely disseminated. Gossip typically occurs in a context of privacy and intimacy and only through and with friends and acquaintances and may or may not be a known fact. It is also conceivable that the initiation of a rumour may be underpinned by some element of 'truth', no matter how obscure or circumstantial the evidence. The extent of the truth or fact is difficult to determine and you may never know if something is a 'white lie' or a 'half truth'. Gossip deals with issues or events of interest to an individual or small group while the parameters of rumour extend beyond a few individuals since its message is of more universal interest.

The purpose or functions served by rumour or gossip are numerous and wide-ranging. Broadly, these are depicted as information, influence and entertainment. The first of these represents an attempt by individuals to better understand their social environment. The second builds on the first by addressing the utilization of information to the individual's benefit. Some contend, for instance, that gossip within organizations may provide a 'survival mechanism' in that it could be one means of humanizing bureaucratic structures. One tangible outcome of this may be related to alleviating excessive levels of employee stress. Finally, rumour or gossip may have entertainment value for its own sake.

Mishra describes different rumour types:

1   *The 'pipe dream' or wish fulfilment.* Such rumours largely express the hopes of those who circulate them. One example might be expressing a possible solution to a work problem that the employee wants to change.
2   *The 'bogey' or anxiety rumour.* These are primarily driven by fear and, consequently, create unease among its recipients. An example of this might be a company takeover and the prospect of redundancies in the not-too-distant future.
3   *The anticipatory rumour.* These are often precipitated by situations of ambiguity. An illustration of this might be whether or not a new general manager will come from within the organization or be appointed from elsewhere.

4   *The aggressive rumour.* Here, women may face disadvantage since they are
    more likely to be the subject of sexual gossip. Sometimes, this may stem from
    a perception that female employees are romantically involved with other
    organizational members for the primary purpose of advancing their careers.

A rumour will tend to dissipate if it becomes irrelevant. Once an event has occurred and
the facts have been established, the rumour becomes superfluous. In addition, rumours
may lose interest among their recipients due to boredom, frustration or simply because
they fail to generate sufficient interest.

In your insider experience and in taking up your reflection you may attend to how engaging in rumour and gossip may evoke something of your *Critical Parent* or the *Spiteful Child*,
and so you respond in a complementary mode. 'Wow! That's what I suspected all along about
that person. Tell me more' or 'I'm not surprised given the way she behaves'. 'Did you hear
the one about ...?' You may, in your *Adult*, choose not to get sucked into that complementary transaction and may cross the transaction by inquiring into the truth of the situation.

THE GRAPEVINE

There are informal communication channels in organizations through which employees pass on information through networks of colleagues and friends. This is typically
referred to as the grapevine, the informal mechanism through which rumour and gossip moves through an organization. It demonstrates a healthy expression of the human
need to communicate because it reflects that employees are interested in their work. The
grapevine is unstructured and not under management's control. It moves in all directions -
upwards, downwards, sideways across and between chains of command. It is dynamic
and varied and even fickle. It goes on all day and continues outside of working hours and
works faster than the formal organizational communication channels. It performs a useful task in supplementing the formal communication channels by allowing people to think
and talk about what they fear will happen and how they might react. In this manner, the
grapevine acts as an early warning system. Management may use it to test how a new
idea will be received. A carefully planned leak from the senior management group provides an opportunity for management to test the water on a potentially explosive plan.

Since the grapevine cannot be held responsible for errors and misinformation, and it
cannot be silenced or suppressed, management needs to provide information through
formal systems of communication so as to minimize any damage done by the grapevine.
Rumours can escalate and so management may need to provide hard facts and as complete information as is possible in order to allay fears and reduce anxiety.

Take a reflective pause to study a rumour or gossip that you experienced in your
organization.

REFLECTIVE PAUSE

Reflecting on your organization think of a rumour or gossip that circulated in your organization via the grapevine:

- What was it about?
- What purpose did it serve?
- How did it circulate?
- Did you believe it? If so, how was it that you found it credible? If you didn't believe it, why not?
- Did others believe it? To what effect?

Standing back from any particular incident, what insights have you about your organization? Can you verify these insights?

HUMOUR AND JOKING

In frontstage activity organizations understand themselves as serious places as they work to sell their product or deliver their service. Humour is a backstage activity that lightens an atmosphere, especially if that atmosphere is very restricted. A shared laugh brings people together and enables them to relax. It can help build relationships and trust as work colleagues enjoy being in their *Child*. It can also be divisive as it may demonstrate an inclusion/exclusion divide, a *Spiteful Child* mode. Who is in on the joke? Who isn't? Does the joke reflect the covert humour and power of an in-group? If jokes are told about other people (i.e. the manager), while they may be funny do they leave the question, are jokes told about me behind my back? If the jokes are based on stereotypes (whether sexist, racist or other groupings) they create a wariness and an inhibition that counters the intended light and collegial atmosphere. If practical jokes are played on people (it tends to be only some people) they may create annoyance and destroy trust.

Sex is a frequent undercurrent of jokes. While in the frontstage or the formal organization sexual stereotyping and explicit reference to gender-related issues is regulated, it is common in a subtle form backstage. Jokes are one such form. Across genders, comments about who fancies whom or where comments are made about appearance, sexual innuendo or stereotyping may be quite destructive. What may appear to some as light teasing may be experienced by others as sexual harassment. Sometimes such teasing goes on for too long or there is little sensitivity as to how an individual is taking it. Within gender groupings, the 'lads' or the 'girls', the conversations about the other gender may be quite unsettling and leave a bad taste, but there may be peer pressure to join in and go along with them.

Take a reflective pause to consider on how humour and joking take place in your organization

---

REFLECTIVE PAUSE

Reflecting on your organization:

- What jokes were told in your hearing recently? What were they about? Were they about the organization and people in it?
- Did you find them funny? Did others? Even though they may have laughed have you a question about how they were received? What is your evidence?
- Are there recurrent jokes that you or others find distasteful? Is the joke teller ever confronted?

Standing back from any particular incident, what insights have you about your organization? Is humour a characteristic of the backstage of your organization? What role does it play in building and maintaining working relationships? Can you verify these insights?

TELLING LIES

Edgar Schein in a provocative article on learning when and how to lie poses a dilemma. On the one hand, as we saw in Chapter 1, the dramatic pattern of experience is grounded in the creation and enactment of social roles where the rules of interaction to preserve the social order require a certain amount of constructive lying where you apply good manners and tact to maintain relationships. Telling the literal truth in many social situations may be very destructive and may destroy necessary working relationships. On the other hand, where management places emphasis on openness, information sharing and organizational learning, lying about results, falsifying financial figures or suppressing unwelcome information are understood as being destructive and, of course, may be illegal. Schein's answer to the dilemma is to posit that lying is not a moral issue in itself. What makes it a moral issue is the intent to be destructive and the degree of harm intended. In Chapter 3 you reflected on how you make value judgements. In the context of this chapter on the organizational underworld, you are being invited to attend to learning how to make a subtle and sophisticated distinction between lying for reasons of good manners or tact, and telling a version of the truth to enhance yourself or put a favourable spin on some event in which you were involved. Do you lie out of your *Adult* or your *Child*?

Take a reflective pause to reflect on the role telling lies plays in the organization in which you are working.

REFLECTIVE PAUSE

Reflecting on your organization:

- What lies do you know are told in your organization? How would you categorize them on a scale from harmless to destructive/illegal?
- What pressure have you experienced to tell a lie? From whom, management or your peers? What did you do?

Standing back from any particular incident, what insights have you about your organization? Can you verify these insights?

THE PROCESS OF DEMOTIVATION

It can be safely assumed that people generally come to a job already motivated and that they are set on the road to demotivation by thoughtlessness and neglect, particularly by management behaviour. Demotivation is where an individual adopts a *Child* stance and, over time, becomes angry at how he/she has been treated, makes various unsuccessful attempts to be seen to work harder and subsequently adopts a disillusioned position. At that point he/she either leaves the organization or adopts a sulky *Child* stance of working the system and grumbling persistently. Leaving the organization may not be a viable option, particularly in an economic recession, so the disillusioned employee may opt to work the system, which is to stay in the organization and exploit it as best as possible for their own self-interest – securing all the benefits available, avoiding all volunteering and extra work and managing to spend as little time as possible doing anything significant. Persistent grumbling is where the individual always complains and grumbles about conditions and how things are in the organization. Some individuals manage to find a niche for themselves in which they create their own private enclave and reduce interdependence with others. Ashforth and Lee describe defensive behaviour as avoiding action by over-conforming, passing the buck, playing dumb, depersonalizing and stalling and avoiding blame by playing safe, justifying and scapegoating. The final option is to collaborate with others who feel the same as they do in creating a collective delusion, which in Merry and Brown's view becomes a neurotic mechanism. So there is blaming, hostility, aggression, anger, feelings of frustration and dysfunctional organizational behaviour that bind people into a collective delusion and serve to relieve the organization of responsibility for confronting and dealing with its problems.

Take a reflective pause to think about whether there is evidence of demotivated employees in your organization. Remember that you cannot get inside the head of another person to judge their motivations. You can make judgements about how your organization works.

REFLECTIVE PAUSE

Reflecting on your organization:

- Do you see evidence of what you understand to be demotivated colleagues who have created their own private enclave of constant grumbling, blaming and complaining? Have they been written off by management and other colleagues?
- Do you observe other colleagues at earlier stages of demotivation? What is your evidence? Are they being noticed? Are the causes being addressed?

Standing back from any particular incident, what insights have you about your organization? Can you verify these insights?

CONCLUSIONS

This chapter has explored some aspects of the organizational underworld, that is what goes on covertly backstage. As an insider you have access to the back region and your insider inquiry opens up understanding of what might be going on. The number of topics that could be covered under this heading is extensive. The handful of topics selected in this chapter is intended to be illustrative rather than comprehensive. The hope is that you will find your own topics, ones that have occurred in your direct experience, that you will pursue them and that you will seek insight into the underworld of your organization. They also provide the opportunity for you to develop insights into your PRIVATE and BLIND panes in how you choose to engage in this underworld.

Managing Cultures

Clegg, S. R., Kornberger, M. and Pitsis, T.

LEARNING OBJECTIVES

This chapter is designed to enable you to:

- Recognize that organizational culture is a more complex phenomenon than it is often thought to be in accounts that assume that all organizations have just one culture

- Understand why managing culture within organizations can be a challenge

- Understand why organizations typically have multiple cultures and subcultures, which makes them less easily manageable by managers

- Distinguish between views of culture as organizationally integrated, differentiated, or fragmented

- Describe how official conceptions of organizational culture often function as a resource for managing, rather than a literal description of the state of affairs

- Explain why the influential work of Geert Hofstede is subject to serious criticism

BEFORE YOU GET STARTED . . .

Unfortunately, it takes just a bit longer for organizational members to change their organization than it takes the organization to change its members. *(Joschka Fischer, past German Foreign Minister)*

INTRODUCTION

Managing the culture of an organization is sometimes presented as an easy task. This chapter will show why that is by no means always the case. For one thing, there often is not a singular organizational culture. For another, whatever cultures exist are often not easily amenable to being managed.

Culture largely comprises the habits, values, mores, and ways of acting – often referred to as the norms – by which people identify themselves and others. Both similarity and difference come into play. Cultural identity is established both by comparison with those whom you see as alike and those whom you see as different, as members of distinct groups. One way of clearly establishing what

Culture represents the totality of everyday knowledge that people use habitually to make sense of the world around them through patterns of shared meanings and understandings passed down through language, symbols, and artifacts.

Norms represent the
tacit and unspoken
assumptions and informal
rules, the meaning of which
people negotiate in their
everyday interactions.

norms are is by breaking them; breaching a norm often means others define the
nature of your deviance from the norm. In other words, you are more likely to
know when you are breaking cultural norms, than when you are practising them.

THE CONCEPTS OF CULTURE

HIGH CULTURE AND THE CULTURES OF EVERYDAY LIFE

What do you think of when you hear the word *culture*? Beethoven, Picasso,
Shakespeare's *Hamlet*, and Tchaikovsky's *Swan Lake*, or Eminem's rhymes, Damien
Hirst's dead animals, *Harry Potter* novels, and *The Lord of the Rings* movies
(Jackson, 2001–2003)? These are all objects of culture. However, culture is not just
'high art'. Some is 'popular' culture such as *Harry Potter*; others are high culture,
such as Shakespeare (although, in his day, Shakespeare was very popular culture).
Culture includes the popular, the everyday, and mundane just as much as the
most elevated cultural products. In fact, everything that is constructed according
to some underlying rule forms a part of culture – no matter whether it is gangsta
rap, Shakespearean sonnets, or the ancient Chinese book/oracle *I Ching*.

Of course, art objects, paintings, popular music, poetry, and other artifacts
are not the only things that are constituted according to rules – so are societies
and organizations. In organizations, everything that marks out the way that we
relate to our habitats, offices, nature, and each other is a part of culture. To put
it in other words, our everyday existence and the ways that we relate to it are
embedded in cultural norms, cultural artifacts, and cultural practices.

Artifacts are those things
with which we mark out
territory: the decorations
and art in a building; the
furnishings and fittings;
the styles of clothes
that people wear; the
types of desks, offices,
and computers that
they use - these are all
artifacts that tell us, subtly,
about the environments
we occupy or are in.

WHAT WOULD YOU DO?

All societies have rules about who can do what to whom and under what circumstances,
or what you can and cannot wear on particular occasions, or which people are allowed
access to specific places and under what circumstances. Given that we all need to eat to live, it
is particularly interesting to consider the rules that surround food. All societies have rules about
what is edible and what is not. How do *you* feel about chicken's feet, a delicacy in Hong Kong;
Witchety grubs, an Australian Koori treat; dog, a perennial favourite in Korea and some other
parts of Asia; rats, sometimes on the menu in China; cow's stomach lining (tripe), popular both in
the north of England and in many parts of Continental Europe; or horsemeat, a German delicacy?
What would you do as a guest? Would you eat the culture you were offered?

Sports make the importance of rules for defining a specific culture clear.
Organizations such as the Royal and Ancient Golf Club of St Andrews are repositories of elaborate rules about membership and members' duties, and enforce
and interpret the rules of the game of golf. The rules of a sport may be more
or less formal. Golf is very formal – it has rules that are constitutive of how it
should be played; but what about skateboarding – how formal is that? Skaters
can have a fairly organized sense about the rules of the game they play. The two
images of skaters, 7.2a and 7.2b, show an informal skate competition in Paris
that was set up on the Pont Louis, a bridge that is closed to traffic which goes
over the River Seine from the Ile de la Cité. The apparatus was composed of found
materials (notably street barriers, which the participants picked up on the street as

IMAGE 7.1   The rules of golf are subject to final interpretation by the gentlemen of the Royal and Ancient Golf Club, St Andrews ('St Andrews' by H. G. Gawthorn)

they sped to the venue on their skates). All the participants understand the rules: the aim, as can be seen from the subsequent pictures, was to clear an obstacle set as high as possible, as stylishly as possible – these were the preferential rules.

When rules are informal, rather than formal, they are often referred to as 'norms'. Norms define culture. These norms are not necessarily what is formally stipulated but are based on what people in the organization actually do. To illustrate this point, in a study of hospitals and the way that people within it dealt with terminally ill patients, the norms revealed that there was a well-established 'officially unofficial' culture that shaped the organization's treatment of those of its patients who departed the organization by dying.

Sudnow's (1967) *Passing On: The Sociology of Dying* compares the culture of two hospitals, one private and one public. One characteristic of both was that most deaths in the hospitals seemed to occur in the mornings. Although Sudnow initially could not figure out why this was the case, he eventually discovered that when death occurred on the night shift, the staff would try not to recognize the fact because of the attendant duties associated with it. Dead bodies are a bureaucratic nightmare; heaps of paperwork and a lot of physical and clean-up work are associated with them. Thus, the shift culture regarded dead bodies as a nuisance best left for the new morning shift to attend to. Hence, deaths peak in the morning, when the new shift clocks on and has to register, statistically, the fact of death.

Culture is a concept with its own complex history that stretches back long before organization theorists began to study it. Consider Image 7.3, showing Traitor's Gate at the Tower of London – the place where traitors, having been transported by barge up the River Thames, entered the tower to await their execution (or, if they were lucky, imprisonment). Traitor's Gate stands as a stark reminder of what might be the consequences of breaking the organizational culture rules in an organization ruled by an absolute authority, such as the Tudor monarchy of Henry VIII. Many of the king's courtiers and two of his wives – Anne Boleyn and Catherine Howard – saw that gate close behind them.

IMAGES 7.2a and 7.2b   Even informal street games have clearly improvised rules

Today, there are still a few CEOs who seem to imagine that they can behave like Tudor monarchs. Many examples were provided at the trial of Lord Conrad Black, the ex-newspaper magnate, accused of using organizational finances as if they were his personal property, and convicted on charges of fraud. Referring to the 'greed of Conrad Black and his complete disregard for his shareholders', Hugh Totten (a partner for the New York law firm Perkins Coie) commented, 'It makes him look like some English Tudor monarch rather than the CEO of a public company with responsibility to shareholders' (Bone, 2007: 45).

In fact, few organizations today have the power of absolute authority. Modern CEOs find it difficult to be absolutist rulers because they do not have the powers of an absolutist monarch but are enmeshed in the rules of complex bureaucratic regulation. Nonetheless, their organizations are just as full of complex culture as any Tudor court. And, like a Tudor court, the cultural rules can often be highly implicit, subtle, and politically charged in interpretations. Tellingly, really great companies do not seem to be like this: they prize collaboration, boundary spanning, and initiative.

CORPORATE CULTURE
AT APPLE

IMAGE 7.3   The basis of the Tudor monarchy's organizational culture of control

ORGANIZATIONAL CULTURE

The earliest approaches to organizational culture actually referred to it using a term from the psychological literature, *organizational climate*. Schein (2002) argues that this term was a precursor to the concept of organizational culture. As Ashkenasy (2003) demonstrates, these roots are pervasive in discussions of organizational culture.

In the contemporary study of organizational culture, a split has opened up between those who maintain a focus on organizations as rational instruments, or tools, and those who see them as patterns of culture oriented around norms, claims to legitimacy, and the symbolism and artefacts that embedded these claims and counter-claims. Business consultants recognize organizational culture's potential for moulding individuals and collaborative relations in the service of management. From the early 1980s questions of culture came into renewed focus, due to a perception in the US and policy circles of the Japanese threat as having organizational (and national) cultural roots. Consultancies mushroomed that claimed to be able to build organizational cultures akin to communities or tight-knit 'clans', replete with images of mutual support, solidarity, and commitment.

More anthropologically oriented researchers were horrified at this instrumental, naïve, and managerialist appropriation of 'culture'. From a more anthropological perspective they were inclined to see culture as a topic in terms of a more conflict-oriented, fragmentary view, questioning the unitary assumptions of managerialist approaches. (For an approach to organizational culture that reflects a more anthropo-logical perspective you can consult Henry Stewart Talks, a series of online audiovisual seminars on Managing Organizations, edited by Stewart Clegg, and choose Talk #9: Managing cultures, by Professor Stephen Linstead of York Management School, UK, if your university supports access to this resource.)

MANAGING CULTURES

Considerations of organizational culture have long been implicit in the development of the field. Parker (2000: 128) notes perceptively that F. W. Taylor, whom we discuss in Chapter 14, sought to create a single utilitarian culture to minimize employee resistance and to maximize productivity – and, of course, to increase profits. However, Taylor in 1911 did not focus explicitly on culture. The earliest explicit research into culture as an object of specific study arose when Roethlisberger and Dickson (1939) argued in what are usually known as the Hawthorne studies that the most significant variables governing the output at the Hawthorne plant appeared to be not physical but social (see also pp. 100; 461–462). As Mouzelis (1967: 99) pointed out, such factors defined the 'culture of the group'.

The Hawthorne studies have been widely discussed and criticized. The series of experiments conducted at the Hawthorne works of the *Western Electric Company*, which mainly assembled telephone equipment, were and still remain 'ground-breaking'. The key research was conducted between November 1924 and February 1933, partly in the midst of the 'Great Depression'. The impact of variance in lighting, work pauses, work duration, payment, rations, and temperature on work output were measured. None of these variables seemed to explain the variations that were observed in workers' performance. Subsequently, something termed the *Hawthorne effect* was held to be responsible: the special managerial attention that attached to the experimental sites was regarded as enough to encourage enhanced performance even as working conditions deteriorated as the variables were changed. The reason given was that the managerial attention created a cultural effect by recognizing the collection of workers in the experimental sites as groups: something subsequently labelled as the culture of an informal organization. (The Hawthorne studies are addressed in Chapter 14.)

Contemporary managers can draw on various types of expert knowledge (psycho-technological and managerial) to manage culture by using comprehensible prescriptions to regulate actions (Kono and Clegg, 1998; Mayo, 1946): job descriptions, manuals of procedures, and mission and vision statements all serve to shape, subtly, the members' sense of their organization's culture. Increasingly, managers seek to secure compliance through shaping employees' attitudes and sentiments (Senge, 1990).

A common managerial assumption, going back to the Hawthorne studies, is that if you can create harmony in terms of expectations and behaviours that flow from the organizational culture, the organization will perform better. However, while some writers have seen culture as the great unifier in organizations, others see it as the great divider.

LEVELS OF CULTURE

Organizational culture comprises the deep, basic assumptions and beliefs, and the shared values that define organizational membership, as well as the members' habitual ways of making decisions, and presenting themselves and their organization to those who come into contact with it.

Schein (1997) offers the most popular definition of organizational culture. He defines it as the deep, basic assumptions and beliefs that are shared by organizational members. Culture is not displayed on the surface; instead, it is hidden and often unconscious. It represents the taken-for-granted way an organization perceives its environment and itself. To clarify the various components of culture in organizations, Schein differentiates between three levels of culture (Figure 7.1).

Level 1 consists of artifacts, including visible organizational features such as the physical structure of buildings and their architecture, uniforms, and interior design. This level is easily observable but does not reveal everything about an organization's culture. Sometimes researchers use the term organizational climate to refer to the more evident and malleable aspects of the organization's environment. For instance, the rich and powerful often use architecture to impress the less fortunate with the magnificence of their wealth. The ways in which these artifacts of power are manifested vary enormously from society to society (see Images 7.4 and 7.5).

IMAGES 7.4 and 7.5   Buildings as artefacts of power designed to awe the populace

Espoused values are a person's or social group's consistent beliefs about something in which they have an emotional investment as they express them; they are articulated in speeches, writings, or other media.

Level 2 comprises espoused values. Values represent a non-visible facet of culture that encompasses the norms and beliefs that employees express when they discuss organizational issues. A mission statement or a commitment to equal employment opportunities is part of this level.

Basic assumptions are defined by Schein as the core, or essence, of culture, represented in difficult to discern, largely unconscious, and tacit frames that subconsciously shape values and artifacts, formed around deep dimensions of human existence such as the nature of humans, human relationships and activity, reality and truth.

The deepest culture – the basic assumptions hidden beneath artifacts and expressed values – is found in level 3. This bull's eye in the dartboard representation of culture is the most important level. It includes the basic assumptions that shape organizational members' worldviews, beliefs, and norms, which guide their behaviour without being explicitly expressed. It is the most influential level because it works surreptitiously and shapes decision-making processes almost invisibly. It is hard to observe and even harder to change. Nonetheless, it is the level that carries the most potential for transformation. (Notice the Freudian influence on these conceptions of culture in terms of unconsciousness and hidden depths)

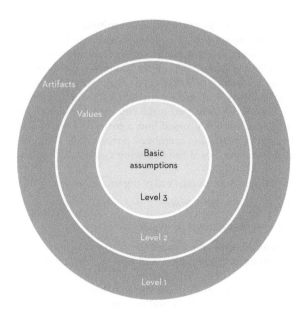

FIGURE 7.1   The levels of culture, according to Schein

STORIES OF STRONG CULTURES

SCHEIN'S CORPORATE
CULTURE

Stories are an important part of organizations; often they circulate as gossip, some-times as part of the informal legends, sagas, and mythologies of the organization and characters deemed important in its history. The key point about stories is that they are transmitted orally through story-telling although they can be recorded and become a part of the official story – think of how Silicon Valley companies such as Apple and Hewlett-Packard started off in garages and grew to become global corporations. Research on corporate cultures has used stories about top leadership that circulated widely in the organization as data. These tales captured something special and unique about the organization and often showed the exemplary quali-ties of the leadership in some way. Phenomena such as myths and legends became important objects for research. The culture became identified with everything from common behavioural patterns to espoused new corporate values that senior management wished to inculcate (Schein, 2002). The researchers who did most to popularize the story-telling approach initially were Peters and Waterman (1982).

PETERS AND WATERMAN: MCKINSEY CHANGING THE WORLD OF ORGANIZATIONS

CONSULTING FIRM
EXAMPLE

Tom Peters and Robert Waterman, two consultants from McKinsey & Company (the multinational consulting firm) who had links to Stanford's Graduate School of Business, offered an account of culture based on an instrumental view of the relation between managerial practice and management knowledge. They promoted the concept that culture that is strong and unifying – which is shared by everyone in an organization – is what makes companies great. It is worth looking at the web pages of any of the big consulting firms, and keying in 'culture', to see how consultancy angles deal with the topic today.

Peters and Waterman's *In Search of Excellence: Lessons From America's Best-Run Companies* was published in 1982. Previously, the central concern characterizing much of management and organization theory had been with organization *struc-ture*. This changed markedly as a result of *In Search of Excellence*, which propelled culture to centre stage in corporate analysis, resulting in related research that we will refer to as *excellence studies*. The message was simple: great companies have excellent cultures. Excellent cultures deliver outstanding financial success. What makes culture excellent is shared core values and presuppositions that are acted on.

Books such as *In Search of Excellence, Corporate Cultures: The Rites and Rituals of Corporate Life* (Deal and Kennedy, 1982) and *Organizational Culture and Leadership* (Schein, 1997) helped make culture a popular and acceptable topic in business. Excellence studies stressed how a pattern of learned and shared basic assumptions framed organization members' perceptions, thoughts, and feelings. Put simply, culture encompassed the following questions:

- How were things done in particular organizations?

- What was acceptable behaviour?

- What norms were imparted to new members?

- What norms were members expected to use to solve problems of external adaptation and internal integration, and which ones did they actually use?

Theorists presumed that if you forged a strong culture that incorporated all organization members in shared beliefs and commitments, everything else – good morale, performance, and results – should follow. Having such a widely shared and integrative culture in organizations is often viewed as a panacea for management and a sure-fire recipe for corporate success.

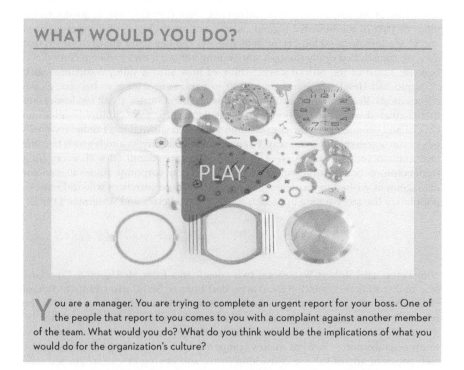

WHAT WOULD YOU DO?

You are a manager. You are trying to complete an urgent report for your boss. One of the people that report to you comes to you with a complaint against another member of the team. What would you do? What do you think would be the implications of what you would do for the organization's culture?

Few management books have been as popular as Peters and Waterman's *In Search of Excellence*. Published in 1982, it has sold many millions of copies worldwide. Its appeal is apparent, packed as it is with anecdotes, lively stories, and lists. According to Peters and Waterman, top management's job was to show leadership through culture

building by making values clear, transmitting them widely, reinforcing them in practice, and backing them up. Formal policies, informal stories, rituals as well as rules,
and constantly practising what you preach should ensure a strong culture. Effective
cultures were also unambiguous, unitary, harmonious, and managerially integrative.
On the other hand, pluralistic cultures that accommodated dissent and conflict were
regarded as dysfunctional and were a sure sign that the culture was unproductive.
Strong leadership that articulated clear values should overcome opposition.

Top managers embraced these arguments, as did many scholars who produced
studies on the keys to excellence in organizations (e.g. Deal and Kennedy, 1982;
Kanter, 1984; 1990; Pascale and Athos, 1981). They argued that improvements
in productivity and quality would accrue when corporate cultures systematically
align individuals with formal organizational goals. Culture was understood as
the glue that should hold organizational objectives and individual needs together.

In Search of Excellence (Peters and Waterman, 1982) and subsequent excellence
studies shaped the world of practice through the authors' consultancy work with
McKinsey & Company (Colville et al., 1999). In fact, although often castigated by
academics because it was popular, Peters and Waterman's (1982) work translated
ideas from quite subtle and complex organization theories to apply them to practical
exigencies. The origin of these theories was the sensemaking perspective of Weick
(1969; 1979; 1995). As Colville et al. (1999: 135) argue, this was reflected in *In Search
of Excellence* through the insights that 'fundamentally … meanings matter' and
'mundaneity is more scarce than people realize' (1999: 136). *In Search of Excellence*
was not simply a publication 'offering advice for addressing pragmatic problems
thought to be relevant to managers, consultants, and other individuals who work in
or with organizations' (Barley et al., 1988: 34). Peters and Waterman (1982) produced
a work that translated unfashionable and highly abstract organization theory into a
form that a wider audience was able to appreciate (Colville et al., 1999).

Peters and Waterman have a nice story to tell. Integrate everyone into one managerially designed and approved culture of excellence and superior performance will
be the outcome. Subsequent researchers (e.g. Denison, 1990) supported this idea.
However, as critics were not too unkind to point out, many of the so-called excellent
companies had in fact become far less successful within 18 months of *In Search
of Excellence* being published. The change in their circumstances did not slow the
rollout of the rhetoric of excellence in management-speak, however. It proliferated
rapidly. Soon, nearly every manager and wannabe manager could be heard talking
about how important searching for excellence was, and many management consultants were only too happy to help design a culture to make this happen.

Despite *In Search of Excellence* being a huge commercial success, it is, ana-
lytically, too one-dimensional, too focused on culture as just one aspect of
organization life, too focused on the stories of top managers, and thus serving
somewhat as propaganda for the managerial elite and their views of the way
culture should be. But millions read it.

IN SEARCH OF EXCELLENCE

EXTEND YOUR KNOWLEDGE

If you want to extend your knowledge of *In Search of Excellence*, the bestselling management
book, read about its scholarly genesis, as discussed in Ian Colville, Robert Waterman and
Karl Weick's (1999) 'Organizing and the search for excellence: making sense of the times in
theory and practice', *Organization* 6 (1): 129–148, which is available at the companion website
https://edge.sagepub.com/managingandorganizations4e, and is a good place to start.
Another resource that is sensible and useful is an *Economist* video: www.economist.com/blogs/

schumpeter/2014/01/business-books-quarterly-corporate-cultureeo, in which there is a well-informed discussion of the travails of changing corporate culture, one that is somewhat more realistic about the difficulties involved than Peters and Waterman. For a laugh, watch the 'Organizational culture change strategy – 5 pillars – Arthur Carmazzi' video on YouTube, which is not intended as a parody of organizational culture consulting – but succeeds in being so.

ORGANIZATIONAL CULTURE

STRONG CULTURES, HOMOGENEITY, AND DISASTER

Research on the demise of England's Barings Bank has shown (Stein, 2000) that too much consensus and homogeneity in an organization can easily lead to blind spots that can be fatal. Barings was the world's first merchant bank, but its proud tradition ceased suddenly in 1995 when it collapsed because of the activities of a 27-year-old trader in its Singapore office, Nick Leeson. Of course, one could blame Leeson personally for the disaster because he was acting unethically (trading speculatively without telling anyone what he was doing, and covering up his tracks as he did so), but this would not explain why Barings collapsed. Rather, it collapsed because he was able to do these things due to a lethal mix of elements in its organizational culture. As Stein (2000: 1227) argues, 'Barings' problem [is located] squarely with the institution rather than with Leeson … the conditions for Leeson's fraud were set in place substantially prior to his arrival at Barings'. They were deeply embedded in the culture of Barings as an organization.

Barings was a very conservative and established bank that recruited its board members from the English aristocracy. Indeed, previous generations of Barings had been governor-generals in colonial Egypt and Kenya. It was the bank of the British monarch's mother. It was just about as Establishment as it was possible for a bank to be.

In the 1980s, the UK government deregulated the banking industry. One consequence was that banks faced more challenges in a more turbulent environment than they had previously. The gentlemen at Barings were not culturally equipped with the trading mentality that the new conditions seemed to suit. Barings decided to employ a risk-taker who was expected to make sense of the new situation: Nick Leeson. He was known as a maverick, someone who told stories about himself that were not always exactly true, as well as someone who liked to drink and gamble. At its worst, these predilections occasionally resulted in unseemly behaviour; as Stein (2000: 1219) writes, 'in a drunken stupor one night, Leeson had exposed his buttocks to several local women in a bar'. In short, he was not seen as the publicly acceptable face that Barings would have preferred to present. But the bank's management agreed that it needed someone different than they were used to hiring if they were to master the challenges ahead. Barings promoted Leeson, and soon he was trading in Singapore with the bank's money – and lost it.

Normally, there are many control mechanisms in place that should ensure that an individual employee could not lose all the company's assets by gambling on the stock market (in the case of Barings, it was £860 million). But Barings management ignored all the signs that Leeson was losing the bank's money. The organizational culture among the gentlemen of the top management team at Barings was strongly homogeneous. Moreover, their bonuses depended on the gains he reported. They had hired him because he was seen to be an entrepreneurial type of person, and they left him to do the job, with very hands-off control. In the past, class and breeding had made strong discipline by management unnecessary. As the Bank of England subsequently reported, there was no clear explanation as to why Barings management did not question why the bank should be apparently lending more than £300 million to its clients to trade on the Singapore Exchange when it had only collected £31 million from clients for those trades. Barings had a strong culture – one in which no one dared to point out that all was not quite what it might seem – which had disastrous outcomes. Leeson described the culture as one in which employees never asked questions because they did not want to appear ignorant. The dominant unofficial culture was one of no questions, despite whatever may have been maintained officially.

MANAGEMENT LEARNING

EXTEND YOUR KNOWLEDGE

The article by Ikujiro Nonaka, Robert Chia, Robin Holt and Vesa Peltokopi (2014) 'Wisdom, management and organization', *Management Learning*, 45 (4): 365–376, which is available at the companion website https://edge.sagepub.com/managingandorganizations4e, begins by outlining many of the spectacular and disastrous recent failures of wisdom, management, and organization in the financial sector of recent times. They go on to examine a particular approach to wisdom that derives from Aristotle, known as phronesis, before outlining the articles that constitute the special issue. Some of these may well be interesting and we strongly advise having a look at the special issue, guided by the introduction.

The case of Barings shows that we should not assume that a dominant culture is always the official one. In some organizations, such as various police services or firms such as Enron and WorldCom, a dominant culture became widespread that was one of corruption. Although such cultures are not 'officially official', their proliferation suggests that formal tolerance enabled them to flourish and to become established as the local norm.

COLLAPSE OF BARINGS BANK

EXTEND YOUR KNOWLEDGE

If you want to extend your knowledge of the Barings Bank case take a look at Ian Greener's (2006) 'Nick Leeson and the collapse of Barings Bank: socio-technical networks and the "Rogue Trader"', *Organization*, 13 (3): 421–441, and Andrew Brown's (2005) 'Making sense of the collapse of Barings Bank', *Human Relations*, 58 (12): 1579–1604, both of which are excellent to read and are available at the companion website https://edge.sagepub.com/managingandorganizations4e, and could be read in conjunction with watching the film, *Rogue Trader* (Deardon, 1999).

THE CULTURE OF MANAGEMENT

In principle, managers who have a taught capacity to understand management should be better able to manage than inspired amateurs. However, we should bear in mind a point made by Mintzberg (1973): in practice, managers change tack every ten minutes or so. One consequence is that managers are more likely to steer with intuitive judgements because managing means doing many things under tight pressure rather than having leisurely opportunities to consult the latest research. Hence, an intuitive ability to understand the different elements of organizational culture that they are working with is an essential prerequisite for the job.

IN PRACTICE

How should practical managers relate to organization and management research?

Managers, as we have seen from Mintzberg's research, are busy people with many demands on their time and consequently limited attention spans. What, then, are they to do with the wealth of knowledge that management researchers have produced? Different authorities suggest different things. Donaldson (1992) would have managers follow the findings of management science. He would want them to be sceptical about popular management recipes, such as the excellence studies promoted. What managers actually do, and what management science says they should do, are sometimes significantly different.

It is a convention of most management science that managers are rational; however, there is a great deal of anecdotal evidence suggesting that managers – even very important ones – are not necessarily as rational as they might seem to be. Our favourite example is one of the most popular of US presidents, Ronald Reagan. A former actor, Reagan used the scripts of films that he knew, such as *Star Wars* (Lucas, 1977–2002), when communicating the sense that he made of the world that he sought to manage. Meanwhile, his wife, Nancy, consulted her astrologer. Do not laugh: for many decision-makers in some economies, such as Hong Kong, the predictions of astrologers or feng shui practitioners are at least as important as those of econometricians or management consultants – and are sometimes as effective.

Nancy Reagan was not the only politician's wife to consult New Age type gurus – Cherie Blair, wife of British Prime Minister Tony Blair, was well known for her penchant for receiving advice from her 'lifestyle coach', Carole Caplin. The *Daily Telegraph* (3 July 2007) contained an interesting story: 'When Asia's rich and powerful need advice' they call on 'a tiny, hunched deaf-mute' soothsayer in her mid-forties called E. Thi, universally known by the nickname ET in Asia. She numbers Thaksin Shinawatra, ex-Prime Minister of Thailand and present owner of Manchester City Football Club, as well as the Burmese Junta, Indonesian Foreign Ministry, and the Nepalese Monarch among her clients.

LIFESTYLE COACH

Some other managers, trained in business schools, may seek to apply some rational models that they dimly remember from their MBA, when they were taught that a culture of 'excellence' was the way to go. They thus replicate lessons from their youth, repeatedly, even though the truths of that time may have become the errors of today. Still others manage their organizational culture by thinking of the most recent columns they read in the press or that last book they bought at the airport on a business trip, or how their mother or father brought them up, or how a winning sports team is managed. Managers in various contexts have different relevancies guiding their culture of managing, and not all are guided by management theories.

The implications for practice: keep an open book and an open mind. As a manager don't rely just on experience or memory. Try and keep in touch with management research as a professional – engage in workshops and executive education, keep refreshing your knowledge. When did you last learn something new and interesting and apply it to practice?

Practising managers' conceptions of what the culture of their organizations are or should be are important. They shape what they regard as 'best practice'. If managers think that a unitary culture will be less troublesome and more supportive of their projects they will apply it as a kind of recipe knowledge. For a while, *In Search of Excellence* seemed to provide a good recipe. The trouble with recipes is that if everybody cooks according to the same script, the lack of variety becomes bland and boring, and there is no innovation in the diet. The lack of innovation applies not only to the competition between organizations but also to organizations in which everyone subscribes to the same culture, enacting the same realities. The more recipes we have to work from, using different approaches, the more skilled we will be in blending experience and ingredients, theory and practice, management and managing. Thus, we would argue for polyphony in preference to strong cultures. Managers are better off with pluralism, better with dissonance, because it offers more space for innovation. If everyone agrees on the direction being steered and the underlying values, such a situation is foolish if they are wrong and their common agreement does not enable them to see the dangers ahead. The *Titanic* was not just a ship; it serves as a metaphor for all those who are secure in the belief that they are unsinkable.

Academics and their students should be sceptics – people prepared to suggest that the old recipes may not necessarily be all that they are cracked up to be. Organizations need renewal, new ideas, new fashions, and new blood. Sometimes sceptics might suggest alternative recipes, whereas other times they might ask whether you really want to use *that* recipe if you want to achieve *that* outcome. Sometimes, they scoff at the recipe. We think that management academics, at their best, should be able to speak out about organizational power without suffering adverse consequences. Some of them are well-paid people, engaged in secure positions, with a privileged access to potentially influential people – their students. As such, they should not be afraid of speaking or writing in ways that represent views that, to paraphrase the economist J. K. Galbraith, challenge the conventional wisdom (Galbraith, 1969).

While experienced managers will rarely know as much about the theory of management as you do as a student, they will probably know a great deal more about a limited practice. Practice is a good basis for learning but not for learning a great deal. It exposes you to real-life problems but they are limited to personal experience. That's why it is often said that there is nothing as practical as a good theory. Some managers may belittle theory. We think they should, if that theory is prescriptive and tells them what they should do. No theory can operate without regard for context. That is why we stress the need always to relate managing – what managers actually do – to the theories, artifacts, and other resources that they manage with. The point of theory in management is not its 'truth' but its use. Even those who object most strongly to 'theory' must be using a theory about the world, however implicit – otherwise they couldn't make sense!

CULTURE IN DISNEYLAND

For anthropologists, those people who are specialists in the study of cultures, usually exotic, strange, and unfamiliar cultures, the enthusiasm for unitary cultures as a source of excellence in organizations might have been surprising. Usually, it is societies whose belief systems are in trouble that seek to re-emphasize symbols and rituals to stress that there are unitary beliefs (Alvesson and Berg, 1992). In doing so, their elites are making a conscious effort to impose value consensus. An example from twentieth-century history is the post-Prague Spring Soviet-backed Husak regime in Czechoslovakia (as it then existed), which was imposed by Soviet tanks in 1968 along with martial law and the overthrow of the Dubcek government. The new policy of the Husak government was actually termed 'normalization'! What is ironic about this is that it took foreign intervention, tanks, troops, and the overthrow of a government – all pretty extraordinary interventions – to create a highly contrived and forcefully imposed 'normalcy'.

Highly developed value integration may be seen as a way of emphasizing underlying basic assumptions – especially when they are under threat. Anthropologically oriented organization researchers are attuned to the politics of symbolic action (Smircich, 2002). Sometimes, from this perspective, one implication is that people might, on occasion, mean more than they say. It would not be surprising if this were the case; the world of organizations usually includes different types of actors, opinions, and conceptions of culture that quite often come into conflict with each other. Organizations are arenas within which many things might happen that put a big smile on top management's faces but there is also much going on that will just as surely wipe the smiles off.

Organizations with friendly public images are often revealed to have elaborate facades. For example, Van Maanen (1991) revealed that Disneyland at that time was not the fun place its marketing promoted; instead, it was an environment with many stressed-out workers, often obnoxious customers, and generally hassled supervisors, all seeking an advantage over others, and using organization resources to do so. Despite this reality, in the 'smile factory' (as Van Maanen calls it), a strong corporate culture sought to make sure that every employee behaved according to Disney's philosophy. Uniforms, education through the University of Disneyland, and an employee handbook embodied this spirit. However, the stressed-out staff found their own way of dealing with the masses of visitors. For especially nasty customers, employees developed informal mechanisms to discipline them. For instance, the 'seatbelt squeeze' on amusement rides was but a 'small token of appreciation given to a deviant customer consisting of the rapid cinching-up of a required seatbelt such that the passenger is doubled-over at the point of departure and left gasping for the duration of the trip' (Van Maanen, 1991: 71). Or bothersome pairs could be separated into different units so that they had to enjoy a ride without each other (the so-called 'break-up-the-party' gambit; Van Maanen, 1991: 72). These and many other unofficial and informal rules and practices were learned and developed on the job and formed a part of the culture of Disneyland. Probably not quite what Walt had in mind, though!

Culture is not just the formally approved ways of doing things; it is also the sly games, informal rules, and deviant subcultures of lower level employees against supervisors and supervisors against lower level employees, women against men and men against women, and creative against management types as well as management types against creatives (Burawoy, 1979; Rosen, 2002; Young, 1989).

ORGANIZATIONAL CULTURE AND GEORGE ORWELL'S *NINETEEN EIGHTY-FOUR*

As we have seen, strong cultures do not necessarily equal good cultures. One of the strongest critiques of the dominant orthodoxy that strong cultures are good cultures came in a scathing article by a British academic, Hugh Willmott, who drew inspiration from Orwell's (1949) most celebrated book, *Nineteen Eighty-Four*, to make sense of corporate culture programmes (Willmott, 2002). In the book, Orwell imagined Oceania, a totalitarian state set in the future. It maintained coercive control through, among other things, making the official parlance of Oceania *Newspeak*, a perversion of the English language. Although Newspeak is based on English, all contentious political words are removed, and, more generally, the vocabulary is much reduced. The purpose of the language is to limit that which can be said and thought. The ultimate aim of Newspeak is to produce a mode of communication that requires no thought on the part of the speakers. This ideal is achieved, in part, through the use of abbreviations that serve to conceal the true meanings of terms. For instance, the Oceania Ministry of Law and Order, where torture occurs, is known as Miniluv. One of the important features of Newspeak is *doublethink*, which refers to the capacity to hold mutually contradictory views at the same time.

So what does the dystopian fiction of a writer who has been dead for half a century have to do with corporate culture? Willmott (2002) argues that Orwell can help us understand what he characterizes as the dark side of the corporate culture project. Willmott regards the language of corporate culture programmes as an attempt at controlling the choices and identities open to employees. He continues the Orwellian analogy by suggesting that the world of corporate culture is plagued by doublethink, in which the values of community and autonomy can be simultaneously celebrated and contradicted. Like the Party member in Orwell's Oceania, the well-socialized, self-disciplined corporate employee is 'expected to have no private emotions and no respite from enthusiasm ... The speculations which might possibly induce a skeptical or rebellious attitude are killed in advance by his early-acquired inner discipline' (Orwell, 1949: 220).

Under the guise of giving more autonomy to the individual than would be the case in organizations governed by bureaucratic rules, corporate culture threatens to promote a new, hypermodern neo-authoritarianism. Working in post-bureaucratic organizations and no longer governed by clear rules, organization members know that as long as they can parrot the corporate line, they can claim to be acting responsibly. Willmott finds this potentially more insidious and sinister than bureaucracy, with its clear formal rules and limits, because it leaves no space for an autonomous professional ethos. There is nothing guiding organization members' action other than the appearance of conformism. Everything must be subordinated to the greater good of the corporate culture. Only within its frame can organization members find freedom and value. However, he does not think it likely that these managerialist fantasies will be easily implementable in practice: they overstate the power of rhetoric and understate the power of the individual's resistance to it.

MAKING UP CULTURE

Much contemporary organizational culture discourse represents a desire by management to enlist workers' cooperation, compliance, and commitment to create an *esprit de corps* with which to limit human recalcitrance at work (Barker, 1998). The rhetoric of control, coupled with a new vocabulary of teamwork, quality, flexibility, and learning organizations, constitutes culture management projects that seek to create culture as a mechanism of soft domination (see also pp. 274–277) through cultural change programmes (Casey, 1995; du Gay, 2000a; Jacques, 1996). At the furthest point, what such thinking about the relation of organization members and organizational culture sought to construct was 'designer employees' (Casey, 1995) – people made up in such a way that they were organizationally most functional. Corporately designed clones, in other words.

IN PRACTICE

Recruiting at Cathay Pacific

The ultimate designer employee is depicted in a Cathay Pacific recruitment advertisement from 1997. The employee is a specific category of organizational subject imbued with an obvious, natural, or acquired demeanour, comportment, and specifications.

Who am I?

I travel the world but I'm not a tourist.

I serve 5-star cuisine but I'm not a chef.

I walk the aisle but I'm not a fashion model.

I care for people but I am not a nurse.

And I do it all from the heart.

Who am I?

I am ...

... a flight attendant with Cathay Pacific and you could be one too! (Cathay Pacific Airways, 1997)

In practice, to what extent has Cathay Pacific, aside from its advertising rhetoric, generated a strong culture among its flight attendants and other staff? (Hint: start from the *Daily Telegraph* online article 'Cathay Pacific crews threaten "no-smile" strike' (28 April 2015))

CATHAY PACIFIC CULTURE

Management practitioners seek to use culture and control to try and frame the subjectivity of their employees – to try and get them to see things with the same set of relevancies that they have as managers. We see this most readily in some post-excellence accounts of quality management, such as the Six-Sigma movement popular in Japan and much of East Asia (Kono and Clegg, 2001). Principles such as *seiri* (putting-in-order), *seiton* (arrange properly), *seiketsu* (cleanliness), *seiso* (cleaning), and *shitsuke* (good behaviour), seen in many plants of Japanese corporations, seek to govern not only the workplace but also the comportment of employees in the workplace (March, 1996). Organizational culture that prescribes norm-defined management techniques and habit-inducing routines seeks to create an obedient and disciplined consciousness around those sets of beliefs and values that the organization favours. Usually these promise a new corporate personhood, a new corporate subjectivity, and even a new corporate embodiment. Think of highly designed conceptions of organizational culture that frame what it means to be an organization member, such as those associated with the advertisement for Cathay Pacific that we saw previously. The employee has to work from the heart; this is what it means to be designed for work as a Cathay flight attendant.

For Casey (1995), a designer culture has the following characteristics:

1. Individual enthusiasm manifested in the values of dedication, loyalty, self-sacrifice, and passion. These values translate into the use of the organizationally approved forms of language, including buzz-terms, as well as a willingness to be part of the team at work, in play and recreation, (joining in at the pub, for instance), and putting in long hours at work – where you earn your salary from 9 to 5 and your promotion from 5 to 9.

2. A strong customer focus, where customers are not just the end-users but employees and other significant stakeholders are thought of as customers.

3. Management discourse is characterized by a language of team and family inclusive of everyone – even if they would prefer not to be a part of the team or family.

4. Finally, there is public display of the designer culture. There will be many artifacts, such as websites, that display images of the culture, such as team photos, team awards, employee of the month, and such like.

Owners and senior managers who have a paternalistic relation to their employees will urge them to be part of the organization family. The use of family metaphors – we're all one big happy family here – is particularly inappropriate. The family metaphor is widely used to try and represent an organizational culture, as for instance when people talk of disloyalty when an employee criticizes the firm or approaches another organization for a position – almost as if they were having an affair! Of course, the whole notion of the organization being metaphorically aligned with a family is suspect. Are managers then parents and employees children? The family metaphor is highly dubious, as we should recognize. Moreover, as many know, not all families are a haven from a heartless world; some are awful places, with institutionalized abuse, violence, and cruelty that are hard to escape. But an idealized notion of family is the one that is usually at work in designer cultures, never the one that takes the sad facts of the family law courts as its empirical compass. Actually, although we cannot choose our families, we can, in principle, choose our organizations. Therefore, we can choose to escape a perverse organization and go elsewhere, but membership in many families does not allow such choice. We suspect that most of you would prefer being exploited by an organization that you can leave easily rather than being held captive in a family (or a family business) that is relatively inescapable. Family bonds are much harder to escape than an employment contract, so here is our advice: beware of employers claiming family ties or suggesting that the organization in which you work is like a family!

WHAT WOULD YOU DO?

Y ou have now learnt quite a bit about management and organizing. Think back to when you were growing up. Given what you know now, in what ways do you think that if you had been in a position to do so you could have improved the culture of your secondary school? What were the best aspects of the culture? What were the worst aspects of the culture? Why?

DIFFERENT PERSPECTIVES ON CULTURE

By now it should be clear that there is a fair degree of ambivalence and controversy about the nature of organizational culture. To try and make sense of the different views about culture and organization one influential writer, Joanne Martin, has devised a sensemaking schema in her book, *Organizational Culture: Mapping the Terrain* (2002). In this book she distinguishes between three perspectives that stress one or other of *integration, differentiation* or *fragmentation*.

THE POLITICS OF MANAGING CULTURE

INTEGRATION PERSPECTIVES

The excellence studies make perfect sense to managers because they provided generic solutions that seemed to be capable of being applied to many problems that could now be reclassified as culture issues. The great strength of the excellent culture perspective was that it seemed to promise the dissolution of all that friction and resistance that managers know they often produce routinely, as a normal part of their work. In the place of conflict it offered integration.

Indeed, some analysts refer to the strong cultures model as an integration perspective. According to Martin and Frost (1996), integration theorists defined *culture* as a phenomenon that was consistent and clear, including in their evidence only manifestations of it that accorded with definitions of a unified culture, thus excising all the plural and non-integrative aspects of the culture.

Integration theorists define *culture* as 'organization-wide agreement with values espoused by top management' (Martin and Frost, 1996: 608). Often, they suggest, such agreement was assumed by researchers only after the views of top management had been sampled! When decisions were not overtly biased by sampling decisions to exclude likely sources of dissenting views, they were often made to exclude any data that seemed to suggest a weak or fragmented culture as an inconsequential margin to the central cultural values. Martin and Frost (1996: 608) are scathing:

Integration characterizes a situation in which everyone shares the same culture and there are no contrary cultures or ambiguities about the culture.

each 'strong' culture was a monolith where every manifestation reinforced the values of top management, employees complied with managerial directives, and preferences were assumed to share these values, and there was, apparently, only one interpretation of the meaning of events shared by all. These studies were designed so integration research would find what it was looking for.

IMPLICATIONS OF INTEGRATION PERSPECTIVES

Many anthropologically inclined researchers were critical of the integrationist findings because they systematically excluded resistance, subcultures, and countercultures from their analysis. These critics saw the integrationist concept of dominant cultures as one that stressed a unitary perspective because it privileged the views of managers of the organization against those for whom a subculture, or even subcultures, might be more important (Willmott, 2002). Only one culture – the official culture – was envisaged. Subcultures may form around the status attributes of the workforce (such as ethnicity, gender, class, and skill) or on the basis of spatial markers (such as where people work and the conditions under which their work is performed). Sometimes, there may be a well-organized counterculture centred on a union or an ethnic subculture, reinforced by a strong sense of community among co-workers. Often this is the case among those who do blue-collar, dangerous work, including dockers, miners, and construction workers.

The integration theorists countered that if you went looking long enough and hard enough for such things as subcultures, you would be sure to find them, especially, the critics continued, if the research consisted of 'focused, non-random samples of lower level employees' and if the process involved 'ignoring (or not searching for) evidence of values shared on an organization-wide basis' (Martin and Frost, 1996: 608). They went on to say that, if properly conducted with appropriate skill, even ethnographers could come to see that deep fundamental values might be shared by a majority of organization members (Schein, 1997).

Predictably, with such disagreement between researchers surfacing in the public arena, the idea that culture might be a quick fix for corporate ills became harder to market. The committed ethnographic researchers were never very interested in the market, anyway. They saw themselves as more akin to anthropologists who practised long-term participant observation and brought tales from the field to the public arena (Van Maanen, 1988).

Organizationally, if, for whatever reasons, you felt unable to bond with the strong cultural values being stressed, you were likely to feel some degree of unease. For instance, many women in organizations felt excluded from implicitly masculinist strong cultures. If work was to become even more of a boy's club as a result of a strong culture, defined by the male elite, these women were not going to be happy with this outcome. Linda Smircich and Joanne Martin, both major American feminist organization theorists, know a thing or two about dominant (masculine) cultures – and about how to resist them. And what they saw in the strong-culture literature raised their feminist hackles; they thought that it seemed to privilege an exclusive club to which leaders could aspire – but the implicit message was that they could succeed only if they were male. Being on the team meant joining in with a world that was masculinized, centred on sports talk, drinking, and blokey inclusiveness. While that was OK for 'the boys' it tended to marginalize 'the girls'. Knowing what it was like to be a female in a world dominated by men, they tried to create a theoretical space within which to make sense of why resistance to dominant masculine culture projects might occur – and not just as a result of poor socialization. They argued that if resistance was an attribute of insufficient socialization, the culture literature was ideological in the extreme.

Ethnography is an approach to research that attempts to understand social phenomena, such as organizational life, as it happens and in its own terms. It involves in-depth interviews, participant observation, and detailed case study, and generally approaches research from the point of view of understanding what the subjects themselves think. It starts from the premise that meanings and understandings are socially constructed.

ETHNOGRAPHY

The differentiation perspective does not expect organizational cultures to be singular totalities but would expect there to be plural conceptions of culture with probable tensions existing among them.

If you opposed the dominant culture, you were automatically a deviant and needed more socialization and training. There was no space from which it might be legitimate and justified to resist.

Smircich (2002) began with methodological criticisms of data based on survey findings. She was particularly critical of the approach to data collection by functionalist researchers. Typically, they had little deep knowledge of the culture that they wrote about, knowledge that should be gained from ethnography and the use of anthropological methods (e.g. living in and mingling intimately with the community being researched). Usually they just administered a questionnaire with a series of questions and Likert-scale response sets. One consequence was that the studies of excellence often ended up being accounts of the espoused values of the top management as if they were the values characterized throughout the organization, rather than being a study of the values actually used by all managers in practice. Thus, these 'excellent' cultures were more often than not top managerial wishes, the fulfilment of which was empirically questionable because the ethnographically rich data that might address it had often not been collected. Much of the best work on organizational culture consists of organizational ethnographies. There is a very good website run by Randy Hodson called the 'Workplace Ethnography Project'. It has a great many references to many different ethnographic studies of work and organizations as well as being a really useful guide to doing ethnographies.

DIFFERENTIATION PERSPECTIVE

Martin (1992a) became particularly concerned with the lack of concordance between researchers from two different perspectives using different methodologies. In the perspective that she classified as 'integration research', the a priori assumptions were that culture was the vehicle of integration for organizations; consequently, that was what was researched. In the perspective that she called 'differentiation research', the assumption was that more than one culture was more likely to be the norm; thus, researchers started with a predisposition to see plural cultures rooted in different experiences within organizations.

Various studies demonstrate that organizations are often unstable and characterized by conflict (Calás and McGuire, 1990; Gregory, 1983; Martin, 1992a; Meyerson, 1991; Riley, 1983). Organizations may have members who share strong values about basic beliefs with some, but not all, of the other members of the organization. There will be cliques and cabals, relatively separate lunch networks, and distinct coffee circles. When these groups are sufficiently clearly articulated in terms of cultures, we refer to them as *subcultures*, which are occupational and professional groups that reflect different interests, tastes, and habits; such subcultures develop alongside whatever may be the formally acknowledged organizational culture (Gagliardi, 1990). Subcultures coexist with other cultures and can become dominant if they can unify adherents through the use of resources, symbols, and other forms of meaning (Clarke et al., 1976). If a subculture reflects a cohesive group and defends plausible ideas, it may become dominant and legitimate (Gagliardi, 1990). If it challenges legitimate values, it becomes a counterculture. Countercultures engage in oppositional political activities (de Certeau, 1988; Scott, 1990).

IMPLICATIONS OF DIFFERENTIATION PERSPECTIVES

The problem with the differentiation perspective, suggest its critics, is that if you expect difference and resistance a priori then you will probably find it. Moreover, if the expectation is that there are irreconcilable interests between different genders, religions, ethnicities or classes then this is not very useful to the manager who has to manage these tensions. Sure, it gives them some intelligence about what the issues are that they might expect but it doesn't promise a solution. On the other hand, it should forearm managers with a degree of scepticism for the highly integrationist solutions and assumptions that are often offered to them by consultants and senior executives out of touch with the realities of the office or shop floor. From this perspective, a little basic sociology should make for better-informed and less naïve managers. If their expectations are that conflicts and tensions are likely to be structurally deep-seated they won't be surprised when they meet examples in practice.

CULTURE: INTEGRATED, DIFFERENTIATED ... AND FRAGMENTED

Martin (1992a) suggests that cultures are always simultaneously somewhat integrated and somewhat differentiated and also somewhat fragmented. An organizational culture might be *integrated* when it reflects a wide consensus, *differentiated* when it is confined to separate subcultures, or *fragmented* when there is little consensus and the situation is essentially ambiguous. Although Martin suggests that these conditions can be found simultaneously at *a given time*, they also provide a framework for depicting changes in organizational culture *over time*, such as in Gouldner's (1954) study of a gypsum plant (see pp. 487). We could easily describe the study's events in terms of a shift from an integrated culture of community to one that became differentiated and then fragmented by the unexpected strike action.

From any perspective that sees organizational culture as more akin to fluid processes than stable value systems, measuring culture would be meaningless. We can understand its fluent and changing nature better through ethnographic case studies. Chan (2003: 313) argues that the 'treatment of culture as a fixed, unitary, bounded entity has to give way to a sense of fluidity and permeability'. He suggests that earlier studies of organizations as essentially 'negotiated orders' (Strauss et al., 1963) are better guides to managerial behaviour. Rather than seeing the organization as a fixed pattern, managers should instead look at the ways that the members of the organization use its resources (including conceptions of its values and culture) constantly to negotiate the sense of what it is that they are doing in and as an organization. In this view, the members of the organization create culture from the mundane, everyday aspects of their work and often use the managerially approved dominant culture as a resource in doing so, but not always in ways that would be approved within its rhetoric (Linstead and Grafton-Small, 2002).

Chan (2003) suggests that culture should be thought of as a way of accounting for what has been done in and around an organization, as a way of making sense of what has been experienced. Thought of in this way, culture is far harder to engineer than the strong-culture perspective suggests. Rather than being just a matter of replacing one set of normative assumptions with an alternative set, producing yet another mission and vision statement, culture consists of loosely negotiated, tacit ways of making sense that are embedded in specific situations in the organization rather than an all-enveloping structure that somehow contains all who are members. Because culture is overwhelmingly situational, culture is usually quite fragmentary, forming around certain emergent issues and then dissolving. Often, managers take different sides on these issues and are thus divided among themselves.

These views are known as the fragmentation perspective. The fragmentation approach shares very little with the normative integration theorists, who argue for the benefits of a strong culture, and the differentiation proponents, who say that a strong culture equals a dominant culture, and a dominant culture is one that subordinates differentiated subcultures.

The fragmentation perspective is suspicious of the desire to make culture clear. According to the fragmentation view, culture is neither clearly consistent nor clearly contested, but likely to be muddled and fragmentary.

The picture represented by fragmentation perspectives is more likely to be one that represents contradictory and confusing cultures battling for the soul of the organization as well as those of its employees. Individuals are more likely to exist in a state of competing cultural commitments, where they are constantly under competing pressures to identify themselves and their organization with rival conceptions of an appropriate cultural identity. In such a situation, 'consensus is transient and issue specific, producing short-lived affinities among individuals that are quickly replaced by a different pattern of affinities, as a different issue draws the attention of cultural members' (Martin and Frost, 1996: 609, citing the work of Kreiner and Schultz (1993) on emergent culture in R&D networks as an example).

IMPLICATIONS OF FRAGMENTATION PERSPECTIVE

Managers schooled in the fragmentation perspective should expect the realities they manage to be complex and ever changing, in process, liquid rather than carved in stone. The good news is that the deep-seated tensions that the differentiation perspective sees may be more fluid than imagined. The bad news is that you never know which issues will emerge as points of coalescence of local interests in antipathy to formal policies and strategies. From this perspective organizational cultures are unpredictable and a pest. They sow confusion for managers rather than being aids to efficient management.

Organizational cultures make us confused, because they overlap and are only partially understood in terms of common sensemaking. Culture is not about a clear, sharp image of corporate and individual identity; it is about ambiguity. Confusion is normal; asking questions about clarity is not. Culture is an artifact of the methods used to investigate it and the assumptions that make such an investigation possible. Realistically, if you cannot define culture clearly, and the people whose culture it is supposed to be do not know what it is, it can hardly be the cure for corporate ills.

Fragmentation studies report a world in which ambiguity provides a protective shroud from the meaninglessness of everyday organizational life. Meyerson (1991) discovered in her study of social workers that:

> ambiguity pervaded an occupation whose practitioners had to operate in a world where the objectives of social work were unclear, the means to these goals were not specified, and sometimes it wasn't even clear when an intervention had been successful or even what success in this context might have meant. (Martin and Frost, 1996: 609)

Cynics might say that this is not surprising, given that the example is social work, an area that is usually under-resourced and that is one in which people have to deal with the many complex problems of often severely dysfunctional clients. However, there are studies of other cultural contexts, which are certainly not resource poor and that have a premium on clarity and detail, in which fragmentary cultures are normal. For example, Weick (1991) discusses a case involving air-traffic controllers in which normal fragmentation produced tragic effects. They were working at Tenerife Airport one foggy night as two jumbo jets maneuvered in their airspace. Pilots, controllers, and cockpit crews struggled to communicate but failed. The barriers of status and task assignment, not to mention the more general problems of languages spoken, all conspired to produce an organizational culture that was mired in fatal ambiguity. When a foggy day met a fragmented culture in the airspace of Tenerife Airport, a disastrous impact occurred. The two jets collided, and hundreds of lives were lost in the atmospheric and the cultural fog. As we mentioned in Chapter 1, cultural cues become particularly acute in organizational handovers.

Culture in organizations and between people in them cannot be ignored. It might not be as manageable as consultants suggest but it has to be understood. Managers need to be practical ethnographers, able to understand what's going on.

CHANGING CULTURES

Suzana Braga Rodrigues is a Brazilian academic who has contributed a number of studies of organizational culture to the literature, drawing on a longitudinal programme of research into a Brazilian Telco as it moved from the public to the private sector (Rodrigues, 2006). She presents a rare historical and contextual account of organizational culture. By focusing on a long slice of time she provides insight into Martin's (1992a; 2000) views of cultural integration, differentiation, and fragmentation as they unfold politically over time. Most studies of organizational culture, including those that focus on the three perspectives, have been cross-sectional and therefore unable to explore in any depth the questions of how and why culture changes in the direction of differentiation or otherwise over time.

Rodrigues shows that institutional forces interact with internal political actors in organizational culture change. Institutions empower or disempower certain categories of actor and create or deactivate the rules that foster alliances and different social formations. When a powerful group or leading coalition supports an organizational culture it tends to be integrated; where there is incapacity by the leading group to satisfy the interests of other groups, fragmentation is likely. The more institutionalized an organization's environment, the more likely it will be that institutional agencies will influence its prevailing culture. In such environments, where external institutional actors control the leadership's mandate from above, power and legitimacy do not necessarily cohere. The dynamics of culture change are seen to centre on the confluence of internal political forces with external institutional parameters. Cultural change is a multifaceted and multilevel process. Whether change pushes culture in organizations in the direction either of cultural integration or differentiation depends on the legitimacy of internal coalitions and their capacity to sustain integrative ideals.

ORGANIZATIONAL
CULTURE CHANGE

EXTEND YOUR KNOWLEDGE

BRANDED REVOLUTIONARIES

Anu Kantola's (2014), 'Branded revolutionaries: circulated gurus as management tools in soft capitalism', *European Journal of Cultural Studies*, 17 (3): 258–274, which is available at the companion website https://edge.sagepub.com/managingandorganizations4e, notes that the call for revolution has become a standard technique in corporate capitalism. Management fashions and gurus turn revolutionary ideas into saleable packages of corporate consulting. The particular focus is on the case of Gary Hamel, the well-known advocate of revolutionary managerial change. Kantola shows how an individual guru becomes a central symbolic pole for the circulation of revolutionary ideas that are promoted by publishing companies, consultancies, universities, and different media that package and disseminate the revolutionary guru. Gurus, revolution, and management, however, are a trinity that cannot escape paradox.

THE TEXTS OF CULTURE

One way of conceiving of culture is to think of it as an unfolding and indeterminate text – something that we can watch at the cinema, like the *Matrix* movies: we may all have an understanding of the film but not necessarily make the same sense (e.g. Chan, 2003). Think of movies that are hard to decipher, that have enigmatic stories, characters, or endings. Often we interpret these differently from our friends.

At the simplest level, the way we come to know organizational cultures is through textual accounts. We look at websites; we read accounts of organizations in magazines and newspapers; or we look at PR material that the company produces. All of these accounts are either literal texts or discourses that are text-like. These texts might be those of researchers or consultants, or they may be managers' artifacts, such as company reports. They could even be what people ordinarily say about the organizations that they work for and know. Sometimes familiarity breeds contempt and the everyday accounts will be very different from the well-turned PR prose!

The ways that we make sense of the social realities of everyday working life in organizations can be thought of as texts. Various accounts and stories abound, with which we seek to enrol and influence others who are trying to do the same to us – they want us to accept their versions of affairs just as we might be committed to our versions. Many different accounts circulate in organizations. There are official accounts, but there are also unofficial and downright scurrilous accounts as well, and only a fool would ever believe just the official story. All of these stories circulate as either literal texts or discourses that are text-like. Such stories are all social constructions with the texts reflecting different accounts that we reflect on in various ways. These texts – whether formal or informal in their production – are fabricated as bricolage made up from what organization stories provide. Using these resources we talk some sense into being as, in doing so, we deny the sense of other accounts or ideas.

Obviously, managers will try and frame, steer, nudge the sensemaking that occurs in organizations. Doing so is a subtle skill, one not easy to practise. It is much more than making pronouncements or telling people what the culture is. It is about being sensitive to different accounts, trying to explain preferred stories in simple and clear terms and trying to win assent to them. It helps if the stories are more plausible of course and not just the imaginings of out of touch executives or consultants who have only a partial, incomplete understanding of the situation.

Managers must expect that managing means they will have to deal with fragmentation. Fragmentation in culture is to be expected when we are trying to capture a certain reality. Social realities are always already textual, composed in words and deeds by different people with different interests. All conceptions of what an organizational culture is will necessarily suppress, silence, and marginalize some elements that some other account might instead privilege. That is, culture acts as a structure around individual behaviour: it constrains what actions you might take and encourages you in particular actions over others – as a result formal, official cultural texts are powerful forces within organizations. They can be used as frames, points of reference, political tools, and orienting devices. People can seek a sense of their self within the documents and texts that imply or state the organizational culture but there is no reason to expect that they will only find direction in the officially approved texts.

The view that organizations should be thought of as complex cultures that can be read in fragments, as incomplete and multifaceted, has become widely associated with postmodernist accounts of culture. Rather than join what Martin and Frost (1996) call the culture war games, postmodern theorists seek to demonstrate the ways that people in organizations engage in strategies in practice that make these games possible (Clegg and Kornberger, 2003). Typical postmodern research accounts of organizational cultures include reflexive analysis by analysts of the culture and sometimes it also includes the voices of research subjects, with their fragmentary, differentiated, or integrative understandings, perspectives often omitted by others (Clegg and Hardy, 1996; Jeffcutt, 1994). Methodologically, postmodern analysis seeks to deconstruct the assumptions that underpin particular accounts of culture and to show that any account of an organizational culture is always an artifact of the assumptions made (Smircich, 2002).

MEASURING NATIONAL CULTURES

If it is a big assumption to think that organizations have a singular culture, how much bigger is the assumption that countries have a singular national culture? And that it can be measured? Some researchers argue that we *can* measure an organization's culture and its effects on performance (see Gordon and DiTomaso, 1992). One prominent researcher along these lines is Ashkenasy (2003), for whom values are the core component of organizational cultures. He says that conceptions of organizational culture are more reliable when they can be measured rather than just described and argues that the concept of a value system allows you to do this. Hofstede (1980) goes one step further: he says that you can measure the values of a national culture.

Geert Hofstede, the writer best known for having measured national culture in terms of values, studied only one organization – but he studied it in over 40 countries! It is now widely known that the unidentified organization that Hofstede (1980) reported on in his book *Culture's Consequences: International Differences in Work-related Values* was the multinational company IBM. He describes culture as 'mental programming', as 'software of the mind', as 'subjective'.

At base, Hofstede's views rely on a definition of values defined as invariant and stable preferences that manifest themselves in any situation, despite other contingencies; these values, it is assumed, are universally shared by the population of a given country, which makes the values recognizably coherent and thus 'national' in character. It is because of their fundamental character that, as in Schein's hierarchy of culture, they frame behaviour and shape artifacts. These values can be elicited by statistical analysis producing the mean scores of answers to self-response survey questions from a small organizational sample of a national population and can be factor analysed as 'dimensions' on which various nations can be contrasted.

Hofstede is a cultural determinist: for him the national culture will determine the shape of the organizational culture. While the population of a nation can be differentiated on many grounds, Hofstede claims that, nonetheless, a national population shares a unique culture. His empirical basis for this claim, however, is a statistical averaging of the principal data – questionnaire responses from IBM employees. It is as a statistical average based on individuals' views, which he calls a 'central tendency' (1991: 253), or 'an average tendency' (1991: 253). In other words, it is a statistical artifact. It has no real root in practice other than an averaging out of data and construction of a mean to represent its totality.

Hofstede's data drew on a data bank of 75,000 employee attitude surveys undertaken around 1967 and 1973 within IBM subsidiaries in 66 countries, which he analysed statistically. He found that the data demonstrated that there were four central dimensions of a national culture, such that 40 out of the 66 countries in which the IBM subsidiaries were located could be given a comparative score on each of these four dimensions. Hofstede (1980) defines these and some subsequently composed dimensions as follows:

1. *Power Distance*: 'the extent to which the less powerful members of organizations and institutions within a country expect and accept that power is distributed unequally' (1980: 98).

2. *Uncertainty Avoidance*: 'the extent to which the *members* of a culture feel threatened by uncertain or unknown situations' (1980: 161).

3. *Individualism versus Collectivism:* Individualism 'stands for a society in which the ties between individuals are loose: Everyone is expected to look after him/herself and her/his immediate family only. Collectivism stands for a society in which *people* from birth onwards are integrated into strong, cohesive in-groups, which throughout people's lifetime continue to protect them in exchange for unquestioning loyalty' (1980: 225).

4. *Masculinity versus Femininity*: Masculinity 'stands for a society in which social gender roles are clearly distinct: Men are supposed to be assertive, tough, and focused on material success. Femininity stands for a society in which social gender roles overlap: Both men and women are supposed to be modest, tender, and concerned with the quality of life' (1980: 297).

The first four definitions were based on questionnaires from IBM employees. Later, in 1991, drawing on research in Hong Kong and Taiwan, he added a fifth dimension:

5. *Long-term Orientation versus Short-term Orientation*: 'Long-term Orientation stands for the fostering of virtues oriented towards future rewards, in particular, perseverance and thrift. Its opposite pole, Short-term Orientation, stands for the fostering of virtues related to the past and present, in particular respect for tradition, preservation of "face" and fulfilling social obligations' (1991: 359).

In 2010, Hofstede et al. (2010) renamed the fifth dimension *Pragmatic versus Normative* and added a sixth dimension:

THE HOFSTEDE CENTRE

6. *Indulgence versus Restraint*: Indulgence stands for a society that allows relatively free gratification of basic and natural human drives related to enjoying life and having fun. Restraint stands for a society that suppresses gratification of needs and regulates it by means of strict social norms.

Hofstede arrived at the original and subsequent national patterns by averaging the means of data collected on individuals in terms of national samples. Consistent patterns were established in terms of national variation – variation according to the means, which were, of course, statistical devices for representing the sum of individual variance. The upshot would be similar to saying that the average Dutch person is taller than the average Chinese person; the statement accepts that the average is a summary device. The average tells you nothing about what any particular Dutch or Chinese person's height may be any more than it informs you about the values they hold. An average of values, although it is economical, is about as meaningful as an average of height. Just as there would be wide variance in the height of any given population so there would be wide variance in the values of that population, a point that is well established in McSweeney's (2002) critique. As he says, Hofstede assumes that it is national cultures that produce the variance in his data but provides no evidence to support the assumption; any other classification made on the basis of another assumption would have done just as well – or as badly – as an explanatory device.

To accept Hofstede's analysis is to assume the cultural homogeneity of nations – that lines on a map inscribe a unitary, patterned, and consistent common culture. In the vast majority of cases in the contemporary world, this is hardly feasible. Neither are there few singularly ethnically, linguistically, and culturally homogeneous countries among the major nations in the world today nor do their boundaries necessarily circumscribe a constant space. For one thing, boundaries change politically. Indeed, one of the countries that Hofstede (1980) treated as a unitary cultural space in his study, Yugoslavia, no longer exists as such – precisely because it was not a unitary cultural space in the first place, as indicated by the horrors of the 'ethnic cleansing' and associated mass murders in the early 1990s that were its major contribution to world affairs. For another thing, in many contemporary countries, modern identities are much more likely to be plural than singular, as shown in hybrid, hyphenated identities such as Anglo-Indian, Viet-Australian, and so on. Will the diversity that the organization's members display in their everyday life not be reflected as diversity in the organization as well?

Citizenship is not a very strong predictor of a common cultural identity as the battles for Scottish independence or the deadly struggles between Shia and Sunni citizens in countries such as Iraq would suggest. The 2014 referendum in the United Kingdom on whether or not Scotland should remain part of the Union, a situation that had prevailed since 1707, led to 45 per cent of the voters (on an 80 per cent turnout of the population) voting for independence rather than continued membership. The United Kingdom is one country but the referendum results and the debates that ensued around the referendum suggest that it would be a grievous error to assume that the one country was characterized by value concordance. On the contrary, Scottish desires for independent nationhood revealed that the construct of the United Kingdom submerged some very strongly divergent values. Elsewhere, as we have seen with the rise of the Islamic State movement in the Middle East, citizenship can be a mask for a fragmented reality of religious beliefs and non-beliefs, linguistic differences, and plural ethnic cultures.

Organizations that want to flourish in the contemporary word would be well advised to sample widely from the differences available to them in terms of personnel rather than hiring for cultural homogeneity. Given this assumption, it is difficult to see that Hofstede has much to offer managers, other than a nostalgia for times when, in most countries, you could rely on a bunch of similar men running things in their interests. You could argue that it is precisely because organizations are able to pick and choose who joins them – through human resource management practices – that they may be said to have specific national cultures (but the countries they operate in also have equal employment and anti-discrimination laws!). In other words, they might select people to fit what they think of as a national culture. Contrary to this viewpoint, however, many organizations have been torn apart by bitter internal conflicts, even when professionally managed by people from the same citizenship, which makes the idea of their having only one culture seem questionable. The highly stylized forms suggested by Hofstede are particularly anachronistic in today's globalized world, such that considering 'nation' as the primal source of identity only makes sense as a piece of political rhetoric, as when a politician talks of what it means to be a member of a national identity – which usually has both an inclusionary and exclusionary focus.

There is an empirical element that might give substance to the claim that nation-states are producers of culture in so far as this happens through the agency of the institutional pressures to which individuals are subjected. While there are multiple regional differences within countries, and we are all becoming more mobile and interconnected, most people have been exposed to a single educational system, that of the country where they grew up. Each country has developed different approaches to educate young people and some of these differences leave a mark in the dispositions of individuals. For instance, your experience as a student in Italy is probably quite similar to that of a student in France but clearly dissimilar to that of an Australian student, not to mention a Chinese or Mexican student. Of course these differences are mediated by other factors (social class, length of studies, other individual experiences, etc.) but each nation tends to produce a more or less coherent institutional setting for education that is likely to leave traces on those who went through the system. Of all the variables that affect identity as it is formed by schooling in national terms it is the stratification of the educational system on more or less hierarchical terms that makes the most difference. Some countries, such as Finland, have only a national system with no private schooling. Others, such as England, Australia, and the United States have systems that are highly stratified both by postcode and by fees. By postcode one means that some schools will draw on much less privileged demographics than others, something that is exacerbated by the existence of fee-paying schools that school students in privilege. In this respect, the composition of the present British Cabinet, the inner circle, of the government, which is not only markedly skewed to elite public schoolboys, but to those that attended Eton, in particular, is notable. It should be evident that very different senses of national culture flow from schools that routinely produce notable elites compared with those that do not. You cannot judge the quality of a nation's schooling by aggregating and then averaging its results without committing what social scientists call an 'ecological fallacy'. The fallacy occurs when you infer that the characteristics of an aggregate (ecological) level also describe those of lower hierarchical levels. The parts do not necessarily have the same characteristics and thus are not represented by those of the whole. Extrapolating from a higher to a lower level does not accurately describe the variances visible at the lower level.

Schooling is obviously important in its contribution to value formation. Other areas of national life may also contribute to a sense of national culture, such as your relationship with politics, the judiciary, or public bureaucracy, which tend to be very different from one nation to the other. All these elements have a strong national imprint that transcends ethnic, regional, class, and religious subdivisions and that ends up affecting business practices. Naturally these aspects are not fixed (as Hofstede seems to imply) but constantly evolving; yet the transformation of institutional systems is slow and one specific generation of people living in the same country is likely to have been exposed to similar influences, albeit refracted through the highly variable experience of being schooled in very different circumstances, affording very different access to types of social capital. Discourses are often transnational (neo-liberalism is a clear case) but there are strong differences in regional adaptations, in which the institutional field that characterizes public sector organizations certainly plays a role. Therefore, while national culture is certainly not integrated as Hofstede suggests, some form of institutionally formed national identity can be found. However, Hofstede's position is ultimately one of romantic conservatism: conservatives insist that every state is based on a notion of a national culture. Historically, such notions feed into and from totalitarian nationalist fantasies. In its extreme form it leads to a view of the predominant cultural space in which the members of other cultures (the 'hyphens') who live in the same space must either respect on the terms that the dominant culture prescribes or accept exclusion or, in extreme cases, be 'ethnically cleansed'.

Geert Hofstede's *Culture's Consequences* is well represented in controversies on the web. For instance, there is a site which includes summaries of Hofstede's work and critiques of it, the most useful of which is McSweeney's (2002) article from *Human Relations*, which is called 'Hofstede's model of national cultural differences and their consequences: a triumph of faith – a failure of analysis'.

HOFSTEDE AT WORK

EXTEND YOUR KNOWLEDGE

Brendan McSweeny is Hofstede's most persistent critic. You can check out his most recent foray against Hofstede in a chapter in a new book on *Transculturalism and Business in the BRIC States: A Handbook* (Sánchez and Brühwiler, 2015). The chapter is called 'Globe, Hofstede, Huntington, Trompenaars: common foundations, common flaws' (McSweeney, 2015). In this chapter he extends his critique to include not only Hofstede but also other arguments that stress that 'national culture' shapes the behaviour of the populations of discrete national territories (countries) both within and outside of organizations (e.g. the decisions and actions of managers and consumers) by also addressing the multi-authored Global Leadership and Organizational Behaviour Effectiveness project (GLOBE) as well as the work of Fons Trompenaars.

SUMMARY

In this chapter we have introduced some key ideas about organizational culture and its discussion in management and organization theory:

- The notion that we can make others do what we want them to do by persuading them to want to do it is one that has a long pedigree. It eventually became formalized as an integrative view of organizational culture, spurred by the remarkable commercial success of *In Search of Excellence* (Peters and Waterman, 1982).

- The 'strong-culture' perspective, even though it is the most popular, is not the only well-developed view of organizational culture.

- Other views see strong cultures as the problem, not the solution, and think of them as dominant rather than empowering.

- More recently, ethnographers have suggested that it may be quite normal for some organizations to have neither a strong nor a dominant culture. On the contrary, culture may be characterized by fragmentation.

- Finally, postmodern theorists suggest that all representations of culture are characterized by such a complex intertextuality – the texts of the subjects, the texts of the organization, and the texts of the authors – that they are better thought of as occasions for further analysis than as in any sense a definitive account of what really happens.

- Managers who are familiar with postmodern thought are at least less likely to be duped into believing that culture is a panacea and might be more sophisticated in the ways that they seek to understand and possibly to use it.

EXERCISES

1. Having read this chapter you should be able to say in your own words what each of the following key terms means. Test yourself or ask a colleague to test you.

○ Culture   ○ Organizational culture

○ Levels of culture   ○ Dimensions of culture

○ National culture

○ Subculture

○ Cultures' consequences

○ Counterculture

2. What are the three levels of culture, and how do they operate?

3. What are the management arguments for a strong culture?

4. What is the difference between seeing a culture as strong and seeing it as dominant?

5. What are the differences between integration, differentiation, and fragmentation accounts of culture?

6. What would postmodernists make of organizational culture?

7. In what ways are contemporary managers good shepherds of their flock in the modern age?

8. Should management academics prescribe organizational cultures?

9. How useful is the construct of national cultures?

10. Think of culture as a multilevel concept, with subcultures, countercultures, and so on: how easy is it to design an organizational culture in such circumstances?

11. Look at the students around you; think of your conversations with them, and discussions in class. To what extent can the variance between their value statements be considered reflective of a 'national culture'?

   i. Why should we be sceptical about accounts that suggest an organization has a national culture?

   ii. How might different assumptions about organization and national culture affect the way that you do your work?

   iii. In what ways is your work, organizationally, shaped by assumptions about your national culture? What are these assumptions? How do they relate to Hofstede's account?

TEST YOURSELF

TEST YOURSELF

Review what you have learned by visiting:
https://edge.sagepub.com/managingandorganizations4e **or your eBook**

   ○ Test yourself with multiple-choice questions

   ○ Revise key terms with the interactive flashcards

CASE STUDY

SEC enacting organizational culture

In the 1980s 'culture' operated as a kind of 'open sesame' concept in management theory. Subsequently it has been heavily criticized. Despite the critics, the concept of culture continues to be widely used by managers and consultants. It signifies processes of importance in organizations that other concepts do not capture so well. A project of 'managing culture' was devised in the year 2000 in collaboration with the Scandinavian engineering consultant company SEC.

Cultural merging

SEC was in a heavy growth period, after mergers and acquisitions of a number of firms. The reasoning behind the mergers was to position the company for the purpose of delivering complete solutions to large engineering projects, which were getting increasingly higher shares of the total project market. The challenges of creating and realizing practical synergies after mergers and acquisitions are all too familiar from the literature. Since 1997 corporations have globally spent well above $5 trillion on mergers and acquisitions, yet in 83 per cent of 700 large mergers the stock price of the combined organization did not rise above those of the single entities.

SEC identified challenges with diverse organizational cultures and work practices in the different companies it had acquired for realizing its ambitions. For example, some of the companies comprised highly specialized, mono-disciplinary, engineers with a much sought-after expert status, and which subsequently had a wide geographical area as their 'field' of work. On the other hand, some companies comprised highly trans-disciplinary engineers with work practices targeted towards complex and often local projects where they had responsibilities for more or less the totality of the project. Thus the project was initiated with the slogan of 'accelerated cultural integration'. In a collaboration between key members of the company and our team of researchers we defined the work tasks implied in the slogan in terms of barriers and enablers for knowledge exchange. The project subsequently focused on methods, concepts, and approaches for accelerated cultural integration after and during the new company mergers and acquisitions.

Rituals of cultural exchange and dissemination

The underlying premise was that faster (than the natural cadence of time would have achieved 'left to its own' social evolution) cultural integration would enable conditions for improving, and lowering the costs of, knowledge sharing. A guiding principle in the project was that culture cannot be dictated through directives and decisions, but rather is enabled through communal practices of everyday work. The basic methods of the project were twofold; first, to facilitate process meetings where top management and local project workers met in all the locations where SEC had offices; and second, to follow closely through interviews two specific projects that SEC was accomplishing at the time, and on the basis of them make two so-called 'learning histories'. We had about 15 process meetings and 20 interviews with top management, middle management, project leaders, and project members. Both in the real-life gatherings and in the learning histories we focused on what we called 'fruitful dilemmas' that SEC employees were facing in daily work activities. Through the 'dilemma doorway' the process meetings provided arenas for people to meet, get to know each other, and exchange different perspectives on significant phenomena and challenging themes. The learning histories, with their intimate project practice focus, provided a possibility to lay down traces and 'sedimentations' in the company from the discussions, perspectives, and practices that the process meetings and the two project cases spurred. Through this work two critical 'sets of oppositional stories' displaying core dilemmas in the company surfaced. We conceived these two 'sets of oppositional stories' as two of the most important myths that were guiding different practices and thus constituting key cultural knowledge in the company.

'Heart surgery – the cheaper the better?'

One of the most important activities in project-based companies like SEC is undoubtedly the process of acquiring and initiating new projects. SEC, like similar companies, lives on

(Continued)

(Continued)

project acquisitions, accomplishment, and satisfactory deliverances, and stories of project creations have naturally a significant place in story-telling practices and thus in the repro-duction of the cultural in the company. The learning histories from SEC focused to a large extent on what might be called the myth of 'project initiation' which in the specific case of SEC was labelled 'Heart surgery – the cheaper the better?' Basically the dilemma of project initiation as unfolded in the myth and displayed in the learning histories stretches along an axis from an understanding of project acquisitions as highly formalized procedures answer-ing 'invitations for tenders' from potential customers, on the one side, to an understanding of acquiring projects through a history of reputation and trust with 'good customers' and intimate personal relationships on the other.

'The flying engineers'

Much of the focus in the SEC project meeting discussions (which we considered as enact-ing rituals enabling cultural exchanges) evolved around aspects of 'the ideal organizational structure' of the company, and practical consequences of the form chosen. Again, dilemmas were at the core, not surprisingly, given the challenges of knowledge sharing after M&A in a distributed environment comprising several large and small former companies, 'inhabited' by engineering experts of different disciplines. For example, the leader of one of the divisions in SEC on several occasions, when discussing priorities, strategies, or challenges, said, 'we cannot make the flying of engineers a business idea!' The contention received mixed applause. Some groups and individuals consented to it, notably the specialized high-status experts, while others expressed their absolute disagreement. The saying pinpointed some of the dilem-mas pertaining to the myth concerning the existence of the 'the ideal organizational form'. In the joint dialogic unfolding of this myth during the project, company members increasingly realized that whatever organizational form you chose to realize, you gain some and you lose some. And like cultural practices that never can be reduced to static structures, you move on.

Questions

1. Is it possible to 'manage culture' at all, or is this a contradiction in terms?

2. Based on your own experience, discuss possible approaches to 'managing culture'.

3. What does culture consist of in this case?

Case prepared by Emil A. Røyrvik, SINTEF Technology and Society.

ADDITIONAL RESOURCES

-   Probably the best way to come to terms with organizational culture is to consult some exemplary studies of it. Peters and Waterman's (1982) *In Search of Excellence: Lessons from America's Best-Run Companies* is the obvious point to start.

-   From a more anthropological and ethnographic perspective, Martin et al.'s (1988) study, 'An alternative to bureaucratic impersonality and emotional labor: bounded emotionality at The Body Shop', is of consid-erable interest because it demonstrates how the distinctive culture of The Body Shop, a cosmetics chain, produces highly committed employ-ees. Many of you have probably been in a Body Shop at some time; now you can read all about what it means in terms of an integrationist organizational culture. Another easily accessible and good narrative account can be found in Van Maanen's (1991) 'The smile factory'. He provides an entertaining account of the corporate culture at Disneyland.

- An excellent account of organizational culture from a detailed ethnographic perspective is Kondo's (1990) *Crafting Selves*, which does a really nice job of unpicking the assumption that Japan has a national culture that easily creates effective and harmonious organizations.

- There is a very thorough analysis of the literature on national cultures in the encyclopedia entry by d'Iribarne (2008).

- Films often provide a detailed insight into organizational cultures. Think of the stress on family values as an integration metaphor in *The Godfather* movies (Coppola, 1972, 1974, 1990) or the emphasis on the sources of gender differentiation in the otherwise seemingly integrated 'organization man' world of the movie *Down With Love* (Reed, 2003) or the *Legally Blonde* movies (Herman-Wurmfeld, 2003; Luketic, 2001).

- Interesting examples of strong organizational cultures and their effects are provided by military/war movies, especially *A Few Good Men* (Reiner, 1992), starring Jack Nicholson, Demi Moore, and Tom Cruise.

- Perhaps one of the most interesting movies ever made about organizational culture is one based on a true story: *Colonel Redl* (Szabo, 1985). Colonel Redl is an outsider in the Austro-Hungarian court at the turn of the nineteenth century. He is part Jewish, part Catholic, part Ukrainian, part Hungarian, and gay. Within this sociopolitical context, he does not fit anywhere into the culture. He manages to pass himself off as a member of the dominant culture; however, he ends up being blackmailed and disgraced, and the culture leaves him with only one organizational option, which occupies the closing reels of the film.

- Both the late Peter Frost and Joanne Martin, whom we have discussed in this chapter, can be seen in short interviews at the companion website https://edge.sagepub.com/managingandorganizations4e

- There is also a film of the Barings Bank disaster caused by Nick Leeson, *Rogue Trader* (Deardon, 1999). This makes particularly interesting viewing, if seen in conjunction with the classic business movie *Wall Street* (Stone, 1987), as an illustration of an organizational culture premised on absolute selfishness and ruthlessness.

PART 7

JOURNALS ON DEVELOPING
WORKPLACE CRITICAL THINKING

How Critical is Critical Thinking?

Shaw, R. D.

Abstract: Recent educational discourse is full of references to the value of critical thinking as a 21st-century skill. In music education, critical thinking has been discussed in relation to problem solving and music listening, and some researchers suggest that training in critical thinking can improve students' responses to music. But what exactly is meant by "critical thinking"? This article explores how critical thinking, when thought of as an outgrowth of Critical Theory and pedagogy concepts, may look very different than our popular definitions of the concept. This reframing of critical thinking requires that students take an active role in questioning and challenging music, education, and the ways in which they may take critical action to pursue change. Examples of critical thinking questions, activities, and curricula are offered, and resources are included for further reading.

Keywords: concept, critical theory, critical thinking, challenge, higher-order thinking, music education, pedagogy, questioning strategies

My seventh-grade band class is wrapping up, and today's rehearsal is coming to an end in an unusual manner. Instead of rehearsing up until the bell rings, we've stopped early to watch YouTube videos of zydeco and jazz musicians from New Orleans. This school is an International Baccalaureate (IB) World School, and the entire seventh grade is involved in an interdisciplinary unit organized around the study of Hurricane Katrina. Students have watched the documentary Hurricane on the Bayou, *studied the weather patterns and erosion of the Louisiana Delta in science class, debated the Federal Emergency Management Agency response in social studies, and written Katrina-centered poetry in English language arts class. In addition to our listening/watching examples, the band will perform John Edmondson's "Jazz Jubilee" and a medley of "When the Saints Go Marching In" and "Just a Closer Walk with Thee" at our concert.*

With the seventh graders out the door, I rearrange music stands and check my e-mail. The sixth-grade band students are entering now, papers in hand. Because they will be performing themes from Dvořák's symphony From the New World *in a few weeks, we studied the New York Philharmonic's 2008 trip to North Korea, during which the orchestra performed the iconic piece. The students have written letters to the White House proposing a goodwill concert for the seventh-grade band in a world "hot spot," and one student hands me his letter. He asks, "Would Iran be too dangerous for our band to travel to?" I start to run through possible questions for the class: Should the New York Philharmonic have traveled to North Korea to perform? What did it mean for them to play "Arirang" for the audience? Are there other times in our country's history that music has played a diplomatic role? Ah, yes! An idea—a "light bulb moment" comes. I do an Internet search using the words Berlin Wall Bernstein, and I start planning the class's next discussion.*

Critical thinking is a concept that has taken on multiple meanings and uses. Authors have written about critical thinking in music education, discussing it in the context of both problem solving and music listening.[1] Critical thinking also is cited as an integral

> *What is critical thinking, and why is it important to music educators? This article suggests ways your students can become a more active part of their own learning.*

Ryan D. Shaw is a doctoral student in music education at Michigan State University, East Lansing. He can be contacted at rydshaw@gmail.com.

DOI: 10.1177/0027432114544376
http://mej.sagepub.com

21st-century skill.[2] But how does critical thinking relate to the fields of Critical Theory and critical pedagogy?[3] Should critical thinking spur action? Can critical teaching practices help music education to become more relevant and central to students' lives?

In the vignette above, the teacher has started down a road toward critical teaching by setting up a particular kind of teaching/learning situation. The notes and rhythms may sound the same as in any other middle school band room, but the students' thinking will be anything but typical. How can the teacher move forward with critical thinking questions? What guiding principles can he draw on to shape his practice?

Some Background

While there are no singular definitions for these three critical arenas, there are some important distinctions and similarities among them. The three areas—theory, pedagogy, and thinking—have separate established literatures and thinkers, but they share the same fundamental concern: that people develop the skills and knowledge necessary to be skeptical and to discern "inaccuracies, distortions, and even falsehoods."[4] Beyond this central focus, important differences abound. Critical theorists primarily are concerned with *transformative social change*, achieved through questioning one's ideology. Critical pedagogues focus more specifically on how educational institutions *perpetuate an unjust status quo* that leads to inequalities. In this sense, critical pedagogy can be thought of as the application of Critical Theory to education.[5]

Critical thinking, as its name indicates, focuses on improving one's thought processes about all areas of life. Critical thinking advocates maintain that people should question "faulty arguments, hasty generalizations, assertions lacking evidence, truth claims based on unreliable authority, ambiguous or obscure concepts."[6] Critical thinking therefore is more inherently "value neutral" than critical pedagogy/theory.[7] While critical thinking authors do not

explicitly discuss power imbalances in society, they implicitly urge the kinds of thought processes that may lead to this kind of questioning. Notable scholars have contributed to the writings that characterize Critical Theory, critical pedagogy, and critical thinking (see the Selected Resources on Critical Theory, Critical Pedagogy, and Critical Thinking sidebar).

Critical Thinking Defined

As mentioned, while critical thinking is accepted broadly as being educationally important, specific definitions are lacking. What is critical thinking and what are critical thinking questions? Psychologist Robert Sternberg defined critical thinking broadly as "the mental processes, strategies, and representations people use to solve problems, make decisions, and learn new concepts."[8] Education professor Michael Scriven and philosopher Richard Paul defined it as "the intellectually disciplined process of actively and skillfully conceptualizing, applying, analyzing, synthesizing, and/or evaluating information gathered from, or generated by, observation, experience, reflection, reasoning, or communication, as a guide to belief and action."[9] Common to these definitions and others is the idea that critical thinking is active rather than passive and is of a higher-order and abstract nature.

With these definitions in mind, it seems clear that not all teacher questioning and student responses are inherently critical. Teachers' questioning procedures can be placed along a spectrum ranging from basic recall to higher-order thinking. This continuum can be illuminated by Bloom's taxonomy of educational objectives, updated recently by Lorin Anderson and David Krathwohl, who studied with Bloom.[10] While there likely is agreement among most music teachers that asking a lower-level thinking question that requires only the recall of facts does not spur critical thinking (e.g., "What's the fingering for B-flat?"), the consensus seems to stop here. Many other less-than-critical questions are sometimes passed off as such.

Level 1: "Neutral" Critical Thinking

Returning to the vignette above, let's consider how the teacher could start to engage students in critical thinking. In the course of rehearsal, the teacher may say to ensemble students, "What are some changes you could make in your performance of themes from the *New World Symphony* to make the band sound better?" According to Bloom's taxonomy, this question is of a higher order than the previous recall question, accessing levels of *understanding* and even up to *analyzing*, depending on the exact discussion procedure. It demands heightened perception and aesthetic awareness, and it even invites student action to remedy perceived limitations in musical performance. This is therefore a critical-thinking question by many popular definitions.

The question is fairly "neutral" in the sense that it is not concerned with social justice. What dimensions would need to be added to move this kind of question toward critical action? While important, this question in its current form (and similar neutral higher-order thinking questions) clearly falls below the threshold set by critical theorists/pedagogues. This question does not address constraints of ideology, and it does not aim at enlightenment in pursuit of emancipatory action. It is not, however, difficult to imagine the classroom discussion moving further in this direction.

Level 2: Moving toward Critical Action

Imagine the teacher posing a different question to the ensemble: "Why do you think an American orchestra would play Dvořák's *New World Symphony* in North Korea?" In the updated version of Bloom's taxonomy, this question falls somewhere around *evaluating* and the highest level, *creating*, since a response demands judgment and synthesis of a number of factors into a new viewpoint.[11] In terms of subject matter, the question is moving away

Selected Resources on Critical Theory, Critical Pedagogy, and Critical Thinking

Critical Theory

- James Bohman, "Critical Theory," *The Stanford Encyclopedia of Philosophy*, Edward N. Zalta, ed. (Spring 2013 Edition). http://plato.stanford.edu/archives/spr2013/entries/critical-theory/

Critical Pedagogy

- Paulo Freire

  Pedagogy of the Oppressed (New York: Seabury Press, 1970).
  Education for Critical Consciousness (New York: Seabury, 1973).

- Henry Giroux

  On Critical Pedagogy (New York: Continuum Press, 2011).

- Michael Apple

  Ideology and Curriculum (New York: Routledge, 1979).

- Edited book

  Critical Theories in Education, Thomas S. Popkewitz and Lynn Fendler, eds. (New York: Routledge, 1999).

Critical Thinking

- Richard Paul

  Critical Thinking: What Every Person Needs to Survive in a Rapidly Changing World (Rohnert Park, CA: Center for Critical Thinking and Moral Critique, 1990).

Music Education Resources

- Book Chapters/Articles

  Douglas Reahm, "Developing Critical Thinking through Rehearsal Techniques," *Music Educators Journal* 72, no. 7 (March 1986): 29–31.

  Lenore Pogonowski, "Developing Skills in Critical Thinking and Problem Solving," *Music Educators Journal* 73, no. 6 (February 1987): 37–41.

  Lenore Pogonowski, "Critical Thinking and Music Listening," *Music Educators Journal* 76, no. 1 (September 1989): 35–38.

  Carol Richardson and Nancy Whitaker, "Critical Thinking and Music Education," in *Handbook for Research on Music Teaching and Learning*, ed. R. Colwell (New York: Macmillan, 1992): 546–57.

  Frank Abrahams, "The Application of Critical Theory to a Sixth Grade General Music Class," *Visions of Research in Music Education* 4 (2004).

  Frank Abrahams, "Transforming Classroom Music Instruction with Ideas from Critical Pedagogy," *Music Educators Journal* 92, no. 1 (September 2005): 62–67.

---

from "neutrality" and toward worldly significance. In and of itself, however, this question is not inherently critical as defined by authors who are critical theorists/pedagogues.

This kind of question moves toward critical action. By hinting at the foundations of critical theory/pedagogy, it easily leads to reflection on the relationship between music and diplomacy and a search for enlightenment through understanding constraints, motivations, and influences. But to be critical in the tradition of critical theory/pedagogy, the line of inquiry would have to continue until students turned an eye on their own circumstances. In a sense, this is a final step toward critical action.

Level 3: Down to Earth

Since critical theorists/pedagogues are concerned with turning an eye on problems in society, critical discussions must connect questioning with students' lives. Music philosopher Thomas A. Regelski noted that in turning critical thinking on students' own circumstances, abstract questions are considered concretely and brought "down to earth."[12] Similarly, music education professor Frank Abrahams suggested that meaningful critical pedagogy empowers students by connecting curriculum to their lives.[13] Consider the possible follow-up questions to the teacher's question about the New York Philharmonic performing Dvořák's symphony *From the New World:* "What music would you pick to communicate the essence of your life in America? Should you have a say in what you express in school or in music class?" The questions have moved from abstract or distant topics and turned toward students' experiences. Now the inquiry has become critical in the tradition of critical theory/pedagogy.

If these levels of critical thinking are not understood, all questioning strategies may be haphazardly grouped together as critical. Acknowledging the difference between higher-order questions, divergent questions with more than one right answer, and critical questions helps music teachers examine their practice and avoid "definition confusion." Acknowledging these differences can also help educators to have productive conversations with one another. When there is a baseline of understanding, discussions can more easily produce meaningful goals and strategies. This understanding has the power to improve teaching.

Full agreement on what is and is not critical thinking may never completely materialize among music educators—and that is okay. By grappling with examples, teachers can make more informed decisions. These examples can effectively help them focus on the questions they really want to ask. For example, teachers may choose to focus questions only on performance, or they may choose to target music's role in society or its relation to their students' circumstances in life.

A "Critical Pedagogy Classroom"

Teaching could look noticeably different if music educators embraced critical pedagogy. Depending on the teacher, changes could occur in the mode of interaction, the subject matter, or both. Due to the complex and "messy" discussions that might ensue, ensemble rehearsals perhaps would be less efficient and therefore less effective in pursuing precision and polished performances. Repertoire might be approached differently. Study of popular band compositions, like "Africa: Ceremony, Song, and Ritual" (Robert W. Smith) and "Variations on a Korean Folk Song" (John Barnes Chance), might consider both inherent elements of the sound (e.g., key and form) and contextual elements surrounding the creation and reception of the music (e.g., nationalistic feelings about music, war, and culture). Students performing Percy Grainger's "Children's March: 'Over the Hills and Far Away'" would not only seek to perform with musical expression and exactness but also would confront the complexity of Grainger's views on race, his mother's troubling struggle with and death from mental illness, and Grainger's reverence for the music of Duke Ellington. And as mentioned above, they would take the crucial step of relating such important issues to their own lives.

Classroom interactions would change. As Abrahams has suggested, infusing music teaching with critical pedagogy means inviting student voice and encouraging students to be critical.[14] Arguments and votes might take place regarding the role of music in the curriculum and the world. Blogs and online forums might be created to host students' critical conversations with one another.[15] Students and teachers might come to embrace a shared mission for their music-making. Performances and performance venues might change to reflect new priorities.

Many music educators might argue that time spent on critical thinking would dilute the precision and polish of performances. Critical pedagogy urges the examination of "uncritical acceptance of and obedience to" ideology, which to some may seem at best a waste of time and at worst an invitation

to classroom chaos.[16] Open-ended, emergent conversations can take time away from music-making and hurt efficiency, which often is prized in music classrooms. Music teachers may believe that these issues and conversations are best left for other classes. This raises important questions about performance goals and what constitutes a musical performance. If musicality is aided by informed and passionate decision making by students who are deeply engaged with musical materials and the richness of the music's context, then critical pedagogy may be considered essential. And performance excellence without active student understanding—if that is even possible—would be frowned on by critical pedagogy advocates. Critical pedagogues would argue that teachers and students must confront issues "head-on," because avoidance of serious topics does not make them disappear. Teachers and students cannot avoid challenging issues because they are embedded in all activities and choices, and schools do not exist in vacuums but are instead microcosms of life filled with an array of challenging ethical debates.[17]

Undoubtedly, some teaching/learning arrangements can more easily incorporate critical pedagogy ideals than others. Teachers who consider their classes to be performance-only ensembles may feel there is no time for critical discussions.[18] But this is a function of teacher perspective more than performance obligations. While some music educators may avoid certain topics and discussions in the pursuit of rehearsal efficiency, they should consider the value of such interactions to students' responses to and understanding of music. Responding is an integral part of the National Core Arts Standards' Create/Perform/Respond framework, and some recent researchers have suggested that critical thinking instruction may improve comprehension.[19]

Some previous articles on this topic have offered some concrete suggestions for putting these ideas into practice. For example, Abrahams offered an eight-step teaching model, and Woodford suggested the most beneficial thing teachers can do is to model critical thinking for students.[20] Small proposed several strategies for teachers, including that they "plan a specific incident of intellectual dissonance."[21] In addition to considering these ideas, teachers can purposefully plan for critical teaching by keeping inquiry and curiosity at the center of their lesson preparation process. Two planning formats are particularly well suited to this inquiry-centered orientation: the CRISPA method and the visual mapping method championed by music education professor Sandra Snow.[22] These planning methods can help set up critical pedagogy by asking teachers specifically to think through the many possible "angles" and entry points into a piece of music or lesson topic. Both

planning formats have inquiry squarely at their core.

Education Oriented toward Action

One can find instances of flourishing educational models that embrace critical ideals. An interesting example of basing curriculum around community engagement and social action exists in Metropolitan Expeditionary Learning School, a public school in New York City.[23] The school was formed in 2010 and follows the "expeditionary learning" model. In this model, curriculum is project based and organized around "learning expeditions." Students participate in community fieldwork and partner with local leaders and community organizations. During a recent three-month expedition, seventh graders were encouraged to consider how "big changes" occur and how ideas spread in society. By the end of the unit, students had designed a media campaign to advocate for alternative taxicab engines in New York City, collaborating with the New York City Taxi and Limousine Commission. In their music classes, music teacher Eric Shieh notes how students turned a critical lens on the "role of blues songs in developing radical consciousness in black Americans."[24]

One of the hallmarks of music programs oriented toward critical pedagogy and action seems to be an emphasis on interdisciplinary study. Shieh notes that while "for many teachers, ideas of the self and the social are generally perceived as the purview of Social Studies or Humanities classes," encouraging students to apply ideas "to their own contexts as agents of change" requires interdisciplinary study.[25] One can find the same emphasis in the International Baccalaureate program, popular at many schools around the world. This program cites critical thinking and "habits of mind" as fundamental to learning and asks teachers to design cross-curricular units of study based on "big ideas" (see vignette).[26] Critical pedagogy does not explicitly demand

these interdisciplinary approaches, but they do seem to evolve naturally from its emphasis on breaking down walls—walls between teacher and student and between curricular subjects.

A Balance of Activities

A music classroom full of critical thinking certainly is atypical but not impossible. The vignette and the other examples mentioned above present just a few of the possibilities that this orientation toward education can encourage. As with any music teaching and learning arrangement, the balance between time spent on practicing skills versus knowledge construction would need to be considered carefully. And for teachers who value relevance and student engagement, a music classroom focused on critical thinking and critical action could make up in significance what it may lack in efficiency. Some authors point to this as an idealized state for education. Music education philosopher Estelle Jorgensen suggested, "Education cannot afford to be trivial and instrumental. Its purpose is to grapple with the central issues of life."[27]

It is important to continue a dialogue in music education about the prevalence or lack of critical thinking in the tradition of Critical Theory and critical pedagogy. An emphasis on awareness, questioning of constraints and systems, and enlightenment and emancipation can be challenging for music teachers, as it may change the nature of classroom interaction in ways that may seem uncomfortable. However, because this kind of critical thinking has the power to make music education more relevant and meaningful for students, it must be taken seriously.

NOTES

1. See Douglas Reahm, "Developing Critical Thinking through Rehearsal Techniques," *Music Educators Journal* 72, no. 7 (March 1986): 29–31; Lenore Pogonowski, "Developing Skills in Critical Thinking and Problem Solving," *Music Educators Journal* 73,

no. 6 (February 1987): 37–41; Lenore Pogonowski, "Critical Thinking and Music Listening," *Music Educators Journal* 76, no. 1 (September 1989): 35–38; Carol Richardson and Nancy Whitaker, "Critical Thinking and Music Education," in *Handbook for Research on Music Teaching and Learning*, ed. R. Colwell (New York: Macmillan, 1992), 546–57.

2. See Partnership for 21st Century Skills, "21st Century Skills Map: The Arts," accessed September 24, 2013, http://p21.org/storage/ documents/ P21_arts_map_final.pdf; The College Board, "Arts Education Standards and 21st Century Skills: An Analysis of the National Standards for Arts Education as Compared to the 21st Century Skills Map for the Arts," August 2011, accessed September 23, 2013, from the National Coalition for Core Arts Standards, http:// nccas.wikispaces.com/file/view/ArtsEduc ationStandards_21stCenturySkills.pdf.

3. Critical Theory can narrowly mean the specific school of thought coming from the Frankfurt School in Germany in the twentieth century, or it can broadly signify a number of critical theories (e.g., critical race theory, feminist theory). I am using Critical Theory in the more narrow sense and capitalizing it accordingly.

4. N. C. Burbules and R. Berk, "Critical Thinking and Critical Pedagogy: Relations, Differences, and Limits," in *Critical Theories in Education: Changing Terrains of Knowledge and Politics*, ed. T. S. Popkewitz and L. Fendler (New York: Routledge, 1999), 46.

5. Ibid.

6. Ibid.

7. It is important to note that critical theorists/pedagogues would say argue nothing is "neutral," since anything that is not working toward critical aims is by definition part of unexamined ideology.

8. Robert Sternberg, "Critical Thinking, Its Nature, Measurement, and Improvement," in *Essays on the Intellect*, ed. Frances R. Link (Alexandria, VA: Association for Supervision and Curriculum Development, 1985), 46.

9. Michael Scriven and Richard Paul, "Defining Critical Thinking," 2008, accessed October 1, 2013, http://www. criticalthinking.org/aboutCT/define_critical_thinking.cfm.

10. See Lorin Anderson and David Krathwohl, *A Taxonomy for Learning, Teaching and Assessing: A Revision of Bloom's Taxonomy of Educational Objectives, Complete Edition* (New York: Longman, 2001); also, Norm Webb, "Research Monograph Number 6: Criteria for Alignment of Expectations and Assessments on Mathematics and Science Education" (Washington, DC: CCSSO, 1997).

11. Anderson and Krathwohl, *A Taxonomy*.

12. Thomas A. Regelski, "Critical Theory as a Foundation for Critical Thinking in Music Education," *Visions of Research in Music Education* 6 (2005), http://www-usr.rider.edu/~vrme/.

13. See Frank Abrahams, "The Application of Critical Theory to a Sixth Grade General Music Class," *Visions of Research in Music Education* 4 (2004); Frank Abrahams, "Transforming Classroom Music Instruction with Ideas from Critical Pedagogy," *Music Educators Journal* 92, no. 1 (September 2005): 62–67.

14. Abrahams, "Transforming Classroom Music Instruction."

15. See Cynthia Johnston Turner, "Another Perspective: Crowdsourcing Our Ensemble Rehearsals," *Music Educators Journal* 100, no. 2 (December 2013): 68–71.

16. Regelski, "Critical Theory," 8.

17. Thomas A. Regelski, "The Ethics of Music Teaching as Profession and Praxis," *Visions of Research in Music Education* 13 (2009), http://www-usr .rider.edu/~vrme/.

18. For example, see the band director quoted in Betty Anne Younker and Maud Hickey, "Examining the Profession through the Lens of Social Justice: Two Music Educators' Stories and Their Stark Realizations," *Music Education Research* 9, no. 2 (2007): 215–27. When asked about the National Standards, he says, "'I don't have time. We are a performance organization, and our number one goal is to get these kids performing. I don't think they are bad,' he continues, 'it's just that they are not part of our program philosophy here'" (p. 219).

19. Daniel C. Johnson, "The Effect of Critical Thinking Instruction on Verbal Descriptions of Music," *Journal of Research in Music Education* 59, no. 3 (2011): 257–72.

20. Abrahams, "Transforming Classroom Music Instruction."

21. Ann R. Small, "Music Teaching and Critical Thinking: What Do We Need to Know?" *Music Educators Journal* 74, no. 1 (September 1987): 48.

22. See P. Bruce Uhrmacher, Bradley M. Conrad, and Christy M. Moroye, "Finding the Balance between Process and Product through Perceptual Lesson Planning," *Teachers College Record* 115, no. 7 (2013); Sandra Snow, "Preparation for Engaged Teaching and Learning in the High School Choral Classroom," *Choral Journal* 51, no. 7 (2011): 10–17.

23. Metropolitan Expeditionary Learning School, "Home Page," accessed September 25, 2013, http://www .metropolitanels.com/MELS/Home.html.

24. Eric Shieh, "'It's Revolutionary!': A Case of Interdisciplinarity in Music Education," in *Listen Out: International Perspectives on Music Education*, ed. Chris Harrison and Sarah Hennessy (London: National Association of Music Educators, 2012), 56.

25. Shieh, "'It's Revolutionary!'" 57.

26. International Baccalaureate, "Middle Years Programme Curriculum," accessed October 24, 2013, http:// www.ibo.org/myp/curriculum/index.cfm.

27. Estelle Jorgensen, "The Artist and the Pedagogy of Hope," *International Journal of Music Education* 27 (1996): 43.

"As a 2006 Harris Poll showed, schools with music programs have significantly higher graduation and attendance rates than those without music programs. For many students, their role in their band, choir, or orchestra, leading and participating in an ensemble toward a shared goal of producing a high-level performance, motivates students to attend school daily. That sense of responsibility as they collaborate with peers who depend on their presence gets students in schools, gets them excited about education."

—"Graduation Rates and Keeping Students 'On Track,'" retrieved September 29, 2014, from http:// www.nafme.org/graduation-rates-and-keeping-students-on-track/

More Alike Than Different: What Generations Value and How the Values Affect Employee Workplace Perceptions

Mencl, J. and Lester, S. W.

Abstract
The purpose of this study was to extend generations research by investigating similarities and differences regarding the importance generations place on the presence of various workplace characteristics. We hypothesized (1) that similarities in the importance of workplace factors between generations would be more prevalent than differences and (2) that the importance of the workplace factors would have consistently similar or different moderating effects among generations on the relationships between employee perceptions of the factors at their organizations and employee attitudes. As expected, results showed the generations were similar on 7 of the 10 work values examined. Findings also revealed similarities and differences between the generations for the factors as moderators, although more differences than similarities were present from these analyses. Implications of these findings as well as directions for future research are discussed.

Keywords
generations, work values, employee attitudes

Today's multigenerational workforce presents a number of opportunities and challenges for managers. With some employees choosing to work into their late 60s and 70s, four generational cohorts are currently working simultaneously. Three of these generations (i.e., Baby Boomers, Generation X, and Generation Y) have the opportunity to work with each other for another decade or more. Although this diversity of perspectives can assist companies in producing well thought-out decisions and increased responsiveness to customers, the diversity also presents complexities in the management of human resource policies and systems to meet employee needs if generations desire different things from their workplace environment.

In the past decade there has been much conjecture and some empirical work on generational differences, however, there is much left to learn (Parry & Urwin, 2011; Twenge, 2010). The current study seeks to replicate and expand upon research on generational differences by addressing two questions in particular: "Are the three prevalent generations in today's workforce actually more similar than different in what they desire in their workplace?" and "How do the similarities/differences in values influence the effects of employee perceptions of these organizational characteristics on attitudinal outcomes by generation?"

Researchers have expressed concern that little empirical research supports generational stereotypes associated with each cohort (e.g., Meriac, Woehr, & Banister, 2010; Macky,

Gardner, & Forsyth, 2008). Several studies have examined proposed generational differences for which findings support generational similarities. For example, Hansen and Leuty (2012) investigated various workplace values among Generation X, the Baby Boomers, and the Silent Generation (also known as Traditionalists), finding only three statistically significant differences out of a possible 20 between two or more generations. Similarly, Cennamo and Gardner (2008) found only two differences between generations for workplace values of the six values that were measured. Other research has compared actual generational differences with perceived generational differences and found that the number of actual generational differences was far fewer than the number of perceived differences (Lester, Standifer, Schultz, & Windsor, 2012). Given these findings, the first objective of the current study is to replicate and extend previous research findings that show similarities for the three youngest generations in the workforce—Generation Y, Generation X, and the Baby Boomers. The

[1]University of Minnesota Duluth, Duluth, MN, USA
[2]University of Wisconsin–Eau Claire, Eau Claire, WI, USA

Corresponding Author:
Jennifer Mencl, Department of Management Studies, Labovitz School of Business and Economics, University of Minnesota Duluth, 1318 Kirby Drive, 365 LSBE, Duluth, MN 55812, USA.
Email: jmencl@d.umn.edu

current study also extends previous work by examining workplace characteristics associated with companies appearing on lists of "best places to work" rather than items that may be stereotypical by generation.

The second objective of the current study is to provide a better understanding of what these actual generational differences mean for employee outcomes. Previous research examining the effects of generation on employee attitudes, such as job satisfaction, organizational commitment, and turnover intention has shown few differences (Benson & Brown, 2011; Cennamo & Gardner, 2008; Costanza, Badger, Fraser, Severt, & Gade, 2012; Deal, Stawiski, Graves, Gentry, Weber, & Ruderman, 2013). We extend the exploration of the ways in which generation influences attitudinal outcomes through a person–organization (P-O) fit perspective and principles of value–percept theory that includes the moderating effect of each workplace value on the relationship between perceptions of the characteristic within the organization and each attitude. By examining the role of generations in this manner, the study provides a more complete perspective of managing employee attitudes beyond the existing literature.

We begin our discussion with a brief review of the generally accepted time periods associated with the three prominent generations in today's workforce. We then provide rationale for which "best places to work" criteria we would expect to see differences and which criteria we would expect to see similarities across generations. After testing whether generations had an influence on employee attitudinal outcomes, we discuss the practical implications of the findings as well as directions for future research.

Literature Review and Hypotheses

Although some discrepancy exists among researchers with respect to generation cut-offs, Baby Boomers are generally viewed as individuals who were born between the years of 1946 and 1964. Generation X was born between the years of 1965 and 1978, and Generation Y was born between the years of 1979 and 2000 (Smola & Sutton, 2002). The belief is that the individuals who grow up during the same time period are influenced by social and historic events and contexts (e.g., the Korean War, The Vietnam War, the end of the Cold War, economic recessions) that shape their values and attitudes in a way that differentiates one generational cohort from another (Jurkiewicz & Brown, 1998; Parry & Urwin, 2011; Sessa, Kabacoff, Deal, & Brown, 2007). However, academic evidence regarding generational differences is mixed (Parry & Urwin, 2011), with much research showing more similarities between generations than differences as previously described. As noted above, such generational differences are more likely to be perceived than actual (Lester et al., 2012).

Characteristics of Interest ("Best Places to Work")

Previous studies investigating generational differences have included a broad range of work-related items, such as perceptions of workplace factors and work values. A study by Benson and Brown (2011) examined nine organizational and work variables including job security, pay-level satisfaction, satisfaction with benefits, promotional opportunities, resource inadequacy, role ambiguity, role conflict, coworker support, and supervisor support. The Work Values Questionnaire and Work Values Scale were used by Cennamo and Gardner (2008) to measure extrinsic, intrinsic, altruistic, status, freedom, and social factors in the workplace. Hansen and Leuty (2012) used the Minnesota Importance Questionnaire in their research that measured 20 value facets categorized into the overarching values of achievement, comfort, status, altruism, safety, and autonomy. Smola and Sutton (2002) examined three work values that included desirability of work outcomes, pride in craftsmanship, and moral importance of work.

This study was designed with the intent of examining similarities and differences between generations using characteristics associated with "best places to work" lists (e.g., *Fortune*'s top 100 companies, *HR Magazine*'s 50 Best Small and Medium Companies). These specific characteristics were chosen for a data collection project being used to identify organizations in a community that were considered good places to work for "young professionals." Although the practitioners involved in the project expected to see differences between generations for most factors, the project provided an avenue to extend previous academic research by showing actual differences versus similarities using "best places to work" characteristics across generations.

The 10 workplace factors selected from the "best places to work" lists included: teamwork and collaboration, flexible work arrangements, a challenging job, involvement in decision making, a financially rewarding job, work–life balance, a climate of diversity, continuous learning, career advancement, and immediate feedback and recognition. While the assumption is made that all of these characteristics are desirable regardless of employee age, we propose that the premium placed on a few of these characteristics will vary by generation. Next, we discuss the four items where we expect to see actual differences.

Actual Differences and Similarities Expected

Diversity Climate. Baby Boomers grew up in a time when the male was often the sole or main breadwinner for the family and when the workplace was more heavily weighted toward a single race (Caucasians). In recent decades, we have seen significant shifts in the demographic makeup of the workforce. For example, with respect to women and minorities in the workplace 50% of women aged 25 to 54 years were in the U.S. workforce in 1970 compared with 75% in 2005, and in 2005, 77% of African American women, 70% of Asian women, and 65% of Hispanic women were in the workforce in the United States (Mosisa & Hipple, 2006). In addition to increased gender and racial/ethnic diversity, globalization has affected the diversity of nationalities in the workforce. Younger employees have also grown up during a time in which gay, lesbian, and transgender issues have received a great deal of attention with respect to workplace diversity and gay marriage has been legalized. Furthermore, the passage of the Americans with Disabilities Act in 1990 is credited to have positively affected the number of individuals with disabilities in the workplace (Smola & Sutton, 2002). These shifts over time that have led to a greater diversification of the workforce have enabled Generation X and, even more so, Generation Y to interact and collaborate with a more diverse workplace than their predecessors. Research findings have shown Generation Y to be considerably more comfortable with diversity (78% of survey respondents) compared with the Baby Boomers (27% of respondents; Hewlett, Sherbin, & Sumberg, 2009). Thus, we expect Generation Y to place a higher importance on a diverse climate compared with other generations and the Baby Boomer generation to report the lowest rating.

Continuous Learning. By being in an environment that supports and fosters ongoing learning, individuals are able to pursue opportunities that ensure their continued employability. Younger generations have grown up in a context where job security was far from assured and downsizing became an accepted management practice (Gowing, Kraft, & Quick, 1998). Therefore, to maintain marketability, younger employees are more likely than older employees to participate in training programs to develop new skills. In addition, a recent review presents research that suggests younger employees are more motivated and willing to engage in continuous learning compared with older employees (Jain & Martindale, 2012). One explanation is that training is less important for the careers of Baby Boomers who have already received promotions to levels in the organizational hierarchy that have satisfied their need for growth. In contrast, members of Generations X and Y are more likely to be seeking promotions and value skill development, especially Generation Y (Wong, Gardiner, Lang, & Coulon, 2008). Another reason that older employees are less motivated to learn is that levels of cognitive processing naturally decline over time and cause learning to occur more slowly. As learning becomes more difficult, individuals are less likely to participate in training activities (Jain & Martindale, 2012). These circumstances taken collectively suggest younger generations will place greater value on a workplace that allows continuous learning compared with older generations, with the greatest importance identified by Generation Y.

Career Advancement. Previous research findings have shown that the number of promotions, as well as the speed of promotions, contribute to career satisfaction for all generations, yet the statistical effect size for career advancement was significantly greater for Generation Y compared with the other generations studied (Dries, Pepermans, & De Kerpel, 2008). Although perceptions of career success are driven by promotions, the importance of promotions becomes less important for employees as they near retirement. For example, members of the Baby Boomer generation who are near retirement age are less likely to be seeking career advancement opportunities compared to employees with decades of working years ahead of them. In addition, a stronger desire for growth arises in part from the perceived expectation associated with Generation Y of finding a perfect job early in their careers as opposed to norms associated with older generations in which individuals should pay their dues prior to any type of advancement (Arnett, 2004). Therefore, we expect career advancement to differ across generations, being valued most by Generation Y and least by the Baby Boomer generation.

Immediate Feedback and Recognition. Generation Y is sometimes referred to as the "me-generation" based on their desire for instant gratification and growing up in a culture in which everyone received a trophy. In addition, Generation Y grew up in a technologically driven environment that has made them accustomed to immediate access to information and instant communication with online connections (e.g., texting, social media outlets; Steele & Gordon, 2006). At work, this translates to a desire to receive detailed feedback from their supervisors on a frequent basis (Crumpacker & Crumpacker, 2007; Herman & Eckel, 2002; Westerman & Yamamura, 2007). Generation X has also been noted to want immediate feedback (Wong et al., 2008), although not as frequently as Generation Y (Glass, 2007; Martin, 2005). In contrast to younger generations, Baby Boomers do not generally share the same need for constant feedback (Glass, 2007). Thus, we expect Generation Y to value immediate feedback and recognition the most among the three generations, followed by Generation X, and then the Baby Boomers.

To summarize the four "best places to work" characteristics for which differences across generations are expected, we hypothesize the following:

Hypothesis 1a: The extent to which employees value diversity, continuous learning, career advancement, and immediate feedback and recognition will vary by generation, with the greatest importance noted by Generation Y and the least importance noted by Baby Boomers.

While we expect generational differences to exist on the aforementioned characteristics, we anticipate a greater number of similarities across the generations in terms of the value placed on other work factors. In the subsequent paragraphs, we discuss the expectation of *no* differences existing between generations on the remaining six workplace characteristics that are summarized into four categories.

Work–Life Balance and Flexible Work Arrangements. As organizations require employees to work more hours and maintain schedules that fall outside the traditional "9 to 5" realm, flexible work arrangements have been a typical practice associated with work–life balance initiatives (Eikhof, Warhurst, & Haunschild, 2007). Generation X and Generation Y have been noted to place a high value on work–life balance (Cennamo & Gardner, 2008; Glass, 2007). And, although Baby Boomers are often known for their strong work ethic and placing a priority on work (Fogg, 2009), they also face nonwork demands such as elder-care responsibilities that make work–life balance a desirable workplace characteristic (Hill, Hawkins, Ferris, & Weitzman, 2001). Recent research comparing Baby Boomers with Generation Y shows similar results for the generations with respect to the importance of work–life balance and flexible work arrangements (Hewlett et al., 2009). Therefore, we expect all three generations to place a similar level of importance on the balance between work and nonwork aspects of their lives regardless of what constitutes one's need for "balance" (e.g., time for hobbies, time to attend children's activities, time with grandchildren, time to take care of aging parents). We also anticipate that the three generations will place a similar level of importance on having flexible work arrangements as a related aspect of achieving a good work–life balance.

Involvement in Decision Making and a Challenging Job. Decentralized decision-making practices in organizations are associated with employee involvement practices that are tied to high-performance work systems (Evans & Davis, 2005). Employee involvement programs, including management-driven initiatives, open-door policies, employee surveys, participative management, employee task forces, and self-managed work teams, all contribute to healthy organizations that realize positive levels of job satisfaction and low levels of turnover (Grawitch, Ledford, Ballard, Barber, 2009; Grawitch, Trares, & Kohler, 2007). When employees become increasingly involved in making decisions that affect the work they do, employees are more empowered (Butts, Vandenberg, DeJoy, Schaffer, & Wilson, 2009) and their jobs become more challenging and more enriched (Luna-Arocas & Camps, 2008).

Job enrichment through autonomy is a well-known predictor in Hackman and Oldham's (1976) job characteristics model that has been empirically tested across generations for several decades. Meta-analyses published in the 1980s examining autonomy and participative decision-making, which involved Baby Boomers as study participants,

showed autonomy was the characteristic most strongly correlated to job satisfaction (Loher, Noe, Moeller, & Fitzgerald, 1985) and was significantly correlated to satisfaction, commitment, and job involvement (Spector, 1986). In recent research that includes Baby Boomers and Generation X as participants (mean age 34 years), the presence of the job characteristics, including autonomy, was positively related to intrinsic motivation and goal commitment (Piccolo & Colquitt, 2006). A study specific to Generation Y employees also showed autonomy contributing to the measure of job characteristics that significantly predicted job satisfaction (Kim, Knight, & Crutsinger, 2009). Based on existing literature, we propose that employees from all generations are likely to desire employee involvement in decision making and, as such, more challenging jobs.

Teamwork and Collaboration. Individuals, regardless of generation, hope to have colleagues who they can get along with and who will support them. Cennamo and Gardner (2008) found supporting evidence for this expectation as their "social" category of work values, which related to interactions with others at work, was the most strongly endorsed by Baby Boomers, Generation X, and Generation Y. Although the nature of experiences with teams may vary, all generations are aware that team-based organizations are a part of today's work environment. Researchers attribute teamwork as a core value of Baby Boomers (e.g., Zemke, 2001). They also recognize that Generation X experienced the advent of widespread downsizing practices in their early careers, and along with that, the realization that in order to do more with less it would be important to function collaboratively. Generation Y employees have gone through school completing projects that were often organized around teams and knowing the value of being supported by those around them as their careers advance (e.g., Tulgan, 2011).

Recent research that examined perceived and actual generational differences provides additional support for similar ratings across generations for the importance of teamwork and collaboration. Lester et al. (2012) found that while there were significant *perceived* differences in the value each generation placed on teamwork (i.e., generations tended to underestimate the value that members of different generations placed on a workplace characterized by teamwork and collaboration) there were no *actual* differences in the desire for teamwork. We expect to replicate the finding in this previous study regarding the actual preferences for teamwork that were similar across generations.

A Financially Rewarding Job. The final characteristic included from the "best places to work" lists is the value placed on a financially rewarding job. Generation-specific research that examined the contribution of salary perceptions to career success showed nearly identical effect sizes for Generation Y ($\eta_p^2 = .74$), Generation X ($\eta_p^2 = .71$), and the Baby Boomers ($\eta_p^2 = .71$; Dries et al., 2008). Although employees may have different expectations regarding their absolute compensation, employees in general want to feel as though they are adequately rewarded by the organization (Pfeffer & Veiga, 1999). As such, we expect that the importance placed on having a financially rewarding job will be rated similarly across generations.

Collectively, we expect the workplace characteristics examined in this study to demonstrate more similarities than differences across the three generations with respect to the perceived degree of importance. We offer the following hypothesis regarding the proposed similarities:

Hypothesis 1b: The extent to which employees value work–life balance, flexible work arrangements, involvement in decision making, a challenging job, teamwork, and a financially rewarding job will not vary by generation.

The Role of Generational Differences on Attitudinal Outcomes

P-O fit scholars would contend that employee perceptions regarding the extent to which their workplace values are met are more important than solely examining the importance placed on these various work factors. P-O fit refers to the extent to which what a person values in the workplace is consistent with the person's perceptions of how well that aspect is provided by the employer (Kristof, 1996). Research shows that the level of congruency between what is valued and what is provided is positively related to various employee attitudes, including job satisfaction, organizational commitment, and turnover intention (Kristof-Brown, Zimmerman, & Johnson, 2005).

Although published findings regarding generations and P-O fit are scarce, a study of organizations in New Zealand showed similarities for the effects of values–supplies discrepancies between generations on four work aspects: intrinsic fit, altruism fit, social fit, and freedom fit (Cennamo & Gardner, 2008). The same study revealed two differences in the discrepancy scores between generations: one difference existed between Generation X and the Baby Boomers for extrinsic fit, and the other difference was present between Generation Y and Baby Boomers for status fit. Drawing on these findings, the second purpose of this article was to further explore values across generations by investigating the effects of those values on employee perceptions and attitudes. In doing so, we examine employee attitudes that are common to both the P-O fit and generations literatures, which include job satisfaction, organizational commitment, and turnover intention.

To more fully understand the combined effects of values and perceptions of workplace characteristics present in employees' organizations, we apply value–percept theory (Locke, 1976). According to value–percept theory, the discrepancy between what a person wants and what a person receives influences job satisfaction, and this relationship is moderated by the importance the person places on the particular item. Therefore, we propose that perceptions of workplace factors will influence employee attitudes, and the relationships will be moderated by the importance of the related items. In addition, based on the generation research summarized above and the previous hypotheses, we expect the moderation effects to vary by generation for the importance items in which a statistically significant difference is found. For all other items, the moderating effect of importance should be similar across generations:

Hypothesis 2: The relationship between the level of work factor fulfillment from an organization and the employee's attitudinal responses will be greater when the importance of that factor is high versus low. These moderating effects will be consistent with the generational similarities and differences in the importance items as specified in Hypotheses 1a and 1b.

Method

Procedure

A Midwestern community's local Chamber of Commerce members were contacted with a request to allow their employees to participate in a data collection project for the Chamber. The intent of the project was to identify organizations in the community that were considered good places to work for "young professionals." The project included an employee survey involving a variety of questions regarding work-related items that all the organizations' employees received. The eight Chamber members that agreed to the request represented government, health care, manufacturing, technology, real estate, and nonprofit organizations.

The current study's lead author, who was referred to throughout the project as the "data collection coordinator," designed the survey and managed the data collection process. The organizational representatives responsible for the survey communications distributed the participation request to their respective employees. The project was designed to draw inferences about young professionals in the community, but all employees were encouraged to complete the survey in order to provide complete comparative data for organizational leaders.

Messages were sent internally so that the organizations maintained control of employee contact information. The initial message included a link to an online version of the survey as well as information that a hard-copy version was

Table 1. Descriptive Statistics by Generation.

	Generation Y	Generation X	Baby Boomers
N	88	144	273
Gender (%)			
Male	24	35	32
Female	76	65	69
Mean age in years (*SD*)	26.99 (3.03)	38.50 (3.88)	53.75 (4.53)
Mean tenure in years in the organization (*SD*)	3.01 (2.44)	7.68 (5.77)	15.94 (5.77)
Employment status (%)			
Full-time	81	84	82
Part-time	19	16	18

available on request. In places where employees did not have regular access to e-mail, messages with the hard-copy survey version were distributed.

To ensure that employee responses were anonymous, the data collection coordinator hosted the online survey, and all completed hard copies of the survey were sent directly to the coordinator in self-addressed postage-paid envelopes. Employees were also informed that their responses would be combined with responses of other employees in reports so that no one would be singled out or identified.

In addition to the items asking subjects to assess the importance they placed on each work-related factor, the survey included a series of related questions about the employees' perceptions of the work factors in their organizations. These questions were used to determine how well the organizations provided study participants with each work-related factor that was rated for its importance, which is consistent with previous research (Cennamo & Gardner, 2008). Scales were selected from published organizational research based on alignment with one or more importance items and reliability statistics. The scales included diversity climate (Pugh, Dietz, Brief, & Wiley, 2008), employee involvement climate (Riordan, Vandenberg, & Richardson, 2005), work design (Morgeson & Humphrey, 2006), work–life balance (Hill et al., 2001; Virick, Lilly, & Casper, 2007), and pay and benefits satisfaction (Heneman & Schwab, 1985). Finally, in order to establish the extent to which the importance items and perceptions of the work-related factors were related to employee attitudes, the survey included measures of job satisfaction (Mitchell, Holtom, Lee, Sablynski, & Erez, 2001), organizational commitment (Allen & Meyer, 1990), and turnover intention (Dupre & Day, 2007).

Sample

In total, 653 employees aged 18 years or older responded to the survey. Age was associated with the year born to classify respondents into generations using Smola and Sutton's (2002) categories. Of the total respondents, 135 were deleted from the data set due to missing data for the "age"

demographic variable. An additional 13 cases representing the Silent Generation (born in 1945 or before) were omitted from the data set due to the small group sample size, resulting in a final sample size of 505 for data analysis. The remaining three generations included Generation Y (born 1979-1994; *n* = 88, 17% of the sample), Generation X (born 1965-1978; *n* = 144, 29% of the sample), and Baby Boomers (born 1946-1964; *n* = 273, 54% of the sample). Demographic information by generation is provided in Table 1.

Measures

Importance of Work-Related Factors (Values). Respondents were given a list of various work-related factors noted to be important to Generations X and Y (Cennamo & Gardner, 2008; Smola & Sutton, 2002) as well as factors related to best places to work (Fulmer, Gerhart, & Scott, 2003; Joo & Mclean, 2006). The list included 10 items: (1) an organization that values diversity, (2) teamwork in the workplace, (3) flexible work arrangements, (4) getting immediate feedback and recognition from my supervisor, (5) work–life balance, (6) having a job that challenges me, (7) a company that provides continual training and development opportunities, (8) that I am involved in decision-making processes that affect my work, (9) being financially rewarded for the work I do, and (10) career advancement opportunities within the company. Participants were instructed to indicate the degree to which each item was important on a scale from 1 (*not important at all*) to 7 (*a must have*), *regardless* of what the person's organization currently offered.

Perceptions of Work Factors in the Organization. Eight measures were used as variables for participants' perceptions of various work factors in their current organizations: diversity climate, social support, feedback and recognition, work–life balance, training and development, decision-making involvement, pay and raise satisfaction, and promotion opportunity (perception measures for flexible work arrangements and having a job that challenges me were not included on the survey since these items were closely related to work–life balance and decision-making

Table 2. Means and Standard Deviations for the Importance Items by Generation.

Variable	Generation Y (n = 86)		Generation X (n = 142)		Baby Boomers (n = 270)	
	M	SD	M	SD	M	SD
An organization that values diversity	5.69	1.17	5.04	1.51	5.43	1.27
Teamwork in the workplace	6.34	0.90	6.17	1.01	6.27	0.82
Flexible work arrangements (e.g., flextime, job sharing, compressed work week)	6.00	1.27	5.88	1.06	5.82	1.04
Getting immediate feedback and recognition from my supervisor	5.73	1.05	5.43	1.11	5.48	1.00
Work–life balance	6.30	1.03	6.17	0.93	6.14	0.88
Having a job that challenges me	6.08	0.83	5.95	0.91	5.97	0.92
A company that provides continual training and development opportunities	6.18	0.97	5.95	1.02	5.95	0.95
That I am involved in decision-making processes that affect my work	6.15	0.93	6.03	1.03	6.16	0.94
Being financially rewarded for the work I do	6.14	0.95	6.12	0.99	6.09	0.87
Career advancement opportunities within the company	6.19	1.06	5.98	0.98	5.83	0.93

involvement measures, respectively). Survey items were selected based on face validity to create scales for the variables, and then the set of items for each variable was entered into exploratory factor analyses to ensure that the items loaded on a single factor. For example, five items of diversity climate were selected for the workplace perception measure (related importance item: an organization that values diversity); all five survey items loaded on one factor. The complete listing of scales and items are provided in the appendix. Items were measured on 5-point scales, and reliabilities ranged from $\alpha = .84$ to .94.

Job Satisfaction. Three items from Mitchell et al. (2001) were used to measure job satisfaction: "all in all, I am satisfied with my job," "in general, I don't like my job" (reverse coded), and "in general, I like working here." Responses ranged from 1 (*strongly disagree*) to 5 (*strongly agree*). Reliability of the measure was $\alpha = .90$.

Organizational Commitment. Affective, normative, and continuance dimensions of organizational commitment were measured using Allen and Meyer's (1990) scales, which consisted of eight items per variable measured on a 5-point Likert-type scale (1 = *strongly disagree* to 5 = *strongly agree*). Sample items include "I would be very happy to spend the rest of my career with this organization" (affective), "if I got another offer for a better job elsewhere I would not feel it was right to leave my organization" (normative), and "I am not afraid of what might happen if I quit my job without having a another one lined up" (continuance; reverse scored). Reliabilities of the scales were affective $\alpha = .89$, normative $\alpha = .80$, and continuance $\alpha = .76$.

Turnover Intention. Three items were used to measure turnover intention (Dupre & Day, 2007): "I will stay with this company for as long as I can" (reverse scored), "I will leave this company if I receive another job offer," and "I plan to leave this organization within the next year." The items were measured using a 5-point Likert-type scale (1 = *strongly disagree* to 5 = *strongly agree*), and high scores indicate a greater likelihood to leave the organization compared with low scores. Scale reliability was $\alpha = .79$.

Results

The means and standard deviations for each of the importance items by generation are provided in Table 2. Table 3 shows the means, standard deviations, and correlations for all variables measured.

A descriptive discriminant analysis (DDA) was conducted to determine whether generational differences among the importance items were present and to identify the items where differences were present. Using DDA to analyze the perceived importance items collectively minimizes the risk for Type I error (Sherry, 2006). Since the number of DDA functions is equivalent to the number of groups minus one, the analysis resulted in two discriminant functions. Function 1 explained 7.4% of the variance in the data, which was statistically significant, Wilks's $\lambda = .926$; $\chi^2(20) = 37.79$; $p < .01$. Function 2 explained 3.2% of the variance in the data, which was statistically significant at a marginal level, Wilks's $\lambda = .968$; $\chi^2(9) = 16.08$; $p = .07$. The effect sizes showed that the importance items contributed to group differences more strongly for Function 1 than Function 2. Both functions were deemed sufficient for further interpretation.

Table 3. Variable Means, Standard Deviations, and Correlations.

Variable	M	SD	1	2	3	4	5	6	7	8	9	10	11	12	13	14	15	16	17	18	19	20	21	22	23	24	25
1. Generation	2.37	0.76	—																								
2. Gender	1.69	0.46	-.04	—																							
3. Imp: Diversity	5.36	1.34	-.02	.23**	—																						
4. Imp: Teamwork	6.25	0.89	-.01	.14**	.51**	—																					
5. Imp: Flexible work arrangements	5.88	1.09	-.06	.13**	.37**	.44**	—																				
6. Imp: Immediate feedback and recognition	5.51	1.04	-.07	.04	.38**	.42**	.35**	—																			
7. Imp: Work–life balance	6.18	0.92	-.06	.01	.34**	.52**	.49**	.43**	—																		
8. Imp: Challenge	5.98	0.90	-.03	.07	.36**	.51**	.41**	.45**	.55**	—																	
9. Imp: Training and development	5.97	0.97	-.06	.10*	.37**	.53**	.44**	.53**	.49**	.62**	—																
10. Imp: Decision making	6.12	0.91	.03	.03	.33**	.43**	.42**	.46**	.48**	.57**	.58**	—															
11. Imp: Financial rewards	6.11	0.92	-.02	-.06	.18**	.39**	.46**	.40**	.51**	.42**	.42**	.43**	—														
12. Imp: Career advancement	5.93	0.98	-.14**	-.04	.23**	.38**	.39**	.48**	.44**	.52**	.59**	.53**	.61**	—													
13. Diversity climate	3.79	0.75	-.21**	-.06	.18**	.22**	.15**	.13**	.15**	.14**	.13**	.06	.05	.07	—												
14. Social support	4.08	0.66	-.09*	.05	.19**	.18**	.10*	.02	.06	.08	.06	.04	.01	.00	.55**	—											
15. Work–life balance	3.71	0.82	-.06	.10*	.04	.11*	.00	.07	-.04	.08	-.01	.01	-.04	-.02	.27**	.29**	—										
16. Feedback and recognition	3.35	0.93	-.09*	.07	.21**	.17**	.14**	.12**	.11*	.13**	.10	.06	.04	.03	.61**	.61**	.30**	—									
17. Training and development	3.68	0.94	-.15**	.02	.19**	.18**	.16**	.12**	.07	.13**	.09	.06	.10	.07	.53**	.46**	.30**	.61**	—								
18. Decision making involvement	4.08	0.73	.02	-.03	.19**	.19**	.12**	.06	.14	.17**	.09	.17**	.05	.03	.49**	.54**	.28**	.58**	.46**	—							
19. Pay and raise satisfaction	3.42	0.93	.12**	.04	.08	.09	.05	.04	.04	.07	.01	.11*	-.15**	-.13**	.23**	.28**	.18**	.35**	.27**	.34**	—						
20. Promotion opportunities	2.79	1.16	-.17**	-.08	.14**	.15**	.10*	.14**	.13**	.16**	.06	.11*	.10	.08	.51**	.40**	.21**	.65**	.49**	.46**	.32**	—					
21. Job satisfaction	4.18	0.75	.06	.11*	.16**	.18**	.11*	.11*	.02	.12**	.08	.09	.04	-.03	.42**	.56**	.44**	.53**	.47**	.57**	.36**	.33**	—				
22. Affective OC	3.55	0.76	.03	.09	.19**	.18**	.13**	.09	.06	.13**	.10*	.14**	-.02	.00	.50**	.61**	.30**	.62**	.53**	.56**	.42**	.44**	.73**	—			
23. Normative OC	3.10	0.59	.07	.03	.03	.13**	-.02	.10*	-.07	.05	.04	.03	-.03	.01	.24**	.24**	.16**	.21**	.23**	.14**	.14**	.15**	.35**	.42**	—		
24. Continuance OC	3.48	0.69	.12**	-.05	-.05	.02	.00	.01	-.02	-.06	-.05	.05	.04	.04	-.11*	-.12**	-.06	-.18**	-.17**	-.02	-.14**	-.07	-.09	.16**		—	
25. Turnover intention	1.98	0.87	-.16**	-.16**	-.08	-.11*	-.03	.00	.01	-.01	.01	-.05	.03	.11*	-.32**	-.40**	-.40**	-.36**	-.34**	-.36**	-.44**	-.19**	-.65**	-.59**	-.44**	-.08	—

Note. Imp. = importance item; OC = organizational commitment.

*p ≤ .05. **p ≤ .01.

Table 4. Standardized Discriminant Function and Structure Coefficients.

Scale	Function coefficient	Structure coefficient (r_s)	Variance (r_s^2, %)
Function 1			
An organization that values diversity	−.227	−.131	1.72
Teamwork in the workplace	−.208	−.042	.18
Flexible work arrangements (e.g., flextime, job sharing, compressed work week)	.332	.247	.10
Getting immediate feedback and recognition from my supervisor	.162	.212	4.49
Work–life balance	.366	.243	5.90
Having a job that challenges me	−.057	.113	1.28
A company that provides continual training and development opportunities	.045	.203	4.12
That I am involved in decision-making processes that affect my work	−.779	−.191	3.65
Being financially rewarded for the work I do	−.511	.102	1.04
Career advancement opportunities within the company	1.099	.598	35.76
Function 2			
An organization that values diversity	.978	.920	84.64
Teamwork in the workplace	−.092	.353	12.46
Flexible work arrangements (e.g., flextime, job sharing, compressed work week)	−.177	.153	2.34
Getting immediate feedback and recognition from my supervisor	.279	.492	24.21
Work–life balance	.009	.217	4.71
Having a job that challenges me	−.112	.244	5.95
A company that provides continual training and development opportunities	−.105	.295	8.70
That I am involved in decision-making processes that affect my work	.026	.283	8.01
Being financially rewarded for the work I do	−.252	.020	.04
Career advancement opportunities within the company	.285	.276	7.62

The eigenvalues for each function indicate the extent to which the function discriminated between groups. In the current sample, the eigenvalues are relatively low ($\lambda_1 = .045$, $\lambda_2 = .033$), indicating that neither function discriminated well between groups. However, further evaluation of the results, including structure coefficients, standardized function coefficients, and the group centroids, provides specific information regarding where differences exist. A structure coefficient represents the bivariate correlation between the item and the function. The squared structure coefficient is the percent of variance the item accounts for in the discriminant function score. The standardized function coefficients are akin to beta coefficients in regression, providing the relative contribution of each item to the discriminant variables created in DDA.

Examination of these values, which are summarized in Table 4, reveals that *career advancement opportunities* was the only item to considerably contribute to Function 1. The standardized function coefficient of *that I am involved in decision-making processes that affect my work* is high whereas its structure coefficient is low. This inconsistency indicates that the item is likely a suppressor variable that is

influencing the discriminant variable through another item. Since the standardized function coefficient of *career advancement opportunities within the company* is greater than 1.0, these two items are closely related. The relationship between the two items is not surprising given that individuals who want to be involved in decision making are likely to desire career advancement opportunities as well. However, in terms of the results, the overinflated contribution of the decision-making item to the variable indicates that the only item for Function 1 in which group differences exist is the importance of career advancement.

The items contributing to Function 2, listed in order of importance, included *an organization that values diversity, getting immediate feedback and recognition from my supervisor,* and *teamwork in the workplace.* Function 2 statistics show the standardized function coefficient for teamwork in the workplace is close to zero, which indicates that the item does not contribute sufficiently to the discriminant variable. Therefore, although the item contributes somewhat to group differences as determined by the variance explained by the item, the effect of the item on the group centroids is minimal.

The group centroids are the means of the discriminant variables for each generation, which tell us the extent to which the groups possess the characteristics that comprise the functions. For Function 1, Generation Y had the highest group centroid ($M = .293$), which is followed by Generation X ($M = .188$) and the Baby Boomers ($M = -.192$). These results indicate that career advancement is more important for Generation Y than for Generation X, and there is an even greater difference between Generation Y and the Baby Boomers. On Function 2, Generation Y had the highest group centroid ($M = .309$) whereas the Baby Boomers was the next highest ($M = .027$) and Generation X had the lowest ($M = -.239$). This finding suggests that Generation Y values diversity and immediate feedback and recognition the most, and Generation X values these work-related factors the least.

Taken together, the DDA results revealed significant generational differences for the importance of career advancement that contributed to Function 1 and marginally significant generational differences for diversity and immediate feedback and recognition that contributed to Function 2. Although Hypothesis 1a was supported for three of the four criteria for which differences were expected, career advancement was the only item that resulted in the expected pattern of differences with Generation Y as the highest and the Baby Boomers as the lowest. Therefore, Hypothesis 1a received partial support. Hypothesis 1b was strongly supported in terms of the characteristics where there were no generational differences.

Given the results of Hypothesis 1, we would expect to see similar variations in the moderation effect of importance on the relationships between perceptions of work factors and attitudinal outcomes specified by Hypothesis 2. Specifically, differences in the moderation effects by generation should be present for the career advancement, diversity, and feedback and recognition importance items. Moderation was investigated using stepwise hierarchical regression analyses in which the continuous predictor variables were centered prior to creating the interaction terms (Baron & Kenny, 1986), and gender was used as a control in the first step of the model. The data set was also split by group to make comparisons between the generations for each moderating effect. The results from the third step of the analyses in which the interaction term is entered into the model are summarized in Table 5.

The results reveal different patterns between the generations regarding the ways in which perceptions of work factors in one's workplace may influence attitudinal outcomes regardless of generational differences of the importance placed on the work-related items. First, for the items for which we would expect to see generational differences, only the *importance of career advancement opportunities within the company* displayed meaningful differences among moderating effects across generations. The importance item did not moderate the relationship between

promotion opportunity and the attitudinal outcomes for Generation Y, two relationships were significantly moderated for the Baby Boomers, and four relationships were significantly moderated for Generation X. The diversity importance item moderated one relationship between diversity climate and an outcome variable for Generation Y (continuance organizational commitment) and one relationship for the Baby Boomers (normative organizational commitment, at a marginal level). No differences in the moderating effects for the generations were found for the *getting immediate feedback and recognition from my supervisor* importance item.

In contrast, we did not expect generational differences to be present among moderating effects for the other importance items. However, different trends in the moderation effects emerged for the importance item related to *training and development opportunities* across the three generations and *being involved in decision-making processes* that differentiated the Baby Boomers from the other two generations. Findings also showed a different moderating effect for the importance of *work–life balance* item. For Generation Y, the item moderated the relationship between perceived work–life balance within the organization and continuance organizational commitment, and for the Baby Boomers the item marginally moderated the effect on affective organizational commitment; no moderating effect was found for Generation X. Given the results, we conclude Hypothesis 2 is somewhat supported, but we find as much meaningfulness in the nonsignificant findings as the statistically significant findings. Our interpretations of the results are discussed in greater detail in the next section.

Discussion

The current study contributes to organizational literature by replicating and extending previous research concerning generational values. Consistent with extant research, the present study's findings demonstrated that generations share more similarities than differences regarding the extent to which work factors are important (e.g., Cennamo & Gardner, 2008; Hansen & Leuty, 2012; Lester et al., 2012). The only three value differences found included career advancement opportunities, diversity climate, and immediate recognition and feedback.

In addition, generational differences were found with respect to the ways that values affected the relationships between perceived fulfillment of work factors and attitudinal outcomes. These differences were most evident with respect to career advancement opportunities within the company, training and development opportunities, and being involved in decision-making processes affecting one's work. By examining relationships between the variables using value–percept theory and a P-O fit perspective, the research provides a novel lens in which to extend organizational research on generations.

Table 5. Moderation Results from Hierarchical Regression Analyses for the Interaction of Perceived Work Factors and Importance Items on Attitudinal Outcomes by Generation.

Workplace perception × Importance item	Dependent variable	Generation Y	Generation X	Baby Boomers
Diversity climate ×	JS	−.01	.00	−.03
An organization that values diversity	AOC	.03	.02	−.03
	NOC	.07	−.11	.10†
	COC	.33**	−.02	−.03
	T/O I	−.16	.02	−.07
Social support ×	JS	.16	−.08	.02
Teamwork in the workplace	AOC	.03	.00	.03
	NOC	−.22†	.04	−.11†
	COC	−.01	−.06	−.03
	T/O I	−.16	.09	−.05
Feedback and recognition ×	JS	.08	.04	.08
Getting immediate feedback and recognition from my supervisor	AOC	.05	−.02	.04
	NOC	.02	.05	−.06
	COC	−.07	−.05	.07
	T/O I	−.13	−.05	−.04
Work–life balance ×	JS	.13	−.02	.05
Work–life balance	AOC	−.02	.06	.11†
	NOC	.03	.12	−.05
	COC	.30*	−.04	.03
	T/O I	−.05	.07	.06
Training and development ×	JS	−.09	.16*	.16**
A company that provides continual training and development opportunities	AOC	−.18†	.18*	.15**
	NOC	−.07	.02	.10
	COC	.25†	.18*	−.03
	T/O I	−.05	−.20*	−.16**
Decision-making involvement ×	JS	.03	.11	.16**
That I am involved in decision-making processes that affect my work	AOC	−.06	−.01	.14**
	NOC	−.09	.06	.09
	COC	.13	−.09	−.05
	T/O I	.02	−.06	−.18**
Pay and raise satisfaction ×	JS	.01	−.05	−.01
Being financially rewarded for the work I do	AOC	−.02	.04	−.01
	NOC	−.22†	.13	−.02
	COC	−.13	−.01	−.06
	T/O I	.09	−.04	−.04
Promotion opportunity ×	JS	.08	.22**	.14*
Career advancement opportunities within the company	AOC	−.01	.14†	.13*
	NOC	.00	.10	.05
	COC	.13	.22*	.00
	T/O I	−.03	−.26**	−.06

Note. Values are beta coefficients for Step 3 of each regression model (moderation effect). JS = job satisfaction; AOC = affective organizational commitment; NOC = normative organizational commitment; COC = continuance organizational commitment; T/O I = turnover intention.
$^\dagger p \leq .10$. $^* p \leq .05$. $^{**} p \leq .01$.

Overall, the findings suggest that the most significant generational difference lies with career advancement opportunities that are more strongly valued by Generation Y compared with Generation X and the Baby Boomer generation.

Career advancement was not only valued to a greater extent by Generation Y, but the moderating effects of the career advancement value item were different as well. Interestingly, however, importance was not a moderator of the relationship between employee perceptions of promotion opportunities and any of the attitudinal outcomes for Generation Y. Instead, statistically significant moderating effects were found for the career advancement value for Generation X and the Baby Boomer generation.

Furthermore, the training and development value and the decision-making value were statistically significant moderators of the respective measures of the employee perceptions and their attitudes for Generation X (training and development item) and Baby Boomers (both value items) whereas no moderating effect was found for Generation Y for these values. These findings suggest that even when no differences are found with respect to the degree of importance placed on work factors, employee perceptions of the factors present in the workplace may still affect how employees think and feel about their jobs and organizations. Importantly, the differences remain less apparent than the similarities between the generations across the items, which further confirms the basic premise of the research.

In addition to supporting the notion that generational similarities may outnumber generational differences, this investigation extended the generational literature in two important ways. First, although similarities did outnumber differences, this study provided additional insight on where generational differences do exist. Specifically, this study builds on Lester et al. (2012) by examining additional and sometimes more narrowly defined characteristics associated with "best places to work." Extensions from the current study include the finding of generational differences on two characteristics not previously examined (i.e., diversity climate and career advancement) and using a narrowly defined characteristic of immediate feedback and recognition rather than recognition more broadly. Previously, Lester et al. (2012) found no actual generational differences on the value attributed to recognition, whereas *immediate* feedback and recognition did prove to be different across generations and most valued by Generation Y in the current investigation. Furthermore, although Generation Y and the Baby Boomers differed in the value they placed on continuous learning in Lester et al.'s (2012) sample, our sample did not demonstrate significant differences in the value placed on continuous learning. These mixed results on continuous learning highlight the need to further examine contextual variables that may enhance or diminish the presence of actual generational differences.

The second important extension of the generations literature provided by this study is the examination of how the importance placed on workplace characteristics by generations moderates the relationship between perceived fulfillment of these desired characteristics (by the organization) and the employee's attitudinal outcomes. Previous research has examined generational differences on work values (e.g., Smola & Sutton, 2002), on perceptions of workplace factors (e.g., Lester et al., 2012), and on employee attitudes

(e.g., Benson & Brown, 2011), but combining these items using value–percept theory had not yet been explored. The moderation results suggest that generational differences and similarities may be complex and may warrant the investigation of interactions between predictor variables.

Strengths and Limitations

Several strengths are present in the research. First, the hypotheses were examined using a large sample size ($N = 505$), which increased the statistical power to detect the present effects. Second, because participants worked in various types of organizations the results are generalizable across organizations. Third, all scale measures had high levels of reliabilities, which increases the accuracy of the results. Fourth, we controlled for gender in the regression analyses, to be consistent with previous research and remove any effects of gender on the outcomes (Cennamo & Gardner, 2008). Although controls are not options in DDA, we conducted multivariate analysis of variance tests with and without gender as a covariate to check for any potential effects of gender on values; the results were not affected by the inclusion of gender as a covariate. Finally, participants were informed that the survey measured perceptions of their organizations and did not know that classifications would be made based on generation. Therefore, the potential for bias with respect to generational differences was minimized.

The limitations of the research include unequal group sizes and organizational climate/perception measures that may not have aligned perfectly with an importance item (e.g., perceived social support was related to the teamwork value). Because unequal sample sizes may affect the results of the DDA, we reviewed the normality of the distribution of the discriminant functions by group (Sherry, 2006). Normality was determined by values within the range of -2 to 2. Function 1 displayed slight nonnormality because of a relatively high-kurtotic distribution (4.14) for Generation Y, and Function 2 displayed nonnormality because of slightly high-kurtotic distributions for Generation Y (2.29) and Generation X (2.64). Therefore, findings should be interpreted with caution, and we recommend that future research use group sample sizes that are more equal and considerably large. Researchers examining the role of generational differences on workplace outcomes are also encouraged to include measures that directly relate to importance items.

Implications for Management and Directions for Future Research

One important implication of the current findings is that managers need be educated about and inform their direct reports about actual generational differences as well as generational similarities rather than making assumptions about differences. Our research results showed differences in career advancement, diversity, and immediate feedback and recognition importance items. Notably, although we had expected a generational difference in continuous learning, we found no difference. This result may be due in part to the recent recession that has caused employees to postpone retirement. In addition, Hewlett et al. (2009) reported that 47% of Baby Boomers they surveyed felt they were in mid-career stages, presumably seeking additional advancement opportunities. Therefore, managers should be careful not to discount the importance of training and development as a work characteristic for Baby Boomers because continuous learning is similarly important to the Baby Boomer generation as it is for Generations Y and X.

In addition, managers should seek to gain insight into what constitutes the importance of similarly rated "best places to work" factors in order to design effective related workplace practices to meet employee needs. For example, preferences for training and development methods will likely vary across the generations, as younger employees grew up using fast-paced technology and older employees are accustomed to face-to-face learning settings.

Furthermore, the findings suggest that managers should also seek to understand how well the organization provides important work-related factors from the employees' perspectives. We strongly recommend to organizational leaders and managers that they use tools such as employee surveys to collect information from their employees on a regular and ongoing basis in order to tailor their human resource management practices more specifically to their existing employees. Gaining this type of insight will allow organizations to provide resources to managers and other employees to support employees on the factors noted to be important to them (e.g., training on how to provide immediate feedback or to mentor younger employees). Organizations can also benchmark other organizations' practices that may have demonstrated success such as Ernst & Young's "Feedback Zone," an online system that allows employees to submit and request feedback at any time, which is tailored to the desire of their Generation Y employees to receive immediate feedback (Hite, 2008).

Taking proactive steps to communicate academic research findings to managers and employees can help eliminate unfounded generational stereotypes and can assist a multigenerational workforce in its efforts to collaborate and build synergies. In the case of the current research, each organization that participated in the research project received tailored report showing the similarities and differences between generations within the organization for the importance items measured. The research findings were also presented in the community in which the data were collected; the study's data collection coordinator gave presentations to two practitioner-oriented professional organizations, and an academic colleague referenced the study in a Chamber of Commerce panel discussion.

Another suggestion for managers is to make sure that they do not assume all employees within a generational cohort value the same things. Managers still need to pay attention to individual difference variables such as gender, personality, and motivational needs when determining the best way to respond in interpersonal situations.

The current research findings support previous research suggesting that the importance placed on a variety of workplace characteristics may be more similar across generations than different, although generations may differ on their workplace attitudes. The findings provide additional support for researchers to further examine the ways that generations are similar in order to facilitate connections between members of generations that have traditionally been perceived as quite different (e.g., Hewlett et al., 2009).

Future research on generations needs to further investigate the "So What?" question in order to determine if and to what extent values and related variables affect workplace outcomes of interest. This study looked at attitudinal outcomes, and future research could better provide additional insights by investigating behavioral outcomes. Other workplace values or more specific aspects of the workplace characteristics should also be examined. For example, future research could explore specific aspects of diversity that are important to reveal more discrete differences and similarities across generations. Finally, although the three generations examined in this study are most prominently represented in today's workplace, it is important to recognize that a new generation will soon be joining the workforce. This next generation, initially labeled as "Generation Z" may bring new intricacies to managing a multigenerational workforce and should be included in future research samples. Our hope is that the findings of this study will spark continued study of an ever-changing work population.

Appendix

Variables Measuring Perceptions of Work Factors in the Organizations

Diversity Climate: $\alpha = .84$

1. My organization makes it easy for people from diverse backgrounds to fit in and be accepted.
2. Where I work, employees are developed and advanced without regard to the gender or the racial, religious, or cultural background of the individuals.
3. Managers demonstrate through their actions that they want to hire and retain and diverse workforce.
4. I feel that my immediate manager does a good job of managing people with diverse backgrounds (in terms of age, sex, race, religion, or culture).

Social Support: α = .87
Items from the work design measure.

1. I have the opportunity to develop close friendships in my job.
2. I have the chance in my job to get to know other people.
3. I have the opportunity to meet with others in my work.
4. My supervisor is concerned about the welfare of the people that work for him/her.
5. People I work with take a personal interest in me.
6. People I work with are friendly.

Feedback and Recognition: α = .90
Items 1 to 3 from work design measure, and items 4 to 6 from employee involvement climate measure.

1. I receive a great deal of information from my manager and coworkers about my job performance.
2. Other people in the organization, such as managers and coworkers, provide information about the effectiveness (e.g., quality and quantity) of my job performance.
3. I receive feedback on my performance from other people in my organization (such as my manager or coworkers).
4. I am satisfied with the amount of recognition I receive when I do a good job.
5. Generally, I feel this company rewards employees who make an extra effort.
6. There is a strong link between how well I perform my job and the likelihood of receiving high-performance appraisal ratings.

Work–Life Balance: α = .86

1. I am easily able to balance the demands of my work and personal/family life.
2. I have sufficient time away from my job to maintain adequate work and personal/family life balance.
3. When I take a vacation, I am able to separate myself from my work and enjoy myself.
4. All in all, I am successful in balancing my work and personal/family life.
5. I often feel drained when I go home from work because of work pressures and problems. (reverse scored).

Training and Development: α = .88
Items from the employee involvement climate measure.

1. I receive sufficient training to do my job.
2. Education and training are integral parts of this company's culture.
3. I have had sufficient/adequate job-related training.

4. If I felt that I needed more job-related training, the company would provide it.

Decision-Making Involvement: α = .94
Items 1 to 3 from the employee involvement climate measure, and items 4 to 9 from the work design measure.

1. I have sufficient authority to fulfill my job responsibilities.
2. I have enough input in deciding how to accomplish my work.
3. I have enough freedom over how I do my job.
4. My job gives me a chance to use my personal initiative or judgment in carrying out the work.
5. My job allows me to make a lot of decisions on my own.
6. My job provides me with significant autonomy in making decisions.
7. My job allows me to make decisions about what methods I use to complete my work.
8. My job gives me considerable opportunity for independence and freedom in how I do the work.
9. My job allows me to decide on my own how to go about doing my work.

Pay and Raise Satisfaction: α = .94
Items from the pay and benefits satisfaction measure.

1. My take-home pay
2. My most recent raise
3. My current salary
4. The raises I have typically received in the past
5. My overall level of pay
6. The size of my current salary

Promotion Opportunities
Item from the employee involvement climate measure.

1. If I perform well, I am more likely to be promoted.

Declaration of Conflicting Interests

The author(s) declared no potential conflicts of interest with respect to the research, authorship, and/or publication of this article.

Funding

The author(s) received no financial support for the research, authorship, and/or publication of this article.

References

Allen, N. J., & Meyer, J. P. (1990). The measurement and antecedents of affective, continuance and normative commitment to the organization. *Journal of Occupational Psychology, 63,* 1-18.

Arnett, J. J. (2004). *Emerging adulthood: The winding road from the late teens through the twenties*. New York, NY: Oxford University Press.

Baron, R. M., & Kenny, D. A. (1986). The moderator-mediator variable distinction in social psychological research: Conceptual, strategic, and statistical considerations. *Journal of Personality and Social Psychology, 51*, 1173-1182.

Benson, J., & Brown, M. (2011). Generations at work: Are there differences and do they matter? *International Journal of Human Resource Management, 22*, 1843-1865.

Butts, M. M., Vandenberg, R. J., DeJoy, D. M., Schaffer, B. S., & Wilson, M. G. (2009). Individual reactions to high involvement work processes: Investigating the role of empowerment and perceived organizational support. *Journal of Occupational Health Psychology, 14*, 122-136.

Cennamo, L., & Gardner, D. (2008). Generational differences in work values, outcomes and person-organisation values fit. *Journal of Managerial Psychology, 23*, 891-906.

Costanza, D. P., Badger, J. M., Fraser, R. L., Severt, J. B., & Gade, P. A. (2012). Generational differences in work-related attitudes: A meta-analysis. *Journal of Business Psychology, 27*, 375-394.

Crumpacker, M., & Crumpacker, J. M. (2007). Succession planning and generational stereotypes: Should HR consider age-based values and attitudes a relevant factor or a passing fad? *Public Personnel Management, 36*, 349-369.

Deal, J. J., Stawiski, S., Graves, L., Gentry, W. A., Weber, T. J., & Ruderman, M. (2013). Motivation at work: Which matters more, generation or managerial level. *Consulting Psychology Journal: Practice and Research, 65*, 1-16.

Dries, N., Pepermans, R., & De Kerpel, E. (2008). Exploring four generations' beliefs about career: Is "satisfied" the new "successful"? *Journal of Managerial Psychology, 23*, 907-928.

Dupre, K. E., & Day, A. L. (2007). The effects of supportive management and job quality on the turnover intentions and health of military personnel. *Human Resource Management, 46*, 185-201.

Eikhof, D. R., Warhurst, C., & Haunschild, A. (2007). Introduction: What work? What life? What balance? Critical reflections on the work-life balance debate. *Employee Relations, 29*, 325-333.

Evans, W. R., & Davis, W. D. (2005). High-performance work systems and organizational performance: The mediating role of internal social structure. *Journal of Management, 31*, 758-775.

Fogg, P. (2009). When generations collide. *Education Digest, 74*, 25-30.

Fulmer, I. S., Gerhart, B., & Scott, K. S. (2003). Are the 100 best better? An empirical investigation of the relationship between being a "great place to work" and firm performance. *Personnel Psychology, 56*, 965-993.

Glass, A. (2007). Understanding generational differences for competitive success. *Industrial and Commercial Training, 39*, 98-103.

Gowing, M., Kraft, J., & Quick, J. (1998). *The new organizational reality: Downsizing, restructuring, and revitalization*. Washington, DC: American Psychological Association.

Grawitch, M. J., Ledford, G. E., Ballard, D. W., & Barber, L. K. (2009). Leading the healthy workforce: The integral role of employee involvement. *Consulting Psychology Journal: Practice and Research, 61*, 122-135.

Grawitch, M. J., Trares, S., & Kohler, J. M. (2007). Healthy workplace practices and employee outcomes. *International Journal of Stress Management, 14*, 275-293.

Hackman, J. R., & Oldham, G. R. (1976). Motivation through the design of work: Test of a theory. *Organizational Behavior and Human Performance, 16*, 250-279.

Hansen, J. I. C., & Leuty, M. E. (2012). Work values across generations. *Journal of Career Assessment, 20*, 34-52.

Heneman III, H. G., & Schwab, D. P. (1985). Pay satisfaction: Its multidimensional nature and measurement. *International Journal of Psychology, 20*, 129-141.

Herman, A., & Eckel, R. (2002). The new American worker: What Generation 'Y' brings to the workplace. *Work Matters, May*, 1-2.

Hewlett, S. A., Sherbin, L., & Sumberg, K. (2009). How Gen Y & Boomers will reshape your agenda. *Harvard Business Review, 87*(7-8), 71-76.

Hill, E. J., Hawkins, A. J., Ferris, M., & Weitzman, M. (2001). Finding an extra day a week: The positive influence of perceived job flexibility on work and family life balance. *Family Relations, 50*, 49-58.

Hite, B. (2008, October 13). Employers rethink how they give feedback. *The Wall Street Journal*. Retrieved from http://online.wsj.com/news/articles/SB122385967800027549

Jain, S., & Martindale, T. (2012, October). *Facilitating continuous learning: Review of research on individual learning capabilities and organizational learning environments*. Paper presented at the annual meeting of the AECT International Convention, *Louisville, KY*.

Joo, B. K., & Mclean, G. N. (2006). Best employer studies: A conceptual model from a literature review and a case study. *Human Resource Development Review, 5*, 228-257.

Jurkiewicz, C. L., & Brown, R. G. (1998). GenXers vs. Boomers vs. Matures: Generational comparisons of public employee motivation. *Review of Public Personnel Administration, 18*, 18-37.

Kim, H., Knight, D. K., & Crutsinger, C. (2009). Generation Y employees' retail work experience: The mediating effect of job characteristics. *Journal of Business Research, 62*, 548-556.

Kristof, A. L. (1996). Person-organization fit: An integrative review of its conceptualizations, measurement, and implications. *Personnel Psychology, 49*, 1-49.

Kristof-Brown, A. L., Zimmerman, R. D., & Johnson, E. C. (2005). Consequences of individuals' fit at work: A meta-analysis of person-job, person-organization, person-group, and person-supervisor fit. *Personnel Psychology, 58*, 281-342.

Lester, S. W., Standifer, R. L., Schultz, N. J., & Windsor, J. M. (2012). Actual versus perceived generational differences at work: An empirical examination. *Journal of Leadership & Organizational Studies, 19*, 341-354.

Locke, E. A. (1976). The nature and causes of job satisfaction. In M. D. Dunnette (Ed.), *Handbook of industrial and organizational psychology* (pp. 1297-1349). Chicago, IL: Rand-McNally.

Loher, B. T., Noe, R. A., Moeller, N. L., & Fitzgerald, M. P. (1985). A meta-analysis of the relation of job characteristics to job satisfaction. *Journal of Applied Psychology, 70*, 280-289.

Luna-Arocas, R., & Camps, J. (2008). A model of high performance work practices and turnover intentions. *Personnel Review, 37*, 26-46.

Macky, K., Gardner, D., & Forsyth, S. (2008). Generational differences at work: Introduction and overview. *Journal of Managerial Psychology, 23*, 857-861.

Martin, C. A. (2005). From high maintenance to high productivity: What managers need to know about Generation Y. *Industrial and Commercial Training, 37*, 39-44.

Meriac, J. P., Woehr, D. J., & Banister, C. (2010). Generational differences in work ethic: An examination of measurement equivalence across three cohorts. *Journal of Business Psychology, 25*, 315-324.

Mitchell, T. R., Holtom, B. C., Lee, T. W., Sablynski, C. J., & Erez, M. (2001). Why people stay: Using job embeddedness to predict voluntary turnover. *Academy of Management Journal, 44*, 1102-1121.

Morgeson, F. P., & Humphrey, S. E. (2006). The Work Design Questionnaire (WDQ): Developing and validating a comprehensive measure for assessing job design and the nature of work. *Journal of Applied Psychology, 91*, 1321-1339.

Mosisa, A., & Hipple, S. (2006). Trends in labor force participation in the United States. *Monthly Labor Review, 129*(10), 35-57.

Parry, E., & Urwin, P. (2011). Generational differences in work values: A review of theory and evidence. *International Journal of Management Reviews, 13*, 79-96.

Pfeffer, J., & Veiga, J. F. (1999). Putting people first for organizational success. *Academy of Management Executive, 13*, 37-48.

Piccolo, R. F., & Colquitt, J. A. (2006). Transformational leadership and job behaviors: The mediating role of core job characteristics. *Academy of Management Journal, 49*, 327-340.

Pugh, S. D., Dietz, J., Brief, A. P., & Wiley, J. W. (2008). Looking inside and out: The impact of employee and community demographic composition on organizational diversity climate. *Journal of Applied Psychology, 93*, 1422-1428.

Riordan, C. M., Vandenberg, R. J., & Richardson, H. A. (2005). Employee involvement climate and organizational effectiveness. *Human Resource Management, 44*, 471-488.

Sessa, V. I., Kabacoff, R. I., Deal, J., & Brown, H. (2007). Generational differences in leader values and leadership behaviors. *Psychologist-Manager Journal, 10*, 47-74.

Sherry, A. (2006). Discriminant analysis in counseling psychology research. *The Counseling Psychologist, 34*, 661-683.

Smola, K. W., & Sutton, C. D. (2002). Generational differences: Revisiting generational work values for the new millennium. *Journal of Organizational Behavior, 23*, 363-382.

Spector, P. E. (1986). Perceived control by employees: A meta-analysis of studies concerning autonomy and participation at work. *Human Relations, 39*, 1005-1016.

Steele, M. J., & Gordon, V. N. (2006). *Advising in a multigenerational workplace*. Retrieved from http://www.nacada.ksu.edu/Resources/Clearinghouse/View-Articles/Generational-issues-in-the-workplace.aspx

Tulgan, B. (2011). Generation Y: All grown up and now emerging as new leaders. *Journal of Leadership Studies, 5*(3), 77-81.

Twenge, J. M. (2010). A review of empirical evidence on generational differences in work attitudes. *Journal of Business Psychology, 25*, 201-210.

Virick, M., Lilly, J. D., & Casper, W. J. (2007). Doing more with less: An analysis of work life balance among layoff survivors. *Career Development International, 12*, 463-480.

Westerman, J. W., & Yamamura, J. H. (2007). Generational preferences for work environment fit: Effects on employee outcomes. *Career Development International Journal, 12*, 150-161.

Wong, M., Gardiner, E., Lang, W., & Coulon, L. (2008). Generational differences in personality and motivation: Do they exist and what are the implications for the workplace? *Journal of Managerial Psychology, 23*, 878-890.

Zemke, R. (2001). Here come the millennials. *Training, 38*(7), 44-49.

Author Biographies

Jennifer Mencl is an Associate Professor of Organizational Behavior at the University of Minnesota Duluth. Her research interests include learning and development, empathy, and ethical decision-making. She has published in journals such as the *International Journal of Selection and Assessment, Journal of Human Resources Education*, and *Journal of Business Ethics*.

Scott W. Lester is a Professor of Management at University of Wisconsin – Eau Claire. His research interests include dyadic trust, the multi-generational workforce, and work-life balance. Scott has published in journals such as the *Academy of Management Journal, Journal of Applied Psychology, Journal of Management*, and *Journal of Organizational Behavior*.

Bridging Cultures: The Academy and The Workplace

Alred, G. J.

This introduction to articles by David Carlone and Laurie K. Lewis et al. argues that the communication advice given by management gurus and in popular press books may reflect the values and practices of the workplace culture, a culture which has contexts and exigencies quite different from those of the academic culture. Generally, the goals of workplace professionals demand that they think in specific, practical, and immediately applicable ways; those of us in the academy must think in terms that are more abstract, conceptual, and long-term. It is understandable, then, that works that might be highly valued by either practitioners or academics can seem entirely irrelevant to the other. And just as understandable, practitioners and academics can easily dismiss or discount the works valued by the other side. Ideally, the best popular press books or gurus would go further than simply aligning themselves with academic scholarship; they could enrich academic scholarship with the experience of savvy workplace professionals.

Keywords: *management gurus, organizational change, Stephen R. Covey, popular press books, academic culture, workplace culture, practitioner advice*

The articles that follow present two perspectives on how ideas about management and change are disseminated in the workplace—one focusing on a single "management guru" and the other examining popular press books. David Carlone (2006), in "The Ambiguous Nature of a Management Guru Lecture," offers an interesting and detailed analysis of a day-long lecture by Stephen R. Covey (1989), consultant and author of the bestselling book, *The 7 Habits of Highly Effective People*. Laurie K. Lewis, Amy M. Schmisseur, Keri K. Stephens, and Kathleen E. Weir (2006), in "Advice on Communicating During Organizational Change," provide an insightful analysis of the dominant themes in popular books on the subject of communication during organizational change. These articles represent a fundamentally important focus for business communication research because our theory and pedagogy must be grounded in a deep and authentic understanding of the powerfully influential ideas that inform workplace practice.

Gerald Alred is a professor of English in the professional writing program at the University of Wisconsin–Milwaukee. He is also an associate editor of JBC. Correspondence concerning this article should be addressed to Prof. Gerald Alred, Department of English, University of Wisconsin–Milwaukee, P.O. Box 413, Milwaukee, WI 53201; e-mail: alred@uwm.edu.

Journal of Business Communication, Volume 43, Number 2, April 2006 79-88
DOI: 10.1177/0021943605285659

These studies reveal at once the validity of the ideas propounded by manage-ment gurus and popular books as well as their limitations and sometimes problem-atic advice. For example, many propositions in the Covey lecture seem sensible and, if practiced, would surely foster productive working relationships. At the same time, as Carlone (2006) concludes, "Covey's lectures simultaneously ease and deepen uncertainty and anxiety." Likewise, some of Covey's strategies, such as "disrupting the ontology" of his listeners, are those many teachers might use to get students to think about issues more deeply. However, few teachers see themselves on a near-religious quest for "transcendent vision," as Carlone reports, or view themselves functioning as something of a spiritual guru, as Covey does.

Lewis et al. (2006) see an ambiguity as well in the popular books they studied. On one hand, popular books often share much with reputable scholarship:

> In our own reading of these books, we noticed a surprising alignment between some of what has been consistently found in the scholarly literature and what is advised in these books. Thus, these books appear to be useful summaries, to some extent, of related scholarly research.

This surprising alignment of principles of popular books with academic scholar-ship could be "by accident," as they suggest. Or it may result in part because some authors of popular books come from the ranks of the academy, or at least hold advanced degrees in the relevant specialties.[1] In what I believe is an insight-ful observation, Lewis et al. (2006) further speculate that the alignment of prin-ciples may be "due to more practice-oriented authors having drawn similar con-clusions as scholars based on different types of evidence."

On the other hand, although they see alignment, Lewis et al. (2006) also find that some of the advice in the popular books is "underspecified and acontextual, and none of it really demonstrates a familiarity with underlying theoretical or even empirical literature." They point out as well that popular books "tended to boil tac-tics for communication down to sound bites and general philosophy." These obser-vations—that practice-oriented authors (or gurus, for that matter) draw conclusions based on different types of evidence and that popular books boil tactics down to sound bites as well as fail to demonstrate familiarity with scholarly literature—are essential to understanding what I see as a cultural difference in the academy and the workplace.

UNDERSTANDING CULTURAL DIFFERENCES

When I reported on a national cultural setting (Alred, 1997b), I said that the term *culture* was problematic but that I would accept *culture* to mean the way a group of people understands reality or the world around them—a shared way of being, eval-uating, and doing—passed from one generation to the next (Limaye & Victor,

1991). Although this definition was intended to describe national cultures, it could describe in many ways the differences in the academy and the workplace.[2]

I reflected on these cultural differences in my introduction to "Essential Works on Technical Communication" (Alred, 2003). Specifically, as I gathered titles from a wide variety of sources, I found a clear dividing line between works valued by academics and those valued by practitioners. Although a handful of works were valued by both academics and practitioners, an overwhelming number of works were recommended exclusively by either practitioner or academic sources (Alred, 2005). Based on my review of those works gathered from practitioner sources, I might agree with Lewis et al. that practice-oriented authors have drawn conclusions based on different types of evidence. But I would also suggest that the workplace requires practitioners to seek fundamentally different ways of responding to their contexts and exigencies—ways that do not require them, for example, to document either their intellectual processes or establish concurrence with scholarly or any other literature.

. . . the workplace requires practitioners to seek fundamentally different ways of responding to their contexts and exigencies . . .

One reason I have learned to appreciate how practitioner contexts and exigencies produce works that I would not necessarily value as an academic is that I have worked closely for more than 30 years with a co-author who spent his entire professional career in business and industry. Charles ("Ted") Brusaw, my co-author on a number of books, has been a professional writer, a corporate trainer, and for many years the manager of technical publications at NCR Corporation's Headquarters in Dayton, Ohio. Although I certainly respect Ted Brusaw for many reasons, I struggled in the past because of our "cultural differences."[3]

Brusaw, whom I regularly invited to speak to my classes, would often say to students, "that never happens in the real world" or "you approach [something] in this way [as if the approach was always right]." Further, when we would meet after he visited my classes, I learned that Ted found it unnatural to spell out processes and rationales that he had internalized in his work at NCR. When we were working on our first book together, *Practical Writing*, he would sometimes suggest boiled down tactics that I viewed initially as arbitrary and simplistic (Brusaw & Alred, 1973). Fresh out of graduate school, I saw everything as complex, contextual, and needing to be supported by theoretical, historical, or empirical literature. Brusaw's approach seemed, as Lewis et al. describe, "underspecified and acontextual," and he was not at all interested in demonstrating a familiarity with scholarly literature.

Even though I was somewhat troubled, I also knew that Brusaw was a successful writer and outstanding manager, and I was impressed at his ability to research, write, organize, and synthesize information. As we worked together, I quickly learned that I was wrong to see his approach as unthinkingly arbitrary and simplistic. Although he had difficulty understanding any need to document his path to the conclusions he developed, he did not passively accept simple-minded solutions. But it took me years to fully understand how Brusaw and his colleagues at NCR constructed what I now think of as "touchstones" (or distilled principles and methodologies) to solve complex problems so they could produce sophisticated documentation within tight deadlines. Their touchstones, which to an outsider might appear as arbitrary and simplistic, were developed through highly specific research using both internal and outside expertise, distilled from a complex historical process of examining rhetorical variables, and documented as operational guidelines rather than narratives of processes or of theoretical models. Working against tight deadlines and within the proprietary constraints of collaborative projects in a competitive corporation, Brusaw had neither the mandate nor the time to document a historical account of his activities. And he certainly did not need to develop conceptual or theoretical frameworks to serve the long-term educational needs of students and future researchers and scholars. Most significant, because Brusaw and his colleagues did not document their methodologies, work, or sources, their processes, contexts, and research materials became invisible as soon as these touchstones were developed.

I would not suggest that Brusaw's processes and those of his NCR colleagues, of course, are typical of all workplace professionals. Nor do I believe that all workplace professionals or authors of popular books necessarily develop similarly valuable touchstones. But then not all published scholarly works provide valuable insights. Given my experience with Brusaw, however, I am not surprised that workplace professionals would find resonance in much of what Covey has to say or would seek nuggets of helpful advice in popular books.

Just as I have learned that those of us in the academy can too quickly reject the seemingly easy and apparently superficial comments of practitioners, Brusaw has told me that his relationship with me has helped him appreciate academic perspectives as well. We have both learned that we have different perspectives, in part because we have had different goals in our work. Brusaw's goal as a manager of technical publications, for example, was to produce usable documentation for very specific products and within tight deadlines. One of my goals as an educator has been to prepare students for lifelong careers that may involve them with future tasks that none of us could imagine. Generally, the goals of workplace professionals demand that they think in specific, practical, and immediately applicable ways; those of us in the academy must think in terms that are more abstract, conceptual, and long-term. It is understandable, then, that works that might be highly valued by either practitioners or academics can seem entirely irrelevant to the other. And just as understandable, practitioners and academics can easily dismiss or discount the works valued by the other side.

TESTING POPULAR ADVICE IN THE WORKPLACE

I wrote in the Introduction to *The St. Martin's Bibliography of Business and Technical Communication* that "theory is necessary to prevent us from being overwhelmed by what is local, particular, and temporal. In turn, pedagogy both mediates practice and transforms our theory" (Alred, 1997a). I would argue that, likewise, practice in the workplace can test theory as well as the advice of gurus and popular books. At the very least, it is an oversimplification to assume that most workplace professionals are gullible and accept the advice of gurus or popular books without reflection, any more than those in the academic community accept uncritically the work of colleagues. And, indeed, the authors of the articles that

---

Generally, the goals of workplace professionals demand that they think in specific, practical, and immediately applicable ways; those of us in the academy must think in terms that are more abstract, conceptual, and long-term.

---

follow also point to the critical awareness of workplace professionals. Lewis et al. (2006) begin their study, for example, with a narrative that reflects the skepticism of many professionals about popular books (Armstrong, 1994):

> I set down my briefcase by my office door and headed around the corner to the coffee and donuts—the last bastion of stability. I poured my coffee and was rummaging through the donuts when Marsha Fillmore, our VP of marketing, brushed by. She shot me a worried look and whispered, "The boss has a new book." . . . Oh no. I quickly forgot about the donuts and walked back to my office. Not another book. (p. 61)

Carlone reports that workplace professionals often attend workshops because they are directed to do so or think they should attend.

One way to determine how popular advice is tested in the workplace, although certainly not the only way, is to search reader comments in Amazon.com about

Covey's *The 7 Habits of Highly Effective People*, particularly those that reflect how a guru's work is received in workplaces. One Amazon.com reader comment, for example, echoes Carlone's point about why workplace professionals attend workshops as well as offers blunt skepticism about Covey's advice: "My boss requires us to take a 2-week course on this book [*The 7 Habits*] as part of the job. I told him I thought the book was over generalized nonsense."[4]

Lewis et al. (2006) observe that popular books are often created as "star vehicles" to launch speaking and promotional tours for their authors (Clark & Greatbatch, 2004, p. 408d). To reach the widest possible audience, ideas are "reduced and simplified into pithy lists, acronyms, concepts, mnemonics, metaphors, and stories that are immediately graspable, understood, and assimilated." Some reader comments on Covey's book not only reflect those observations but also offer serious reservations. The following Amazon.com reader criticisms are typical:

> Being well-read in self-help literature, I would conclude that the "7 habits" represents an up to date effort to re-represent old ideas and theories that have been around since common sense was invented. . . . I am left with some mixed feelings about this book and I can see the same from the reviews posted here: You either love it or you hate it. . . . Basically, I liked Covey's messages about being principle-centered and so forth. However, he seemed to "beat a dead horse" referring over and over again to basic, character-based, lighthouse-guiding principles over and over again in an irritatingly repetitive way.

> This book has seven platitudes we have learned at our mother's knee.

> I just finished reading this book, and have to say it was a serious let-down in light of the [positive] reviews. Let me save you some time and money: 1) You are responsible for your own life, so do something about it. 2) Make a plan for yourself. 3) Focus on what's important. 3) [sic] You reap what you sow—so sow well. 4) Seek mutually beneficial relationships. 5) Have empathy and be considerate to others. 6) Be cooperative. 7) Take care of yourself—mind, body, and soul. Ground-breaking stuff, isn't it?!?! Mr. Covey is a wealthy man for this?! Hmmmmmmm.

MEETING PRACTITIONER NEEDS

Although some practitioners may be highly skeptical, at the same time many participants and readers would seem to approach guru workshops or popular books positively, thinking that they will give the tactics a try and see how they work. Or perhaps they see popular books or a Stephen Covey lecture as potentially useful in finding touchstones or in learning a process for making useful shortcuts to recurring workplace challenges. Many Amazon.com reviewers, for example, even when they agree with those reader critics who say Covey provides nothing new, nevertheless find Covey's interpretation useful:

Stephen R. Covey managed to repackage an ethical and moral tradition thousands of years in development and make it meaningful to a late twentieth century, secular audience.

This work organizes and encapsulates years of good advice into a simple program for practical use.

Covey certainly borrows from other gurus in this work, but puts it together nicely in a way that makes sense and keeps you interested.

Other readers suggest that Covey provides motivation for their work in a time of change.

[*The 7 Habits*] give us the security to adapt to change and the wisdom and power to take advantage of the opportunities that change creates.

7 habits allows me to stay focused even when I feel everything is out of control.

I learned how to manage myself and manage my relationships with others.

Indeed, some of Covey's concepts seem worthwhile even when he presents them with mnemonic aphorisms like "Seek First to Understand, Then to Be Understood." In fact, that precept seems one that could be usefully practiced in

---

Ideally, the best popular press books or gurus would go further than simply aligning themselves with academic scholarship; they could enrich academic scholarship with the experience of savvy workplace professionals.

---

academic departments as well as in business offices. I also find it particularly interesting that, although some practitioners object to repetitiveness in popular books, one of the works Lewis et al. cite points out the value of repetition (Duck, 1998):

It is important for the messages to be consistent, clear, and endlessly repeated. If there is a single rule of communication for leaders, it is this: when you are so sick of talking about something that you can hardly stand it, your message is finally starting to get through. (p. 61)

Some workplace professionals, of course, may overzealously embrace the advice of gurus and popular books, but many workplace professionals are quite savvy, as these postings from Amazon.com suggest:

> One guy in our office was so taken with it [Covey's book] that he drove everyone
> around him crazy with the delegation and time management aspects that his super-
> visor finally told him to knock it off. Seems he was delegating too much.

> There is NO PROOF what so ever that this book [*The 7 Habits*] helps anybody. In
> fact I made a bet with my boss. I told him if I could guess at least 5 out of the 7 hab-
> its without having read or looked at the book; [sic] I wouldn't have to go to the two-
> week course. I guessed 5 of them.

Ideally, the best popular press books or gurus would go further than simply
aligning themselves with academic scholarship; they could enrich academic
scholarship with the experience of savvy workplace professionals.

BUILDING ON THESE STUDIES

Understanding the cultural differences in the workplace and the academy is
important not only in the interpretation of workplace studies but also in research
that would build on or parallel the two articles that follow. The Covey study could
be enriched, for example, through interviewing participants of a Covey lecture to
answer significant questions.

- How many people have read Covey's book before coming to the lecture?
- What percentage of the participants were fans of Covey's *7 Habits* before attending
  the workshop?
- Do participants approach a Covey lecture with modest or focused expectations?
- To what extent are participants savvy about or skeptical of the rhetorical strategies of
  Covey and others?
- How many participants were "forced" to attend by managers who were excited about
  the book or tips?
- What were the participants' general reactions to the workshop or what aspects of
  Covey's methodology did participants find useful a month or a year later?

It would be interesting to compare the books with the lectures of other popular
speakers to determine how the rhetorical strategies of lectures and books are
similar or distinctive. Does the Covey book, for example, "simultaneously ease
and deepen uncertainty and anxiety" in the same way as the lecture? Does the
Covey book have as much potential as the lecture to create the "liminoid event"
that Carlone (2006) describes?[5] Covey seems as much a motivational speaker or
latter-day Dale Carnegie as a management guru. Perhaps further studies could
focus on gurus who are more specifically management oriented.

The Lewis et al. (2006) study could be extended by examining how managers
read popular management guides. We know from the past 30 years of research that
proficient readers do much more than passively absorb writing, sequentially decoding sentences and pages as if they were machines. Readers are much more creative.
They draw inferences as they read, and they term their own concepts; they make
meanings as they read, and the meanings they make are often surprising leaps of

imagination. In other words, readers remember not only what we tell them but also what they tell themselves (Flower, 1981). Readers also choose the information they believe is useful to them as they read, based on their needs (Alred, Oliu, & Brusaw, 1991). We also know that readers bring their own stores of knowledge into play as they attempt to shape possible text meanings (Schoenbach, Greenleaf, Cziko, & Hurwitz, 1999). Based on reading theory and studies, we might ask a number of important questions:

- Do those in workplaces "cherry pick" advice from books as Lewis et al. recommend?
- Just how do popular books meet the needs of workplace professionals?
- Do readers in different fields use different strategies for assessing popular advice?
- What are the key issues for readers? motivation? time management? personal relationships in the workplace?

My review of Amazon.com reader comments is rather cursory: Perhaps a more careful and detailed study of reader comments from Amazon.com and other sites would be helpful in answering key questions about popular books like Covey's *The 7 Habits*. In addition, Lewis et al. (2006) suggest that change is a central theme in popular management books. In fact, they say, "Organizations appear to be drawn—almost cult-like—to embrace constant change." Some intercultural theorists see change as a dominant theme of U.S. culture (Jandt, 1998). What other facets of guru lectures or popular books might reflect U.S. cultural themes?

Generally, those of us in the academy need research that helps us understand how the principles we teach conflict or align with the advice that workplace professionals encounter in influential popular books and in the advice of management gurus. We need to know the answers to such questions both so that research can inform theory and so that our pedagogy enables our students to be wise consumers of popular advice.

NOTES

1. Stephen R. Covey holds an MBA from Harvard and, according to his biography, he taught as a professor of business management and organizational behavior at Brigham Young University, where he earned a doctorate in church history and doctrine.

2. I am generally troubled by the application of the term *culture* to groups outside of historical national contexts, as in the culture of stamp collectors or certain types of music enthusiasts. Often, such applications of culture tend to trivialize the truly pervasive nature of national cultures and the ubiquitous infrastructures that support cultural themes and practices. It is unfortunate that no other term describes as well this understanding of the academy and the workplace.

3. I would like to thank Ted Brusaw for reading this article and continuing to give me the benefit of his workplace experience.

4. For specific URLs for the Amazon.com customer reviews, contact the author.

5. Carlone describes a liminoid event as a middle phase in a secular rite of passage from "ineffective" to "effective."

REFERENCES

Alred, G. J. (1997a). *St. Martin's bibliography of business and technical communication.* New York: St. Martin's Press.

Alred, G. J. (1997b). Teaching in Germany and the rhetoric of culture. *Journal of Business and Technical Communication, 11,* 353-378.

Alred, G. J. (2003). Essential works on technical communication. *Technical Communication, 50,* 585-616.

Alred, G. J. (2005). Academic and practitioner perspectives on essential works in technical communication. *ATTW Bulletin, 15,* 11-13.

Alred, G. J., Oliu, W. E., & Brusaw, C. T. (1991). *The professional writer: A guide for advanced technical writing.* New York: St. Martin's Press.

Amazon.com Customer Reviews. Retrieved November 27, 2005, from http://www.amazon.com/gp/product/customer-reviews/0743269519

Armstrong, W. W. (1994). The boss has read another new book! *Management Review, 83*(6), 61-63.

Brusaw, C. T., & Alred, G. J. (1973). *Practical writing: Composition for the business and technical world.* Boston: Allyn & Bacon.

Carlone, D. (2006). The ambiguous nature of a management guru lecture: Providing answers while deepening uncertainty. Journal of Business Communication, 43.

Clark, T., & Greatbatch, D. (2004). Management fashion as image-spectacle. *Management Communication Quarterly, 17,* 397-424.

Covey, S. R. (1989). *The 7 habits of highly effective people: Restoring the character ethic.* New York: Simon & Schuster.

Duck, J. D. (1998). Managing change: The art of balancing. In *Harvard Business Review on change* (pp. 55-83). Boston: Harvard Business School Publishing.

Flower, L. (1981). *Problem-solving strategies for writing.* Orlando: Harcourt.

Jandt, F. E. (1998). *Intercultural communication: An introduction* (2nd ed.). London: Sage.

Lewis, L. K., et al. (2006). Advice on communicating during organizational change: The content of popular press books. Journal of Business Communication, 43.

Limaye, M. R., & Victor, D. A. (1991). Cross-cultural business communication research: Hypotheses for the 1990s. *Journal of Business Communication, 28,* 277-299.

Schoenbach, R., Greenleaf, C., Cziko, C., & Hurwitz, L. (1999). *Reading for understanding.* San Francisco: Jossey-Bass.

Association between Just World Beliefs and Perceptions of Counterproductive Workplace Behaviors

Stieger, S., Kastner, C. K., Voracek, M. and Furnham, A.

Summary.—320 adults rated 48 counterproductive workplace behaviors (CWBs) on a 9-point scale, from petty to serious offense, and also completed the Just World Beliefs scale. Ratings of the seriousness of the CWBs indicated considerable variability in perceptions, with theft and physical violence rated most strongly. A factor analysis yielded five interpretable factors. Older participants were more likely to rate as more serious all counterproductive workplace behaviors.

Over the past few years, the increasing interest and research on counterproductive workplace behaviors (CWBs) has resulted in a number of books (e.g., Furnham & Taylor, 2004) and edited volumes (e.g., Fox & Spector, 2004; Griffin & O'Leary-Kelly, 2004). CWBs are defined as acts with similar characteristics which are intended to harm an organization or its stakeholders (e.g., clients, customers; Spector & Fox, 2005). Very specific issues have been examined, often motivated by the desire on the part of organizations to reduce CWBs. Indeed, it is possible to discern two dominant issues in the related contemporary literature (Robinson & Bennett, 1995). The first is related to attempts to classify and measure CWBs. For instance, there have been various attempts to devise valid structured interviews (e.g., Blackman & Funder, 2002) and self-report questionnaires (e.g., Hakstian, Farrell, & Tweed, 2002; Jones, Brasher, & Huff, 2002; Marcus, Schuler, Quell, & Hümpfner, 2002) that measure CWBs. Researchers have tended to either develop taxonomic models and devise questionnaires to measure them or else "identify" the different types of CWBs by factor analyzing scales.

There are various lists of CWBs. For example, Fox and Spector (1999) listed 27 items grouped into four factors (minor, serious, personal, and or-

[1]Address correspondence to Stefan Stieger, Department of Basic Psychological Research, School of Psychology, University of Vienna, Liebiggasse 5, 1010 Vienna, Austria or e-mail (stefan.stieger@univie.ac.at).

DOI 10.2466/09.16.17.PR0.108.2.606-616   ISSN 0033-2941

ganizational), while Marcus and colleagues (2002) listed 74 items grouped into four factors (absence/withdrawal, substance abuse, aggression, and theft/property violations). In a similar vein, Bennett and Robinson (2000) listed 28 CWBs divided into behaviors harmful to the organization and harmful to the individual. A more recent example is Spector, Fox, Penney, Bruursema, Goh, and Kessler's CWB Checklist (2006), which comprises 45 items in five factors (sabotage, withdrawal, production deviance, theft, and abuse). There is no clear consensus about how these phenomena should be defined and measured, although most of these questionnaires have good reliability and validity (Ones, Viswesvaran, & Schmidt, 1995; Ones, Viswesvaran, & Reiss, 1996).

The second research theme in this area has been to try to understand individual and organizational correlates of CWBs (Robinson & Bennett, 1995). The general question asked is when and why do certain people commit CWBs, while others do not. There is an extensive literature from a social psychological perspective (e.g., Greenberg, 2002), as well as from a more trait-based perspective (e.g., Mount, Ilies, & Johnson, 2006) on this topic. A meta-analysis examining correlations of the Big Five personality traits and counterproductive behaviors found that all five personality dimensions were related only to some CWBs, deviant behaviors, and turnover (i.e., voluntary quits and discharges; Salgado, 2002). There is also a growing literature on personality disorders and CWBs (e.g., Babiak, 1995; Babiak & Hare, 2006).

The concept of just world beliefs was introduced by Lerner (1980). "Individuals have a need to believe that they live in a world where people generally get what they deserve. The belief that the world is just enables the individual to confront his physical and social environment as though they were stable and orderly. Without such a belief it would be difficult for the individual to commit himself to the pursuit of long range goals or even to the socially regulated behavior of day-to-day life. Since the belief that the world is just serves such an important adaptive function for the individual, people are very reluctant to give up this belief, and they can be greatly troubled if they encounter evidence that suggests that the world is not really just or orderly after all" (Lerner & Miller, 1978, pp. 1030–1031). Logic suggests that if there is no belief in a just world, there would be less perceived chance of retribution for poor behavior and of personal rewards for good behavior. Meta-analytic evidence proposes that perceived justice in organizations is related to CWBs (Cohen-Charash & Spector, 2001). Therefore, it seems potentially interesting to analyze whether individuals not believing in a just world engage more frequently in CWBs.

The present study focuses on two features of this literature. The first is perceived seriousness of individual CWBs. The second is the relationship between just world beliefs and CWBs. Although research has identified many CWBs, criteria for what constitutes a CWB are not agreed upon. CWBs seem to be associated with interpersonal coldness. They also are associated with serious organizational problems. These are grouped and assumed to be of equal importance, although factor analytic work suggests that it is the seriousness of the behavior as much as the precise nature of the behavior that best serves as a grouping variable (Fox & Spector, 1999). In this study, the perceived seriousness of nearly 50 frequently discussed CWBs is the focus. The aim is to assess a lay perspective of CWBs. Participants' ratings of these CWBs will make examination of a factor structure possible. In addition, the individual difference correlates of perceptions will be examined, including demography (sex, age, education), personal ideology (religious and political beliefs), as well as belief in a just world.

There are inevitably differences in what individuals consider to be CWBs and how serious they deem those behaviors to be. Thus, some people would consider joking, practical pranks, and using "inappropriate" language to be normal or even healthy, while others might see these as relatively serious CWBs. This study was designed to assess correlates of these differences. Three groupings of individual difference data were considered: (1) demographic differences—sex, age, and education; (2) "ideology" based on religious and political beliefs; and (3) perceptions of a just world. It was anticipated that all three sets of individual difference factors would be correlated with perceptions of CWBs and that a factor analysis of ratings would yield a coherent and interpretable factor structure.

METHOD

Participants

There were 320 participants (152 men, 168 women; M age = 30.7 yr., SD = 12.7). Most were Catholic (76.9%), 7.8% were Protestant, and 15.3% were of other religions, atheist, or agnostic. For the vast majority (97.5%), German was their mother tongue. Just over a half (58.8%) had a postsecondary school diploma, while 20.3% had postgraduate education. Almost exactly half of participants' parents had completed secondary school education (mothers 48.8%, fathers 49.0%). Around one-quarter were single (26.9%) or married (22.5%), while the others were in a relationship (47.5%). Asked "How religious are you?" on a 7-point scale (1: Not at all, 7: Very), the mean rating was 3.16 (SD = 1.55). Political orientation ("What is your political orientation?") was rated between 1: Strongly right-wing and 7: Strongly left-wing; the mean score was 4.65 (SD = 1.23). Regarding their employment status, three-quarters (76.3%) described themselves as employees, while 7.8% were supervisors, 7.2% mid-ranking managers, and 3.4% high-ranking managers. They had worked for their organizations from less than 1 yr. to 40 yr. (M = 6.3, SD = 8.9).

Measures

Personal workplace observation.—Participants were asked to rate their pride in the organization on a 5-point scale (1: Not at all, 5: Very); the mean was 3.69 (*SD*=1.08). They were also asked to rate how much CWBs occurred in their organization (1=None, 5=A lot); the mean was 2.70 (*SD*=1.18).

Counterproductive workplace behavior.—A 48-item questionnaire was developed based on a variety of sources including Bennett and Robinson's 18-item measure (2000) of workplace deviance, 27 items from Spector (1975), the 74 items on counterproductive behavior listed by Marcus and colleagues (2002), and the recent checklist developed by Spector and colleagues (2006). Participants were asked to rate the seriousness of these counterproductive workplace behaviors on a 9-point scale with anchors 1: Petty offense and 9: Serious offense.

Belief in a just world (Rubin & Peplau, 1975).—This is a 20-item scale that has 11 items related to belief in a Just world (e.g., "Basically, the world is a just place") and nine related to belief in an Unjust world (e.g., "I've found that a person rarely deserves the reputation he has"). Participants had to state whether they agreed or disagreed with the statements on a 9-point scale (1: Disagree, 9: Agree). Higher mean subscale scores reflect a stronger belief in a just or unjust world, respectively. This scale was one of the first in this area and is probably the most widely used in research on just world beliefs (Furnham, 2003).

Results

Table 1 shows the mean ratings of the seriousness of the behaviors. Four items' mean ratings were near 8 on the 9-point scale: two referring to theft (Items 7 and 21) and two to physical violence (Items 31 and 33). In all, 13 items' mean ratings were above 7, and four were lower than 5. The latter items concerned use of time (Items 13 and 15), inappropriate attire (Item 46), and waste of materials (Item 1).

These ratings were then treated with a varimax-rotated factor analysis (principal components; scree plot criterion; see Table 1). Five factors emerged which together accounted for about 50% of the variance. The first factor, which had 16 items, was labeled Social Interaction, as items concerned issues like insults, bad jokes, ignoring a person, hiding information, and falsely attributing blame. The second factor had 12 items and concerned Cheating (by working slower, less, etc.). The third factor had 9 items and concerned Rule-breaking by bad, slothful, or inappropriate behavior. The fourth factor involved more serious behaviors like violence, theft, and sabotage, hence the factor was called Serious Demeanors. The final factor with two items was called Inappropriate Behavior.

TABLE 1
MEANS AND STANDARD DEVIATIONS AS WELL AS VARIMAX ROTATED FACTOR ANALYTIC RESULTS ON THE SERIOUSNESS OF COUNTERPRODUCTIVE WORKPLACE BEHAVIORS

Item	M	SD	F1	F2	F3	F4	F5
38. Insulted or made fun of someone at work.	6.41	1.78	.76	.13	.01	.04	.23
24. Refused to help someone at work when asked for assistance.	6.27	1.74	.76	.11	.17	.09	-.11
22. Made fun of someone's physical deformity (e.g., facial disfigurement).	6.87	2.01	.73	-.06	.21	-.03	.11
23. Deliberately ignored someone at work.	5.24	2.11	.72	.14	.14	-.10	.02
17. Made fun of someone's personal life.	5.56	2.10	.71	-.06	.13	-.09	.18
34. Did something to make someone at work look bad.	6.74	1.57	.71	.11	.00	.12	.07
27. Blamed someone else for an error s/he made.	7.30	1.49	.68	.10	.03	.25	-.18
29. Verbally abused a subordinate at work.	6.80	1.58	.68	.01	-.07	.27	.08
25. Withheld needed information from someone at work.	6.92	1.52	.67	.12	.23	.35	-.16
16. Insulted a fellow employee about his/her poor job performance.	5.57	1.82	.66	.04	.26	-.07	.17
36. Played a prank to embarrass at work.	5.06	2.20	.65	.31	-.09	-.09	.35
26. Purposely interfered with someone at work doing his/her job.	5.05	1.82	.59	.28	.15	.05	.00
35. Took credit for the work of a colleague at work.	7.36	1.52	.58	.27	-.06	.29	-.15
28. Started an argument with someone at work.	6.14	1.84	.58	.16	.20	.12	.12
30. Made an obscene gesture to someone at work.	6.02	2.04	.55	.11	.01	.11	.31
32. Hid something so someone at work could not find it.	5.78	2.16	.51	.32	.11	.09	.24
15. Left work earlier than is allowed.	4.84	2.09	.19	.74	.19	.02	.11
13. Took a longer break than is allowed.	3.41	1.96	.14	.73	.31	-.12	.14
39. Worked on a personal matter instead of work for the company.	5.70	1.83	.20	.66	-.03	.27	.03
18. Took supplies or tools home without permission.	5.38	2.16	.07	.65	.15	.16	.08
20. Put in to be paid for more hours than s/he worked.	6.89	1.65	.17	.64	.14	.32	-.20
19. Tried to look busy while doing nothing.	5.68	1.78	.33	.62	.17	.16	-.17
42. Intentionally worked slower than s/he could have.	5.37	1.77	.28	.51	.26	.19	.18
1. Purposely wasted the company's materials or supplies.	4.79	2.12	-.05	.47	.18	.06	.01
46. Wore inappropriate (seductive/over-casual) clothing to work.	4.08	2.07	.20	.45	.21	.06	.42
37. Looked through a coworker's private mail or property without permission.	6.04	2.29	.35	.43	-.10	.09	.16

(continued on next page)

Note.—F1 = Social Interaction; F2 = Cheating; F3 = Rule-breaking; F4 = Serious Demeanors; F5 = Inappropriate Behavior.

TABLE 1 (CONT'D)
MEANS AND STANDARD DEVIATIONS AS WELL AS VARIMAX ROTATED FACTOR ANALYTIC
RESULTS ON THE SERIOUSNESS OF COUNTERPRODUCTIVE WORKPLACE BEHAVIORS

Item	M	SD	F1	F2	F3	F4	F5
6. Purposely dirtied or littered his/her surroundings at work.	5.64	1.98	.10	**.42**	.38	-.01	.11
5. Stayed home from work and said s/he was sick when s/he wasn't.	6.93	1.81	-.06	**.42**	.38	.17	-.01
9. Was nasty or rude to a client/customer.	7.27	1.54	.17	.02	**.66**	.21	.05
3. Told people outside the job what a lousy organization s/he worked in.	5.66	2.18	.08	.17	**.66**	-.02	.03
10. Refused to take an assignment when asked by a supervisor.	6.57	1.86	.02	.23	**.63**	.12	-.05
11. Arrived late at an appointment or meeting without permission.	5.80	1.90	.13	.37	**.53**	.03	.18
12. Failed to report a problem with the intention of making it worse.	7.25	1.56	.20	.01	**.52**	.31	-.25
4. Being late to work without permission.	5.88	1.87	.07	.43	**.49**	-.07	.04
14. Purposely failed to follow instructions.	6.46	1.57	.14	.37	**.49**	.26	-.13
2. Spent too much time daydreaming.	5.35	1.80	.10	.37	**.45**	.10	-.03
8. Started, or continued, a damaging or harmful rumor at work.	6.29	2.04	.35	.10	**.38**	-.02	.32
47. Sabotaged the organization's tools or equipment.	7.39	1.63	.10	.18	.21	**.66**	.00
21. Took money from the company without permission.	8.55	0.91	.07	.23	.08	**.60**	-.08
40. Falsified a receipt to get reimbursed for more money than s/he spent on business expenses.	7.88	1.51	.04	.44	.06	**.57**	.01
44. Used an illegal drug or consumed alcohol on the job.	7.96	1.58	-.09	.16	.21	**.56**	.44
33. Physically attacked someone at work.	8.34	1.10	.30	-.21	-.11	**.53**	.12
43. Discussed confidential company information with an unauthorized person.	7.52	1.55	-.01	.24	.28	**.52**	.24
31. Threatened a subordinate at work with violence.	8.15	1.13	.45	-.07	-.13	**.52**	.15
48. Threatened to expose a scandal at the firm.	7.47	1.64	.23	.06	.37	**.46**	.08
7. Stole something belonging to the company.	8.08	1.46	-.13	.31	.25	**.38**	.19
45. Made an inappropriate sexist remark or joke at work.	6.51	2.10	.36	.08	-.07	.24	**.68**
41. Made an inappropriate ethnic, religious, or racial remark or joke at work.	6.44	2.25	.39	.01	-.04	.11	**.61**
Eigenvalues			8.49	5.64	4.02	3.66	2.27
Variance explained, %			17.7	11.7	8.4	7.6	4.7
M			6.19	5.37	6.21	7.92	6.48
SD			1.27	1.27	1.13	0.85	1.92
Cronbach's α			.93	.86	.81	.78	.74

Note.—F1 = Social Interaction; F2 = Cheating; F3 = Rule-breaking; F4 = Serious Demeanors; F5 = Inappropriate Behavior.

In order to examine demographic and belief correlates of the rated seriousness of the behaviors, seven scores were computed: a Total score which indicated the participants' perceptions of the overall seriousness of the behaviors; a computed Most Serious score, the mean for the 13 behaviors with mean ratings higher than 7; the mean ratings for items loading on each of the five factors.

Next, the Just World questionnaire was scored to obtain both Just and Unjust scores for each person. Internal consistency reliabilities for the subscales (Cronbach alphas) were Just .59 and Unjust .70. The Pearson correlation between the Just and Unjust scores was $r = -.20$ ($p < .001$; $95\% CI = -.31$, $-.09$). Subsequently, seven regressions were computed for Total, Most Serious, and the five-factor scores, each with seven predictor variables: demography (sex, age, and education), ideology (religious and political belief), and Just World beliefs (Just and Unjust). Table 2 shows that all the regressions were statistically significant, but they explained only small to moderate amounts of the variance in ratings of Total CWB ratings (2% to 14%). Some variables were consistently statistically significant predictors across all the regressions; others were rarely statistically significant. Sex and age were statistically significant predictors in four of the regressions and political beliefs in three; religious belief and Just World belief were not statistically significant predictors in any regression.

The first regression for Total score was an index of how seriously participants took all the 48 items in general, related to the predictor variables. Betas for all three demographic variables were statistically significant: in general, less well educated, older females had the highest scores. Considering the Most Serious scores, the two significant predictors were sex and political beliefs, with women and those with scores indicating more right-wing (conservative) political beliefs rating the items higher.

When looking at the regressions for each of the five-factor scores, results showed some similarities but also differences. The only variable that accounted for significant variance in participants' ratings of the seriousness of Social Interaction (Factor 1) was age. Older people rather than younger people gave higher ratings to these items. Age and education had statistically significant betas on Factor 2, Cheating. Older, less educated people had higher mean ratings on these items. A similar pattern emerged for Factor 3, Rule-breaking. Older, more conservative, and less educated people rated these items higher. Only one variable accounted for significant variance in Factor 4, Serious Demeanors. Women's mean rating for these items was higher. Finally, sex and political beliefs were significantly associated with Factor 5, Inappropriate Behavior, with women and those who characterized their political beliefs as more liberal having higher mean ratings.

TABLE 2
Regression of Demographics (Sex, Age, Education), Ideology (Political Orientation and Religiousness), and Just World Beliefs onto Ratings of Total and Most Serious Counterproductive Workplace Behaviors and Five Factors

Independent Variable	Total			Most Serious			F1			F2		
	r	β	t	r	β	t	r	β	t	r	β	t
Sex	.11*	.13	2.35*	.13*	.14	2.47*	.08	.10	1.76	.07	.08	1.51
Age	.24†	.21	3.62‡	.09	.06	0.98	.15†	.16	2.66†	.33†	.28	5.05‡
Education	-.15†	-.13	-2.30*	-.06	-.05	-0.90	-.09	-.07	-1.23	-.21†	-.19	-3.63‡
Religious belief	.10	.02	0.26	.05	-.02	-0.32	.00	-.05	-0.74	.18†	.08	1.39
Political belief	-.12*	-.06	-1.02	-.13*	-.13	-2.14*	-.02	.00	-0.01	-.15†	-.04	-0.65
Unjust world	.05	.04	0.61	-.03	-.04	-0.74	.10	.08	1.33	.01	-.01	-0.18
Just world	.08	.05	0.79	.06	.04	0.66	.00	.08	-0.02	.11*	.05	0.88
$F_{7,312}$	4.70‡			2.11*			2.08*			8.50‡		
Adj R^2	.08			.02			.02			.14		

Independent Variable	F3			F4			F5		
	r	β	t	r	β	t	r	β	t
Sex	.03	.06	1.12	.14*	.15	2.57*	.20†	.19	3.47†
Age	.20‡	.14	2.44*	.07	.03	0.55	.00	.05	0.85
Education	-.17†	-.14	-2.56*	-.02	-.02	-0.36	.08	.08	1.38
Religious belief	.12*	.02	0.40	.08	.02	0.25	.01	.02	0.37
Political belief	-.22‡	-.17	-2.88†	-.13†	-.12	-1.95	.18†	.18	3.15†
Unjust world	.03	.03	0.45	-.07	-.08	-1.28	.09	.09	1.60
Just world	.12*	.07	1.27	.09	.07	1.14	-.07	.00	-0.06
$F_{7,312}$	5.12‡			2.34*			4.18‡		
Adj R^2	.08			.03			.07		

Note.—Males coded 1, females 2. Total = mean rating on all items; Most Serious = mean of 13 items with mean ratings higher than 7; F1 = Social Interaction; F2 = Cheating; F3 = Rule-breaking; F4 = Serious Demeanors; F5 = Inappropriate Behavior. * $p < .05$, † $p < .01$, ‡ $p < .001$.

Discussion

Most studies on counterproductive workplace behaviors (CWBs) have been concerned with their classification as well as their individual correlates and consequences. This study focused on subjective perceptions of the seriousness of 48 CWBs. The data showed that participants clearly differentiated their perceptions of CWBs' seriousness on the 9-point scale with mean item ratings ranging from 3.41 ("Taking a longer break than is allowed") to 8.55 ("Stealing company money"). Standard deviations showed sufficient variability in the responses of the participants.

The behaviors rated most serious were in rank order: the theft of money (Item 21), physically attacking someone at work (Item 33), threatening with violence (Item 31), and stealing something (Item 7). Theft and violence, therefore, appear to be considered the most serious behaviors. A few CWBs were considered minor; four had mean ratings <5.0. It is unclear which behaviors should be classified as counterproductive workplace behaviors, and whether that definition might vary from one nation or organization to another. Thus, working less hard and taking a few minutes extra at a break or wearing too casual clothes may seem normal, natural, and perfectly acceptable to many. One issue that may be relevant is the rank or status of the person making the judgment. That is, it may well be that managers make different judgments compared to employees. Indeed, a *post hoc* analysis revealed that managers ($n = 34$) judged CWBs as more serious than employees, although the effect was not statistically significant (manager: $M = 6.6$, $SD = 0.83$; employee: $M = 6.3$, $SD = 0.94$; $t_{247} = 1.59$, $p = .11$, Cohen's $d = 0.20$). This needs to be addressed in future research by aiming for a larger subsample of managers.

This study showed that the selected 48 items had five interpretable factors similar to those found in other studies. Thus, some counterproductive workplace behaviors are about interpersonal behavior, others about invasions of privacy, and still others about serious criminal issues like theft and violence. Among the variables examined, there were few statistically significant individual correlates of factor scores. For example, Just World beliefs and religiousness appear not to be related to CWB ratings. It should be kept in mind that religiousness was assessed with a single item measure; using a validated multi-item scale might reveal an association. There was some indication that those participants who were women, older, less well educated, and described themselves as politically more conservative tended to rate CWBs higher. These results raise the question as to what, if any, individual difference factors like personality, values, or ethical positions are related to perceptions of counterproductive workplace behaviors. It may well be that most of these behaviors are consistently rated and that whole cultures share their evaluations of what are counterproductive behaviors in the workplace.

REFERENCES

BABIAK, P. (1995)   When psychopaths go to work: a case study of an industrial psycho-path. *Applied Psychology, 44*, 171-188.

BABIAK, P., & HARE, R. D. (EDS.) (2006)   *Snakes in suits: when psychopaths go to work.* New York: Regan Books.

BENNETT, R. J., & ROBINSON, S. L. (2000)   Development of a measure of workplace deviance. *Journal of Applied Psychology, 85*, 349-360.

BLACKMAN, M. C., & FUNDER, D. C. (2002)   Effective interview practices for accurately assessing counter-productive traits. *International Journal for Selection and Assessment, 10*, 109-116.

COHEN-CHARASH, Y., & SPECTOR, P. E. (2001)   The role of justice in organizations: a meta-analysis. *Organizational Behavior and Human Decision Processes, 86*, 278-321.

FOX, S., & SPECTOR, P. E. (1999)   A model of work frustration-aggression. *Journal of Organizational Behavior, 20*, 915-931.

FOX, S., & SPECTOR, P. E. (EDS.) (2004)   *Counterproductive work behavior: investigations of actors and targets.* Washington, DC: American Psychological Association.

FURNHAM, A. (2003)   Belief in a just world: research progress over the past decade. *Personality and Individual Differences, 34*, 795-817.

FURNHAM, A., & TAYLOR, J. (2004)   *The dark side of behaviour at work.* Basingstoke, UK: Palgrave.

GREENBERG, J. (2002)   Who stole the money, and when? Individual and situational determinants of employee theft. *Organisational Behavior and Human Decision Processes, 89*, 985-1003.

GRIFFIN, R. W., & O'LEARY-KELLY, A. M. (EDS.) (2004)   *The dark side of organizational behavior.* New York: Jossey-Bass.

HAKSTIAN, A. R., FARRELL, S., & TWEED, R. G. (2002)   The assessment of counter-productive tendencies by means of the California Psychological Inventory. *International Journal of Selection and Assessment, 10*, 58-86.

JONES, J. W., BRASHER, E. E., & HUFF, J. W. (2002)   Innovations in integrity-based personnel selection: building a technology-friendly assessment. *International Journal of Selection and Assessment, 10*, 87-97.

LERNER, M. J. (1980)   *The belief in a just world: a fundamental delusion.* New York: Plenum.

LERNER, M. J., & MILLER, D. T. (1978)   Just world research and the attribution process: looking back and ahead. *Psychological Bulletin, 85*, 1030-1051.

MARCUS, B., SCHULER, H., QUELL, P., & HÜMPFNER, G. (2002)   Measuring counter productivity: development and initial validation of a German self-report questionnaire. *International Journal of Selection and Assessment, 10*, 18-35.

MOUNT, M., ILIES, R., & JOHNSON, E. (2006)   Relationship of personality traits and counterproductive work behaviors: the mediating effects of job satisfaction. *Personnel Psychology, 59*, 591-622.

ONES, D. S., VISWESVARAN, C., & REISS, A. D. (1996)   Role of social desirability in personality testing for personnel selection: the red herring. *Journal of Applied Psychology, 81*, 660-679.

ONES, D. S., VISWESVARAN, C., & SCHMIDT, F. L. (1995)   Integrity tests: overlooked facts, resolved issues, and remaining questions. *American Psychologist, 50*, 456-457.

ROBINSON, S. L., & BENNETT, R. J. (1995)   A typology of deviant workplace behaviors: a multidimensional scaling study. *Academy of Management Journal, 38*, 555-572.

Rubin, Z., & Peplau, L. A. (1975)   Who believes in a just world? *Journal of Social Issues,* 31B, 65-89.

Salgado, J. F. (2002)   The Big Five personality dimensions and counterproductive behavior. *International Journal of Selection and Assessment,* 10, 117-125.

Spector, P. E. (1975)   Relationships of organizational frustration with reported behavioral reactions of employees. *Journal of Applied Psychology,* 60, 635-637.

Spector, P. E., & Fox, S. (2005)   A model of counterproductive work behavior. In S. Fox & P. E. Spector (Eds.), *Counterproductive work behavior: investigations of actors and targets.* Washington, DC: American Psychological Association. Pp. 151-174.

Spector, P. E., Fox, S., Penney, L. M., Bruursema, K., Goh, A., & Kessler, S. (2006)   The dimensionality of counterproductivity: are all counterproductive behaviors created equal? *Journal of Vocational Behavior,* 68, 446-460.

Accepted March 24, 2011.

PART
8

JOURNALS ON KNOWLEDGE AND
INFORMATION MANAGEMENT FOR
THE WORKPLACE

PART
8

JOURNALS ON KNOWLEDGE AND
INFORMATION MANAGEMENT FOR
THE WORKPLACE

Holistic Views of Knowledge Management Models

Yang, B., Zheng, W. and Viere, C.

The problem and the solution. Based on a newly developed holistic theory of knowledge and learning, this article critically evaluates selected models of knowledge management (KM) and proposes a holistic KM model. Most existing KM models tend to narrowly define knowledge from conceptual and perceptual perspectives and fail to recognize affectual knowledge such as values and visions. Furthermore, most models view KM as a linear or cyclical process and thus fail to identify the multidimensional nature of the knowledge dynamics between individuals and organizations. Implications of the holistic model for human resource development are discussed.

Keywords: *holistic theory; knowledge management; organizational learning*

Knowledge management (KM) and related terms such as organizational learning and learning organization have become buzzwords in business practices and popular research topics in the field of human resource development (HRD). The central concept among these terms is knowledge. Compared with the wide usage of the term *knowledge*, a clear definition of an organized framework revealing and integrating the underlying structure of knowledge theories has received inadequate attention in the literature. Tsoukas and Vladimirou (2001) contend that "Organizational knowledge is much talked about but little understood" (p. 973).

Authors' Note: The research was partially supported by a grant from the National Science Foundation of China (NSFC Project No. 70725005).

Advances in Developing Human Resources Vol. 11, No. 3 June 2009 273-289
DOI: 10.1177/1523422309338584

There is an increasing body of literature on KM, and yet limited comparative theoretical integration exists. One notable effort by Argote, McEvily, and Reagans (2003) suggests an integrative framework for organizing the literature on KM. This framework consists of two dimensions, KM contexts and outcomes. Knowledge creation, retention, and transfer represent KM outcomes. The KM contexts are reflected in units (individuals, groups, or organizations) and the relationships between units and the nature of knowledge itself (tacit vs. explicit). It has been observed that existing theoretical frameworks of KM can be categorized into one of three contexts. Some frameworks emphasize the properties of the units themselves (Cohen & Levinthal, 1990), some recognize the importance of the relationships between units (Crossan, Lane, & White, 1999), and yet others call attention to the nature of knowledge such as tacitness (Nonaka & Takeuchi, 1995). Overall, although several comprehensive frameworks for organizing KM theories have appeared in the literature, two shortcomings exist relevant to the purpose of the article at hand. First, many existing frameworks have not yet been fully developed because the interactions between key components of knowledge are not identified nor described, which leads to incomplete views of KM. Second, no effort was made to critically examine the prevalent KM theories in the literature.

KM theory and practice deserves attention in HRD literature because KM is fundamentally aligned with HRD. According to McLean and McLean (2001),

> HRD is any process or activity that, either initially or over the long-term, has the potential to develop adult's work-based knowledge, expertise, productivity, and satisfaction, whether for personal or group/team gain, or for the benefit of an organization, community, nation, or ultimately the whole of humanity. (p. 322)

Because of the shared focus on the development of work-based knowledge, KM deeply aligns with this definition and purpose of HRD and shares applicability beyond the organizational level to the national and global levels. As a field of study and practice, HRD professionals need to have a clear concept of knowledge and develop powerful KM principles so as to improve practice.

The purpose of this article is to comparatively examine the major models of KM in the literature from an integrative and holistic perspective. This article has two related objectives. First is to demonstrate the utility of a newly developed holistic theory that takes an integrative perspective of knowledge and therefore could inform models of KM. Second, the article aims to critically examine major models of KM and illuminate differences that have a practical impact for KM and HRD.

Theoretical Foundation

To manage knowledge, our understanding of what knowledge consists of is essential. In this section, we introduce an emergent model of KM based on Yang's (2003) model of holistic learning.

Three Knowledge Facets

Yang (2003) proposed a holistic learning theory that defines knowledge as a construct with three distinct and interrelated facets—implicit, explicit, and emancipatory knowledge. This article builds on this perspective and uses three different terms for purposes of clarity—perceptual, conceptual, and affectual knowledge. *Perceptual knowledge* refers to personal kinesthetic understanding of the world through direct experience and involvement in a particular situation. *Conceptual knowledge* indicates abstract concepts and a scheme of interrelated concepts that may be transferred across situations. *Affectual knowledge* is individuals' sentiment attached to certain objects. Knowledge is viewed as human beings' awareness and understanding about reality gained through personal familiarity, cognitive and mental processing, and emotional affection. The facets of knowledge are different aspects of the way through which we get to know the physical, social, emotional, and spiritual world.

A Dialectic Perspective of the Three Knowledge Facets

Although classifying human learning into three domains (i.e., cognitive, psychomotor, and affective) is not new (Bloom, Englehart, Furst, Hill, & Krathwohl, 1956), the holistic theory views that all of these three facets or dimensions are interrelated. Yang (2003) posits that all of the three facets are present in all learning processes, even though not all of them need to undergo a change for learning to happen. Furthermore, the holistic theory calls for a dialectical perspective of the three knowledge facets. On one hand, there are some intrinsically different characteristics of the three knowledge facets; they seem to be different and contradictory, like the two faces of a coin. On the other hand, they interact with each other and become indivisible when we take a holistic perspective. They occur by default whether we recognize them or not. All of the three facets are necessary components of the whole.

The holistic learning theory asserts that the construct of knowledge consists not only of the three facets but also of three knowledge layers (Yang, 2003). The knowledge layers include foundation, manifestation, and orientation. The first layer is a stratum of foundation or premise, which serves as the basis for our knowing and determines the boundary. Foundation includes those tacit assumptions that have been taken for granted as valid and are not normally requiring proof. We have to accept certain assumptions to know and act. This layer indicates our epistemological beliefs. The second layer is manifestation that represents the outcomes of our knowing. The third layer is the orientation of our knowing, which defines the direction and tendency of knowing action. The third layer indicates the driving forces of our learning process.

Organizational Knowledge

The holistic theory further suggests that learning is not only an individual activity but also a social phenomenon (Yang, 2003). An individual learner has

Table 1: Holistic Theory of Organizational Knowledge

Knowledge Layers	Knowledge Facets		
	Technical	**Practical**	**Critical**
Foundation	Institutionalized Conceptual Knowledge (System and Structure)	Collective Perceptual Knowledge (Process and Practice)	Dominated Affectual Knowledge (Value and Vision)
Manifestation	Rules, regulations, policies, standard operation procedures, technical specifications, formal communication channels and formats	Shared experiences, social norms, customs, conventions, shared understandings, intuitions, insights, routines, technical know-how	Mission awareness, managerial philosophies, sense of social responsibilities, morale, ethical and moral standards, and spirituality
Orientation	Rationality (reflected as efficiency and optimization)	Reality (reflected as effectiveness and flexibility)	Liberty (reflected as productivity and responsibility)

to interact with his or her immediate social group or organization within certain social and cultural contexts. The holistic theory posits that group or organizational knowledge has three corresponding facets—technical, practical, and critical knowledge. Similar to individual knowledge, group and organizational knowledge can be viewed as a social construct with three facets, and each of them has three layers. Table 1 lists the three layers of group and organizational knowledge in three domains. The first facet of group and organizational knowledge is technical knowledge, which is demonstrated in a formal system and structure. Technical knowledge is institutionalized conceptual knowledge of individual members (Crossan et al., 1999). Technical knowledge is manifested by those establishments such as formal rules, regulations, policies, standard operation procedures, technical specifications, and formal communication channels and formats. The orientation of technical knowledge is efficiency and optimization, which is one of the major driving forces of organizations. In other words, the main function of technical knowledge of an organization is to produce maximum products and services with efficient use of available resources for a clearly defined mission. Once technical knowledge is acquired and established in a group or in an organization, it influences an individual employee's behavior mainly through the rational driving force within the domain of conceptual knowledge.

The second facet of group and organizational knowledge is practical knowledge, which can be identified in organizational processes and practices. It is manifested as perceptual or implicit knowledge that has not been (or cannot be) incorporated into formal organizational systems. Examples of practical knowledge include shared experiences, social norms, customs, conventions, shared understandings, intuitions, insights, routines, and technical know-how. Practical knowledge also includes individual employees' knowledge that has not been incorporated into the formal system, such as their awareness of market changes. Organizational learning of practical knowledge can be facilitated by action-oriented activities such as socialization, conversation and dialogue, and some interactive systems (Crossan et al., 1999). Practical knowledge is oriented toward effectiveness and flexibility, one of the driving forces for a group or organization to function. A group or organization's practical knowledge is a collection of its members' knowledge that has been proven to be workable in practice.

The third facet of group and organizational knowledge is critical knowledge, which is based on the foundation of organizational value and vision. Critical knowledge can be defined as the dominant affectual knowledge of its members. Because individuals tend to possess diverse values and visions of their own and have different understandings about organizational issues, the formation and change of critical knowledge generally involve organizational power and politics. It also activates and defines individual and organizational interests and ethics. Critical knowledge is manifested by those less stable but vital elements such as mission awareness, managerial philosophies, organizational politics and power distribution, economic gain, and ethical and moral standards in the workplace. Critical knowledge is largely determined by the sense of social responsibility and it interacts directly with individual employees' affectual knowledge.

A Holistic KM Model

On the basis of the above review, we propose that KM can be viewed as a process of managing change in the dimensions of technical, practical, and critical knowledge in an organization, as well as managing the dynamic interactions of the three dimensions of knowledge. In other words, KM encompasses the creation, transferring, and use of the three dimensions of knowledge and the facilitation of the transformation of one facet of knowledge to another. We think that organizations need to manage in both epistemological and ontological dimensions. Figure 1 depicts a new model of KM that describes the dynamic interactions among the three knowledge facets at both the individual and organizational levels.

There are nine KM processes in the realm of epistemological dimensions: socialization, systematization, transformation, formalization, routinization, evaluation, orientation, deliberation, and realization. Socialization encompasses the processes of organizational members' creation of new practical knowledge from their actual experience in order to become fully participating and effective

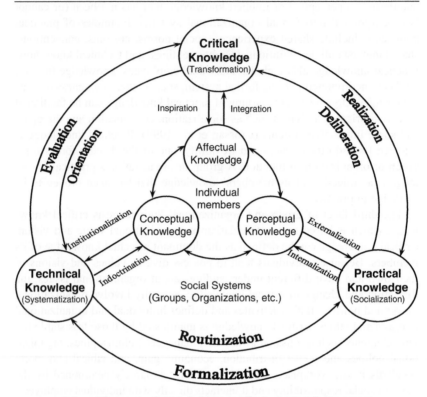

FIGURE I: A Holistic Framework of Knowledge Management

members in a community of practice. Systematization is a process of systematizing technical knowledge gained from organizational members into a system with explicit rules and systems. Transformation is a process of changing an organization's fundamental values and visions by leading it toward internal productivity and social responsibility. Formalization is a process of articulating, transferring, and formalizing practical knowledge into a structured organizational system. As results of this KM process, employees' roles are structured and their activities are governed by formal rules and procedures. It converts intangible knowledge into tangible explanations by embedding practical knowledge gained from practice into new rules, systems, or structures. Conversely, routinization is a process of implementing technical knowledge into practical knowledge. It is the process of using rules and systems in a specific work context so that such explicit rules and requirements become regular and conventional procedures. Evaluation is a process of determining the values and guiding principles of organizational members on the basis of reasoning, shared rules, and structures (changing from technical knowledge to critical knowledge). Conversely, orientation is a process of justifying organizational rules and regulations based on the values and guiding principles held by members. Deliberation is the process of making collective meanings and beliefs from organizational members' actual experience. Conversely, realization is a process of realizing organizational values by putting them to the test of practical knowledge.

There are six KM processes in the realm of ontological dimensions: *institutionalization, indoctrination, externalization, internalization, inspiration*, and *integration*. Institutionalization is a process of translating effective conceptual knowledge from individual members as part of normal and structured organizational system. It aims at establishing action guidelines applicable to daily activities. Indoctrination is a process of transmitting formal requirements and regulations to all organizational members. Externalization is a process of converting individual members' implicit knowledge into shared practical knowledge in a community of practice. Internalization is a process of making practical knowledge such as routines and mental models digestible to organizational members. Inspiration is a process of uniting organizational members through shaping and aligning with members' values, visions, and aspirations. Integration is a process of developing shared attitudes, values, visions, and aspirations among organizational members through mutual adjustment.

A Comparative Review of Selected KM Models

Knowledge Creation Model

Nonaka and Takeuchi (1995) propose a knowledge creation model. This model describes the creation and dissemination of knowledge throughout an organization as embodied within its "products, services and systems" (Nonaka & Takeuchi, 1995, p. 3). According to the theory, knowledge moves on two ontological dimensions (individuals to organizational) and on two epistemological dimensions (tacit and explicit). Tacit knowledge is characterized as more difficult to formalize and communicate because it is often intimately tied to action and experience. Explicit knowledge is the knowledge that can be put into words, written down, modeled, and relatively easily transferred. The modes of knowledge conversion include socialization (from tacit to tacit knowledge), externalization (from tacit to explicit knowledge), combination (from explicit to explicit knowledge), and internalization (from explicit to tacit knowledge). The progression on the ontological dimension ranges from the individual at one end and moves to team, group, organization, and beyond in a spiral-like fashion "when the interaction between tacit and explicit knowledge is elevated dynamically from a lower ontological level to higher levels" (Nonaka & Takeuchi, 1995, p. 57). The knowledge-creation process for this model contains fives steps—sharing tacit knowledge, creating concepts, justifying concepts, building an archetype, and cross-leveling knowledge (Nonaka & Takeuchi,

1995; von Krogh, Ishijo, & Nonaka, 2000). Enabling of knowledge creation organizationally is promoted by examining barriers, establishing conditions by creating an enabling context, and by establishing organizational enablers (von Krogh et al., 2000). On the basis of their model, Nonaka and Takeuchi (1995) suggest that organizations need to mobilize tacit knowledge and facilitate the socialization, combination, externalization, and internalization process through which knowledge can be created.

The knowledge creation model recognizes the potential nature of tacitness of the knowledge and provides useful concepts of the dynamic interactions between explicit and tacit knowledge. However, there are several limitations associated with this model. First, despite its illustration of the knowledge creation process between individuals and organizations, this model does not differentiate individual and organizational knowledge. Therefore, it fails to acknowledge the characteristics of knowledge at different organizational levels. In practical terms, how to manage individual knowledge and how to manage organizational knowledge may be different and yet this model does not point to differential treatment when it comes to different levels of knowledge. Second, this model suggests that knowledge creation is a spiral process and implies that all types of knowledge have to go through a tacit–explicit process. In fact, much tacit knowledge cannot be externalized and the learners have to participate in a community of practice to gain such knowledge. Therefore, the limitation of externalization should be recognized. For example, most professional schools require their students to fulfill practicum (i.e., to gain tacit knowledge) in addition to formal schooling (i.e., to acquire conceptual or explicit knowledge). Third, this model fails to recognize a third facet of knowledge, affectual or emancipatory knowledge. Learning and knowledge creation should not be isolated from emotion, motivation, and perceived needs. Managing knowledge does not occur in a value-free context. Knowledge managers should always be aware of the values, beliefs, and guiding principles of organizational members that influence their willingness and decision to exert efforts in KM activities.

The 4I Framework of Organizational Learning

Crossan et al. (1999) observe that despite a growing popularity, there has been little convergence among organizational learning theories. This model, also referred to as the 4I framework, contains four process stages of organizational learning that consist of *intuiting, interpreting, integrating*, and *institutionalizing*. Each of the 4I process stages are conceptualized at the individual, group, and organizational levels. Together, the stages and levels and their interactions are explicated to improve organizational learning for the underlying purpose of strategic renewal in organizations.

In Crossan et al.'s (1999) model, the central proposition states that the four *I*s (intuiting, interpreting, integrating, and institutionalizing) are related in "feed-forward and feedback processes across the [organization] level." (p. 523). In the framework, intuiting and interpreting occur at the individual level. Intuiting refers to subconscious recognition of the pattern and/or possibilities that are implicit to a personal experience that leads to the development of tacit knowledge. For Crossan et al., interpreting is largely a cognitive act and progressively conscious act of explaining, through words and/or actions, a cognitive map with insights or ideas to one's self and to others as change from previous understanding and/or actions. As learning progresses from individual learning toward group learning, a process of integration begins to occur. Crossan et al. refer to the process of integrating as developing shared understanding among individuals and with the outcome of taking shared and coordinated actions through mutual adjustment. Institutionalizing refers to the process of ensuring that routinized actions occur as an organization strives to leverage the knowledge created by individuals or informal communities. This model provides a systematic and dynamic model of organizational learning that includes processes and levels, focusing on the flow of knowledge from implicit to explicit, and from the individual to the group. On the basis of their model, Crossan et al. propose that managers need to be aware of the facilitators and inhibitors of the four processes, paying particular attention to systems such as reward systems, information systems, resource allocation systems, strategic planning systems, and structure. However, no further suggestions were offered.

From the perspective of Yang's (2003) holistic theory, the foundation or premise generally represents, in part, an epistemological belief system. The holistic theory defines knowledge as a social construct with three distinctive and interrelated facets—conceptual, perceptual, and affectual knowledge. The knowledge facets provide visibility into an epistemological basis for the holistic theory that calls for acknowledging a dynamic interplay in the creation of knowledge between empirical–analytic, interpretive, and critical epistemologies (Yang, 2003). Crossan et al.'s (1999) 4I framework does not fully explicate the foundations of the framework with respect to highlighting epistemologies or knowledge facets. The framework does begin to illustrate the roles of explicit and implicit knowledge, but stops short of acknowledging an affectual or emancipatory facet.

Both frameworks, 4I model and the holistic theory, however, advance propositions related to learning processes. Crossan et al.'s (1999) intuiting process is closely related to gaining implicit knowledge at the individual level. Interpreting in the framework represents developing cognitive maps and is similar to conceptualization in the holistic theory. However, the interpreting process centers on the cognitive domain and the role of the affective domain and emancipatory knowledge equivalent is not defined or mentioned. Integration in Crossan et al.'s framework refers to shared understanding by group members that results in coherent, collective actions. This learning process reflects the dynamic relationships between the individual and the group. However, the holistic theory suggests that the integration of individual knowledge does not always occur in the cognitive and explicit domain but can also occur in the behavioral and implicit domains, through processes such as transferring knowledge hard to express into formal language and symbols, and emancipatory knowledge into its values and consequently change its critical knowledge. Likewise, both models incorporate the concepts embodied by Crossan et al.'s notion of the *institutionalizing* process but differ when moving beyond the conceptual, in the continued interplay of perceptual and affectual knowledge.

The major weakness of the 4I model is its failure to recognize the nature of knowledge. Because the 4I framework does not distinguish the three facets of knowledge and clarify its epistemological knowledge basis, it fails to capture some of the key organizational learning activities. For example, the holistic theory suggests that changing an organization's values and visions is a vital learning process and that it is critical knowledge that interacts with individuals' shared values and critical knowledge. Rules and procedures can be institutionalized but cannot guarantee the desired change and the coherence of individual values.

Information-Space Model

Boisot (1998) proposes that individual knowledge is the sum of our mental models and through these mental models we process data and information to bring about actions and change. Boisot contends that knowledge is essentially a set of patterns stored in the memory that helps us make sense of the world. He further categorizes knowledge along three dimensions of codification, abstraction, and diffusion. These three dimensions make up the information-space (I-Space) for capturing the distribution of knowledge in organizations. In terms of codification, knowledge is either codified or uncodified. Codified knowledge refers to the knowledge that is represented by language or other systems. Codified knowledge is easily transmittable from one human agent to another. On the contrary, uncodified knowledge is highly dependent on the implicit expertise of the human agent. The second dimension, abstraction, describes the extent to which knowledge is abstracted from the concrete and observable information. Knowledge with higher abstraction is believed to be constructed through building relationships of less abstract knowledge (Boisot, 1998). The third dimension is diffusion. This refers to the extent to which knowledge is available among human agents. Boisot suggests that organizations need to decide on their codification and abstraction strategies on the basis of their respective circumstances.

Boisot's (1998) three-dimensional I-Space model bears similarities with the holistic model. The codification dimension is similar to Yang's (2003) distinction between conceptual and perceptual knowledge, because conceptual knowledge can be easily codified by language or other systems and thus can be transmitted from one agent to another. On the other hand, perceptual or implicit knowledge is usually not verbalized or codified through other means. As regards the diffusion dimension, the holistic model elucidates three levels along this dimension: individual, group, and organization.

The holistic model proposes three dimensions of knowledge: conceptual, perceptual, and affectual. Boisot's (1998) model considers the explicit (codified) and implicit (uncodified) dimensions but does not consider the affectual dimension. Elements of the affect factor is recognized in his model as the perceptual and conceptual filters that influence what data and information human agents turn into knowledge. However, Boisot fails to accommodate these filters into his model of knowledge. The holistic model takes into consideration these filters and offers a third category of knowledge—affectual or emancipatory knowledge. This affectual knowledge is defined as the objectives and missions that guide our actions. In Boisot's model, the perceptual and conceptual filters are such knowledge that dictates what knowledge human agents take in and spread as well as what direction human actions take. The holistic model absorbs this affectual knowledge into the nature of knowledge, contrary to Boisot's model that externalizes these filters. The reason for internalizing the filters into the arena of knowledge is consistent with Boisot's definition of knowledge—a set of patterns stored in memory that helps us make sense of the world (Boisot, 1998). These filters as conceptualized by Boisot are previous patterns that exist in the human mind in understanding the world. When it comes to managing knowledge, leaving out the affectual dimension of knowledge may lead knowledge managers to focus too much on the technical aspects of knowledge—its level of abstraction, codification, and diffusion. The alignment or misalignment of these aspects of knowledge with the values and guiding principles of organizational members ultimately decides the effectiveness of KM.

Learning With Knowledge Cycle Model

A large portion of the past literature focuses on KM processes. Demerest (1997) builds a KM model that consists of four stages: knowledge construction, knowledge dissemination, knowledge use, and knowledge embodiment. Soliman and Spooner (2000) modify this model and proposed a five-stage KM chain. Their five stages are as follows: create knowledge, capture knowledge, organize knowledge, access knowledge, and use knowledge. Based on their models, Rowley (2001) suggests a model, the Learning with Knowledge Cycle (LK cycle), that consists of knowledge articulation, knowledge repository updating, knowledge access, knowledge use, and knowledge revision. According to Rowley, the cycle applies to both explicit and implicit knowledge, which means that these stages are equally applicable to both explicit and implicit knowledge.

These KM process models contribute to the conceptualization of the development of knowledge from the individual to the organizational level, but they offer only a macro picture of KM. Although they are useful in grouping different organizational activities into different KM processes, these models do not account for the dynamic relationships and interactions of the components of knowledge. Nor do they describe how knowledge moves from one stage to another. In practice, the interrelations among people or units often affect the learning process. The rigid segregation of the flow of actions and events into static stages is inadequate to direct practice effectively.

Rowley (2001) includes explicit and implicit knowledge in the LK model. However, she posits that both explicit and implicit knowledge go through the processes discussed in the model. This proposition puts an indiscriminate face on explicit and implicit facets. As implicit knowledge is something hard to formalize and communicate because of the familiarity that has yet to be articulated, it is difficult, if not impossible altogether, to make a convincing case that the evaluation, dissemination, use, and revision of such unarticulated knowledge can be done the same way for explicit knowledge. How can some unarticulated, unverbalized, and shapeless knowledge be measured and weighed? Different types of knowledge need to be managed differently. For example, a more social approach needs to be implemented when managing the tacit, not-yet-articulated knowledge, whereas a more codified approach should be used when managing explicit knowledge.

Another inadequacy is similar to that of Boisot's model. The affectual aspect of knowledge is not given sufficient attention. Rowley (2001) claims that the LK cycle model embraces the social construction of knowledge, but it actually follows a mechanical approach of disregarding the value orientation of individuals or interrelations of people, which is in the realm of the affect aspect of knowledge.

Holistic Comparison of KM Theories

Throughout this review of selected knowledge theories, several themes were found to be systemic across most theories reviewed. The themes include knowledge facets, knowledge conversion between knowledge facets, distinguishing organizational levels, and knowledge creation and learning processes. Not all theories contained these structures and this will be highlighted.

Knowledge Facets

The knowledge facets, when described, generally referred to the epistemological source of knowledge. As shown in Table 2, nearly all theories referenced or in a major way addressed the contribution of implicit and explicit knowledge as described in the review. Yang (2003) exclusively argued for the inclusion of critical knowledge facet as a vital holistic component of knowledge.

Table 2: A Comparison of KM Models—Epistemological Sources of Knowledge

KM Models and Proponents	Knowledge Facets and Dimensions		
	Practical (Implicit, Perceptual)	**Technical (Explicit, Conceptual)**	**Critical (Affectual, Emancipatory)**
Knowledge Creation Model (Nonaka & Takeuchi, 1995)	X	X	–
Knowledge Cycle Model (Demerest, 1997)	O	O	–
Information Space Model (Boisot, 1998)	X	X	–
4I Framework (Crossan, Lane, & White, 1999)	X	X	–
Holistic Theory (Yang, 2003)	X	X	X

Note: X = major focus; O = minor focus; – = not discussed.

Leveraging the critical (affectual) facet of learning, practitioners may be able to develop initiatives leading to productive and transformative learning environments, facilitate cultures that fully support knowledge sharing, and organizational participants that are more motivated to use new knowledge.

Knowledge Conversion Between Knowledge Facets

Knowledge conversion in KM literature is the movement of knowledge from one facet to another. As shown in Table 3, whether or how the theory discusses knowledge conversion is a reflection of the theory's focus on its dynamic nature in relation to knowledge facets and epistemological sources. For example, by arguing for the critical facet, Yang (2003) has illuminated exponentially more sources of learning in the conversion of knowledge.

Distinguishing Organizational Levels

HRD literature contains a long history of addressing organizational levels in theory and practice approaches. Several KM theories distinguished the influence of the organizational levels, shown in Table 4, in the knowledge development process. Yang (2003) addresses the organizational level in a unique way by defining the technical knowledge, practical knowledge, and critical knowledge as organizational knowledge amplified through their respective knowledge facets. Overall, how a knowledge theory manages the organizational levels appears to have significant bearing on the theory's structure.

Table 3: **A Comparison of KM Models—Dynamic Conversion Between Knowledge Facets**

KM Models	Knowledge Facet Conversion
Knowledge Creation Model	Four modes: socialization (from tacit to tacit knowledge), externalization (from tacit to explicit knowledge), combination (from explicit to explicit knowledge), and internalization (from explicit to tacit knowledge)
Knowledge Cycle Model	Does not address
Information Space Model	Alludes to implicit-to-explicit conversion in the codification stage of process
4I Framework	Not directly addressed, but the intuitive stage of process reflects implicit learning, whereas institutionalizing may refer to conversion to explicit from implicit
Holistic Theory of KM	Nine modes: socialization (implicit to implicit), formalization (implicit to explicit), routinization (explicit to implicit), systematization (explicit to explicit), orientation (explicit to critical), evaluation (critical to explicit) transformation (critical to critical), realization (critical to implicit), and deliberation (implicit to critical)

Table 4: **A Comparison of KM Models—Ontological Dimensions of Knowledge**

	Ontological Dimensions		
Theory	Individual	Group or Social	Organizational
Knowledge Creation Model	X	X	X
Knowledge Cycle Model	–	–	–
Information Space Model	–	–	–
4I Framework of Organizational Learning	X	X	X
Holistic Theory of KM	X	X	X

Note: X = major focus; – = not discussed.

Following this line of thinking, we have identified six modes of KM as discussed in the previous section.

Conclusion

This article examines milestone KM models from a holistic perspective. Most of the models reviewed in the article touch on but do not incorporate an important aspect of knowledge—affectual or critical knowledge. Most models do recognize the importance of organizational culture, relations among people or units, and other emotional factors, which demonstrate their agreement that this affectual facet of knowledge is indispensable because it describes people's or organizations' values, assumptions, and other knowledge that dictates the direction of their action. However, they do not integrate this facet into their KM models and so fail to provide a holistic account of what is happening and what ought to be. In addition, most existing KM models are at the conceptualization stage, and measurements and propositions have not undergone empirical examination. The next step is to generate indicators and measures from the KM models and subject them to empirical testing.

The holistic model of KM highlights the equal importance of the three facets of knowledge: conceptual, perceptual, and affectual. We think that explicit and implicit knowledge correspond to cognitive and behavioral domains that have received abundant consideration in past research, but the affectual knowledge is either totally neglected or externalized to be an environmental factor instead of something innate to a person or an organization's knowledge base. The practical implication of this view is that personal values or organizational culture is dealt with separately from rules, regulations, or experiences. However, in real life, personal values go hand in hand with a person's knowledge as a whole, and an organizational culture permeates every aspect of the organization's repertoire of knowledge. The artificial separation of affectual knowledge from others would lead to partial organizational solutions.

Within organizations, knowledge improvement initiatives may vary in several ways. For example, KM may be led by an exclusively titled knowledge manager empowered at the organizational level or by individuals at the group level within communities of practice, and to some degree just about everyone in an organization has a role to play in managing knowledge (Davenport & Prusak, 2000). In a review of 31 KM projects, Davenport and Prusak (2000) report differences between KM initiatives as some were centralized at the corporate level or decentralized in an organizational subunit, some were self-funded or funded as part of broader initiatives, and KM projects varied whether the program's aims are fundamental to an organization's existence or simply peripheral to the organization. However, all KM projects had in common identifiable knowledge objectives and a focus on knowledge outcomes rather than just data or information and have a clearly appointed leader managing them (Davenport & Prusak, 2000). Consequently, effective KM projects need to build a strong base of affectual knowledge that serves as a basis for creating, sharing, and using two other facets of knowledge. For example, existing studies have demonstrated that trust played a crucial role in the context of knowledge sharing (He, Fang, & Wei, 2009; Liao, 2009). In practice, HRD professionals need to first establish an organizational climate of trust and pay attention to affectual knowledge before a KM system is introduced. This may include designing and launching organization development interventions that assess organizational members' attitudes about knowledge, communicating and preparing organizational members for the advent of KM initiatives, and involving organizational members in developing measures and metrics that are meaningful to their contexts. KM or HRD practitioners may be able to develop initiatives that more fundamentally use the critical facet to produce more productive and transformative learning environments, facilitate cultures that fully support knowledge access and sharing, and organizational participants that are more motivated to use new knowledge.

Because of the theorized interconnected nature of the knowledge facets according to the holistic model, all programs to facilitate knowledge creation, sharing, and use would be affected by technical (conceptual), contextual (perceptual), and critical (affectual) facets regardless of whether KM leaders have awareness or take actions for each facet. Most of the KM models reviewed in this article included implicit and explicit facets, but no model includes the critical (affectual) facet except for the holistic model. KM and HRD professionals need to be cognizant of the interconnected nature of the three facets of knowledge and correspondingly adopt a holistic approach to leverage the dynamic interrelations among the three facts. For example, practices need to be created that could help organizational members systematize their actual experience in the organizational life into explicit knowledge that the whole organization can share. Same things need to happen to help organizational members align their beliefs and their actual experiences as well as with their espoused knowledge. KM and HRD professionals need to take advantage of the interconnections of the three facets of knowledge and facilitate the interpenetration of the three facts so that knowledge could be consistently transferred and maximally utilized.

Overall, the holistic model of KM combines the affectual aspect with the conceptual and perceptual aspects of knowledge and so offers a more complete picture for practitioners when dealing with organizational issues and challenges. Technical (conceptual), practical (perceptual), and critical (affectual) aspects all need to be considered at the same time.

References

Argote, L., McEvily, B., & Reagans, R. (2003). Managing knowledge in organizations: An integrative framework and review of emerging themes. *Management Science, 49*(4), 571-582.

Bloom, B. S., Englehart, M. D., Furst, E. J., Hill, W. H., & Krathwohl, D. R. (1956). *Taxonomy of educational objectives, Handbook I: The cognitive domain*. New York: David McKay.

Boisot, M. (1998). *Knowledge assets: Securing competitive advantage in the information economy*. Oxford, UK: Oxford University Press.

Cohen, W. M., & Levinthal, D. (1990). Absorptive capacity: A new perspective on learning and innovation. *Administrative Science Quarterly, 35*, 128-152.

Crossan, M. M., Lane, H. W., & White, R. E. (1999). An organizational learning frame-work: From intuition to institution. *Academy of Management Journal, 24*, 522-537.

Davenport, T. H., & Prusak, L. (2000). *Working knowledge.* Boston: Harvard Business School Press.

Demerest, M. (1997). Understanding knowledge management. *Journal of Long Range Planning, 30*(3), 374-384.

He, W., Fang, Y., & Wei, K. (2009). The role of trust in promoting organizational knowledge seeking using knowledge management systems: An empirical investiga-tion. *Journal of the American Society for Information Science & Technology, 60*(3), 526-537.

Liao, L. F. (2009). Knowledge-sharing in R&D departments: A social power and social exchange theory perspective. *International Journal of Human Resource Management, 19*(10), 1881-1895.

McLean, G., & McLean, L. (2001). If we can't define HRD in one country, how can we define it in an international context? *Human Resource Development International, 4*(3), 313-326.

Nonaka, I., & Takeuchi, H. (1995). *The knowledge-creating company: How Japanese companies create the dynamics of innovation.* New York: Oxford University Press.

Rowley, J. (2001). Knowledge management in pursuit of learning: The Learning with Knowledge Cycle. *Journal of Information Science, 27*(4), 227-237.

Soliman, F., & Spooner, K. (2000). Strategies for implementing knowledge manage-ment: Role of human resource management. *Journal of Knowledge Management, 4*(4), 337-345.

Tsoukas, H., & Vladimirou, E. (2001). What is organizational knowledge? *Journal of Management Studies, 38*, 973-993.

von Krogh, G., Ishijo, K., & Nonaka, I. (2000). *Enabling knowledge creation: How to unlock the mystery of tacit knowledge and release the power of innovation.* New York: Oxford University Press.

Yang, B. (2003). Toward a holistic theory of knowledge and adult learning. *Human Resource Development Review, 2*(2), 106-129.

Baiyin Yang (yangby@sem.tsinghua.edu.cn) is a professor and chair of Human Resources and Organizational Behavior at Tsinghua University (China). His research interests include adult and organizational learning, program planning and evaluation, power and influence tactics, cross-cultural studies of learning and organizational behavior, and quantitative research methods.

Wei Zheng (wzheng@niu.edu) is an assistant professor of HRD at Northern Illinois University. Her research interests lie in social dynamics of KM and innovation, strate-gic HRD, and international HRD.

Chris Viere (cviere@orgdevelopment.com) is a Ph.D. Candidate in HRD at the University of Minnesota. His research interests include KM, organizational learning, and the role of HRD in implementing and using information technology.

This refereed journal article is part of an entire issue on HRD's Role in Knowledge Management. For more information or to read other articles in the issue, see Gary N. McLean, Yonjoo Cho, and Eunsang Cho (2009). HRD's Role in Knowledge Manage-ment. (Special issue). *Advances in Developing Human Resources, 11* (3).

26

Knowledge Management Process: A Case Study of NTPC and POWERGRID

Pandey, K. N.

Abstract

The pre-dominance of power in infrastructure industry is a pivotal one and with the emergence of knowledge economy, it is imperative to use knowledge as an asset in power industry. Largely, knowledge-driven processes have occupied the central place in power industry as well. This necessitates that knowledge management is implemented in letter and spirit in this industry. Knowledge management processes are the most crucial part of knowledge management. This article outlines the knowledge management processes through an empirical study of the two leading power companies of India that is, NTPC and POWERGRID. The study has been carried out in these two companies by using secondary and primary data collected from various published sources besides from the companies under study.

Keywords

Knowledge management, knowledge processes, knowledge capitalization, NTPC Ltd., POWERGRID, public sector undertaking

Introduction

It is a universally acknowledged truth that knowledge economy has pervaded the entire world and 'Indian knowledge economy has definitely identified knowledge firms as the primary driver' (Richter and Banerjee, 2003, p. 2). The massive growth in information technology and knowledge transfer across the boundaries of the organization and eventually the nation has provided a major impetus to the phenomenon of globalization (Cheng, 2004; Green and Ruheler, 1995). Organizational knowledge sharing has gained recognition against this backdrop as one of the most important keys to performance in organization. Successful organizations today reward employees for seeking and sharing organizational knowledge, thereby creating a 'knowledge pull'—a grass root desire, among employees to tap into their organizations intellectual resources (Hauschild et al., 2001). The onus on organizations to develop and maintain effective knowledge sharing practices that can transcend organizational and natural boundaries is even more given the globalization of business today. Apropos this, it attains importance that the entire gamut of knowledge management at organizational level is studied in detail from six points of view (i) theoretical aspects of knowledge management; (ii) processes of knowledge management;

---

*Chief Manager (HRD), Power Grid Corporation of India Ltd, Gurgaon & Ph.D. Student, School of Management Studies, Indira Gandhi National Open University, New Delhi.

(iii) organizational and social aspects of knowledge management; (iv) managerial aspects of knowledge management; (v) technological aspects of knowledge management and (vi) application specific knowledge management (Schwartz, 2006). However, this article limits itself to the processes of knowledge only and that too in two leading power Public Sector Undertakings (PSUs) in India.

> In India, public sector organizations are those where more than 51 per cent of equity in a company rests with the central or state governments. The major objective of setting up public enterprises was to facilitate economic growth through industrialization and infrastructure development. It was envisioned that creation of such enterprises would result in income redistribution, employment generation, promotion of small scale and ancillary industries and balanced regional development. The private sector, on the other hand, is run for private profit and not controlled by the state. (Chawla and Joshi, 2010, p. 811).

NTPC and POWERGRID are two PSUs who are the industry leaders in the power generation and power transmission in India and because of these both of the companies have been selected for this study.

Rationale

This article aims at bringing the live phenomena of knowledge processes of NTPC and POWERGRID. It entails that the knowledge management processes of these two Indian power companies will provide the information and fact which can be further used by other power companies in India. Even professionals engaged in the knowledge management implementation will find it relevant and useful. The future researchers may refer to this case study for culling out general patterns which could be emulated by power industry as a whole, particularly in India.

Literature Survey

As an organization or for that matter, a society proceeds towards knowledge economy, they make their living from knowledge creation and knowledge application (Gottschalk, 2007). This movement entails the usage of knowledge in various forms, stages, situations and purposes. If we treat knowledge management as the chief driver of knowledge economy *tabula rasa*, we have to chart out various processes of knowledge management. The perusal of reading material, articles, books and research reports of various scholars including electronically available literature, knowledge management processes may be delineated under eight heads viz. knowledge creation, knowledge acquisition, knowledge collation, knowledge storage and use, knowledge dissemination, knowledge sharing, knowledge reuse and synthesis along with knowledge capitalization.

Knowledge Creation

The business transactions and activities create huge amount of data and information. In order to create value and remain in competitive advantageous position the firms have to create knowledge. 'Creating knowledge requires the existence of a person or group of people who come up with new ideas, new concepts, innovative product or process etc' (Ceptureanu and Ceptureanu, 2010, p. 150). 'Thus, knowledge creation involves a people dimension, technology dimension and the processes that link the people and technology' (Wickramasinghe, 2006, p. 333). Geisler and Wickramasinghe (2009) summarized this aspect when they narrated that 'two conceptual streams of thought have emerged that describe knowledge creation either as a people or technology centric process' (pp. 44–45). They further report that Nonaka's 'people-centric knowledge spiral' is the most widely used framework for knowledge creation through socialization, combination, externalization and internalization.

> It is almost an axiom that knowledge creation in firms lies at the heart of competitive advantage that 'firms learn', 'firms know' etc. have become common place expressions in much of the strategy and KM literature. However, it is not firms as such that learn and firms themselves do not process knowledge. So-called 'firm-knowledge' is composed of knowledge sets controlled by individual assets. (Foss and Mahnke, 2003 p. 86)

'Spender's people centric model' (Newell et al., 2002) corresponds with Nonaka's tacit knowledge which is part of SECI model proposed by Nonaka. Newell et al. have also quoted about Blacker's 'people-centric approach' which depicts that knowledge can exist in several forms (encoded, embedded, embodied, encultured, embrained). By looking at various people centric models and approach, we may infer that different organizations require different models and no single model can be quoted 'to fit all' kinds of firms.

In addition to people centric approach some researchers have concluded that 'technology-centric' approach may also be used by way of mechanistic method which enables knowledge discovery in databases through data mining tool. Fuller and Wilson (2006, p. 188–189) reported through their research that 'using case classification accuracy as the criteria neural networks have typically outperformed traditional parametric techniques (for example, discriminant analysis, logistic regression) as well as other non-parametric approaches (for example, various inductive learning systems such as ID3, C4.5, CART, etc.). This also takes care of creation of knowledge by using IF-THEN rules from trained feed-forward neural network used in classifiers. Neural network is basically a form of artificial intelligence in which a computer simulates the way human brain processes information. Possibly, this imposes limitations to neural network technique of knowledge creation and brings to the fore the centrality of the people centric approach'.

The latest research reported in the area of knowledge creation (Desouza and Paquette, 2011, p. 99) states that,

> [T]he creation of knowledge occurs in many dynamic forms. Most often, it is through humanistic means, such as formal training, living through new experiences, or talking with people who share similar interest. Technical mechanisms also assist in the knowledge creation process, such as knowledge management systems, data warehousing and data mining activities. Therefore, the significance of the employee and supporting knowledge management technologies has grown substantially over recent decades. Organizations now live (or die) by their ability to create knowledge, innovate and generate value with new knowledge.

Knowledge Acquisition

Knowledge acquisition is an activity which explores the possibility of finding expertise which should be acquired from outside through 'relationship with customers, suppliers, competitors and partners in co-operative ventures' (Probst et al., 2002). It means it is the prerequisite of knowledge acquisition to 'identify the required knowledge domains in alignment with the KM strategy, locate the source of this knowledge and acquire the required knowledge' (Shukla and Srinivasan, 2002, p. 41). It underlines the importance of the outside view which, 'is really a fresh view, which brings with it confidence that new order and sound logic can be applied through knowledge so that an organization can actually improve. Wherever the outside view comes from, it must be based on knowledge' (Mathews, 2000, p. 10). Of late, firms have been seen increasingly interested in inter-firm relations and want to develop proximity with outside world.

Martinez–Cavas et al. (2012, p. 64) have reported that 'the resource-based view of the firm points that intangible resources that are valuable, rare, imperfectly imitable and not substitutable in the long-term provide a competitive advantage for organizations'. They further state that this, 'knowledge-based view of the firm also asserts that more innovative firms must leverage their acquisition capabilities to update their knowledge capital constantly to match new environmental conditions'. With this in view, firms should have their skills and ability through repeated interaction to reorganize and evaluate the pertinent external knowledge.

Business intelligence related technical tools can help companies in acquiring knowledge from other companies besides browsing the World Wide Web and Google Scholar and Wikipedia which have become axiomatic these days. Environmental scanning is also required by companies to devise new goals and strategies. However, apropos knowledge management the Competitive Intelligence becomes more useful. Parker and Nitse (2006, p. 44) have brought to the fore this fact more clearly when they write that 'Competitive Intelligence' (CI) is a process for gathering usable knowledge about the external business environment and turning it into the intelligence required for tactical on strategic decisions. The two are strongly connected because gathered CI has no long-term value unless an effective KM process is in place to turn the information into something usable.

Knowledge Collation

Collation stands for comparison and analysis of two or more sources of information. Its connotations cover calibration also because calibration involves comparing some measurement against a given standard. The codification and classification of the knowledge objects, synthesizing them, making them meaningful and relevant for the target group and adopting the knowledge to the 'firm-specific' needs form the objectives of collation (Shukla and Srinivasan, 2002). Knowledge collation is a must before it is relegated to repositories. In fact, two major categories—critical and not-critical should be ideally created before the nuances of knowledge collation are brought into play. The personnel who are responsible for collation or systems of collation should have an 'awareness of organizational challenges' (Martins and Meyer, 2012).

Knowledge management processes require a structured, 'coordinated system for managing knowledge effectively' (Xu and Wang, 2006). This is required in both forms of knowledge—tacit and explicit. 'While explicit knowledge can be identified more easily, and systems and procedures can be developed to deal with it, for example through feedback and training, dealing with tacit knowledge poses a greater challenge' (Goldsmith and Pillai, 2006, p. 314). These researchers offer a solution to these problems by suggesting that for collation of knowledge two types of memories—trans-active and mechanistic may be used.

Trans-active memory refers to the set of individual memory systems in combination with their inter-communications, trans-active memory exists as a property of a group as group members share their memories through their interactions with each other and with external memory devices. *Mechanistic memory* refers to information accessed from mechanical systems. A part of trans-active memory can be conceptualized as overlapping with tacit knowledge. Codifying such trans-active memory and systematizing it will enable the creation of inter-active procedures that could assess the level of miscalibration of users. (Goldsmith and Pillai, 2006, p. 314)

Knowledge Storage and Use

Once knowledge has been created, acquired or collated, it is to be stored in repositories so that individuals, groups and organization can have access to it.

> Empirical studies have shown that while organizations create knowledge and learn, they also forget (i.e. do not remember or lose track of the required knowledge). Thus the storage, organization and retrieval of organizational knowledge, also referred to as organizational memory, constitute an important aspect of effective organizational knowledge management. (Gottschalk, 2007, p. 33)

Knowledge storage may be done in a hard copy form and electronically enabled tools, both. The documents in hard copy form may include 'memos, reports, presentations, articles and so forth and put it into a repository where it can be easily stored and retrieved' (Davenport and Prusak, 2000, p. 146). These documented knowledge are 'to be integrated in the natural IT organizational environment' (Levy, 2011, p. 588). Researchers (Allameh, et al., 2011, p. 1214) have concluded that,

> [N]ew creating knowledge is not enough and mechanisms are needed to store acquired knowledge and retrieve it when needed. The concept of organizational memory is a great solution in this regard. Organizational memory includes knowledge residing in various component forms that may include written documentation, structured information stored in electronic databases, codified human knowledge stored in expert systems, documented organization procedures and processes and tacit knowledge acquired by individuals and network of individuals.

In this stage, the organization should classify the filtered knowledge and add it to the organizational memory (Benbya et. al., 2004, p. 212).

For storage and retrieval perspective, the repositories may be classified into three main categories— (i) external knowledge, (ii) structured internal knowledge and (iii) informed internal knowledge (Davenport and Prusak, 2000). Some of the aspects of these repositories should be supported by 'an infrastructure capable of supporting the creation and maintenance (.......) and an environment that enables the cultivation and facilitation of knowledge sharing and organizational learning' (Al-Hawamadeh, 2005, p. 22). Documentary repository becomes handy in this regard because it is computer based application for storing and retrieving documents in an organized way. It is generally equipped with a search engine that uses keyword matching and similar techniques to locate and retrieve documents of potential interest to users. Storing knowledge may also be done through a number of other means such as knowledge portal, learning reviews, knowledge cafes, after action reviews, document libraries knowledge clusters, expert locator, knowledge bases (Wikis), etc. Storage in the electronic memory provides unlimited storage capacity and the facility of digitalization.

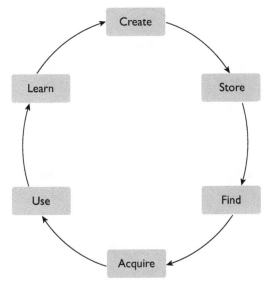

Figure 1. The Knowledge Life Cycle
Source: Wikipedia.

The greater aim of knowledge storage is, in fact, its use in organization by personnel who require knowledge and want it at the right time and at the right place. In present time, the application and utilization of knowledge is the sole purpose of knowledge management so that 'reinvention of wheel' could be avoided and time and cost could be saved. The knowledge life cycle depicts 'use' of knowledge prominently as elaborated in Figure 1.

Some of the techniques used by personnel while applying knowledge include peer assist, communities of practices (CoPs), blogs, advanced search, mentor–mentee, apprenticeship, etc. Many of the firms apply 'pull technique' and 'push technique' also for the use of knowledge. No matter how many resources an organization forms into creating highly sophisticated knowledge systems, the question looms: will people use them? For any knowledge base or intranet to draw users, it has got to be 'better' at helping them find information than the systems and networks with which they are already comfortable and familiar. Having a solid framework and processes for making organizational knowledge available will ultimately ensure that people will use the information (Bukowitz and Williams, 1999, p. 75; O'Dell, 2004, pp. 12–13) concludes in her research through a reified figure as reproduced below that 'Knowledge Management is successful when information and knowledge move through the stages in future and are actually used.' This reification has been delineated in Figure 2.

Knowledge Dissemination

Knowledge dissemination has been known by various terms such as knowledge translation, knowledge transfer and knowledge exchange. It has been defined as the transfer of knowledge within and across

Figure 2.
Source: O'Dell, C. (2004).

settings, with the expectation that the knowledge will be 'used' conceptually (as learning, enlightenment, or acquisition of new perspectives or attitude) or instrumentally, (in the form of modified or new practices). There are, however, those who see dissemination as having other legitimate outcomes. Some of these outcomes include: (i) increased awareness; (ii) ability to make informed choices among alternatives; and (iii) the exchange of information; materials or perspectives. Dissemination is delivering and receiving of knowledge by engaging an individual in the process of transfer of best practices, lessons learned, innovations made or improved processes, etc., within the context of an organization. The relationship of key elements of dissemination leading to knowledge utilization as propagated by Asian Development Bank (2009) is depicted in Figure 3.

The knowledge dissemination may be done through using information and communication technologies, human based social interactions and systems or through pathways and media based means and library means.

Knowledge Sharing

Knowledge sharing is that process which enables the knowledge held in individuals or groups to be transferred to others in an organization so that it could be applied for the improvement or creation of new products, services and processes (Van den Hooff and Ridder, 2004). The knowledge sharing process has been categorized into two main types of usage 'personal advice usage' and 'electronic document usage' (Haas and Hansen, 2007). The personal advice usage includes the direct contact between individuals

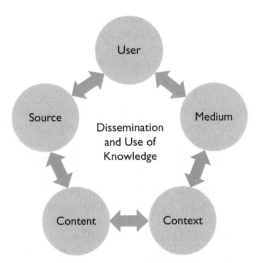

Figure 3. Dissemination and Use of Knowledge
Source: Asian Development Bank (2009).

when they meet, by phone or via e-mail, whereas electronic document usage covers sharing of electronic documents which can be used as stand-alone resources. However, sharing as a process entails 'the act of placing knowledge by one at the disposition of others. Its ramifications include that it is a voluntary effort through which one gives and receives knowledge and develops a continuity of previous knowledge to the new knowledge which is to be innovated' (Camelo-Ordaz et al., 2011). Knowledge sharing has also been depicted as 'solicited knowledge sharing' and 'voluntary knowledge sharing' (Teng and Song, 2011). The environmental antecedents to knowledge sharing such as culture, structures and technology may vary as per the choice of solicited or voluntary types.

It has also been argued that explicit knowledge can be shared easily whereas tacit knowledge is 'inherently difficult to share because it is socially embedded' and sticky (Osterloch and Frey, 2000). In fact, explicit knowledge because of its being already documented can be shared without any problem. However, tacit knowledge requires the help of mentor–mentee, apprenticeship, person-to-person contact, face-to-face communication, deputizing and other factors such as trust, respect and friendship in order to be shared. Two important tools—namely, narrative and story have been found to be of immense help in sharing the tacit knowledge (Connell, 2006; Snowden, 2006). A narrative is an account of connected events. It may also be said that it is the part of a fictional work that tells the story, as distinct from the dialogue. Snowden (2006, p. 680) has stated that, 'One of the important aspects of narrative and one of the reasons it works is that it creates a higher resonance of new concepts of ideas with existing patterns than exist in the human mind'. The narrative explains three aspects of knowledge—information flow, namely, abstraction, codification and diffusion. It is because of these properties that narratives become so handy for sharing the tacit knowledge. Narratives have also been found as 'sense-making devices' presenting holistic practices and their context.

In juxtaposition to narrative,

[S]tories can be seen as one of the ways in which we can encode data about our environment, both personal and organizational. A particular strength of storytelling for knowledge management lies in its capacity not only to represent such sets of data, but also to offer some insights into the complex interrelationships between such data elements. In an organizational context, these interrelationships might help us to make sense of the organization (Connell, 2006, p. 721).

A distinction has been drawn between 'the notion of narratives and the concept of story by taking "story" as the more specific and narrative as the basic and more general notion. This means that all stories are narratives but not all narratives are stories' (Geiger and Schreyogg, 2012, p. 99).

'Knowledge Translation' is yet another tool which is gaining momentum for sharing of knowledge especially in Canada in the realm of clinical discourse. Some define the sharing of experiential knowledge as 'Knowledge management' and the sharing of research, facts and findings as 'knowledge transfer', coupled with *translation*, which includes exchange, brokering, interaction, or, mobilization.

Knowledge mobilization is putting available knowledge into active service to benefit society. It may be knowledge that has been gathered through systematic study or through experience. Both the research knowledge and experiential wisdom are worth sharing to the benefit of others. It is an obligation and a right to share and to have access to beneficial knowledge.

Enablers and Barriers to Knowledge Sharing

At this juncture, it is pertinent to have a look at the enablers and barriers to knowledge sharing. A number of scholars have delved in detail in these two areas. First, an attempt has been made to delineate the enablers. Enablers can be useful on two levels—individual and organizational. At individual level emotional state poised towards knowledge sharing becomes very important. The pride moves an individual towards eagerness and willingness both to share his or her knowledge. The hubristic pride enables an individual 'to share out of the wish (—) for the collective interest' (Williams and De Steno, 2008). 'It implicitly assumes a utopian view of benevolent co-operators who voluntarily give up personal knowledge without appropriate award' (Lam and Ford, 2010, p. 52). Motivation plays a pivotal role in knowledge sharing. Hedonic and extrinsic motivators reinforce the propensity for knowledge sharing. Hedonic motivator inculcates individual knowledge sharing whereas extrinsic can help the group or organization to part with the tacit knowledge.

In case of organization the knowledge sharing culture is required. Training and career progression are to be ensured by an organization to exhort the personnel to share the knowledge. Other human resource management related factors such as incentive, reward and recognition, job-rotation, job-shadowing, acknowledging the contribution of the individual's normative attitude towards sharing are to be placed properly. Organizations can also take recourse to formation of cross-functional teams by bringing expert and knowledgeable personnel together for a better understanding of the know-how and skill of others. 'Cross-functional co-operation promotes knowledge sharing, because it is associated with the perception of individuals on the collective use of the shared knowledge in pursuing common interest of the team' (Ghobadi and D'Ambra, 2012, P. 286). Contextual factors at the organizational level such as 'trust', management support and learning are equally required to enable people to share their knowledge. An organization may also have to form 'Expert networks' to function as catalyst on the demand-side that is, individual's knowledge seeking behaviour of people (King, 2006).

The barriers to knowledge sharing emanate from cultural differences and problems related with communication. In a path breaking study Lindsey (2006, P. 503) prepared an exhaustive list of barriers to knowledge sharing which is depicted in Annexure-I.

In addition to the above some barriers such as 'no physical proximity to colleagues', 'unusability of knowledge', 'perception of knowledge as power', 'unawareness about who knows the relevant knowledge' and 'thought to be perceived as fool' are also reported which hinder the knowledge sharing (Cabrera and Cabrera, 2002; McLaughlin et al., 2008). It is to be pointed out here that if the knowledge-sharing context undergoes a change, the barriers to knowledge sharing may also change.

Knowledge Reuse and Synthesis

Knowledge reuse stands for use of knowledge more than once. It entails that it is such a process by which 'an entity is able to locate and use shared knowledge' (Majchrzak et al., 2004) Oshri (2006, P.487) defines knowledge reuse as 'processes [which] emphasize the centrality of knowledge within an organization by aligning information systems and communication technologies with human activity and organizational mechanisms, such as learning processes and organizational structures'. There are four types of reuses of knowledge viz. 'shared work producers'; 'shared work practitioners'; 'expertise-seeking novices'; and 'secondary knowledge miners'. Besides this the process of knowledge includes six stages: (i) approach for reuse; (ii) search for reusable ideas; (iii) scanning the reusable ideas; (iv) evaluating reusable ideas; (v) conducting the in-depth analysis of reusable ideas and selecting one which is most appropriate and; (vi) use the idea (Majchrzak, et al., 2004).

> There are three major roles in the knowledge reuse process: *Knowledge producer* – the originator and documenter of knowledge, who records explicit knowledge or makes tacit knowledge explicit, *knowledge intermediary*— who prepares knowledge for reuse by eliciting it, indexing it, summarizing it, sanitizing it, packaging it, and who performs various roles in dissemination and facilitation, and *knowledge consumer*—the knowledge reuser, who retrieves the knowledge content and applies it in some way (Markus, 2001, P. 61).

In addition to these the knowledge reusers have to apply social mining for discovering patterns and codifying reusable experiences (Akoumianakis, 2009).

In order to ensure reuse of knowledge the same is to be synthesized in repositories of the organization. Different types of knowledge reusers perceive the role of repositories in different ways therefore the synthesis becomes equally important apropos knowledge.

> The knowledge synthesis is a social as well as an individual process-sharing. Tacit knowledge requires individuals to share their personal beliefs about a situation with others. At that point of sharing, justification becomes public. Each individual is faced with the tremendous challenge of justifying his or her beliefs in front of others—and it is this need for justification, explanation, persuasion and human connection that makes knowledge synthesis a highly fragile process. (Vat, 2006, P. 533)

The challenge is how to design the infrastructure to enable spontaneous knowledge capture and transfer so as to turn the scattered diverse knowledge into well structured knowledge for reuse. Knowledge management architecture accommodating individual learning, organizational learning and intellectual property management put together may offer a viable solution to this conundrum.

The technique of building a 'knowledge tree' which includes all knowledge subjects, and explicitly marking the branches to be retained and those to be pruned is said to be an important practice in synthesis of knowledge. Finally, knowledge is to be integrated into routines and business processes of the organization as it makes its reuse more facilitating. Levy (2011, p. 588) has mentioned it succinctly when she says that,

> The knowledge documented is to be integrated in the natural IT organizational environment. Yet, it was found to be very convenient, when such infrastructure was not available to document the information and knowledge using a WIKI system. The WIKI's structure enables usage of a template, enabling light as well as tight connections between the items documented, and is suitable for integration within other existing intranet sites, as each page is a unique URL. Furthermore, the structure of WIKI suits the nature of the knowledge documented, as it does not cover all topics, rather the more important ones, forming a net with holes in between.

Knowledge Capitalization

In the twenty-first century, economic and social development depends increasingly on knowledge rather than labour and capital.

> The most common denominator of the changing economic structure is a shift away from an economy driven and governed by material inputs into the productive process and its organization, toward an economy in which the transformations of productive and distributive processes are increasingly determined by symbolic or knowledge based inputs. (Stehr, 2005, pp. 124–125)

Capitalization, especially of knowledge has become even more urgent in the present financial and economic crisis. It stands for taking the 'chance to gain advantage' from existing knowledge of a firm. The point of focus today is knowledge and service production with more emphasis being laid on knowledge capital. This capitalization of knowledge stimulates key stakeholders to transform individual and institutional experience and knowledge into capital which can be used in future.

Machlup (2005, p. 46) has pondered over the issue of knowledge capitalization in terms of stock when he states that,

> A fundamental distinction is commonly made between stocks and flows, usually with reference to goods, to capital funds, to money. The distinction also applies to knowledge. At any moment of time, there is a stock of knowledge; during any period of time there is a flow of knowledge.

So far as this stock is concerned, it includes the 'recorded knowledge' [Explicit] & 'knowledge in the mind' [Tacit]. 'Knowledge as an economic good exhibits major limitations in terms of radical uncertainty, non-appropriability and non-rivalry in use. Much economic analysis has explored the implications with respect to tradability of knowledge' (Antonelli and Teubal, 2010, p. 98). The capitalization of knowledge is usually analyzed by taking recourse to external socio-economic factors.

The process of knowledge capitalization involves the selling or producing economic added value in the knowledge for which it must be completely understandable and reproducible by both the inventor or others. Viale (2010, p. 31) narrates the process of capitalization in his seminal work by stating that,

> The generation of economic value can be said to be 'direct' when one sells the knowledge for some financial, material or behavioural good. The generation of economic value is considered 'indirect' when it allows the production of some material or service goods that are sold on market. The direct mode comprises the role of personal know-how, such as in the case of a plumber or of a sports instructor. It also comprises the sale of intellectual property, as in the case of patents, copyrights or teaching. The indirect mode comprises the ways in which organizational, declarative or procedural knowledge is embodied in goods or services. The economic return in both cases can be financial (for example, cash), material (for example, the exchange of consumer goods) or behaviour (for example, the exchange of personal services.

Venture capital is a concrete example of 'knowledge-driven capitalization of knowledge' because it is a capital which is invested in a business project which involves large element of risk that can be taken care of by knowledgeable experts because it is a capital provided to early-stage, high potential, high risk, growth oriented and start-up companies (Ruhnka and Young, 1987). True private equity investments began to emerge in United States when knowledge economy started emerging (Ante, 2008). This was further strengthened apropos knowledge process of Law firms (Austin, 2010). It shows that knowledge capitalization is an important and probably the end process of knowledge management.

Knowledge Audit

A great body of current Knowledge Management literature refers to the Knowledge Audit as the very first and possibly the most important step of a knowledge management strategy. It entails the fit of knowledge management strategy with overall business strategy of the company. Knowledge management audit should follow normal audit pattern thereafter.

> The knowledge audit serves to help the audited unit to determine if it 'knows what it knows' and 'knows what it doesn't know' about its existing knowledge state. It will also help it to unearth what it should know to better leverage knowledge for business and competitive advantage. This enlightenment sets the agenda for the knowledge management initiative, programme and implementation. (Paramasivan, 2003, p. 499)

Cases

NTPC: A Company profile (Adapted from NTPC website ntpc.co.in)

India's largest power company, National Thermal Power Corporation (NTPC) was set up in 1975 to accelerate power development in India. A public sector undertaking of the Government of India, it is one of the pioneers in power generation in India. NTPC is emerging as a diversified power major with presence in the entire value chain of the power generation business. NTPC was ranked 341st in the 2010, Forbes Global 2000' ranking of the World's biggest companies. NTPC became a Maharatna company in May 2010, one of the only few companies to be awarded this status.

Be in the generating capacity or plant performance or operational efficiency, NTPC's Installed Capacity and performance depicts the company's outstanding performance across a number of parameters.

	No. of Plants	Capacity (MW)
NTPC Owned		
Coal	16	30,855
Gas/Liquid Fuel	7	3,955
Total	23	34,810
Owned by JVs		
Coal & Gas	7	4,364
Total	30	39,174

NTPC has demonstrated the highest ever growth in the history and the same has been briefly touched upon a few highlights:

1. 2,820 MW commissioned in 2011–2012, the highest ever in a single year, surpassing the previous year's capacity addition record of 2,490 MW.
2. 9,610 MW added during 11th Plan period ending March 2012, exceeding the Plan target.
3. Highest ever capex of ₹ 159.94 billion in 2011–2012 with group capex of ₹ 199.73 billion.
4. 2,160 MW added in the first quarter of 2012–2013.
5. 6,870 MW added in the past two years which is almost 20 per cent of the total capacity added since inception of NTPC.
6. Three 660 MW Super Critical Units commissioned and declared commercial at Sipat, the higher efficiency reduces CO_2 emissions substantially.
7. 7,041 MW of work awarded since January 2012.
8. 16,000 MW under construction.

Strong Operational Performance and Challenges

Operating one of the largest fleets in the world consisting of 120 units (only NTPC units) on commercial operation, Company's operational excellence is at par with world standards with high levels of capacity utilization and reliability through use of latest technologies and best practices. Some of the operational highlights of 2011–2012 are:

1. 6 out of 15 coal stations had Plant Load Factor (PLF) of over 90 per cent.
2. 27.4 per cent share of NTPC group in total power generated in India, thus maintaining leadership position in the power sector.
3. 85 per cent PLF achieved by the coal based stations as against the national average of 73.32 per cent.
4. 89.5 per cent availability factor.

NTPC is committed to bring about continuous improvement in generation efficiency to scale still higher levels of performance.

Sound Financials

NTPC's robust growth and operational excellence translate into sound financials. Prudent management of financial resources ensures that the fundamentals of the company remain strong and are leveraged for further growth and higher returns. Some of the financial highlights for the year 2011–2012 are:

1. Total revenue crossed ₹ 600 billion reaching ₹ 648.3065 billion, an increase of about 13 per cent over 2010–2011.
2. The net profit increased and stood at ₹ 92.2373 billion.
3. Paying highest ever dividend of 40 per cent.
4. Ranked 5th among all the listed companies in terms of PAT for 2011–2012.
5. Resounding success in raising USD 500 million from the international bond market which was oversubscribed more than five times with participation of over 200 investors, indicating robust confidence in NTPC among the international investors.

The Momentum Gets Stronger in 2012–2013

The overall growth and excellence achieved in the year 2011–2012 has led NTPC into still higher gear of performance as demonstrated in the results during the first quarter of year 2012–2013 as compared with the corresponding quarter of the year 2011–2012. Some of the highlights are:

1. Commissioned 2,160 MW capacity (NTPC Group).
2. Generation growth has been 7.80 per cent as against all India growth of 6.40 per cent.
3. Total revenue increased by 11 per cent to ₹ 168.45 billion.
4. Profit After Tax increased by 20 per cent to ₹ 24.99 billion.
5. Capex increased by 83 per cent to ₹ 39.78 billion.

During the year 2012–2013, NTPC Group has declared 2,320 MW capacity on commercial operation.

Thus, despite the numerous challenges and hardships being faced by the economy and the sector, NTPC is marching ahead with strong results with the help of well conceived strategies.

POWERGRID: At a glance (Adapted from POWERGRID website www.powergridindia.com)

Power Grid Corporation of India Limited (POWERGRID), the Central Transmission Utility (CTU) of India, was incorporated on October 23, 1989 under the Companies Act, 1956. POWERGRID was conferred the coveted *Navratna* status by the Government of India in May 2008 in recognition of its contribution to the Indian power sector and *numero uno* in transmission of power in country and the potential to become a global power major.

POWERGRID started its commercial operation in 1992–1993. The transmission assets along with manpower posted in the transmission system of various Central/Central-State Joint Venture Organizations such as NTPC, NHPC, NEEPCO, NLC, NPC, THDC, SJVNL, etc. were transferred to POWERGRID in phased manner till 1994. The RLDCs transferred from Central Electricity Authority (1994 to 1996) were modernized and National Load Despatch Centre (NLDC) established by 2009, (presently transferred to POSOCO), a fully owned subsidiary of POWERGRID.

The growth of the Company may be seen in terms of lifelong turn-over, profit, assets and manpower of the ratio as given below beginning 1992–1993 up to 20.10.2011:

	1992–1993	2010–2011	Growth in %
Line length (ckt. km.)	22228	82335	370%
Turnover (Rupees in billions)	6.34	91.00	1335%
Profit (Rupees in billions)	2.37	26.97	1037%
Assets (Rupees in billions)	35.21	593.52	1330%
Manpower (Personnel)	61.67	97.75	58%

On amalgamation of seven companies with different culture, different rules and regulations which metamorphosed into one culture that is, POWERGRID culture with one set of rules and regulations for all employees. They have not lost even a single man day since their inception and they have been making profit also since beginning. This situation placed them in a unique position which has also manifested itself in our evolution in various areas of operation.

In the two decades of its existence, POWERGRID has scaled up its transmission network manifold to cater to the increased generation capacity addition. The company has established a transmission network of about 95,846 ckt. km and 157 substations having more than 1,44,303 MVA of transformation capacity. Compare this with POWERGRID at the onset of its commercial business in 1992–1993 operating 22,220 circuit km and 42 substations having transformation capacity of 12,200 MVA. POWERGRID has maintained its gigantic transmission network at an average liability of 99.94 per cent comparable to the best international standards.

Such outstanding track record has given an impetus to POWERGRID's financial as well. In FY 2011–2012, POWERGRID achieved a turnover of ₹ 107.85 billion and a net profit of ₹ 32.55 billion, an increase of 19 per cent and 21 per cent respectively over the previous year. In order to bolster revenue streams and to remain a financially progressive organization in emerging market conditions, POWERGRID has diversified into synergetic businesses such as consultancy assignments at the national and international levels in transmission, distribution, telecom, etc.

The uneven distribution of energy resources in the country has necessitated development of a strong National Grid. Towards this, a perspective transmission plan has been evolved by POWERGRID for strengthening the regional grids and to enhance the inter-regional power transfer capacity of National Grid presently. National Grid with an inter-regional power transfer capacity of about 28,000 MW has already been established and the company plans to enhance the inter-regional power transmission capacity to 32,200 MW by March 2013.

POWERGRID has undertaken several technological innovations aimed at conserving Right-of-Way (ROW), minimizing impact on natural resources and human habitat and cost effectiveness in evacuation of power from the future generation projects. Having established the 765kV AC in the country, the company has taken leadership initiative to develop 1200kV system, the highest in the world, indigenously. A 1200kV UHVAC test station along with a 1200kV test line is being established at Bina in Madhya Pradesh as a collaborative effort with equipment manufacturers, for indigenous development of 1200kV equipments in India. Towards induction of the next voltage level in HVDC, POWERGRID has already started implementation of 800kV, 6000MW HVDC Bi-pole line from north-eastern region to northern region (Agra), which shall be the first of its kind (+800kV HVDC line) having the largest power carrying capacity and transmitting power over a distance of more than 2,000 km. These are pioneering initiatives even globally.

POWERGRID diversified into telecom business by leveraging the country wide transmission infrastructure and has established all India Broadband Telecom network of about 25,000 km with reliability of 99.99 per cent. Expansion is in progress for another 33,000 km. POWERGRID is the only service provider in the country having pan India overhead optic fibre network on its extra high voltage transmission lines. The network covers over 200 cities and towns providing connectivity to all metros, major cities and towns including remote areas of Jammu and Kashmir and north-eastern states. POWERGRID is also in the process of implementing state-of-the-art Multi Protocol Label Switching (MPLS) enabled network across the country.

Objective

The objectives of the study are twofold: (i) to delineate the processes of knowledge management in NTPC and POWERGRID, and (ii) to find out the tools that are enabling the knowledge management processes in these two companies to come into being and getting strengthened besides creating 'ripple effect'.

Methodology

In this study, we have depended on the classification of knowledge management aspects by Schwartz (2006) and Knowledge Management Assessment Tool published by American Productivity and Quality Center & Arthur Anderson Consulting (1995) for narrowing at knowledge management processes. Primary data and secondary data in case of NTPC and POWERGRID were collected for analysis. While studying knowledge management processes in NTPC and POWERGRID, the observation and interview were used as research tools. In case of NTPC the 'Knowledge Management Implementation in NTPC: an Indian PSU' (Goel et al., 2010) and 'A Study of Knowledge Management Practices and Organizational Citizenship Behaviour in NTPC' by George (2012) were taken as repositories of secondary data.

Since this researcher is an executive in POWERGRID and that too in Knowledge Management Cell itself 'observation' as a tool of data collection was used more intentionally because it 'entails systematic noting and recording of events, behaviour and artifacts (objects) in the social setting chosen for study' (Marshall and Rossman, 2006, p. 98). The focus group interview of the team for knowledge management in NTPC and members of Task Force for Implementation of Knowledge Management in POWERGRID respectively was conducted because it is 'often used for concept screening and refinement' (Zikmund, 2003) besides structured interviews since 'structured interviews are those conducted when it is known at the outset what information is needed' (Sekaran and Bongie, 2010, p. 188). The secondary data sources were also used while studying NTPC and POWERGRID. The methodology has got an exploratory tinge. The case study research method was opted because it is 'an enquiry that investigates a contemporary phenomenon within its real life context' (Yin, 2003, p. 13) and it delineates 'a human activity embedded in the real world' (Gillham, 2005, p. 1). Woodside (2010) opines that case study method provides 'the nuance necessary for capturing the thinking/doing process'. This method was also taken recourse to because NTPC and POWERGRID are in the industry of power and thus 'generalization takes place in the minds of reader/consumer of the case study' (McLeod, 2010, p. 35).

Analysis and Results

The creation of knowledge in NTPC and POWERGRID has been through Research & Development Department of NTPC and Technology Development Department of POWERGRID. The creation of tacit knowledge has been taking place in the minds of their personnel which get posted in the knowledge management portal under LAKSHYA in NTPC and Knowledge Bank in POWERGRID. Both of the companies have been using knowledge management technology through information and communication technology tools. So far as the acquisition of knowledge is concerned, the two companies under study have been found to take benefit of their networking with suppliers, stakeholders, vendors, customers, regulators and power traders. So far as the collation of knowledge nuggets is concerned, NTPC and POWERGRID are undertaking this exercise by maintaining and updating their knowledge management portals.

The storage of knowledge is being done in the repositories, databases, electronic devices and libraries by both NTPC and POWERGRID. Executives in NTPC are increasingly using 'SAP System which provides a provision of knowledge management also. NTPC considers its KM Portal as the backbone of the KM System and helps the usage of knowledge throughout the Company in a big way.' (George, 2012). The usage of knowledge is having progressive and increasing trends in POWERGRID as well. POWERGRID has got the task to 'Share—Implement and maintain knowledge sharing systems on KM Portal (like groupware, bulletin boards, meetings, etc.) and disseminate (to the relevant target groups)' (POWERGRID, 2010).

The dissemination of knowledge in NTPC and POWERGRID is taking place through their KM portals, leaflets, various publications and house journals. POWERGRID has published its knowledge maps & matrices (POWERGRID, 2011) NTPC has been disseminated knowledge through their 'Domains of Operation & Maintenance, Engineering, Corporate Planning, Business Excellence, Commercial, Consultancy, Environment as utilization and afforestation, IT, Materials & Contract, Medical & Health Services, Project Construction & Erection, R&D, R&M, R&R & CSR, Safety, Vigilance & Finance' (NTPC, Lakshya accessed on 16.10.2012). The dissemination of tacit knowledge in these companies is ensured through various training programmes, workshops, seminars, video conferencing, email and other mimeographs of seminars, etc. The sharing of knowledge in these companies is ensured through mentor–mentee programmes, cross functional teams, inter-departmental committees, project teams, induction training and project completion reports.

The reuse of knowledge has been the mainstay of NTPC and POWERGRID as they plan and expeditiously implement Power projects by using this process NTPC and POWERGRID both have formed various (CoPs) along its their business verticals of Operation & Maintenance of transmission assets, Project Management, Grid Management, Telecom and Consultancy and the business enablers of Human Resource Management, Finance & Information Technology. These CoPs are ensuring the reuse of knowledge and in this field, POWERGRID is in leading position. However, the reuse of knowledge in both of these companies has not reached the maturity stage.

The capitalization of knowledge in POWERGRID is only in its policy as depicted in their Policy Manual which reads 'Monitor usage, assess/measure the benefits of the knowledge management in terms of the specified knowledge goals, get feedback, review and renew the knowledge bases (including identification of new knowledge to be captured), and embed knowledge into the organization's value creating activities (services and/or information).' (POWERGRID, 2010). However, NTPC has also finalized its policy in this area but did not publicize it.

The knowledge audit is an effort to understand where an organization stands in terms of knowledge management and its knowledge assets. 'Knowledge audit assesses what knowledge assets are possessed by a specific organization. By knowing what knowledge is possessed, it is possible to find the most effective method of storage and disseminations' (Liebowitz, 2000). Ideally, it should take place at the beginning itself.

However, NTPC and POWERGRID both did not undertake this exercise as a process of knowledge management formally.

The stages of knowledge management processes in NTPC and POWERGRID have been charted out in the flow chart in Figure 4.

Both NTPC and POWERGRID have entered the 'third generation' of Knowledge Management especially that of the knowledge management processes. However, the traits of third generation are not crystallized and stabilized because they lack unbound focus, innovation and knowledge capitalization. These power majors are striving towards meeting these conditions nevertheless.

In a nutshell, the bases of knowledge management processes in NTPC and POWERGRID are deeply rooted in their knowledge portals which depicts that knowledge management technology is the fountain head of their knowledge management processes. Intranet of these companies is primarily supported by information technology which plays a pivotal role in such a milieu. Since these companies are PSUs where the so-called top management is basically middle management, the knowledge sharing, use, reuse and capitalization have still not formed the part of the culture and repertoire of organization capital. In view of this, these companies need the impetus and fillip from top management that is, the administrative ministry viz. Ministry of Power, Government of India.

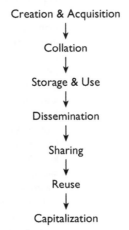

Figure 4.

Source: Developed by the author.

Conclusion

The entire gamut of knowledge management processes of NTPC and POWERGRID has come of age and it may be emulated by other power companies in India. Awareness about these processes should be created in a big way in NTPC and POWERGRID to develop the knowledge sharing culture. (At this stage, NTPC should go for Knowledge Audit so that they could get an in-depth understanding of the dynamics of knowledge management processes and may improve on the short comings and pitfalls especially in view of the fact that POWERGRID has partially conducted this while preparing its Knowledge Maps and Matrices [POWERGRID, 2011]).

Annexure–I

Barriers to Knowledge Sharing

absorptive capacity of receiving unit	feeling that the knowledge fits current context
access to the knowledge	fear of:
ambiguity regarding	becoming redundant
ethical situations	distortion or omission of information
knowledge seekers	exploitation once knowledge is shared
peers	losing confidentiality
reward	losing power once knowledge is shared
supervisor support	losing resources once knowledge is shared
the knowledge-sharing task	penalty if knowledge is shared
professional goals	risk
appropriate communication mode	global constraints including culture
appropriateness of the sharing channel	high costs of knowledge search
availability of:	hostile attitude toward knowledge sharing
dynamic channels to share knowledge	improper feedback
knowledge-sharing technology	inability to understand non-verbal cues
static channels to share knowledge	inability to voice relevant knowledge
time to dedicate to knowledge sharing	inappropriate physical appearance
communication direction	informal social groups or cliques
communication frequency	information overload
communication of organizational vision	internal resistance to knowledge sharing
communicator's lack of credibility	know-it all attitude
compatibility of legacy systems	knowledge-sharing structures match compatibility
sharing systems	of the organization's style
confidence in the knowledge	knowledge-sharing system simplicity
cultural differences	knowledge workers have a local orientation
defensiveness for gaining knowledge	lack of:
desire to retain information ownership	a knowledge-sharing facility
differences in perception of workers	clarity and conciseness
discontinuity in progress towards goals	common ground
effectiveness of sharing channel	contextual clues

(Appendix I continued)

(Appendix I continued)

effectiveness of the sharing system
efficiency of the sharing system
either-or thinking
emotional reactions to sharing
employees can identify the knowledge
richness of transmission channels
existing resources sufficient to share
expected:
  associations with other shares
  contribution to the organization
  recognition for sharing knowledge
  rewards for sharing knowledge
obvious link between sharing and the business'
  problems
operating environmental factors
org. communicates good achievements
overly competitive attitude
passive listening
perceived value of source's knowledge
perception that knowledge will be of worth
personality conflicts
physical distance between workers
physical noise and distractions
poor communication skills (lack of)
poor organization of ideas
poor spatial arrangements
power and status relationships
prejudice or bias
prematurely jumping to conclusions
preoccupation with an ongoing task
prevention of free riders
professional cultures
proprietary knowledge
proprietary thinking
questionable accuracy of information
receiver perceives enhanced efficacy

interest in the subject matter
motivation to participate
reciprocity
subject-matter knowledge
trust
understanding of technical language
willingness to share
local problem constraints
measurement of knowledge transfer
memory loss
motivational disposition of source
multiple languages used by knowledge workers
resistance to change
satisfactory content of the sharing transaction
self-interest
sender must establish legitimacy
sense making
skepticism toward sharing
specialization of jobs
specialized languages and methodologies
state of mind
status or position
strengthened group identity
strengthened personal responsibility
structural barriers in hierarchical organizations
tendency of the receiver to evaluate
time limitations
too many gatekeepers
understanding of the context
unit goals
unit subculture
unwillingness to listen
usability of the knowledge
use of a network that motivates participation
user friendliness of knowledge-sharing
system

Annexure–II

Task Force for Implementation of Knowledge Management in POWERGRID, interviewed on 15.10.2012

Sl. No.	Name of Department	Name & Designation of Committee Members
1.	Information Technology	Ms. Kumud Wadhwa, Chief Manager
2.	Corporate Planning	Mr. A J Rao, Chief Manager
3.	Engineering	Mr. A K Singh, Dy. Chief Design Engineer
4.	Finance	Ms. Prataksha, Chief Manager
5.	Operation Services	Mr. V K Bhaskar, Chief Manager
6.	System Operation	Ms. Minaxi Garg, Chief Manager
7.	Human Resources	Mr. K N Pandey, Chief Manager

Annexure–III

Questions used in Focus Group Discussion and Structured Interview:

- Do you have any mechanism for knowledge-creation in your company?
- Please list initiatives currently used in your company to gather, share and retain knowledge.
- Do you use knowledge sharing mechanism? If so, how?
- Have you got networks in place for dissemination of knowledge?
- Which are the tools used by your company for knowledge dissemination?
- Whether information for use across different establishments of your company is available to your personnel?
- Have you developed a mechanism for effective cataloguing and archiving for your knowledge portal?
- Do you ensure targeting knowledge provisions towards decision taking by your employees?
- Do you practice job-rotation for your personnel in R&D and Technology Development Department?
- How do you ensure reuse of knowledge in your company?
- Have you devised any mechanism for knowledge capitalization in your organization?
- Since you people have taken the mantle of knowledge management implementation across the length and breadth of your company, which are the knowledge management processes you use in your company?

Rerferences

Akoumianakis, D. (2009). Practice-oriented toolkits for virtual communities of practice. *Journal of Enterprise Information Management, 22*(3), 317–345.

Al Hawamadeh, S. (2005). *Knowledge management: Cultivating knowledge professionals.* Oxford: Chandos Publishing.

Allameh, S.M. et al. (2011). Examining the impact of KM enablers on knowledge management processes, Procedia Computer Science 3. Retrieved 21 July 2012, from www.Elsevier.com/locate/procedia

American Productivity & Quality Center and Arthur Anderson Consulting. (1995). *Knowledge management assessment tool.* Retrieved from http://kwork.org./white_papers/Kmat/html

Ante, S.E. (2008). *Creative capital: Georges doriot and the birth of venture capital.* Cambridge, MA: Harvard Business School Press.

Antonelli, C., & Teubal, M. (2010). Venture capitalism as a mechanism for knowledge goverance. In R. Viale & H. Etzkowitz (Eds), *The capitalization of knowledge.* Cheltenham, UK and Northampton, MA: Edward Elgar.

Asian Development Bank. (2009). *Disseminating knowledge products.* Retrieved 27 July 2012, from Google.com

Austin, S. (2010). Law firms offer discounts, play matchmaker. *The Wall Street Journal*, 9 September 2010.

Bukowitz, W.R., & Williams, R.L. (1999). *The knowledge management fieldbook.* Great Britain: Pearson Education Ltd.

Cabrera, A., & Cabrera, E.F. (2002). Knowledge sharing dilemmas. *Organisation Studies*, *23*, 687–710.

Camelo-Ordaz et al. (2011). The influence of human resource management on knoweldge sharing and innovation in Spain: The mediating role of affective commitment. *The International Journal of Human Resource Management*, *22*(7), 1442–1463.

Ceptureanu, S., & Ceptureanu, E. (2010). Knowledge creation/conversion process. *Review of International Comparative Management*, *11*(1), 150.

Chawla, D., & Joshi, H. (2010). Knowledge management initiatives in Indian public & private sector organizations. *Journal of Knowledge Management*, *14*(6), 811–827.

Cheng, X. (2004). Culture as a special technology in globalization. In S. Cullenburg & P.K. Pattanaik (Eds), *Globalization, culture and the limits of the market: Essays in economics & philosophy.* New Delhi: Oxford University Press.

Connell, N.A.D. (2006). Organisational storytelling. In D.G. Schwartz (Ed.), *Encyclopedia of knowledge management.* Hershey: Idea Group Reference.

Davenport, T.H., & Prusak, L. (2000). *Working knowledge: How organisations manage what they know.* Boston, MA: Harvard Business School Press.

Desouza, K.C., & Paquette, S. (2011). *Knowledge management: An introduction.* London: Facet Publishing. (p. 99).

Foss, N.C., & Mahnke, V. (2003). Knowledge management: What can organisational economics contribute. In M.E. Smith & M.A. Lyes (Eds), *The Backwell Handbook of Organisational Learning and Knowledge Management* (p. 86). Malden, MA: Blackwell Publishing.

Fuller, C.M., & Wilson, R.L. (2006). Extracting knowledge from neural networks. In D.G. Schwartz (Ed.), *Encyclopedia of knowledge management* (pp. 188–189). London: Idea Group Reference Hershey.

Geiger, D., & Schreyogg, G. (2012). Narrative in knowledge sharing: Challenging validity. *Journal of Knowledge Management*, *16*(1), 97–113.

Geisler, E., & Wickramsinghe, N. (2009). *Principles of knowledge management: Theory, practice and cases.* New York, NY: M.E. Sharpe, Armonk. (pp. 44–45).

George, T.E. (2012). A study of knowledge management practices & organizational citizenship behaviour in NTPC. *Tattva Journal*, *2*(1), July 2012, 17–27.

Ghobadi, S., & D'Ambra, J. (2012). Knowledge sharing in cross-functional teams. *Journal of Knowledge Management*, *16*(2), 285–301.

Gillham, B. (2005) *Case Study Research Methods.* London and New York, NY: Continuum.

Goel, A., Sharma, G.R., & Rastogi, R. (2010). Knowledge management implementation in NTPC, an Indian PSU. *Management Decision*, *48*(3), 383–395.

Goldsmith, R.E., & Pillai, K.G. (2006). Knowledge calibration. In D.G. Schwartz (Ed.), *Encyclopedia of knowledge management.* Hershey: Idea Group Reference.

Gottschalk, P. (2007). *Knowledge Management Systems.* Hershey: Idea Group Publishing.

Green, C., & Ruheler, K. (1995). Globalization, borderless worlds and the Tower of Babel: Metaphors gone awry. *Journal of Organizational Change Management*, *8*(4), 55–68.

Haas, M.R., & Hansen, M.T. (2007). Different knowledge, different benefits: Toward – a productivity perspective on knowledge sharing in organizations. *Strategic Management Journal*, *28*, 1133–1153.

Hauschild, S., Licht, T., & Stein, W. (2001). Creating a knowledge culture. *The Mckingey Quarterly*, *1*(1), 74–81.

King, W.R. (2006). Knowledge sharing. In D.G. Schwartz (Ed.), *Encyclopedia of Knowledge Management.* Hershey: Idea Group Reference.

Lam, A., & Lambermont Ford, J. (2010). Knowledge sharing in an organizational context. A motivation-based perspective. *Journal of Knowledge Management*, *14*(1), 51–66.

Levy, M. (2011). Knowledge retention: Minimizing organizational business loss. *Journal of Knowledge Management, 15*(4), 582–600.

Liebowitz, J. (2000). The knowledge audit. *Knowledge and Process Management, 7*(1), 3–10.

Lindsey, K.L. (2006). Knowledge sharing barriers. In D.G. Schwartz (Ed.), *Encyclopedia of Knowledge Management.* Hershey: Idea Group Reference.

Machlup, F. (2005). Stocks and flows of knowledge. In R. Grundmann & N. Stehr (Eds), *Knowledge: Critical concepts* Vol. III (Knowledge & the Economy). London and New York, NY: Routledge.

Majchrzak, A. et al. (2004). Knowledge reuse for innovation. *Management Science, 50*(2), 174–188.

Markus, M.L. (2001). Towards a theory of knowledge reuse: Types of knowledge reuse situations and factors in reuse success. *Journal of Management Information Success, 18*(1), 57–93.

Marshall, C., & Rossman, G.B. (2006). *Designing qualitative research.* Thousand Oaks, CA, London and New Delhi: SAGE Publications.

Martinez–Cavas, R. et. al (2012). Knowledge acquisition's mediation of social capital-firm innovation. *Journal of Knowledge Management, 16*(1).

Martins, E.C., & Meyer, W.J. (2012). Organisational and behavioral factors that influence knowledge retention. *Journal of Knowledge Management, 16*(1).

Mathews, M.L. (2000). *Knowledge-driven profit improvement: Implementing assessment feedback using PDK action theory.* London; New York, NY: St. Lucie Press.

Mclaughlin, S. et al. (2008). Barrier impact on organisational learning within complex organisations. *Journal of Knowledge Management, 12*(2), 107–123.

McLeod, J. (2010). *Case study research: In counseling & psychotherapy.* Los Angeles, CA and London: SAGE.

Newell, S.M. et al. (2002). *Managing knowledge work.* New York, NY: Palgrave.

National Thermal Power Corporation (NTPC) (2012). *Lakshya (Knowledge Portal).* Retrieved 16 October 2012, from www.ntpc.co.in

O'Dell, C. (2004). *The executive's role in knowledge management.* New Delhi: Tata McGraw Hill.

Oshri, I. (2006). Knowledge reuse. In D.G. Schwartz (Ed.), *Encyclopedia of Knowledge Management.* Hershey: Idea Group Reference.

Osterloch, M., & Frey, B. (2000). Motivation, knowledge transfer, and organisational forms. *Organisation Science, 11*, 538–550.

Paramasivan, T. (2003). Knowledge audit. *The Chartered Accountant, November 2003.*

Parker, K.R., & Nitse, P.S. (2006). Competitive intelligence gathering. In D.G. Schwartz (Ed.), *Encyclopedia of Knowledge Management.* Hershey: Idea Group Reference.

POWERGRID. (2010). *Knowledge Management Policy.* Gurgaon: Power Grid Corporation of India Limited.

———. (2011). *Knowledge maps & matrices.* Gurgaon: Power Grid Corporation of India Limited.

Probst, G. et al. (2002). *Managing knowledge building blocks for success.* West Sussex: Wiley.

Richter, F., & Banerjee, P. (2003). *The knowledge economy in India.* New York, NY: Palgrave Macmillan.

Ruhnka, J.C., & Young, J.E. (1987). A venture capital model of the development process for new ventures. *Journal of Business Venturing, 2*(2), (Spring 1987), 167–184.

Schwartz, D.G. (2006). *Encyclopedia of knowledge management.* Hershey: Idea Group.

Sekaran, U., & Bongie, R. (2010). *Research methods for business: A skill building approach.* New Delhi: Wiley India (P) Ltd.

Shukla, A., & Srinivasan, R. (2002). *Designing knowledge management architecture: How to implement successful knowledge management programs.* New Delhi, Thousand Oaks, CA and London: Response Books. A Division of SAGE Publications.

Snowden, D. (2006). Narrative. In D.G. Schwartz (Ed.), *Encyclopedia of knowledge management.* Hershey: Idea Group Reference.

Stehr, N. (2005). The texture of knowledge societies. In R. Grundmann & N. Stehr (Eds), *Knowledge: Critical concepts* Vol. III (Knowledge & the Economy). London and New York, NY: Routledge.

Teng, J.T.C., & Song, S. (2011). An exploratory examination of knowledge sharing behaviors solicited and voluntary. *Journal of Knowledge Management, 15*(1), 104–117.

Van den Hooff, B., & Ridder, J.A. (2004). Knowledge sharing in context: The influence of organisational commitment, communication, climate and CMC use on knowledge sharing. *Journal of Knowledge Management, 8*(1), 117–130.

Vat, K.H. (2006). Knowledge synthesis framework. In D.G. Schewartz (Ed.), *Encyclopedia of knowledge management.* Hershey: Idea Group Reference.

Viale, R. (2010). Knowledge driven capitalisation of knowledge. In R. Viale & H. Etzkowitz (Eds), *The capitalization of knowledge* (pp. 31–73). Cheltenham and Northampton, MA: Edward Elgar.

Wickramasinghe, N. (2006). Knowledge creation. In D.G. Schwartz (Ed.), *Encyclopedia of knowledge management.* Hershey: Idea Group Reference.

Williams, L.A., & De Steno. (2008). Pride and perseverance: The motivational role of pride. *Journal of Personality and Social Psychology, 94*(6), 1007–1017.

Woodside, A.G. (2010). *Case study research: Theory, methods, practice.* United Kingdom: Enerald.

Xu, D., & Wang, H. (2006). Integration of knowledge management and e-learning. In D.G. Schwartz (Ed.), *Encyclopedia of knowledge management.* Hershey: Idea Group Reference.

Yin, R.K. (2003). *Case study research: Design and methods.* Thousand Oaks, CA, London and New Delhi: SAGE Publications.

Zikmund, W.G. (2003). *Business research methods.* Australia, UK, USA.: Thomson South-Western.

Use of Knowledge Management for Competitive Advantage: The Case Study of Max Life Insurance

27

Joshi, H., Farooquie, J. A. and Chawla, D.

Abstract

In the Asian subcontinent, the insurance business is highly competitive. The Indian insurance industry too witnessed tremendous growth and competition in the last few years. Both public and private insurance companies are currently facing two main challenges: struggling to retain their customer base and knowledge loss resulting from employee turnover. Insurance companies are realizing that efficiently managing its customer and employee knowledge and utilizing the same in designing insurance products and services is a key to survival. While effective knowledge management (KM) has been acknowledged as the key driver for new knowledge and new idea generation, the fact that academics still write about it and organizations are actively pursuing the concept makes us believe that this trend is going to continue in future too. This article discusses the KM planning and implementation journey undertaken by Max Life Insurance Company Limited, India. The company not only has successfully implemented KM but also has plans to roll out the project in other group companies. The case presents instances and examples of how the company has used KM for real business improvements with measurable outcomes. It also investigates the critical success factors for KM implementation using secondary and primary data collected from published literature besides the company under study. The study will be beneficial to organizations that are willing to implement KM but do not have a clear idea of how to proceed with it. It also provides directions for future research and implications for global managers for having KM into place.

Keywords

Knowledge management, Max Life Insurance, case study, India

[1] Assistant Professor, International Management Institute, New Delhi India.
[2] Professor, Department of Business Administration, Aligarh Muslim University, Aligarh, Uttar Pradesh, India.
[3] Distinguished Professor and Dean (Research), International Management Institute, New Delhi, India.

Corresponding author:
Himanshu Joshi, Assistant Professor, International Management Institute, B-10 Qutab Institutional Area, New Delhi 110016, India.
E-mail: himanshu@imi.edu

Introduction

As the head of the knowledge management (KM) initiative, Vikrant recalled the early days when he was asked to prepare a roadmap to enhance knowledge creation, sharing and application at Max Life Insurance. As a quality champion who strongly believed in ideas and innovation, the initial thrust was on identifying the existing knowledge-oriented activities which the company was involved in. The company had a knowledgeable resource pool, but it was limited to individuals and small teams. There was no formal and structured way of knowledge sharing and dissemination, and it was left to the individuals and teams to document or share knowledge. However, the company has come a long way in using KM for enhancing performance.

In this article, we examine the Max Life Insurance KM initiative and best practices adopted by the organization for making KM a success. The article is divided into various sections starting with review of literature, research objectives, methodology, KM initiative–background, best practices identification, approval and replication, critical success factors and conclusions and recommendations. The following sections presents a summary of the review of literature conducted to determine the topics studied by researchers under the domain of KM to identify research gaps and objectives of the study.

Review of Literature

The last few years witnessed an increasing belief among managers that effective management of knowledge is a key dimension for achieving and sustaining competitive advantage. Knowledge management is gaining popularity among large organizations. It allows organizations to share, capture, organize and store internal company knowledge and intellectual capital. It is a way of finding, understanding and using knowledge to create value (O'Dell, 2004). Recent studies show that the rationale behind KM popularity is the need for innovation and differentiation, proliferation of technology and changing stakeholder's expectations (Fernandez & Sabherwal, 2010; Grossman, 2006; Major & Cordey-Hayes, 2000; Massa & Testa, 2009; Prieto & Smith, 2006). Yet, not all organizations have achieved business benefits from their KM initiative (Davenport, DeLong & Beers, 1998), and high failure rates of such programmes raise serious doubts about their ability to improve knowledge flows (Mehta, Oswald & Mehta, 2007). However, organizations which have been persistent with the initiative have been able to derive multiple business benefits. Consulting companies, IT companies and R&D organizations have known this for years (Davenport & Prusak, 1998), but other firms in oil, steel and consumer products are recognizing the importance of knowledge assets as the source of their success (Birkinshaw, 2001). Both large- and small-sized organizations have benefited from the initiatives.

Dilnutt (2002) discusses three KM initiatives in Asia Pacific region. In the first case, a major Australian bank faced the challenge to improve its product support services provided through its call centre. The call centre consultants relied on paper-based procedures which resulted in inaccuracies and delays. A knowledge-based approach was followed involving determining what knowledge was needed, from where it was sourced and how it was presented. In the second case, an Australian fund manager recognized the opportunity to create a proactive orientation towards compliance. Compliance managers were always seen firefighting and it was decided to reengineer the total compliance management function which involved restructuring the information flow between stakeholders. A compliance monitoring system along with guidelines database was developed to enable managers to be up to date with compliance requirements. In the third case, a government treasury organization responsible for providing high-quality advice to the cabinet on economic issues was unable to respond to the demands as information was not readily accessible. To address the problem, the organization clustered improvements around people, process, technology, knowledge sources and project management. In all the three organizations, a common methodology was followed. First, discovering what knowledge is important to the business; second, structuring and prioritizing the knowledge and finally, validation of business cases and implementation of KM project. Wong and Aspinwall (2006) have presented the results of KM implementation in a small company in Hampshire, UK. This company provides business consultancy and software development services. Prior to KM, the company faced issues related to information organization, categorization, dissemination and relevance of existing knowledge. As an approach to KM, the company identified key knowledge areas or domains and established ownership and established roles for knowledge-related tasks. As a result of the initiative, the consultants were able to generate proposal documents quickly by leveraging on existing domain-specific knowledge, lessons learnt and best practice repositories. In India, Wipro Technologies Limited, Infosys Technologies Limited, Tata Steel Limited, Tata Consultancy Services Limited, etc. to name a few, have successfully adopted and implemented the concept of KM.

At the heart of conceptualizing and implementing KM initiative are people, processes and technology. Mehta et al. (2007) describe and discuss how Infosys Technologies Limited—a Global Most Admired Knowledge Enterprise (MAKE)—faced a lack of knowledge flow while implementing a programme aimed at continuously improving their core business processes. The company initiated a KM programme with people processes and technology as the three pillars to support the five-stage KM maturity model. The vision was that every instance of learning within Infosys should be available to every Infosys employee (Garud & Kumaraswamy, 2003). Another MAKE winner, Wipro Technologies initiated the KM programme in 2000. The KM initiative at Wipro has its roots in the continuous quality improvement programme that Wipro started to benchmark itself against the top international standards. The projects undertaken by the company were getting complex with increasing demand of shorter delivery cycle from customers. The stakes were high and KM was seen as a necessity rather than an option for success. However, Wipro officials knew that there is no single approach or single mantra which guarantees success of a KM initiative. Therefore, they focused on identifying the right set of business needs and leveraging existing investments in people and systems to deliver the right value (Rajakannu, 2008).

Another IT giant, TCS, started KM initiative with a vision to enhance the stakeholder value by enabling it to be a knowledge-centric organization through capturing, sharing and application of knowledge. TCS felt the need to initiate KM so as to inculcate shared learning among its employees by providing access to the existing knowledge assets. The model has three basic pillars or key foundation areas (KFAs): People (people and culture); Process (process, policy and strategy); and Technology (technology and infrastructure). The first pillar 'People' addresses the mindset of the people; second pillar 'Process' facilitates and guides the effort of people to capture and use the knowledge in the organization for achieving business results; and the last pillar 'Technology' acts as an enabler in helping people deriving the maximum out of KM initiative (Mohanty & Chand, 2007). Yajnik (2014) has studied KM implementation in two Indian organizations, a leading fast-moving consumer goods (FMCG) company and a leading chain of retail stores. The retail chain company uses various IT tools such as e-learning, video library, online quizzes, data warehousing and mining, Moodle open source and wikis. The FMCG company uses Microsoft SharePoint tool, enterprise portal names as 'MILAP' for KM. It also uses rewards and recognition as incentive for KM adoption.

Example of KM implementation in Indian IT companies is common; however, other sectors are catching up fast. Among power companies in India, NTPC and Power Grid KM processes can be discussed in eight heads, namely knowledge creation, acquisition, collocation, storage and use, dissemination, sharing, reuse and synthesis and capitalization (Pandey, 2014). Globally as well as in India, more and more insurance companies are using KM to provide access to relevant knowledge and its sources at the right time, place and format. Babu and Bhide (2012) believe that the benefits of KM can be seen across the insurance value chain—right from reducing time to market for new product launches, improving agent productivity through collaboration tools, increasing customer satisfaction through established frequently asked questions (FAQs)/self-help documents and reducing operating costs by streamlining and standardizing internal processes.

The review of literature reveals that although there are many empirical researches conducted to compare the extent of KM implementation at industry or sector level, there is not enough qualitative work done. Barring few Indian IT companies and manufacturing companies, not much has been done and documented in the domain of KM. Therefore, this case study builds on this research gap.

Research Objectives

1. To conduct an in-depth study of KM implementation at Max Life Insurance and identify key success factors.
2. To determine how Max Life Insurance used KM for attaining competitive advantage.

Methodology

This article employs a case study method. This is a qualitative research methodology often used by researchers in gathering rich, contextual data. An exploratory study was carried out by conducting an in-depth review of literature followed by a series of 10 personal interviews using an interview template (Appendix 1). The questions asked were primarily related to KM planning and implementation activities, constructs of KM and its impact on performance. According to Kvale (1996), the most common number of interviews for a qualitative research study tends to be between 5 and 25, due to the time and resources constraints. Hence, a sample size of 10 was deemed sufficient for face-to-face interviews. Interviews were chosen because more in-depth information can be obtained. Face-to-face interviews can be regarded as an interpersonal role situation in which an interviewer asks respondents questions designed to obtain answers pertinent to the objective of the study (Powell, 1998). Notes were made during the interviews. These interviews were audio recorded and later converted into transcripts.

Personal Interviews Sample Description

The sample comprised senior and middle executives (chief technical officers (CTOs), vice-presidents, directors, managers, project leaders, etc.) who have experienced KM implementation in Max Life Insurance (see Appendix 2 to read more about the company). The age of the respondents ranged from 32 to 50 years. On an average, the working experience of the participants ranged from 4 to 30 years.

The data collected from personal interviews were subjected to content analysis to bring out the common constructs discussed. Germain (2006) believes that content analysis of transcripts will result in certain number of themes which can subsequently be cross-checked with literature, and as a result, the themes can be conceptually grouped into constructs and sub-constructs. The following steps (Powell & Renner, 2003) were used to examine the qualitative information:

- Step 1: Understanding the data collected
- Step 2: Focus the analysis

- Step 3: Categorize the information
- Step 4: Identify the relationship within and between constructs
- Step 5: Conceptualizing the themes together

The data collected were analyzed in order to get an overall understanding of KM initiative at Max Life Insurance Limited and identify best practices adopted by the company corresponding to various KM dimensions. The findings from the analysis of data are divided into various sections and discussed below.

Knowledge Sharing before KM Initiative

The company has a strong emphasis on human capital and considers it to be its competitive advantage. It believes that people are the biggest asset and hence lays a strong emphasis on employee-friendly practices leading to high levels of employee engagement and motivation. Recognizing the importance of knowledge sharing and dissemination, the company embarked upon the KM journey in 2010. However, this recognition did not come easy. How the company went about realizing the need for KM is truly inspiring. The journey presents the realities and complexities of making KM work in a real world.

Like most companies that came up during the Internet era or the new economy era, the challenge at Max Life Insurance was to manage data and information generated from different sources. The company, due to its huge geographical footprint, faced the risk of 'islands of information' and 'reinvention of wheel'. The scope and scale of operations required massive synergies across different operational zones. With over four million customers across various products, more than 7,500 employees and 35,000 advisors, the challenge was to devise a mechanism by which pockets of knowledge held by few people could be made available at an organizational level. For example, specialized knowledge with respect to actuarial, oncology, etc. was available with only few people. In addition, knowledge was being shared which was primarily through emails, phone, seminars, conferences, etc. However, most of it was ad-hoc, sporadic, unstructured and left to the discretion of individuals and teams. Another challenge was attrition rate. As one senior official puts it,

> When people join a company, they acquire the knowledge, use it and then leave the company for better prospects. One can always talk to the individual informally and try to capture some knowledge but not 100 percent can be captured. Therefore, formal systems, structures and process need to be defined to prevent knowledge loss.

Dilnutt (2002) experienced a similar trend while discussing three KM initiatives involving two major Australian-based financial institution and a government treasury organization. In all the three cases, most of the organizational knowledge remained locked in the heads of the individuals and did not percolate out of the functional areas. To compound the problem was the high turnover rate (23–25 per cent), thereby draining corporate memory and creating a productivity slump. According to Davenport et al. (1998), to transfer tacit knowledge from individual into a repository, organizations usually use some sort of community-based electronic discussion. According to Aujirapongpan, Vadhanasindhu, Chandrachai and Cooparat (2010), studies using the resource-based capability perspective show that an appropriate technology must be in place for effective KM and a robust technology platform can enable the flatter organizational structures.

In all this while, the insurance sector was witnessing explosive growths over last few years, as a result of which people from diverse industries were joining Max Life. There was a growing feeling among the top management that the key to growth and sustainability is quality, speed and innovation. The company needed an initiative which could help them achieve this. The KM initiative in that sense aligned beautifully with the overall vision of the organization. As one official explained,

> We are a billion dollar company with 7500 employees, operations spanning 300 locations. Unless we adopt KM and adopted it very well, our aspiration to be the most admired or excellent organization cannot be met. We may continue to do it informally in an ad hoc way, but unless we put a structure around it and encourage and motivate our employees, its full value can't be realized.

Roadmap to KM

The first step was to identify where the company was in terms of knowledge creation, sharing and application and its internal capabilities to manage knowledge. It also involved identifying current activities which could be classified as KM. This helped in identifying current strengths and gaps. Scoping of the initiative is a crucial step for documenting the capabilities and resource requirements of the KM system. The KM journey involved formulating the KM objectives and developing understanding of its alignment with the overall business objectives. This is followed by preparing a business case for KM, identifying potential knowledge champions or subject matter experts (SME), defining the roles and responsibilities and getting the necessary buy-in and budget approvals from the top management. This stage also involved creating awareness about the KM initiative among different stakeholders, and planning and designing the initiative. Figure 1 presents how KM planning and scoping was done at Max Life Insurance Company Limited.

As part of the KM initiative, the company developed a road map for 3 years. The KM team comprised a programme management team, a steering team (head of quality and service excellence, CTO), SMEs from various function and a project team. The steering team was responsible for reviewing the progress of the work done by the core team every week and every month. The KM initiative follows a project management approach wherein the focus is on timelines, budgets and scheduled reports to capture compliance and aberrations.

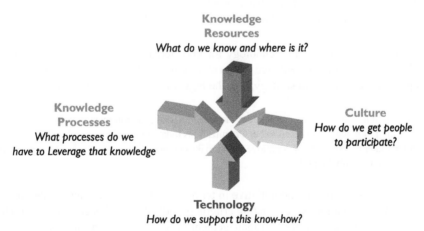

Figure 1. KM Planning and Scoping

Source: Max Life Insurance Limited.

While embarking on the KM journey, the KM also studied KM implementation at various organizations including Bharti Airtel Limited and Wipro Technologies Limited to learn from their experience. Both the core team and the project team comprise people who have experience in KM implementation at these two organizations. This helped the organization in terms of sharing and introducing the KM best practices to other employees.

The next step was identifying the resource requirements and developing and testing of the KM infrastructure. Max Life Insurance developed Knowledge Bridge which is a KM and collaborative suite that offers opportunities for documentation and collaboration. Documentation allows the users to create logical segmentation of files into centralized folders and sub-folders along with drag and drop functionality. The versioning feature allows and maintains a version history and change of version on editing. The tag-based search feature allows mapping of related content and enables easy search. The workflow feature allows automated approval workflow and provides the workflow status for documents. The applications also provide role-based secure access, metadata and comment storage. Other collaborative tools include wikis, blogs, discussion threads, calendar and links. The idea behind introducing such innovative tools was to get out of a system involving multiple level of hierarchy and stages of approvals and empower employees to practice self-service and decision making.

The technology behind Knowledge Bridge is a worldwide intranet accessible to employees and company advisors. The network enables people to submit and retrieve best practices all the time enabling them to communicate and coordinate their efforts in real time. The collaborative tools allowed users to create communities of practice. To ensure better acceptability, the organization implemented KM as a pilot in some select key process and then demonstrated the success stories. The objectives of Knowledge Bridge are

- To share knowledge in multi-location and multi-transaction business environment
- To develop a centralized repository to store and retrieve knowledge
- To give everyone access to central knowledge repositories
- Allow for time and space shifting—making it available 24 hours a day, 7 days a week
- To ensure version control and workflow-based knowledge system
- To allow a robust and easy to use search and navigation capability
- Facilitate virtual collaboration and discussion forums
- Offer flexibility in KM processes based on requirements of function/department

Development of the platform and technology for knowledge creation, sharing and application was half the task done. The next major challenge was to make employees use the tool effectively. What would work well, a push strategy or a pull strategy, was the bigger question. A senior executive added,

The whole paradigm has shifted from employee at the receiving end and employer at the giving end. Organizations cease to be the kind of places that it used to be. Organizations today have to be very vibrant places to keep attracting and retaining talent. Today it's the employee who makes choices. It has to be a bottom-ups approach. In this kind of paradigm, it can only be pull.

The next stage involves evaluating the initiative in terms of its business impact. As the initiative was in the early part of implementation, no evaluating criteria or indicators had been thought of. However, the process owner acknowledged that the top management gets excited when they can see a dollar value behind the KM initiative. The plan is to create dollar benefit in future. This is needed to justify the spending and business benefits derived.

The company has developed its own methodology that, based upon experience and research, has proven to reliably lead to desired/better business results. Whenever any new idea or innovative practice is submitted, it is evaluated based on its contribution to improving an organizations performance and efficiency in three specific areas. This measurable impact is approved by finance based on the revenues which could be attributable to the best practice and cost savings due to higher efficiency of operations. The second impact assessment is based on the degree to which the best practice improves customer experience, for example, key result area (KRA) scores, increased E-SAT (Gallup scores) which refers to employee satisfaction and engagement scores and improved work ethics. The third dimension is the ease of system implementation.

Best Practice Identification: The Replication Funnel

The company has created social and technology-driven platforms, such as idea submission, surveys, discussion forums and audits, to capture best practices and ideas. A best practice has to go through a quality check funnelling or filtering process for approval. Once approved, the best practice needs to be replicated. The value of a best practice is determined not just by the quality of idea but also by its frequency of replication. There are hundreds of ideas submitted throughout the organization but only a selected few are considered as best practices. A similar approach was discussed by Wong and Aspinwall (2006) wherein, in the first instance, the company looked at what information was currently residing in the organization and an assessment was carried out to determine its relevance. This was followed by establishing the structure of each of the new knowledge areas for better search and retrieval. The process for the selection is presented in Figure 2.

Best Practice Approval Workflow

The first stage is where a new idea/suggestion is uploaded on the KM platform 'Maxters'. The submitted idea is sent to the supervisor for approval. Once approved, it is posted as a best practice which is sent for quality check by single point of contact (SPOC). In case there are any questions or feedback, the same is sent back to authors for revisions and resubmission. If the idea is approved, it goes finally to the SME for determining the possible financial impact. Once this is determined, the idea becomes a best practice which is published on Maxters. At this stage, the best practices are available to all for viewing and possible replication. These best practices are also shared with the SMEs of other group companies if they are found to be relevant. The objective is to inculcate the practice of cross-fertilization and sharing of ideas and best practices not within one company but between the group companies. This workflow is shown in Figure 3.

Critical Success Factors

There is no single right or wrong way to implement KM. However, there are certain factors which play a critical role in determining how well a KM initiative is implemented. Birkinshaw (2001) has defined the following five basic guidelines to make KM work: map the knowledge flows in the organization, map the stocks of knowledge and use them to encourage sharing of best practice, focus efforts on mission-critical rather than nice-to-have knowledge, raise the visibility of KM activities and use incentives to institutionalize new knowledge sharing activities. Huang and Lai (2014) found individual

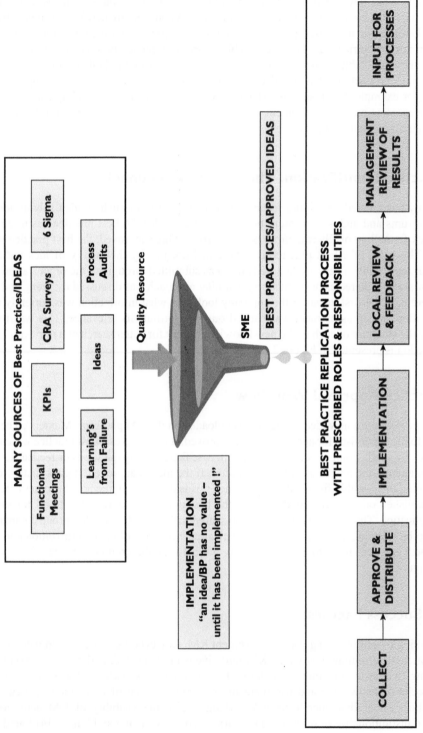

Figure 2. Best Practice Filtering and Replication Process

Source: Max Life Insurance Limited.

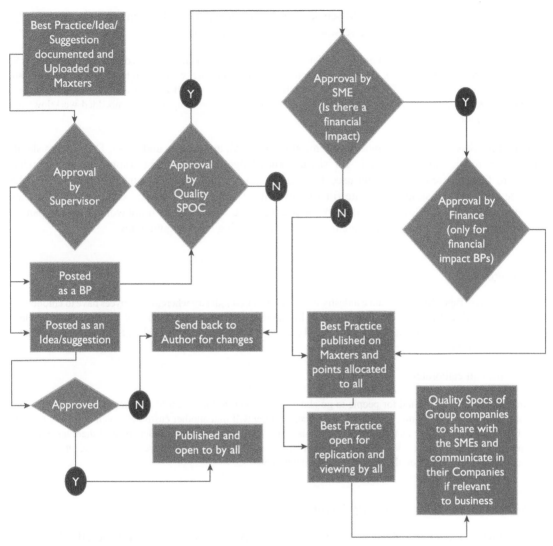

Figure 3. Best Practice Approval Workflow

Source: Max Life Insurance Limited.

characteristics, KM characteristics and organizational characteristics as critical success factors for KM implementation in Life Insurance companies in Taiwan. With respect to Max Life Insurance Company, the following critical success factors emerged from the data collected.

KM Process

Fundamentally, there are few things that have been part of the company DNA ever since its beginning. It has a deep-rooted quality focus which involves properly written down documented formal processes available in digital form. From the KM perspective, this inherent attribute helps in keeping the knowledge submission up to date and facilitate version control. A senior manager explains,

> Rather than having different truths, it's crucial to have one version which is a verified and a reliable source. So we intend to make KM as a single point source of information. Further, we are also trying is to integrate some of the work flows in KM. For example, in compliance, we send out self reading and self learning material wherein employees can get themselves self certified. The ideas is to integrate and embedded workflows that people can use.

The KM process comprises knowledge submission, retrieval, application and reuse. The process should be simple, quick and user friendly for sharing knowledge and enhancing community membership. Standard formats are designed and used for creating knowledge inventory and maximize knowledge sharing. The process should facilitate filtering of content and ensure stringent content quality control through approval workflow and matrix. Although there are standard KM frameworks, the company is implementing KM in a project management style and evolving its own guidelines.

KM Culture

> Vikrant says, Typically an insurance industry is a rejection based industry wherein employees have to emotionally tough to survive. These employees because of the nature of job go through a range of emotions including high levels of stress. Therefore, making them excited enough to contribute to the knowledge base of the organization is a real challenge.

As one official elaborates,

> In our company it's normal for people to go aboard few time times in a year to celebrate success. I don't think cash rewards will make much sense for them because they will find another customer which translates in terms of more incentives and meeting their targets rather than contributing into KM. But some of them have lifelong inspiration to meet a senior leader or getting on a platform where they are recognized. So intrinsic motivators like public appreciation, pat on the back are valued much more.

Indicators for Knowledge Sharing Culture

The following are some indicators as identified by Max life Insurance to measure effectiveness of organizational culture:

- Culture of openness—celebrating each other's success
- Engage people by valuing what they know
- Measures and incentive programmes to reward and recognize knowledge contributions
- Culture of best practice sharing and replications
- Best performing teams share and others replicate

KM Technology and Platform Evolution

Choosing the right technology platform is crucial for the success of the KM initiative. Babu and Bhide (2012) believe that technology platforms that support enterprise content management (ECM), collaboration tools, e-learning platforms and business process management (BPM) system are core requirements of any KM solution to manage the insurance value chain. The company initially developed an intranet called 'Sangam'. However, because of its static functionality, the company moved on to develop an improved version on open source platform which was named as 'Knowledge Bridge'. As part of the KM infrastructure, the idea is to develop active knowledge networks, communities of practice (CoPs) and centres of excellence. The technology includes a robust search engine and sufficient storage for knowledge repository. However, for the past 2 years, with increasing user base and enrolment, the company's existing KM infrastructure was not scalable enough to support the load. The technology team at Max, realizing the limitation of the platform, designed a better platform known as 'Maxters'. This platform was developed keeping in mind the increasing user base and customers emerging preferences in terms of products feature and capabilities. The new platform is based on the lines of popular social media platform wherein users can share messages, photos, videos, invite friends, etc.

At the moment, the tool is being evolved as a people engagement tool across the group companies. Apart from that, the platform can also be used to share documents and files not only within the company or function but also across all the group companies. There are different levels of access control for users. By default all users get a read only access. The site-manager moderates and approves all content posted by respective interest groups or functions in the micro-site. Finally this is shared with all users through common dashboards.A senior officer explained, 'The success of this platform will depend on how many actually use the platform. As of December 2012, there are 5000 users and we have an ambitious target of increasing this to 10000 by end of 2013.' The company is also planning to introduce a web traffic analysis tool to determine how users are spending time on Maxters. This includes the traffic patterns from various group companies, feature or section most visited, time spent by users, etc.

Human Resources

For the success of the KM initiative, team selection and composition are crucial. Individuals who are good with meeting and communicating with others, outgoing and extrovert are obvious choices. They should be able to excite and energize others. An official explains,

> We have identified some people who are known as SPOC (Single point of contact). Call them the catalysts, influencers or the change agent these people are passionate about the work they do and have good inter-personal skills. Largely people who are into HR, training or quality fit well into that role.

The organization has also identified SMEs who are experts in their domain. In insurance industry, there are many processes and some of them can be very complicated. Therefore, domain experts, for example, underwriting experts, claim settlers, analytic experts, etc. are important part of the process. Their role is to identify and approve best practices and also ensure that the body of knowledge is current. Employees also play a key role as knowledge contributors and knowledge users (communities of practice). It is also important to identify a KM leader who can garner top management support and strategic commitment towards KM.

Evaluation and Continuous Improvement

No initiative is considered successful unless its impact on the organization is determined. At Max, impact assessment and evaluation is treated as a centralized function wherein the focus is on continuous

BEST PRACTICE

Name of Function	Agency Sales (North-2)
Best Practice Description	Improving Case Size
Process Owner/Project Leader	Sanjeev Meghani
Process Champion	Anil Misra
Process	Sales Process

SECTION 1: BACKGROUND/KEY BUSINESS ISSUES

Case Size is a critical parameter which has a huge impact on MNYL Revenue. Case Size had come across as a major area of focus in UP. This project has helped agency to meet it's strategic goal of revenue enhancement which has further contributed in achieving overall objectives of business at large. This will also build our conviction with the employees for doing our business in the right manner. Case Size enhancement also means better renewal generation for the region.

When this project was initiated in Mar 2009 the Case Size was ₹ 15415 and required immediate attention, then "Central Eastern U.P. Agency Sales Team" has taken it as the scope of this project with a CTQ to improve Case Size from ₹ **15415 to ₹ 18000 by 15-Dec 2009**.

SECTION 2: APPROACH/SOLUTION

A well planned DMAIC approach was taken & a cross-functional team was involved to drive and achieve the goal. Following were the actions implemented:-

- R&R for Office Heads on achieving 120%.
- New agent launch to be reviewed by MPML-R (RM) with Office Heads (7-FOD's) in weekly Con Calls.
- Same policy applied by same person to be accompanied by a customer acknowledgement (letter).
- Saturday Drill on Employer – Employee cases & Business cases like HUF, MWPA – AM-Ops & OH's will keep the records.
- No approval on below 9 points for recruitment of agent advisor. (Also at zonal level a restriction made by ZVP that maximum limit for <9-pointer approval would be 5% that

SECTION 3: BUSINESS RESULTS

- Case Size increased to ₹ 17723 (YTD) ₹ 18261 (Mean).
- Revenue enhancement of ₹ 7.0133 Cr (annually)

Performance With Special Product (Smart Express)

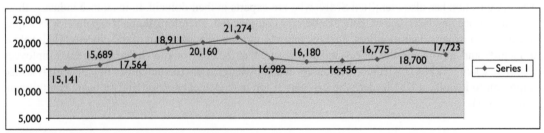

Figure 4. Best Practice Template and Dashboard

Source: Max Life Insurance Limited.

Table I. The K-point Grid

Document Type	Knowledge Points to Originator	Approver I (supervisor)	Approver 2 (quality SPOC)	Approver 3 (SME)	Approver 4 (finance)
Implemented Best Practice	50	10	10	20	20
Replicated Best Practice	100 for replicator 50 for source	10	10	20	20

Source: Max Life Insurance Limited.

improvement of processes. The company has devised ways to link knowledge submissions to key performance indicators (KPIs) for creation of best practices and sharing with others. The basis for incentives is the extent to which knowledge is created and reused. The company has also done cost–benefit analysis in terms of broader business benefits, such as cost savings and enhanced productivity. The computation of points is based on point allocations done for the originator, replicator, supervisor, quality SPOC, SME and finance. A simple illustration for point computation is shown in Table 1. It can be seen that for every instance of best practice replication, the replicator as well as the originator is incentivized along with the approving authorities.

Road Ahead

Knowledge management in a decent size company to take routes, prosper and really start creating enormous amount of benefit takes some time. Depending on the organizational culture, capabilities, leadership and people, it may vary from organization to organization. Max Life Insurance has started reaping the benefits of its KM efforts. More than 100 best practices have been identified and being used by companywide employees. With its increasing customer base and adding of new employees, advisors and newer locations and geographies, there is a greater reliance on KM for knowledge capture, dissemination and application. They are learning fast. However, with increasing employee and client enrolment, the scalability of the solution is something the promoters of KM are concerned about. They are also thinking if the existing KM solution features and functionality would meet the expectations of the users for 2–3 years down the line. As part of an annual assessment cycle carried by Max Group, the team identified KM initiative at Max Life Insurance as a best practice. They are also evaluating the possibility of expanding the initiative as a corporate-wide initiative in its other six group companies. However, this move has its own set of challenges. The system should be able to handle 18,000 users across the six companies. Will the same solution work for the entire group and help it in offering consistent experience or services to its customers? How much of the application needs to be centralized and decentralized and distributed? Who would be responsible and accountable for the success of the initiative? What kind of resources would be needed?

Knowledge management in any organization is an evolutionary process and the journey is never complete. As many organizations embark on this journey, Max Life has also started with focused pilots, and even though the journey is about 5 years old, Max Life leadership believes that it is still a stage of evolution. Currently, all the necessary support systems have been put in place including technological platforms, resource allocation is done through an annual budgeting process and human resources have been allocated with dedicated as well as part-time allocation to the role to drive the initiative to higher levels of adoption. Senior leaders are ensuring that adequate and proper rewards and recognition schemes are in place to encourage and support the right behaviour for sharing and adopting knowledge by generously contributing into the programme by all employees. Various awards have been constituted to promote accelerated business results through a culture of knowledge creation, sharing and replication across Max group companies. The top management or the chief executive officer (CEO) recognition (top knowledge contributor award, top knowledge leader award) is to reward leading contributors and KM leaders. There are also rewards in the form of knowledge points which are redeemable. Appreciation letters are also given by leadership.

Conclusions and Recommendations

The most important conclusion drawn from this case study is the importance of culture and leadership which provides a backdrop to the knowledge creation, sharing and application behaviour.

Knowledge management is not a simple game, and to play it effectively, there are no simple remedies. For KM to be successful, an overall understanding of the organization including its processes, culture, information technology, people, etc. is important. Knowledge management is much more than just information technology and therefore synergy between the business leadership and IT leadership is a must. In addition, emerged from the discussion was the fact that KM planning and design, KM implementation and evaluation, technology in KM, culture in KM, leadership in KM and structure in KM are important requirements to ensure KM initiatives to succeed.

Max Life Insurance Company had created an integrated KM approach, which involved defining KM objectives and activities matrix. They had also formally defined and documented what KM is and what it is expected to do. Therefore, organizations should have a clear idea of the business problems they are trying to address using KM. If objectives are not stated clearly, the KM effort tends to become just like any other initiative forced on employees for no apparent reason. For example, if the problem is related to employees spending lot of time in duplicating efforts or reinventing the wheel, then it is important to list it down as one of the KM objectives. Next, organizations should find answer to the question, 'Are we presently doing anything to prevent duplication of efforts?' Organizations should also develop clarity in terms of resources needed for preventing duplication of efforts. As a matter of fact, it is very important that the top management is convinced. Therefore, it is recommended that organizations should identify a process for pilot and run it in project mode, that is, form a team, identify technology needed, performance measures, duration of project, etc. The success of the future of KM project depends upon how well the team is able to demonstrate small successes.

It is recommended that organizations while implementing KM pilot should define the organizational strategy 'Push' or 'Pull' and the means by which it is going to be achieved. For example, push strategy could include mandates, such as compulsory submission of ideas or pull could include rewards and recognition, pat on the back, etc. Whatever be the strategy, push or pull or a combination of both, it is important to document experiences and share it in the form of best practices for possible replication and adoption. One of the ways of doing this is capturing the knowledge and experience of senior people (organizational anchors) through interviews and discussion when they are retiring. It is also recommended that the organizations should be mindful of the need for analyzing the KM impact on behavioural (teamwork, sharing, etc.) and financial improvements. This includes identifying the business processes where practices can be replicated and making KM integral to individual and team performance evaluation. A simple method could be computing a KM score for each individual and using it while evaluating annual performance.

From the knowledge-sharing perspective, information technology plays a crucial role in filtering, categorizing and sharing of knowledge with multiple stakeholders. For example, idea generation, submission, filtering and conversion into best practice may involve multiple stakeholder efforts. These efforts can be minimized using technology. For example, to increase the accuracy and classification of knowledge, automated software can be used. It classifies incoming stream of new knowledge and shares it with those who need it. It is recommended that since not all knowledge and data are of the same value, it needs to be prioritized and therefore, it is important to identify data that need to be maintained centrally and controlled. This is where intranet and extranet technology can be readily used. Technology can also be used to develop directory of SMEs to help in finding people in the organization who have specific knowledge. Use of technology in KM initiative can help in enhancing organizational performance. It is recommended to adopt IT tools and technologies which are relevant to the organization.

Knowledge management is much more than mere application of technology. Only a small fraction in the whole KM initiative is technology, rest is non-technical issues. Organization culture determines the extent to which KM activities can influence performance. It is the role of the leader to plan KM initiatives taking into consideration the existing culture and ensuring that KM influences culture. It is important that a nonthreatening culture is cultivated and supported so that employees are not inhibited from sharing ideas. Organizations, therefore, need to create a supportive and collaborative culture which may require redesigning organizational value and introduction of incentive schemes. However, just incentive schemes may not work. It is important to provide coaching and mentoring and also finding time to implement KM. If KM stacks upon the existing workload, people may find it difficult to cope up with their existing workload and may lose interest.

It is also important that organizations must identify a KM leader with strong project management skills—leadership is one of the most important pillars for successful KM implementation. Knowledge management leader is one who ensures that the KM initiative ultimately realizes its objectives. As KM initiative encompasses different functions and departments, the KM leader requires not only good project management but also change management skills. The individual should have a broader understanding of the organization and should have excellent people skills. Therefore, selection of KM leader is crucial.

It is obvious from the above recommendations that the success of KM initiative mandates a structure which eases the flow of information. The KM leader needs to define reporting structures which allows for free flow of ideas. While initiating a KM programme, it is recommended to include plan on how to govern and structure the KM initiative.

Finally, it is recommended that managers should align their KM initiatives with enhancing organizational performance by developing the right kind of metrics to track the progress. This could include the use of indicators (financial and non-financial) to distinguish between individual and team members' contribution to the KM initiative.

As part of the next phase, all best practices will be mandated for submission only through Maxters and not through other modes, such as email, physical copies, etc. All best practices across the group will be shared between the quality team members and points redemption (K-shop) will be expedited. Moving into the next phase would be challenging yet exciting. As KM head, Vikrant had a bigger role to play, that is, streamlining knowledge flows across group companies. Would the challenges be similar or different? Could there have been a better way to implement KM? If yes, what could have been done differently, would the next phase require additional manpower and technical capabilities and who would be responsible to making it a success in group companies? What kind of IT infrastructure would be needed to support the KM group initiative? With these thoughts in mind, his car came to a screeching halt. He had reached home.

Implications for Global Managers

As managers around the globe increasingly face the challenges of handling KM issues, it becomes important for them to understand how effective KM can be planned around critical organization issues. For example, fortune 500 companies lose an enormous amount of money every year by failing to share knowledge. With this in mind, the case discusses the roadmap adopted by Max Life Insurance Company Ltd., as well as what managers can do to make the KM initiative successful.

This research provides a roadmap to implementing KM in organizations. It is important for global managers to acknowledge that KM needs to be implemented as a project wherein it needs to have a strategy and a plan, objectives and deliverables, allocated team, budget, timelines and setting up of accountability. Irrespective of the size of the organization, location or nature of products and services offered, KM offers competitive advantage. Research work on KM have cited KM to work in all major industries like manufacturing, services, financial, banking, insurance, oil and gas, pharmaceuticals, retail, legal, etc. and also across globe.

Managers are bombarded with constant stream of data, and the data overload makes KM increasingly more important. Failure to derive knowledge from data can handicap managers in their quality of decision making. In addition to the theoretical implications, this research has potential implications for practicing managers. Knowledge management as a philosophy cannot survive and achieve intended results unless the initiative is formally planned and developed. This is particularly important for companies which are continuously innovating and generating new ideas and competing globally. Creating structure and opportunities for knowledge creation and sharing is extremely crucial; however, the role of technology in knowledge dissemination cannot be discounted. The cultural differences across countries are to be recognized, understood and managed accordingly. It is also important to build mechanisms for rewarding and recognizing knowledge-sharing behaviour. Further, it is vital to have a high-level sponsor or project champion during the implementation, as KM brings along with it changes which are bound to face resistance. It is important to set up the agenda for change as high priority among practicing mangers in other departments. An impact analysis of KM efforts or KM audit needs to be conducted to identify the strengths and gaps in the current processes. In this way, organizations can ensure that employees treat KM as an important organization-wide initiative and make efforts so that it becomes integrated into the typical working patterns of employees.

This case illustrates a series of interventions taken by Max Life Insurance that can serve as a reference for implementing KM in the enterprise across the globe. The approach includes developing a KM planning and implementation process along with knowledge metrics. In the long run, the approach can transform an organization into a knowledge enterprise, which will fuel innovation and new idea generation to help organizations achieve enhanced knowledge creation and dissemination for sustainable competitive advantage.

Acknowledgements

The case study is part of an outcome of a PhD thesis entitled 'Knowledge Management Practices and Performance in Indian Industry: Manufacturing Versus Service' done under the supervision of Dr Jamal A. Farooquie, Professor, Aligarh Muslim University, Aligarh and Dr Deepak Chawla, Distinguished Professor, International Management Institute, Delhi.

This case is based upon the study of an actual organization; however, the names of the individuals mentioned in the case are fictitious. Nevertheless, the business context is real, images and tables used are from company sources and the learning's based on the feedback received from the respondents are real in nature.

The authors are grateful to the anonymous referees of the journal for their extremely useful suggestions to improve the quality of this article. Usual disclaimers apply.

Appendix I

Interview Template

KM Planning

- 'KM is a fad and it's nothing more than hype'. How do you react to that?
- So you all strongly believe that KM works. What was the need for planning such an initiative?
- Before you started this initiative, how was knowledge being managed in the organization? Cite an example of how it's being handled differently now?
- Where does KM fit in your vision and overall strategy?

KM Implementation

- Have you developed/followed a framework to list out KM activities and milestones?
- Which departments/groups are responsible for KM? Who owns it (IT/HR/Finance/Marketing)?
- Did you face change management issues?
- If yes, then what role did leadership play in overcoming change issues?

KM Infrastructure

- What kind of resource allocation (human, technology, financial, time, etc.) has been allocated to facilitate KM?
- Do you have any technology in place to access/share crucial insights or lessons learnt?

KM Sharing/Culture

- 'Culture is crucial in KM success?' How do you encourage people to share knowledge?
- Do you reward knowledge-creating and knowledge-sharing behaviours?

Knowledge Management Structure

- What kind of KM structure do you promote in your organization?
- What structures are most appropriate for KM?

Knowledge Management Impact/Assessment

- To what extent, do you think KM has achieved its objective?
- How do you monitor/assess whether KM is happening?
- Has KM influenced any policy-level changes?
- How do you measure the impact of KM on performance? What are the performance indicators used? Have you identified both financial and non-financial indicators?

Knowledge Management Improvement

- Have you developed feedback mechanism across all levels? How do you process this feedback into action?
- Do you follow what other individuals/organizations are doing in KM? How has it helped?

Knowledge Management Critical Success Factors

- What are the CSF which contributes to success and sustainability of KM initiative?
- Are there any 'Do's' and 'Don'ts' related to KM?

Appendix 2

About Max Life Insurance Company

Max Life Insurance, an India-based Life Insurance Company is in the business of offering life insurance solutions. The company started its operations in 2001. It is headquartered in New Delhi, India, and is one of the largest non-bank private sector insurers. Its network comprises more than 7,500 employees, more than 35,000 advisors who offer 24 insurance products across more than 1,000 cities of India. The company is one of the six companies under the Max Group of companies. Others are Max Healthcare (MHC), Max Bupa Health Insurance (MBHI), Antara, Max Neeman Medical International (MNMI) and Max Specialty Films (MSF). Max Healthcare is a leading provider of health care services including patient care, scientific research and medical education. The vision of Max Life Insurance is to become the most admired Life Insurance Company for all stakeholders through the guiding values which include caring, credibility, collaborative and excellence. The goal is to use knowledge effectively to develop an ability to consistently perform at a higher level, better than the competitors. The thrust is on developing a knowledge-based network that enables all stakeholders in the value chain to submit process, store and disseminate vital knowledge. The company which has sold more than 5 million policies since inception relies on KM for continuously replenishing the organizational knowledge repository.

References

Aujirapongpan, S., Vadhanasindhu, P., Chandrachai, A., & Cooparat, P. (2010). Indicators of knowledge management capability for KM effectiveness. *VINE, 40*(2), 183–203.

Babu, M., & Bhide, P. (2012). How can insurance organizations cash in on knowledge management? *The Malaysian Insurance Institute*. Retrieved 20 February 2015, from http://www.infosys.com/industries/insurance/Documents/insurance-organizations-cash.pdf

Birkinshaw, J. (2001). Why is knowledge management so difficult? *Business Strategy Review, 12*(1), 11–18.

Davenport, T.H., DeLong, D.W., & Beers, M.C. (1998). Successful knowledge management projects. *Sloan Management Review, 39*(2), 43–57.

Davenport, T.H., & Prusak, L. (1998). *Working knowledge: How organizations manage what they know*. Cambridge, MA: Harvard Business School Press.

Dilnutt, R. (2002). Knowledge management in practice—Three contemporary case studies. *International Journal of Accounting Information Systems, 3*(2), 75–81.

Fernandez, I.B., & Sabherwal, R. (2010). *Knowledge management—Systems and processes*. Armonk, NY, London: M.E. Sharpe.

Garud, R., & Kumaraswamy, A. (2003). *Infosys: Architecture of a scalable corporation* (No. RG 2003). Leanard N. Stern School of Business, New York University, NY RG 2003.

Germain, M.L. (2006). *Stages of psychometric measurement development: The sample of the generalized expertise measure (GEM)*. Paper presented at the Academy of Human Resource Development International (AHRD) Conference, Symposium 42-2, Columbus, Ohio, 22–26 February 2006(pp. 893–898). Retrieved 20 January 2012, from http://www.eric.ed.gov/PDFS/ED492775.pdf

Grossman, M. (2006). An overview of knowledge management assessment approaches. *The Journal of American Academy of Business, 8*(2), 242–247.

Huang, Li-Su, & Lai, Chend-Po. (2014). Critical success factors for knowledge management implementation in life insurance enterprises. *International Journal of Management and Marketing Research, 7*(2), 79–89.

Kvale, S. (1996). *Interviews: An introduction to qualitative research interviewing.* London, UK: SAGE Publications.

Major, E., & Cordey-Hayes, M. (2000). Knowledge translation: A new perspective on knowledge transfer and foresight. *Foresight, 2*(4), 411–423.

Massa, S., & Testa, S. (2009). A knowledge management approach to organizational competitive advantage: Evidence from the food sector. *European Management Journal, 27*(2), 129–141.

Mehta, N., Oswald, S., & Mehta, A. (2007). Infosys technologies: Improving organizational knowledge flows. *Journal of Information Technology, 22*(4), 456–464.

Mohanty, K.S., & Chand, M. (2007). 5iKM3—knowledge management maturity model, Tata Consultancy Services Whitepaper. Retrieved 27 February 2007, from http://www.tcs.com/SiteCollectionDocuments/WhitePapers/5iKM3KnowledgeManagementMaturityModel.pdf

O'Dell, C. (2004). *The executive's role in knowledge management.* Houston, TX: American Productivity and Quality Center.

Pandey, K.N. (2014). Knowledge management processes: A case study of NTPC and PowerGrid. *Global Business Review, 15*(1), 151–174.

Powell, W. (1998). Learning from collaboration: Knowledge and networks in the biotechnology and pharmaceutical industries. *California Management Review, 40*(3), 228–240.

Powell, E.T., & Renner, M. (2003). Analyzing qualitative data. University of Wisconsin-Extension, Madison, Wisconsin. Retrieved 20 November 2011, from http://learningstore.uwex.edu/assets/pdfs/G3658-12.pdf

Prieto, I.M., & Smith, M.E. (2006). Dynamic capabilities and the role of organizational knowledge: An exploration. *Information Systems Research, 15*(5), 500–510.

Rajakannu, M. (2008). Wipro collaboration and KM journey. Wipro Technologies Whitepaper. Retrieved 18 August 2008, from http://www.wipro.com/webpages/insights/kmjourney.htm

Wong, K.Y., & Aspinwall, E. (2006). Development of a knowledge management initiative and system: A case study. *Expert Systems with Applications, 30*(4), 633–641.

Yajnik, N.M. (2014). Case studies of knowledge management in India. *Global Management Journal, 6*(1), 5–11.

PART 9

JOURNALS ON DEVELOPING RELATIONSHIPS AND WORKPLACE ACHIEVEMENT

Capacity and Capability Building for National HRD: A Multilevel Conceptual Framework

Alagaraja, M. and Githens, R. P.

Abstract
Human resource development (HRD) scholars have grappled with the question of developing theoretical and conceptual frameworks that capture the complexities of building human capital capacity and capability at a national level. Relying on national HRD (NHRD) and international development literatures, we develop a multi-level framework for understanding capacity and capability building that is useful for assessing national development priorities for countries in general. We theorize that NHRD priorities must consider the simultaneous development of financial, industrial, and workforce capacities at the national, organizational, and individual levels. The conceptual framework considers positive as well as negative NHRD synergies that can emerge from linking financial, industrial, and workforce capacities to capability-building efforts at the national, organizational, and individual levels. In doing so, the framework contributes to the NHRD-model-building approaches in the extant HRD literature.

Keywords
national HRD, workforce development, foundations of HRD, international HRD

The field of human resource development (HRD) has a dominant focus on training and development for enhancing learning and performance in organizational contexts (Swanson & Holton, 2009). In addition, other streams of HRD literature recognize the importance of a macro-level focus on workforce development for long-term

[1]University of Louisville, KY, USA
[2]University of the Pacific, Sacramento, CA, USA

Corresponding Author:
Meera Alagaraja, Organizational Leadership and Learning, College of Education and Human Development, University of Louisville, 347, CEHD, Louisville, KY 40292, USA.
Email: meera.alagaraja@louisville.edu

development of human resources at the national level (Lynham & Cunningham, 2006; McLean, 2012). This focus puts national human resource development (NHRD) as a dominant driver in national and global contexts where the impact of macro-level economic, technological, socio-cultural, and political forces shapes the development of human resources for achieving economic growth, renewal, and in more recent times, toward recovery as well. Thus, the design, formulation, and implementation of HRD strategies can create a robust multi-level platform conducive for national growth and prosperity for countries in general (Cho & McLean, 2004; Lynham & Cunningham, 2006).

Utilizing single or cross-country comparisons, NHRD scholars identified macro-level contextual factors in developing unique NHRD strategies (Lynham & Cunningham, 2006). However, theory or model-building efforts in NHRD to date remain underexplored (Alagaraja & Wang, 2012b). The reality is that the context of HRD exists in the interplay of individuals, organizations, and national forces in all countries. In this article, we present a multi-level framework by conceptualizing additional levels of analysis to address an important gap in the NHRD-model-building literature. Such a focus suggests alternative pathways for examining NHRD strategies, challenges, and opportunities facing countries today.

Scope of NHRD

Several HRD scholars examined opportunities and challenges that enable or hinder the long-term development of human resources at the national level (Cho & McLean, 2004; Lynham & Cunningham, 2006). This literature expands the traditional lens of HRD, which primarily focused on individual, team, and organizational contexts. HRD supports economic development strategies by promoting job growth and employment through enhancing training and development as well as skill development, specifically, in organizational contexts. The traditional lens, however, fails to consider marginalized and vulnerable sections of the adult workforce that have little to no access to basic skills training, education, or retraining (Torraco, 2007). In today's global economic environment, it is imperative for HRD to not only focus on workforce development, skill development, and training of employees within the private sector but also emphasize the development of skills at the regional and national levels by considering training/retraining of the partially employed, underemployed, unemployed, as well as new entrants to the labor force. Thus, an NHRD perspective provides an opportunity for taking a broader multi-level view for designing, assessing, and investigating national development priorities of countries in general (Ardichvili, Zavyalova, & Minina, 2012).

For the purpose of this article, NHRD is defined as strategies, programs, and policy development initiatives that target capability building as well as capacity building of human resources at the national level (Cho & McLean, 2004). This definition is useful for two reasons. First, the definition identifies different NHRD *capability*-building strategies by targeting individuals through education, training, and development. Capability building focuses on assisting individuals through skill development, vocational education and training, as well as educating and advancing the adult workforce (Kuchinke, 2010). These capability-building efforts elaborate on the demographic compositions of people, including geographic considerations (e.g., rural vs. urban), gender, age educational attainment, ethnicities, skills acquired, and employment mobility. It also includes the degree to which individuals are able to exercise "freedoms" to lead a livelihood of their choice (Kuchinke, 2010; Sen, 1999). Capability-building efforts at the individual level affect organizations and collectively, the nation as a whole.

Second, *capacity*-building efforts emphasize protecting and building natural resources, industrial and financial capacities, as well as consideration of workforce development capacities that can foster an NHRD environment for accelerating productivity and growth (McKinsey Quarterly, 2012). Recent NHRD publications discuss capacity building by linking national strategic goals with the planning of higher education systems, technical and vocation education systems, and workplace training and development programs (Ardichvili et al., 2012; Arthur-Mensah & Alagaraja, 2013; Rana & Ardichvili, 2015). While a full elaboration of human development efforts such as health, access to food, water, nutrition, and housing is beyond the scope of NHRD, we see developing industrial infrastructure, financial capacities, as well as natural resources as important for fostering NHRD environments conducive for competitive growth. Specifically, we adopt NHRD-literature-based classification of countries as advanced, transitioning, and emerging markets (Lynham & Cunningham, 2006). This classification scheme accounts for countries' competitive positioning in the global economy.

Purpose Statement

The development of multi-level conceptual frameworks is important for the following reasons. Policy makers predominantly adopted economic development models from developed countries. This left out emerging market contexts experiencing socio-economic transformations and as such cannot be adequately addressed through existing NHRD models (Alagaraja & Wang, 2012a). There is also limited literature examining the evolution of NHRD strategy development explaining HRD priorities in the contexts of advanced countries that are undergoing declining growth, slow economic recovery, and/or shifts in demographic compositions (McKinsey Quarterly, 2012). Third, current NHRD "model examples" emphasize economic, social, and cultural development as the core foundation for comparing and assessing NHRD strategies across different countries (Cho & McLean, 2004; McLean, 2012). Furthermore, the emergent cross-country comparison models of HRD at the national level emphasize economic development as the foundation of their assessment efforts. These models reflect the growth of a broad consensus that NHRD is critical for achieving economic and social development outcomes (Storberg-Walker, 2009).

Building on the NHRD literature, we attempt to focus on capacity- and capability-building efforts aimed at integrating national, organizational, and individual interests. The goal of the article was to develop a multi-level framework for examining NHRD strategies for countries including advanced, transitioning, and emerging markets. A multi-level framework helps identify additional components that are important and necessary for developing NHRD strategies. We do not intend to argue that common NHRD strategies would be universally beneficial for all countries. Rather, countries may reap possible benefits of developing alternative NHRD strategies from identifying additional levels of analysis as a conceptual starting point for building an NHRD framework.

To do so, the article addresses two main questions: First, what additional considerations of NHRD strategies address HRD challenges faced in advanced, transitioning, and emerging market economies at the national level? Second, what are the HRD challenges faced by the countries at the national, organizational, and individual levels? *By attending to these questions, we develop a multi-level framework that offers an expanded view of NHRD strategy formulation and design, as well as suggest direction for future NHRD research and practice.*

Review of NHRD Models in the Literature

As our focus was on NHRD model building, we used the following literature bases: (a) country-level HRD strategy, (b) country-level human resource management (HRM) strategy, and (c) national HRD/HRM models and frameworks as predetermined criteria to conduct the literature review. These search criteria were utilized using EBSCO, Google Scholar, and ABI/Inform. We narrowed our search to focus primarily on articles that conceptualized the development of NHRD models and frameworks. The final result elicited 21 articles both from HRD and in disciplines outside HRD, such as labor economics, public policy, and HRM.

The NHRD literature from HRD publications focused on priorities and policies for a number of advanced, transitioning, and emerging market economies (Lynham & Cunningham, 2006). This literature enhanced our understanding of the concept of NHRD as well as debates regarding its theoretical foundations (McLean, 2012; McLean, Lynham, Azevedo, Lawrence, & Nafukho, 2008; G. G. Wang & Swanson, 2008; J. Wang & Wang, 2006). Other NHRD models continued the investigation of political and socio-cultural systems (Cho & McLean, 2004; Cunningham, Lynham, & Weatherly, 2006; Lynham & Cunningham, 2006) and expanded the theoretical knowledge base of NHRD. These models were helpful in identifying core NHRD characteristics that were necessary for developing policies, program recommendations, and implications for policy makers.

Early models from the non-HRD literature had a more narrow focus on conducting cross-country comparisons. For example, education-led systems (formal, informal, enterprise-led, vocational educational systems) formed the basis of comparative assessment in the United States, United Kingdom, France, and Germany (Calloids, 1994; Furth, 1985; Green, 1991). Other models in this stream of literature focused on strengthening conceptual and theoretical understanding through empirical investigations. For example, scholars examined the effects of occupational and labor markets on vocational- and enterprise-led education systems in Germany, France, Brazil, and Japan (Koike & Inoki, 1990). A second focus in the literature examined historical and cultural influences on industry and vocational education systems in the United States, France, Germany, Austria, Switzerland, and Japan (Castro & Alfthan, 1992). Furthermore, scholars investigated the role of the government in vocational and workplace training at the regional levels in Singapore, Taiwan, and South Korea (Ashton, Green, James, & Sung, 1999). Another approach focused on institutional arrangements and relationships between (a) labor markets, (b) industries, (c) existing educational and skill development systems, and (d) the utilization of national skills development through partnerships between the government- and private-sector organizations in North American and European countries (Ashton, Sung, & Turbin, 2000). These non-HRD models consider the development of human resources at the national level. The inclusion of these models in our review strengthens the limited NHRD-model-building literature in HRD. Therefore, the non-HRD models were considered as NHRD models in this article. Building on the HRD and NHRD approaches, contributions from HRD also began to focus on conducting cross-country comparisons for examining economic, social, cultural, and political opportunities in emerging market economies such as China, India, Ghana, and Brazil (Alagaraja & Wang, 2012a; Arthur-Mensah & Alagaraja, 2013; Hasler, Thompson, & Schuler, 2006; Ke, Chermack, Lee, & Lin, 2006).

In the HRD literature, Cho and McLean (2004) classified countries based on the central role of government in economic development. Five emerging NHRD classifications describe centralized NHRD, transitional NHRD, government-initiated NHRD, decentralized/free market NHRD, and small-nation NHRD models based on the extent to which the government played a central to almost decentralized role in NHRD. More recently, Alagaraja and Wang (2012a) developed a cross-country comparison model tracing the evolution of economic transformation elaborating on the social, political, and cultural systems prevalent in India and China.

The dominant focus of NHRD models in the HRD and non-HRD literature considers national economic development as a starting point for conducting country comparisons. The models identified a variety of national priorities such as education-led systems, linkages between labor markets, employers as well as public institutions that support work-based learning systems (Ashton et al., 2000). Second, NHRD strategies are contextual and differ in the ways in which they are designed, formulated, and implemented. Third, NHRD models were primarily developed in one of the following national economic contexts: advanced, transitioning, and emerging markets, which limit their broad applicability across these contexts. These models support the established NHRD view that there is no single path toward achieving economic growth and prosperity (McLean, 2012). Finally, NHRD strategies and policies are likely to be more effective when they also consider the dynamic impact of social, political, cultural, and economic systems on education, labor markets, and coordination of alliances among stakeholder institutions (e.g., government, private-, and public-sector organizations; Alagaraja, Kotamraju, & Kim, 2014). These findings reveal the plurality of NHRD strategies that are often developed through diverse contexts.

The current NHRD literature, although providing important insights into the issues, challenges, and opportunities facing different countries, suffers from several limitations.

First, it is fragmented across several research streams such as HRD, public policy, and labor economics. Second, although there is consensus regarding the analysis of macro-level factors such as national-level economic, political, and cultural systems, identification of micro-level factors at the organizational and individual levels can yield rich insights into the selection of certain NHRD strategies. Second, even though several scholars explore NHRD cross-country comparisons, they fail to provide a systematic framework through which NHRD strategies can be organized, examined, and understood (Alagaraja & Wang, 2012a). We address these limitations by proposing a multi-level conceptual framework as they relate to enhancing resource capacities and capability-building efforts.

Developing a Multi-Level Conceptual NHRD Framework

We argue that examination of both micro-level and macro-level NHRD factors is essential. Such an approach considers the interdependence of economic, social, politi-cal, and cultural systems in considering how countries mobilize human resource capacities and enable capability building at the national, organizational, and individual levels. A multi-level framework offers ways to consider policies, practices, and skills that are distinct and appropriate for the three levels of analysis (e.g., national policies, organizational policies and practices, individual skills and knowledge). Such an approach also considers the interaction effects between policies, practices, and skills at the three levels, which can identify ways for creating value. Further examination of the three levels from a HRD perspective can be useful in addressing existing discrep-ancies in the NHRD-model-building literature.

First, we build on the established view in HRD that considers capability building as consisting of primarily three interacting levels: individual, team, and organization (Swanson & Holton, 2009). In our model, we respond to the call of NHRD scholars to describe interorganizational networks and associations between government and private-sector programs that target capability building of individuals (Hawley & Taylor, 2006).

Second, HRD aims for the alignment of human resource capacity with strategic and operational goals to meet individual, team, organizational, and societal objectives. When considering how human resource capacity goals are met on a national scale, HRD programs, initiatives, policies, and even practices cannot successfully occur without necessary investment of industrial and financial resources. According to Jacobs and Hawley (2009), "Workforce development is the co-ordination of public and private sector policies and programs that provide individuals with the opportunity for a sustainable livelihood and helps organizations achieve exemplary goals, consis-tent with the societal context" (p. 2543). When examining NHRD contexts, it is appro-priate to consider financial and industrial resources in addition to the socio-cultural, political, and educational systems. All of these exist in a symbiotic relationship that fosters the development of individual capabilities, spurs economic growth, and ensures sustainability. This perspective of NHRD suggests that countries have an array of common choices and value implications that can be identified by conceptualization of additional levels of analysis when making decisions or responding to external forces with respect to NHRD strategy.

Al-Zendi and Wilson (2012) define capacity building as the "potential for using resources effectively" (LaFond & Brown, 2003, p. 7). In their view, capacity building identifies important resources that offer opportunities for growth at national, organizational, and individual levels. They identified financial, manufacturing, and education as three broad resource capacities that can improve the performance capabilities at the national, organizational, and individual levels.

Their proposed conceptual model viewed these resource capacities as bottlenecks or constraints that can prevent or block the growth and development of an organization, individual, or even a nation state. According to them, financial, manufacturing, and educational "bottlenecks" can prevent the full utilization of HRD. The triage of "bottlenecks" must be overcome for achieving community and national development (p. 1). Their model suggests that NHRD strategies must involve the consideration of these resource factors from a constraining capacity perspective.

We reframed Al-Zendi and Wilson's (2012) model of "bottlenecks" as areas of capacity that need to be developed. Instead of focusing on bottlenecks, we considered the importance of examining resources or capacities from a development perspective that views each resource capacity and their interaction effects as fully functioning and sufficiently complementary. We also broadened the terminology of the resource capacities to increase their applicability to advanced, transitioning, and emerging market countries. Therefore, we adopted industrial capacities to refer to manufacturing bottlenecks, and "workforce capacities" replaced "educational bottlenecks" to identify resources capacities that would work in various types of economies.

We identify (a) financial capacity, (b) industrial capacity, and (c) workforce capacity as three *capacity development* factors that influence *capability* building at the national, organizational, and individual levels. The multi-level framework of NHRD is presented as a matrix (see Figure 1) that considers each of these factors. These intersections are essential to consider because the factors interact with others continuously. Within "emerging markets," "transitional," or "advanced" economies, each country relies on similar NHRD resources (i.e., financial, industrial, workforce capacities) to advance growth and development by building capabilities at multiple levels (i.e., individual, organizational, national). Later in this article, we identify NHRD strategy alternatives in which capacity–capability complementarities can be organized in Figure 1.

We contend that development of workforce capacity exists in dynamic relationship with financial and industrial capacities. A skilled workforce is not needed to work in the formal economy in the absence of financial capacity, nor could financial and industrial capacity development occur successfully in the absence of a skilled workforce. The multi-level framework is focused on three interrelated resource capacity factors as they most directly interact with individual, organizational, and national capability-building efforts (as opposed to issues related to basic sustenance). This scope helps avoid confusion with larger concepts such as human development. The identification of NHRD factors is not necessarily exhaustive. They serve as conceptual and select representations of plausible NHRD strategies. As such, they are useful as a starting point toward building a multi-level NHRD framework.

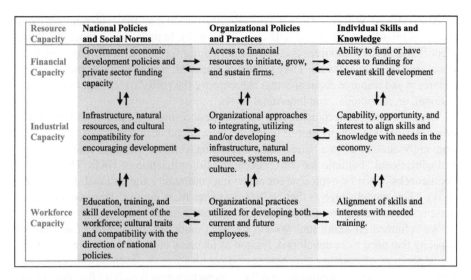

Figure 1. Multi-level contextual framework for considering NHRD.
Note. NHRD = National HRD.

In the subsequent sections, we offer definitions of the basic concepts that are used in the multi-level framework. These definitions present an explanation of how countries value and build financial, industrial, or workforce capacities at the national, organizational, and individual levels. We do so by adopting a linear approach and begin first by defining financial, industrial, and workforce capacities at the national level.

National Policies and Social Norms

Macro-level national policies and social norms comprise an *enabling environment* that influences organizational- and individual-level capability building through "policies, legislation, power relations, and social norms" (United Nations Development Programme, 2008, p. 6). Cho and McLean's (2004) country classification suggests the overarching role of national policies and social norms, which influence the NHRD trajectory of different countries. Thus, for example, when national governments (e.g., China, India) formulate the overall strategy for "planning, implementing, and assessing HRD policies" at the state and regional levels, NHRD strategy becomes a centralized activity (Cho & McLean, 2004, p. 383). This centralized model is also rooted in a strong collectivist nature (Cho & McLean, 2004), which explains the critical influence of social norms on the NHRD trajectories of different countries. In contrast, countries such as the United States have adopted national policies of the free market economic system, which reinforce individualistic orientations toward employee- and organizational-level capability-building efforts.

National Financial Capacity

We define national financial capacity as the willingness of a country to invest in national-, organizational-, or individual-level capability-building efforts and generate returns from these investments. Thus, countries can differ in how they attribute value to certain forms of financial investments in organizations and individuals. For example, some emerging market economies tend to focus on building newer and more grassroots forms of financial capacity building, especially for the rural poor who have limited resource availability (e.g., micro-credit programs in Bangladesh; World Bank, 2008).

Successful utilization of financial capacity at the national level is based on economic development policies for encouraging development. The financial capacity for a country can be treated as an NHRD investment that can lead to economic performance differences across the globe as well as internally within different states and regional cities (McKinsey Quarterly, 2012). Financial capacity at this level represents how a nation acquires or builds those financial resources that they expect will help make better investments in the global as well as internal markets. These financial resources can range from large finance programs for major investments at the national level to the much smaller operating loans that are made available for small businesses, including loans that fund micro-level enterprises and individuals. As an example of national financial capacity building, the World Bank (2013) advocates the development of consistent and predictable procedures for protecting lenders, including establishment of credit registries. According to their perspective, borrowers' and creditors' rights must be clearly delineated to create a more equitable and transparent process. Furthermore, the World Bank report (2013) suggests that the financial capacity of a country is strengthened when minority investors have rights to lawsuits and access to information about organizational finances.

National Industrial Capacity

Industrial capacity at the national level includes the infrastructure, regulatory environment, natural resources, as well as cultural compatibility for encouraging development of different types of industries in diverse geographic regions. Some industries are inherently more compatible with certain countries than others. Geographical location and natural resources are the two major drivers of industries such as mining, agriculture, maritime, and tourism. Other industries are dependent on culture compatibility with the local region. For example, the development of a traditional Western-style resort in an indigenous region may not be compatible with the dominant culture of that region. Another example is that multilingualism in a region may open opportunities for a wider variety of industries. Due to excellence in math and science, some Asian countries may have a higher industrial capacity for some industries in the technology sector (OECD, 2014).

The regulatory environment is another key aspect to consider in allowing for the development of large, medium, small, and even micro-firms. Regulatory burdens include a myriad of requirements, including complying with permits for property attainment, acquiring permits required to open businesses, complying with labor regulations, submission of tax forms, completing procedures for import/exports, and for resolving problems such as enforcement of contracts (World Bank, 2013). Some countries have streamlined processes for completing such requirements (e.g., Singapore, Hong Kong, New Zealand), whereas others require visits to multiple agencies and offices, various forms, and long wait times for approval (World Bank, 2013). Countries with stringent requirements require connections and/or bribes to successfully navigate the labyrinth of regulations (World Bank, 2013). Unwieldy and difficult-to-navigate regulatory systems involve direct costs, labor costs, as well as compliance and opportunity-related costs, which dis-incentivize investments in certain national contexts.

One of the least fixed of these aspects of national industrial capacity is infrastructure because infrastructure such as communication technologies can be developed and enhanced in most locations in the world. The emergence of off-site customer service centers in places such as India and the Philippines has resulted in improved quality and reduced costs (Jacobs & Hawley, 2009). Investments in infrastructure offer ways of reaching out to rural populations and also demand that NHRD strategies invest in enhancing access to training for adult populations. Of course, cultural, social, and political barriers sometimes prevent the development of adequate infrastructure for some industries. If financial and workforce capacity is not in place, additional changes can arise in the utilization and development of industrial capacity.

National Workforce Capacity

National workforce capacity is dependent upon primary, secondary, and postsecondary education, as well as other formal and informal systems that encourage training by employers and non-governmental organizations (NGOs). The development of workforce capacity is interdependent with financial development and industrial capacity development. Misalignment among any of three factors can lead to national economic problems. For example, if these formal or informal systems do not match the needs of employers, it can result in underemployment (i.e., excess supply of workers in some fields), worker shortages, or lack of supply of workers. For instance, Panama is an example of a country experiencing impressive economic and industrial growth without an adequately educated citizenry to fill those roles (Bureau of Economic and Business Affairs, 2012; Githens, Albornoz, Gonzalez, Rocco & Wiggins-Romesburg, 2014; International Monetary Fund, 2013; Schwab, 2013). This shortage has resulted in many professional positions being filled with foreigners (Mattson & Teran, 2011).

Postsecondary (or tertiary) education spans the public and private sectors and ranges from short-term technical certificates or courses to university doctoral degree programs. In addition to educational programs occurring in educational and training institutions, national policies can help encourage employer-based learning initiatives. Such initiatives range from worker pipeline programs developed in partnership with public institutions to apprenticeship programs that are independent of colleges and universities, to programs that fund or support the development of existing employees. European countries have strong traditions of apprenticeship programs, in which government incentives are provided for employers paying apprentices during on-the-job training and classroom instruction (Steinberg & Gurwitz, 2014). In the United States, apprenticeship programs have lagged, particularly outside of traditional occupations such as building trades. The U.S. federal government has recently implemented new initiatives designed to expand such workforce development programs outside of traditional occupations.

In some countries, coordinated efforts between private- and public-sector enterprises as well as the state have led to the formation of formally led educational systems that are geared toward addressing specific and unique demands of the markets. For instance, the formation of the national skills development corporation (NSDC) in India came about as a result of formal partnerships where workforce training and development address the needs and demands of a number of industries across diverse sectors (Alagaraja, 2012). Availability and accessibility of programs remain a common theme, particularly in regard to in-demand and growing occupations. The manner in which education providers respond to employers is a crucial link in this relationship between individual, organizational, and national levels (Ghosh & Githens, 2011). In some cases, evidence suggests that higher education institutions lack responsiveness to employers and individuals by not creating programs for in-demand and growing occupations, which hampers efforts to create workforce readiness (Githens, Sauer, Crawford, Cumberland, & Wilson, 2014). Lack of availability of such programs hampers efforts to create workforce readiness.

Workforce readiness is determined in part by social norms. For example, perceptions of employer needs are sometimes removed from actual employer needs. An example is the U.S. perception of the need for or the social desirability of attaining bachelor's degrees. There have been public proclamations from political leaders regarding the desirability of credentials leading to jobs as opposed to only focusing on broader-focused bachelor's degrees (The White House, 2014). In addition, job forecast data indicate mixed findings regarding the need for bachelor's degree (Carnevale, Smith, & Strohl, 2010). Evidence consistently supports the economic viability of many certificate programs as being superior to bachelor's degree for some students in terms of job earnings and likelihood of success (Jacobson & Mokher, 2009).

National-level policies and social norms shape financial, industrial, and workforce capacities. Our analysis contributes to the NHRD literature more specifically by providing an explanation of how different countries are willing to invest in developing financial, industrial, and workforce capacities as well as attribute different values and expectations from these resource investments. These national-level policies and social norms in turn facilitate and/or hinder firms from achieving a position of competitive advantage in the global, national, and regional markets. In what follows, we explore how differences in national development strategies lead to the idiosyncratic nature and development of organizational policies and practices.

Organizational Policies and Practices

One of the primary contributions of the HRD field has been to consider how human expertise can be aligned with organizational needs. Various scholars have emphasized aspects such as learning (Marsick & Watkins, 1994) or performance (Swanson & Holton, 2009), which can benefit the individual, organization, and/or society (e.g., McLean & McLean, 2001; Swanson & Holton, 2009). An organization can have extremely skilled and knowledgeable individuals, but those same individuals can be unfulfilled, dissatisfied, or unproductive when various conditions exist. For example, if individuals are not in the right jobs, work in dysfunctional teams or systems, or feel unsupported by their manager, then individual knowledge and skills are of little benefit (Alagaraja & Shuck, 2015).

The mechanisms for NHRD value creation at the organizational level stem from the continuous alignment of financial, industrial, and workforce capacities. An organization's performance depends on the successful functioning and alignment of all aforementioned factors as well as on the identification of conditions that support the alignment of these capacities under which organizations are able to position themselves to create unique value in their markets. Our analysis aims to address how firms leverage financial, industrial, and workforce capacities for achieving firm performance.

Organizational Financial Capacity

The organizational financial capacity of the firm offers a means of understanding how organizations make decisions regarding resource investments for not only creating customer value but also optimizing their operating costs. The deployment of human resources in this context becomes an important factor. Both the fields of HRD and HRM offer evidence identifying the impact of human resource practices on firm performance. More recent investigations on the topic have established evidence of linking HRD practices, while emphasizing the importance of leadership for enhancing alignment and improving organizational performance (Alagaraja, Cumberland, & Choi, 2015). In the last two decades, there has been an increasing emphasis on the investigation of HRD practices, policies, and systems and their linkage to firm performance (Alagaraja, 2013). This empirical stream of research offers further evidence that investments in the people-related management practices enhance financial performance of organizations. However, stand-alone improvements and financial investments in HRD practices and policies cannot create additional product and service value without enhancements in the industrial capacity of the organization in terms of the culture, infrastructure, and systems. This is discussed below.

Organizational Industrial Capacity

Organizations develop, utilize, or integrate the infrastructure, natural resources, policies, practices, and their unique organizational culture to meet their objectives

(Mintzberg, 1979; Schein, 2010; Uhl-Bien, Marion, & McKelvey, 2007). Strategic planning and execution of those plans by leaders can lead to success or failure of organizations. Some of these activities and processes involve the interface between the organization and the larger system, while others involve internal development (Katz & Kahn, 1966).

A common conceptualization of the theoretical foundations of HRD provides systems theory as a foundation for the field, along with economics and psychology (Swanson & Holton, 2009). Despite this common conceptualization, consideration of the interface between national infrastructure, natural resources, dominant cultural values and norms has not been a focus in the HRD literature. Deep consideration and openness to working in concert with these aspects is essential due to the interconnectedness of these capacities under which organizations operate (McGuire, Garavan, O'Donnell, & Watson, 2007). A more common emphasis in HRD research has been the development of internal culture, policies, and practices to align human potential and organizational performance. In particular, organization development (OD), when used as a HRD process, has the ability to enhance the alignment of workforce capacity with organizational goals. This occurs through the "system wide application and transfer of behavioral science knowledge to the planned development, improvement, and reinforcement of the strategies, structures, and processes that lead to organization effectiveness" (Cummings & Worley, 2009, pp. 1, 2). More recent approaches in organizational development and change have prompted the adoption of performance improvement and non-training interventions as a means for enhancing organizational industrial capacity (Hale, 2012).

Organizational Workforce Capacity

Organizational workforce capacity can be enhanced through the design, development, and implementation of HRD practices such as training and performance appraisal (Swanson & Holton, 2009). In fact, the effect of individual HRD practices on firm performance as well as the effect of interrelated HRD practices suggest how organizations can leverage the full capacity of their workforce (Swanson & Holton, 2009). Employer preferences for experience, industry certification, or formal degree attainment vary based on job type, sector, and size of the organization (Bartlett, 2004, 2012).

In addition, organizations can help foster cultures in which informal and incidental learning is encouraged through routine and non-routine work experiences (Marsick, Watkins, Callahan, & Volpe, 2008). Support for workforce capacity development through learning and performance interventions may improve the organization's position in the market. By investing in workforce development, organizations improve on ways to create value.

In turn, expansion of workforce capacity can further support financial capacity and potentially establish a stronger market position for firms. We also contend that when organizational-level capabilities are aligned to national-level policies and social norms, they develop stronger capacities for making NHRD investments than other competitors (Hawley & Taylor, 2006). Finally, in addition to financial, industrial, and workforce capacity improvements at the organizational level and complementary linkages to national policies and social norms, we focus our analysis on individuals' skills and knowledge, which can create differential levels of NHRD value at national and organizational levels.

Individual Skills and Knowledge

In the previous sections, we addressed that leveraging unique NHRD investments creates capabilities at the national and organizational levels. Decisions on talent acquisition, management, and retention in organizations are made on the basis of existing internal and external organizational-level resource capacities. Yet, the historical development of individual skills and knowledge in the HRD literature was primarily conceptualized as an individual endeavor. For instance, the adult education literature has advocated the need for helping individual citizens acquire basic as well as integrated skills (Comings, Reder, & Sum, 2001). Within the context of the HRD research literature, the development of human resources has been examined extensively at the individual level (Swanson & Holton, 2009). However, using the multi-level framework presented in this article, we conceptualize individual-level capability development as existing in tandem with (a) organizational policies and practices, and (b) national policies and social norms. When considering individual skills and knowledge as a discrete category for national HRD, it is clear that the interplay of financial, industrial, and workforce capacities plays a role in determining individual choices and outcomes concerning learning and performance.

Individual Skills and Financial Capacity

Investments in education and training are essential across national contexts as they facilitate economic growth and success (Ashton et al., 2000). Funding levels vary across countries at the primary, secondary, and postsecondary levels. In some countries, abundant funding for a high-quality education at all levels is obtained from government sources (e.g., Germany, Finland), whereas in other countries (e.g., Chile, United States, United Kingdom, Canada) funding for some or all of levels of education comes from individual resources (Ashton et al., 2000). The need for individual investment highlights access issues in some contexts, particularly among individuals from lower-income families or among those living in poverty. The recent global economic meltdown and slow recovery have contributed to the long-term escalation of costs for education and skill development due to declining government support for higher education. These declines have resulted in escalating student loan debt and have hindered other opportunities for access to educational opportunities (e.g., United States). Access to education matters, and as noted by the World Bank (2013), national economic performance can be attributed to having or not having better opportunities to education. We, therefore, need to consider the connection between individual-level educational outcomes and the financial capacity at the organizational and national levels.

Individual Skills and Industrial Capacity

In the previous section, we discussed the impact of individual skills development as a stand-alone resource that not only enhances but that is also enhanced by financial capacity. In addition to the potential stand-alone improvements, return on NHRD investments can be enhanced when individual-level skill development is aligned with industrial capacity. Competitive advantages are sustainable when individual and organizational capabilities continuously shift and respond to market demands. Individual capabilities can enhance industrial capacity when skill development is linked to organizational value creation. We suggest that the intersection of individual skills and industrial capacity can create an effective production of organizational value that results in the development of new products, services, technologies, and social media trends. As Toner (2011) suggests, the accumulation of skills, education, knowledge, and innovation is critical to national development. These in turn enhance existing industrial capacities in new, innovative, and disruptive ways. However, disruptive technologies change or diminish the value of NHRD investments on individuals, as new and different skills may be demanded (Levy & Murnane, 2004). The multi-level conceptual framework implies the effects of negative complementarities as NHRD strategies evolve and develop over time.

Individual Skills and Workforce Capacity

Decisions regarding the development of workforce capacity at the individual level result from cultural, family, and economic factors (Toner, 2011). Individual choices and paths result from the interplay of personal characteristics, background, expectations, interests, goals, and learning experiences (Lent, Brown, & Hackett, 2000). Recent NHRD literature has begun to explore access and opportunities for low-income individuals and those with limited educational backgrounds (Alagaraja et al., 2014). This literature argues the importance of supply and demand of labor as crucial for national economic performance. For instance, the notion of jobs-for-life has become a relic of the past in most countries and sectors, thus placing increasing onus on the individual for acquiring new skills which can further compound existing disparities among disadvantaged and marginalized populations. Furthermore, in the context of the rapidly changing global environment, the acquisition of new skills does not guarantee an adequate fit of the individual with their job. These trends suggest that workforce capacity building from an individual-level perspective has limited influence on wages and has negatively affected the quality of work life experienced by millions of workers in advanced as well as emerging economies.

The limited inclusion of immigrants (Neuman & Ziderman, 2003), disabled youth, and older workers (Kammermann, 2010) also creates additional barriers for building workforce capacity at the individual level. Put together, a fluctuating and uneven supply and demand in the labor market (Baqadir, Patrick, & Burns, 2011), mismatch of jobs, qualifications and interests (Béduwé & Giret, 2011) negatively affect workforce capacity building at the organizational and national levels. Lack of financial resources as well as opportunities for skill and capability development highlights the contextual influences of the national policies, organizational practices, societal, as well as cultural norms. Thus, the broader organizational and national strategies inform the design, development, and institutionalization of qualification and credentialing standards that are important and necessary for NHRD resource creation.

Discussion

To better understand and evaluate NHRD strategies, we need to distinguish the variation that occurs in what countries do in terms of capability building and how they focus their efforts on enhancing resource capacities. Relying primarily on a review and integration of NHRD published in HRD and non-HRD literatures, we present a multi-level framework that integrates financial, industrial, and workforce capacity building with national, organizational, and individual capabilities and outcomes. By adopting a multi-level framework, we place a primary focus on how countries acquire, develop, and manage their NHRD investments. The conceptual framework also offers broad multi-lateral approaches for sustaining financial, industrial, and workforce development initiatives by integrating HRD policies and cultural norms at the national, organizational, and individual levels.

The multi-level framework is useful for assessing national development priorities for countries in general and expands understanding of NHRD models, and adds to the existing NHRD-model-building literature in the following ways: first, the multi-level framework assists in making comparative assessments beyond the traditional categorization as advanced, transitioning, or emerging countries. Existing NHRD model examples elucidate the reasons for variations in the economic development across different national and market contexts (e.g., Cho & McLean, 2004; McLean, 2012). Furthermore, these NHRD models emphasized socio-cultural transformations that also affected NHRD strategies of countries in general. Our framework utilized the prevalent NHRD models as a starting point and further identifies financial, industrial, and workforce capacities and the alignment or misalignment between them as an important determinant of how countries resolve their NHRD priorities. The framework, therefore, strengthens existing efforts of comparing NHRD strategies from the literature. We attempt to address the need for examining NHRD factors at various levels and offer a platform for examining NHRD strategies of countries. Furthermore, this classification helps examining the underlying rationale of the NHRD investments countries commonly undertake for improving economic, socio-cultural, and educational outcomes.

Importantly, the framework identifies how countries attribute value and invest in building financial, industrial, or workforce capacities at the national, organizational, or individual levels. In turn, these investments create diverse NHRD opportunities, challenges, and issues unique to each country. Furthermore, the conceptual framework considers positive as well as negative complementarities that can emerge from linking financial, industrial, and workforce capacities to national, organizational, and individual-level capability-building efforts and outcomes. For example, an overemphasis on building financial, industrial, and workforce capacities at the organizational level can affect NHRD investments at the national and individual levels (e.g., United States). In turn, the reduced investments in national and individual levels can lead to economic recession and delay recovery, which can affect financial, industrial, and workforce capacity in the long term.

The accumulation of skills, education, knowledge, and innovation (Toner, 2011) enhances existing industrial capacities in innovative ways that can change how countries attribute value to NHRD investments. The use of technologies in today's world is a prime example of the impact individuals can enhance, change, or disrupt existing investments in financial and industrial resource capacities. The implication is that new technologies help in expanding or creating new resource capacities that are yet to be fully elaborated. However, the development of new technologies can also reduce existing jobs, increase unemployment, and cause economic recession. Thus, negative complementarities arise out of the development of just one resource capacity. To address this, countries need to consider how strategic choices affect individuals and organizations, and as such the efforts deepen the understanding of NHRD strategy formulation and implementation over time.

The conceptual framework attempts to enrich the existing literature on NHRD models in HRD literature by emphasizing the interdependent interactions that occur when countries prioritize specific NHRD capacity- and capability-building efforts. A possible limitation of the study is that the model presented simplifies the real-world nuances in terms of NHRD differences that can exist. We recognize that NHRD strategies are likely to be driven by macro-level contextual factors (e.g., cultural norms), in addition to idiosyncratic factors (e.g., demographics), and suggest these as areas for future research.

Implications for NHRD Policy, Practice, and Research

The conceptual framework has important implications for NHRD policy, practice, and research. More recent conceptualizations of NHRD in the HRD literature emphasize the importance of addressing macro-level NHRD factors such as economic, political, and socio-cultural challenges at the regional, state, and national levels. We contribute to this established view by offering a multi-level framework for examining the interdependent linkages of NHRD capacity- (i.e., industrial, financial, workforce) and capability-building efforts at the national, organizational, and individual levels. Our conceptual framework offers NHRD strategy alternatives primarily in terms of enhancing capacity and capability building. There are other factors that can potentially influence NHRD strategy in countries that future research could potentially explore.

Specifically, the multi-level conceptual framework suggests that alignment of NHRD capacity- and capability-building efforts can create positive or negative complementarities or some combination of both. These complementarities affect national economic, socio-cultural, and educational outcomes. As we have presented in this article, the country-specific factors provide for unique assessments of NHRD strategy. Because we more explicitly identify the country-level factors, our conceptualization allows NHRD policy makers to better understand and influence investments in enhancing a specific resource capacity. Given the increasing trend toward globalization, countries have begun to adopt NHRD practices from one another with relative ease. For example, the recent economic recession and slow recovery have affected the ways in which advanced, transitioning, and emerging markets are responding to protect or expand their existing financial, industrial, and workforce capacities.

Private-sector organizations have proactively demonstrated their interest and involvement in regional workforce development initiatives. For example, Toyota, Siemens, and other organizations leverage linkages with higher educational institutions such as community colleges and education boards to develop their workforce (Alagaraja et al., 2014; Symonds, Schwartz, & Ferguson, 2011). Emerging markets such as India have begun to institutionalize private-sector partnerships with the federal government such as the NSDC to enhance current labor needs and predict future workforce development pipeline (Alagaraja, 2012). The NSDC has institutionalized formal partnerships with private organizations, professional industry associations, and various levels of governments to identify and create alternative pathways for developing India's workforce. In the global race of economic success, countries have begun to adopt NHRD best practices and strategies to ensure that their citizens are not left behind. These trends suggest that NHRD strategies will continue to focus on developing their workforce capacity at the national (e.g., NSDC), organizational (e.g., Siemens), and individual levels as a way to enhance their industrial capacity to compete in global markets. Specifically, the framework suggests that alignment of workforce development strategies must also consider capacity building of industrial and financial resources.

Policy makers, trade organizations, NGOs, educational systems, and employers can use the concepts presented in this framework in considering the interrelationships between the various factors (Jacobs & Hawley, 2009). Future research can test this model through empirical research at the individual, organizational, or national level. Possibilities for research include analysis of the relationship between multiple factors. Current research has primarily focused on analyzing relationships within one level of analysis (e.g., examining relationship of skills/education to earnings, relationship between organizational learning and training to organizational performance). Building on the past research, new studies could examine relationships at multiple levels (e.g., organizational training programs' impact on state- or national-level economic outcomes). This strand of research has important implications for NHRD policy makers looking to create collaborative public–private and cross-sectoral partnerships involving social enterprises, governmental, non-governmental, and for-profit organizations. The direct effects of encouraging such hybrid linkages connect private-sector-focused HRD outcomes (e.g., organizational-level training and development) with NHRD outcomes (e.g., national-level social and economic development outcomes). The indirect effects of such partnerships can also be controversial because such outcomes may sometimes be viewed as being good for the business and private sector but undermine overall national capacity and capability development. For example, private-sector policies regarding the inclusion of workers based on specific skills and competencies in the workforce can sometimes be viewed as controversial that has long-term implications for building the internal workforce capacity of a country. Therefore, a national-level focus on skill and capacity building can help address organizational policies that sometimes limit or exclude marginalized and vulnerable population groups such as older workers or workers with disabilities. Overall, an NHRD focus can help better manage the supply and demand of workforce skills and capabilities in the labor market.

Our recommendation for NHRD policy makers, practitioners, and researchers would be to recognize this inherent tension between organizational- and national-level HRD outcomes and find ways to reward collaborative partnerships that spur national development. We would like to caution readers that these recommendations are not universal; in every country, the nature of collaborative partnerships would be diverse involving complex arrangements with multiple stakeholders at regional, state, and national levels. Research, theory, and models from the leadership, OD, and organization theory literatures can complement what we have presented in this article.

Finally, we elaborate on the implications of the article for NHRD theory. We build on the established HRD view that considers capability building as consisting of primarily three interacting levels—individual, team, and organization. In the context of NHRD, we identify individual, organization, and national as three distinctive levels that interact to affect NHRD outcomes over the long term. This is a theoretical addition to the NHRD literature. It is crucial for HRD scholars to continue their efforts in building NHRD models and conducting empirical research that addresses the importance of leveraging existing resource capacities and linking these to national-, organizational-, and individual-level capability-building efforts. Finally, our treatment of the capacity- and capability-building efforts as fairly homogeneous constructs in the model is another area, which can be further developed in future research. We contend that developing human resources at the national level will continue to gain priority among employers, governments, and individual citizens. NHRD will continue to gain priority as the countries, organizations, and individuals compete globally for economic survival and success in the future.

Declaration of Conflicting Interests

The author(s) declared no potential conflicts of interest with respect to the research, authorship, and/or publication of this article.

Funding

The author(s) received no financial support for the research, authorship, and/or publication of this article.

References

Alagaraja, M. (2012). National human resource development in practice: An interview with MV Subbiah. *Human Resource Development International, 15*, 515-524.

Alagaraja, M. (2013). Mobilizing organizational alignment through strategic human resource development. *Human Resource Development International, 16*, 74-93.

Alagaraja, M., Cumberland, D., & Choi, N. (2015). The mediating role of leadership and people management practices on HRD and organizational performances. *Human Resource Development International, 18*, 220-234.

Alagaraja, M., Kotamraju, P., & Kim, S. (2014). A conceptual framework for examining HRD and NHRD linkages and outcomes: Review of TVET literature. *European Journal of Training and Development, 38*, 2-20.

Alagaraja, M., & Shuck, B. (2015). Exploring organizational alignment-employee engagement linkages and impact on employee performance: A conceptual model. *Human Resource Development Review, 14*, 17-37.

Alagaraja, M., & Wang, J. (2012a). Development of a national HRD strategy model: Cases of India and China. *Human Resource Development Review, 11*, 407-429.

Alagaraja, M., & Wang, J. (2012b). Reflections on the invited response dominant themes in current NHRD research. *Human Resource Development Review, 11*, 437-442.

Al-Zendi, D., & Wilson, J. P. (2012). Capacity development and human resource development. In J. P. Wilson (Ed.), *International human resource development: Learning, education and training for individuals and organizations* (3rd ed., pp. 215-239). London, England: Kogan Page.

Ardichvili, A., Zavyalova, E. K., & Minina, V. N. (2012). National human resource development strategies: Comparing Brazil, Russia, India, and China. In J. P. Wilson (Ed.), *International human resource development: Learning, education and training for individuals and organizations* (pp. 177-193). London, England: Kogan Page.

Arthur-Mensah, N., & Alagaraja, M. (2013). Exploring technical vocational education and training systems in emerging markets: A case study on Ghana. *European Journal of Training and Development, 37*, 835-850.

Ashton, D., Green, F., James, D., & Sung, J. (1999). *Education and training for development in East Asia: The political economy of skill formation in newly industrialized economies.* London, England: Routledge.

Ashton, D., Sung, J., & Turbin, J. (2000). Towards a framework for the comparative analysis of national systems of skill formation. *International Journal of Training and Development, 47*, 8-25.

Baqadir, A., Patrick, F., & Burns, G. (2011). Addressing the skills gap in Saudi Arabia: Does vocational education address the needs of private sector employers? *Journal of Vocational Education & Training, 63*, 551-555.

Bartlett, K. R. (2004). *The signaling power of occupational certification in the automobile service and information technology industries.* St. Paul, MN: National Research Center for Career and Technical Education.

Bartlett, K. R. (2012, November). *A theoretical review of the signaling role of certifications in career and technical education.* Paper presented at the Association for Career and Technical Education Research Annual Conference, Atlanta, GA.

Béduwé, C., & Giret, J. F. (2011). Mismatch of vocational graduates: What penalty on French labour market? *Journal of Vocational Behavior, 78*, 68-79. doi:10.1016/j.jvb.2010.09.003

Bureau of Economic and Business Affairs. (2012). *2012 investment climate statement: Panama.* Washington, DC: U.S. Department of State.

Calloids, F. (1994). Converging trends amidst diversity in vocational training systems. *International Labor Review, 133*, 241-260.

Carnevale, A. P., Smith, N., & Strohl, J. (2010). *Help wanted: Projections of job and education requirements through 2018.* Lumina Foundation. Washington, DC: Georgetown University, Center on Education and the Workforce.

Castro, C., & Alfthan, T. (1992). *Five training models* (Occasional Paper No. 9). Geneva, Switzerland: ILO.

Cho, E., & McLean, G. N. (2004). What we discovered about NHRD and what it means for HRD. *Advances in Developing Human Resources, 6,* 382-393. doi:10.1177/1523422304266090

Comings, J., Reder, S., & Sum, A. (2001). *Building a level playing field: The need to expand and improve the national and state adult education and literacy systems* (Occasional Paper). Cambridge, MA: National Center for the Study of Adult Learning and Literacy.

Cummings, T. G., & Worley, C. G. (2009). *Organization development and change* (9th ed.). Cincinnati, OH: South-Western College Publishing.

Cunningham, P. W., Lynham, S. A., & Weatherly, G. (2006). National human resource development in transitioning societies in the developing world: South Africa. *Advances in Developing Human Resources, 8,* 62-83.

Furth, D. (1985). *Education and training after basic schooling.* Paris, France: OECD.

Ghosh, R., & Githens, R. P. (2011). Online contract training: Applying organization theory to reconcile competing missions within community colleges. *Human Resource Development Review, 10,* 180-197.

Githens, R. P., Albornoz, C., Gonzalez, L. E., Rocco, T. S., & Wiggins-Romesburg, C. (2014). Development of human resources in Central and South America. In R. Poell, T. S. Rocco & G. Roth (Eds.), *Routledge companion to HRD* (pp. 413-424). London, England: Routledge.

Githens, R. P., Sauer, T. M., Crawford, F. L., Cumberland, D. M., & Wilson, K. B. (2014). Online workforce development in community colleges: Connection with community, institutional, and governance factors. *Community College Review, 42,* 283-306. doi:10.1177/0091552114534724

Green, A. (1991). The reform of post-16 education and training and the lessons from Europe. *Journal of Education Policy, 6,* 327-339.

Hale, J. (2012). *The performance consultant's fieldbook: Tools and techniques for improving organizations and people.* San Francisco, CA: Jossey-Bass/Pfieffer.

Hasler, M. G., Thompson, M. D., & Schuler, M. (2006). National human resource development in transitioning societies in the developing world: Brazil. *Advances in Developing Human Resources, 8,* 99-115.

Hawley, J. D., & Taylor, J. C. (2006). How business associations use interorganizational networks to achieve workforce development goals: Implications for human resource development. *Human Resource Development International, 9,* 485-508.

International Monetary Fund. (2013). *Panama* (IMF Country Report No. 13/88). Washington, DC: Author.

Jacobs, R. L., & Hawley, J. D. (2009). The emergence of "workforce development": Definition, conceptual boundaries and implications. In R. Maclean & D. Wilson (Eds.), *International handbook of education for the changing world of work* (pp. 2537-2552). Bonn, Germany: Springer.

Jacobson, L., & Mokher, C. (2009). *Pathways to boosting the earnings of low-income students by increasing their educational attainment.* Washington, DC: Hudson Institute Center for Employment Policy.

Kammermann, M. (2010). Job or further training?: Impact of the Swiss Basic Federal Vocational Education and Training (VET) Certificate on the careers of low achieving young people. *Education+ Training, 52,* 391-403. doi:10.1108/00400911011058334

Katz, D., & Kahn, R. L. (1966). *The social psychology of organizations.* New York, NY: Wiley.

Ke, J., Chermack, T. J., Lee, Y.-H., & Lin, J. (2006). National human resource development in transitioning societies in the developing world: The People's Republic of China. *Advances in Developing Human Resources, 8,* 28-45. doi:10.1177/1523422305283056

Koike, K., & Inoki, T. (1990). *Skill formation in Japan and South East Asia.* Tokyo, Japan: University of Tokyo Press.

Kuchinke, K. P. (2010). Human development as a central goal for human resource development. *Human Resource Development International, 13,* 575-585.

LaFond, A., & Brown, L. (2003). *A guide to monitoring and evaluation of capacity building: Interventions in the health sector in developing countries* (MEASURE Evaluation Manual Series). Chapel Hill: UNC Carolina Population Center.

Lent, R. W., Brown, S. D., & Hackett, G. (2000). Contextual supports and barriers to career choice: A social cognitive analysis. *Journal of Counseling Psychology, 47,* 36-49.

Levy, F., & Murnane, R. J. (2004). *The new division of labor: How computers are creating the next market.* New York, NY: Russell Sage Foundation.

Lynham, S. A., & Cunningham, P. W. (2006). National human resource development in transitioning societies in the developing world: Concept and challenges. *Advances in Developing Human Resources, 8,* 116-135. doi:10.1177/1523422305283150

Marsick, V. J., & Watkins, K. E. (1994). The learning organization: An integrative vision for HRD. *Human Resource Development Quarterly, 5,* 353-360.

Marsick, V. J., Watkins, K. E., Callahan, M. W., & Volpe, M. (2008). Informal and incidental learning in the workplace. In M. C. Smith & N. DeFrates-Densch (Eds.), *Handbook of research on adult learning and development* (pp.570-600) New York, NY: Routledge.

Mattson, S., & Teran, A. (2011, September 6). Education trap threatens Panama's economic boom. *Reuters.* Retrieved from http://www.reuters.com/article/2011/09/06/us-panama-education-idUSTRE7857D420110906

McGuire, D., Garavan, T., O'Donnell, D., & Watson, S. (2007). Metaperspectives and HRD: Lessons for research and practice. *Advances in Developing Human Resources, 9,* 120-139.

McKinsey Quarterly. (2012, November). *Manufacturing the future: The next era of global growth and innovation.* Retrieved from http://www.mckinsey.com/insights/manufacturing/the_future_of_manufacturing

McLean, G. N. (2012). Invited response observations on modeling NHRD strategy. *Human Resource Development Review, 11,* 430-436.

McLean, G. N., Lynham, S. A., Azevedo, R. E., Lawrence, J. E. S., & Nafukho, F. M. (2008). A response to Wang and Swanson's article on national HRD and theory development. *Human Resource Development Review, 7,* 241-258. doi:10.1177/1534484308316486

McLean, G. N., & McLean, L. (2001). If we can't define HRD in one country, how can we define it in an international context? *Human Resource Development International, 4,* 313-326.

Mintzberg, H. (1979). *The structuring of organizations: A synthesis of the research.* Englewood Cliffs, NJ: Prentice Hall.

Neuman, S., & Ziderman, A. (2003). Can vocational education improve the wages of minorities and disadvantaged groups? The case of Israel. *Economics of Education Review, 22,* 421-432. doi:10.1016/S0272-7757(02)00094-8

Organisation for Economic Co-Operation and Development. (2014). *PISA 2012 results in focus: What 15-year-olds know and what they can do with what they know.* Paris, France: Author.

Rana, S., & Ardichvili, A. (2015). Cambodia and the ASEAN economic community: Opportunities, challenges, and implications for human resource development. *Reconsidering Development, 3,* 38-55.

Rao, T. V. (2004). Human resource development as national policy in India. *Advances in Developing Human Resources, 6,* 288-296. doi:10.1177/1523422304266075

Schein, E. H. (2010). *Organizational culture and leadership* (4th ed.). San Francisco, CA: Jossey-Bass.

Schwab, K. (2013). *The global competitiveness report 2013-2014: Full data edition*. Geneva, Switzerland: World Economic Forum.

Sen, A. (1999). *Development as freedom*. New York, NY: Oxford University Press.

Steinberg, S. A., & Gurwitz, E. (2014). *Innovations in apprenticeship: 5 Case Studies that illustrate the promise of apprenticeship in the United States*. Washington, DC: Center for American Progress.

Storberg-Walker, J. (2009). Integrative literature reviews: Heterodox economics, social capital, and HRD: Moving beyond the limits of the neoclassical paradigm. *Human Resource Development Review, 8*, 97-119.

Swanson, R. A., & Holton, E. F., III. (2009). *Foundations of human resource development* (2nd ed.). San Francisco, CA: Berrett-Koehler.

Symonds, W. C., Schwartz, R. B., & Ferguson, R. (2011). *Pathways to prosperity: Meeting the challenge for preparing young Americans for the 21st century*. Boston, MA: Pathways to Prosperity Project, Harvard Graduate School of Education.

Toner, P. (2011). *Workforce skills and innovation: An overview of major themes in the literature*. Paris, France: OECD.

Torraco, R. (2007). Low-skilled adults in the United States: A case of human resource underdevelopment. *Human Resource Development Review, 6*, 343-352.

Uhl-Bien, M., Marion, R., & McKelvey, B. (2007). Complexity leadership theory: Shifting leadership from the industrial age to the knowledge era. *The Leadership Quarterly, 18*, 298-318.

United Nations Development Programme. (2008). *Capacity development practice note*. Retrieved from http://www.undp.org/content/dam/aplaws/publication/en/publications/capacity-development/capacity-development-practice-note/PN_Capacity_Development.pdf

Wang, G. G., & Swanson, R. A. (2008). The idea of national HRD: An analysis based on economics and theory development methodology. *Human Resource Development Review, 7*, 79-106. doi:10.1177/1534484307311415

Wang, J., & Wang, G. G. (2006). Exploring national human resource development: A case of China management development in a transitioning context. *Human Resource Development Review, 5*, 176-201. doi:10.1177/153448430628727

The White House. (2014). *Remarks by the President on opportunity for all and skills for America's workers*. Retrieved from http://www.whitehouse.gov/the-press-office/2014/01/30/remarks-president-opportunity-all-and-skills-americas-workers

World Bank. (2008). *Bangladesh: Financial services for the poorest*. Washington, DC: Author.

World Bank. (2013). *Doing business 2014: Understanding regulations for small and medium-size enterprises*. Washington, DC: Author.

Author Biographies

Meera Alagaraja is an assistant professor at the University of Louisville. Her research and consulting expertise focus on workplace spirituality, leadership, and talent management. Her research publications in *Human Resource Development Quarterly, Human Resource Development Review*, and *Human Resource Development International* emphasize the role and importance of HRD in the implementation of strategies such as Lean. Her prior experience in India and the U.S. involved the implementation of Lean and Six Sigma strategies in manufacturing companies. She interacted with more than 200 senior executives from both countries to understand, support, and contribute to organization development and change. This work resulted in research and practitioner publications. She has worked and consulted for healthcare sector companies in the U.S. and India.

Rod Patrick Githens is an associate professor and assistant dean for Sacramento Programs in the Gladys L. Bernerd School of Education at University of the Pacific. His primary research interests center around fostering humane, accessible, and diverse workplaces. Prior to beginning his faculty career, he worked for several years in the corporate sector doing HRM and HRD work. He continues to consult with various types of organizations through his consulting practice, Githens and Associates.

Using Work-Integrated Learning to Enhance Career Planning among Business Undergraduates

Jackson, D. A.

Abstract

Effective career planning among undergraduates is increasingly important amid competitive graduate labour markets and high levels of graduate underemployment. Students must be able to set clearly defined career objectives and be equipped to identify suitable development pathways to achieve their career goals. This study examined the impact of work-integrated learning on student career planning. It focused on the completion of an elective work placement by 102 business undergraduates in a Western Australian university. The study adopted a qualitative approach and used structured reflections to examine how the placement influenced students' career objectives, developed their self-awareness in the context of career planning, and helped them identify personal development strategies to improve their employment prospects. Drawing on social cognitive career theory, the study advances our understanding of how work-integrated learning can shape undergraduate career objectives and improve currently weak levels of student engagement with career planning. Implications for future career counselling are discussed.

Keywords

Career planning, work-integrated learning, work placement, student, business

Introduction

Effective career planning involves setting clearly defined career objectives and strategies for achieving them (Gould, 1979). The modern worker must successfully interpret and navigate a myriad of evolving career opportunities, adapting and up-skilling themselves to the changing needs of industry (Lent, 2013). Despite career management provision evolving far beyond individual counselling and sometimes being embedded in undergraduate curriculum (Watts, 2006), students are often undecided about where they are heading and what avenue to pursue postgraduation (McKeown & Lindorff, 2011). Given highly competitive graduate labour markets (Graduate Careers Australia (GCA), 2016) and elevated levels of graduate underemployment and unemployment (Karmel & Carroll, 2016), it is increasingly important for students to be proactive and focused in their career planning (Segers & Inceoglu, 2012).

Work-integrated learning (WIL) is one platform that can give clarity to students on which career objective to pursue and how. It enables students to develop an understanding of effective professional practice through integrating their learning across practice and education settings (Billett, 2011). While grounded in the theory of experiential learning (Kolb, 1984), Billett asserts the two settings may produce different experiences and learning, which the student will come to associate and reconcile (or perhaps reject) through reflection and critical evaluation. This provides a rich, and superior, learning experience and affords deep insight into student's intended profession and world of work. There has been some attention to the typology of WIL (see, for example Sattler, Wiggers, & Arnold, 2011) and acknowledgement that it can take many forms. These include 'immersed' models – such as internships, placements, and practicums – and others where individuals might not be physically based in the work setting for prolonged periods – such as industry-based projects and simulations.

WIL provides insight into the realities of a profession (Daniel, 2010) and affords students the opportunity to experiment with their professional identity (Trede, Macklin, & Bridges, 2012). It can influence career choice (see Anderson et al., 2012)

Corresponding author:
Denise A Jackson, School of Business and Law, Edith Cowan University, 2.361b, 270 Joondalup Drive, Joondalup, WA 6027, Australia.
Email: d.jackson@ecu.edu.au

and assists students with developing career self-management skills (see, for example Pegg, Waldock, Hendy-Isaac, & Lawton, 2012; Smith et al., 2009). The overarching aim of this study is to explore the influence of WIL on career planning, motivated by an apparent lack of research in this area and weak levels of student engagement with career planning processes (see McKeown & Lindorff, 2011; Pegg et al., 2012). Being a phenomenological study, it explores the experiences of students who participate in WIL and seeks to address the following research objectives: (i) to examine the influence of WIL on career objectives; (ii) to explore key factors which students learn about themselves, in the context of career planning, during their WIL experience; and (iii) to examine how WIL helps students identify and evaluate strategies for improving themselves and their employment prospects.

The study adopts a qualitative approach and uses the structured reflections of 102 business undergraduates undertaking WIL in a Western Australian university. The focus is on students gaining work experience through immersion in a professional setting relevant to their degree studies, termed a work placement. The study contributes to existing literature in two ways. First, it advances our understanding of the factors that underpin undergraduate career objectives and how WIL might influence these. Second, it draws on social cognitive career theory (SCCT) (Lent, Brown, & Hackett, 1994); exploring how WIL can improve career planning among students. The paper is structured to review relevant literature, followed by an overview of methodology and presentation of results. Findings are discussed in respect to implications for stakeholders, before the concluding remarks.

Background

Career planning

Career planning involves setting goals, identifying strategies, and establishing an action plan, with associated timelines, required to successfully achieve the intended career objectives (Zikic & Klehe, 2006). It can be interpreted through the theoretical lens of the DOTS model of career development (Watts, 2006) which comprises the four elements of decision-making learning, opportunity awareness, transition learning, and self-awareness. In particular, career planning aligns with the dimension of decision-making learning. Setting career goals or objectives gives the individual direction and stability and is associated with higher levels of commitment, perseverance, and resilience to changing conditions (see Seibert, Kraimer, Holtom, & Pierotti, 2013). It can, however, be 'a tricky proposition, especially in the context of an uncertain, changing, and sometimes unkind environment' (Lent, 2013, p. 6). There has been an increasing shift towards intensive global

competition and complex working structures (Yuhee & Takeuchi, 2016) and a rise in part-time, project-based, and contract-based working with increased job mobility and less organisational career development (see Lent, 2013). Lent argues workers are expected to adapt to the evolving needs of the organisation and role, requiring effective career planning to remain competitive.

The call for career planning is amplified by the shift to the boundaryless career (Arthur & Rousseau, 1996) where individuals are no longer focused on the 'organisational' career but now seek opportunities across different organisations. The modern career is increasingly characterised by multiple job changes, horizontal career movement, and global mobility (Foundation for Young Australians (FYA, 2015), requiring fine-tuned skills in career self-management and a clear idea of long-term aspirations and how they will be achieved (Coetzee & Beukes, 2010). Further, many of the roles with which our curricula align could radically change in the coming years due to automation (FYA, 2015) and students must stay abreast of shifts and trends in the labour market. Students also need to consider how they can differentiate themselves from the growing pool of recruits to enhance their chances of graduate-level employment. To source suitable opportunities and access the hidden job market, they need a personal brand and must be networked and connected (Bridgstock, 2016). Never before has career planning been so important to our students.

Role of WIL

WIL integrates academic learning and real-world experience and capitalises on self-reflection and industry feedback (Smith, 2012). There has been significant attention to the benefits of WIL, suggesting it enhances student self-confidence (Lowden, Hall, Elliott, & Lewin, 2011), improves their non-technical skills (Australian Workforce and Productivity Agency (AWPA), 2013), and provides them with a unique insight into the conduct and behaviour associated with a particular profession (Woodley & Beattie, 2011). WIL offers professional development for the host organisation's staff through their mentoring of participating students (AWPA, 2013) and allows industry to direct student learning and identify talent prior to graduation (Wilson, 2012). It presents a collaborative opportunity for students, educators, and industry to develop graduate work readiness, for which they are all responsible (Jackson, 2016).

In this study, SCCT's basic interest and choice model of career counselling (Lent, Brown, & Hackett, 2000) is drawn upon to interpret how WIL can enhance career planning. SCCT asserts that choice of career is influenced by an individual's beliefs of whether they are capable of succeeding in a particular career (self-efficacy), their expectations of the outcomes they can achieve (outcome expectations), and personal goals. Objective and perceived environmental variables will influence career development, such as personal characteristics, labour market conditions, and recruitment bias. Lent (2013) argues there are six obstacles that might prevent the development or implementation of a suitable career plan. These are a lack of identifiable career interest, perceived or actual skill limitations, problematic career outcome expectations, difficulty in framing career goals, environmental barriers, and lack of environmental support. The model is aligned to developing life preparedness, which 'can lead to the use of proactive strategies to manage barriers, build supports, and otherwise advocate for one's own career-life future' (Lent, 2013, p. 7). Lent argues that career counselling should focus on identifying barriers to achieving goals and developing strategies to manage them, and fostering agency and resilience among students.

It would make sense that WIL generates career interest among participating students and allows them to evaluate their commitment to a particular career. There is evidence that WIL assists students in establishing career objectives through observing and experimenting with different roles in their intended field. Previous studies (see Chen & Shen, 2012; Daniel, 2010; Hughes, Mylonas, & Benckendorff, 2013) have also noted the role of WIL in clarifying career goals and making students aware of the capabilities required for their intended career. Usher (2012) found WIL helped students to better understand pathways leading to their career

objective through immersion in the professional community of practice (Zegwaard & Coll, 2011), including career discussions with seasoned professionals and workplace colleagues. Indeed, McIlveen et al. (2011) found that all four DOTS model dimensions were featured in the WIL programmes delivered by careers provision 36 Australian universities, although decision-making learning was least apparent. There appears, however, to be relatively little discussion of how WIL might help students recognise barriers to their aspirations and identify support systems for achieving career plans.

Method

Participants

One hundred and two students completing a work placement, an elective component of their business undergraduate degree programme in a Western Australian university, participated in the study. All were in the latter stages of their degree and had successfully applied to participate in the placement programme. The programme attracts academic credit and combines 100–150 hours of relevant work experience with on-campus sessions and assessments, including reflective activities and an e-portfolio. Students were assigned to placements based on their course major and/or chosen area of interest with only a small proportion sourcing their own placement opportunity. Participant characteristics are summarised in Table 1. Approximately 70% of the

Table 1. Summary of participant characteristics (N = 102).

Characteristic	Subgroup	Semester 1		Semester 2		Total	
		N	Valid %	N	Valid %	N	Valid %
Age	Less than 20 years	1	2	9	17.3	10	9.8
	20–24 years	33	66	27	51.9	60	58.8
	25–29 years	9	18	9	17.3	18	17.6
	30 years and over	7	14	7	13.5	14	13.7
Gender	Male	11	22	19	36.5	30	29.4
	Female	39	78	33	63.5	72	70.6
Specialisation	Human Resources Management	8	16	7	13.5	15	14.7
	Finance/Accounting	14	28	14	26.9	28	27.5
	Marketing, Public Relations and Advertising	5	10	14	26.9	19	18.6
	Tourism, Hospitality, Recreation and Events	15	30	9	17.3	24	23.5
	Management and other	8	16	8	15.4	16	15.6
Sector of host organisation	Public sector	8	16	7	13.5	15	14.7
	Private sector	35	70	36	69.2	71	69.6
	Not for profit	7	14	9	17.3	16	15.7
Residency status	Domestic	38	76	45	86.5	83	81.3
	International	12	24	7	13.5	19	18.7

sample were female, the majority were aged between 20 and 24 years and most completed their placement in the private sector. Participants were studying and working in a range of different disciplines within the field of business.

Procedures

Students participating in the work placement programme were required to write a structured, assessed reflection in the final weeks of their placement. All 111 students enrolled in the programme were invited by email to share their reflection for research purposes, of which 102 agreed. Data were collected during May 2016 (first semester, $N = 50$) and then October 2016 (second semester, $N = 52$).

Measures

Phenomenology intends to capture the experiences of individuals and their interpretation of them (Taylor, 1993) and is suited to examining the experiences of those in professional practice (Adams, Daly, Mann, & Dall'Alba, 2011). Structured reflections were used to investigate students' career objectives and plans, as well as how their WIL experience influenced these. Reflection is integral to WIL, and reflective writing forms a core element of the business undergraduate programme; thus, students are well versed in this when entering the placement programme. First, students were asked to reflect on, in 800 words, what is their career objective and how, if at all, this changed since during their work placement. Second, they were asked to outline the three main things they have learned about themselves, within the context of their intended career. Finally, they were asked to define five action points for improving themselves and their chances of securing a graduate-level job, and to explain how these placement highlighted these and how they plan to address them in the next 12 months.

Analysis

The 102 reflections were thematically analysed to enhance our understanding of the influence of WIL, more specifically the work placements, on career planning. Using the basic principles of qualitative research (see, for example Mishler, 1990), the first semester's reflections ($N = 50$) were reviewed and individual responses were assigned to various themes using an inductive coding approach. A detailed coding scheme was developed and the resulting framework of themes included an explanation of each. This framework was used to analyse the second semester reflections ($N = 52$) using deductive coding processes. While the thematic analysis for the second semester sample was not confined to the original themes, there was little difference in the data with only one new theme added and no original ones revised. This methodology

of combined inductive and deductive analysis can produce clear and rigorous results (Fereday & Muir-Cochrane, 2008).

To enhance rigour, the analysis of the first semester's reflections was repeated by an independent research assistant trained in qualitative research methods. Individual responses were revisited for the few areas of difference until consensus was reached. The analysis of the second sample of reflections was repeated by a different research assistant, also trained in qualitative research methods and familiarised with the developed framework of themes. Again, data were re-examined for the very few areas of difference until consensus was reached. Trustworthiness was enhanced (see Merriam, 1995) through analysing data over two different time periods, conducting multiple analyses and keeping an audit trail, which detailed decisions made and issues encountered during the analysis.

Results

Themes identified in the analysis are summarised in Table 2 for each of the following subsections: choice of personal career objective, how self-awareness in the

Table 2. Summary of themes.

Area of exploration	Themes
Choice of career objective	Personal gratification
	Opportunity for promotion
	Collaborative working
	Promotes well-being
	Scope for professional development
	Organisation type and size
	Experience for self-employment
	Utilises personal strengths
Enhanced self-awareness, in relation to career planning, during WIL	Emphasised commitment and suitability to intended career
	Better understanding of required non-technical capabilities
	Better able to benchmark capabilities and identify areas for improvement
	Enhanced self-confidence in pursuing career
Action points for personal development	Become more self-confident
	Improve non-technical and discipline-related capabilities
	Become more proactive
	Gain more practical experience
	Improve ability to self-manage career
	Achieve better work–life balance
	Undertake more professional development, including further study

WIL: work-integrated learning.

career planning context was developed during WIL, and action points for personal improvement.

Career objective

Identified themes were interpreted in the context of literature relevant to WIL and career management. First, in relation to personal career objectives, there were a number of underlying themes in student responses. Approximately one-quarter of students chose their career based on personal gratification and were drawn towards doing something they had a passion for and where they felt they could make a difference. Gaining intrinsic satisfaction through mentoring others and striving for sustainability featured strongly in this theme. This aligns with Allan, Owens, and Duffy's (2016) findings of the importance of seeking meaningful work and the value undergraduates place on this as part of their career counselling. It also supports evidence of millennials' motivation to pursue a career which offers satisfaction gained from altruistic behaviour and contributing to societal good (Deloitte, 2016).

Fifteen per cent of students stated opportunity for promotion was pivotal and underpinned their career objective, cognisant with other studies exploring career aspirations and desired progression among the younger generations (Deloitte, 2016). Being able to work in a team environment was important to six students when deciding their career objective. This is positive, despite the small proportion, as collaborative mindset and desire for ongoing learning are both important for operating successfully in the new economy (FYA, 2015). Approximately 20% of students were very broad in their consideration of career objective and specified only the field – such as Marketing – they wished to enter. Given students were placed in a placement opportunity aligned with their study major/field, it is perhaps surprising they did not further refine their objective post-placement. On balance, developing a broad skill set which can be transported across different working contexts is considered critical to surviving the future demise of certain occupations (FYA, 2016) and could prove a useful strategy for employment.

It was evident that some students focused more on where they wished to work when considering their career objective. Around 10% specified high profile, larger organisations as their ideal destination, perceiving them as more dynamic and offering better opportunities for working overseas and/or interstate. This preference for larger organisations among new graduates is well documented (Deloitte, 2015) and their global outlook is applauded given the need for international mobility (FYA, 2015). Two students stated their career objective was to work for an organisation which offered a healthy environment, work–life balance, and promoted well-being, documented as important among millennial workers (Deloitte, 2016).

Seven students wished to gain sufficient experience to achieve their ultimate goal of running their own business, important given entrepreneurship enables future graduates to create their own work. For 15% of the students, their career objective was defined by a strong desire to utilise their personal strengths and undertake work which they excelled in, drawing on skills and knowledge acquired during their degree programme. Interestingly, only two students explicitly stated pursuit of a financially rewarding career as their underlying objective. A global survey of millennials revealed that pay and financial benefits are the key driver in career decisions (Deloitte, 2016) and Eagen et al. (2014) found financial reward was far more important to commencing college students than developing a meaningful 'philosophy of life'.

Influence of WIL on career objectives

Just over 40% of the students had a long-established career objective, perhaps through current and prior work experience, which was not changed by their work placement. The remaining 59% believed WIL influenced their objective although this was in a variety of ways. Just under one-half of the sample found the work placement strengthened and clarified their career objective. The experience affirmed their intended pathway through exposure to the various work environments in which their profession operates; experiencing different aspects of their intended profession through their undertaking of projects and tasks; and raising awareness of the skills, knowledge requirements, and expectations of their intended profession. One student simply felt 'my placement has made me feel more comfortable about the job field I am about to enter into'.

Nine students declared their placement made them realise they no longer wished to pursue their original career objective. These students found the experience either highlighted elements of their intended role which they did not enjoy or find rewarding, such as working in an office or completing tasks that did not appeal to them, or required capabilities which they did not possess or felt would be difficult for them to master. One student, for example, stated

> Now at the end of my internship, I feel like I must go a completely different way in terms of a career, as a career in business does not seem to excite me and make me feel like I am making a difference.

Three students found the placement created uncertainty about where they were heading, which they had not experienced previously, due to realising the range of options available within their field. An equal number found the work placement emphasised that their capabilities exceeded their expectations and, as a result, upgraded their career objective to a higher status role.

There was an overwhelming sense among students who believed that WIL somehow influenced their career objective that the experience took them one step closer to making the right career decision. One student commented, for example, 'the more experience I got, the closer I had got to determining which area is suitable for my future job. This created changes in my awareness of planning activities and led me to set out better objectives'. This applied to even those where the work placement created uncertainty about their original career objective as the experience had highlighted varying options and the need for more careful consideration on which pathway to pursue. This finding aligns with Drysdale, Frost, and McBeath's (2015, p. 150) assertion that WIL can 'broaden their knowledge about the careers available in their field of study, allowing them to become more cognisant of many possible occupations and less certain about one specific career path'. Again, this is not a bad thing given the need for new graduates to be flexible and open to working in different roles and contexts.

Self-awareness in relation to career planning

In regards to what the students learned about themselves during their work placement in the context of career planning, four themes emerged (see Table 2). First, just over one-quarter of the students found the placement emphasised their level of commitment and suitability to their intended career pathway. One observed, 'my placement has taught me that I am more interested, passionate and committed than I initially thought and has allowed me to confirm the career direction I wish to take'. As noted previously, the placement strengthened the desire for most students to achieve employment in their intended area while, for others, it highlighted they might be better suited to a different type of role. This involved assessing their suitability to the expectations and characteristics of the working environment associated with their career objective, including sector, organisation size, working hours, and the ability to work from home.

Second, almost all of the students felt the work placement helped develop mastery in at least one non-technical capability considered important for graduate employment. Working effectively as part of a team within a business environment featured in the comments of 17% of the sample. Approximately 10% spoke of their increased ability to adapt to and work effectively in a culturally diverse environment and 15% of levels of professionalism in relation to dressing appropriately, conducting themselves appropriately, being respectful, and managing confidentiality. This connection with their professional self was expressed by one student,

I found that I naturally developed a professional persona when creating connections with other members

in the group, instead of shying away as I do more usually, I began to break away from my shell and adapt to meet the needs around me.

Self-management – spanning multitasking, time management, and working autonomously – was mentioned by just under one-fifth of the sample. Approximately 30% commented on their greater willingness to try new things, be adaptable, and embrace change. Development in these areas might enhance career progression as flexibility, global outlook, confidence, curiosity, and having a collaborative mindset are inherent to succeeding in today's economy (Chartered Accountants, 2016). Also positive was around one-quarter noting the work placement had aided their understanding of the importance of and their ability to communicate effectively. One stated, 'after 100 hours of internship I started to realise that building rapport and consistent communication are effective approaches to creating a functional team'. Other areas were an improved ability to adhere to expected ethical practice (6%), being accountable (7%), giving and receiving feedback (16%), conducting research (10%), managing stress (4%), and following instructions (5%).

Third, approximately one-half found the placement improved their understanding of personal skill deficiencies and areas requiring development to attain graduate employment. Despite their workplace learning, some felt they needed to improve in aspects of technical expertise and/or non-technical skill and admitted they had overestimated their capabilities prior to placement, a tendency common among students due to 'not knowing what they don't know' (Smith, Ferns, & Russell, 2014). One student admitted, 'It is hard to admit that improvements need to be made, but in reflection, the improvements are always beneficial and provide interesting challenges'. Approximately 10% of all students felt they lacked the confidence and self-trust to apply their disciplinary skills and identified this as an area for development. One realised, 'if I do not push myself to be more confident, appear more confident or proactive, it will affect my performance'. Two believed they did not have a sufficiently diverse mix of skills to be competitive in the labour market, while four others commented on their lack of industry knowledge and poor understanding of the external environment relevant to their profession.

Fourth, and contrary to the third theme, around one-third believed they had underestimated their ability to function effectively in the workplace and found they already possessed the required capabilities for their intended career. One student commented, 'I was not mindful of the importance of study until I got to work placement. Even though the study from university mostly is conveyed based on theory, it is useful in processing tasks in the real workplace'. As these students reflected on an emerging sense of their own capabilities, some reported enhanced confidence arising from the placement. They commented on how their degree had given them a solid base of knowledge for their chosen career and how they were confident in their ability to perform to the standards expected by industry. As one eloquently stated, 'I am as smart as I want to be, I just have to find a particular point within the work that I enjoy or can do well'.

Students seemed to understand how resilient they actually were with one stating, 'I am emotionally stronger than I thought – discipline is a hard thing to learn but I believe through my work experience I have learned to overcome and go beyond my conventional self-doubts'. Student exposure to contemporary working practices appears, therefore, to not only have provided valuable insight of what is required of them postgraduation but also gave them confidence in meeting the demands and challenges of the new world of work.

Action points for personal improvement

Students identified a number of action points, summarised in Table 2, for improving themselves and their chances of graduate-level employment. They cited several aspects of their WIL experience as useful in defining these action points. First, observing and interacting with seasoned professionals in an authentic setting gave them insight into expected standards against which they could benchmark their own capabilities. The usefulness of career counselling in the workplace was noted by students, in addition to informal and formal feedback from workplace mentors, supervisor(s), and peers, which helped them to gauge their performance, strengths, areas for improvement, and developmental pathways. Reflective assessments and activities during on-campus sessions were deemed to encourage students to consider their preferences and future career direction. Professional networking opportunities with internal and external stakeholders were considered vital in providing the 'bigger picture' and how their profession relates to the external environment.

Self-confidence. Approximately one-third stated they needed to become more self-confident with one commenting, 'over the course of the next year I will focus on having a "can do" attitude with a willingness to learn above and beyond what is required of me'. Students cited several ways of achieving this, including trying not to overthink things; watching inspirational videos and reading strategies on developing confidence; attending more networking events and interacting more with clients; being more focused on the positives; aligning body language and signals with high levels of confidence; undertaking additional work placements; seeking feedback from peers and colleagues; deliberately placing oneself in unfamiliar situations; and practicing calming techniques in

circumstances which placed them outside of their comfort zone.

Skill development. The majority of students noted the need for up-skilling in at least one skill area, and there were many instances where students acknowledged the benefits of reflecting on their capabilities. One, for example, stated 'the placement highlighted to me that it is okay to have weaknesses and that working on my strengths is important to improve myself'. Approximately one-half commented on the need to improve their communication skills, aligning with effective communication being one of the most highly demanded skills among graduate employers (GCA, 2016) and critical for success in the new economy (FYA, 2016). Strategies for improvement included reading more books, articles, and newspapers; making eye contact when conversing with others; practising 'small talk' and how to make conversation; attending workshops and seminars; proactively engaging in discussions and debates; practicing writing professional emails and public speaking; and enrolling in classes dedicated to business English.

Thirty per cent commented on needing to improve their discipline-related skills, achieved by obtaining more industry-related qualifications; asking more questions relevant to given tasks; reading literature relating to their intended profession; undertaking professional development; and researching skills relevant for their profession. Almost one-half of the sample acknowledged they needed to improve their information technology skills with deficiencies predominantly noted in software specific to their profession, design, social media, and Google analytics. The dominating approach to up-skilling was researching the most utilised software and then undertaking formalised training – online or otherwise – to attain proficiency. This finding is interesting, given digital literacy is considered pivotal for future ways of working (FYA, 2016).

Further developing time management and organisation skills were noted by approximately one-third of the sample and strategies for improvement included breaking down tasks, setting goals and milestones, having regular progress reviews, establishing a routine, prioritising tasks, delegating tasks as needed, reducing procrastination, keeping a diary, taking more precise notes, avoiding unnecessary distractions, and managing sleep patterns. Two other key areas were team working and generating new ideas. The 10% of students commenting on the former did not align with the overwhelming priority employers associate with this skill (GCA, 2016), or perhaps students felt their collaborative working skills were sufficiently developed. Strategies for improvement included practising listening skills, gaining more work experience, and attending relevant workshops. Generating new ideas was noted by almost one-fifth of the sample, aligning with the expectation that entering graduates are able to contribute in the workplace and become tomorrow's leaders (Trede et al., 2012). Students proffered a number of strategies for up-skilling, including learning to communicate new ideas effectively, engaging in continuous learning and development, reflective journaling, attending workshops, gaining additional experience, staying current with best practice, and thinking outside the box.

There were several areas for improvement noted only by a handful of students. Eight felt they needed to become more self-aware, which could be achieved through self-assessments, possibly in combination with peer and 360 degree reviews, striving for excellence and constantly searching for ways to better oneself, focusing on one's strengths, and developing ways to uncover weaknesses. The same number noted the need to become more professional in terms of presentation and attitude, attained through observing and 'copying' seasoned professionals. Five felt they should improve on their critical evaluation skills through completing 'brain games', mathematical puzzles, and reading more books, while two wanted to develop their project management skills through relevant training. Emotional intelligence was acknowledged as an area for improvement by five students, achieved by attending training on better recognising and managing emotions, and volunteering in diverse organisations. Finally, only five students commented on developing their leadership and management skills, perhaps highlighting a disconnection with the importance assigned by industry as 14% of Australian graduate employers identify leadership skills as their most important selection criteria (GCA, 2016).

Being proactive. Approximately one-third of students felt they needed to be more proactive and learn to show more initiative to improve their career prospects. This included taking responsibility for their actions, requesting feedback, and exhibiting self-motivation. New graduates are often accused of being spoon-fed and one student's comment emphasises this, 'I am going to stop asking questions about a problem until I am a hundred per cent certain that I cannot do it'. Demonstrating initiative is highly regarded by industry (Lowden et al., 2011) and, anecdotally, a key characteristic sought in WIL students. Strategies identified to achieve enhanced initiative were fairly broad and included updating industry knowledge so one felt better equipped to take the lead in certain situations; sourcing academic and professional mentors; working on finding solutions to problems without assistance; giving more attention to detail in future work; and requesting feedback more regularly to improve skills and capabilities in the long term, thus being able to work more autonomously in the future.

Practical experience. Students noted the importance of gaining more practical experience through employment, volunteering, and additional internships. Although only 30% stated this as a key strategy, undertaking relevant work experience featured in other themes such as increasing self-awareness and improving one's skills. The importance of relevant work experience to enhancing graduate employment prospects is well documented (see, for example Department of Employment, 2016). Fifth, 28% of students realised the importance of developing industry knowledge through volunteering work, using library and internet resources to research industry practices, attending relevant events and workshops, subscribing to industry news, enrolling in a mentor programme, and undertaking training to that particular industry.

Career self-management. Almost all of the students believed enhanced career self-management skills would improve their job prospects, aligning with their asserted connection with graduate employability (Bridgstock, 2009) and employment outcomes (Pegg et al., 2012). There were a number of sub-themes and associated strategies within career management. Building professional networks and developing networking skills were noted by almost one-half of the sample as key to improving employment prospects, cognisant with literature acknowledging their importance for graduate success and navigating the new work order (Bridgstock, 2016). A broad range of strategies were noted, which included developing or improving one's personal brand; being more proactive in social media (such as LinkedIn); allocating more time and effort to connecting with other professionals through industry events, career fairs, volunteering work, and professional association membership; participating in an industry mentoring programme; creating a blog; and nurturing existing professional contacts. One student confidently stated,

> creating an authentic personal brand can help me to attract new opportunities and gain recognition in my future career. The best way to start with is by making a self-assessment of values and skills and to define how I want to be perceived by people.

Just under 10% of students felt they needed to become more career focused by setting goals and actively pursuing strategies to achieve them. Approximately 20% felt it is important to seek guidance from career counsellors through attending seminars and/or individual sessions to improve their interview skills, resume, and cover letter writing techniques. While most commented on seeking support from university career services, some realised the value of advice from experienced professionals. Eight noted the benefit of strong job search skills and their desire to develop different techniques, in particular using online platforms. Finally, five noted the importance of developing resilience by 'staying focused on wanting a graduate job and gravitating towards positivity and success... (retaining a) "don't let one failed attempt get you down" mentality'.

Work–life balance and professional development. Around 18% of students believed achieving a better work–life balance to be a valuable action point for professional success. This could be attained by making time for family and friends, and undertaking physical activities before or after work. There was acknowledgement of the different demands on their time with one student stating, 'I have realized that I'm in the developing stage in balancing my personal life, work and studies; where being on-call for my casual jobs has greatly impacted on my time management'. Finally, an equal portion of students stated their career prospects would improve by continuing their studies with a focus on both professional qualifications and broader postgraduate tertiary qualifications.

Implications

WIL appears to be helpful in addressing four of SCCT's six inhibitors to career planning: lack of identifiable interest, skill limitations, problematic outcome expectations, and difficulty in framing career goals. WIL's exposure to professional ideology enables students to explore their career interests in the context of more informed outcome expectations. Findings suggest WIL largely generated student interest in their career with most having some notion, albeit broad, of their career objective. Grounded in experiential learning theory, quality WIL incorporates activities where students gain feedback and reflect on their skill capabilities and limitations (Smith, 2012). Academic mentors and host organisations helped students to identify skill gaps and pathways to improve to expected levels for graduate employment. Through direct exposure to the professional environment, WIL students developed a more detailed understanding of what their intended career involves and framed their goals and objectives accordingly. Underpinned by a pedagogy of reflection, WIL augmented self-awareness and encouraged students to evaluate their commitment to their intended career. This, in combination with enhanced disciplinary expertise and non-technical capabilities, means students who complete WIL often experience greater self-confidence in pursuing their career objective.

Career development learning, certainly in the WIL space, could be extended to focus on the remaining two inhibitors to effective career planning: environmental barriers and lack of environmental support. Findings indicate a vast array of strategies for personal development emerged during the students' WIL experiences. Reflective processes and observing and interacting with established professionals, among other things, enabled students to identify useful action points to aid their employment prospects and resilience in highly competitive graduate labour markets. Their consideration of action points prompted students to reflect on both areas for improvement and inhibitors to graduate-level employment in their desired field.

Career planning should not be imparted to WIL students as an isolated event but something that is fluid and requiring ongoing consideration and adaption in line with environmental factors and personal preference (Smith et al., 2009). Identifying action points to achieve career plans could become integral to WIL assessment and reflective activities, emphasising the need to regularly review and revisit formed plans. Contingency planning might help students learn to understand that career planning is confounded by the reality of resource limitations and environmental factors (Lent, 2013) and can be affected by unplanned events (Seibert et al., 2013). A graduate suffering financial hardship, for example, might simply need to take any job – or might be diverted to an alternative pathway – rather than pursue the career they would most like to enter. As suggested by Lent, students could undertake a form of contingency planning where they identify support mechanisms and coping strategies – drawing on both newly formed and established networks – for managing the unexpected.

Rather than encouraging WIL students, and others, to focus narrow-mindedly on one particular career, encouraging them to be adaptable, resilient, and alert to opportunities, which might assist in reaching their career goals, as well as factors which might cause a change in direction, could be particularly useful (Lent, 2013). In line with this, many of the development strategies identified by WIL students were broad and not specific to their career intentions. The value of, for example, enhancing their self-confidence and improving their non-technical skills can be transferred across different work contexts and are worthy action points for most entry-level positions. Encouraging students to develop a career action plan that encompasses broad objectives and can therefore be responsive to changing economic conditions and any resource limitations could prove highly beneficial (see FYA, 2016).

Importantly, the highlighted benefits for future career planning can only be harnessed for a broad spectrum of students with increased employer engagement in WIL. Industry is often reluctant to participate in work placements due to concerns with mentoring and supervisory capacity and insufficient resourcing, resulting in an imbalance in the supply and demand of work placements (Department of Industry, 2014). While educators must articulate the importance of effective career planning to students, providing access to authentic WIL opportunities to help develop career planning skills – and general work readiness – is the responsibility of all stakeholders. As outlined in Australia's National Strategy for WIL (Universities

Australia et al., 2015), educators, industry, and the government must work together to upscale WIL and harness the benefits for more students.

Finally, findings highlight the importance of innovative forms of WIL – such as incubator centres to foster start-ups among students (see Universities Australia, 2016) – in developing entrepreneurial capabilities among students. While it is true that entrepreneurs tend to be older (Ardagna & Lusardi, 2010), the expressed desire among some students to gain experience necessary to start their own business highlights the need for greater emphasis on self-employment during undergraduate education, particularly given the cohort is business students. Although innovative, WIL is attracting increasing attention, more understanding is needed of its influence on professional networking and career self-management in comparison with more immersed models.

Concluding remarks

Findings affirm that WIL, the intersection of academic and workplace learning, can play a valuable role in engaging students with meaningful career planning processes. It can assist with clarifying career objectives, enhancing self-awareness in the context of career planning, and can help students identify development pathways to improve graduate employment prospects. It is important to note this particular WIL programme is reasonably resourced and regularly evaluated to ensure adherence to quality principles in WIL design and delivery, such as those outlined by Smith (2012). This helps to avoid common issues such as inadequate workplace supervision and poor student preparation prior to placement, which might mediate the positive influence of WIL on career planning. In alignment, there are some caveats to the largely positive results of the study. First, students in this study were assigned to placement opportunities that aligned with their study major and which were rigorously vetted to ensure they offered meaningful and relevant work experience. Sourcing meaningful work as part of their career counselling is important to students (Allan et al., 2016) and they should undertake placements which align with their career intentions. Without this, the positive results of this study might not be replicated.

Second, students had elected to participate in WIL and had undergone a fairly rigorous selection process to gain entry onto the programme. This may have meant a more career-motivated sample who were committed to exploring their career aspirations and/ or who had already defined the career objectives they wished to experiment with. Third, it is important to acknowledge there are often barriers to certain student groups undertaking WIL which may mediate its positive influence on career planning. In addition to international and mature students, these include those of lower socio-economic status, who have mental illness or a disability, and who are single parents (see Peach et al., 2016). While demonstration of sound work ethic is the determining factor of entry onto this particular WIL programme, it is possible that these marginalised groups opted not to apply due to inhibiting factors such as the cost of clothing, travel, and childcare (Brough, Correa-Velez, Crane, Johnstone, & Marston, 2014).

Fourth, students in this study completed a minimum of 100 hours in the workplace and were nearing the completion of their degree programme. The latter might mean they were more inclined to be actively considering their career and exploring the impact of WIL on career planning in earlier stages of study might be useful. As WIL is often undertaken in the later stages of the degree, it should be complemented with other initiatives – such as individual career counselling and/or embedded career development learning – as career planning should start early (Bridgstock, 2009).

Limitations of the study are that, first, data were collected only from one university using one single method (online survey), although at two separate time points, which might raise concerns with common method variance (Podsakoff, MacKenzie, Lee, & Podsakoff, 2003). The generalisation of results might be limited as the sample comprised only business students and there might be variations in career decision-making by discipline (Daniels, Stewart, Stupnisky, Perry, & LoVerso, 2011). Finally, it was not possible to capture data on socio-economic status for this particular cohort, and therefore any mediating influence on the relationship between career planning and WIL could not be assessed.

Nevertheless, the study provides a useful insight into how the work placement can influence a student's career planning through the theoretical lens of SCCT. It explores the link between career development learning and WIL which, despite their corresponding importance for graduate employability, remains a research area in relatively infancy. It provides a foundation for future studies exploring the influence of other forms of WIL and variations across different disciplines. Examination of earlier stages of study and different length WIL programmes will be useful in assessing the transferability of findings, as would be comparing the clarity of career objectives and the level and quality of action planning between students completing WIL and those who are not. Investigating the mediating influence of contextual variables – such as those identified in SCCT (Lent et al., 2000) – on career planning in the WIL context would be useful. Finally, replicating the study in a core WIL programme would further enrich our understanding of the role of WIL and future career counselling interventions.

Declaration of Conflicting Interests

The author(s) declared no potential conflicts of interest with respect to the research, authorship, and/or publication of this article.

Funding

The author(s) disclosed receipt of the following financial support for the research, authorship, and/or publication of this article: The author received a strategic research grant from the School of Business and Law, Edith Cowan University, to support the research.

References

Adams, R., Daly, S., Mann, L., & Dall'Alba, G. (2011). Being a professional: Three lenses into design thinking, acting, and being. *Design Studies, 32*(6), 588–607. https://doi.org/10.1016/j.destud.2011.07.004

Allan, B., Owens, R., & Duffy, R. (2016). Generation me or meaning? Exploring meaningful work in college students and career counselors. *Journal of Career Development*, 1–17. https://doi.org/10.1177/0894845316667599

Ardagna, S., & Lusardi, A. (2010). Explaining international differences in entrepreneurship: The role of individual characteristics and regulatory constraints. In J. Lerner, & A. Schoar (Eds.), *International differences in entrepreneurship.* (pp. 17–62). Chicago, IL: University of Chicago Press.

Arthur, M., & Rousseau, D. (1996). Introduction: The boundaryless career as a new employment principle. In M. Arthur, & D. Rousseau (Eds.), *The boundaryless career.* (pp. 3–20). New York, NY: Oxford University Press.

Anderson, E., Johnston, N., Iles, L., Mcrae, N., Reed, N., & Walchli, J. (2012). Co-operative education and student recruitment, engagement and success: Early findings from a multi-institutional study in British Columbia. *Journal of Cooperative Education and Internships, 46*, 58–76.

Australian Workforce and Productivity Agency. (2013). *Information and communications technology workforce study*. Canberra, Australia: AWPA.

Billett, S. (2011). *Curriculum and pedagogic bases for effectively integrating practice-based experiences*. Sydney, Australia: Australian Learning and Teaching Council.

Bridgstock, R. (2009). The graduate attributes we've overlooked: Enhancing graduate employability through career management skills. *Higher Education Research and Development, 28*(1), 31–44. https://doi.org/10.1080/07294360802444347

Bridgstock, R. (2016). *Graduate employability 2.0: Social networks for learning, career development and innovation in the digital age.* Retrieved from http://www.graduateemployability2-0.com/resources/articles/

Brough, M., Correa-Velez, I., Crane, P., Johnstone, E., & Marston, G. (2014). *Work-integrated learning in social work and human services. Assessment of financial stress associated with student placements.* Springvale, Australia: ACEN.

Chartered Accountants. (2016). *The future of work: How can we adapt to survive and thrive?* Sydney, Australia: Chartered Accountants.

Chen, T., & Shen, C. (2012). Today's intern, tomorrow's practitioner? The influence of internship programmes on students' career development in the Hospitality Industry. *Journal of Hospitality, Leisure, Sport & Tourism Education, 11*(1), 29–40. https://doi.org/10.1016/j.jhlste.2012.02.008

Coetzee, M., & Beukes, C. (2010). Employability, emotional intelligence and career preparation support satisfaction among adolescents in the school-to-work transition phase. *Journal of Psychology in Africa, 20*(3), 439–446. https://doi.org/10.1177/103841621001900203

Daniel, R. (2010). Career development and creative arts students: An investigation into the effectiveness of career theory and WIL experiences on practice. *Australian Journal of Career Development, 19*(2), 14–22. https://doi.org/10.1177/103841621001900203

Daniels, L., Stewart, T., Stupnisky, R., Perry, R., & LoVerso, T. (2011). Relieving career anxiety and indecision: The role of undergraduate students' perceived control and faculty affiliations. *Social Psychology of Education, 14*(3), 409–426. https://doi.org/10.1007/s11218-010-9151-x

Deloitte. (2015). *Mind the gaps: The 2015 Deloitte millennial survey*. London, UK: Deloitte.

Deloitte. (2016). *The 2016 Deloitte millennial survey: Winning over the next generation of leaders*. London, UK: Deloitte.

Department of Employment. (2016). *The household, income and labour dynamics in Australia survey: Selected findings from waves 1 to 14*. Melbourne, Australia: Melbourne Institute of Applied Economic and Social Research.

Department of Industry. (2014). *Engaging employers in work integrated learning: Current state and future priorities*. Richmond, Australia: PhillipsKPA.

Drysdale, M., Frost, N., & McBeath, M. (2015). How often do they change their minds and does work-integrated learning play a role? *Asia-Pacific Journal of Cooperative Education, 16*(2), 145–152.

Eagen, K., Stolzenberg, E., Ramirez, J., Aragon, M., Suchard, M., & Hurtado, S. (2014). *The American freshman: National norms fall 2014*. Los Angeles, CA: Higher Education Research Institute, UCLA.

Fereday, J., & Muir-Cochrane, E. (2008). Demonstrating rigor using thematic analysis: A hybrid approach of inductive and deductive coding and theme development. *International Journal of Qualitative Methods, 5*(1), 80–92. https://doi.org/10.1177/160940690600500107

Foundation for Young Australians. (2015). *The new work order: Ensuring young Australians have the skills and experience for the jobs of the future*. Melbourne, Australia: FYA.

Foundation for Young Australians. (2016). *The new work mindset: 7 new job clusters to help young people to navigate the new work order*. Melbourne, Australia: FYA.

Gould, S. (1979). Characteristics of career planners in upwardly mobile occupations. *Academy of Management Journal, 22*(3), 539–550. https://doi.org/10.2307/255743

Graduate Careers Australia. (2016). *Australian graduate survey 2015: The report of the 2015 graduate outlook survey*. Melbourne, Australia: GCA.

Hughes, K., Mylonas, A., & Benckendorff, P. (2013). Students' reflections on industry placement: Comparing four undergraduate work integrated learning streams. *Asia-Pacific Journal of Cooperative Education, 14*(4), 265–279.

Jackson, D. (2016). Conceptualising graduate employability: The construction of pre-professional identity in the higher education landscape of practice. *Higher Education Research and Development, 35*(5), 925–939. https://doi.org/10.1080/07294360.2016.1139551

Karmel, T., & Carroll, D. (2016). *Has the graduate labour market been swamped?* Adelaide, Australia: National Institute of Labour Studies, Flinders University.

Kolb, D. A. (1984). *Experiential learning.* Englewood Cliffs, NJ: Prentice Hall.

Lent, R. (2013). Career-life preparedness: Revisiting career planning and adjustment in the new workplace. *The Career Development Quarterly, 61*(1), 2–14. https://doi.org/10.1002/j.2161-0045.2013.00031.x

Lent, R. W., Brown, S. D., & Hackett, G. (1994). Toward a unifying social cognitive theory of career and academic interest, choice, and performance. *Journal of Vocational Behavior, 45*(1), 79–122. doi: https://doi.org/10.1006/jvbe.1994.1027

Lent, R., Brown, S., & Hackett, G. (2000). Contextual supports and barriers to career choice: A social cognitive analysis. *Journal of Counseling Psychology, 47*(1), 36–49. https://doi.org/10.1037//0022-0167.47.1.36

Lowden, K., Hall, S., Elliot, D., & Lewin, J. (2011). *Employers' perceptions of the employability skills of new graduates.* London, UK: Edge Foundation, University of Glasgow, SCRE Center.

McIlveen, P., Brooks, S., Lichtenberg, A., Smith, M., Torjul, P., & Tyler, J. (2011). Perceptions of career development learning and work-integrated learning in Australian higher education. *Australian Journal of Career Development, 20*(1), 32–41. https://doi.org/10.1177/103841621102000105

McKeown, T., & Lindorff, M. (2011). The graduate job search process – A lesson in persistence rather than good career management? *Education + Training, 53*(4), 310–320. https://doi.org/10.1108/00400911111138479

Merriam, S. (1995). What can you tell from an N of 1: Issues of validity and reliability in qualitative research. *PAACE Journal of Lifelong Learning, 4,* 50–60.

Mishler, E. (1990). Validation in inquiry-guided research: The role of exemplars in narrative studies. *Harvard Educational Review, 60*(4), 415–443. https://doi.org/10.17763/haer.60.4.n4405243p6635752

Peach, D., Moore, D., Campbell, M., Winchester-Seeto, T., Ferns, S., Mackaway, J., & Groundwater, L. (2016). *Building institutional capacity to enhance access participation and progression in work integrated learning (WIL).* Canberra, Australia: Learning and Teaching Support Unit.

Pegg, A., Waldock, J., Hendy-Isaac, S., & Lawton, R. (2012). *Pedagogy for employability.* York, UK: Higher Education Academy.

Podsakoff, P., MacKenzie, S., Lee, J., & Podsakoff, N. (2003). Common method biases in behavioral research: A critical review of the literature and recommended remedies. *Journal of Applied Psychology, 88*(5), 879–903. https://doi.org/10.1037/0021-9010.88.5.879

Sattler, P., Wiggers, R., & Arnold, C. (2011). Combining workplace training with postsecondary education: The spectrum of Work-Integrated Learning (WIL) opportunities from apprenticeship to experiential learning. *Canadian Apprenticeship Journal, 5.*

Segers, J., & Inceoglu, I. (2012). Exploring supportive and developmental career management through business strategies and coaching. *Human Resource Management, 51*(1), 99–120. https://doi.org/10.1002/hrm.20432

Seibert, S., Kraimer, M., Holtom, B., & Pierotti, A. (2013). Even the best laid plans sometimes go askew: Career self-management processes, career shocks, and the decision to pursue graduate education. *Journal of Applied Psychology, 98*(1), 169–182. https://doi.org/10.1037/a0030882

Smith, C. (2012). Evaluating the quality of work-integrated learning curricula: A comprehensive framework. *Higher Education Research and Development, 31*(2), 247–262. https://doi.org/10.1080/07294360.2011.558072

Smith, C., Ferns, S., & Russell, L. (2014). *Assessing the impact of work integrated learning on student work-readiness.* Canberra, Australia: Office of Learning and Teaching.

Smith, M., Brooks, S., Lichtenberg, A., McIlveen, P., Torjul, P., & Tyler, J. (2009). *Career development learning: Maximising the contribution of work-integrated learning to the student experience.* Wollongong, Australia: University of Wollongong.

Taylor, B. (1993). Phenomenology: One way to understand nursing practice. *International Journal of Nursing Studies, 30*(2), 171–179. https://doi.org/10.1016/0020-7489(93)90066-4

Trede, F., Macklin, R., & Bridges, D. (2012). Professional identity development: A review of the Higher Education literature. *Studies in Higher Education, 37*(3), 365–384. https://doi.org/10.1080/03075079.2010.521237

Universities Australia, BCA, ACCI, AIG, and ACEN. (2015). *National strategy on work-integrated learning in university education.* Canberra, Australia: UA.

Universities Australia. (2016). *Submission to the inquiry into innovation and creativity: Workforce for the new economy.* Canberra, Australia: Universities Australia.

Usher, A. (2012). Measuring work-integrated learning: The development of the meta-competency test. *Journal of Cooperative Education and Internships, 46*(1), 5–15.

Watts, A. (2006). *Career development learning and employability.* Learning and Employability Series Two. York, UK: Higher Education Academy.

Wilson, T. (2012). *A review of business–university collaboration.* London, UK: Department for Innovation and Skills.

Woodley, C., & Beattie, S. (2011). Communal reflections on the workplace: Locating learning for the legal professional. *Asia-Pacific Journal of Cooperative Education, 12*(1), 19–30.

Yuhee, J., & Takeuchi, N. (2016). Gender differences in career planning and success. *Journal of Managerial Psychology, 31*(2), 603–623. http://dx.doi.org/10.1108/JMP-09-2014-0281

Zegwaard, K., & Coll, R. (2011). Using cooperative education and work-integrated education to provide career clarification. *Science Education International, 22*(4), 282–291.

Zikic, J., & Klehe, U. (2006). Job loss as a blessing in disguise: The role of career exploration and career planning in predicting reemployment quality. *Journal of Vocational Behavior, 69*(3), 391–409. https://doi.org/10.1016/j.jvb.2006.05.007

PART 10

JOURNALS ON MANAGING PROJECTS IN THE ORGANISATION

Lessons from Management 101: Learning to Manage Ourselves

Miller, J. A.

Abstract

The Management 101 Project continues to shape our understanding of what's essential to an introductory general education course in management. Our ongoing challenge is to integrate responsibilities to people (Who needs to learn? Everybody.), to best practices (How can we best learn? Active, experiential methods.), and to the contents of our discipline (What do and don't we need to learn? Effective projects + efficient methods + caring communities.).

Keywords

experiential learning, organization as classroom approaches, teaching and learning, management learning, performing to learn, general education

> For the first time in human history, we will have to learn to take responsibility for managing ourselves. . . . [T]he achievers, and I don't mean millionaires, but rather the ones who want to make a contribution, who want to lead a fulfilling life, and want to feel that there is some purpose in their being on this earth [. . .] will have to learn something which, only a few years ago, a very few super achievers ever knew. They will have to learn to manage themselves, to build on their strengths, to build on their values.
>
> —Peter Drucker, 1998

---

¹Bucknell University, Lewisburg, PA, USA

Corresponding Author:
John A. Miller, 1177 Pendleton Circle, The Villages, FL 32162, USA.
Email: jmiller@bucknell.edu

Our job as educators—in Management 101 (MG101) as in Management Education in general—is to help each other learn to manage ourselves. MG101's methods are grounded on experiential learning assumptions: We learn best when we need to know; we learn most from making sense of our own decisions and actions; we continue to test, refine, and confirm understandings; and, in the process, we learn about how best we can keep learning. The MG101 first-generation report (Miller, 1991) focused primarily on how the faculty learned to make the course work. The current MG101 teaching team's report (Hendry et al., in this issue) updates descriptions of the machinery we needed to create, borrow, and test. What follows is a summary of lessons that we are learning and challenges we face in our efforts to understand and manage critical relationships among people (Who needs to learn?), pedagogical methods (How can we best learn?), and the essential contents of our discipline (What do and don't we need to learn?) in MG101.

Who Needs to Learn?

Our motivating commitment has been to address the learning needs of undergraduate students enrolled in colleges and universities that aspire to educate their graduates for responsible participation in major economic, political, and social institutions. From the outset, our challenge was to respond to specific problems inherent in building on undergraduate students' needs, experiences, developmental levels, career goals, and collaboration skills. Few students other than management majors will have any other formal management education before taking on managerial leadership roles in key institutions of our society, including health care, governmental, educational, religious, and other community and social service institutions. And, many who plan careers as doctors, lawyers, politicians, teachers, and journalists would not have time for—much less be caught dead in—a "business school." In addition, MG101 needed to offer engaging, memorable, and positive learning experiences for students who lack significant full-time work experience, informed commitments to any particular career paths, and prior formal management education while serving also as an academically responsible foundation for prospective majors in management subdisciplines, consistent with "Common Body of Knowledge" (CBK; now "basic business disciplines and concepts"; AACSB, 2013, p. 12).

MG101 is designed to provide a comprehensive survey of our discipline's principles, practices, and problems that can serve as a general education course for *everybody*. It aims to develop practical perspectives on management as a system of concepts and methods useful to anyone in any collaborative enterprise. MG101 is designed, above all, to serve as a liberating experience in organization and management. How free can we be if we do not know how to set and achieve our own objectives?

We Are All Teachers Here

MG101 continues to generate learning opportunities beyond those we hoped to provide for our students and for faculty colleagues at Bucknell and in sister institutions. Among the most important are effects on the undergraduate management curriculum beyond the introductory course, supportive teaching/learning relationships with multiple stakeholders on campus and in the community beyond MG101, and demanding, often urgent learning agendas for us, the teacher-scholars directly responsible for the course.

BSBA (Bachelor of Science in Business Administration) students learn to use MG101's active learning processes to establish support networks that shape both friendship and working relationships in campus organizations and in subsequent courses. More important, MG101 builds an integrative conceptual framework that helps BSBA students make comprehensive sense of the discipline, make informed decisions about majors, and place functional area topics in context. Instructors in midlevel functional area and capstone-level problem (case), policy, and leadership seminar courses report that they use and reinforce themes and vocabularies from MG101 (Gruver & Miller, 2011) to leverage students' understandings of their subject matter's relationships to other areas and to larger system-level issues. Students who already know MG101 basics about functions that cross all projects understand that Marketing/Finance/Operations/Accounting/Information Systems/Human Resources only make sense as interacting components of all organizations.

MG101 companies are temporary project organizations (Kenis, Janowicz-Panjaitan, & Cambré, 2009) embedded in a strong and supportive institutional context. From the course's earliest years, we asked for and received informal support and advice from friends and colleagues in campus offices. Relationships among students, course faculty and staff, and university officers have evolved into regular institutional arrangements, with significant learning opportunities for us and for the institution. MG101 continues to enrich the campus community.

The managerial rationale for our service project requirement—beyond altruism, community development, diversity awareness, and other frequently cited goals of service-learning networks (Eyler & Giles, 1999; Furco, 2011)—is straightforward and explicit: A realistically complex, multidivisional (hybrid-matrix) organization design offers both leadership and "followership" opportunities for a large enough number of company members to make the need for formal management processes self-evident. Professional service agency administrators regularly serve as critical evaluators of service project plans and as both temporary team members and supervisors for on-site project activities; they provide powerful insights into the needs of special populations in the community. More important, service clients and agencies give us opportunities to reflect on contrasts that students observe between the priorities and administrative practices of managers in for-profit and not-for-profit organizations.

We all learn from close and supportive relationships with experienced, professional colleagues and administrators on campus and in the larger community. They, and many others, are all teachers here, too. But our MG101 experience confirms an even broader interpretation, well beyond the peer-learning cliché—"students learn more from each other. . ." For us, "We are all teachers here" is the central feature of every company member's job. That applies, above all, to the course's faculty and teaching assistants.

It Is Our MG101 Project

MG101 has become an integrated project organization—a *real-world-organization-as-classroom*—in which all its members, however differentiated or temporary, contribute to accomplishing our common purposes. MG101 began to feel like and identify itself as its own MG101 project organization (not just a single-semester "class" with "teachers" for and about somebody else, much less a product to be sold to student "customers") when our teaching assistants began to serve as members of the course's Board of Directors, effectively expanding their staff support roles in simple structures to take on middle line and technostructure roles in our increasingly complex professional bureaucracy (Mintzberg, 1980). We all needed each other, especially those closer to campus cultures, peer relationships, and the realities of student life than teachers could be, to help bridge conventional teacher–student gaps, and to help us learn richer, easier, more *human* ways to work with each other in complex systems (Conklin, 2013).

Each term and each MG101 company provides opportunities for MG101 faculty members to learn new lessons about how to manage ourselves as a team. Participants are continually surprised to discover who "we" are, and what we bring, individually and collectively, to each other in this collaborative enterprise. MG101 directly confronts seldom-discussed issues about the realities of working with *people*, especially in large introductory classes, as if all the participants' individual and interpersonal characteristics either do not or should not matter in providing essential learning opportunities about real organizational life.

The faculty's learning agendas—in particular regarding finance and accounting, operations, information systems, and other functional specializations—were especially stretched during and at the end of design phases, when companies presented complex operating plans for board approval and operating capital loans. MG101 forces faculty members responsible for the course to struggle continually to identify and fill the gaps in our respective educations and experiences. We have all become general education students.

In the process of coping with our own learning needs, as we watch ourselves enacting key principles of organizational differentiation and integration ("nobody needs to know everything"), the broader lesson is that our own MG101 project's experiential learning adventure mirrors—and explicitly models—that of our student organizations.

How Can We Best Learn?

Learning to observe and describe, to reflect, and to design needs to take place in community (Rogers, 2002). To talk with each other efficiently in ways that would capture the complexity of learning in MG101, we needed to adopt accessible short-hand terminology to describe our experiential learning model in a manner consistent with best experiential project practice (Argyris & Schön, 1978), the "three fundamental steps [of reflective practice]" (Gallos, 2008, p. 163), and "normal" Scientific Method (Kuhn, 1970). We adopted a straightforward three-phase [→ Perform → Reflect→ Design →] learning cycle model that MG101 companies learned quickly to use as a framework for "experienced reflection" (Mintzberg, 2005) and to help us describe, explain, and manage the course's learning processes. We learned how to manage the scope and frequency of [→ P → R → D →] cycles so that we could observe and describe "what just happened" as reliably and validly as possible. We learned to extend time horizons of experiential learning cycles *backwards and forwards from key performances*—and to embed "mini-cycles" within nests—so we could then collaborate in "making sense" (Weick, 1995, as cited in McNamara, 2015) of those observations and developing action plans that could appropriately guide subsequent experience—or, at least, provide valid data for new Reflection and Redesign.

We learned from colleagues' reports at sister institutions about important local, campus, and community operational realities that shape our methods, and how institutional policies, instructional schedules, academic calendars, staff characteristics, resources, norms, and demographics support this work. We drew practical lessons from MG101 company experiences with developing technologies, and (in particular) through critical incidents around interpersonal, intergroup, and other stakeholder relationships. Need-to-know/ just-in-time (Hake, 1998) logics of experiential project management taught us lessons about selecting and organizing topic sequences, so we could rearrange textbook reading assignments, find supplementary technical notes and essays, and schedule "guest experts" accordingly. We borrowed familiar journalists' "who, what, when, where, why" checklists, three-point essay-writing guidelines, and several storytelling techniques (Boje, 1995; Campbell, 1968) in structured lab notes, journals, and writing assignments to help link recursive cycles into coherent and memorable lessons. We continue to refine an integrated sequence of individual and collaborative storytelling activities that can coherently anchor learning in the course's repetitive experience patterns. Storytelling and story-writing assignments force us to reflect critically on interpersonal and intergroup relationships and patterns among events we are experiencing, and to test the relevance of course concepts and methods to solving problems and making sense of our own experiences. Above all, because stories make sense, they help create lasting memories.

An ongoing operational problem is how to manage the timing and sequencing of project activities, milestones, and deadlines through a well-defined series of project, interpersonal and group processes (Cohen, 1976; Putzel, 2007), and team developmental phases (Tuckman & Jensen, 1977). We reorganized subject matter so that we could continuously discern and label linked patterns of causes and consequences, from short to long time horizons and from beginning to end, within and across phases. Borrowing concepts from literatures on group processes, organization development, and project management, we defined clear milestones for strategy decisions, operating plan and capital loan approvals, and project implementation. Transition ceremonies, formally including authority delegations and performance assessment milestones, invariably become critical turning points in participants' stories.

What Do and Don't We Need to Learn?

MG101's subject matter task is to select, organize, and transform essential ideas from a rich, complex, and fragmented body of knowledge—embodied in our disciplinary texts, journals, course syllabi, program curricula, and a torrent of cases and anecdotes from popular media—so that its themes will serve as a coherent and valid foundation for further learning and responsible action. The bane of our existence—as of every teacher in every discipline—has been provocatively dubbed *Anupholsteraphobia*—"the fear of the lack of coverage."[1] What should we leave out?

While our topic selection criteria surely include scholarly consensus on what students should learn, compelling "need-to-know-*now*" dominates both our content-selection and topic-organization criteria. As they worked on projects, students consistently taught us about the contents they did and did not need to know. They did not need to know many details of the traditional subject matter. Instead, they needed much more useful tools and more tightly organized sets of complex concepts.

In the process of reordering topic sequences to meet project needs, we were forced to think through apparent redundancies, ambiguities, and contradictions in CBK terminology; to supplement CBK content learning materials with borrowings from other disciplines; and to borrow and to invent new, more abstract, and general labels and vocabularies for efficient communications about course content. To help manage our companies' *initial formation tasks*, for example, we needed to introduce topics typically spread across later chapters in CBK texts, including group processes, community building, communication styles, interviewing and active listening, motivation, organization development, and organizational norms and culture, and then provide more extended essays on these topics again later, when relevant, especially during the *project performance* phase.

We had the more challenging task of organizing topics to provide essential support to companies in dealing with project strategy and policy-making phases. Although we found materials on power sources and organizational politics, group decision making, leadership, stakeholders, conflict, negotiation, and project planning in standard texts—typically distributed across apparently unrelated chapters—assembling them into a coherent and useful set of readings, lectures, and discussion agendas required extensive borrowings from other literatures, including Political Science and Public Administration (e.g., Parliamentary Procedure, Policy/Administration, Theories of Democracy). For the design and operations phases, we needed specific "best practice" materials from intermediate-level functional area texts (Strategic Positioning and Targeting; Market Research, Critical Paths, Job Design, Performance Appraisal, Managerial Accounting).

Our experiences convinced us of the inadequacy of a wide variety of two-dimensional frameworks—for example, Efficiency/Effectiveness, Formal/ Informal, Directive/Participative, Initiating Structure/Consideration, Authoritarian/Democratic, Mechanistic/Organic, Task/Social, X/Y, and so on. We found powerful confirmation in the work of colleagues on stories or metaphors—"market, bureaucratic and clan control" (Ouchi & Price, 1978), "frames" (Bolman & Deal, 2008), "images" (Morgan, 2006)—that provide umbrella generalizations by capturing and organizing familiar historical and contemporary content literatures. We discovered that we needed *at least* three distinct, consistent, and coherent narrative threads to provide conceptual scaffolds useful for performance description, meaningful reflection, and sound design. Based on student and colleague reactions, we developed a three-category/metaphor model that we use to organize and transform traditional introductory management textbook tables of contents, as follows:

Effective Projects/Tournaments: Competitive Markets, Contests, Wars, Games; Conflict; Missions, Movements, Strategies, Ends; Stakeholders, Audiences, Classes; Negotiation, Coalitions and Allies; Pooled Results; Influence, Power, Authority; Leadership; (Organizational) Politics; Debate, Vote, Decision-Making Rules.

Efficient Methods/Tools: Machines, Technologies; Scientific Method, Rationality, Systems, Control, Cybernetics; Operations, Sequential Interdependencies; Algorithms, Programs, Means, Tactics; Organization Structure; Design, Bureaucracies, Functions, Delegation; Tasks, Roles, Skills; Sustainability

Caring Communities/Tribes: Living Systems, Social Systems; Generations, Families, Parents, Siblings, Clans, Tribes, Cultures, Nations; Groups, Teams; Trust, Reciprocity, Relationships, Members, Belonging; Identities, Personalities, Needs, Motives, Attitudes, Habits; Diversity; Norms, Socialization, Ethics; Networks

We use the three themes—Effectiveness, Efficiency, Community—to provide a readily available, memorable, face-valid set of category labels—a vocabulary "checklist" that helps us organize performance descriptions, critical reflections, design principles, action plans, and assessment criteria throughout the course. Management education can help us learn to manage ourselves when we can share a vocabulary that usefully describes and explains how organizations learn to manage themselves and then commit ourselves to work continually to refine and share that vocabulary.

Our ongoing content challenges are to understand how these stories can help us usefully make sense of *here and now*; why and how those stories are different from, augment, or conflict with each other; and how they might need to be edited or rejected, generating new stories and creating higher level, integrative meanings. Our greatest content challenge is that we need to know what we need to know *now*, so we can put aside the rest for someone else, or for later . . . or forever.

Conclusions: Performing to Learn

The MG101 project demonstrates that *all* the participants in an introductory general education course can work with each other successfully enough to carry out a variety of relatively complex projects. More important, they can learn to talk sensibly enough about that work to be confident about taking on even more challenging projects.

The most important lesson we have learned is not simply that our *how* decisions affect *what* we learn. It was, before anything else, that our work to make content-learning goals fit need-to-know experiential methods forces us both to better understand our discipline's subject matter and more effectively help each other learn it. To restate our MG101 project's most general lesson: To help each other think, decide, and act usefully about content, process, and people decisions, we need to understand them as a single, coherent system. In managing, ends and means and people entail each other. The main content challenge is then to attend to them, reflect on them, and act on all three of them *together.*

MG101 certainly does not imply that formal management education is a prerequisite to successful organizational leadership—much less that principles and methods developed to fit in any set of specialized institutions, including MG101, can be applied thoughtlessly in other organizational settings—in order to have some confidence in our potential value to people who will work in any setting. Our work, however, starts by observing that every organization—indeed, every polity, every community, and every family—depends on the willingness and the competence of its members to collaborate in managing. If we understand anything about what it takes to design and manage organizations, we have clear obligations to figure out how to demystify the principles and make them accessible to everybody. Above all, if we do not trust in the generality or the accessibility of the basic management principles and techniques we have learned, we have an obvious responsibility to test the limits of those ideas. Our challenges are continuously to rethink not only our methods and our concepts but also our audiences.

Management education is an essential component of everybody's general education. Our job, like everybody's job, is to help each other learn to manage ourselves. If evidence of our effectiveness is summarized in the world's breaking news headlines, historical records, and our own daily project diaries, there is clearly no end to the urgent work we need to do.

> The things we have to learn before we do them, we learn by doing them. (Aristotle)

Declaration of Conflicting Interests

The author declared no potential conflicts of interest with respect to the research, authorship, and/or publication of this article.

Funding

The author received no financial support for the research, authorship, and/or publication of this article.

Note

1. Thanks to Randy Bass, my Carnegie Academy for SoTL colleague: https://www. pinterest.com/pin/217087644508038579/

References

AACSB. (2013). *AACSB assurance of learning standards: An interpretation.* Retrieved from http://www.aacsb.edu/~/media/AACSB/Publications/white-papers/wp-assurance-of-learning-standards.ashx

Argyris, C., & Schön, D. (1978). *Organizational learning: A theory of action perspective.* Reading, MA: Addison Wesley.

Boje, D. M. (1995, August). Stories of the storytelling organization: A postmodern analysis of Disney as "Tamara-Land." *Academy of Management Journal, 38,* 997-1035.

Bolman, L. G., & Deal, T. E. (2008). *Reframing organizations: Artistry, choice, and leadership* (4th ed.). San Francisco, CA: Jossey-Bass.

Campbell, J. (1968). *The hero with a thousand faces.* Princeton, NJ: Princeton University Press.

Cohen, A. R. (1976). Beyond simulation: Treating the classroom as an organization. *Journal of Management Education, 2,* 13-19.

Conklin, T. (2013). Making it personal: The importance of student experience in creating autonomy-supportive classrooms for millennial learners. *Journal of Management Education, 37,* 499-538.

Drucker, P. (1998). All-Academy Symposia Special Address. *Academy of Management Annual Meeting.* San Diego. [Extended and edited versions of this address have been published as *Managing Oneself* in *Harvard Business Review,* Boston: Harvard Business School Publishing Corporation, March 1999, and reprinted frequently as a *Harvard Business Review Classic,* Drucker Institute, Drucker Foundation, and *HBR* monographs, and elsewhere.]

Eyler, J., & Giles, D. E., Jr. (1999). *Where's the learning in service-learning?* (Jossey-Bass Higher and Adult Education Series). San Francisco, CA: Jossey-Bass.

Furco, A. (2011, May). *Securing student success through service-learning.* Keynote address at the Community College National Center for Community Engagement 20th Annual National Conference, Scottsdale, AZ.

Gallos, J. V. (2008). Making sense of organizations: Leadership, frames, and everyday theories of the situation. In J. V. Gallos (Ed.), *Business leadership: A Jossey-Bass reader* (pp. 161-179). San Francisco, CA: Jossey-Bass.

Gruver, W. R., & Miller, J. A. (2011). *Teaching the unteachable? Leadership studies at Bucknell University.* Retrieved from http://dx.doi.org/10.2139/ssrn.1874113

Hake, R. R. (1998). Interactive-engagement versus traditional methods: A six-thousand-student survey of mechanics test data for introductory physics courses. *American Journal of Physics, 66,* 64-74.

Hendry, J. R., Hiller, T. B., Martin, E. C., & Boyd, N. M. (2017). Context and pedagogy: A quarter-century of change in an introductory management course. *Journal of Management Education, 41,* 346-384.

Kenis, P., Janowicz-Panjaitan, M., & Cambré, B. (Eds.). (2009). *Temporary organizations—Prevalence, logic and effectiveness.* Cheltenham, England: Edward Elgar.

Kuhn, T. (1970). *The structure of scientific revolutions* (2nd ed.). Chicago, IL: University of Chicago Press.

McNamara, L. A. (2015). *Sensemaking in organizations: Reflections on Karl Weick and social theory*. Retrieved from https://www.epicpeople.org/sensemaking-in-organizations/

Miller, J. A. (1991). Experiencing management: A comprehensive, "hands-on" model for the introductory undergraduate management course. *Journal of Management Education, 15,* 151-169.

Mintzberg, H. (1980). Structure in 5's: A synthesis of the research on organization design. *Management Science, 26,* 322-341.

Mintzberg, H. (2005). *Managers not MBAs: A hard look at the soft practice of managing and management development.* Oakland, CA: Berrett-Koehler.

Morgan, G. (2006). *Images of organization.* Thousand Oaks, CA: Sage.

Ouchi, W. G., & Price, R. (1978). Hierarchies, clans, and theory Z: A new perspective on organization development. *Organizational Dynamics, 7*(2), 25-44.

Putzel, R. (2007). XB: New-paradigm management of the classroom as a complex organization. *Journal of Business and Leadership: Research, Practice, and Teaching, 3*(1), 136-143.

Rogers, C. (2002). Defining reflection: Another look at John Dewey and reflective thinking. *Teachers College Record, 104,* 842-866.

Tuckman, B., & Jensen, M. (1977). Stages of small-group development revisited. *Group Organization Management, 2,* 419-427.

Weick, K. E. (1995). *Sensemaking in organizations* (Vol. 3). Newbury Park, CA: Sage.

PART 11

JOURNALS ON UNDERSTANDING AND ENGAGING IN THE CUSTOMER EXPERIENCE

PART 11

JOURNALS ON UNDERSTANDING AND ENGAGING IN THE CUSTOMER EXPERIENCE

Customer Value Management

Kotler, P.

Abstract

A company's job is to create superior customer value in the mind of the customer. Be aware that the customer's sense of value may differ from the company's sense of value. A customer is interested in more than the physical product. The customer also pays attention to the service level, guaranties and warranties, financing arrangements, return policies — all making up the total product. The challenge is to help the customer perceive more total value than the total cost of acquisition and usage.

Keywords

Value, customer value, total product, customer journey, touchpoints

It has become a marketing mantra that the marketer's job is to create, produce and communicate customer value. The marketer is not to create what he or she thinks is value to the customer but what the customer will perceive as value. A pen company might produce a pen whose ink lasts longer than any other competitor's pen, but this is not a value to customers who throw away or lose most pens.

We have to distinguish between what a product is supposed to do and what a customer actually wants to achieve. Professor Ted Levitt long ago said that a customer does not want to buy and own a drill; he or she wants to 'buy' a hole. We need to distinguish between a function (drilling) and a desired outcome (a hole). A movie goer buys a box of popcorn but what the customer actually wants is something to munch for most of the movie. That's why popcorn outsells candy bars in most movie theatres.

Professor Clayton Christensen makes the point that a customer is not just buying a product; the customer is actually 'hiring' a product to produce an outcome. A product is a tool for producing a valued service that will produce a valued outcome.

[1] Kellogg School of Management, Northwestern University, Global Hub, Evanston, Illinois, US.

Corresponding author:
Philip Kotler, Kellogg School of Management, Northwestern University, Global Hub, 2211 Campus Drive, Evanston, Illinois-60208, US.
E-mail: pkotler@aol.com

A product is too narrow a view of what it takes to create value for the customer. There are dozens of patented mousetraps that are all capable of capturing a mouse. But the real value is for the mousetrap manufacturer to claim that he or she can help the buyer know what cheese is best to use and where the mousetrap should be placed.

We must replace the idea of a physical product with the idea of a 'total product' that includes a whole set of services. The car buyer is not only choosing a particular car but also a particular dealer and manufacturer. The contract specifies a set of services that will come with the car, such as parts replacement, regular maintenance, a manual, an advisory service and so on. The car buyer will form a certain image of the seller and a set of expectations about the performance of the car and the seller.

Every offer is a bundle of physical and service attributes. The attributes will create a different perceived value and weighting among different prospective buyers. The job of a salesperson is to probe or intuit what a particular buyer might see as the value and weights of the different attributes.

The real challenge for the marketer is to quantify the value of the company's offer in relation to the best competitor's offer. The marketer has to show that his or her product delivers more value in the particular customer's mind than is offered by competing products.

The need to quantify the value of an offer is especially important in the BtoB (Business-to-Business) world. BtoB buyers are trained purchasing agents who are hard-nosed about the facts in a purchasing situation. The procurement person wants hard facts about the performance of a product and its services and its supplier. The procurement person does not want his or her boss to criticize why he or she chose a particular branded product and supplier. Hard facts matter. The marketer's job is to create the value, calculate it, communicate it and capture a reasonable share of the created value.

The BtoB marketer needs to develop and deliver the right narrative to the buyer that the buyer can use when he or she explains his or her brand purchase preference to his or her associates. The product he or she chooses will be of interest to his or her manufacturing associate, his or her finance associate and even to his or her associate who worries about environmental issues. The BtoB marketer must help the procurement person explain his or her preferred choice to a lot of other involved parties in his or her company. The job of the salesperson is to 'document and demonstrate' the 'total cost of ownership' that the procurement person can use with his or her associates.

Some marketers are moving from proving that their offer minimizes the 'total cost of ownership' to emphasizing 'the total profit added' by the marketer's offer. Whichever concept is used, it needs to be put in monetary terms. BtoB buyers need a financial metric to help them make their purchase decision.

Quantifying the financial value in a BtoC (Business-to-Consumer) situation is more difficult. Consumers use a less rational framework in making their purchase choices. They are influenced more by emotional forces and make many decisions on low-cost items in a habitual or impulsive way. The challenge to the marketer is to study the different 'consumer journeys' and 'touchpoints' that are encountered in a particular buying situation and look for insights that can be turned into a distinctive competitive strategy. The consumer marketer must look for ways to reduce the consumer's decision time or reduce customer cost or risk.

Consumer marketers must specify the consumer need that they are trying to satisfy and the relevant competitors who are trying to satisfy the same need. They need to identify the consumer set that would have this need and their other characteristics. They must decide on the differences to build into their offer. They must be sure that each difference is a relevant difference; otherwise it adds an unnecessary cost.

Every touchpoint during the consumer's journey provides a 'moment of truth' about the product. The marketer needs to identify and remove any negative moments of truth. Broadly, the consumer will experience three major moments of truth: when he or she attempts to buy the product, when he or she later uses the product and finally when he or she considers disposing of the product. The consumer marketer must keep this in mind.

The marketer's major challenge occurs when the customer likes the product but complains that the price is too high. The marketer can decide to

- Leave the price as it is but explain how the offer at its present price offers the lowest total cost of ownership.
- Leave the price as it is but offer an additional incentive, such as free shipment or a warranty.
- Offer to lower the price by removing some feature of the offer to reduce the buyer's cost.
- Offer a straight discount off the price.

All said, the marketer's job is to be a 'value merchant'. The marketer must provide leadership in 'customer value management'.

Operationalizing Relative Customer Value

Keiningham, T., Aksoy, L. and Cadet, F.

Abstract

The construct of "value" has been central to explaining economic exchange since the time of Adam Smith. Despite its central importance, debate still exists as to what value entails. Absent a comprehensive understanding of value, researchers and managers have grappled with how to measure and manage value. Not surprisingly, absent a definition, no comprehensive, robust approach has emerged.

We argue that value first must be viewed as a dual construct, i.e. value to the customer and value to the firm, that must be balanced to be sustainable. Given that value to the customer is clearly assessed as relative to competitive alternatives, we also argue that any robust measurement of value must account for competitive alternatives.

We propose applying recent research on the use of relative metrics in linking to share of category spending as the foundation of assessing value to the customer (particularly since customers in most categories divide their spending across competing firms). This allows firms to assess the monetary value customers' assign to their offerings, and to estimate changes in this value from different market actions. As value to the firm is ultimately about the net present value of customers' economic contributions to the firm, this allows firms to balance value to the customer with value to the firm.

Keywords

Value, share of wallet, relative metrics, Zipf's Law, Wallet Allocation Rule, Zipf distribution

[1] J. Donald Kennedy Endowed Chair in ECommerce and Associate Professor of Marketing, St. John's University Peter J. Tobin College of Business, Queens, NY, US.
[2] Associate Dean of Undergraduate Studies and Professor of Marketing, Fordham University Gabelli School of Business, Hughes Hall, East Fordham Road, Bronx, NY, US.
[3] Assistant Professor of Marketing, St. John's University Peter J. Tobin College of Business, Queens, NY, US.

Corresponding author:
Timothy Keiningham, J. Donald Kennedy Endowed Chair in ECommerce and Associate Professor of Marketing, St. John's University Peter J. Tobin College of Business, 8000 Utopia Parkway, Queens, NY 11439, US.
E-mail: keiningt@stjohns.com

Introduction

Maximizing customer value is the core aim of firms. Nonetheless, managers (and customers) do not agree on what value means, which begs the question, 'How do you manage what you cannot define?' There are two key reasons for the problem. First, customer value is a dual construct (Kumar & Reinartz, 2016). For firms, customer value is ultimately defined as the monetary contributions a customer provides to the firm. We argue that this contribution must be considered relative to customers' spending levels at competing organizations. Specifically, how do customers divide their share of category spending? For customers, it is their 'perceptions' of relative value (i.e., the value offered by the firm relative to competitive alternatives). Specifically, how do customers' perceive that competing firms rank (from best to worst) in delivering value to them?

The end goal is to have firms' and customers' views of value aligned. This has proven to be no easy task. Recent scientific discoveries, however, shed light on how to make this a reality.

What Is Value?

Value, the 'relative worth, utility, or importance' of something (*Merriam–Webster*, 2017), has been a core principle of economics since the time of Adam Smith (O'Donnell, 1990). Value is believed to be imperative to economic exchange and business strategy (Porter, 1991), which is not surprising given that its definition is often intertwined with commerce. Yet despite value being a lynchpin of economics, there are multiple schools of thought regarding what actually constitutes value. In fact, the differing ways in which economists view the construct of value has resulted in schisms in economic and political schools of thought (Hunt & Lautzenheiser, 2015).

Consumers have even more diverse, abstract and idiosyncratic notions of what constitutes value. Zeithaml (1998, p. 13) found consumers' definitions of value tend to fall into one of four groups: '(1) value is low price, (2) value is whatever I want in a product, (3) value is the quality I get for the price I pay, and (4) value is what I get for what I give'. The problem with these different consumer perceptions of value is that they interact with different constructs that drive customers' purchasing decisions.

Given that centuries of economic thought and debate has not resulted in a consensus on what constitutes value and that customers have divergent definitions of value, it is easy to understand why no method of value 'assessment' has gained widespread acceptance among managers. There have, however, been serious efforts to change that. Perhaps the most widely used value metric by managers since the 1990s is customers survey-based responses to a 'worth what paid for' question (Bowden, 1998; Clark et al., 1999; Kordupleski & Vogel, 2015; Varki & Colgate, 2001). For example, Gale (1994, p. 80) recommended using the following question to gauge value; 'Considering the products and services that your vendor offers, are they worth what you paid for them?' While the logic behind such an approach clearly follows the common refrain that value equals benefits minus costs (e.g., Barnes, Blake, & Pinder 2009), such metrics 'presume that consumers carefully calculate the give and get components of value, an assumption that did not hold true' in Zeithaml's (1988, p. 17) investigation. The popularity of measuring value using 'worth what paid for' as a key performance indicator has waned significantly since the 1990s, however, with most managers instead tracking customer satisfaction and recommend intention to help managers assess their primary objective from value measurement and management to customer loyalty (Aksoy, 2013).

Currently, when value is used in a management context, it typically describes the monetary value of the customer to the company. For example, assessing customer lifetime value (CLV), that is, the economic contributions of a customer to a firm or brand over her lifetime, has become a high profile topic for both managers and researchers (e.g., Kumar, Venkatesan, Bohling, & Beckmann, 2008).

This shift from a focus on customers' perceptions of value provided by a firm to a firms' evaluation of the economic contribution of the customer to the company points to an important fact regarding customer value—it is a dual concept. Customers must perceive that the firm provides value to them, and customers must also provide value to the firm (Kumar & Reinartz, 2016). In a thorough review and synthesis of the customer value literature to date, Kumar and Reinartz (2016) clearly spelled out what constitutes value 'to' and 'from' the customer, with implications for best practice implementation by managers. Simplistically, Kumar and Reinartz (2016) proposed that the ideal situation is one where customers' perceptions of value provided by the firm and CLV are modelled together to arrive at pricing decisions that align the two notions of value.

Without question, the approach proposed by Kumar and Reinartz (2016) represents an ideal scenario that allows both the customer and the firm to achieve a sustainable optimal value. Operationally, however, this approach would appear to be limited to a small percentage of firms.[1] Specifically, CLV measurement and management (as currently proposed in the literature) requires several years of detailed customer-level transaction data for all firm–customer interactions (e.g., George, Kumar, & Grewal 2013). While clearly that is ideal, it is unrealistic for most firms.

Additionally, even if this approach could be simplified, it typically does not directly account for the impact of competition. Only in an Orwellian *Big Brother* environment is it possible to envision that managers possess detailed customer-level transaction data for competitor–customer transactions within an industry category. Therefore, now (and for the foreseeable future) managers must infer competitor-based purchases from customers' firm-based buying behaviours. As a result, this necessitates surmising the reasons for these predicted competitor-based purchases based largely upon knowledge of the function of the item and its selling price relative to competitors, or based upon customer survey feedback.

Relative Metrics as a Measure of Value

Michael Porter (1991) argues, 'At the broadest level, firm success is a function of two areas: the attractiveness of the industry in which the firm competes and its relative position in that industry' (pp. 99–100). Therefore, a firm's strategy is dependent upon the way that the firm 'configures and links the many activities in its value chain relative to competitors' (p. 102). Given this, it is impossible to accurately gauge value absent an understanding of the 'relative position' of the discrete activities within a firm's value chain vis-à-vis competitive alternatives.

Bradley Gale (1994) introduced a method of Customer Value Analysis (CVA) that attempted to address this fundamental truth. Feuss (2010, p. 1) described the methodology as follows:

> Within AT&T, the specific measure that conferred predictive power came to be known as Customer Value Added (CVA). Outside AT&T, this measure has become known as Relative Customer Value (RCV) or the Customer Value Ratio (CVR). It is a relative measure; that is, it is a measure of the perceived value of a firm's products or services relative to the perceived value of its competitors' products or services. Relative measures are generally expressed as ratios. The numerator of the Customer Value Ratio is the firm's customers' average rating of the value of its services. At AT&T, the denominator is the firm's competitors' customers' average rating of the value of their services.

Specifically, the relative value metric proposed by Gale (1994) is calculated by determining a firm's average rating level to customers' responses to a 'worth what paid for' survey question. This is similarly done for the competition by determining the average rating level to competitors' customers' responses to a 'worth what paid for' survey question. The firm's average rating level is then divided by a competitor's average rating level (or the average of all competitors) to determine the Customer Value Ratio (CVR).

On the surface, there are several intuitive and attractive features of this approach. Mean rating levels are easy to calculate for the firm and its competitors, ratios take competition into the assessment of firm performance and findings tend to be relatively easy to communicate to the organization.

Unfortunately, despite many good features, there are several serious problems with this methodology. At a fundamental level, the type of survey-based metrics tracked to calculate the ratios lack the necessary properties to do so. While it is possible to calculate means, these numbers are based open ordinal data, as opposed to ratio data. In particular, the lack of a 'true zero point' means that the scales cannot be multiplied or divided. As a result, they are not appropriate for calculating ratios.

The approach also had serious methodological flaws in the structure of the basic calculations that dramatically impacted interpretation of the results (Keiningham & Vavra, 2001, pp. 42–43). As a result, despite its widespread use in the mid-1990s, this approach fell out of favour for most firms (Keiningham, Aksoy, Cooil, & Andreassen, 2008), and with it the widespread attempt by managers to directly assess customer-perceived relative value.

A Renewed Call for Relative Metrics

As CVA use declined, managers shifted their focus to other metrics proposed to link to customer behaviour and firm performance, most notably customer satisfaction, the Net Promoter Score (Reichheld, 2003) and the Customer Effort Score (Dixon, Freeman, & Toman, 2010). Unfortunately, none of these metrics linked well with customers' share of category spending, aka share of wallet (Keiningham, Gupta, Aksoy, & Buoye, 2014). This is particularly important since how customers divide their spending among competing brands in a category provides the most tangible signal of their perceptions of the relative value these firms provide. The inability of these new metrics to link to share of wallet strongly suggests that (as currently measured and analysed) they still lacked the discriminating power to gauge customers' relative perceptions of value.

Recent research by Hofmeyr, Goodall, Bongers and Holtzman (2008), however, dramatically improved the ability of perceptual metrics to link to customers' share of wallet allocations. Customers' share of category spending followed their relative ranked perceptions of the brands they used per Zipf's Law (Zipf, 1949). In other words, by knowing whether a customer considered a brand his/her first, second, third (and so on) choice, researchers could predict his/her share of category spending with a high degree of accuracy. Moreover, the best approach for determining rank was to have customers provide ratings to a superordinate perceptual/attitudinal metric (e.g., satisfaction, recommend intention, etc.) for all brands used by a customer in a category because of the need for it to be easy to have ties (i.e., two or more brands ranked equally).

This discovery led to other simpler approaches based upon Zipf's Law (e.g., Keiningham et al., 2011; Louw & Hofmeyr, 2012), most notably the Wallet Allocation Rule (Keiningham, Aksoy, Williams, & Buoye, 2015). These approaches have been vetted in multiple scientific investigations and shown to be robust across customer characteristics, industries and countries (e.g., Aksoy, 2014; Buoye, 2016; Keiningham, Buoye, & Ball, 2015; Keiningham, Cooil, et al., 2015; Louw & Hofmeyr, 2012).

One clear message relevant to the hunt for the best metric to gauge value is that from a managerial perspective, the effort is almost certainly misplaced. Research finds that all traditional perceptual/attitudinal metrics designed to gauge customers' overall perceptions of a brand's offering perform about the same when used to gauge a customer's relative ranking of the brands he uses. That is because all perceptual/attitudinal metrics designed to gauge customers' overall assessment of a firm/brand are measuring the same underlying construct (Hayes, 2008).

Instead the focus should be on aligning a customer's value to the firm with a customer's perceptions of the value provided by the firm/brand. This is the fundamental argument of Kumar and Reinartz (2016). But for this alignment to become a widely adopted corporate strategy, it requires an approach that can be easily used by most firms, not only those with detailed customer-level purchasing data over multiple years. The research of Hofmeyr et al. (2008) and Keiningham, Cooil, et al. (2015) offers a promising approach for aligning value 'to' and 'from' the customer. Using a relative ranked 'worth what paid for' metric (or some other superordinate perceptual/attitudinal metric) as the primary assessment of customer perceived value should strongly link with the share of category spending provided by customers to the firm/brand, using either the Wallet Allocation Rule approach of Keiningham, Aksoy et al. (2015) or the Zipf distribution approaches of Hofmeyr et al. (2008) and Louw and Hofmeyr (2012). And because share of wallet is easily translated into money spent with a firm/brand and its competitors, value to the firm represents a meaningful economic metric.

For managers, this approach has the advantage of being easy to implement. It merely requires surveying customers regarding the perceptions of the various brands that they use in a category. And it has the added benefit on making it relatively easy to identify the key drivers of value for a firm and its competitors (Buoye, Keiningham, Williams, & Aksoy, 2014).

Current State of Practice

Many firms already use Zipf-based approaches to gauge share of wallet (the core component of our proposed 'customer value to firm'). Typically, however, these firms do not realize that this is the case. That is because they are part of the underlying algorithms for several market research firms' brand equity and customer experience offerings (e.g., Rockbridge, 2017; TNS, 2017). Often, however, the predicted share of wallet from these models is not linked to individual customer spending levels. As a result, managers using these products often do not make the connection between share of category spending and economic value.

Of course, it should also be noted that many firms have legacy systems in place that managers have invested the company's money, and their time and credibility. Moreover, despite the simplicity of Zipf-based approaches to most researchers, managers often find them difficult to understand. By contrast, the legacy systems used tend to be models of great simplicity (e.g., satisfaction, repurchase intention, Net Promoter Score). Little (2004, p. 1855) observed that in such cases, managers tend to avoid models they view as complex and 'revert to models of great simplicity'.

Nonetheless, there are numerous examples of firms adopting this approach, although most consider their efforts to be proprietary and confidential (e.g., top 5 hotel chain, top 4 credit card payments processor, top 5 investment bank, etc.). A great public example of using this new approach can be seen in the study conducted through the Filene Business Institute by Aksoy (2013), where the Wallet Application Rule was applied to credit unions. This study found that for credit unions to gain share of wallet from their bank competitors (i.e., capture additional value from their customers), credit union managers must first understand precisely why their members feel the need to use these institutions (value provided to the customer). Although the most important driver of satisfaction for credit unions was found to be in-bank service, it was not the most important driver of rank for credit union members (that being competitiveness of fees). In another study, this approach was also applied regarding consumers' credit card decisions (Aksoy, Keiningham, Buoye, & Ball, 2017). Again, with this approach, managers were able to identify differentiating attributes that influence customers' perceptions of their rank vis-à-vis competition, and thereby grow share, thus aligning value to and from the customer.

Conclusion

Customer value has long been regarded as the raison d'être of economic exchange. Unfortunately, this recognition has provided little strategic guidance for managers because of the inherent difficulty creating a measurement and management process that could align value 'to' and 'from' the customer. To date, this ability has been limited to a small number of firms that possessed detailed customer purchasing behaviour data over several years.

The discovery of the Wallet Allocation Rule and Zipf distribution-based approaches, however, provides managers with a relatively easy technique to create that alignment. As a result, value measurement and management can take its rightful place as the core strategic aim of companies. And because drivers of value can be easily identified, managers can allocate resources to those areas that drive improved share of wallet and reduce customers' perceived need to use the competition.

Note

1. This should not be taken as a denigration of the Kumar and Reinartz (2016) approach, but rather as a reflection of the operational realities of most firms.

References

Aksoy, L. (2013). How do you measure what you can't define? The current state of loyalty measurement and management. *Journal of Service Management, 24*(4), 356–381.
———. (2014). Linking satisfaction to share of deposits: An application of the Wallet Allocation Rule. *International Journal of Bank Marketing, 32*(1), 28–42.
Aksoy, L., Keiningham, T. L., Buoye, A., & Ball, J. (2017). Linking satisfaction to credit card decisions: An application of the Wallet Allocation Rule. *International Journal of Bank Marketing, 35*(2), 205–219.
Barnes, C., Blake, H., & Pinder, D. (2009). *Creating and delivering your value proposition: Managing customer experience for profit*. London, UK: Kogan Page Publishers.
Bowden, P. (1998). A practical path to customer loyalty. *Managing Service Quality, 8*(4), 248–255.
Buoye, A. (2016). An examination of relative satisfaction and share of wallet: Investigating the impact of country and customer characteristics. *Journal of Service Theory and Practice, 26*(3), 297–314.
Buoye, A., Keiningham, T. L., Williams, L., & Aksoy, L. (2014). Understanding what it takes to be number 1. In J. Kandampully (Ed.), *Customer experience management: Enhancing experience and value through service management* (pp. 327–345). Dubuque, IA: Kendall Hunt Publishing Company.

Clark, L. A., Cleveland, W. S., Denby, L., & Liu, C. (1999). Competitive profiling displays. *Marketing Research, 11*(1), 24–33.

Dixon, M., Freeman, K., & Toman, N. (2010). Stop trying to delight your customers. *Harvard Business Review, 88*(7/8), 116–122.

Feuss, W. (2010). *Fundamentals of customer value analysis* (William Feuss & Associates white paper). Retrieved 14 April 2017, from http://williamfeuss.com/Inc-1.pdf

Gale, B. (1994). *Managing customer value: Creating quality and service that customers can see.* New York, NY: The Free Press.

George, M., Kumar, V., & Grewal, D. (2013). Maximizing profits for a multi-category catalog retailer. *Journal of Retailing, 89*(4), 374–396.

Hayes, B. E. (2008, October). Customer loyalty 2.0. *Quirk's Marketing Research Review, 57,* 54–58. Retrieved 15 April 2017, from http://businessoverbroadway.com/wp-content/uploads/2011/01/BOB_Customer_Loyalty_2.0_Quirks.pdf

Hofmeyr, J., Goodall, V., Bongers, M., & Holtzman, P. (2008). A new measure of brand attitudinal equity based on the Zipf distribution. *International Journal of Market Research, 50*(2), 181–202.

Hunt, E. K., & Lautzenheiser, M. (2015). *History of economic thought: A critical perspective* (3rd ed.). London, UK: Routledge.

Keiningham, T. L., Aksoy, L., Cooil, B., & Andreassen, T. W. (2008). Linking customer loyalty to growth. *MIT Sloan Management Review, 49*(4), 51–57.

Keiningham, T. L., Aksoy, L., Buoye, A., & Cooil, B. (2011). Customer loyalty isn't enough. Grow your share of Wallet. *Harvard Business Review, 89*(10), October, 29–31.

Keiningham, T. L., Aksoy, L., Williams, L., & Buoye, A. (2015). *The Wallet Allocation Rule: Winning the battle for share.* Hoboken, NJ: John Wiley and Sons.

Keiningham, T. L., Buoye, A., & Ball, J. (2015). Competitive context is everything: Moving from absolute to relative metrics. *Global Economics and Management Review, 20*(2), 18–25.

Keiningham, T. L., Cooil, B., Malthouse, E. C., Lariviere, B., Buoye, A., Aksoy, L., & De Keyser, A. (2015). Perceptions are relative: An examination of the relationship between relative satisfaction metrics and share of wallet. *Journal of Service Management, 26*(1), 2–43.

Keiningham, T. L., Gupta, S., Aksoy, L., & Buoye, A. (2014). The high price of customer satisfaction. *MIT Sloan Management Review, 55*(3), 37–46.

Keiningham, T. L., & Vavra, T. G. (2001). *The customer delight principle: Exceeding customers' expectations for bottom-line success.* Chicago, IL: McGraw-Hill.

Kordupleski, R. E., & Vogel, W. C. (2015). The right choice: What does it mean? Groundbreaking research from the early days of customer value management. *Journal of Creating Value, 1*(1), 3–22.

Kumar, V., & Reinartz, W. (2016). Creating enduring customer value. *Journal of Marketing, 80*(6), 36–68.

Kumar, V., Venkatesan, R., Bohling, T., & Beckmann, D. (2008). Practice prize report—The power of CLV: Managing customer lifetime value at IBM. *Marketing Science, 27*(4), 585–599.

Little, J. D. C. (2004). Comments on 'models and managers: The concept of a decision calculus': Managerial models for practice. *Management Science, 50*(12) supplement, 1854–1860.

Louw, A., & Hofmeyr, J. (2012). Reality check in the digital age: The relationship between what we ask and what people actually do. In D. S. Fellows (Ed.), *3D digital dimensions 2012 ESOMAR publication series volume S355.* Amsterdam: ESOMAR.

Merriam–Webster. (2017). *'Value', Merriam–Webster online dictionary*. Retrieved 28 March 2017, from https://www.merriam-webster.com/dictionary/value

O'Donnell, R. (1990). *Adam Smith's theory of value and distribution: A reappraisal*. New York, NY: Palgrave Macmillan.

Porter, M. E. (1991, Winter). Towards a dynamic theory of strategy. *Strategic Management Journal, 12* (Special Issue), 95–117.

Reichheld, F. F. (2003). The one number you need to grow. *Harvard Business Review, 81*(12), 46–55.

Rockbridge. (2017). *MaxShare*. Retrieved 9 June 2017, from https://rockresearch.com/maxshare/

TNS. (2017). *Conversion model*. Retrieved 9 June 2017, from http://www.tnsglobal.com/what-we-do/by-expertise/brand-communication/conversion-model

Varki, S., & Colgate, M. (2001). The role of price perceptions in an integrated model of behavioral intentions. *Journal of Service Research, 3*(3), 232–240.

Zeithaml, V. A. (1998). Consumer perceptions of price, quality, and value: a means-end model and synthesis of evidence. *Journal of Marketing, 52*(3), 2–22.

Zipf, G. K. (1949). *Human behavior and the principle of least effort*. Cambridge, MA: Addison-Wesley.

PART 12

JOURNALS ON WORKPLACE CULTURE AND ORGANISATIONAL EFFICIENCY

PART 12

JOURNALS ON WORKPLACE CULTURE AND ORGANISATIONAL EFFICIENCY

The Impact of National Culture on Informal Learning in the Workplace

Kim, S. and McLean, G. N.

Abstract

The purpose of this article was to identify how differing cultural factors affect informal learning in the workplace. We have introduced concepts and reviewed studies on informal learning and national culture based on an extensive literature review on the factors influencing informal learning, particularly based on five Hofstede's dimensions of national culture. Findings suggest that adult education and workplace learning professionals need to attend to cultural influences and efforts at indigenization when foreign theories or practices are adopted.

Keywords

informal learning, national culture, workplace learning, indigenization, Hofstede

Informal learning is the most prevalent way of acquiring knowledge or skill in the workplace (Ellinger, 2005; Leslie, Aring, & Brand, 1998). Several studies have shown that people gain and transfer knowledge more effectively and frequently in informal learning situations than in traditional formal training (Ellinger, 2005; Enos, Kehrhahn, & Bell, 2003; Marsick, 2003). Recently, interest in informal learning has increased among corporations and human resource development (HRD) or workplace learning professionals with a change in the learning paradigm from traditional instructor-driven events to constant knowledge acquisition (Paradise, 2008).

However, most workplace learning theories and practices have been developed in the United States and some developed Western countries and have enormously

[1]Texas A&M University, College Station, TX, USA
[2]McLean Global Consulting, St. Paul, MN, USA

Corresponding Author:
Sehoon Kim, Texas A&M University, 544 Harrington Tower 4226, College Station, TX 77842-4226, USA.
Email: caoman00@tamu.edu

influenced workplace learning throughout the world (McLean, 2010; McLean & McLean, 2001). Moreover, workplace learning settings and needs cannot be fully identified without exploring associated cultural perspectives (Felstead, Fuller, Jewson, & Unwin, 2009). Despite the increasing necessity for reflection of cultural influence in learning (Merriam, Caffarella, & Baumgartner, 2007) and indigenous development of theories and programs in the current global setting, there have been only a few theories developed using appropriate cultural considerations (McLean, 2010).

As cultural context influences developing, implementing, and evaluating workplace learning (Felstead et al., 2009; Marquardt, Berger, & Loan, 2004), professionals who are in non-Western countries or who address and support culturally diverse workforces may need to consider different results in various cultures when they adopt theories or programs developed on a different cultural foundation from those of the recipients. Informal learning is not an exception to this reality. Even in the dominant culture, such as the United States, culturally different approaches in training and development have been on the rise because of the diversity in the workforce (Marquardt et al., 2004).

Ways of accelerating informal learning and its influencing factors have been intensively and extensively studied and developed among western countries, especially in recent years (Berg & Chyung, 2008; Kyndt, Dochy, & Nijs, 2009; Lohman, 2006). Informal learning occurs in an individual, in interactions among individuals, in organizations, and within the broader environment (Marsick & Watkins, 2001). All these contexts are closely related to culture. As informal learning is gaining more attention in workplaces (Marsick, 2006), it is important to identify how informal learning varies in different cultural contexts and how it affects individual learning.

The purpose of this article was to explore the impact of national culture on informal learning in the workplace. To this end, we identified what is known to date from studies that have examined cultural variables relevant to the practice and outcomes of informal learning in the workplace. The major factors that influence informal learning were analyzed according to five of Hofstede, Hofstede, and Minkov's (2010) seven national culture dimensions: power distance, individualism versus collectivism, masculinity versus femininity, uncertainty avoidance, and long-term versus short-term orientation (Hofstede & Bond, 1988; Hofstede et al., 2010). Indulgence versus restraint and monumentalism versus self-effacement, the most recently proposed dimensions (Hofstede et al., 2010), were excluded because very little literature addressing these dimensions was found for this study. Through examples in various cultural settings, we identified differences in informal learning in the workplace based on national cultures.

Theoretical Background

The theoretical background for this article focuses on the three primary areas under exploration: informal learning in the workplace, national culture, and Hofstede's cultural dimensions.

Informal Learning in the Workplace

In the workplace, informal learning is a type of experiential learning that can occur in both institutional and noninstitutional contexts (Marsick & Watkins, 1990). People learn informally from their previous experiences to understand the context of problems or to produce solutions by organizational intentions or personal curiosities. Thus, informal learning can happen anywhere in the workplace if people are motivated to learn and are given such opportunities by their organization (Marsick & Watkins, 2001).

Although the concept of informal learning has theoretical roots from Lewin (1935) and Dewey (1938), who emphasized individual experience and interactions between learners and their environment (Conlon, 2003), *informal learning* was introduced by Knowles (1950). He divided learning into four types based on the perspective of locus: of control unintended, self-directed, mediated, and authority directed. Informal learning mainly appears in the first three types (Knowles, Holton, & Swanson, 2011).

Recently, studies on informal learning have combined learning at the individual level with organizational learning in the workplace (e.g., W. Choi & Jacobs, 2011; Reardon, 2010). Because employees learn mostly from informal activities and interactions, Leslie et al. (1998) claimed that 70% of learning is from informal learning, Marsick and Watkins (1990) claimed 80%, and Sorohan (1993) claimed 90%. Several studies have been conducted to determine how workplace informal learning can be controlled to increase performance or to identify what affects its occurrence (e.g., Ellinger, 2005; Eraut, 2004; Skule, 2004). Table 1 shows the major factors influencing informal learning categorized by individual, peer-to-peer, organizational, and environmental levels.

National Culture

Hofstede (2001) regarded culture as "the collective programming of the mind that distinguishes the members of one group or category of people from another" (p. 9). He stated that each individual belongs to various groups that have various levels of culture from organizational to national. The shared culture among a group of people appears as basic assumptions or deeply-held convictions; values; and behaviors and practices, symbols, rituals, and artifacts that are easily observed (Schein, 1997).

National culture is a collection of common ways of thinking and acting in a country, distinct from other countries (Marquardt et al., 2004). Hofstede et al. (2010) argued that there are two reasons why national culture is frequently used in the social sciences. First, nations contain strong forces toward integration of language, mass media, laws, education, politics, sports, and economy. Second, one of the purposes of cross-cultural research is to enhance inter-nation collaboration.

However, one might question whether artificial country borders are appropriate for assigning culture to a nation might involve obviously different groups that have a dissimilar history, language, customs, and religion. The population of some countries consists of diverse ethnic groups with different cultures. Moreover, there may be much

Table 1. Factors Influencing Informal Learning.

Level	Examples	Factors Influencing Informal Learning
Individual	• Self-directed learning • Trial and error • Modeling	• Confidence (Lohman, 2006) • Interest in profession (Berg & Chyung, 2008; Lohman, 2006) • Endurance for changing (Eraut, 2004; Skule, 2004) • Previous experience (Eraut, 2004; Marsick, Volpe, & Watkins, 1999) • Professional capability (Berg & Chyung, 2008) • Job satisfaction (Berg & Chyung, 2008; W. Choi & Jacobs, 2011) • Accessibility (Berg & Chyung, 2008; Ellinger, 2005; Lohman, 2000, 2006)
Peer to peer	• Mentoring • Coaching • Teaming	• Climates of collaboration, sharing, and trust (Ellinger, 2005, Eraut, 2004, Lohman, 2006; Marsick et al., 1999) • Feedback of people (Berg & Chyung, 2008; Ellinger, 2005; Eraut, 2004; Jeon & Kim, 2012; Lohman, 2000, 2006) • Supervisor's support and encouragement (W. Choi & Jacobs, 2011; Ellinger, 2005; Lohman, 2006; Marsick et al., 1999; Skule, 2004) • Opportunities to meet professionals (Ellinger, 2005; Eraut, 2004)
Organization/ environment	• Job assignment • Human resource system • Career development policy	• Learning support system (Berg & Chyung, 2008; W. Choi & Jacobs, 2011; Lohman, 2006) • Reward (Berg & Chyung, 2008; Lohman, 2006; Skule, 2004) • Challenging and valuable work (Berg & Chyung, 2008; Jeon & Kim, 2012; Marsick et al., 1999) • Learning culture (Ellinger, 2005; Reardon, 2010) • Time and space (Ellinger, 2005; Lohman, 2000, 2006; Marsick et al., 1999)

shared cultural traits across nations. Thus, in this article, our focus is not on what are included in each national culture, but, rather, how different cultural traits influence informal learning in the workplace using a national culture frame regardless of the cultural stereotypes of a nation.

Table 2. Dimensions of National Culture According to Hofstede.

Dimension	Description
Power distance	The extent to which power is distributed equally or unequally
Collectivism/individualism	The extent to which relationship between individuals is loose or tight
Femininity/masculinity	The extent of assertiveness or modesty
Uncertainty avoidance	The extent to which individuals feel threatened by ambiguous or unknown situations
Long-term/short-term orientation	The extent to which individuals think and behave for future rewards or present values

Source. Hofstede et al. (2010).

Hofstede's Cultural Dimensions

Hofstede (2001) developed four cultural dimensions in 1972 by surveying IBM employees in 72 countries and updated them in 2001. Hofstede's original four dimensions of national cultures are power distance, collectivism/individualism, femininity/masculinity, and uncertainty avoidance. He identified a fifth dimension, long-term/short-term orientation while using the Chinese Values Survey (Hofstede & Bond, 1988). Recently, he identified sixth and seventh dimensions: indulgence/restraint and monumentalism/self-effacement. These emerged from his collaboration with Minkov using the World Values Survey (Hofstede et al., 2010). In this article, we do not address the two recently identified dimensions because of a lack of literature on them. Table 2 displays features of the five other dimensions.

This cultural framework is regarded as the most practical among the major cultural dimension approaches (Gannon, 2004). Many scholars have recognized that Hofstede's (Hofstede et al., 2010) cultural dimensions provided a useful theoretical tool for researchers and practitioners and opened the door for them to make use of culture in training, learning, development, and management (Chapman, 1997; Meyer et al., 2012; Schröder, 2000; Taras, Steel, & Kirkman, 2012; Teekens, 2000). According to Google Scholar, the two editions of his book, *Culture's Consequences*, which describe his cultural dimensions, have been cited more than 30,000 times.

However, some scholars have criticized this cultural frame regarding its research design and assumptions. McSweeney (2002) and Schwartz (1994) questioned the sample characteristics of Hofstede's research design and said that it may not be appropriate to generalize the results of research about a corporation to each national culture. Smith (2002) disagreed with the quantitative approach to measure cultures. Taras et al. (2012) found that many results in Hofstede's research are outdated due to more rapid culture change than Hofstede anticipated. We are uncomfortable with the label that Hofstede chose for the Feminine/Masculine dimension, because it reinforces gender stereotypes. Nevertheless, as Hofstede has chosen to stay with this label in spite of criticisms about it, we have chosen to use it because of its familiarity to readers familiar with Hofstede.

There are several models widely referred to in research to understand and distin-guish cultures, such as the framework of Hofstede (2001), Schwartz (1994), and Global Organizational and Behavioral Effectiveness (GLOBE; House & Javiddan, 2004). We employed Hofstede's dimensions for our analyses because this taxonomy focuses on values in a group of people, while GLOBE deals mainly with behavioral and managerial practices (Meyer et al., 2012). Furthermore, most previous research that dealt with culture in education and human resources adopted Hofstede's taxon-omy. As the focus of this study is not on the dimensions themselves, but on informal learning associated with cultures, adopting a more widely used cultural classification helps clarify the influences of culture.

Research Questions

The purpose of this article was to explore how national cultures influence informal learning in the workplace based on a literature review. Among the informal learning factors, those related to original human nature and individuality were excluded in our research. Hofstede et al. (2010) proposed that culture is distinguished from both inher-ited human nature, such as physical and emotional functioning, and personal unique-ness, such as experience, opportunity, and ability. For example, professional capability or previous task experience may not be significantly dependent on culture. As such, we formulated the following research questions:

> **Research Question 1:** Does national culture result in differences in the factors influencing informal learning, such as self-confidence, commitment, feedback, collaborative relationships, rewards, challenging tasks, change, and time and space?
> **Research Question 2:** How are the factors influencing informal learning affected by each of the five dimensions of national culture?

Method

We conducted a literature review of peer- and non–peer-reviewed articles, book chap-ters, and books. Keywords used in the database search were culture, cross-cultural, informal learning, and each factor of informal learning (self-confidence, commitment, feedback, time and space, collaborative relationship, reward, challenging tasks, and change). The literature was searched based on publication after 1988, when Hofstede's fifth dimension was proposed (Hofstede & Bond, 1988), to 2012. Relevant literature was identified through the electronic library system of our university, EBSCO, Science Direct, the search system of the Korean Education and Research Information Service, Google Scholar, and references found in identified articles. In total, 74 articles, dis-sertations, book chapters, and books were reviewed to address the research questions for this study.

Although few references directly identified informal learning associated with cul-tural contexts, we found several applied intercultural studies related to the factors of informal learning (e.g., self-confidence, commitment, feedback) in HRD, as well as psychology and management. Hence, the literature for this study included not only informal learning studies, but also cultural or cross-cultural studies in which the factors of informal learning were involved. The identified literature was reviewed focusing on how each factor of informal learning is effectuated in the workplace with cultural differences or cross-cultural contexts. For content analysis, after the initial review of the literature, we segmented relevant information found in the literature into a unit of the identified informal-learning factors. Then, the segments were sorted according to the five cultural dimensions to be analyzed in the findings section. Our cultural background (one is from East Asia and the other from North America with extensive global experience) led us to focus a culturally analytical lens on informal learning.

Findings

We found that informal learning may work differently based on national cultures. The factors influencing informal learning were analyzed according to five Hofstede's (Hofstede et al., 2010) dimensions of national culture selected for this article.

Power Distance

In organizations, the relationship between managers and subordinates shows the extent of power distance. If an organization is in a small power distance country, employees are more likely to have an equal relationship with their supervisors. In contrast, in high power distance countries, there is more likely to be a clearly unequal relationship. Hofstede et al. (2010) explained that, in a large power distance setting, unequal power occurs from the hierarchical system, and people most desire a supervisor who is a "benevolent autocrat or good father" (p. 73). In low power distance countries, subordinates have power despite their unequal roles and regard their supervisor as a consultant who helps, supports, and guides them.

In the workplace, informal learning is enhanced, personally, when an individual is proactive in making decisions about his or her work and development (Marsick & Watkins, 2001) and, organizationally, when supervisory support and a cooperative work environment are provided (Skule, 2004). Therefore, individuals are positively or negatively influenced in their informal-learning activities based on the situated power distance environment because it relates to relationships with supervisors and peers and to self-initiative for learning.

In informal learning, the supervisor's feedback facilitates and expands employees' creativity and knowledge. However, unlike lower power distance found in many western countries, in large power distance cultures, employees are likely to perceive feedback as interference or oppression of their autonomy. In their study with bank employees from 28 different countries, Bochner and Hesketh (1994) found that, in large power distance cultures, employees described the relationship with their supervisor as less open, close, and direct. Employees in a large power distance society tend naturally to accept a supervisor's interrupting behavior because of the contextual relationship with their supervisor (Chun, 2008), recognizing support and feedback from superiors not as suggestions but as important directions or commands (White & Thobo-Carlsen, 2002). In addition, Lehmann (2009) argued that communications between supervisors and employees are usually one-way in large power distance cultures, such as Thailand and Kenya, where questions from subordinates are not acceptable, and this may lead to a negative impact on motivating individuals' learning and change in the workplace.

As for collaborative relationships that enhance informal learning through active knowledge exchange and reciprocal cooperation, Y. S. Kim (2003) found that, in large power distance cultures, such as Korea, hierarchy is based on age, gender, and position and sometimes inhibits emerging team learning because this power may weaken or erode individual autonomy to choose collaboration and learning. Thus, he suggested that workplace learning practitioners may need to encourage supervisors to understand the effects of their power and avoid one-way commands in a team setting. Jiacheng, Lu, and Francesco (2010) surveyed employees in 10 Chinese and 10 U.S. organizations on knowledge sharing and reported that employees reacted differently according to nationality. Chinese employees in larger power distance contexts revealed acquiescence to knowledge sharing with fear of punishment, whereas U.S. employees did not worry about the consequences and autonomously participated in knowledge sharing.

Lehmann (2009) pointed out that close relationships between supervisors and subordinates can be a key means not for development but for an individual's success in a large power distance culture because it often relates to hiring, promotion, and financial rewards. In a similar vein, H. M. Choi (2004) found that employees in a large power distance culture often focused on face saving for their supervisors because they believed that it affects the relationship between them and leads to better support and recognition for the employee in the workplace.

Power distance affects learning culture, as people become accustomed to different learning approaches in terms of self-directedness and learning sources. Through a survey with 855 managerial- or professional-level employees, Ralston et al. (2008) found that U.S. employees showed much higher scores on self-direction than those from Russia, Japan, and China. This is consistent with the findings of Kirkman and Shapiro (2001) that self-management is negatively related to large power distance. In such cultures, employees are inclined to expect knowledge and expertise to come from a prominent person with status and power (Rao, 2011). Thus, they prefer to learn from experts or a verified learning source using an appropriate learning protocol. Dirani (2009) identified, in Lebanon, a large power distance country, that people are used to respecting a teacher and giving that role strong authority. Students are used to listening and taking notes, not asking questions or discussing.

Time for learning can also be an issue in such cultures. A report of Organisation for Economic Co-operation and Development ([OECD], 2004) reported that employees in Korea, who work around 2,400 hours a year (34% more than the U. S. average), usually start their work at 8 a.m. and end at around 10 p.m. or later. They often have dinner during work to stay late because they should be at their desks waiting for their superiors to leave. This extra time appears, however, not to add to the productivity of the workers (S. Kim, Park, & McLean, 2012).

Collectivism Versus Individualism

In individualistic cultures, individuals are expected to behave for their personal interest, whereas, in collectivist cultures, group benefit is more important than private benefit (Hofstede, 2001). Thus, individual performance is the most important matter of concern (Hofstede et al., 2010). On the other hand, people from collectivist cultures may look on the organization as a family in which reciprocal responsibilities of guaranteeing security and loyal devotion exist. They think harmony in their organizations or groups is more important than any other value (Hofstede et al., 2010).

Relationships between individuals influence how and the extent to which peer-to-peer interactions occur in organizations, one of the major sources for informal learning (Ellinger, 2005; Eraut, 2004; Marsick et al., 1999). Thus, we can expect active informal learning through close relationships with colleagues. Moreover, in relationships with supervisors, expectations, support, encouragement, and recognition from supervisors tend to motivate individual learning as well as commitment to informal learning activities (Berg & Chyung, 2008; Eraut, 2004; Lohman, 2000; Skule, 2004).

On the other hand, with respect to feedback, Shipper, Hoffman, and Rotondo (2007) found that, in strong collectivist cultures, feedback is not valued because criticism is normally avoided, and individuals are afraid of breaking harmony of the group because of their negative feedback. Stone-Romero and Stone (2002) also warned that negative feedback can be dysfunctional in collectivist cultures in spite of its necessity for the organization. If people prefer only positive feedback, some realities that are unfavorable but necessary could be distorted or hidden. Collectivists share knowledge to achieve harmonious relationships with other employees in the organization while individualists share because of individual values (Jiacheng et al., 2010).

Peer-to-peer interactions in informal learning also reveal different aspects according to culture. Compared with people from individualistic cultures, collectivists tend to prefer working on a team to working alone and have more informal contact with coworkers (Bochner & Hesketh, 1994). Several cross-cultural studies comparing collectivistic cultures with the United States (recognized as a high individual culture) showed that Hispanic (Sanchez & Gunawardena, 1998), Korean (Lim, 2004), Chinese (Bennett, 1999), and Puerto Ricans (Triandis et al., 1988) favored collaborative group activities rather than in-group competition. Through a qualitative case study, Kubo, Saka, and Pam (2001) discovered that, although Japanese organizations have a vertical structure in which peers need a manager's permission to cooperate with each other because of a strong and inflexible hierarchical structure, sharing information or knowledge in informal ways frequently occurs in this culture. After-work hours are important for them to build deep relationships and interactions. This phenomenon is usually observed in other collectivistic Asian cultures. In Korean organizations, informal networks that are formed by drinking together after work, often excluding females (Kang

& Cho, 2007), affect formal work relationships, as well, such as support and information exchange (Jung, 1996; M. Y. Kim, 2007).

It seems that collectivistic cultures have the strength of collaborative group activities compared with individualistic culture. However, several studies have shed light on the relationship between outcomes and collaborations in different cultures. Ramburuth and McCormick (2001) found that Asian cultures (collectivistic) revealed higher motivations in group activities but a lower level of strategies for the project than Australian (individualistic). This supports the findings in Teng (2007) and Trumbull et al. (2000) that people from an individualistic culture performed better in jobs making group decisions and completing group tasks than did collectivists. Although collectivists showed more collaboration, they focused more on building relationships in the group than on the goal. In this regard, Valiente (2008) warned that, in collectivistic cultures, employees may fail to distinguish between what needs to be done to complete the task and how to behave in group activities.

The extent of relationships among individuals closely relates to expectancy or preference for rewards to facilitate informal learning. While western cultures of individualism use individual reward to motivate people's behavior, collectivist cultures, as in East Asia, have strong interdependent traits, regarding performance in social or group obligations and responsibilities as a priority over personal rewards (Markus & Kitayama, 1991). Collectivistic employees are often motivated when their group or organization succeeds or is rewarded (Lee & Semin, 2009), and they emphasize individually equal allocation of rewards in the group (Hui et al., 1991).

Environmental or organizational change provides learning opportunities for people in informal ways because the change expands meetings with the addition of new people, ideas, and experience, which enhances learning (Marsick & Watkins, 2001). Opinions on how this dimension influences people's perspective of taking on change are divided. One perspective is that individuals from individualistic countries are apt to engage, set maximum goals, and prefer to take risks to achieve personal development goals (Crowe & Higgins, 1997) and more easily accept and follow changes (Liberman, Idson, Camacho, & Higgins, 1999). However, individuals from collectivistic cultures generally prefer safety and security and are likely to favor minimum goals and are reluctant to take risks (Crowe & Higgins, 1997). They desire the status quo (Liberman et al., 1999). Hsee and Weber (1999), however, disagreed with this position, based on their investigation of Chinese and U.S. participants. They argued that in the collectivistic culture, China, people are more risk-seeking than those in the individualistic culture, the United States, because they can cope with risks or change with their family or group members helping each other. Through this cooperation, people increase learning.

Moreover, Hooker (2003) argued that each nation has different characteristics on space, an informal learning factor. According to Hooker, Germany (strong individualism) has a strong sense of private space. Offices should be surrounded by sound-proof partitions, and the doors are normally closed. On the other hand, the Japanese (strong collectivism) sense of privacy is opposite to Germany's. They are used to sharing rooms with other people and feel comfortable with paper partitions in their offices.

Therefore, when HRD practitioners enhance informal learning, the locus where learning occurs should be carefully considered according to culture.

Femininity Versus Masculinity

Femininity–masculinity is about how aggressive or nurturing a culture is. In the workplace, a feminine culture emphasizes insight, serenity, and consensus while a masculine culture focuses on performance, competitiveness, and achievement (Hofstede, 2001). In feminine cultures, employees expect equal benefits, prefer more leisure to more money, and think that a humanized job needs cooperation with other people, whereas those from masculine cultures take equitable benefits for granted, desire more money than more leisure, and consider humanization of work coming from rich job contents (Hofstede et al., 2010).

In masculine cultures, people are likely to have stronger willingness to challenge at work, which relates to self-concept, affecting work performance and achievement. Self-concepts that influence confidence and efficacy for work are main factors influencing informal learning (Eraut, 2004; Lohman, 2006). Thus, attitudes toward learning may differ across cultures. In addition, individuals from masculine cultures are more responsive to cheerful, honored, and proud emotions related to their work and to the competitive environment there, whereas those reflecting feminine cultural traits are more likely to be open to relaxed, peaceful, and comfortable emotions (Higgins, 1997).

For example, in the research with the Australian and South Asian samples, Niles (1995) found that students from Australia (a masculine culture) recognized competition and reaching the top as the central motivations for learning, whereas social approval, such as caring about a family's expectations and relationship with the instructor, significantly motivated the achievement of South Asian students (feminine culture). Bennett (1999) discovered that employees in the United States who showed strong masculinity were negatively associated with attitudes toward human development. Bing and Ai-Ping (2008) found that Chinese adult learners had a higher level of assertiveness and competition in its masculine culture than Malaysian learners (feminine culture). The Chinese learners more seriously recognized the importance of exams and academic success for their career development than did the Malaysian learners.

Uncertainty Avoidance

Uncertainty avoidance reflects how stressed people are in uncertain and unclear situations (Hofstede, 2001). In the workplace, employees from strong uncertainty avoiding cultures are relieved when they are provided with formal rules, regulations, detailed directions, and explicit duties, whereas people from low uncertainty avoidance cultures feel restricted and uncomfortable in the same setting. Hofstede et al. (2010) concluded that individuals prefer less change, more rules, busier work, and more formalization in strong uncertainty-avoiding countries, while those from low uncertainty avoidance cultures reveal greater acceptance of change, more autonomy, only essential work, and acceptance of ambiguity.

In light of these different traits, individual informal learning carried out intentionally, such as self-directed learning, may be influenced by these cultural attributes as people from strong uncertainty avoidance countries easily feel anxious with an informal and self-controlled learning environment. They may feel comfortable when structured and predicted learning settings are provided and when there are definite, correct answers in the learning situation (Bing & Ai-Ping, 2008; Hofstede et al., 2010; Rao, 2011). Olaniran (2009) warned that the learning concepts of Web 2.0, in which an individual learns any knowledge by interacting with anybody at any time in the web environment, could be limited to certain cultures because of a lack of relationships between teacher and student and also the extent of the need for self-learning control. He also argued that learning by online technology, on which informal learning also relies, threatens some people and creates anxiety. People in Korea, a strong uncertainty-avoiding country, also have a tendency to prefer formal teaching and learning situations in which learning occurs based on an instructor (H. Kim, Kwon, & Pyun, 2008).

There is an argument that individual learning style is influenced by some traits of national culture, including uncertainty avoidance. Yamazaki and Kayes (2005) examined cultural differences in learning styles and found that Japanese managers who revealed high uncertainty avoidance preferred concrete experience and reflective observations, while U.S. managers with low uncertainty avoidance relied mainly on abstract conceptualizations and active experiments. This is consistent with Hoppe (1990), who surveyed 1,544 adult learners from 19 countries and found that the reflecting style was more associated with strong uncertainty avoidance, whereas the thinking style was more related to weak uncertainty avoidance.

Long-Term Versus Short-Term Orientation

Although time frame orientation is a measure based on the teachings of Confucius, a Chinese philosopher, this is not all about Confucian values (Hofstede et al., 2010). Rather, long-term versus short-term orientation posits "persistence and thrift reflect an orientation toward the future" versus "personal stability and tradition seen as a static orientation toward the present and the past" (Hofstede et al., 2010, p. 239). In the workplace, strong short-term orientation cultures emphasize leisure time, quick profits, and present performance, while employees from long-term orientation cultures pursue self-discipline and hard work, prefer position to earnings, and worry about benefits 10 years in the future (Hofstede et al., 2010).

As for informal learning, learning motivation and purposes vary in this dimension. In strong long-term orientation cultures, individuals are likely to learn for future positions, jobs, and unexpected change. They stress personal growth and social competence through which personal life circumstances and social status can be changed (Zhu, Valcke, & Schellens, 2008). On the other hand, people from short-term orientation cultures may view learning as a solution to confronting challenges and as a performance tool. They tend not to plan for future learning outcomes but focus on present interests (Rao, 2011). Briley (2009) found that East Asians with strong long-term orientation have an inclination to concentrate not only on the present, but also on the past and future, while North Americans with strong short-term orientation regard the present as most important. He argued that East Asians have a more complex structure when they make decisions because of the tendency of considering experience and anticipating the future, whereas North Americans have a relatively simple thinking model, as they believe that their destiny is up to themselves and is based on present decisions. Individuals who have a long-term orientation are generally open to various types of learning methods and are well-adjusted in the learning environment because their major interest is not learning itself but the results from the learning that contribute to future goals (Chuang, 2012). Thus, in long-term orientation cultures, informal learning may be expected to be strategic for self-development but far from improving work performance. Supervisors may look at self-learning as just a hobby, not as a work-related activity and inhibit individuals from being involved in learning. In short-term orientation cultures, informal learning could be practical for current jobs or problems but far from long-term development.

Conclusions

Learning begins with experience (Jarvis, 2006) and is increased by the relationship between a learner and models from whom the learner likes to imitate (Bandura, 1986). Thus, where individuals have lived and those with whom they grew up play a critical role in how they learn. In this article, to identify cultural impact on informal learning, we investigated how factors influencing informal learning work in different cultural contexts based on Hofstede's (Hofstede et al., 2010) national culture dimensions. Through a literature review, we analyzed influences of culture on major factors of informal learning: self-confidence, commitment, feedback, time and space, collaborative relationships, rewards, challenging tasks, and change.

Our findings point to ways that informal learning is influenced by each national cultural dimension. Regarding the power distance dimension, attitudes on feedback, involvement in knowledge sharing, self-directedness, and preference for learning source may be different by the degree of sensitivity in the relationship with people who have power. People from a collectivistic culture are likely to prefer group activities to activities focused on individual values and goals compared with people from individualistic culture. In feminine cultures, individuals tend to care about social approval (e.g., expectation, relationship) within the team, learning group, or organization, whereas, in masculine cultures, they are usually goal oriented and tend to emphasize learning outcomes. Depending on the extent of uncertainty avoidance, individuals may show a different level of anxiety about the self-controlled learning environment. In strong uncertainty-avoidance cultures, more specific and clear guidelines may be necessary for the learning activities, while more autonomy is acceptable (or demanded) in weak uncertainty-avoidance cultures. In long-term orientation cultures, motivations and goals for learning are generally for future success or change. However, people from short-term orientation cultures are likely to find their learning motives in present problems or imminent work performance rather than self-development.

Although we found cultural differences in informal learning and described them according to each cultural dimension, it may be a little early to conclude what is the best way for a certain culture to enhance informal learning. As a culture has a tendency to consist of several layers of traits and those layers are interwoven, individual behaviors, attitudes, beliefs, or values regarding informal learning may be influenced by multiple cultural traits. For example, we can analyze self-directed learning from several cultural aspects, such as power, preference for collaboration, assertiveness of the learning environment, tolerance of uncertainty, and whether the motivation for learning is current or for the future.

This article has limitations. First, what we searched was literature written only in English and Korean because of our linguistic skills, and this led to a limited review. Second, despite our efforts, this article could not cover all factors affecting informal learning but only some of the major ones. Third, although our study is based on the assumption that factors of informal learning may work differently in various cultural contexts, we did not explore the possibility that the factors themselves might be different in different situations. We could not suggest solutions for building indigenous theories or practice for every culture, obviously, but we have highlighted the necessity of considering cultural differences. Finally, by selecting Hofstede's construct of culture, we had to accept his perspective that culture is contained within country boundaries, a concept that we reject but had to accept given the void of any other available model for such an analysis.

Recommendations for Theory and Practice

Although most theories and concepts in workplace learning originated in the west, its concepts and practices have spread over the world. As globalization increases, workplace learning practitioners face cross-cultural challenges. Practitioners need to be cautious about adopting practices from other cultures, as has often been the case with concepts. They need to create expectations of academics within their culture for research that is culture specific, with clearer implications of how certain workplace learning practices will work within that culture.

Likewise, informal learning theories and research tools built in one culture might not be applicable in different cultural settings, because each ethnic group and country has disparate contexts (McLean, 2010). If workplace learning professionals adopt foreign theories or programs without any cultural consideration at customizing, they may pay a high price. In the organization, workplace learning professionals should be aware of employees' cultural backgrounds and reflect this knowledge in their learning interventions. If the employees are from multiple cultures, cultural similarities and differences in informal learning may need to be clarified. Previous cross-cultural studies and practices or experts on culture can help identify the traits of the target cultures. A pilot test may be necessary to see beforehand if the newly adopted practice tools work well in different cultures.

Moreover, workplace learning professionals should also avoid creating cultural stereotypes of individuals. The cultural differences in informal learning in our article are not about individual but group (nation) distinctions. This means that the overall ways and results of informal learning in one culture may differ from those with other cultural dimensions. Some people, however, may show different behaviors regarding informal learning from their national culture because individual variability exists.

Recommendations for Future Research

More studies on cultural differences and their impact on adult learning are necessary. Research should be conducted based on its own cultural context and not relied solely on the research done in other cultural contexts.

We propose, first, in-depth research focusing on each factor influencing informal learning according to cultures. Although some factors, such as feedback and collaborative relationships, have been frequently explored in cross-culture studies in education, management, and psychology, few studies that have examined other informal-learning factors (e.g., perception of change or challenging work) combined with culture were found. For instance, Chang, Chen, Huang, and Yuan (2012) studied from a cognitive learning aspect how individuals react over cross-cultural challenges that were entirely different from their previous experiences. Based on their conceptual framework, further studies may examine how differently informal-learning processes occur when individuals face challenges in different cultural contexts.

Second, how informal learning is associated with formal learning in various cultural contexts may also be explored. Informal and formal learning are complementary, and they influence each other (W. Choi & Jacobs, 2011). However, in this study, our research foci did not include the relationship with formal learning. To understand workplace learning better, it is necessary to study not only formal and informal learning separately but also their relationships in various settings.

Third, future research can focus on what is commonly shared regarding learning across ethnic groups or nations. Most cultural or cross-cultural studies have emphasized differences by cultures. However, those differences may be clearer when we identify shared cultural traits. Unlike the general expectation, recent studies have revealed that perceptions of learning and preferred learning methods between adult learners from East Asia and the West are not significantly different, but their different specific-learning situations cause different learning approaches (Chuang, 2012; Zhu et al., 2008).

Fourth, future research on informal learning may include diverse research methods. Through comparison studies, the effectiveness of each type of informal learning in different cultures may be analyzed. If what is different between cultures is clarified, it will help workplace learning practitioners to determine where employees need learning support. Case studies that cover informal-learning practices in various cultural settings are also needed. These case studies will form a basis for further research development on informal learning. In their qualitative study on informal learning of young anticapitalists, for example, Hemphill and Leskowitz (2012) explored the distinctive learning activities of the unique cultural group considering their national culture and history.

Last, we need to examine informal learning in the workplace from an interdisciplinary perspective. As learning is not a distinct variable from inner or outer circumstances in the organization, such as productivity, economy, members, culture, and society (Felstead et al., 2009), an integrative approach to understanding workplace learning may be necessary instead of regarding it solely as a cognitive psychology phenomenon. Future research may explore informal learning through a combination of multiple aspects, including not only psychology but also technology, policy, anthropology, and sociology.

Authors' Note

An earlier version of this article was presented at the AHRD International Conference 2010, in Shanghai, China.

Declaration of Conflicting Interests

The author(s) declared no potential conflicts of interest with respect to the research, authorship, and/or publication of this article.

Funding

The author(s) received no financial support for the research, authorship, and/or publication of this article.

References

Bandura, A. (1986). *Social foundations of thought and action*. Englewood Cliffs, NJ: Prentice Hall.

Bennett, R. H., III. (1999). The relative effects of situational practices and culturally influenced values/beliefs on work attitudes. *International Journal of Commerce and Management, 9*, 84-102.

Berg, S. A., & Chyung, S. Y. (2008). Factors that influence informal learning in the workplace. *Journal of Workplace Learning, 20*, 229-244.

Bing, W., & Ai-Ping, T. (2008). The influence of national culture toward learners' interaction in the online learning environment: A comparative analysis of Shanghai TV University (China) and Wawasan Open University (Malaysia). *Quarterly Review of Distance Education, 9*, 327-339.

Bochner, S., & Hesketh, B. (1994). Power distance, individualism/collectivism, and job-related attitudes in a culturally diverse work group. *Journal of Cross-Cultural Psychology, 25*, 233-257.

Briley, D. A. (2009). Looking forward, looking back: Cultural differences and similarities in time orientation. In R. Wyer, C. Chiu, & Y. Hong (Eds.), *Understanding culture: Theory, research, and application* (pp.311-328). New York, NY: Talyor & Francis.

Chang, W., Chen, C. L., Huang, Y., & Yuan, Y. (2012). Exploring the unknown: International service and individual transformation. *Adult Education Quarterly, 62*, 230-251.

Chapman, M. (1997). Preface: Social anthropology, business studies, and cultural issues. *International Studies of Management & Organization, 26*(4), 3-19.

Choi, H. M. (2004). *Supervisors's reactions according to performance and face-saving behaviors of subordinates* (Unpublished master's thesis, Chungang University, Korea). Retrieved from http://www.riss.kr

Choi, W., & Jacobs, R. L. (2011). Influences of formal learning, personal learning orientation, and supportive learning environment on informal learning. *Human Resource Development Quarterly, 22,* 239-256.

Chuang, S. (2012). Different instructional preferences between Western and Far East Asian adult learners: a case study of graduate students in the USA. *Instructional Science, 40,* 477-492.

Chun, H. D. (2008). *Influence of transformational leadership and learning organization on organizational learning competence* (Unpublished doctoral dissertation, Kyunghee University, Korea). Retrieved from http://www.riss.kr

Conlon, T. J. (2003). A review of informal learning literature, theory and implications for practice in developing global professional competence. *Journal of European Industrial Training, 28,* 283-295.

Crowe, E., & Higgins, E. T. (1997). Regulatory focus and strategic inclinations: Promotion and prevention in decision-making. *Organizational Behavior and Human Decision Processes, 69,* 117-132.

Dewey, J. (1938). *Experience and education.* New York, NY: Collier Books.

Dirani, K. M. (2009). Measuring the learning organization culture, organizational commitment and job satisfaction in the Lebanese banking sector. *Human Resource Development International, 12,* 189-208.

Ellinger, A. D. (2005). Contextual factors influencing informal learning in a workplace setting: the case of "reinventing itself company. *Human Resource Development Quarterly, 16,* 389-415.

Enos, M. D., Kehrhahn, M. T., & Bell, A. (2003). Informal learning and the transfer of learning: How managers develop proficiency. *Human Resource Development Quarterly, 14,* 369-387.

Eraut, M. (2004), Informal learning in the workplace. *Studies in Continuing Education, 26,* 247-273.

Felstead, A., Fuller, A., Jewson, N., & Unwin, L. (2009). *Improving working as learning.* New York, NY: Routledge.

Gannon, M. (2004). *Understanding global cultures: Metaphorical journeys through 28 nations, clusters, and continents* (3ed ed.). Thousand Oaks, CA: Sage.

Hemphill, D., & Leskowitz, S. (2012). DIY activists: Communities of practice, cultural dialogism, and radical knowledge sharing. *Adult Education Quarterly, 63,* 57-77.

Higgins, E. T. (1997). Beyond pleasure and pain. *American Psychologist, 52,* 1280-1300.

Hofstede, G. (2001). *Culture's consequences: Comparing values, behaviors, institutions, and organizations across nations.* London, England: Sage.

Hofstede, G., & Bond, M. H. (1988). The Confucius connection: From cultural roots to economic growth. *Organizational Dynamics, 16*(4), 4-21.

Hofstede, G., Hofstede, G. J., & Minkov, M. (2010). *Cultures and organizations: Software of the mind.* New York, NY: McGraw-Hill.

Hooker, J. (2003). *Working across cultures.* Palo Alto, CA: Stanford University Press.

Hoppe, M. H. (1990). *A comparative study of country elites: International differences in work-related values and learning and their implications for management training and development.* Unpublished doctoral dissertation, University of North Caroline at Chapel Hill, NC.

House, R. J., & Javidan, M. (2004). Overview of GLOBE. In R. J. House, P. J. Hanges, M. Javidan, P. W. Dorfman, & P. Gupta (Eds.), *Culture, leadership, and organizations: The GLOBE study of 62 societies* (pp. 9-28). Thousand Oaks, CA: Sage.

Hsee, C. K., & Weber, E. U. (1999). Cross-national differences in risk preference and lay predictions. *Journal of Behavioral Decision Making, 12*, 165-179.

Hui, C. H., Triandis, H. C., & Yee, C. (1991). Cultural differences in reward allocation: is collectivism the explanation? *British Journal of Social Psychology, 30*, 145-157.

Jarvis, P. (2006). *Towards a comprehensive theory of human learning.* London, England: Routledge.

Jeon, K., & Kim, K. (2012). How do organizational and task factors influence informal learning in the workplace? *Human Resource Development International, 15*, 209-226.

Jiacheng, W., Lu, L., & Francesco, C. A. (2010). A cognitive model of intra-organizational knowledge-sharing motivations in the view of cross-culture. *International Journal of Information Management, 30*, 220-230.

Jung, Y. A. (1996). Relation between performance-based culture and male dominance in the workplace. *Women's Studies Review, 13*, 295-319.

Kang, H. R., & Cho, M. Y. (2007). Comparison of career success models between male and female employees. *Korean Journal of Management, 15*(2), 1-38.

Kim, H., Kwon, D. B., & Pyun, C. (2008). Korean corporate HRD in transition: issues and challenges. *Human Resource Development International, 11*, 81-89.

Kim, M. Y. (2007). *A study on relationships at work and learning & adaptation of female early careers* (Unpublished master's thesis, Yonsei University, Korea). Retrieved from http://www.riss.kr

Kim, S., Park, S. Y., & McLean, G. N. (2012). *Long work hours in Korea.* Paper presented at the International Conference of the Academy of Human Resource Development, Istanbul, Turkey.

Kim, Y. S. (2003). Learning one's way to implementing learning teams in Korea: The relationship between team learning and power in organizations. *Advances in Developing Human Resources, 5*, 64-83.

Kirkman, B. L., & Shapiro, D. L. (2001). The impact of cultural values on job satisfaction and organizational commitment in self-managing work teams: The mediating role of employee resistance. *Academy of Management Journal, 44*, 557-569.

Knowles, M. (1950). *Informal adult education.* New York, NY: Association Press.

Knowles, M. S., Holton, E. F., & Swanson, R. A. (2011). *The adult learner* (7th ed.). Burlington, MA: Butterworth-Heinemann/Elsevier.

Kubo, I., Saka, A., & Pam, S. (2001). Behind the scenes of knowledge sharing in a Japanese bank. *Human Resource Development International, 4*, 465-485.

Kyndt, E., Dochy, F., & Nijs, H. (2009). Learning conditions for non-formal and informal workplace learning. *Journal of Workplace Learning, 21*, 369-383.

Lee, A. Y., & Semin, G. R. (2009). Culture through the lens of self-regulatory orientations. In R. Wyer, C. Chiu, & Y. Hong (Eds.), *Understanding culture: Theory, research, and application* (pp. 299-310). New York, NY: Talyor & Francis.

Lehmann, S. (2009). Motivating talents in Thai and Malaysian service firms. *Human Resource Development International, 12*, 155-169.

Leslie, B., Aring, M. K., & Brand, B. (1998). Informal learning: The new frontier of employee development and organizational development. *Economic Development Review, 15*(4), 12-18.

Lewin, K. (1935). *A dynamic theory of personality.* New York, NY: McGraw-Hill.

Liberman, N., Idson, L. C., Camacho, C. J., & Higgins, E. T. (1999). Promotion and prevention choices between stability and change. *Journal of Personality and Social Psychology, 77,* 1135-1145.

Lim, D. H. (2004). Cross cultural differences in online learning motivation. *Educational Media International, 41,* 163-175.

Lohman, M. C. (2000). Environmental inhibitors to informal learning in the workplace: A case study of public school teachers. *Adult Education Quarterly, 50,* 83-101.

Lohman, M. C. (2006). Factors influencing teachers' engagement in informal learning activity. *Journal of Workplace Learning, 18,* 141-156.

Markus, H. R., & Kitayama, S. (1991). Culture and the self: Implication for cognition, emotion, and motivation. *Psychological Review, 98,* 224-253.

Marquardt, M., Berger, N., & Loan, P. (2004). *HRD in the age of globalization.* New York, NY: Basic Books.

Marsick, V. J. (2003). Invited reaction: Informal learning and the transfer of learning: How managers develop proficiency. *Human Resource Development Quarterly, 14,* 389-395.

Marsick, V. J. (2006). Informal strategic learning in the workplace. In J. Streumer (Eds.), *Work-related learning* (pp. 51-69). Dordrecht, Netherlands: Springer.

Marsick, V. J., Volpe, M., & Watkins, K. E. (1999). Theory and practice of informal learning in the knowledge era. *Advances in Developing Human Resources, 3,* 80-95.

Marsick, V. J., & Watkins, K. E. (1990). *Informal and incidental learning in the workplace.* London, England: Routledge.

Marsick, V. J., & Watkins, K. E. (2001). Informal and incidental learning. *New Directions for Adult and Continuing Education, 89,* 25-33.

Merriam, S. B., Caffarella, R. S., & Baumgartner, L. M. (2007). *Learning in adulthood: A comprehensive guide* (3rd ed.). San Francisco, CA: Jossey-Bass.

McLean, G. N. (2010). The need for indigenous theory and practice in human resource development in Thailand. *NIDA HROD Journal, 1,* 1-19.

McLean, G. N., & McLean, L. D. (2001). If we can't define HRD in one country, how can we define it in an international context? *Human Resource Development International, 4,* 313-326.

McSweeney, B. (2002). Hofstede's model of national cultural differences and their consequences: A triumph of faith—A failure of analysis. *Human Relations, 55,* 89-118.

Meyer, J. P., Stanley, D. J., Jackson, T. A., McInnis, K. J., Maltin, E. R., & Sheppard, L. (2012). Affective, normative, and continuance commitment levels across cultures: A meta-analysis. *Journal of Vocational Behavior, 80,* 225-245.

Niles, S. (1995). Cultural differences in learning motivation and learning strategies: A comparison of overseas and Australian students at an Australian university. *International Journal of Intercultural Relations, 19*(3), 369-385.

Olaniran, B. A. (2009). Culture, learning styles, and web 2.0. *Interactive Learning Environments, 17,* 261-271.

Organistion for Economic Co-operation and Development. (2004). *Clocking in and clocking out: Recent trends in working hours.* Retrieved from http://www.oecd.org/datao-ecd/42/49/33821328.pdf

Paradise, A. (2008). Informal learning: Overlooked or overhyped? *T+D, 62*(7), 52-53.

Ralston, D. A., Holt, D. H., Terpstra, R. H., & Kai-Cheng, Y. (2008). The impact of national culture and economic ideology on managerial work values: a study of the United States, Russia, Japan, and China. *Journal of International Business Studies, 39,* 8-26.

Ramburuth, P., & McCormick, J. (2001). Learning diversity in higher education: A comparative study of Asian international and Australian students. *Higher Education, 32,* 333-350.

Rao, P. (2011). E-learning in India: The role of national culture and strategic implications. *Multicultural Education & Technology Journal, 5*, 129-150.

Reardon, R. F. (2010). The impact of learning culture on worker response to new technology. *Journal of Workplace Learning, 22*, 201-211.

Sanchez, I., & Gunawardena, C. N. (1998). Understanding and supporting the culturally diverse distance learner. In C. C. Gibson (Ed.), *Distance learners in higher education* (pp. 47-64). Madison, WI: Atwood.

Schein, E. (1997). *Organizational culture and leadership*. San Francisco, CA: Jossey-Bass.

Schröder, R. (2000). The international student in the international classroom, in H. Teekens (Ed), *Teaching and learning in the international classroom* (pp. 48-56). The Hague: Netherlands Organization for International Cooperation in Higher Education.

Schwartz, S. H. (1994). Beyond individualism/collectivism: New cultural dimensions of values. In K. Uichol, H. C. Triandis, C. Kagitcibasi, S.-C. Choi, & G. Yoon (Eds.), *Individualism and collectivism: Theory, method, and applications* (pp. 85-119). Thousand Oaks, CA: Sage.

Shipper, F. M., Hoffman, R. C., & Rotondo, D. (2007). Does the 360 feedback process create actionable knowledge equally across cultures? *Academy of Management Learning & Education, 6*, 33-50.

Skule, S. (2004). Learning conditions at work: a framework to understand and assess informal learning in the workplace. *International Journal of Training and Development, 8*, 8-20.

Sorohan, E. (1993). We do: Therefore, we learn. *Training and Development, 4*(10), 47-52.

Stone-Romero, E. F., & Stone, D. L. (2002). Cross-cultural differences in responses to feedback: Implications for individual, group, and organizational effectiveness. *Research in Personnel and Human Resources Management, 21*, 275-331.

Taras, V., Steel, P., & Kirkman, B. L. (2012). Improving national cultural indices using a longitudinal meta-analysis of Hofstede's dimensions. *Journal of World Business, 47*, 329-341.

Teekens, H. (2000). *Teaching and learning in the international classroom*. The Hague: Netherlands Organization for International Cooperation in Higher Education.

Teng, L. Y. W. (2007). Collaborating and communicating online: A cross-bordered intercultural project between Taiwan and the US. *Journal of Intercultural Communication, 13*. Retrieved from http://www.immi.se/intercultural/nr13/teng-2.htm

Triandis, H. C., Bontempo, R., Villareal, M. J., Asai, M., & Lucca, N. (1988). Individualism and collectivism: cross-cultural perspectives on self-ingroup relationships. *Journal of Personality and Social Psychology, 54*, 323-338.

Trumbull, E., Rothstein-Fisch, C., & Greeneld, P.M. (2000). *Bridging cultures in our schools: New approaches that work*. Retrieved from www.web.wested.org/online_pubs/bridging/welcome.shtml

Valiente, C. (2008). Are students using the wrong style of learning? *Active Learning in Higher Education, 9*, 73-91.

White, C. J., & Thobo-Carlsen, R. (2002). Cultural differences and managers' perceptions of work-related attributes. *Human Resource Development International, 5*(2), 235-239.

Yamazaki, Y., & Kayes, D. C. (2005, August). *Expatriate learning: Exploring how Japanese managers adapt in the United States*. Paper presented at the annual meeting of the Academy of Management, Honolulu, HI.

Zhu, C., Valcke, M., & Schellens, T. (2008). A cross-cultural study of Chinese and Flemish university students: Do they differ in learning conceptions and approaches to learning? *Learning and Individual Differences, 18*, 120-127.

Author Biographies

Sehoon Kim, GPHR, is a PhD student in the department of Educational Administration and Human Resource Development at Texas A&M University. He previously worked in the HR field in Korea for several years. His research interests include work hours, cross-cultural issues, talent management, and socialization.

Gary N. McLean, EdD, PhD hon., is president of McLean Global Consulting, Inc., a family business. As an OD practitioner, he works extensively throughout the world. He also teaches regularly at universities in Thailand, Mexico, and France. He was formerly a senior professor and executive director of international human resource development programs at Texas A&M University and is professor emeritus at the University of Minnesota. He has served as president of the Academy of Human Resource Development and the International Management Development Association. His research interests are broad, focusing primarily on organization development and national and international HRD (gary.mclean@mcleanglobal.com).

Work and Culture: Approaching Cultural and Work Psychology

Bendassolli P. F.

Abstract

In this article, we aim to explore the potential consequences of an approach to the theme of work that lies between culture psychology and work psychology. We argue that culture and work, considered as entities, have suffered from a process of mutual distancing over the course of history. Our first argument is to show the fallacy underlying this distancing, by arguing that culture is not an entity, but rather a process by which we use signs as tools to mediate our relationship with the environment and to regulate our own action in irreversible time. We also argue that work is a sign-mediated activity that occurs through culture. Most importantly, we advance the urgency of considering work as a cultural phenomenon, whose specific role is to make culture by getting things transformed into objects. The second argument we put forward is that work is a meaning-making complex. We further develop this concept by claiming that work should be analysed at the general level of the semiotic principles of meaning-making.

Keywords
Culture and work, meaning-making, work meaning, meaningfulness in work

For a work psychologist and some researchers dealing with work issues, the first encounter with researchers in the field of the Cultural Psychology (CP) of semiotic mediation (e.g. Valsiner, 2007, 2014)[1] can be unsettling. First and foremost, this is due to an awkward absence. For instance, from a search for the years 1995 to 2016 in the most important journal in the field, *Culture & Psychology*, using the keywords 'culture' and 'work' in all search fields, we retrieved 595 papers, of which only three deal with work-related topics, namely: professional learning (Daniels, 2011), stress (Kirkegaard & Brinkmann, 2015) and youth unemployment

Corresponding author:
Pedro F Bendassolli, Universidade Federal do Rio Grande do Norte, Departamento de Psicologia, Avenida Salgado Filho, S/N 59078-970, Natal/RN, Brazil.
Email: pbendassolli@gmail.com

(Pultz & Hviid, 2016). We also found some mention of work in Valsiner (2015a), although this analysis is not exactly about work but rather about the emergence of novelty in organizational dynamics. Another quasi-exception is Valsiner (2007), in which we can find two or three paragraphs devoted to work (as a goal-oriented activity and as a support for socialization).

Beyond that absence, the unsettled feeling most likely arises because, habituated to a certain anthropology inspired by Marxism (despite the probability that this 'Marxist tone' may already have become outmoded to many work psychologists), we tend to think of work as a central activity in human lives. Many of us belonging to the field of Work Psychology (WP) think that work is a good candidate for being able to embody the high-level psychological functions that are so important to CP (e.g. Bendassolli & Gondim, 2014, 2016; Clot, 1999; Dejours & Deranty, 2010). As a consequence, work should be considered as the first choice route through which human beings grasp and master nature and transform it (and itself) by infusing this dynamics with meaning.

The roots of the unsettled feeling regarding CP probably go much deeper. CP tries to be one type of meta-psychology, or a general psychology, as Valsiner (2015b) has already designated it. It is intended to analyse culture from the perspective of the human agent trying to make sense of the fact of living in an irreversible time and being unable to escape from the semiosphere that he or she has built and that enables him or her to deal with the present, digging into the past through the lenses of an anticipated future.

Actually, the reason why we would expect CP researchers to devote more attention to work probably comes from precisely this far-reaching *corpus* and ambition to be a general psychology for our times, and a contra-hegemonic psychology – since we believe that work is the 'perfect' field for someone trying to do nonmainstream psychology, considering all the political and social challenges currently associated with work that compel psychology to position itself, for instance, against some negative side effects of the current neo-liberal ideology (unemployment, untenable work conditions and moral harassment, among other issues). So we can ask: why has this new general psychology almost never chosen work as a topic of interest? Is it because work is not considered part of the culture? By chance, could CP somehow be caught by the same process that lead to some mechanistic views splitting culture & work in the Western intellectual tradition?

However, we can take advantage of this unsettling feeling of being at the threshold of a general-but-non-work-inclusive psychology. The feeling can move us one step forward, to foster at least two critical reflexions. First, concerning the perspective that always thought of work as being a vital and central sphere of our lives – i.e. work centrality, both psychological centrality (work determines who we are, our identity, our self-value and our existential sense) and social and moral centrality (our character relies on work/job we perform). Indeed, CP may not have fully considered work in its formulations because it is envisaged as only one context among many for theoretical inquiry. For instance, could work be a fundamental phenomenon like psychological development (a major topic studied by CP)?

Or might work be only a context for applying theoretical frameworks developed in other, more basic or general psychology? As we discuss in this article, the answers to these questions depend on the distinct levels at which the theorization process is supposed to be connected to the selected phenomenon that is under investigation.

Second, a reflection on the tendency to think of work as something related primarily to the economic sphere, where it becomes a means of producing goods and services. This tendency considers work only in its capacity as a *job*, i.e. a particular form of organizing work (as an activity) under capitalistic conditions. While the previous perspective generalizes (work as something all-embracing or work centrality), this one goes in the opposite direction by holding that work is only an instrumental set of actions through which people get by. The corollary of the 'great transformation' (Polanyi, 1971) that work underwent in the last two centuries was the sharp split between culture and economy, the latter supposedly being ruled by extra-cultural principles. Since then, research on work and on culture have followed different paths, with countless attempts to build a bridge between them yet *while considering each of them as unique and bounded entities.*

This brings us to the main objective of this article, which is to advance the argument that *work is a cultural phenomenon.* We believe that this theoretical repositioning of work as a cultural phenomenon may contribute to surmounting two supposedly antagonistic views: on the one hand, the view according to which work is 'a determining cause of' culture (work centrality); and, on the other hand, the view that work is 'determined' by culture (work as a by-product of culture). We posit that this antagonism creates artificial boundaries and vertical hierarchies between two phenomena that are deeply connected, as well as rigid borders between the CP and WP domains. We set forth two supportive arguments.

The first is that the position occupied by work in relation to culture should once again be reconsidered. Therefore, our first task will be to try to reconsider the work–culture relationship, drawing on the CP axiom of the *centrality of the experiencing person* and the overwhelming role of signs. The second argument advances the concept of work as a *meaning-making complex.* Based on the idea of the generality of the semiotic mediation process (Valsiner, 2014), we will present and discuss the constitutive elements of such a complex. We will try to show how, as a meaning-making complex, work plays both a psychological (personal culture) and a social (collective culture) function.

Culture against work

Just over 40 years ago, the sociologist Daniel Bell, recognized for his analysis of so-called post-industrial societies, admitted that the relationship between socioeconomic structures and culture was the most complicated subject in his field (Bell, 1972). He also asserted that Marx's idea of culture as a 'reflection' of economy had been supplanted by the increasing autonomy assumed by culture, given a radical social change in the image of the artist as a powerful tastemaker. Culture had thus become a self-defining entity and, at some point, had begun to *stand against* (as an 'adversary', in Bell's words, p. 30) the social structure defined by economics, technology and occupation. In Bell's text, culture is nearly synonymous with *art*. Work (bound to economy) appeared to be an alien activity in this new cultural landscape.[2] This kind of analysis extends through time and is still present, in a more expansive scope, in cultural studies and beyond.[3]

In a similar context, two positions need to be highlighted regarding the work–culture relationship. The first position is posited by Habermas (1975) in a remarkable essay that reflects upon Marx's materialistic theory of work and its role in explaining social evolution. According to Habermas, work can be analysed in terms of three distinct actions: instrumental, strategic and communicative. But, according to him, the strategic action features more prominently than the other two actions in Marx's thesis about the central role of work in explaining social evolution. Habermas casts doubt on this role assigned to work. If we want to understand the *specifically human* mode of reproduction of life, we need to consider communication-based domains, such as family or kinship. In other words, we need to understand the role played by *language*. Accordingly, we may conclude that work (instrumental and strategic action-driven) and culture (communicative action-driven) are ruled by different rationalities. This position has opened a huge debate over the last decades concerning the role of language in the world of work.

The second position follows a similar thought, although with a hermeneutical tone. Paul Ricoeur (1955), in a piece devoted to discussing *parole* (speech) and work, went much further than Habermas by straightforwardly asserting that '(. . .) the essence of language escapes to the nature of work: the language signifies; it does not produce' (p. 252). This position is quite illustrative of the humour of other post-hermeneutical thinkers, despite variations over time in their positions. In ontological terms, work is not in the same position as culture-as-a-language-domain. Culture and, more specifically, language are the key tenets in the endeavour to define the human condition. We can find this notion in existentialism as well, as evidenced by Heidegger (1977) and his discussion on the colonization of the world of life (to use a Habermasian expression) by the technological spirit of modernity, where work can roughly be placed. It would be absurd to think that Heidegger's 'Being' should be envisaged through the lens of work (despite his brilliant discussion on craftsmanship).

Work against culture

On the opposite end of this discussion, authors, particularly from the materialistic spectrum, are concerned with regarding work in an ontological capacity as defining our humanity. Certainly, Marx's colossal oeuvre comes immediately to mind here. Even though it is beyond the scope of our current analysis to present an in-depth discussion of Marx, we nonetheless highlight the fact that work occupies a central role in his theorization about capitalism, and especially in his view about what defines a human being. According to Marx, work is the basis of the process of *hominization.* This theoretical positioning of work can be seen in the writings of contemporary Marxist scholars. In what follows, we will discuss one of these scholars in particular: György Markus embedded in the French materialistic sociology. Although not a universally well-known *penseur*, he still serves as an example of the tradition that has advanced the sense of work centrality.

Markus is the author of the 1982 book *Langage et production* (Language and production), specifically devoted to dismantling the limits of materialism in its dealing with language. Bakhtin (1986) and Lukács (1980) are also committed to this approach, albeit with a much wider perspective (see also Lecerde, 2006). In his work, Markus argues against what he denominates the linguistic paradigm, according to which language is the universal source of all human forms of objectifications. He asserts that this hermeneutical approach misses the point about the real possibility of developing a practical attitude toward society, understood in its totality. Markus opposes this paradigm with what he calls the paradigm of production, which addresses a fundamental demand: to recognize that material production ought to stand as the cornerstone of our intellectual drive to interpret *all* the manifestations of social life.

At this point, we can identify two ideal positions embedded in this intellectual heritage, despite the caricature-like portrait, we have presented of it. To use a metaphor, the first position places culture (art, communicative rationality, language) above work, and the other places work above culture (paradigm of production). The above/below positioning is meant in the sense of a causal and transitive determination, wherein above is the *explanans* and below the *explanandum*. In between these two positions, we can identify tensions springing from the issue of what place should be assigned to work in our narratives, i.e. the idea of the centrality of work *ipso facto*. However, we also need to ask the following question: Why should work occupy such a high-level position in a supposedly social or even psychological value hierarchy? The same applies to culture: Should we regard culture as a kind of circular metaphor wherein we could locate a stable and bounded centre? Or is culture like a *container* of all human actions (including work)?

Culture reconsidered

The two positions about work and culture that we have just depicted rely on an underlying conception according to which culture is an *entity* and work is understood (if at all) only as *abstract work*. As ideal types of work–culture relationships, we probably cannot find them in their pure form in reality, but even so, they symbolize an ongoing essentialist view that derives from Plato, as well as an essentialist and a prosopopoeial view since culture seems to be defined as a person.

When we proposed using the word *relationship* to further discuss the two phenomena (work and culture), in the introduction of this article, could this have revealed our own underlying conception of two bonded entities: culture AND work? What might the nature of this relationship be? Might it be a hyphen-like relationship (culture–work) or an interspace/liminal zone (something like culture↔work)? If the latter, could this interspace be inclusive, in the sense of an 'inclusive separation' as advanced by Valsiner (2014)? We believe that recasting some core ideas from CP may help us advance towards an idea of interspatial inclusion/liminality, or at least help us to add new insights to this wide-ranging, ancient but still open-to-debate controversy.

The first and certainly the most important of these concepts is the concept of culture. From the perspective of semiotic CP, neither is culture an entity nor can it be grasped as a state-like phenomenon (a point-like sign, see Valsiner, 2007). Culture is a process, a realm of different products of the mind, such as meanings, tools and symbols. As a corollary, it is also assumed that culture has no agency. Instead, *it is the agent that acts* – this is the fundamental position of CP about the centrality of the experiencing person (personology – see Stern (1938). The agent invents tools and signs and metasigns that regulate, in turn, this same action of making use of tools and signs (Valsiner, 1999). As Valsiner (2014) puts it, 'Culture does not cause anything, yet human beings operating though culture in goals-oriented ways re-organize their worlds' (p. 35).

Culture, as long as it is composed of signs, offers us a challenge: neither can we avoid or escape from these signs nor can we react to culture as if it were an invisible gas acting upon us – as something standing outside us. Culture is inside us; it is not an environment (at least not in the sense of a natural or given one). Culture is the result of the central human ability to make meaning (and to be overdetermined by it), which is used by the agent to encode the environment and infuse it with meaningfulness.

Additionally, signs have the double function of distancing us from the here-and-now and, at the same time, of making us forget their own existence. The latter function can be responsible for the fact that we do not need to think all the time about how to act in specific situations or settings. Of course, this would be completely different in a crisis situation, in transitions, or when signs help us, as goal-driven agents, in our endless effort to anticipate the future and negotiate the tensions and ambiguities that we face in the irreversible time.

Work through culture

However, the same take-for-granted characteristic of living through signs may be epistemologically misunderstood, giving rise to the above/below metaphor. Culture and work cannot be placed in a transitive above/below position because, first, culture has no centre as long as it is not an entity and, second, we cannot put ourselves (as meaning-making agents) above or below signs, either in onto-logical terms (as some truth beyond the signs – our 'true self', as Wittgenstein denounced when he discussed the myth of private language) or in methodological terms (linear causality – signs as entities causing our behaviour outwardly, from above). All we can do is keep moving and inventing sign hierarchies that, despite having been created by ourselves, may take control over us in a process of semiotic regulation. In the same way, work should not be placed above culture because work is a sign-regulated activity as well, caught in the same ambiguous and uncertain nature of signs (no 'centre', no bounded border). So, how should the interspace between culture and work be envisaged from a (cultural) psychological point of view?

If we understand culture as a semiosphere and follow the assertion that culture is, at same time, inside us (by internalization) and is made by us through externalizations – for instance, externalizations through work – in an in-between dynamics (inner-outer) (Valsiner, 2007, 2014), or interspace, then culture and work are embodied in the same generic process of meaning-making through signs. They cannot be considered to be entertaining a *causal relationship* between them, at least not a linear, one-path, causality. Culture and work relate with each other in an inclusive separation mode as this concept has been developed in CP (Valsiner, 2004). Their borders are made by signs, and these signs move all the time as a result of the agent actions of irreversible time.

Turning back to our idea of interspace and liminality, we can advance the following: (a) Researchers need to conceptualize the phenomenon under investigation by using discriminating strategies. Such a conceptualization shows that culture and work are only apparently separate entities, due to the operation of intellectual and discursive processes; we will develop this claim in the next section. (b) At the level of the semiotic processes, however, both work and culture are hyper-generalized signs (Valsiner, 2014), i.e. all-embracing ones, providing the context for other meaningful concepts and connections.

Elaborating further on this topic, we claim that the interspace between culture and work corresponds to a dynamic process of meaning-making, with permeable boundaries between the two. At a more general level, culture operates as a catalytic sign, bringing to the acting person symbolic tools in the form of suggestions, contra-suggestions and myths (and counter-myths), constraining the flux of their possible actions (circumvention signs) or promoting other actions (promoter signs) (Valsiner, 2014). In its way, work is an activity carried out *through* culture. This means that when we are engaged in work, we are catalysed by culture, in the sense of making use of these symbolic tools and adopting some direction for our own actions.

For instance, the formal education through which a future professional is prepared to perform specific tasks corresponds to a series of symbolic resources made available to her in the form of instructions, norms, procedures and how-to advice. These are normally embedded in books and are also co-produced in the process of interacting with professors, other professionals and colleagues. While working, this same professional is also supported by a body of accumulated knowledge (not necessarily a formal one) that canalizes her efforts towards some goals and shapes her actions in order to reach these goals. As a sign, culture mediates the relation between the subject and the parts of reality to be transformed through work as an activity. Our challenge in the next sections is to further discuss what exactly culture *is* within work and what work *is* within culture. We tackle the issue by advancing the thesis of work as a *meaning-making complex*.

Work as a liminal concept?

Before developing the argument that work should be considered a meaning-making complex within culture, we need to set forth some crucial epistemological issues related to the similarities and distancing in the CP↔WP 'in-between' zone, or put in other words, between work and culture interspace taken in a disciplinary level. To a certain extent, CP and WP can be seen as much closer than they might appear at first glance. Indeed, there seem to be some crucial and strategic points of intersection between them, which might be surprisingly familiar to some branches of work psychologists – for instance, to those working on the Psychodynamics of Work (Dejours, 2013) and on the Clinic of Activity (Clot, 1999), approaches that have both been developed in the French work psychology context. In both cases, work is understood as supporting crucial psychological functions.

One example of the previous assertion can be gleaned from a chapter of Valsiner's last book (2014, chapter 7), even if he never uses the word *work*, nor any of its synonyms, in this chapter, the goal of which is to discuss how *culture is made through objects*. The similarity shows up immediately, considering that the primary goal of work, useful labour (Marx, 1887), is to mediate the exchanges between human beings and nature toward making (useful) objects to afford human life and, at same time, embody culture. We extract four core ideas from Valsiner's (2014) chapter:

- We *make* things. And through those things we *modify ourselves*. Furthermore, we *decide upon the fate of things we have made* – keep them or abandon, adore them, destroy them or pass them on to others (...). These three notions – make, modify and maintain – are sufficient to specify how the human species differs from most others (...) (p. 135, emphasis in the original);
- It is educating the perception-action system – the eye, the ear and, most importantly, the hand – that has made it possible to create and maintain the enormous overload of human-created objects (...) (p. 136);
- In the invention and manufacture of human tools is the functional fit of the material and the goal of a human-made thing that mattered. The very first act of creating a cultural tool (...) required transcending the immediate affordances of the things (p. 141);
- We turn things in objects. These objects do not merely exist – they *resist* our efforts to act upon them (p. 153, emphasis in the original).

Looking at a famous passage from Marx's *The Capital* that has probably inspired some work psychologists in their definition of work (even if indirectly), we can observe a similar 'sign field', despite the word *labour* being used in this case. Marx (1887) wrote:

> Labour is, in the first place, a process in which both man and Nature participate, and in which man *of his own accord* starts, regulates, and controls the material re-actions between himself and Nature. He *opposes* himself to Nature as one of her own forces,

setting in motion arms and legs, head and hands, the natural forces of his body, in order to appropriate Nature's productions *in a form adapted to his own wants.* By thus acting on the external world and changing it, he at the same time *changes his own nature.* (. . .) what distinguishes the worst architect from the best of bees is this, that the architect *raises his structure in imagination before he erects it in reality.* (p. 128, emphasis added)

Comparing these extracts, we feel as though we are looking at the same (or broadly similar) phenomenon (X = work), but described with a CP-proper narrative (Y) rather than with a similar (but still non-overlapping) narrative of the sort we use in some branches of WP, inspired by this theoretical repertory drawn from Marx (Z), here used just as a prototypical example. Could this similarity exist simply because we can posit a single, shared phenomenon and then compare the narratives *qua* equivalents (Y ↔ Z → X)? This question is of vital significance in order to improve our understanding of the *liminalities* between CP and WP regarding work as a cultural phenomenon.

Work< >Non-work

At a first level of analysis, as we have already suggested, we can say that these liminalities exist due to distinct uses of theoretical tools – an epistemological issue. Employing different narratives to build upon the phenomenon is a current practice in science. These tools canalize the researcher's attention to some parts of the phenomena, which are then used as facts, and not to others. Phenomena are objectified (or externalized) into language through the process of sign construction and its oppositions (A< >non-A). As a consequence, researchers themselves operate *through* culture as a sign, being guided by culture as a reservoir of symbolic resources. In the same process, they also make culture through their externalizations.

Therefore, at a semiotic level of analysis, we can assert that culture has acted over time as a catalyst in the process of making distinctions between work< >non-work. In this case, there is not only an epistemological issue at stake, but also a 'work of culture', to use an Obeyesekere (1990, p. 55) key concept. Researchers are oriented by culture to use certain sign complexes rather than others.

The same could be said about the current difficulties faced by people in general in trying to define what work is and what it is not – for example, in between the family/work borders, formal/informal, home-based/organizational-based, retirement/non-retirement and paid/non-paid work borders. These borders have practical implications. For instance, if someone considers that work at home is not work at all, they can accept the work much more than they would if they described the situation as an invasion of work into family time. And the opposite also seems to be true: conceiving work as home-based implies that there is no invasion of work into one's private life, since it is inwardly reconstructed as a home activity. In this process, the borders of what work means are enlarged in such a way as to include, for instance, parenting and housekeeping.

However, if the borders between work< >non-work are at least partly determined by the way that researchers (and people in general), catalysed by culture,
make meanings and come up with conceptual distinctions, how can we define work
in a broader sense, as a cultural phenomenon? At this point, we reach the second
argument brought up in the introduction, concerning our understanding of work as
a meaning-making complex.

The meaningful functions of work

As a cultural phenomenon, and from a CP point of view, work could be said to be
an arena for an individual's process of making meaning out of her relation with the
environment. Through work (mediated by signs), organisms pre-adapt themselves
to this environment, by anticipating the future in the present. At this level, we must
bear in mind a crucial difference between work as a job, i.e. as a particular arrangement that emerged together with the capitalist system in the 19th century (that is to
say, a specific cultural arrangement), and work as a meaning-making activity, by
which we struggle not only to survive as a species or individuals but also as culture-
making, future-oriented creatures.

It follows from this definition that work is a cultural phenomenon, because it
plays the function of making culture through objects, engaging human agents in
goal- and means-directed activities aimed at transforming the natural environment
into an *Umwelt* (Chang, 2009), i.e. an agent-centred environment. Through work,
agents also *resist* the *affordance* of these same objects (a stand against, or
Gegenstand) (Valsiner, 2014, p. 153) when their action faces an obstacle and they
create a counter-action (resistance) to the obstacle. Work encapsulates a specific
meaningful setting in which active human agents make meanings and use them to
regulate their activity. Once built, these meanings are then incorporated into the
collective culture.

By defining work in this way, we are introducing a major distancing from some
current approaches in WP. For instance, there is an entire branch of research on
the 'meaning of work' (e.g. Meaning of Work International Research Team
(MOW), 1987). Overall, research based on MOW's model is focused on meaning
qua quasi-static predicates – e.g. work is a way to make money, work represents
suffering, work is a source of self-realization, among others. These predicates are
cultural markers concerning what work means, and they are important elements
qua social representations.

Researchers need to go beyond this manifest level and get into the meaning-
making level as a general semiotic process of organisms relating to their environment. Otherwise, it would be difficult to explain an agent's actions or even
high-level psychological processes embedded in work as a cultural phenomenon,
as a meaning-making complex. In the next sections, and based on Figure 1, we will
spell out three features of this complex: (a) the role of the active agent, (b) the role
of signs in work as a mediated activity and (c) the core process by which things
(nature) are transformed into objects (culture).

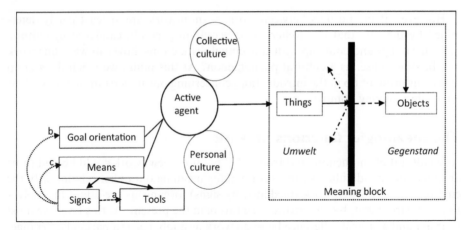

Figure 1. Work as a meaning-making complex.
Source: Elaborated by the author based on Valsiner (2007, 2014).

Work as an agent-driven activity

The model proposed in Figure 1 assumes that the person is the active builder of meaning, and, in the case of work, is the active agent that *invests herself* in a goal-oriented activity through which things get transformed into objects. In this sense, work is a specific set of actions implying a movement of the agent from inside to outside herself, toward other persons, things and the activity itself – triggered by internal meaning structures and canalized by external norms, constraints and pro-moter and circumvention signs. Work is a multi-directed activity (Clot, 1999).

The person brings culture, both personal and collective culture, to her work. She works *through* culture, and culture is made *through* work. Therefore, the active agent enters into work embedded in two, non-isomorphic manifestations of culture. The personal culture is related to the singularity and uniqueness of the person. It is built through a constructive process of internalization. This process draws on the semiotic material (symbolic resources; Zittoun, 2007) available in the meaningful environment where the person lives (her *Umwelt*).

In contrast, through a constructive externalization process, the person transposes the semiotic material (inner meaning structures based on value and hyper-generalized affective field signs) to the realm of external action. Through externalization, the agent objectifies meaning into actions, at the same time infusing the collective culture with new meanings. In turn, the collective culture is the stock of symbolic resources available for action. In WP, we can find a similar idea in the *genre professionnel* (professional genre; Clot, 1999, 2009). Such a *genre* represents all the norms, obligations and references, i.e. the collective memory, of a specific *métier* that canalizes action in work. In the present context, we could also 'trans-late' Clot's professional genre as semiosphere.

Work as a meaningful setting

The large box in Figure 1 depicts our main idea of work as a meaning-making process. It is based on Valsiner's (2007) re-elaboration of Vygotsky's Method of Double Stimulation. As can be seen in the figure, work implies a non-linear relationship between things and objects, sustained by the goal-directed action of the agent in a meaningful setting fed by semiotic elements – tools and signs. By making use of signs, the active agent regulates the selection or construction of tools (Figure 1(a)), makes meaning for the act of pursuing the goal (Figure 1(b)), and makes meaning for the persistence (motivation) towards the goal (Figure 1(c)). The goal pursued can be established by the agent herself (auto-determination) or by others (hetero-determination). Even when hetero-determined, this goal needs to make sense to the agent.

To say that work takes place in a meaningful setting means that the agents need to deal with a complex semiotic situation, with impediments or resistances, tensions, ambiguities and sometimes opposing possibilities in the course of their action. However, these elements are not 'objective' ones, in the sense of something that could be 'isolated' in the work environment or inside the personality of the agent. They are *intrinsic* to the activity and are *meaningful* by nature. They are not given, but continuously elaborated and re-elaborated by the agent through dialogical processes. This positioning is quite different, for instance, from the 'work conditions' tradition in WP. This tradition usually thinks of work as taking place in objective settings, where several elements, such as work load, psychosocial risk factors, temperature, luminosity, technology, organizational culture and so on, can be found. These elements are believed to *act upon* the agent.

In a different direction, we assert that the work setting is a meaningful one because the agent needs to struggle with meaning blocks, not simply with objective and 'natural' constraints. Meaning blocks are meaningful barriers interposed in the course of the process of getting things transformed into objects. Meaning blocks may originate from several sources. The collective culture is one such source, as long as it brings to the work setting, by means of the agent, different semiotic situations.

For instance, this meaning block could play a circumvention role (Valsiner, 2014), when a particular direction of feeling or thinking is reversed or suppressed in the stream of consciousness. As a consequence, a range of possible action courses (ACs) that could come along with the transformation process (things → objects) are not observed. The agent needs to struggle with the opposition between the emerging AC 1 and non-AC 1, with sign oppositions, and with the ambiguous meanings attached to them. We provide some examples to clarify this idea. First, an individual who is faced with different options in a decision-making process needs to choose one direction instead of another, each of these with practical implications and sometimes irreversible ones. Second, even if an organization offers its workers a series of prescriptions regarding the 'correct' way to accomplish the tasks assigned to them, there is a range of possibilities that emerge as the workers actually engage themselves during the course of the task accomplishment.

Ultimately, it is up to the workers to decide the more suitable way to approach some of these tasks, based on their previous experiences, their imagination, their decision-making or even trial and error. Some work psychologists differentiate between *prescribed work* (usually prescribed by the organization) and *real work*, meaning what happens while people are trying to figure out how exactly to carry out their work (Bendassolli & Gondim, 2016). For some researchers (e.g. Dejours, 2013), work dynamics can be analysed based on this gap between prescription and reality.

Similarly, Clot (1999) draws a line between the realized activity (course of action effectively pursued) and the *réel de l'activité* (the real of the activity), the latter representing all the possible courses of action not followed by the agent, but still alive in the agent's mind, *qua* potentialities. As a consequence, work psychologists should focus not only on what has happened in work (past), but mostly on what could or should happen (future). Work can be done by means of equally possible courses of action; there is no best or the only correct way to perform a task. In this sense, work is not merely a matter of applying technical prescriptions (i.e. of following normative instructions regarding how correctly have the tasks done) – if it were only this, what would then remain for the person to do that a machine couldn't do better? It is not an accident that a lack of autonomy to shape work according to the worker's imagination, competencies and desires is frequently reported as a core element hindering the promotion of healthier job conditions (e.g. Dejours, 2013).

The second possibility is that of the meaning block playing a promotion role. In this case, the agent's action can be canalized by the collective culture signs in such a way as to help her accomplish the action (the straight arrow). Similarly, the process of facing the meaning block can lead to innovative and creative forms of work, i.e. ways of dealing with the activity of transforming things into objects (see the bypassing path in Figure 1). In this latter case, the meaning block is re-invented by the agent. In both cases, how can culture foster action in work through meaning blocks? The more basic way in which this could happen is through the use of tools (and also language). Sometimes a meaning block is noticed, for instance, in the process of learning how to use a new technology and in the resistances and difficulties implied by this task. There is a twofold developmental process at play here, since the person learns not only how to use and apply such a technological tool in her activity, but also how to improve this tool or even the activity itself. A tool is a material example of a culturally (meaningful) embedded device that can foster work accomplishment. Another example can be found in the relation between some musical composers and the craftsman in charge of creating new musical instruments, when the song is fit to the material tools that bring it into reality (Sennett, 2008).

Additionally, the meaning block could be a zero-sign-type (Valsiner, 2014) block. In this case, the agent could decide to give up on the situation (the arrows pointing to outside of the plane in Figure 1). This could be a conscious decision, based on an evaluation of the situation, but it could also be a forced decision, in which case we might expect to observe psychological consequences – negative ones, like work suffering. What could make one person interpret a meaning block as a challenge to be overcome (fuelling her action towards a surmounting action), while another considers it an insurmountable endeavor? One traditional attempt is to look for the answer in interindividual differences. Take work stress as an example. Why do some people become stressed, which sometimes even evolves to burnout, while others do not? Some researchers believe that this happens because people respond differently to the *same* or *similar situations* (e.g. tough work conditions) based on their psychological backgrounds – for instance, their personalities (for a review, see Clot & Gollac, 2014). In other words, the situation remains the same, while the manifestations of stress are different because people are different (personal variability). The problem with this approach is that it ignores the inherently meaningful nature of the impediments workers face in reality (the meaning blocks). These are not the same for all people, nor are they 'objective', in the sense of being something out of the reach of the agent's interpretation when using signs.

Things< >objects

What does it mean to say that things get transformed into objects? Why do we claim that this distinction should be at the core of the work meaning-making complex? This distinction probably goes back to Aristotle's concept of four causes, posited in volume II of his *Metaphysics* (Falcon, 2015). The first cause, the material one, is roughly tantamount to 'thing' – for instance, the plaster of a statue. In Peirce's (1935) terms, the thing could be associated with the Rhema concept, i.e. with the possibility. In Marx (1887), as we have seen in the quotation above, things are embedded in the realm of Nature (with a capital 'N'). Something similar is at play in Valsiner's (2014) interpretation, with the assertion that inanimate things have no intentionality and then advancement of the concept of *Gegenstand* – a projection of the agent into the object that resists.

The essential idea behind our comprehension of the thing is that it lies in a non-differentiated state or in a quasi-differentiated one. Consider the plaster in our previous example. What is the form of the plaster without further human intervention? Chemically, it is a powder produced by heating gypsum, a mineral. In a sense, it contains in itself a set of possibilities that depend on what the agent decides to do with it and, obviously, also on its natural (invariable) proprieties (we can't make a plane with plaster – unless we are interested in a toy plane). Only the agent (the Aristotelian efficient cause) is able to 'recast' the plaster from this undifferentiated realm and take it to the realm of meaning (the final cause) – for instance, as a statue, as complex detailing for use in room interiors, or through the creation of a mural painting, such as Michelangelo's Sistine Chapel ceiling. An object is, thus, the outcome of working on a thing as mediated by culture and guided by a purposeful goal.

The transformation of things into objects is a fundamental high-level psychological operation, mediated by signs. We move from the realm of possibilities (material cause) to the realm of intended forms or objects (the final cause). To a work psychologist, the most important point here is the fact that this entire process *only happens* because of the agentive power of the person – because of her hands, eyes and arms, to put it as Marx did, but also because of her imagination and inner personal culture. In the act of engaging in the transformative process (work) through culture, the agent is at the same time internalizing meanings (signs), using tools and other culture-based devices and externalizing new meanings through new objects.

Before materializing her thoughts in a book, a writer may have no clear idea of what her book is going to be (maybe she has only 'things', in a metaphorical sense, or undifferentiated elements to be built upon – memories, feelings, vague ideas, etc.). When this vague content (the things) is transformed by means of her hands (by handwriting or typing) into letters, sentences and an entire narrative, we can then say that we have an object, in the sense of something with a cultural meaning or purpose, to be used by other people (in this case, with the potential consequence of producing new feelings or ideas in the reader's mind).

However, this transformation process does not take place without resistance. There is no work without struggle. Things and objects resist our actions. As a consequence, work implies an effort of the agent against things in order to get them transformed into objects. This resistance, as we have tried to show, can be strengthened by circumvention meaning blocks, or it can be tackled by promotion meaning blocks. In both cases, the agent operates *through* culture. The active role played by nature, or by our striving efforts to transform nature into an *Umwelt* (Chang, 2009), forces us to counter-act nature in order to create, transform or even destroy culturally formed objects. The thing< >object border is kept moving due to work. In sum, we can posit that work as an activity helps us in determining the borders between nature and culture, if we consider that things 'pertain' to nature and objects to culture.

Conclusion

Our goal in this article was to approach CP and WP by discussing what work means. We have argued that work and culture have suffered a process of mutual distancing over history. Culture is sometimes posited in an 'above' position in relation to work, associated with high-level values (creativity, innovation, meaning). In contrast, work is sometimes considered as the most important domain of human lives (the realm of practical concerns and a means to afford our material life, culture being a 'manifestation' of the objectivations of the means of production). We have denounced the fallacy underlying both perspectives by arguing that culture is not an entity, but a process by which we use signs as tools to mediate our relationship with the environment and to regulate our own action in irreversible time. At same time, we have also claimed that work is not an entity. Work is a sign-mediated and regulated activity occurring *through* culture. Most importantly, we have advanced the urgency of considering work as a cultural phenomenon whose specific role is to make culture by getting things transformed into objects.

We have also put forward the concept of work as a meaning-making complex. This means that work is an activity that takes place in a meaningful setting, where we can identify signs acting as meaning blocks. These meaning blocks can play the role of promoter signs, circumvention signs or zero signs. However, despite the role played, these signs operate as mediators in the process of getting things transformed into objects. Finally, we have proposed that thing< >object borders are kept moving due to work, as long as nature plays an active role of resistance against the agent's attempts to make culture through objects.

Our analysis in this article seems to point to several fruitful implications or challenges of this first attempt to bring cultural and work psychology closer together. First, there is a methodological implication that starts with a shift from the traditional quantitative methods that are widely used in WP. These methods are based on generalizations from cumulative data derived from samples, and these generalizations overshadow the singular cases (the acting person), since the researcher's interest lies in discovering patterns and general regularities. In order to grasp the characteristics of work as a cultural phenomenon, methods need to be designed that respect the meaningful nature of this phenomenon. For instance, adopting analysis of the microgenetic and mesogenetic level implied in all the paths followed by the agent in her struggle with meaning blocks (Figure 1). Meaning shifts should then be detected, registered and associated with the agent's psychological dynamics in work. How do they deal with the resistances? Which strategies do they mobilize in this process? How do they develop new abilities and meanings through struggling with the process of transforming things into objects? How can this process be enhanced by the way people use signs (including tools)? These are only a few key questions that an idiographic methodology could address.

The second implication we would like to mention is related to the extension of the personology approach in the realm of work. On the one hand, this approach casts doubts on the 'fetish' of transforming signs (and sign complexes) into entities. Signs are empty without an agent. One consequence of this kind of consciousness about *who* actually *acts* (*through* signs) is a move from the notion of institutionalized work (prescribed work, as might be said by French ergonomists) to an agentive or personology-based notion of work. On the other hand, work is by and large a technical domain, in the sense of an arena occupied by several 'players', each of them pursuing institutionalized interests (from business to politics). Additionally, work is a battlefield between organizations (and their legal representatives) and workers, generally in an asymmetrical relationship. In this context, to use an expression of Clot (2008), we are sometimes in the presence of *travail sans l'homme* (work without a subject). How to reconcile a personology approach with an institutionalized version of work is quite a large challenge for WP. We think this should be somehow discussed beyond the *agency vs. structure* mindset.

Finally, the last implication is connected to an emphasis on meaning-making rather than only on 'meanings of work'. We think that the widespread feeling of emptiness in current work contexts is not related to the lack of 'meaning', but just the opposite: it is related to the overdetermination of meaning. Today it easier than ever to find books, magazines, advisers, consultants, 'gurus' and other prophets trying to selling us the 'latest discovery' in the matter of 'happiness at work'. The more people seek to find meaning in work, the more they seem to lose it. Why this is happening? Why is the number of empty activities, or 'empty labour' (Paulsen, 2014), visibly growing around the world, especially in highly advanced societies? At the same time, why there are an increasing number of people, especially young people, who are no longer willing to work – the so-called 'NEET generation' (neither work nor study)? Do they not see 'meaning' in working? Would work be a pointless activity to them? These are all questions that a meaning-making WP could try to address in future developments.

Acknowledgement

I am grateful for the feedback I have received from Jaan Valsiner and Dany Boulanger.

Declaration of conflicting interests

The author(s) declared no potential conflicts of interest with respect to the research, authorship, and/or publication of this article.

Funding

The author(s) disclosed receipt of the following financial support for the research, authorship, and/or publication of this article: This study was funded by Coordenação de Aperfeiçoamento de Pessoal de Nível Superior (CAPES, Brazil) (Grant number: 99999.007367/2015-05).

Notes

1. We do not include in this comment the activity theory tradition, broadly inspired by Vygotsky's work. As examples, we could mention Engeström (1999) and Y. Clot (in France; e.g. Clot, 1999, 2008, 2009).
2. A different perspective on culture and work was developed by members of the Frankfurt School. There are also a number of studies about this relationship using 'cultural critic' as a base level. See, for instance, du Gay's (1996) critique of Marx's theory of the meaning of work; Arendt's (1958) attempt to bring together work and culture by distinguishing labour, work and action; and studies on the changing nature of the self in new cultural practices related to work (Beck, 2002; Sennett, 2000).
3. Examples of such extension are visible in studies of post-material society (Inglehart, 1990); cultural emergence studies (Bonnell & Hunt, 1999); and – in a more fashionable way – studies that combine culture and economy, labelled under the generic 'creative industries' umbrella (Caves, 2000).

References

Arendt, H. (1958). *Human condition*. Chicago: UCP.

Bakhtin, M. (1986). *Marxism and the philosophy of language*. Boston: Harvard University Press.

Beck, U. (2002). *Individualization*. London: Sage.

Bell, D. (1972). The cultural contradictions of capitalism. *Journal of Aesthetic Education, 6*(1), 11–38.

Bendassolli, P. F., & Gondim, S. M. (2014). Significados, sentidos e função psicológica do trabalho [Meaning, meaningfulness and psychological function of work]. *Avances en Psicologia Latinoamericana, 32*(1), 131–147.

Bendassolli, P. F., & Gondim, S. M. (2016). Cliniques du travail et réalisme critique: Dialogues et implications. *Nouvelle revue de psychosociologie, 21*(1), 131–142.

Bonnell, V. E., & Hunt, L. (1999). *Beyond the cultural turn*. California: University of California Press.

Caves, R. (2000). *Creative industries*. Cambridge, MA: Harvard University Press.

Chang, R. S. (Ed.). (2009) *Relating with environment: A new look at Umwelt*. Charlotte: Information Age Publishers.

Clot, Y. (1999). *La fonction psychologique du travail*. Paris: PUF.

Clot, Y. (2008). Le travail sans l'homme? Paris: La Découverte.

Clot, Y. (2009). *Travail et pouvoir d'agir*. Paris: PUF.

Clot, Y., & Gollac, M. (2014). *Le travail peut-il devenir supportable?* Paris: Armand Colin.

Daniels, H. (2011). Analyzing trajectories of professional learning in changing workplaces. *Culture & Psychology, 17*(30), 359–377.

Dejours, C. (2013). *Travail vivant*. Paris: Bayard.

Dejours, C., & Deranty, J.-P. (2010). The centrality of work. *Critical Horizons, 11*(2), 167–180.

Engeström, Y. (1999). Activity theory and individual and social transformation. In Y. Engeström, R. Miettinen, & R. L. Punamäki (Eds.), *Perspectives on activity theory* (pp. 19–38). Cambridge: Cambridge University Press.

Falcon, A. (2015). Aristotle on Causality. In E. N. Zalta (Ed.), *The Stanford encyclopedia of philosophy*. Retrieved from http://plato.stanford.edu/archives/spr2015/entries/aristotle-causality (accessed 25 November 2016).

Gay, P. (1996). *Consumption and identity at work*. London: Sage.

Habermas, J. (1975). Towards a reconstruction of historical materialism. *Theory and Society, 2*(3), 287–300.

Heidegger, M. (1977). *The question concerning technology*. New York: Harper.

Inglehart, R. (1990). *Culture shift in advanced industrial society*. Princeton: Princeton University Press.

Kirkegaard, T., & Brinkmann, S. (2015). Rewriting stress: Toward a cultural psychology of collective stress at work. *Culture & Psychology, 21*(1), 81–94.

Lecerde, J. J. (2006). *A Marxist philosophy of language*. Leiden: Brill.

Lukács, G. (1980). *Ontology of social being*. New York: Merlin Press.

Markus, G. (1982). *Langage et production*. Paris: Dénoel.

Marx, K. (1887). *The capital* (Volume I). Retrieved from: https://www.marxists.org/archive/marx/works/download/pdf/Capital-Volume-I.pdf (accessed 25 November 2016).

Meaning of Work International Research Team (MOW). (1987). *The meaning of work*. London: Academic Press.

Obeyesekere, G. (1990). *The work of culture*. Chicago: University of Chicago Press.

Paulsen, R. (2014). *Empty labor: Idleness and workplace resistance*. Cambridge: CUP.

Peirce, C. S. (1935). *Collected papers of Charles Sanders Peirce*. Cambridge: Harvard University Press.

Polanyi, K. (1971). *The great transformation*. New York: Beacon Press.

Pultz, S., & Hviid, P. (2016). Imagining a better future: Young unemployed people and the polyphonic choir. *Culture & Psychology*, Online First. doi: 10.1177/1354067X16660853.

Ricoeur, P. (1955). *Histoire et verité*. Seuil: Paris.

Sennett, R. (2000). *The corrosion of character*. New York: W. W. Norton & Company.

Sennett, R. (2008). *The craftsman*. London: Penguin.

Stern, W. (1938). *General psychology from the personalist standpoint*. New York: Macmillan.

Valsiner, J. (1999). I create you to control me: A glimpse into basic processes of semiotic mediation. *Human Development, 42*, 26–30.

Valsiner, J. (2007). *Culture in minds and societies*. London: Sage.

Valsiner, J. (2014). *An invitation to cultural psychology*. London: Sage.

Valsiner, J. (2015a). Negotiating novelty. In R. Garud, B. Simpson & A. Langley, et al. (Eds), *The emergence of novelty in organizations*. New York: OUP.

Valsiner, J. (2015b). What is new general psychology and why do we need it? [Lecture 1]. Retrieved from http://www.sv.uio.no/english/research/doctoral-degree/summer-school/oss-schedule.html (accessed 25 November 2016).

Zittoun, T. (2007). The role of symbolic resources in human lives. In J. Valsiner, & A. Rosa (Eds.), *The Cambridge handbook of sociocultural psychology* (pp. 342–361). Cambridge: CUP.

Author biography

Pedro F Bendassolli is a work psychology professor at the Universidade Federal do Rio Grande do Norte, Natal/Brazil. Currently is a visiting professor (pos-doc fellow) at the Centre for Cultural Psychology, Aalborg University, Denmark. In the past years, he has developed studies on psychosocial mechanisms involved in the meaning-making process in work, their nature, dimensions, determinants, and consequences. For further information, visit his website: http://www.pedrobendassolli.com.

Culture Wars in the Workplace? Cultural Antecedents of Workers' Job Entitlement

Wallace, M. and Leicht, K. T.

This article revisits Hunter's (1991) culture wars thesis and applies it to an institutional arena that has received comparatively little attention in the culture wars debate—the contemporary American workplace. The authors ask to what extent cultural divisions originating in four broad cultural domains (i.e., social equality, social freedom, multiculturalism, and gender equity) permeate the workplace and impact workers' views of the property rights of jobs. That is, do cultural values originating in the larger society affect workers' evaluations of managerial prerogative to make unilateral decisions in the best interests of the firm without regard to workers' claims to their jobs? Or, conversely, do such cultural values shape workers' sense of job entitlement that jobs should be protected in times of changing technology, declining demand for a firm's product, or other organizational and market imperatives? The authors use data from the Indiana Quality of Employment Survey to examine several hypotheses surrounding this debate. The results suggest that the relationship between cultural values and specific, work-based ideologies are more complicated than Hunter's original formulation might suggest; that is, there are complex and nonobvious relationships between these four domains of American cultural life and workers' views concerning job entitlement. These relationships are not significantly mediated by organizational and occupational characteristics normally associated with workplace attitudes. The results speak to broader debates about the role of structure and culture in the sociology of work and the complexity of the ideological landscape of American working life.

Keywords: *cultural values; the workplace*

INTRODUCTION

It has been over a decade since James Hunter's (1991) pathbreaking book *Culture Wars* attempted to map the major fault lines in the cultural landscape of late 20th century American society. Hunter's work pointed to a moral

Authors' Note: *This article was presented at the annual meetings of the American Sociological Association in August, 2001. We wish to thank* Work and Occupations

WORK AND OCCUPATIONS, Vol. 31 No. 1, February 2004 3-37
DOI: 10.1177/0730888403259827
© 2004 Sage Publications

struggle over the expansion of pluralism in political and social affairs, the disintegration of religious consensus about core values in public life, and the polarization of religious discourse between fundamentalists and progressives. These themes were echoed in part by other observers (Bellah, Sullivan, Swidler, & Tipton, 1991; Wuthnow, 1988, 1989). Hunter argued that this religiously-centered struggle fundamentally transformed the cultural boundaries of five major institutions: the family, education, the media, law, and electoral politics. Yet, he noted that this struggle permeated every aspect of American social life in the 1990s.

Although many aspects of Hunter's argument cannot be adjudicated empirically—indeed, this is the very characteristic that gives it such vitality—the outcome holds potentially deep consequences for the content of American life. In his original work, Hunter had little to say about the impact of the American cultural war on the workplace or economic institutions more generally. Yet, the 2 decades since Reagan's breaking of the Professional Air Traffic Controllers Organization strike have witnessed dramatic changes in the organization of work (see the collection in Cornfield, Campbell, & McCammon, 2001; see also Boyett & Conn, 1992; Leicht, 1998). These changes make the workplace a fertile ground for the exploration of Hunter's culture wars thesis.

In this article, we ask whether, in the wake of radical workplace changes of the 1990s, clashing moral visions have impacted core values about the economic order of American society. We investigate the cultural antecedents of one of the most contentious dimensions of American capitalism, what Leicht and Wallace (1988, 1990) termed the *property rights of jobs.* The property rights of jobs represents a continuum between *managerial prerogative* (i.e., the proprietary rights of employers and managers to run their companies as they see fit without regard for workers' job security) and *job entitlement* (i.e., workers' rights to claim entitlement to their jobs in the face of economic downturns, technological change, or employers' quests for increasing productivity). We contend that growing cultural divisions centering on four major tenets of American society—social equality, social freedom, multiculturalism, and gender equity—have penetrated the discourse of workplace politics and shifted perceptions of workers' job property rights. These cultural forces, which are largely exogenous to the workplace, are resilient factors that shape workers' views of job entitlement even after controlling for other plausible explanations.

---

editor Dan Cornfield, two anonymous reviewers, and several who commented at our ASA presentation in 2001 for their helpful comments on previous versions of this article.

WHY STUDY CULTURAL VALUES AND JOB ENTITLEMENT?

We can think of at least three compelling reasons for this study. First, recent research has documented dramatic changes in the organization of work (Cornfield et al., 2001) and the heightened politicization of economic life in the United States (cf. Aronowitz & DiFazio, 1994; Phillips, 1993). These changes have occurred in dramatic fashion in other parts of the world as well (cf. Blom & Melin, 2003; Frenkel, 2003; Perlow, 2001; Webster & Omar, 2003; Wharton & Blair-Loy, 2002). In the 1990s, many Americans' faith in their economic institutions had been shaken by downsizing (Gordon, 1996), outsourcing and "lean" work strategies (Cappelli et al., 1997; Hodson, 2002; Kalleberg, 2003), the growing use of contingent workers (Moore, 1996), technological displacement of workers (Dunkerley, 1996; Rifkin, 1996), deunionization (Edwards, 1993), declining or stagnant real earnings (Sennett, 1998), and the breakdown of the social contract between business and labor (Rubin, 1996; Wallace & Brady, 2001). The demise of the long-standing American promise of continuing prosperity, good jobs at decent wages, and stable work careers has engendered new fears among the middle class about the prospects for achieving the American dream (Newman, 1993; Wallace, 2003). As a result, job insecurity and economic uncertainty have become such pervasive features of American working life that they undermine the meritocratic ideology that shapes perceptions of labor markets and social inequality. Previous research on job entitlement (Leicht & Wallace, 1988, 1990) used a resource perspective to portray it as largely a consequence of factors that left workers vulnerable to the uncertainties in the labor market. The new insecurity in the labor market has widened the spectrum of workers experiencing vulnerability and thus has rendered discussions of job entitlement more timely than ever (cf. *New York Times*, 1996; Smith, 2001).

Second, despite the initial popularity of Hunter's culture wars thesis, subsequent research has called into question some of its key assumptions (cf. Evans, 1997; Hoffmann & Miller, 1997, 1998). For example, DiMaggio, Evans, and Bryson (1996) used the General Social Survey from 1974 to 1994 to show that Americans' attitudes on a range of topics such as women's roles in society, racial integration, and crime and justice have not become more polarized since the 1970s as Hunter's argument would suggest. However, they did find evidence of polarization in attitudes on abortion and, to a lesser extent, on views of the poor. Similarly, Davis and Robinson (1996, p. 780) found that "most Americans occupy a middle ground between the extremes of religious orthodoxy and moral progressivism" on a range of issues. They found that religious orthodoxy strongly impacted issues closely related to gender and the family as Hunter would argue, but that the impact of ortho-doxy did not carry over to broader societal issues of racial inequality and eco-nomic inequality. The upshot of these counterarguments is that American society is not as socially and politically polarized as culture war advocates would suggest and that the connection between religiously-based cultural values and societal attitudes is more complex and multidimensional. Our analysis incorporates these insights first, by uncoupling cultural conserva-tism from religious orthodoxy and recognizing that cultural values take on a life of their own in the determination of social attitudes and second, by devel-oping a strategy to empirically assess the multidimensional impact of cultural values on social attitudes. We find that cultural divisions are indeed relevant for understanding workers' attitudes toward job entitlement, but their effects are more complex than a simplistic culture wars argument would allow.

Third, our analysis contributes to the ongoing structure-culture debate that is prominent throughout sociology and especially lively in the sociology of work. For instance, Lincoln and Kalleberg's (1990) comparative study of U.S. and Japanese work organizations offered compelling evidence that differences in a variety of organizational resources accounted for well-established differences in organizational commitment and job satisfaction between U.S. and Japanese workers. However, equally convincing argu-ments attributed the diverging attitudes of U.S. and Japanese workers to larger societal differences in the cultures of the two countries such as differ-ences in the role of the individual and the group, the desire for consensus, and deference to authority (cf. Dore, 1973; Nakane, 1970; Takezawa & Whitehill, 1981). Analyses in other national contexts suggest that there are pervasive cultural differences in preferences for alternative workplace arrangements (cf. Blom & Melin, 2003; Frenkel, 2003; Perlow, 2001; Webster & Omar, 2003; Wharton & Blair-Loy, 2002).

Similarly, the structuralist perspective has heavily influenced previous analyses of job entitlement. For instance, Leicht and Wallace (1988, 1990) showed that job entitlement was linked to the presence or absence of organi-zational resources such as plant size, levels of supervision, workplace tech-nology, and unions. Job entitlement was also related to personal characteris-tics such as age, sex, and race that tapped vulnerabilities in the workplace. In this study, we explicitly investigate the cultural side of job entitlement by analyzing the impact of four broad cultural values on workers' sense of en-titlement to their jobs.

In the next section, we discuss the property rights of jobs in greater detail. We then turn to a discussion of how these four cultural divisions in the work-place might affect attitudes about job property rights. Finally, we conduct an empirical investigation of these relationships and end with a discussion of the implications of our research.

THE PROPERTY RIGHTS OF JOBS

In two earlier analyses, Leicht and Wallace (1988, 1990) examined the relationship between workplace characteristics and workers' evaluations of the property rights of jobs. The property rights of jobs refer to the degree to which workers perceive themselves to have an implicit right to their jobs that approximates the legal and ethical status of the property rights of capital (Leicht & Wallace, 1988, p. 191). They conceptualize the property rights of jobs as a continuum with two extremes; job entitlement and managerial prerogative. The *job entitlement* pole of the continuum maintains that workers' jobs are a virtual right of corporate citizenship that should not be jeopardized by changes in technology, demand for a firm's product, or other organizational and market imperatives. The *managerial prerogative* pole of the continuum holds that human resource allocations fall exclusively within the jurisdiction of management and are not open to worker input. From a pro-worker perspective, job entitlement thus represents the progressive dimension and managerial prerogative represents the conservative dimension of this concept. Though job property rights have not been researched extensively, we think that conflicts over job property rights are central to many public and academic debates on work and the labor process (cf. Carnoy, 2000; Collom, 2001, 2003; Gordon, 1996; Hodson, 2001).

Leicht and Wallace's research on job entitlement supported what they called a *vulnerability* hypothesis of the property rights of jobs. Those employees in relatively disadvantaged workplaces with little corporate protection or who represented vulnerable and underrepresented groups in the labor market were more likely to support job entitlement conceptions of the property rights of jobs. Those workers with corporate protection and in relatively advantaged positions in the labor market were more likely to support managerial prerogative conceptions of the property rights of jobs. In this research, we use the vulnerability hypothesis to anticipate and interpret the effects of the various control variables in the models.

CULTURAL DIVISIONS AND
THEIR IMPACT ON JOB ENTITLEMENT

In this section, we identify four cultural divisions originating in the larger society that have penetrated the American workplace and are likely to have had an impact on workers' perceptions of job entitlement. These divisions revolve around four values that are deeply embedded in the fabric of American life—social equality, social freedom, multiculturalism, and gender equity—each represents the terrain for the culture wars of recent years. Divisions between progressives and conservatives over these core values are ultimately about who gets ahead and who is left behind in American society. These cultural values have growing resonance for the workplace, particularly in an era of increasing job insecurity, because work is a central institution for distributing rewards in society. Thus, we anticipate that divisions over these core values will have consequences for workers' perceptions of job entitlement.

Our conceptualization of these cultural divisions and how they operate in the labor market suggest that there might not be a simple linear relationship between liberalism, conservatism, and job entitlement. In the ensuing discussion, we sketch both conservative and progressive sides of each of the four cultural divisions in American society. Then, in the analysis, we conceptualize each cultural division as a bipolar dimension with *conservative* and *progressive* poles and ask whether opposite poles might have similar or dissimilar impacts on job entitlement.

Social equality is the progressive notion that, to some extent, equality is a desirable outcome and that all citizens should receive equal treatment despite their skills and abilities. This value is premised on the foundation of equal treatment in the political arena but, for progressives, extends also to the economic arena to include equality of access to jobs, housing, health services, child care, and economic security. In extreme versions, progressives extend the principle of social equality to include not only equality of access, but also equality of outcomes in the stratification system. Hence, they contend that the state has a central role in regulating the excesses of the market, redistributing income, and guaranteeing some semblance of economic equality in society (cf. Amenta, 1998; Skocpol, 2000; in another context, see Webster & Omar, 2003).

Conservatives contend that economic rewards should be allocated by the market, not by government intervention. Hence, they promote a laissez-faire, market-driven interpretation of social and economic outcomes that leaves little room for policies that consciously promote social equality. In fact, conservatives hold a meritocratic view of society in which economic rewards are distributed as a direct function of one's abilities and contributions to society as determined by the market. Therefore, social and economic *in*equality is a natural outcome of the market and a sign of a healthy system. Of consequence, policies designed to ameliorate the harsher outcomes of the market are seen as harmful, because they disrupt the natural equilibrium of the market (cf. Carnoy, 2000; Friedman & Friedman, 1980).

The principle of social equality has long been a contentious feature of modern capitalism manifested most clearly in debates over the role of the welfare state. Legislation regarding social security, welfare, unemployment benefits, universal health care, child labor, workplace safety, job training, minimum wages, and family leave are but a few examples of work-related outcomes that have hinged on debates and alternative interpretations of the social equality principle (cf. Esping-Andersen, 1996; Marsden, 1999). In an era of downsizing and job insecurity, the social equality principle has fueled arguments in some quarters that employers have a moral, if not legal, responsibility to safeguard the jobs of their employees. Hence, we expect those with progressive views toward social equality will support job entitlement, whereas those with conservative views will not.

Social freedom, in constitutional terms, is the principle that all citizens should be free to pursue "life, liberty, and happiness" unencumbered by restrictions related to race, national origin, religion, or other status identities. Conservatives regard this as the quintessential expression of individual liberties and as an extension of the principles of a laissez-faire market. They typically construe social freedom as individual freedom from government constraints in the personal lives of citizens. Individual actors, free to pursue their own personal gain, achieve the maximum welfare for themselves and for society as a whole. Radically conservative interpretations of this principle underlie the ideologies of underground militia groups and other antigovernment activists. Conservatives also hold that social freedom implies individual responsibility, and that individuals should bear the costs of their own misjudgements, poor planning, and mistakes (cf. Mead, 1992; Murray, 1984). Thus, the principle of social freedom reinforces the conservative view of a meritocratic society in which individuals rise to the level of their own talents and abilities or sink to the level of their own frailties and shortcomings.

However, as Giddens (1994) and others pointed out (see also Carnoy, 2000; Leicht, 1998), the principal of social freedom in late 20th century neoconservative thought contains within it a potential contradiction. The patriarchal nuclear family, traditional sexual mores, and cultural and religious conservatism are viewed as the fabric that holds American society together, including the so-called "new economy" (cf. Boyett & Conn, 1992). However, by championing laissez-faire freedoms in economic life, conservatives unleash forces that undermine the very social institutions that they claim hold American society and culture together. At a minimum, these contradictions complicate the relationship between ultraconservative expressions of social freedom and job entitlement leading to the phenomenon of Pat Buchanan-Republicans, ultraconservatives who express sentiments of isolationism in foreign policy with job protectionism in domestic economic policy. Hence, we also expect ultraconservative expressions of social freedom, as typified by Buchananites, to be positively related to job entitlement conceptions of job property rights.

Of course, historically, the principle of social freedom has not been extended with equanimity to all social groups in American society. Racial and ethnic minorities, immigrants, the poor, the youth culture, religious minorities, women, gays and lesbians, and persons with physical disabilities have, with varying success, struggled to attain the protections of social freedom (cf. Quadagno, 1994). With the backing of progressives, these groups have sought to use the machinery of government to extend the mandate of social freedom to groups that have been left behind in American society. In so doing, progressives have openly used identity politics to transform the meaning of social freedom to encompass freedoms of excluded social groups and identities, not individuals per se. Historically, progressives have championed the working class as one such excluded group. New Deal era legislation declaring workers' rights to unionize and bargain collectively, and subsequent legislative gains by organized labor and the working class resulted in large part from progressive efforts to extend the principle of social freedom beyond the comfort zone of business elites and other conservatives (cf. Amenta & Halfmann, 2000). Because extending social freedoms in the late 20th century is identified with progressive causes, we contend that progressive expressions of social freedom will be positively related to job entitlement conceptions of job property rights.

Multiculturalism is the principle that cultural diversity is to be celebrated and that society is made stronger by the contributions of people from different backgrounds, nationalities, and races. Progressives contend that American society is composed "from many strands" (Lieberson & Waters, 1988), and that persons of all races and ethnic heritages contribute to the promise of America.

Yet, the legacy of multiculturalism in America is ambivalent and littered with setbacks. The debate over multiculturalism is central to what Myrdal (1944) called the *American Dilemma* and provides the subtext to numerous defining episodes in the American experience from the Civil War to the civil rights movement to affirmative action. Although conservatives typically endorse the ideology that American society is a "melting pot"—a notion of dubious merit given the actual experience of racial and ethnic minorities in this country—they are quick to exclude groups that do not conform to their image of assimilation (cf. D'Souza, 1995). Hence, persons several generations removed from their Northern or Southern European descent are deemed upstanding examples of the multicultural heritage of America, whereas African Americans and more recent immigrants from Asia, Oceania, Latin America, and Africa are viewed as outsiders or interlopers. Groups who assimilate quickly and willingly and shed all traces of their cultural origins are welcome, whereas groups who maintain their cultural identity and language cannot conceal their physical differences from Whites or are otherwise slow to "Americanize" are deemed foreigners who are accepted grudgingly, at best (cf. Buchanan, 2002). Periodic revivals of extremist conservative groups such as the Ku Klux Klan, the John Birch society, McCarthyites, and skinheads attest to the recurrent nativistic undertones in American society.

For 3 decades, the multicultural debate in the workplace has centered on progressively inspired affirmative action and the conservative backlash against it. Yet in recent years, threats posed by foreign competition to many U.S. industries, immigrant labor (legal and illegal), and global trade policies such as NAFTA and GATT have heightened nativist tendencies in American society (for analyses and reviews, see Tomaskovic-Devey & Skaggs, 1999; Waters, 1999; Wilson & Jaynes, 2000). Prospects of job loss to lower-paid workers in foreign countries or to legal or illegal alien workers in this country have exacerbated the concerns of American workers about their jobs. Therefore, in an era of deindustrialization and increased job insecurity, multiculturalism has had an ironic backlash effect on expressions of job property rights, which pushes more workers to adopt views of racial and cultural intolerance, particularly toward foreigners coming to America to seek economic opportunity.[1] In turn, we hypothesize that conservative expressions of multiculturalism (i.e., those opposing further cultural diversity in American life) are positively associated with job entitlement conceptions of job property rights, whereas progressive expressions of multiculturalism have a negligible impact.

Gender equity is the principle that women and men should have equal rights and opportunities in society. Although equality of the sexes has been a recurring theme in American history, the impetus of the women's movement in the 1970s opened new doors for women in education, politics, and other arenas of social life. Gender constitutes perhaps one of the most public arenas of cultural conflict between conservatives and progressives. Conservatives generally endorse traditional gender roles for women that center on domestic duties in the household and a subordinated economic role to men. In recent years, discussions about women's advancement in the labor market have been entangled in debates about "family values," a conservative buzz word

TABLE 1: Hypotheses for the Effects of Cultural Values on Job Entitlement

Pole	Conservative	Progressive
Social equality	−	+
Social freedom	+	+
Multiculturalism	+	NA
Gender equity	NA	+

for keeping women in their traditional roles. Many of the same cultural contradictions in late 20th century conservative thought about social freedom are
echoed in discussions and debates surrounding changes in gender roles (cf.
Carnoy, 2000).

Progressives, on the other hand, advocate greater opportunity for women
in the labor market and greater equity in job rewards with men. In fact,
women have made impressive gains in the labor market to the point that
Hochschild (1989, p. 239) called women's movement into the paid labor
force "the basic social revolution of our time." Although barriers to women's
advancement and total equality persist (see Gerstel & McGonagle, 1999;
Maume, 1999; Spalter-Roth & Deitch, 1999), women have made steady
inroads toward equality, and the gender gap in opinions about gender equality has narrowed (Shirley & Wallace, in press). Yet despite the gains made by
women in recent decades, gender equity, like multiculturalism, is still a divisive issue in the contemporary labor market. We suspect, however, that the
perception that equality for women is desirable and likely to be associated
with a more inclusionist view of the labor market that is consistent with
endorsing job entitlement conceptions.

Our hypotheses about the impact of the four cultural divisions on job entitlement are summarized in Table 1.

In the following analysis, we examine these hypotheses, using a unique
data set collected in the late 1990s during a time of radical workplace change.
In addition to assessing the relationships among wider cultural values and the
property rights of jobs, we also assess the extent to which workplace characteristics mediate these relationships.

DATA AND METHODS

The data for our analysis come from the Indiana Quality of Employment
Survey (IQES), which was conducted between April and July of 1996 under
the auspices of the Center for Social Research at Indiana University's Institute of Social Research. The IQES consisted of telephone interviews with

workers in the state of Indiana who were 18 years of age or older and who worked for 20 hours or more in nonfarm employment. A list-assisted, random-digit dialing system was used to compile the telephone numbers. Screening was conducted to identify households fitting the sampling frame; in households where multiple persons met the sampling criteria, a computer algorithm randomly selected the respondent for the survey. A total of 705 respondents completed the survey, resulting in an 84% response rate. Some 51 cases were dropped from the analysis due to missing data on one or more variables, resulting in a sample size of 654 respondents.

The 1996 IQES was modeled after the 1973 and 1977 Quality of Employment Surveys (QES). Like the original QES surveys, the IQES includes questions about workers' jobs, their employers, their attitudes about their work, their marital status and family situation, their housework and child care responsibilities, and sociodemographic characteristics. One major difference is that the IQES was confined to the state of Indiana instead of being a national sample. However, as a large, midwestern, industrial state, Indiana's industrial, occupational, and demographic structures are fairly representative of the United States as a whole. However, we note that Indiana has a larger manufacturing base (24% vs. 15% of employment) and fewer service occupations (24% vs. 29%) than the national sample. Indiana also has a higher White population than the United States as a whole (91% vs. 83%).

Our analyses consist of ordinary least squares (OLS) regression analyses of job entitlement. We also examine relationships between our cultural values and three other salient workplace outcomes (job satisfaction, organizational commitment, and job autonomy) to display the unique association between job entitlement and its relationship to cultural forces outside the workplace. Our analyses utilize two-tailed tests at the .05, .01, and .001 levels of significance. We also display significance levels at $p \leq .10$ to indicate the relationships that approach the conventional levels of significance.

VARIABLES

DEPENDENT VARIABLE

The dependent variable, *job entitlement*, is a three-item scale that taps respondents' beliefs that workers are entitled to keep their jobs in the face of companies' needs to increase their productivity, make technological changes, or downsize their work forces to maintain profitability. The first two items in this scale are almost identical to items in Leicht and Wallace's (1988; 1990) original scale, and the third is a new item that addresses the recent problem of downsizing. We use the label "job entitlement" because higher scores on the scale correspond with the job entitlement pole of the property rights continuum.

Characteristics of the job entitlement scale are provided in Table 2. Panel A shows the three Likert items used in the scale along with frequency distributions and descriptive statistics for each item. Respondents who *disagree* with these statements receive higher scores on the job entitlement scale. On balance, the respondents in the 1996 sample expressed slightly more favorable attitudes toward the two kindred job entitlement items compared to the responses of Leicht and Wallace's respondents from 14 years earlier. This came as a surprise because the IQES utilizes a representative sample of all workers in the economy, whereas Leicht and Wallace's original respondents were mostly blue-collar workers in manufacturing firms (both surveys were conducted in Indiana). This suggests that, if anything, changes in the labor market over the past 2 decades have only heightened workers' sense of entitlement to their jobs.

Panel B of Table 2 shows that the correlations among the three items in the scale are moderately high, between .45 and .55. Panel C shows the scale characteristics of the job entitlement scale. The three items scale as a single factor with an Eigenvalue of 2.04 and an alpha of .77 suggests that the three items comprise a satisfactory scale.

KEY INDEPENDENT VARIABLES

Our theoretical discussion identified four dimensions of the cultural landscape that might have relevance for job entitlement: *social equality, social freedom, multiculturalism,* and *gender equity.* We tap these four dimensions with four Likert items from the IQES:

> *Social equality*: Everyone should receive a livable income regardless of their skills and abilities.
> *Social freedom*: People should be able to live whatever lifestyle they choose as long as it doesn't hurt anybody else.
> *Multiculturalism*: It's too easy for people from other countries to come and live in the United States.
> *Gender equity*: All in all, family life suffers when the woman has a full-time job.

Descriptive statistics for these four items are shown in Table 3. Progressive responses are indicated by *agreement* with the first two items and *disagreement* with the second two items. The descriptive statistics in Panel A indicate that respondents express fairly progressive views (that is, item means are greater than the scale midpoint of 2.5) about social equality and social free-

TABLE 2: Characteristics of the Job Entitlement Scale

Panel A. Descriptive Statistics of Items in the Job Entitlement Scale

	(1) Strongly Agree	(2) Somewhat Agree	(3) Somewhat Disagree	(4) Strongly Disagree	Mean	SD
Item 1: Companies must become more productive even if it means that some workers must lose their jobs.[a] (*Job Loss*)	108 (15.5%)	297 (42.6%)	166 (23.8%)	121 (17.3%)	2.43	.95
Item 2: If new technologies can do workers' jobs more efficiently, it is OK for a company to lay off employees.[a] (*Layoffs OK*)	65 (9.3%)	231 (33.1%)	208 (29.8%)	186 (26.7%)	2.74	.95
Item 3: It's OK for a company to downsize its workforce to increase its profits.[a] (*Downsizing*)	60 (8.6%)	210 (30.0%)	215 (30.7%)	209 (29.9%)	2.82	.96

Panel B. Correlations Among Items in the Job Entitlement Scale

	Job Loss	Layoffs OK	Downsizing
Job Loss	1.00		
Layoffs O.K.	.55	1.00	
Downsizing	.45	.55	1.00

Panel C. Scale Characteristics of the Job Entitlement Scale

	Loading	h^2
Job Loss	.812	.660
Layoffs OK	.856	.733
Downsizing	.807	.651

Eigenvalue = 2.04
Alpha = .77

a. Percentages do not sum to 100% due to a few respondents who responded "Neither Agree nor Disagree" (scored 2.5).

TABLE 3: Characteristics of Cultural Values Items

Panel A. Descriptive Statistics of Cultural Values Items and Correlations With Job Entitlement

	(1) Strongly Disagree	(2) Somewhat Disagree	(3) Somewhat Agree	(4) Strongly Agree	Mean	SD
Item 1: (Social equality)[a]: Everyone should receive a livable income regardless of their skills and abilities.	97 (13.9%)	142 (20.3%)	256 (36.7%)	199 (28.5%)	2.80	1.00
Item 2: (Social freedom)[a]: People should be able to live whatever lifestyle they choose as long as it does not hurt anybody else.	91 (13.0%)	121 (17.2%)	208 (29.6%)	280 (39.9%)	2.97	1.04

	(1) Strongly Agree	(2) Somewhat Agree	(3) Somewhat Disagree	(4) Strongly Disagree	Mean	SD
Item 3: (Multiculturalism)[a,b]: It's too easy for people from other countries to come and live in the United States.	284 (40.7%)	219 (31.4%)	135 (19.4%)	55 (7.9%)	1.95	.96
Item 4: (Gender equity)[a,b]: All in all, family life suffers when the woman has a full-time job.	179 (25.5%)	250 (35.6%)	133 (18.9%)	138 (19.6%)	2.33	1.06

Panel B. Correlations Among Cultural Value Items

	Social Equality	Social Freedom	Multiculturalism	Gender Equity
Social equality	1.00			
Social freedom	.23	1.00		
Multiculturalism	.02	-.02	1.00	
Gender equity	-.01	.14	.12	1.00

Panel C. Factor Analysis of Cultural Value Items

	Factor 1 Loading	h^2	Factor 2 Loading	h^2
Social equality	.76	.58	-.09	.01
Social freedom	.79	.62	.13	.02
Multiculturalism	-.13	.02	.74	.55
Gender equity	.17	.03	.74	.55
Eigenvalue	1.25		1.13	
Alpha	.37		.21	

a. Percentages do not sum to 100% due to a few respondents who responded "Neither Agree nor Disagree" (scored 2.5).
b. Items 3 and 4 have been rekeyed so that high scores reflect "progressive" orientations on the values.
*$p \le .05$. **$p \le .01$ (two-tailed tests).

dom, but comparatively *un*progressive views about multiculturalism and gender equity. Panel B of the table displays zero-order correlations among the four cultural values items. The correlations among these four variables are fairly low, the highest among them being .23 between social equality and social freedom. This suggests that the four items tap distinctive dimensions of the cultural landscape and should exert independent effects on job entitlement.

This impression is reinforced by the factor analysis in Panel C. This factor analysis yields two significant factors that distinguish social freedom and social equality from multiculturalism and gender equity. However, the reliabilities from scales constructed with these factors are unsuitably low (.37 and .21, respectively), suggesting that the four cultural values items tap separate and unique dimensions and that responses on one do not have any particular relationship to responses on another. Overall, the results in Table 3 are consistent with prior research (Davis & Robinson, 1996; DiMaggio et al., 1996), which suggests that cultural disagreements in American society do not neatly sort people into distinctive "camps" reflecting traditional and progressive social attitudes.

We previously hypothesized that some of the relationships between the cultural values items and job entitlement might be nonlinear, and that some of their strongest effects on job entitlement might occur at the extremes, either the conservative or progressive poles (see Table 1). We find preliminary support for these hypotheses in Table 4 that presents mean job entitlement scores for each category of the four cultural values measures. In the last column, we present zero-order correlations between each of the cultural values items and job entitlement. The results provide modest support for our hypotheses. Social equality shows the strongest tendency toward a positive linear relationship with job entitlement — a correlation coefficient of .26 with the lowest values for job entitlement at the conservative pole (2.28) and the highest values at the progressive pole (2.92). Social freedom shows a bimodal pattern that is more clearly nonlinear (despite a significant −.08 correlation) with the highest values of job entitlement at the conservative (2.70) and progressive (2.78) poles. With respect to multiculturalism, the highest value for job entitlement occurs at the conservative pole (2.88) and shows no clear pattern among the remaining three responses. Yet, on the strength of the high score at the conservative pole, a significant correlation of −.20 between multiculturalism and job entitlement occurs. Finally, gender equity shows a bimodal distribution (similar to social freedom) with the two highest scores at the conservative (2.73) and progressive (2.87) poles. These results are largely consistent with the hypotheses outlined in Table 1. Only the relatively high score for the conservative pole of the gender equity cultural value is

TABLE 4:   Mean Job Entitlement Scale Scores by Scores on Cultural Values Measures

Cultural Values	Mean Job Entitlement Scores				
	Conservative Pole		Progressive Pole		Correlation With Job Entitlement
	(1) Strongly Disagree	(2) Somewhat Disagree	(3) Somewhat Agree	(4) Strongly Agree	
Everyone should receive a livable income regardless of their skills and abilities. (*social equality*)	2.28	2.55	2.66	2.92	.26**
People should be able to live whatever lifestyle they choose as long as it does not hurt anybody else. (*social freedom*)	2.70	2.49	2.59	2.78	-.08*
	(1) Strongly Agree	(2) Somewhat Agree	(3) Somewhat Disagree	(4) Strongly Disagree	
It is too easy for people from other countries to come and live in the United States. (*multiculturalism*)	2.88	2.55	2.47	2.55	-.19**
All in all, family life suffers when the woman has a full-time job. (*gender equity*)	2.73	2.54	2.60	2.87	.06

*$p \leq .05$, two-tailed test.   **$p \leq .01$, two-tailed test.

unanticipated. In total, these results suggest that the relationships between cultural divisions and job entitlement are complex and cannot easily be classified as originating from only conservative or progressive influences.

These preliminary results suggested that we needed to specify the cultural values variables in a manner that captures the nonlinear, bipolar aspects of these variables and their impacts on job entitlement. In our regression model, we transform the cultural values measures into a series of dummy variables that classify respondents who identify with the extremes of each item (i.e., the conservative and progressive poles) in contrast to those with attitudes toward the middle two responses (the reference category). In addition to accounting for the likely nonlinearity in the relationship between cultural values and job entitlement, this specification allows us to focus on the distinctive relationships impacting those respondents who have strongly conservative or progressive opinions about the cultural values.

CONTROL VARIABLES

We control for several variables that represent possible competing explanations for variations in job entitlement. First, our analysis controls for three measures that capture contextual dimensions of respondents' employment and residential situations. First, *median household income* taps the degree of affluence in the community of residence and is specified as the median household income in the respondent's zip code. This measure taps dimensions of consumerism, social status, and affluence that are recognized as visible signs of success in American society. Living in higher-income communities should lead respondents to think they have made it by the standards of American society and make them less inclined to assert claims for job entitlement. Second, *occupational earnings* measures the average weekly earnings of incumbents of the respondent's three-digit occupation. Working in high-earnings occupations should assure workers of continued prospects for employment success and should have a negative impact on job entitlement. Third, the *local unemployment rate* measures the rate of unemployment in the respondent's county of residence. Because high unemployment is indicative of diminished employment prospects and economic uncertainty, it should heighten expressions of job entitlement among workers. Hence, we expect *negative* relationships between median household income, occupational earnings and job entitlement, and a *positive* relationship between local unemployment and job entitlement.

Next, we control for three sociodemographic variables. Consistent with the resource approach used in earlier research (Leicht & Wallace, 1988, 1990), we expect workers who are in more vulnerable positions in the labor market to express higher degrees of job entitlement. Hence, workers who are female, non-White, and in mid-career are demographically more vulnerable should express greater support for job entitlement. We operationalize these variables as follows. The respondents' *sex* is coded 1 for women, 0 for men. *Race* is a dichotomous variable coded as 1 for non-Whites and 0 for Whites. *Age* is coded in years, transformed to reflect the expected curvilinear effect between age and job entitlement. The original age variable was transformed into z-scores, the z-scores were squared to generate a variable with only positive values, then we took the square root of these values to return the variable to the original z-score metric, but retaining the all-positive values. This allows us to use a single variable to tap the expected curvilinear effects of age on job entitlement. With the uncertainties of the current labor market, workers in mid-career are increasingly threatened with downsizings or layoffs that lead them to be highly concerned about their job security. Hence, we expect middle-aged workers to express higher levels of job entitlement than younger and older workers. A negative effect for the curvilinear age variable would be consistent with this "inverted-U" hypothesis.

Next, we consider five human capital measures that tap various dimensions of skill and experience that workers bring to their jobs. *Education* is the number of years of formal schooling. *Employer tenure* is measured as years of employment with one's current employer. Longer tenure with a single employer is a good indicator of de facto job security and should limit strong expressions of job entitlement. *Autonomy* is a three-item scale ($\alpha = .69$) asking workers about their agreement with the three following items (a) "I have a lot of say about what happens on my job," (b) "It is basically my own responsibility to decide how my job gets done," and (c) "My job gives me a lot of freedom about how I do my work." We expect a negative effect of autonomy on job entitlement because autonomous workers are generally secure in their employment situations. We also include two measures of skill: *occupational skill*, which taps the general level of skill incumbent in the occupation,[2] and *substantive complexity*, which indexes the skill inherent in the job itself.[3] Both measures are expressed curvilinearly in a manner similar to the age variable described previously. We expect that workers who have skill levels in the middle ranges will be most vulnerable in the new economy, because they have made a large enough investment in their skill resources to have a stake in their current jobs, but not enough to feel secure in their employment prospects. Hence, we anticipate a negative relationship between the curvilinear specifications of occupational skill and substantive complexity and job entitlement.

Finally, we control for a number of organizational variables that represent various types of resources that should have an impact on workers' job entitlement. First, we include a measure of *employer size* that is the number of employees working in the respondent's organization, transformed by natural logarithms to account for the expected nonlinear impact of size on job entitlement. We expect a negative impact of employer size on job entitlement. Second, we include a measure of *organizational scope*, which is coded as a dichotomous variable coded 1 for employers that are national or international in scope (operationally defined as having additional operations outside the state of Indiana) and 0 for employers that are local or whose other operations are exclusively within the state. Our expectations for this variable are uncertain. On the one hand, organizations that are national or international in scope command considerable resources that might be deployed to enhance the employment situation and job security of workers. This would suggest a negative impact of organizational scope on job entitlement. On the other hand, in the new global economy, organizations that are national or international are typically on the leading edge of the spatial restructuring of work (Wallace & Brady, 2001) and will often move to new locations in search of more desirable work force arrangements. This tends to undermine the job security of workers in those organizations and suggests that such workers' concerns would translate into higher degrees of job entitlement (see also Carnoy, 2000).

We also include a dichotomous measure indicating whether a worker is a *union member* (1). We expect a positive effect of union membership on job entitlement because unions are important agents in the politicization of work inequities. Unions are likely to raise the consciousness of their workers about entitlement to their jobs in the face of companies' efforts to raise productivity, make technological changes, or downsize their workforces. We also include a direct measure of technological change based on answers to the question: "Since you began your present job, how much change has there been in the technology you use on your job?" Answers were coded as 1 (*none at all* or *not very much*); 2 (*some*); and 3 (*very much*). Because technological change exacerbates uncertainties about workers' roles and job security, we expect it to be positively associated with job entitlement.

We also tap dimensions of organizations that reflect workers' positions in the authority structure or chances for advancement. *Number of workers supervised* is based on responses to the question: "How many workers do you supervise directly and indirectly?" This measure parsimoniously captures the extent of workers' supervisory or administrative roles in the organization. *Promotion likelihood* is based on workers' responses to the question: "In the next five years, how likely are you to be promoted?" with responses 1 = *very unlikely*, 2 = *somewhat unlikely*, 3 = *somewhat likely*, and 4 = *very likely*. We expect workers who supervise other workers and with high chances of promotion to have ample organizational resources that reduce their support for job entitlement.

ANALYSIS

Table 5 presents the main analysis, an OLS regression analysis of job entitlement. Our goal is to examine the relationship between job entitlement and the progressive and conservative poles of the four cultural values. We view cultural values as variables that are largely exogenous to the workplace and mediated by the control variables described previously. Hence, we conduct a stepwise regression in which we enter the cultural values measures in Equation 1, contextual variables in Equation 2, sociodemographic controls in Equation 3, human capital variables in Equation 4, and organizational variables in Equation 5. In each step, we are interested in the extent to which cultural values persist as determinants of job entitlement and also the degree to which their effects are mediated by the inclusion of the control variables.

Model 1 presents the effects of the cultural values measures by themselves. The relationships among the cultural values measures and job entitlement are largely consistent with our hypotheses. As expected, those with progressive attitudes on the social equality scale strongly support job entitlement, and those with conservative attitudes on social equality are strongly against it. The results for the remaining cultural values measures reflect the nonlinear patterns we found in Table 4: Those expressing *both* progressive and conservative orientations on social freedom support job entitlement; those with conservative attitudes on multiculturalism support job entitlement, and those with progressive attitudes on gender equity support job entitlement. Also worth noting, those with progressive attitudes on multiculturalism do not necessarily support job entitlement, and those with conservative attitudes about gender equity do not necessarily oppose it. These results suggest that relationships between cultural attitudes acquired outside the workplace and attitudes regarding work are present, but far from straightforward.

In column 2, we add the contextual variables, which are also largely exogenous to the workplace, and find that each has significant effects on job entitlement in the expected direction. Median household income and occupational earnings are negatively related to support for job entitlement, and the local unemployment rate is positively related. Moreover, the inclusion of these variables adds significantly to the explanatory power of the model (R^2 increases from .148 to .220). Controlling for local context reduces the effects of some of the cultural values variables, but the statistical significance levels

TABLE 5: Determinants of Job Entitlement (N = 654), Unstandardized Regression Coefficients (Standardized Coefficients in Parentheses)

Value	(1)	(2)	(3)	(4)	(5)
Cultural values					
Social equality—progressive pole	.234*** (.134)	.174** (.099)	.172** (.098)	.176** (.100)	.148* (.084)
Social equality—conservative pole	-.465*** (-.200)	-.429*** (-.185)	-.382*** (-.165)	-.362*** (-.156)	-.356*** (-.154)
Social freedom—progressive pole	.133* (.082)	.117^ (.072)	.110^ (.068)	.107^ (.066)	.095 (.059)
Social freedom—conservative pole	.222* (.092)	.223* (.093)	.218* (.091)	.216* (.090)	.179* (.074)
Multiculturalism—progressive pole	-.137 (-.046)	-.085 (-.029)	-.109 (-.037)	-.094 (-.032)	-.102 (-.035)
Multiculturalism—conservative pole	.313*** (.195)	.257*** (.160)	.255*** (.158)	.209*** (.130)	.199*** (.124)
Gender equity—progressive pole	.269*** (.136)	.282*** (.143)	.278*** (.141)	.293*** (.148)	.297*** (.150)
Gender equity—conservative pole	.108 (.059)	.119^ (.065)	.088 (.048)	.077 (.042)	.075 (.041)
Contextual variables					
Median household income[a]	—	-.108** (-.106)	-.117** (-.116)	-.106** (-.105)	-.095** (-.094)
Occupational earnings[b]	—	-.596*** (-.176)	-.522*** (-.154)	-.355** (-.105)	-.334* (-.099)
Local unemployment rate	—	.076*** (.133)	.068*** (.120)	.063** (.111)	.058** (.102)
Sociodemographic variables					
Sex (1 = women)	—	—	.161** (.101)	.157** (.099)	.178** (.112)
Race (1 = non-White)	—	—	.187* (.073)	.216* (.084)	.228* (.088)
Age (curvilinear)	—	—	-.112* (-.082)	-.111* (-.081)	-.096^ (-.070)

	Model 1	Model 2	Model 3	Model 4		Model 5	
Human capital							
Education	—	—	—	-.037**	(-.104)	-.035*	(-.098)
Employer tenure	—	—	—	-.003	(-.038)	-.000	(-.000)
Autonomy	—	—	—	-.085*	(-.075)	-.073^	(-.064)
Occupational skill (curvilinear)	—	—	—	-.127*	(-.084)	-.127*	(-.084)
Substantive complexity (curvilinear)	—	—	—	-.059	(-.045)	-.058	(-.044)
Organizational variables							
Employer size (logged)	—	—	—	—		-.021^	(-.075)
Organizational scope (1 = national or international)	—	—	—	—		.124^	(.078)
Union member (1 = union member)	—	—	—	—		.174*	(.081)
Technological change	—	—	—	—		.062^	(.064)
Number of workers supervised	—	—	—	—		-.003*	(-.090)
Promotion likelihood	—	—	—	—		-.027	(-.039)
Constant	2.379	2.718	2.744	3.561		3.491	
R^2	.148	.220	.239	.266		.289	

a. The coefficient of median household income is multiplied by 10,000.
b. The coefficient of occupational earnings is multiplied by 1,000.
*$p \leq .05$, two-tailed test. **$p \leq .01$, two-tailed test. ***$p \leq .001$, two-tailed test. ^$p \leq .10$, two-tailed test.

of their coefficients are largely unaffected. However, there are two exceptions to this pattern: The progressive pole of the social freedom value is reduced in significance to $p < .10$, and the conservative pole of the gender equity value becomes (temporarily) significant at the same level. The latter finding is consistent with the pattern revealed in Table 4. These results suggest that some portion of the effects of cultural values on job entitlement is mediated by local economic conditions and circumstances. For instance, even though it remains strongly significant, the impact of anti-immigrant attitudes (i.e., the conservative pole of multiculturalism) on job entitlement is partly shaped by conditions of declining affluence, lower earnings, and local unemployment conditions. Despite all these changes, the six hypothesized effects for the cultural values variables remain statistically significant and in the predicted direction.

In column 3, we add the sociodemographic controls and find that the R^2 for the model increases modestly from .220 to .239. As expected, women, non-Whites, and middle-aged workers express support for job entitlement. All these results are consistent with the vulnerability hypothesis found in previous research (Leicht & Wallace, 1988, 1990), although the age effect requires some explanation. The significant negative coefficient for age indicates that middle-aged workers are more supportive of job entitlement than younger or older workers. We believe this finding is largely consistent with the realities of the contemporary labor market in that middle-aged workers are most threatened by job dislocations due to deindustrialization, downsizing, and other radical workplace changes. The inclusion of the sociodemographic variables has relatively little net impact on the effects of the cultural values, except for a modest reduction (from $-.185$ to $-.165$) in the conservative pole of the social equality value. The upshot of these results is that sociodemographic characteristics are important in shaping attitudes about job entitlement, but only a small portion of the impact of cultural values on job entitlement is attributable to these sociodemographic characteristics.

In column 4, we add the human capital variables and witness another moderate increase in R^2, from .239 to .266. Again, we find support for our expectations about these variables and continued support for our main hypotheses. Workers with higher levels of education express lower degrees of job entitlement. Similarly, autonomy shows a negative, significant effect, indicating that workers in less autonomous jobs express the highest degrees of job entitlement. Also, occupational skill shows the expected inverted-U relationship with job entitlement. This latter effect indicates that workers with occupational skill levels in the middle ranges (i.e., those for whom job loss poses the greatest risk) are most likely to endorse job entitlement. Employer tenure and substantive complexity show effects in the expected directions, but their coefficients are not statistically significant. It is important to note that even de facto job security as evidenced by employer tenure does not reduce the sense of job entitlement as one might expect it to in a more robust labor market. Again, we witness only modest changes in the net effects of the cultural values variables. The only substantial change is a reduced effect of the conservative pole of multiculturalism (.158 to .130). More important, the significance levels of the eight cultural values remain unchanged in this step of the analysis.

Finally, in column 5, we add the organizational variables to the analysis and find that R^2 increases from .266 to .289. The effects of these variables generally conform to our expectations though not all of them achieve statistical significance. As expected, union membership and technological change ($p < .10$) positively affect endorsements of job entitlement. In addition, organizational scope, about which we were uncertain, shows a positive and significant ($p < .10$) impact on job entitlement. This can be interpreted as meaning that workers who have employers that are national and international in scope feel vulnerable to the job loss that accompanies the spatial restructuring of work and hence endorse job entitlement. Employer size ($p > .10$) and number of workers supervised show the expected negative effects on job entitlement. Not surprisingly, one's position in the authority structure, as shown by workers supervised, is negative and has the strongest impact on job entitlement of any variable in this set. The effect of promotion likelihood, while in the expected direction, fails to achieve statistical significance. Looking at the net effects of the cultural values measures suggests only a modest portion of the relationship between cultural values and job entitlement is mediated through workers' organizational experiences and locations. However, one of these effects, the progressive pole of social freedom, falls out of statistical significance altogether. This suggests that, net of other variables in the model, organizational locations are, at best, only modestly operable as intervening mechanisms between larger cultural values and job entitlement.

Taken together, these results suggest that there are many factors that are important for shaping workers' attitudes about job entitlement, but that some of the key factors are cultural value sets that workers bring with them from outside the workplace. These cultural values, shaped not only by experiences at work but also by myriad other experiences in everyday life, are resilient and durable factors in shaping workers' views about entitlement to their jobs. Moreover, the impacts of these variables are only partially mediated by contextual, sociodemographic, human capital, and organizational variables. Excepting the progressive pole of gender equity, which actually gets stronger as controls are added to the model, the cultural values variables are partially mediated by the other variables. The amount of mediation varies from 19.4%

TABLE 6: Correlations Among Job Entitlement, Organizational Commitment, Job Satisfaction, and Job Autonomy

	(1)	(2)	(3)	(4)
Job entitlement	1.00	−.16**	−.12**	−.17**
Organizational commitment		1.00	.60**	.45**
Job satisfaction			1.00	.39**
Job autonomy				1.00

*p ≤ .05, two-tailed test. **p ≤ .01, two-tailed test. ***p ≤ .001, two-tailed test.

(social freedom, conservative pole) to 37.3% (social equality, progressive pole). The overall results suggest that cultural values provide a kind of buffer against the uncertainties of workplace change and an interpretive lens for workers to evaluate the impact of worker dislocations or inequities.

One reviewer of an earlier version of this article suggested that the impact of the cultural values on job entitlement might be an artifact of the way in these variables are connected to other common workplace attitudes or experiences. We present two analyses that address this concern. First, Table 6 examines zero-order correlations between the job entitlement scale and three frequently used measures of workplace outcomes: job satisfaction, organizational commitment, and job autonomy. Job entitlement shows a significant, but modest, negative correlation with all three of these workplace concepts. Generally, workers who express high values of job entitlement have relatively low levels of job satisfaction, organizational commitment, and job autonomy. This pattern is consistent with Leicht and Wallace's (1988, 1990) original conception that relatively vulnerable workers with few resources will express a desire to protect their jobs from the uncertainty of managerial decisions. Yet more important, job entitlement is shown to be conceptually and empirically distinct from these traditional workplace concepts exhibiting much lower correlations with these concepts than the correlations among them. The perceived right of entitlement to a secure job is clearly distinct from whether one is happy in it, committed to one's employer, or free of direct supervision in carrying out one's tasks.

We show further support for the conceptual distinctiveness of job entitlement from other workplace outcomes in Table 7. Here, we show OLS regression estimates of job satisfaction, organizational commitment, and job autonomy that are identical to those estimated for job entitlement in Table 6. We show two models, the first with regression estimates for just the cultural values variables and the second adding the control variables. Out of 48 possibly significant coefficients for the cultural values variables both before and after

TABLE 7: Determinants of Job Satisfaction, Organizational Commitment, and Autonomy (N = 654), Unstandardized Regression Coefficients (Standardized Coefficients in Parentheses)

	Job Satisfaction		Organizational Commitment		Autonomy	
	(1)	(2)	(3)	(4)	(5)	(6)
Cultural values						
Social equality—progressive pole	-.098 (-.062)	-.063 (-.040)	-.032 (-.022)	.030 (.021)	-.017 (-.011)	.033 (.021)
Social equality—conservative pole	.187* (.089)	.160* (.076)	.134^ (.071)	.085 (.045)	.093 (.046)	.079 (.039)
Social freedom—progressive pole	-.093 (-.064)	-.054 (-.037)	-.055 (-.042)	-.004 (-.003)	-.067 (-.047)	-.034 (-.024)
Social freedom—conservative pole	.033 (.015)	.081 (.038)	-.041 (-.021)	-.015 (-.008)	-.045 (-.021)	-.023 (-.011)
Multiculturalism—progressive pole	-.007 (-.003)	-.070 (-.026)	.018 (.007)	-.051 (-.021)	.105 (.039)	.036 (.014)
Multiculturalism—conservative pole	-.113^ (-.078)	-.033 (-.023)	-.096^ (-.073)	-.072 (-.006)	-.149* (-.105)	-.119* (-.084)
Gender equity—progressive pole	.048 (.027)	.020 (.011)	-.027 (-.017)	-.055 (-.034)	.024 (.014)	.030 (.017)
Gender equity—conservative pole	.058 (.004)	.042 (.026)	-.002 (-.001)	.040 (.027)	.010 (.007)	.029 (.018)
Contextual variables						
Median household income[a]	—	-.005 (-.006)	—	.009 (.011)	—	-.007 (-.008)
Occupational earnings[b]	—	.140 (.046)	—	.150 (.054)	—	.560*** (.188)
Local unemployment rate	—	.013 (.026)	—	.013 (.028)	—	-.002 (-.003)
Sociodemographic variables						
Sex (1 = women)	—	.107^ (.075)	—	.067 (.052)	—	-.110^ (-.079)
Race (1 = non-White)	—	-.166^ (-.072)	—	-.151* (-.072)	—	.011 (.005)
Age (curvilinear)	—	.079^ (.065)	—	.099* (.088)	—	.035 (.029)

(continued)

TABLE 7 (continued)

	Job Satisfaction		Organizational Commitment		Autonomy	
	(1)	(2)	(3)	(4)	(5)	(6)
Human capital						
Education	—	.012 (.038)	—	.023* (.081)	—	-.002 (-.006)
Employer tenure	—	.001 (.007)	—	.007* (.096)	—	.003 (.044)
Autonomy	—	.357*** (.349)	—	.345*** (.371)	—	—
Occupational skill (curvilinear)	—	-.015 (-.011)	—	-.047 (-.038)	—	.044 (.033)
Substantive complexity (curvilinear)	—	-.076^ (-.064)	—	-.083* (-.076)	—	-.077^ (-.065)
Organizational variables						
Employer size (logged)	—	-.018 (-.072)	—	-.021* (-.093)	—	-.057*** (-.237)
Organizational scope (1 = national or international)	—	-.040 (-.028)	—	-.066 (-.051)	—	.029 (.020)
Union member (1 = union member)	—	.069 (.036)	—	-.013 (-.007)	—	-.219** (-.116)
Technological change	—	.057^ (.066)	—	.029 (.037)	—	.068* (.080)
Number of workers supervised	—	-.000 (-.003)	—	.003 (.017)	—	.002^ (.064)
Promotion likelihood	—	.093*** (.151)	—	.116*** (.207)	—	.032 (.053)
Constant	3.248	1.508	3.364	1.485	3.285	3.150
R^2	.030	.237	.014	.301	.019	.168

a. The coefficient of median household income is multiplied by 10,000.
b. The coefficient of occupational earnings is multiplied by 1,000.
*$p < .05$, two-tailed test. **$p \leq .01$, two-tailed test. ***$p \leq .001$, two-tailed test. ^$p \leq .10$, two-tailed test.

adding the control variables, only seven are statistically significant at the .10 level or greater. Of these, only two cultural variables (the conservative pole of social equality for job satisfaction and the conservative pole of multicultural-ism for autonomy) maintain significance at the .05 level or greater after add-ing controls. Clearly, as one would expect, there is no strong empirical con-nection between the cultural values and these other workplace attitudes. The relative absence of effects for the cultural values measures in these models suggests that job entitlement is uniquely connected to larger cultural values and disagreements about equality and justice.

DISCUSSION

Our results provide partial support for all six hypotheses we developed and strong support (after the inclusion of controls) for five of them. These relationships between cultural processes and job entitlement exist net of a series of contextual, sociodemographic, human capital, and organizational characteristics that serve as plausible alternative explanations of job entitle-ment. Of our four cultural values, only the relationship between social equal-ity and job entitlement approximates a linear relationship. Job entitlement is positively associated with the progressive pole of gender equity, and the con-servative poles of social freedom and multiculturalism.

Thus, our results lend support to a modified version of Hunter's culture wars argument. We do not find evidence for polarized "camps" that sharply divide the labor force in their views about job entitlement. And we do not explicitly explore the religious bases of moral conservatism and progressiv-ism. Yet, we find that a mélange of cultural forces is important in shap-ing workers' views on job entitlement. Indeed, the three strongest variables in the final model for job entitlement are three of the cultural variables—the conservative pole of social equality, the progressive pole of gender equity, and the conservative pole of multiculturalism (with standardized coefficients of −.154, .150, and .124, respectively). These effects are net of a myriad of demographic, contextual, and organizational characteristics that normally affect conventional workplace attitudes (see Table 7), suggesting that larger cultural and societal forces have important and independent influences on workers' attitudes about their jobs and managerial decisions about them.

CONCLUSION

In this article, we have extended the debate surrounding "culture wars" to the workplace. We have argued that the broader cultural clash between conservatives and progressives in the wider society has implications for perceptions of and support for the property rights of jobs in the workplace.

Our analysis suggests a more complex picture of cultural divisions than suggested by Hunter. For example, we find that cultural factors are multidimensional and that they mostly impact job entitlement in a nonlinear fashion. Only social equality seems to approximate a linear pattern, but even so, the negative impact of the conservative pole is nearly twice the magnitude of the positive impact of the progressive pole. Each of the other cultural values only has significant impact at one extreme or the other, supporting the case for nonlinearity. Moreover, our results indicate that holding culturally progressive views does not uniformly lead to support for the progressive notion of job entitlement. Likewise, cultural conservatism, specifically with regard to social freedom and multiculturalism, sometimes forms the basis for endorsing job entitlement. Both of these findings, which might seem implausible on the surface, are consistent with our theorizing. The positive impact of the conservative pole of social freedom can be thought of as the "Buchanan effect" shared by conservative Republicans who endorse both isolationism in foreign policy and job protectionism in domestic economic policy. The positive effect of the conservative pole of multiculturalism is consistent with persons who reject cultural pluralism, particularly because of anxieties about the threats posed by immigrants, and who also endorse job entitlement as a form of protectionism against immigrant workers.

Our analysis points to an "interventionist" orientation, as opposed to any overtly religious orientation, as a common mechanism for translating cultural forces into support for job entitlement. For instance, progressive orientations toward social equality and gender equality share with job entitlement an "interventionist" view of progressive social action. In other words, endorsing the goals of social equality and gender equity is likely to be linked not only to job entitlement but also to a broader agenda of progressive economic issues such as health care reforms, minimum wage laws, and progressive taxation. On the other hand, the conservative orientation toward multiculturalism suggests a similar interventionist stance that is also consistent with job entitlement. Our measure of multiculturalism can essentially be construed as a measure of support for immigration. American workers have historically had an ambivalent stance toward immigration, typically viewing it as part of a managerial effort to maintain a supply of cheap, foreign labor to compete with U.S. workers for jobs. Although there is debate about the overall effects of immigration on U.S. labor markets, the negative effects on unskilled workers are well-documented (cf. Waters, 1999; Wood, 1995). In this sense, support for limits on immigration is an expression of vulnerability in the labor market; hence, endorsing job entitlement suggests support for government intervention to restrain the unbridled flow of immigrant labor.

How the conservative orientation toward social freedom can be reconciled with an interventionist approach requires some discussion. We start by noting that differences between conservative and progressive interpretations of social freedom essentially boil down to prioritizing individual rights versus group rights in society. Innately, conservatives believe in the sanctity of individual rights and the importance of the market as the key mechanism for allocating success or failure in society. They oppose government efforts to extend social freedoms to women, minorities, gays, or other marginalized status groups. In their view, government actions that protect or extend social freedom are harmful interventions that disrupt the natural order of things. Ordinarily, they believe that society would be better served by a minimalist approach that allowed individuals to succeed or fail on their own merits rather than legislating social outcomes. How does such a conservative view align with support for job entitlement? We believe that the ultraconservative passion for leaving social outcomes to unfettered market forces stops at the border. On a macro level, such views translate into support for isolationism in foreign affairs and protectionism in the domestic economy. In other words, when global market forces result in challenges to American business interests and massive job loss for American workers, as they did during the 1980s and 1990s, these market conservatives become interventionists of a different stripe. Because they view decreases in product demand, changing technologies, and downsizing as by-products of America's declining role in the global economy, they are more likely to endorse measures to maintain tariffs on foreign products and to protect Americans' jobs. This leads many with conservative orientations on social freedom to support the progressive idea of job entitlement.

Aside from the specific findings regarding the cultural processes underlying job entitlement, our analyses also speak to broader debates in sociology about the relative importance of culture and structure in the sociology of work. This study balances out the structural emphasis of previous studies of job entitlement (Leicht & Wallace, 1988, 1990) by showing how cultural factors also matter. More important, our analysis shows that the cultural values that workers carry with them from outside the workplace have important consequences for attitudes and orientations they acquire at work. These orientations include promising new research that examines cross-cultural norms toward time management and the workplace (cf. Epstein & Kalleberg, 2001; Jacobs & Gerson, 2001; Perlow, 2001; Thompson & Bunderson, 2001) in addition to continued work on managerial control over access to jobs, careers, and workplace opportunities. We think that rather than being posed as competing alternatives, structural and cultural interpretations should be combined to better understand changing forces in the workplace. The study of these changes, along with a fuller appreciation of their structural and cultural underpinnings, returns the sociology of work to its central mission of understanding work as a crucial nexus of social organization and social action. We think combining these perspectives to investigate the determinants of job entitlement and managerial prerogative goes a long way toward understanding the origins of conflict and consensus in the workplace. We hope future research on these topics will adopt such a combined approach.

Finally, our article contributes to the ongoing literature on the sources of conflict and consensus in the workplace (see also Hodson, 2001, 2002). The property rights of jobs taps a deep-seated source of conflict between management and workers that is worthy of further investigation. Whether one endorses the managerial prerogative to structure jobs and determine employment in the best interests of the company or the job entitlement perspective that workers' jobs are a virtual right of economic citizenship and why are central questions that run through much of the literature in the sociology of work. These questions have never been more relevant than they are now as workers' jobs seem more insecure and depreciated than ever. We hope that future researchers will continue the analysis of job entitlement and related topics in the workplace.

NOTES

1. The theme of multiculturalism has many dimensions including racial and cultural diversity among U.S. citizens as well as immigration of people from different nationalities, races, and ethnicities. In this article, our measure of multiculturalism focuses on "people from other countries (who) come and live in the United States" because this measure is most salient for understanding the threat to domestic U.S. workers posed by outsiders. Moreover, the threat posed by immigrants cuts across different racial and ethnic groups among U.S. workers.

2. The occupational skill measure is a scale consisting of eight attributes of skill appended to respondents' three-digit occupational codes. These attributes are: occupational socioeconomic index (SEI), occupational score on handling of data, occupational score on dealing with people, occupational reasoning score, occupational score on math usage, occupational score on specific vocational preparation (SVP), average education in an occupation, and percentage of occupational incumbents with a college degree. This occupational skill measure achieved an alpha level of .88.

3. The substantive complexity measure consists of a scale in which respondents were asked to respond to the following three items: (a) "How long did it take you to learn the key aspects of your job: a few hours (=0.5); a day (=1.0); a few days to a week (=1.5): several weeks (=2.0); 2 to 5 months (=2.5); 6 months to 1 year (=3.0); a few years (=3.5); and 5 years or more (=4.0)"; (b) "My job requires a high degree of skill: strongly disagree (=1.0); somewhat agree (=2.0); some-

what agree (=3.0); and strongly agree (=4.0)"; and (c) "I am constantly learning new things on my job: strongly disagree (=1.0); somewhat agree (=2.0); somewhat agree (=3.0); and strongly agree (=4.0)." This scale produced an alpha of .66.

REFERENCES

Amenta, E. (1998). *Bold relief: Institutional politics and the origins of modern American social policy.* Princeton, NJ: Princeton University Press.

Amenta, E., & Halfmann, D. (2000). Wage wars: Institutional politics, WPA wages, and the struggle for U.S. social policy. *American Sociological Review, 65*, 506-528.

Aronowitz, S., & DiFazio, W. (1994). *The jobless future.* Minneapolis: University of Minnesota Press.

Bellah, R., Sullivan, W. M., Swidler, A., & Tipton, S. M. (1991). *The good society.* New York: Knopf.

Blom, R., & Melin, H. (2003). Information society and the transformation of organizations in Finland. *Work and Occupations, 30*, 176-193.

Boyett, J. H., & Conn, H. B. (1992). *Workplace 2000: The revolution shaping American business.* New York: Plume.

Buchanan, P. J. (2002). *The death of the west: How dying populations and immigrant invasions imperil our country and civilization.* New York: Thomas Dunne Books.

Cappelli, P., Bassi, L., Katz, H., Useem, M., Knoke, D., et al. (1997). *Change at work.* New York: Oxford University Press.

Carnoy, M. (2000). *Sustaining the new economy: Work, family, and community in the information age.* New York: Russell Sage Foundation.

Collom, E. (2001). Social inequality and the politics of production: Identifying potential supporters of economic democracy. *Sociological Forum, 16*, 471-501.

Collom, E. (2003). Two classes and one vision? Managers' and workers' attitudes toward workplace democracy. *Work and Occupations, 30*, 62-96.

Cornfield, D. B., Campbell, K. E., & McCammon, H. J. (2001). (Eds.). *Working in restructured workplaces: Challenges and new directions for the sociology of work.* Thousand Oaks, CA: Sage.

Davis, N. J., & Robinson, R. V. (1996). Are the rumors of war exaggerated? Religious orthodoxy and moral progressivism in America. *American Journal of Sociology, 102*, 756-787.

DiMaggio, P., Evans, J., & Bryson, B. (1996). Have Americans' social attitudes become more polarized? *American Journal of Sociology, 102*, 690-755.

Dore, R. (1973). *British factory-Japanese factory: The origins of diversity in industrial relations.* Berkeley: University of California Press.

D'Souza, D. (1995). *The end of racism: Principles for a multiracial society.* New York: Free Press.

Dunkerley, M. (1996). *The jobless economy? Computer technology in the world of work.* Cambridge, UK: Polity.

Edwards, R. (1993). *Rights at work: Employment relations in a post-union era.* Washington, DC: Brookings Institution.

Epstein, C. F., & Kalleberg, A. L. (2001). Time and the sociology of work: Issues and implications. *Work and Occupations, 28*, 5-16.

Esping-Andersen, G. (1996). (Ed.). *Welfare states in transition: National adaptations in global economies.* London: Sage.

Evans, J. (1997). Worldviews or social groups as the source of moral value attitudes: Implications for the culture wars thesis. *Sociological Forum, 12*, 371-404.

Frenkel, S. J. (2003). The embedded character of workplace relations. *Work and Occupations, 30*, 135-153.

Friedman, M., & Friedman, R. (1980). *Free to choose: A personal statement*. New York: Harcourt Brace Jovanovich.

Gerstel, N., & McGonagle, K. (1999). Job leaves and the limits of the Family Medical Leave Act: The effects of gender, race, and family. *Work and Occupations, 26*, 510-534.

Giddens, A. (1994). *Beyond left and right: The future of radical politics*. Stanford, CA: Stanford University Press.

Gordon, D. M. (1996). *Fat and mean*. New York: Free Press.

Hochschild, A. R. (1989). *The second shift*. New York, NY: Avon Books.

Hodson, R. (2001). *Dignity at work*. Cambridge, UK: Cambridge University Press.

Hodson, R. (2002). Management citizenship behavior and its consequences. *Work and Occupations, 29*, 64-96.

Hoffmann, J. P., & Miller, A. S. (1997). Social and political attitudes among religious groups: Convergence and divergence over time. *Journal for the Scientific Study of Religion, 36*, 528-546.

Hoffmann, J. P., & Miller, A. S. (1998). "Denominational influences on socially divisive issues. Polarization or continuity?" *Journal for the Scientific Study of Religion, 37*, 528-546.

Hunter, J. D. (1991). *Culture wars: The struggle to define America*. New York: Basic Books.

Jacobs, J. A., & Gerson, K. (2001). Overworked individuals or overworked families? Explaining trends in work, leisure and family time. *Work and Occupations, 28*, 40-63.

Kalleberg, A. L. (2003). Flexible firms and labor market segmentation: Effects of workplace restructuring on jobs and workers. *Work and Occupations, 30*, 154-175.

Leicht, K. T. (1998). Work (if you can get it) and occupations (if there are any)? What social scientists can learn from the end of work and radical workplace change. *Work and Occupations, 25*, 36-48.

Leicht, K. T., & Wallace, M. (1988). The property rights of jobs: Job entitlement versus managerial prerogative in manufacturing firms. *Research in Social Stratification and Mobility, 7*, 189-221.

Leicht, K. T., & Wallace, M. (1990). Work organization, business culture and job entitlement in the United States and Japan. *Comparative Social Research, 12*, 177-208.

Lieberson, S., & Waters, M. C. (1988). *From many strands: Ethnic and racial groups in contemporary America*. New York: Russell Sage Foundation.

Lincoln, J. R., & Kalleberg, A. L. (1990). *Culture, control and commitment: A study of work organization and work attitudes in the United States and Japan*. Cambridge, UK: Cambridge University Press.

Marsden, D. (1999). *A theory of employment systems: Microfoundations of societal diversity*. New York: Oxford University Press.

Maume, D. J., Jr. (1999). Glass ceilings and glass escalators: Occupational segregation by race and sex differences in managerial promotions. *Work and Occupations, 26*, 483-509.

Mead, L. M. (1992). *The new politics of poverty: The nonworking poor in America*. New York: Basic Books.

Moore, T. S. (1996). *The disposable workforce: Worker displacement and employment instability in America*. New York: Aldine de Gruyter.

Murray, C. A. (1984). *Losing ground: American social policy, 1950-1980*. New York: Basic Books.

Myrdal, G. (1944). *An American dilemma: The Negro problem and modern democracy*. New York: Harper.

Nakane, C. (1970). *Japanese society*. Berkeley, CA: University of California Press.

Newman, K. S. (1993). *Declining fortunes: The withering of the American dream*. New York: Basic Books.

New York Times. (1996). *The downsizing of America*. New York: Times Books.

Perlow, L. A. (2001). Time to coordinate: Toward an understanding of work-time standards and norms in a multi-country study of software engineers. *Work and Occupations, 28*, 91-111.

Phillips, K. P. (1993). *Boiling point: Republicans, Democrats, and the decline of middle-class prosperity*. New York: Random House.

Quadagno, J. S. (1994). *The color of welfare: How racism undermined the war on poverty*. New York: Oxford University Press.

Rifkin, J. (1996). *The end of work: The decline of the global labor force and the dawn of the post-market era*. New York: Putnam.

Rubin, B. A. (1996). *Shifts in the social contract: Understanding change in America society*. Thousand Oaks, CA: Pine Forge Press.

Sennett, R. (1998). *The corrosion of character: The personal consequences of work in the new capitalism*. New York: W. W. Norton.

Shirley, C., & Wallace, M. (in press). Domestic work, family characteristics, and earnings: Re-examining gender and class differences.

Skocpol, T. (2000). *The missing middle: Working families and the future of American social policy*. New York: W.W. Norton.

Smith, V. (2001). *Crossing the great divide: Worker risk and opportunity in the new economy*. Ithaca, NY: ILR Press.

Spalter-Roth, R., & Deitch, C. (1999). "I don't feel right sized; I feel out-of-work sized": Gender, race, ethnicity and the unequal costs of displacement. *Work and Occupations, 26*, 446-482.

Takezawa, S., & Whitehill, A. M. (1981). *Work ways: Japan and America*. Tokyo: Japan Institute for Labor.

Thompson, J. A., & Bunderson, J. S. (2001). Work-nonwork conflict and the phenomenology of time: Beyond the balance metaphor. *Work and Occupations, 28*, 17-39.

Tomaskovic-Devey, D., & Skaggs, S. (1999). An establishment-level test of the statistical discrimination hypothesis. *Work and Occupations, 26*, 422-443.

Wallace, M. (2003). *Middle class fears in the new economy*. Unpublished manuscript.

Wallace, M., & Brady, D. (2001). The next long wave: Spatialization, technocratic control, and the restructuring of work at the turn of the century. In I. Berg & A. L. Kalleberg (Eds.), *Sourcebook on labor markets: Evolving structures and processes* (pp. 101-135). New York: Plenum.

Waters, M. (1999). Immigrant dreams and American realities: The causes and consequences of the ethnic labor market in American cities. *Work and Occupations, 26*, 352-364.

Webster, E., & Omar, R. (2003). Work restructuring in post-apartheid South Africa. *Work and Occupations, 30*, 194-203.

Wharton, A. S., & Blair-Loy, M. (2002). The "overtime culture" in a global corporation: A cross-national study of finance professionals' interest in working part-time. *Work and Occupations, 29*, 32-63.

Wilson, F. D., & Jaynes, G. (2000). Migration and the employment and wages of native and immigrant workers. *Work and Occupations, 27*, 135-167.

Wood, A. (1995). How trade hurt unskilled workers. *Journal of Economic Perspectives, 9*, 57-80.

Wuthnow, R. (1988). *The restructuring of American religion: Society and faith since World War II*. Princeton, NJ: Princeton University Press.

Wuthnow, R. (1989). *The struggle for America's soul: Evangelicals, liberals, and secularism*. Grand Rapids, MI: Eardmans.

Impact of Corporate Culture on the Relationship between Efficient Technology Transfer and Business Performance

Nguyen, T. D. N. and Aoyama, A.

Abstract

This study focuses on the impact of corporate culture on the relationship between efficient technology transfer and a firm's business performance, emphasizing a firm's productivity and innovation capacity.

Exploratory factor analysis (EFA), confirmatory factor analysis (CFA) and structural equation modelling (SEM) multi-group analysis are used to analyze structured survey data from 223 Japanese manufacturing subsidiaries in Vietnam. The results indicate that efficient technology transfer has a 40 per cent positive effect on a firm's productivity and a 29 per cent positive effect on its innovation capacity. Corporate culture produces significant differences in the effects of efficient technology transfer on business performance. The higher value the company places on learning, encourages staff to participate in decision making and accepts risk, the higher the success of a firm's business performance with the efficiently transferred technology.

Keywords

Corporate culture, efficient technology transfer, business performance, Japanese subsidiaries, Vietnam

Introduction

The global economy is changing under increasingly competitive and cooperative business conditions. Business activities continue to thrive because individuals tend to become more cohesive and they gravitate towards each other. They look ahead and understand the trends and forces that create new innovative values within the corporate culture mindset amid changes in the management environment, technology, society and the marketplace.

Vietnam is no exception; the Vietnamese government is making increasing efforts to become an important part of the international market. The country is transitioning from a centralized plan economy to a market economy by attracting foreign direct investment (FDI), which has been recognized as an appropriate approach to synergize the intercultural potential for international integration. Accordingly,

Nguyen Thi Duc Nguyen (Corresponding author), Research Organization of Science and Technology, Ritsumeikan University, 525-8577 Noji-higashi 1-1-1, Kusatsu Shiga, Japan. E-mail: ntducnguyen@yahoo.co.jp
Atsushi Aoyama, Graduate School of Technology Management, Ritsumeikan University 525-8577 Noji-higashi 1-1-1, Kusatsu Shiga, Japan. E-mail: aoyama@mot.ritsumei.ac.jp

Japanese companies have been investing in Vietnam since the early 1990s; they have ranked third in terms of approved foreign investment projects and ranked first in terms of the implementation rate (Fukunaga, 2010). However, the achievement of the management and business performance of Japanese manufacturing companies has been a difficult and complicated process. Although the companies intensified their efforts to transfer technology and management experience from the host country, they were unable to achieve high efficiency in productivity and quality in the early years (Nguyen et al., 2012). Meschi (1997) pointed that most of the obstacles mentioned in international projects can be traced back to differences in national and organizational culture. In reality, during the implementation of international technology transfer, the incoming corporate culture and transferred technology must be integrated into the existing organizational structure and long-term competition strategy in most countries. Actually, corporate culture is not always what the strategic leaders and the chief executives of an organization think or mention in annual reports, and Japanese companies are no exception to these constraints. Therefore, the following questions are raised: What is the role of efficient technology transfer in achieving successful business performance by mainly emphasizing on a firm's productivity and innovation capacity? Does corporate culture formed through synergizing the intercultural potential of long-term cooperation have any effect on translating efficient technology transfer into the firm's long-term business performance?

At the same time, few academic studies have been conducted in Vietnam, and problems related to cross-cultural technology transfer are still being discovered. Cross-cultural technology transfer research specifically focusing on Japanese firms in Vietnam is inadequate. Therefore, in order to address the current shortcomings of cross-cultural technology transfer research, this study uses a structured survey to investigate the real-life context of 223 Japanese manufacturing subsidiaries in Vietnam. Exploratory factor analysis (EFA), confirmatory factor analysis (CFA), and structural equation modelling (SEM) multi-group analysis are employed for validating the measurement scales, and testing the hypotheses. The perspective of organizational learning that links the learning process with its knowledge acquisition and knowledge application outcomes is used to underpin the definition of efficient technology transfer. It is defined as changing potential behaviours or potentially using the acquired knowledge within the organization (Huber, 1991), resulting in changed ways of improving performance (Buckler, 1998), developing or acquiring new knowledge or skills to respond to internal or external stimuli and enhancing organizational effectiveness (Sadler-Smith et al., 2001). Correspondingly, the viewpoint of efficiency and effectiveness defined by Bernolak (1997) as cited in Tangen (2005) is considered the proper measure for this study in evaluating a firm's business performance from learning and execution.

Accordingly, technology transfer is herein defined as a specific knowledge transfer in the context of cultural differences and as the phenomenon of geographic expansion of production activities. Thus, it is the process of transferring technological knowledge and know-how across organizational borders from more- to less technologically developed countries so that the recipients effectively acquire, absorb, and apply the new knowledge to reach the same levels of production activities and management as those at the original organizations (Ando et al., 2005; Bozeman, 2000; Derakhshani, 1984; Williams and Gibson, 1990; Yamashita, 1991).

This article is organized as follows (see Figure 1): After briefly offering the prevailing situation in cross-cultural technology transfer in the first section, the second section reviews the research to date about the consequence of technology transfer and defines the operational concepts of corporate culture, efficient technology transfer, and business performance (specifying a firm's productivity and innovative capacity) and their measurement scales. The third section proposes the hypotheses on the relationship

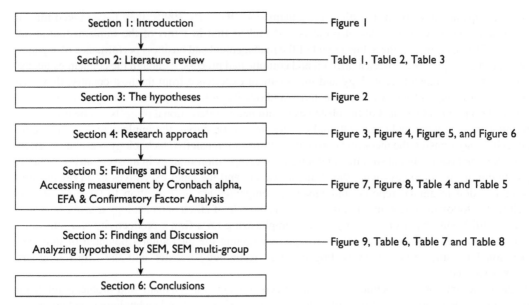

Figure 1. Article Structure

between efficient technology transfer and business performance and on the effect of corporate culture on the above relationships. The fourth section describes the research approach, including survey design, sampling techniques and the methods for analysis including EFA, CFA and SEM multi-group analysis. The fifth presents the findings and discusses the significant differences in the effect of corporate culture on the relationship between efficient technology transfer and a firm's business performance, emphasizing on the firm's productivity and innovative capacity. Finally, the sixth section offers practical conclusions.

Literature Review

This section presents the research to date regarding: (*a*) the consequence of technology transfer; and (*b*) operational concepts and measurement scales, including corporate culture, efficient technology transfer and firm's business performance.

Consequence of Technology Transfer

Previous studies on cross-cultural knowledge and technology transfer have addressed various aspects of operational performance including transferred technology and knowledge, such as organizational learning effectiveness (Cavusgil and Yavas, 1984; Inkpen, 2000; Le and Evangelista, 2007); productivity or revenue and market share (Caves, 1974; Xu, 2000; Yin and Bao, 2006); competitive advantage (Liao and Hu, 2007; Rodriguez and Rodriguez, 2005); operational efficiency, employee productivity, market share, market penetration, product quality and customer satisfaction (Cui et al., 2006; Dhanaraj et al., 2004; Lane et al., 2001; Tsang et al., 2004); technological capabilities (Kumar et al., 1999; Madanmohan et al., 2004); human resources, business and general performance (Lyles and Salk, 1996); and potential for innovation (Guan et al., 2006; Kotabe et al., 2007).

Overall, most studies on operational performance with the transferred technology have insufficiently focused on the effects of efficient technology transfer on the firm's business performance in terms of the firm's productivity and innovation capacity. The role of corporate culture on these relationships has particularly received little attention. In addition, technology transfer can be considered as the process of transferring knowledge, which involves understanding the process of how efficient knowledge transfer significantly affects the business performance of subsidiaries, and thus it merits further examination. Therefore, this study takes advantages to address the shortcomings in literature by investigating the impact of corporate culture on the relationship between efficient technology transfer and a firm's business performance, emphasizing productivity and innovative capacity.

Operational Concepts and Measurement Scales

Corporate Culture Concept

Current literature offers several operational definitions of organizational culture, also called corporate culture, but there is no strong consensus on the definition (Palanisamy, 2007); the similarities and compatibilities among the definitions are aplenty. Corporate culture is mostly considered as one of the primary factors in determining behavioural norms in the workplace and shaping companies' value systems. Each company has its own specific corporate culture that is rooted in its goals, strategies, structure and approaches to business activities, and this differs from the culture of other companies (Schein, 1996).

This study defines corporate culture as: (*a*) the convergence of a company's management and employee shared practices, core beliefs, attitudes, standards, codes and behaviour models through mutual learning and interactions in the cultural difference context, leading co-workers to think and act similarly (Kilmann et al., 1985; Schein, 1996; Steinwachs, 1999); and (*b*) the hybridization of intercultural potential to exploit home and host advantages and minimize differences in management practice from the originating cultures (Nguyen and Aoyama, 2012). Indeed, the notions of hybridization and crossvergence are used better in explaining human resource management practices and their diffusion across countries (Mamman et al., 2009). In this study, corporate culture is particularly concerned with the synergy of Japanese and Vietnamese management practices and beliefs. Accordingly, the perspectives of organizational culture and learning orientation provided by Hurley and Hult (1998) are exploited to measure corporate culture concept through five dimensions, as follows: (*a*) individual learning and development; (*b*) participative decision making that encourages employees to participate in the process; (*c*) power sharing (the internal and external information exchange and interaction that reduces focus on turf, politics and status); (*d*) tolerance for conflicts; and (*e*) support and collaboration (openness and collegial support, helping employees cooperate and readily offering needed help). Then, the expression of these original measurement scales is finally modified to fit the characteristics of Japanese manufacturing companies in Vietnam through in-depth interviews for easily understanding and answering the survey questions (see Table 1).

Efficient Technology Transfer Concept

The concept of efficient technology transfer is addressed from various perspectives. Technology transfer herein is particularly viewed through an organizational learning lens as the process of acquiring, accumulating, and applying technical knowledge by efficiently transferring technology into production activities, which requires concise measurements to properly evaluate the efficiency of the transfer.

Table 1. Corporate Culture Measurement Scale (CORCUL)

Code	Scale Items
CORCUL1	Our company culture places value on learning
CORCUL2 (*)	Our company evaluates staff performance primarily on working process rather than outcomes.
CORCUL3	Our company encourages staff to participate in the decision-making process.
CORCUL4	Our company transmits accurate and timely internal and external information about business operations.
CORCUL5 (*)	Our company accepts conflicts.
CORCUL6	Our company accepts risk.
CORCUL7	Our staff cooperates with each other and readily offers needed help.

Source: Prepared by the authors.
Note: Items marked (*) were eliminated from the final analysis.

Therefore, this study considers the viewpoint of product development skills (Mansfield et al., 1982), knowledge acquisition and application, and professional standards improvement (Lin, 2007) to be the most applicable factors; these were adjusted based on the interviews with Japanese and Vietnamese managers to fit the actual situations of Japanese manufacturing subsidiaries in Vietnam.

As a result, efficient technology transfer concept mastered in this study is concentrated on acquiring technological knowledge from a partner, enhancing knowledge application, increasing the motivation for further study and improving innovative capacities to provide process and product quality (see Table 2).

Business Performance Concept

Measuring organizational performance is a considerable task, because it is strongly related to the behaviour of managers and employees (Lee and Choi, 2003). The ultimate operation of any business usually leads to measurable performance.

Table 2. Efficient Technology Transfer Measurement Scale (EFFKNO)

Code	Scale Items	Referenced Source
Through long-term technology transfer implementation process:		
EFFKNO8(*)	Every Vietnamese technical staff member has fully learned exclusive knowledge.	Lin, 2007
EFFKNO9	The technical information and knowledge of the Vietnamese technical staff have improved significantly.	Lin, 2007
EFFKNO10	The operating skills to manufacture quality products of the Vietnamese technical staff have increased greatly.	Newly developed
EFFKNO11	The motivation for further study of the Vietnamese technical staff has increased greatly.	Newly developed
EFFKNO12	The Vietnamese technical staff has good ability to improve product quality.	Newly developed
EFFKNO13(*)	The Vietnamese technical staff members who were trained in intensive technological knowledge have stayed with our company for a long time.	Newly developed

Source: Prepared by the authors.
Note: Items marked (*) were eliminated from the final analysis.

This study aims at the view of efficiency and effectiveness, which the definition of Bernolak (1997) as cited in Tangen (2005) is considered as the proper measure to evaluate an efficiency of company's business performance achievements resulting from learning and execution. They closely relate to the efficient use of resources where performance decreases when resources are not used optimally and strongly entails meeting customer requirements effectively. Accordingly, the aspects of business performance specifying at firm's productivity and innovation capacity are addressed.

First, in the context of globalization, the competition in quality, on-time delivery, and price is tight (Golhar and Deshpande, 1999; Kaplan and Norton, 1996); therefore, firm's productivity is assessed not only through financial performance but also through the firm's ability to meet customer requirements, specifically on: (*a*) the level of a firm's response to customer requirements for quality products (Lee et al., 2001), price, timely delivery (Tran and Bui, 2009) and quick response to customer problems; and (*b*) financial performance in terms of revenue growth (Chenhall and Langfied-Smith, 2007; Lee et al., 2001; Lin and Germain, 2003; Miller, 1991), net profit growth (Chenhall and Langfied-Smith, 2007; Lin and Germain, 2003; Miller, 1991), and market share growth (Lin and Germain, 2003). Then, the view of a firm's innovation capacity (INN) is captured from the idea of Miller (1991) regarding a company's ability to frequently bring innovative products to the market. In addition, the continuous process innovation ability is newly developed to measure this aspect.

Briefly, this study divides business performance (FIRPER) into three features (see Table 3): (*a*) level of response to customer requirements (PROSat); (*b*) financial performance (PROFin); and (*c*) innovation ability (INN). Among these, the first and the second features form the operational construct of a firm's advance productivity (PRO).

Table 3. Business Performance Measurement Scale (FIRPER)

Code		Scale Items	Referenced Source
PROSat	PERQUA14	Our company provides quality products that meet customer requirements.	Lee, Lee, and Chang, 2001
	PERPRI15	Our customers accept our products' prices.	Tran and Bui, 2009
	PERTIM16	Our company ensures timely delivery.	Tran and Bui, 2009
	PERSER17	Our company quickly responds to customer complaints.	Newly developed
PROFin	PERFIN18	In comparison with the general state of the industry, our company's revenue growth over the past three years has been good.	Miller, 1991; Lee, Lee, and Chang, 2001; Lin and Germain, 2003; Chenhall and Langfied-Smith, 2007
	PERFIN19	In comparison with the general state of the industry, our net profit growth over the past three years has been good.	Miller, 1991; Lin and Germain, 2003; Chenhall and Langfied-Smith, 2007
	PERFIN20	In comparison with the general state of the industry, our market share growth over the past three years has been good.	Lin and Germain, 2003
INN	PERINN21	Our company has had continuous product innovations over the past three years.	Miller, 1991
	PERINN22	Our company has had continuous process innovation over the past three years.	Newly developed

Source: Prepared by the authors.

Framework of Analysis

Efficient Technology Transfer and Firm's Business Performance, etc.

Based on the organizational learning view, acquiring knowledge is closely related to the outcomes of using the knowledge. Technology transfer that specifically includes knowledge transfer is considered one of the factors contributing to a firm's business performance. Accordingly, a substantial transfer of technology can enhance the competitive advantage (Liao and Hu, 2007; Rodriguez and Rodriguez, 2005), influence company productivity (Caves, 1974; Xu, 2000), increase the local industry's capacity for technological development (Kumar et al., 1999; Madanmohan et al., 2004; Markusen and Venables, 1999), increase innovation potential (Guan et al., 2006; Kotabe et al., 2007) and facilitate the economic growth of the host country (Blomstrom, 1990). In addition, intra- and cross-firm knowledge transfer and acquisition have a significantly positive effect on human resources, and both business and general performance (Lyles and Salk, 1996) affect operational efficiency, employee productivity, business performance in terms of market share, product quality and customer satisfaction (Cui et al., 2006; Dhanaraj et al., 2004; Lane et al., 2001; Tsang et al., 2004) and increase the recipient firms' productivity (Yin and Bao, 2006).

Consequently, the following hypotheses are proposed (see Figure 2): Efficient technology transfer has a positive effect on business performance in term of a firm's productivity (H1a) and innovation capacity (H1b).

The activities of cross-cultural knowledge transfer and technology transfer always take place in the context of corporate culture. Because corporate culture promotes an active exchange of ideas, information transfer has happened in a general atmosphere of inventiveness, creativity and willingness to pursue new opportunities (Miles, 1978 cited in Menon and Varadarajan, 1992). Therefore, corporate culture is considered as one of the factors that shape managerial behaviour and contribute to efficient technology transfer. Moreover, knowledge-oriented corporate culture is pointed out as the most important factor contributing to successful knowledge transfer and knowledge management (Davenport and Prusak, 1998). In addition, strong corporate culture can have a significant impact on a firm's long-term economic performance (Heskett and Kotter, 1992). Thus, higher-level innovativeness connects with an organizational culture that emphasizes learning, development and participative decision making (Hurley and Hult, 1998). Particularly, corporate culture works toward the process of minimizing cultural differences and their impact on technology transfer through management practices that directly convince local behaviour and address the mindset of the home and host staff (Nguyen and Aoyama, 2012; Nguyen et al., 2012).

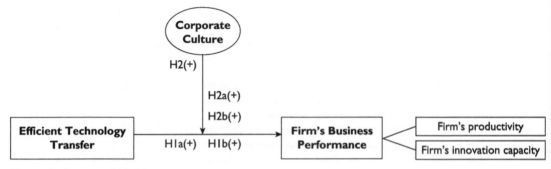

Figure 2. Conceptual Model

Source: Prepared by the authors.

Research Approach

Survey Design

The survey questionnaire was divided into two main parts.

The first part consisted of two cover letters, in both Japanese and English, written by a research supervisor and primary researcher. The letters provided organizational leaders information such as: (*a*) the study's focus, managerial implications and long-term benefits of the expected outcomes; (*b*) extreme significance of their contributions in ensuring this work's success; and (*c*) strong commitment of presenting collected data in statistical form solely for academic research purposes and of briefly reporting the results upon request on the completion of the study.

The second part included brief instructions to answer the questions; that is choosing any of the numbers in between 1 and 5 according to the strength of feelings and the best represented perceptions about the mentioned issues. The options of returning the response, a list of questions consecutively written and carefully translated in English, Vietnamese and Japanese, and the expected deadlines were referred. The questionnaire's wording, structure and configuration were checked by academic professionals and presented to three university academics in the cross-cultural technology transfer field. Next, the pre-test version was exchanged with seven key Japanese and Vietnamese executives who were each fluent in all the three languages and had an average of 11 years' experience in international technology transfer. The final version was sent to the Japanese subsidiaries in Vietnam in the form of a hard copy, a soft copy and a Google online survey for optimal convenience in feedback. In cases of discrepancies, explanations of all questions was provided through email, phone calls and face-to-face conversations. The key informant approach, one representative production manager or other relevant executive of each investigated company, which is more popular in organizational research than the use of multiple informants, was appropriate to apply in this study (Wilson and Nielson, 2000). Therefore, production managers or other relevant executives who know their companies' technology-transfer activities very well were preferably targeted.

The questionnaire was rated on a five-point Likert scale, the most commonly used question format for assessing participants' opinions (Dumas, 1999) and one that has also been recently applied in other organizational research in Vietnam (for example, Tran and Bui, 2009). The key informants were required to choose their level of agreement with each item.

Sampling

This study focuses on the impact of transferring technology on the business performance and on the role of corporate culture on the above correlation for Japanese companies invested in manufacturing activities in Vietnam. Therefore, the sample population was Japanese manufacturing subsidiaries in Vietnam, and the unit of analysis was the organization. The investigation of each focal unit was aimed at the engineering production department, the primary interest area of this study.

The sample framework was identified from Mori's (2010) 2010–2011 Japanese Companies in Vietnam and HEPZA's (2009) 2009–2010 Enterprises Directory. Among more than 1,000 companies, 905 companies were targeted.

Sampling techniques and methodologies of mailing surveys follow the phone, mail contact and follow-up methods recommended in Dillman's Total Design Method (1978). First, the survey was sent out nationwide via express mail. Then, three–five days after the mail was sent, direct phone calls were placed to confirm that the survey had been received, to answer questions, to express hope that the contact would contribute to the research and provide either the online survey link or the survey file, depending on the company's preference. At the same time, personal information such as e-mail or cell phone number was requested to further build the relationship. In particular, managers were asked to send the survey to other executives to increase the number of responses. In many cases, the primary researcher or a manager selected business cards from close contacts for immediate photocopying and obtaining the phone contacts. The official thank you letter was written carefully and it contained a promise to report the aggregated findings once the study was completed. A reminder letter with a replacement survey questionnaire was mailed three weeks after the initial mail was sent. Direct phone contacts helped to increase the feedback.

The survey was conducted from February to May 2012. A total of 223 companies responded (response rate of 24.64 per cent): 70 electric and communication companies (31.39 per cent); 73 machinery/transport companies (32.74 per cent); 27 companies manufacturing daily necessities (12.11 per cent); and 53 chemical treatment companies (23.77 per cent). Among which, 84 responses (37.67 per cent) came from companies in the key northern industrial zones such as Nomura-Haiphong, Que Vo, Tien Son, Thang Long, Noi Bai, Dong Van and Quang Minh,; and 139 responses (62.33 per cent) came from companies in the key southern technology parks and export processing zones, such as Amata, VSIP, Bien Hoa-Dong Nai, My Phuoc, Tan Thuan and Linh Trung. These companies have an average experience of 8.96 years of operating with transferred technology and an average of 915 employees. Key informants are between 40 and 50 years of age and have an average experience of 8.15 years in international technology transfer.

Overall, the study's sample size of 223 companies[1] exceeded the expected 200 cases from the research method based on experience; and therefore, the sample size was considered to be large enough to obtain reliable analysis while employing an SEM approach, a method employed in large-sample distribution theory (Kline, 1998). Moreover, this sample size is considered reasonable and manageable because low response rates are common in surveys.

EFA Method

EFA is first used to assess and refine the preliminary scales. The principal axis factoring in EFA with Promax rotation with the criterion of eigenvalue ≥ 1 is employed to appropriately determine the number of extracted factors. Next, Cronbach's alpha coefficient is exploited to assess the reliability of the scales. In addition, various supplementary assessments are also conducted on the data: (*a*) no item is allowed to load too high or low on more than one factor as to indicate a unidimensional measurement (Anderson and Gerbing, 1988); (*b*) all items comprising a scale must load highly on one factor to indicate good discriminant validity (Hair et al., 1998); and (*c*) factor loading ≥ 0.50; item-total correlation ≥ 0.35; Cronbach's alpha ≥ 0.60 (Hair et al., 1998); and total variance extracted ≥ 50 per cent (Gerbing and Anderson, 1988).

CFA Method

CFA is conducted to finalize the scales validity with the considered criteria: (*a*) scales achieve unidimensionality if the corresponding measurement model has overall fit, including the latent construct and its designated items (Steenkamp and Van Trijp, 1991). A chi-squared statistic with a p-value >0.05 is a key required indicator of overall model fit (Hair et al., 1998); (*b*) the scale values demonstrate convergent validity if the regression coefficients of all standardized variables ≥0.60 and have statistically significant p-values of <0.05 (Anderson and Gerbing, 1988); (*c*) the composite reliability of scales is satisfactory at CR ≥0.60 (Hair et al., 1998); and (*d*) the scale achieves discriminant validity between concepts when the measurement model achieves overall fit and correlation coefficients among concepts of r < 1 with statistically significant p-values (Steenkamp and Van Trijp, 1991).

SEM Multigroup Analysis

SEM multi-group analysis is applied to determine the moderating effect of corporate culture on the relationship between efficient technology transfer and business performance. The multi-group analysis method used in this study includes both unconstrained (measurement components, and the relationships between the research concepts in the theoretical model are not bound) and partially constrained structure models (measurement components are not bound, but the relationship between the research concepts in the theoretical model is set equally for the two groups). In Figures 3 and 5, the model path coefficients were freely estimated for each group, whereas in Figures 4 and 6, the coefficients were partially constrained to be equal across the two groups. A comparison of these two models showed significant

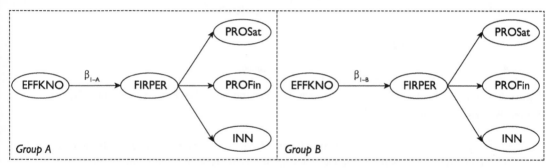

Figure 3. Unconstraint Model of Efficient Technology Transfer and a Firm's Business Performance

Source: Prepared by the authors.

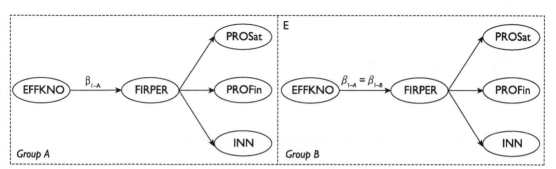

Figure 4. Constraint Model of Efficient Technology Transfer and a Firm's Business Performance

Source: Prepared by the authors.

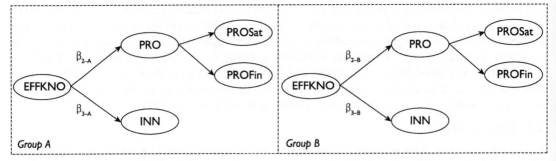

Figure 5. Unconstraint Model of Efficient Technology Transfer and Firm's Productivity/Innovation Capacity
Source: Prepared by the authors.

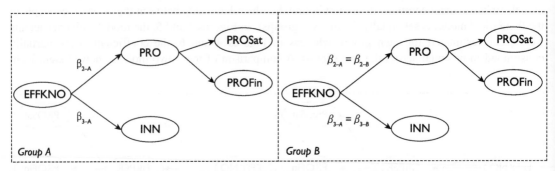

Figure 6. Constraint Model of Efficient Technology Transfer and Firm's Productivity/Innovation Capacity
Source: Prepared by the authors.

differences in corporate culture in the hypothesized path coefficients between efficient technology transfer and a firm's business performance in terms of productivity and innovation ability.

The sample is categorized into high and low corporate culture groups, Group A and B, based on their ratings on this construct. Those with ratings above the median form the high-corporate culture group while those below the median form the low-culture group. To ensure measurement invariance between the two groups, variables that do not meet the criteria of EFA and CFA evaluation are eliminated.

Findings and Discussions

This section presents the results and discussions on EFA and CFA scale assessment and hypotheses test.

Assessing the Reliability of Measurement Scales by the EFA Method

By preliminary assessment of the measurement scales of corporate culture, efficient technology transfer and business performance, the following items that were unsatisfactory with EFA's criteria had to be deleted from the original scale: two items in the corporate culture construct, regarding evaluation primarily on working process rather than outcomes (CORCUL2) and accepting conflicts (CORCUL5), and one item regarding long-term employee tenure with the company after intensive technology training (EFFKNO13) on the efficient technology transfer scale. The reliability indices of constructs in the conceptual model are presented in Tables 4 and 5.

Assessing the Validity of Measurement Scales by the CFA Method

In line with the CFA's criteria, the business performance measurement scales satisfied the evaluation criteria for a multidimensional scale and yielded at chi-square = 55.48 (p = 0.00); TLI = 0.96; CFI = 0.97; RMSEA = 0.08; df = 24, reflecting the validity of each scale (see Figure 7). The final overall measurement model yielded the following measurement indices: chi-square = 189.65 (p = 0.00); TLI = 0.97; CFI = 0.97; RMSEA = 0.05; df = 129, showing the adequate overall fit (see Figure 8). One item in

Table 4. Reliability Indices for Corporate Culture and Efficient Technology Transfer Construct Based on Preliminary Scale Assessment (EFA) and Scale Validity (CFA)

Sample size: N = 223			Preliminary Assessment (EFA)		Scale Validity (CFA)		Standardized
Coded item	Mean	Std. Dev.	Factor Loading	Item-Total Correlation	Factor Loading	Item-Total Correlation	Regression Weights
Corporate culture							
CORCUL1	3.704	0.887	0.724	0.665	0.724	0.665	0.733
CORCUL2	—	—	—	—	—	—	—
CORCUL3	3.771	0.847	0.804	0.728	0.804	0.728	0.791
CORCUL4	3.731	0.788	0.814	0.738	0.814	0.738	0.812
CORCUL5	—	—	—	—	—	—	—
CORCUL6	3.507	0.810	0.632	0.585	0.632	0.585	0.627
CORCUL7	3.812	0.766	0.765	0.701	0.765	0.701	0.778
Eigenvalue			3.242		3.242		
Variance extracted			64.838%		64.838%		
Cronbach's alpha			0.862		0.862		
Composite reliability					0.865		
Efficient technology transfer							
EFFKNO8	—	—	0.531	0.499	—	—	—
EFFKNO9	3.928	0.700	0.851	0.774	0.834	0.762	0.848
EFFKNO10	3.924	0.728	0.916	0.816	0.929	0.837	0.910
EFFKNO11	3.744	0.767	0.782	0.713	0.788	0.734	0.793
EFFKNO12	3.812	0.729	0.686	0.635	0.685	0.646	0.696
EFFKNO13	—	—	—	—	—	—	—
Eigenvalue			3.288		2.963		
Variance extracted			65.768%		74.070%		
Cronbach's alpha			0.862		0.881		
Composite reliability					0.887		

Source: Prepared by the authors.
Note: In Table 4, the items with '—' is eliminated from the analysis.

Table 5. Reliability Indices for Business Performance Construct Based on Preliminary Scale Assessment (EFA) and Scale Validity (CFA)

| Sample size: N = 223 | | | Preliminary Assessment (EFA) Scale Validity (CFA) | | | | Standardized |
| | | | Factor Loadings | | | Item-Total | Regression Weights |
Coded Item	Mean	Std. Dev.	1	2	3	Correlation	(CFA-Scale Validity)
PERQUA14	4.072	0.762	0.790	−0.039	0.012	0.706	0.769
PERPRI15	3.955	0.752	0.861	0.013	−0.096	0.740	0.798
PERTIM16	4.175	0.789	0.808	−0.030	0.078	0.757	0.836
PERSER17	4.157	0.702	0.654	0.090	0.054	0.670	0.749
PERFIN18	3.744	0.807	0.092	0.886	−0.098	0.779	0.873
PERFIN19	3.583	0.945	−0.116	0.910	0.071	0.781	0.879
PERFIN20	3.543	0.820	0.053	0.665	0.052	0.678	0.731
PERINN21	3.565	0.867	−0.071	0.000	0.991	0.777	0.844
PERINN22	3.659	0.823	0.130	0.024	0.742	0.777	0.921
Eigenvalue			4.546	1.468	1.029		
Variance extracted			50.516	16.308	11.436	Total Variance extracted = 78.260%	
Cronbach's alpha			0.867	0.863	0.874		
Composite reliability			0.868	0.869	0.876		

Source: Prepared by the authors.

the efficient technology-transfer construct, fully learned exclusive knowledge (EFFKNO8), had to be eliminated from the original scale to improve the overall fit of the model.

Efficient Technology Transfer and Firm's Business Performance

First, the standardized regression coefficient between efficient technology transfer and firm's productivity is 0.63 (p = 0.00), which supports the hypothesized relationship between efficient technology transfer and business performance in term of a firm's productivity (H1a). Then, the standardized regression coefficient between efficient technology transfer and a firm's innovation capacity is 0.54 (p = 0.00), validating the positive correlation between these concepts (H1b). Overall, the results of the path analysis on the structural model and the hypotheses indicate that efficient technology-transfer performance contributes to 40 per cent of a firm's productivity and 29 per cent of a firm's innovation capacity (see Figure 9). These results provide interesting additional information compared with the work of Tran and Bui (2009) on manufacturing enterprise in Vietnam, which revealed that managerial factors contribute to 55 per cent of a firm's productivity.

Therefore, to achieve successful business performance, international managers should focus on executing methodical, efficient practices. They must then create a new learning culture that promotes sharing the intercultural values of Japan and Vietnam in successful business performance. Managerial activities should focus on improving Vietnamese technical staffs' knowledge, operating skill, ability to manufacture quality products, meet customer requirements, ensure timely delivery and quickly respond to customer complaints. The challenge for Japanese and Vietnamese executives is to motivate the staff through the spirit of learning and working. Efforts should directly affect growth in revenue, net profit, and market share as well as product and process innovation ability, all of which contribute to maintaining the competitive advantage of Japanese manufacturing subsidiaries in Vietnam.

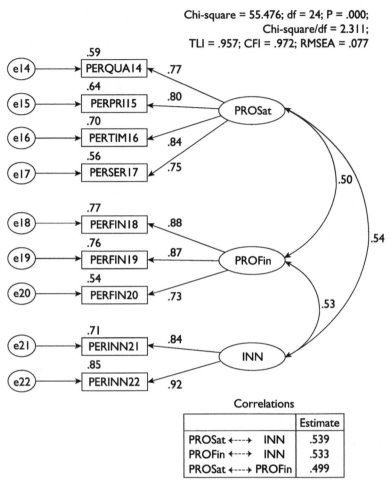

Figure 7. CFA for Business Performance

Source: Prepared by the authors.

The Effect of Corporate Culture on the Relationship between Efficient Technology Transfer and Firm's Business Performance

To assess the effect of corporate culture on the relationship between efficient technology transfer and a firm's business performance, the sample is categorized into high and low corporate culture groups based on their ratings on this construct: above the median (n = 170 companies) forms the high corporate culture group, and below the median (n = 53 companies) forms the low corporate culture group.

On the moderating variable of corporate culture, when binding the regression coefficient β from efficient technology transfer performance to firm's business performance in the theoretical model (β_{1-A} = β_{1-B}); to firm's productivity (β_{2-A} = β_{2-B}); and to firm's innovation capacity (β_{3-A} = β_{3-B}), equally across both two business groups, the value of df increases one degree of freedom (from 127 to 128) and the chi-square also increases. Chi-square tests between the partially constrained and unconstrained structure

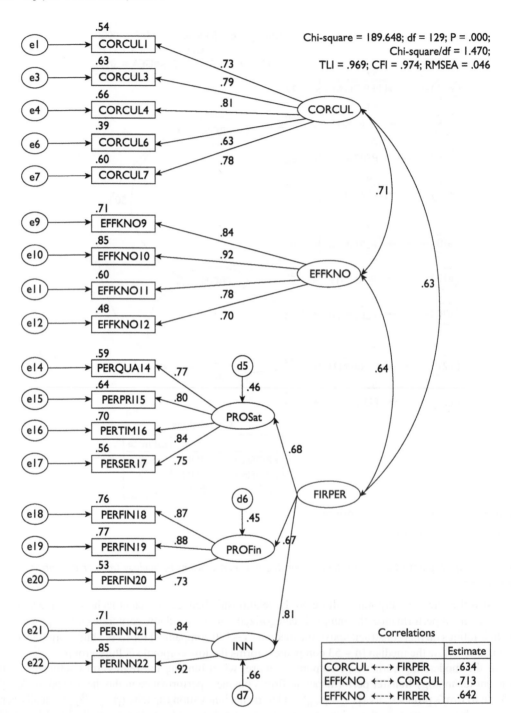

Figure 8. The Total Measure Scale Validity by CFA

Source: Prepared by the authors.

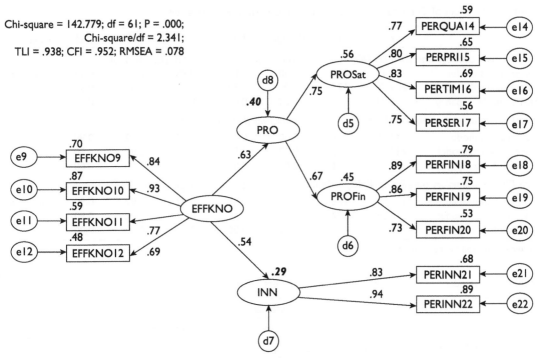

Chi-square = 142.779; df = 61; P = .000;
Chi-square/df = 2.341;
TLI = .938; CFI = .952; RMSEA = .078

Figure 9. Results of Testing Hypotheses of Efficient Technology Transfer and a Firm's Productivity and Innovation Capacity

Source: Prepared by the authors.

models, using the Maximum Likelihood estimation method, show results of p (Δχ2 corresponding with Δdf) 0.02 for business performance; 0.03 for firm's productivity; and 0.01 for firm's innovation capacity (see Table 6). The discrepancy meets the statistically significant p-value of <0.05 (Byrne, 2001). Therefore, hypothesis of corporate culture producing significant differences in the effects of efficient technology transfer on a firm's business performance (H2) is supported..

In addition, based on the results of unstandardized estimation on moderating effect of corporate culture on the relationship of efficient technology transfer and firm's business performance in Table 7, there are significant discrepancies meeting the statistically significant p-value of <0.05 among groups high and low corporate culture. Therefore, the hypothesis of higher corporate culture, higher positive effect of efficient technology transfer on firm's productivity is supported (H2a). Similarly, the hypothesis of higher corporate culture and a higher positive effect of efficient technology transfer on a firm's innovation capacity is also supported (H2b). Thus, the higher corporate culture, the more the company can use efficiently the transferred knowledge for achieving business performance on both firm's productivity and innovation capacity.

Furthermore, by analyzing the moderating effects of each scale item of the corporate culture construct on the hypothesized relationships, the findings presented in Table 8 support that: (a) the more the company places value on learning, encourages staff to participate in the decision-making process and

Table 6. The Effect of Corporate Culture on the Hypothesized Relationships

	χ^2	df	P-value	NFI	RFI	IFI	TLI	Result
H2: *Efficient technology transfer (EFFKNO)* → *Firm's business performance (FIRPER)* $(\beta_{1-A} = \beta_{1-B})$								
Constrained model	215.11	128	0.00	0.88	0.85	0.95	0.93	Supported
Unconstrained model	209.70	127	0.00	0.88	0.85	0.95	0.93	
Significant discrepancy	5.41	1	**0.02**	0.00	0.00	0.00	0.00	
H2a: *Efficient technology transfer (EFFKNO)* → *Firm's productivity (PRO)* $(\beta_{2-A} = \beta_{2-B})$								
Constrained model	247.55	128	0.00	0.85	0.82	0.92	0.90	Supported
Unconstrained model	242.59	127	0.00	0.85	0.82	0.92	0.90	
Significant discrepancy	4.97	1	**0.03**	0.00	0.00	0.00	0.00	
H2b: *Efficient technology transfer (EFFKNO)* → *Firm's innovation capacity (INN)* $(\beta_{3-A} = \beta_{3-B})$								
Constrained model	248.91	128	0.00	0.85	0.82	0.92	0.90	Supported
Unconstrained model	242.59	127	0.00	0.85	0.82	0.92	0.90	
Significant discrepancy	6.32	1	**0.01**	0.00	0.00	0.00	0.00	

Source: Prepared by the authors.

Table 7. Unstandardized Estimation on Moderating Effect of Corporate Culture

	Unconstrained Model								Constrained Model			
	Low Corporate Culture				High Corporate Culture							
Hypothesized Relationship	m	SE	CR	p	m	SE	CR	p	m	SE	CR	p
(H2): EFFKNO→FIRPER	0.38	0.09	4.01	0.00	0.95	0.28	3.44	0.00	0.48	0.09	5.26	0.00
(H2a): EFFKNO→PRO	0.33	0.11	2.94	0.00	0.91	0.28	3.21	0.00	0.46	0.10	4.47	0.00
(H2b): EFFKNO→INN	0.50	0.11	4.59	0.00	1.11	0.26	4.21	0.00	0.65	0.10	6.54	0.00

Source: Prepared by the authors.

accepts risk, the higher the firm's business performance in terms of firm's productivity and firm's innovation capacity with the efficiently transferred technology; (*b*) the more the company transmits accurate and timely internal and external information about business operations, the more the company achieves the firm's productivity from using the transferred knowledge efficiently, though, the significant discrepancy in achieving the firm's innovation capacity has not been statistically perceived; and (*c*) the more the staff cooperates with each other and readily offers help, the more the positive changes in achieving a firm's productivity and innovation capacity with the efficient transferred technology, but the discrepancy does not meet the statistically significant. These outcomes can be explained by cultural difference traits between Japanese and Vietnamese management styles from the perspectives of collectivism and power distance in leading technology transfer and business performance (Nguyen et al., 2012).

Indeed, once efficient technology transfer is achieved, the corporate culture is created and facilitates technology transfer performance; of course efficient technology transfer leads firm's productivity performance. Interestingly, corporate culture herein has ability enhancing the positive relationship of efficient technology transfer and firm's business performance. In fact, companies have the corporate culture highly emphasizing on learning culture, they exploit effectively the advantages of Vietnamese culture with high attention on learning to have distinguished individual initiative and take the chance of high power distance in management. At the same time, the learning culture is also supported by Japanese

Table 8. Moderating Effect of Each Scale of Corporate Culture on the Hypothesized Relationship

	df	Efficient technology transfer → firm's productivity	Efficient technology transfer → firm's innovation capacity
		Chi-square	Chi-square
CORCUL1: Company culture places value on learning			
Constrained model	128	248.97	250.53
Unconstrained model	127	243.85	243.85
Difference	1	5.12	6.68
P value		**0.02**	**0.01**
Result		Supported	Supported
CORCUL3: Encouraging staff to participate in the decision-making process			
Constrained model	128	254.06	253.23
Unconstrained model	127	249.37	249.37
Difference	1	4.69	3.86
P value		**0.03**	**0.05**
Result		Supported	Supported
CORCUL4: Transmitting accurate and timely operating information to internal/external business			
Constrained model	128	231.93	229.65
Unconstrained model	127	226.37	226.37
Difference	1	5.56	3.28
P value		**0.02**	0.07
Result		Supported	Not Supported
CORCUL6: Accepting risk			
Constrained model	128	303.63	304.18
Unconstrained model	127	293.90	293.90
Difference	1	9.73	10.29
P value		**0.00**	**0.00**
Result		Supported	Supported
CORCUL7: Cooperating each other and readily offering help			
Constrained model	128	260.10	260.95
Unconstrained model	127	258.71	258.71
Difference	1	1.38	2.24
P value		0.24	0.14
Result		Not Supported	Not Supported

Source: Prepared by the authors.

culture in high in the masculinity dimension which stressesd on training. Even though technology is successfully transferred and the company can manufacture with manual, guidelines, acquired knowledge and skills and, etc., but in the actual operating process, some troubles and innovative matters need to be handled for fitting in with local manufacturing conditions. The workers have to learn more and try to make experiments, accepting risks in changing at once,; but those workers can make invaluable decisions for better operational management along with their minds. Therefore, a learning culture promotes a higher firm's higher productivity and firm's innovation capacity performance. Furthermore, once the accurate internal and external information about business operations is transmitted quickly, the corrective action and preventive action is timely conducted in a timely manner and adjusted; the higher firm's attains a higher productivity performance is reached. However, the information about business operations, especially, the exclusive technological information which needs to be protected for competition is transmitted more; though, there has not been found the significant change in firm's innovation capacity. Furthermore, another point could be that the important root driving firm's innovation capacity is the wisdom in the co-workers' mindset. The knowledge and skills through learning process and practices are absorbed into the employee's wise mind, were continuously lead process innovation and frequently bring innovative products to the market. In addition, although the both Japanese and Vietnamese cultures share the same collectivism spirit which especially devotes to given help; but the more the focus on offering the needed help is, the more the individual's creativity is limited.. Actually, the cultural collectivism dimension provides both positive and negative impacts on efficient technology transfer and business performance (Nguyen et al, 2012; Nguyen and Aoyama, 2012), that are eliminated each other, and balanced their impacts on business performance. Therefore, although the more the staff cooperates with each other and readily offers help, possibly, the lesser the firm's productivity and innovation capacity significantly obtain with the efficient transferred technology.

Consequently, corporate culture produces significant differences in the effects of efficient technology transfer on business performance in general and on a firm's productivity and innovation capacity in particular. Therefore, to shift from a low- to a high corporate culture, companies must place value on learning. Organizational learning and knowledge-sharing and management are a prerequisite for promoting innovation and creation of new knowledge (Dasgupta and Gupta, 2009). Besides, encouraging staff to participate in the decision-making process and openly transmitting accurate, timely internal and external information about business operations are very important. After recruitment, staff should be trained carefully and managers must carefully monitor the work in detail. International executives should be aware of the benefits of corporate culture and transmit its spirit and know-how to their staff so that they thoroughly understand why a corporate culture is crucial for efficient business performance. An organization which lacks a corporate culture for knowledge learning, sharing, creation and dissemination has a serious situation for the competitiveness at the firm, industry and country level (Pillania, 2006). In addition, although there are many techniques for creating corporate culture—including assessing which features should be copied from Vietnamese culture, which aspects should be kept from Japanese culture through technology transfer, and which angles should be newly created to fit with intercultural cooperation—all are considered to be intelligent strategies of organizational management.

These strategies challenge the vision and the ability of professionals and expatriates to evaluate opportunities based on which cultural differences bring conflicts and which can provide synergy benefits.

Conclusions

This study obtains statistical evidence about the role of corporate culture on two aspects of cross-cultural technology transfer: (*a*) efficient technology transfer has a 40 per cent positive effect on business performance in terms of a firm's productivity, and a 29 per cent positive effect on business performance in terms of a firm's innovation ability; and (*b*) corporate culture produces significant differences in the effects of efficient technology transfer on a firm's business performance, particularly on firm's productivity and firm's innovation capacity. The higher the corporate culture, the higher the success of a firm's business performance (in terms of firm's productivity and firm's innovation capacity) with the efficiently transferred technology; especially: (*a*) the higher the company places value on learning, encourages staff to participate in the decision-making process, and accepts risk, the higher the success of a firm's business performance (in terms of firm's productivity and firm's innovation capacity) with the efficiently transferred technology; (*b*) the more the staff cooperates with each other and readily offers help, the more the positive changes in achieving firm's productivity and innovation capacity with the efficient transferred technology, but the discrepancy in changing is not large enough to meet the statistically significant; and (*c*) the more the company transmits accurate and timely internal and external information about business operations, the more the company achieves firm's productivity from using the transferred knowledge efficiently; though, the significant discrepancy in achieving firm's innovation capacity has not been statistically perceived.

Furthermore, in this study, the advantages of the powerful multivariate technique with structural equation modelling (SEM) (Alavifar et al., 2012) are utilized as the means of data analysis to focus mainly on analyzing the impact of corporate culture on the relationship between efficient technology transfer and a firm's business performance, emphasizing firm's productivity and firm's innovation capacity. Based on a conceptual approach and statistical technique, the meaning of structural equation modelling (SEM) and multiple regression analysis basically have similarities, and parameter estimates will be identical or very close in testing the relationships of independent and dependent variables. However, the conceptual model in this study is built on three latent variables with several indicators— corporate culture construct, efficient technology transfer construct and business performance construct; that are measured on the basis of the strength of feelings and the best representing perceptions for self-assessment methods. In order to measure, and assess the hypothesized relationships, these measurements cannot be measured and validated without the contamination of measurement error. Additionally, for latent variables with several indicators, especially, the firm's business performance construct which is the latent variable with multiple indicators of the same construct, structural equation model analysis approach helps to naturally handled measurement errors. In this case, with regression analysis, multiple indicators cause collinearity problems and small increments in variance also accounted for. Therefore, the two-phase approach of both exploratory factor analysis and confirmatory factor analysis in SEM and SEM multiple analysis are properly used to derive reliability of measured variables and internal consistency measures of reliability and to result the construct validity of measurement and hypotheses assessment.

Accordingly, the above results through the SEM analytical method in this study shape the following comprehensive issues. First, based on the discovered discrepancy value of corporate culture in efficiently translating technology transfer into business performance, company executives, including those of Japanese manufacturing subsidiaries, should exploit the powerful advantages of corporate culture in developing sustainability. Although minds cannot be managed, they can be transformed by inspiring leaders who spread new visions that advocate new meanings and lines of thinking (Browaeys and Price, 2008). Therefore, Japanese and Vietnamese executives should proactively engage in developing appropriate management interventions, mastering employee beliefs, and values, and moving the company forward. Second, international expatriate managers and corporate practitioners should pay attention to evaluating current corporate culture and practicing hybrid management to set the goals for timely improvement. They will then benefit from the value of using transferred technology to achieve efficient business performance within their specific cross-cultural contexts. Third, although there are many ways of creating corporate culture, it is considered intelligent management strategy for each company to consider which features should be copied from Vietnamese culture, which should be retained from Japanese culture, and which angles should be newly created to fit with intercultural cooperation. These strategies challenge the talent of professionals and expatriates in evaluating opportunities based on considering which cultural differences bring conflicts and which can hybridize to provide benefits. Fourth, management practices that emphasize on corporate culture can help gradually alter staff behaviour and mindset, the foundation for improvement and innovation activities. This calls for managers and executives to be open-minded and have a strategic vision to lead the company in the globally competitive arena. Finally, all things considered, even though this study makes an effort respond to the lack of understanding regarding the impact of corporate culture on the relationships of efficient technology transfer and a firm's productivity and innovative capacity; however, further research should extend the investigation on (*a*) how corporate culture affects business performance; (*b*) which management practices help to form corporate culture; (*c*) whether corporate culture controls the effect of management practices on efficient technology transfer; (*d*) how corporate culture can reduce the impact of cultural difference on technology transfer; and (*e*) during technology transfer, which managerial elements from the host country's national culture should be adjusted and which should be maintained. Accordingly, the alternative technique of both qualitative comparative analysis and quantitative analysis applied successfully in recently cross-cultural research could be appropriate for examining corporate cultural values.

In addition, Vietnamese companies, particularly Japanese companies in Vietnam, are sensitive about openly providing financial information; thus, this study applies perceptual self-assessment methods to measure business performance. Even though objective and subjective financial assessments showed close relationships and gave similar results (Chenhall and Langfield-Smith, 2007; Dess and Robinson, 1984; Geringer and Hebert, 1991; Lyles and Salk, 1996); the objective assessment of performance is the most practical and provides the ideal measurement of performance. Likely, the measurement of the variables in corporate culture, efficient technology transfer is based entirely on the perceptions of possibly just one key informant from each of the 223 participating organizations. The validity of such subjective data is also questionable. Also, the key informant approach as representative agent of the investigated company, which is more popular in organizational research than the use of multiple informants (Wilson and Nielson, 2000); though, the number of respondents is the same as that of the 223 companies, the unit of analysis is not just the organization but also the individual. Therefore, researchers conducting organizational studies in Vietnam face the challenge to conduct further studies with an objective approach and useful outcomes to add more empirical evidence to the regional understanding of Japanese management practices regarding technology transfer.

Acknowledgement

We gratefully acknowledge the generous grant in aid for international research activities provided by the Ritsumeikan Kokusaiteki research fund, and the Japanese Ministry of Education, Science and Culture. We would also like to express our deep gratitude to the Vietnamese production managers and Japanese executives of Japanese manufacturing subsidiaries in Vietnam. We sincerely thank to Prof. Atsushi Abe, Prof. Bui Nguyen Hung and Dr. Tran Thi Kim Loan for their kind support. Last but not least, we are grateful to the anonymous referees of the journal for their extremely useful suggestions to improve the quality of the article.

Note

1. Using the collected data from 223 companies, this study applies the SEM analyzing techniques, incorporating SPSS 16.0 and AMOS 16.0 software through the two-phase approach of both EFA and CFA and SEM multiple group analysis.

References

Alavifar, A., Karimimalayer, M., & Anuar, M.K. (2012). Structural equation modeling vs multiple regression: The first and second generation of multivariate techniques. *IRACST—Engineering Science and Technology: An International Journal (ESTIJ)*, 2(2), 326–329.

Anderson, J.C., & Gerbing, D.W. (1988). Structural equation modeling in practice: A review and recommended two-step approach. *Psychology Bulletin, 103*(3), 411–423. Retrieved from http://dx.doi.org/10.1037//0033-2909.103.3.411

Ando, T., Kawashima, M., & Kan, K. (2005). *Chugoku no gijutsu hatten to gijutsu iten: Riron to jisshou (Technology development and technology transfer in China: Theoretical and empirical analysis)*. Kyoto: Minerva Shobo.

Blomstrom, M. (1990). *Transnational corporations and manufacturing exports from developing countries*. New York: United Nations.

Bozeman, B. (2000). Technology transfer and public policy: A review of research and theory. *Research Policy, 29*(4–5), 627–655. Retrieved from http://dx.doi.org/10.1016/S0048-7333(99)00093-1

Browaeys, M., & Price, R. (2008). *Understanding cross-cultural management*. Harlow, Tokyo: Financial Times Prentice Hall.

Buckler, B. (1998). Practical steps towards a learning organization: Applying academic knowledge to improvement and innovation in business process. *The Learning Organization, 5*(10), 15–23.

Byrne, B.M. (2001). *Structural equation modeling with AMOS: Basic concepts, applications and programming*. Mahwah, NJ: Lawrence Erlbaum Associates Publishers.

Caves, R.E. (1974). Multinational firms, competition and productivity in host-country markets. *Economica, 41*(162), 176–193.

Cavusgil, S.T., & Yavas, U. (1984). Transfer of management know-how to developing countries: An empirical investigation. *Journal of Business Research, 12*(1), 35–50. Retrieved from http://dx.doi.org/10.1016/0148-2963(84)90036-5

Chenhall, R.H., & Langfield-Smith, K. (2007). Multiple perspectives of performance measures. *European Management Journal, 25*(4), 266–282.

Cui, A.S., Griffith, D.A., Casvugil, S.T., & Dabic, M. (2006). The influence of market and cultural environmental factors on technology transfer between foreign MNCs and local subsidiaries: A Croatian illustration. *Journal of World Business, 41*(2), 100–111. Retrieved from http://dx.doi.org/10.1016/j.jwb.2006.01.011

Dasgupta, M., & Gupta, R.K. (2009). Innovation in organizations: A review of the role of organizational learning and knowledge management. *Global Business Review, 10*(2), 203–224.

Davenport, T.H., & Prusak, L. (1998). *Working knowledge: How organizations manage what they know*. Boston, MA: Harvard Business School Press.

Derakhshani, S. (1984). Factors affecting success in international transfers of technology: A synthesis, and a test of a new contingency model. *Developing Economies, 22*(1), 27–46. Retrieved from http://dx.doi.org/10.1111/j.1746-1049.1984.tb00650.x

Dess, G.G., & Robinson, R.B.J. (1984). Measuring organizational performance in the absence of objective measures: The case of the privately-held firm and conglomerate business unit. *Strategic Management Journal, 5*(3), 265–273.

Dhanaraj, C., Lyles, M.A., Steensma, H.K., & Tihanyi, L. (2004). Managing tacit and explicit knowledge transfer in IJVs: The role of relational embeddedness and the impact on performance. *Journal of International Business Studies, 35*(5), 428–442.

Dillman, D.A. (1978). *Mail and telephone surveys: The total design method*. New York: Wiley.

Dumas, J. (1999). *Usability testing methods: Subjective measures, Part II—Measuring attitudes and opinions*. American Institutes for Research. Retrieved from http://www.upassoc.org/html/1999_archive/usability_testing_methods.html

Fukunaga, Y. (2010). Shifting FDI trends in Vietnam: Broadening beyond manufacturing base to consumer market. *Economic Review*, *5*(4), 1–11.

Gerbing, W.D., & Anderson, J.C. (1988). An update paradigm for scale development incorporating unidimensionality and its assessments. *Journal of Marketing Research*, *25*(2), 186–192.

Geringer, J.M., & Hebert, L. (1991). Measuring performance of international joint ventures. *Journal of International Business Studies*, *22*(2), 249–263.

Golhar, D.Y., & Deshpande, S.P. (1999). Productivity comparisons between Canadian and US TQM firms: An empirical investigation. *International Journal of Quality and Reliability Management*, *16*(7), 714–722.

Guan, J.C., Mok, C.K., Yam, C.M., & Pun, K.F. (2006). Technology transfer and innovation performance: Evidence from Chinese firms. *Technological Forecasting and Social Change*, *73*(6), 666–678. Retrieved from http://dx.doi.org/10.1016/j.techfore.2005.05.009

Hair, J.F., Anderson, R.E., Tatham, R.L., & Black, W.C. (1998). *Multivariate data analysis* (5th ed.). Upper Saddle River, NJ: Prentice Hall.

HEPZA. (2009). *Danh ba doanh nghiep: Cac khu che xuat—Khu cong nghiep Thanh pho Ho Chi Minh va mot so tinh phia Nam 2009—2010 (Enterprise directory: Export processing zones—Industrial zone in Ho Chi Minh city and some southern provinces)*. Ho Chi Minh City: HEPZA.

Heskett, J., & Kotter, J. (1992). *Corporate culture and performance*. New York: The Free Press.

Huber, G.P. (1991). Organizational learning: The contributing processes and the literature. *Organization Science*, *2*(1), 88–115.

Hurley, R.F., & Hult, G.T.M. (1998). Innovation, market orientation, and organizational learning: An integration and empirical examination. *Journal of Marketing*, *62*(3), 42–54.

Inkpen, A.C. (2000). Learning through joint ventures: A framework of knowledge acquisition. *Journal of Management Studies*, *37*(7), 1019–1043.

Kaplan, R.S., & Norton, D.P. (1996). Using the balanced scorecard as a strategic management system. *Harvard Business Review*, *74*(1), 75–85.

Kilmann, R.M.J., Saxton, M.J., & Serpa, R. (1985). Introduction: Five key issues in understanding and changing culture. In R.H. Kilmann, M.J. Saxton & R. Serpa (Eds), *Gaining control of the corporate culture* (pp. 17–43). San Francisco, CA: Jossey-Bass.

Kline, R. (1998). *Principles and practice of structural equation modeling*. New York: Guildford.

Kotabe, M., Dunlap-Hinkler, D., Parente, R., & Mishra, H. (2007). Determinants of cross-national knowledge transfer and its effect on firm innovation. *Journal of International Business Studies*, *38*(2), 259–282.

Kumar, V., Kumar, U., & Persaud, A. (1999). Building technological capability through importing technology: The case of Indonesian manufacturing industry. *Journal of Technology Transfer*, *24*(1), 81–96.

Lane, P.J., Salk, J.E., & Lyles, M.A. (2001). Absorptive capacity, learning, and performance in international joint ventures. *Strategic Management Journal*, *22*(12), 1139–1161.

Le, N.H., & Evangelista, F. (2007). Acquiring tacit and explicit marketing knowledge from foreign partners in IJVs. *Journal of Business Research*, *60*, 1152–1165. Retrieved from http://dx.doi.org/10.1016/j.jbusres.2007.04.006

Lee, C., Lee, T., & Chang, C. (2001). Quality/productivity practices and company performance in China. *International Journal of Quality and Reliability Management*, *18*(6), 604–625.

Lee, H., & Choi, B. (2003). *Knowledge management enablers, processes, and organizational performance: An integrative view* and *empirical examination. Journal of Management Information System*, *20*(1), 179–228.

Liao, S.H., & Hu, T.C. (2007). Knowledge transfer and competitive advantage on environmental uncertainty: An empirical study of the Taiwan's industry. *Technovation*, *27*(6–7), 402–411. Retrieved from http://dx.doi.org/10.1016/j.technovation.2007.02.005

Lin, W.B. (2007). Factors affecting the correlation between interactive mechanisms of strategic alliance and technological knowledge transfer performance. *The Journal of High Technology Management Research*, *17*(2), 139–155. Retrieved from http://dx.doi.org/10.1016/j.hitech.2006.11.003

Lin, X., & Germain, R. (2003). Organizational structure, context, customer orientation and performance: Lessons from Chinese state-owned enterprises. *Strategic Management Journal, 24*(11), 1131–1151.

Lyles, M.A., & Salk, J.E. (1996). Knowledge acquisition from foreign parents in international joint ventures: An empirical examination in the Hungarian context. *Journal of International Business Studies, 27*(5), 877–903. Retrieved from http://dx.doi.org/10.1057/palgrave.jibs.8490155

Madanmohan, T.R., Kumar, U., & Kumar, V. (2004). Import-led technological capability: A comparative analysis of Indian and Indonesian manufacturing firms. *Technovation, 24*(12), 979–993. Retrieved from http://dx.doi.org/10.1016/S0166-4972(03)00030-0

Mamman, A., Baydoun, N., & Adeoye, B. (2009). Transferability of management innovation to Africa. A study of two multinational companies' performance management system in Nigeria. *Global Business Review, 10*(1), 1–31.

Mansfield, E., Romeo, A., Schwarts, M., Teede, D., Wagner, S., & Brach, P. (1982). *Technology transfer, productivity, and economic policy.* New York: W.W. Norton and Co. Inc.

Markusen, J.R., & Venables, A.J. (1999). Foreign direct investment as a catalyst for industrial development. *European Economic Review, 43*(2), 335–356. Retrieved from http://dx.doi.org/10.1016/S0014-2921(98)00048-8

Menon, A., & Varadarajan, P.R. (1992). A model of marketing knowledge use within firms. *Journal of Marketing, 56*(4), 53–71.

Meschi, P.X. (1997). Longevity and cultural differences of international joint ventures: Toward time based cultural management. *Human Relations, 50*(2), 211–227. Retrieved from http://dx.doi.org/10.1177/001872679705000207

Miller, D. (1991). Stale in the saddle. *Management Science, 37*(1), 34–52.

Mori, M. (2010). *Betonamu Nikkei kigyonenkan 2010–2011 nendoban (Japanese companies in Vietnam 2010–2011).* Bangkok, Thailand: Comm Bangkok Co. Ltd. Retrieved from http://www.hellothai.com/joho/JV.htm

Nguyen, T.D.N., & Aoyama, A. (2012). Does the hybridizing of intercultural potential facilitate efficient technology transfer? An empirical study on Japanese manufacturing subsidiaries in Vietnam. *Asian Social Science, 8*(11), 26–43. Retrieved from http://dx.doi.org/10.5539/ass.v8n11p26

Nguyen, T.D.N., Takanashi, C., & Aoyama, A. (2012). Can efficient technology transfer be achieved through a corporate culture? A study on Japanese manufacturing subsidiaries in Vietnam. *International Journal of Business and Management, 7*(7), 24–39. Retrieved from http://dx.doi.org/10.5539/ijbm.v7n7p

Palanisamy, R. (2007). Organizational culture and knowledge management in ERP implementation: An empirical study. *Journal of Computer Information Systems, 48*(2), 100–120.

Pillania, R.K. (2006). State of organizational culture for knowledge management in Indian industry. *Global Business Review, 7*(1), 119–135.

Rodriguez, J.L., & Rodriguez, R.M.G. (2005). Technology and export behaviour: A resource-based view approach. *International Business Review, 14*(5), 539–557. Retrieved from http://dx.doi.org/10.1016/j.ibusrev.2005.07.002

Sadler-Smith, E., Spicer, D.P., & Chaston, L. (2001). Learning orientations and growth in smaller firms. *Long Range Planning, 34*(2), 139–158. Retrieved from http://dx.doi.org/10.1016/S0024-6301(01)00020-6

Schein, E.H. (1996). Three cultures of management: The key to organizational learning. *Sloan Management Review, 38*(1), 9–20.

Steenkamp, J.B.E.M., & Van Trijp, H.C.M. (1991). The use of LISREL in validating marketing constructs. *International Journal of Research in Marketing, 8*(4), 283–299. Retrieved from http://dx.doi.org/10.1016/0167-8116(91)90027-5

Steinwachs, K. (1999). Information and culture—The impact of national culture on intonation processes. *Journal of Information Science, 25*(3), 193–204.

Tangen, S. (2005). Demystifying productivity and performance. *International Journal of Productivity and Performance Management, 54*(1), 34–46.

Tran, T.K.L., & Bui, N.H. (2009). Tac dong cua cac yeu to quan ly den nang suat doanh nghiep (Impact of managerial factors on firm productivity). *Tap chi phat trien khoa hoc va cong nghe (Science and Technology Development), 12*(15), 73–86.

Tsang, E.W.K., Nguyen, D.T., & Erramilli, M.K. (2004). Knowledge acquisition and performance of international joint ventures in the transition economy of Vietnam. *Journal of International Marketing, 12*(2), 82–103.

Williams, F., & Gibson, D.V. (1990). *Technology transfer: A communication perspective*. Newbury Park, CA: Sage Publications.

Wilson, D.T., & Nielson, C.C. (2000). Cooperation and continuity in strategic business relationships. *Journal of Business-to-Business Marketing, 8*(1), 1–24. Retrieved from http://dx.doi.org/10.1300/J033v08n01_01

Xu, B. (2000). Multinational enterprises, technology diffusion, and host country productivity growth. *Journal of Development Economics, 62*(2), 477–493. Retrieved from http://dx.doi.org/ 10.1016/S0304-3878(00)00093-6

Yamashita, S. (1991). *Transfer of Japanese technology and management to the ASEAN countries*. Tokyo: University of Tokyo Press.

Yin, E., & Bao, Y. (2006). The acquisition of tacit knowledge in China: An empirical analysis of the 'supplier-side' individual level' and 'recipient-side' factors. *Management International Review, 46*(3), 327–348.